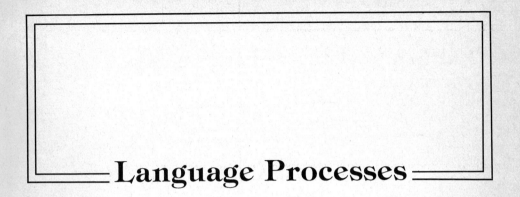

Language Processes

Language Processes

Vivien C. Tartter

Rutgers University

HOLT, RINEHART AND WINSTON

*New York / Chicago / San Francisco / Philadelphia
Montreal / Toronto / London / Sydney
Tokyo / Mexico City / Rio de Janeiro / Madrid*

The publishers and editors wish to thank the following review-
ers for their contributions: Peter Gordon, Harvard University;
Jola Jakimik, University of Wisconsin-Madison; Mark Sieden-
berg, McGill University; David McNeil, University of Chicago;
Marvin J. Honzie, University of Virginia; David Townsend;
Deborah Keller-Cohen, University of Michigan; and Sheila
Blumstein, Brown University.

Library of Congress Cataloging-in-Publication Data

Tartter, Vivien C.
  Language processes.

  Includes bibliographies and index.
  1. Linguistics.   2. Language and languages.
I. Title.
P121.T315   1986   410   85-14026

ISBN 0-03-063589-6

CBS COLLEGE PUBLISHING
Holt, Rinehart and Winston
The Dryden Press
Saunders College Publishing

To my teacher, advisor, colleague, and friend—Sheila Blumstein

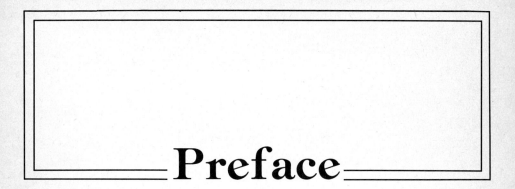

Preface

Psycholinguistics is an interdisciplinary field, with contributions from cognitive psychology and linguistics, and also from communication sciences, philosophy, artificial intelligence, ethology, comparative psychology, behavioristic psychology, neurology, and clinical psychology. Students of psycholinguistics, too, may come from any of these areas and may have limited experience in the others.

This book is designed to reflect the inherently interdisciplinary nature of the field, discussing the data, methods, and insights of the various disciplines, integrating the contributions, and yet maintaining the identities of the individual disciplines so their approaches are clear. It is aimed at anyone interested in language and language processes regardless of how limited a background he or she might have in the relevant disciplines. Thus, many chapters provide basic material before presenting sophisticated issues. The novice may need to study the basic material while the non-novice may wish to skim or skip to the more advanced material. Those with good linguistic backgrounds, for example, probably can skip the chapters on syntax and phonology (4 and 6), while those with strong backgrounds in various areas of psychology may choose to skip discussions of reinforcement principles, factor analysis, experimental design principles, etc. (found in sections of chapters 2 and 3).

I have organized the book in two halves around one dominant issue: defining language and how it is shaped by the social, perceptual, and cognitive constraints of its users. The first half contains, for the most part, material found in traditional psycholinguistics books: semantics and processing of word meaning, syntactic descriptions and their reality for processing (together with processing of meaning in propositions), phonology and speech perception and production. For each level of language there is one chapter dealing with language structure as reflected in philosophy, linguistics, and/or behavioristic psychology, followed by a chapter dealing with language processing, as reflected in artificial intelligence, and cognitive psychology. The chapters on speech are more detailed than is typical for psycholinguistics books and there may be readers therefore who wish to select from the sections in these chapters. There are isolated sections of some subsequent chapters that assume knowledge of speech processes (speech development in Chapter 9, phonological rules in Genie's speech in Chapter 10, analogies to "Is speech special?" in ASL in Chapter 11, and speech perception in aphasia in Chapter 12), and these may be eliminated also without substantially affecting the continuity of the chapters.

After providing a background in language, the book moves to the central theme of defining language, leaving this until readers have sufficient background to evaluate for themselves the various controversies and alternative schemes surrounding language definition. Chapter 8 presents animal communication systems and human non-language communication systems as contrasts and analogies for human language, provides controversial criteria for recognizing language, and then applies these criteria to evaluate the attempt to teach nonhuman animals some form of human language.

Subsequent chapters of the book treat language and language processes in people with language experience different from that of the normal hearing adult: "normal" children (Chapter 9), children deprived of an appropriate language model through abandonment, neglect, or the combination of deafness and parents advocating strictly oral education (Chapter 10), individuals whose primary communication is through the visual-gestural modality, ASL (Chapter 11), individuals with brain damage, principally aphasia (Chapter 12), and individuals with personality disorders (principally schizophrenia). Each of these chapters asks whether the communication system described constitutes language according to the criteria established in Chapter 8, and whether and in what ways the systems are deviant from normal adult speech. Most of these chapters are also used to infer biological and environmental factors responsible for normal language skills—either because the changed constraint does not alter language profoundly or because it does. Examples of the first are schizophrenia, which results in deviant communication but normal language structure and processing, or sign language, which makes use of a less usual mode of communication, but surprisingly this does not affect acquisition, basic structural properties of language, or language processing apart from the speech-to-sign change. Examples of the second are the great difference in structure and processing of primary language acquired after puberty—which suggests the viability of the critical period notion—or the structure and processing of language by aphasics, which indicates the normal neural underpinnings of language and the biological independence of language "modules" such as syntax and semnatics. The chapters in the second half of the book are written to be relatively autonomous, so instructors or readers may select from them as interest indicates.

Because of the central interest in biology shaping language structure, I have restricted inquiry to *primary* language—the language one thinks in. Unlike some books, therefore, this book contains no chapters on reading and writing or on second language acquisition, interesting areas no doubt, but acquiring a foreign language involves skills that have been shaped by primary language processes. Likewise artificial languages, like signed English, are discussed only minimally, and then in contrast to their primary language counterparts.

My principal interest in writing this book was to communicate the fun and excitement I find in psycholinguistic research. Every chapter is accompanied by its own reference list to facilitate searches for additional reading in the chapter's subject area. Many chapters include boxes and/or exercises with interesting (and relevant) language examples, demonstrations, or side issues to provoke additional consideration. Controversies are presented as such with, as far as possible, arguments presented on many sides of the issue together with guidelines for rational evaluation. Readers are then urged to resolve the issue for themselves. Finally, in this regard, I have tried to present some issues, which appear at the moment to be resolved, from a historical perspective—as in behavioristic approaches to language or the early stages of transformational theory. These have been resurrected partly because I think they still provide valuable insights, partly because history can repeat itself in science too and they may some day again be actively considered, and partly because I think the importance and excitement of new truths and methods can be appreciated only in light of the old ways.

It is my profound hope that through open discussion of controversy, emphasis on methods of analysis and criticism, presentation of psycholinguistics from the diverse perspectives of its various researchers, and encouragement of active involvement, readers will be stimulated to continue thinking about language and its processing well after they have completed this book. The first course I had in psycholinguistics added a major dimension to my life and I would like to pass that gift on.

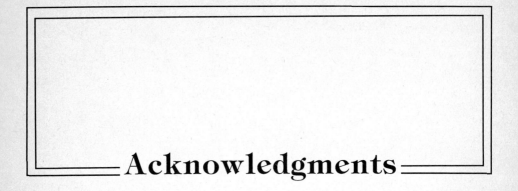

Acknowledgments

I would like to first thank my husband, Paul, for pushing me to write this book when I hesitated initially, and for his support for the two-and-half years I labored over it. I am also grateful beyond words to Arty Samuel and Dane Harwood, who went through multiple drafts of the manuscript and provided outstanding critiques and stimulated me to think in ways I had never considered. Thanks also to Richard Meier, who reviewed the final draft, and my husband, Paul, and parents, John and Trudy Rothman, who critiqued most of the first draft and helped point out ways to make it more comprehensible to the educated layman. I am grateful to Mark Blechner for critiquing much of the manuscript in galleys, and to anonymous reviewers of selected chapters.

Individual chapters were critiqued by friends and colleagues whom I would also like to thank. Chapters 6 and 7 benefited form discussions with Chris Shadle on acoustics and Marion Macchi on speech perception research. Chapter 8 and sections of other chapters dealing with comparative psychology and behaviorism were substantially improved by comments from and discussions with Bill Whitlow. Richard Meier helped shape my thinking and manuscript on ASL, Chapter 11. Sheila Blumstein brought me up-to-date on aphasia and her comments improved both chapters 12 (aphasia) and 13 (schizophrenic language). And Mark Blechner substantially improved Chapter 13 by his critical editing, assistance in discovering the relevant literature, and discussions with me of Freudian theory and clinical views of schizophrenia and split personality. As is usual, I followed suggestions selectively and take exclusive responsibility for what I have written—but I am extremely grateful for the time and learning these friends shared.

The debt I owe my undergraduate teachers, especially Sheila Blumstein and Dick Millward who inspired me with a resilient love for linguistics, psycholinguistics, and cognitive psychology, as well as academia in general, is most gratefully acknowledged. Thanks also to my graduate adviser, Peter Eimas, for his guidance in thinking, experimental methodology, and research.

Special thanks are also due to John Silberman for his advice on the process of publishing at the onset of the project, and of course to my editors, Alison Podel, Theresa Bowers, and Biodun Iginla, for their help throughout.

Contents

1

Perspectives on Language   1

2

Meaning   15

3

Semantic Memory   42

4

Syntax   85

5

Sentence Processing   133

6

Speech   175

7

Speech Perception and Production   209

8

Language: A Human-Specific Accomplishment?   263

9

Acquisition of the First Language 319

10

Human Communication in the Absence of a Language Model 376

11

Sign Language as a Primary Language 402

12

The Dissolution of Language: Brain Damage 448

13

Language Changes from Personality Disorders 485

14

Retrospectives on Language 514

1

Perspectives on Language

What makes human beings special? Answers to that question through the ages have usually begun with "language." Because of language, we, perhaps alone, can consider the abstract, the nonimmediate, and the unreal. We can also communicate across generations, and this has allowed us to build on the knowledge of others, constructing a civilization with features distinct from those of any other animal group. In fact, most other features that have at various times been considered uniquely human—religion, tool use, and the ability to imagine death—depend in some way on language.

In the twentieth century, language as a uniquely human endowment has been seriously challenged. More has become known about principles of learning, suggesting that many seemingly complex language phenomena may have the same basis as simple reflex associations. The increased use of sophisticated computers in areas thought to be restricted to intelligent humans has raised (although at times, lowered) the probability that language may be programmable and therefore producible by machine and not unique to humans. Increased study of natural animal communication systems has indicated that some properties of natural language exist in nonhuman communication, which in turn has raised the question of what are the defining and special characteristics of human language. And finally, research in animal learning and in language itself has suggested that language may not require exclusively human skills.

This book explores a variety of data on the issue of whether language is special. The book is aimed at defining human language and how it is shaped by the perceptual and cognitive constraints of its users. The first section discusses normal language processes, and the second, the consequences of the breakdown of social, perceptual, or cognitive influences on the shape of language.

The Fascination of Language

Besides its potential for distinguishing humans from other species, language may be distinct from other behaviors for many reasons. Once we know a language, we have a symbol system that seems to affect our mental organization radically. Thinking seems to take place through language, and more specifically, in the particular language *we* happen to speak. This notion leads us to address speakers of a foreign language more loudly and slowly, "with an unshaken confidence that the English tongue [is] somehow the mother tongue of the whole world, only the people [are] too stupid to know it ..." (*Little Doritt,* p. 875). On a more serious note (if you have never seriously thought about the language of thought, see Box 1.1) it has been claimed that: (1) thinking is impossible without language (Rieber and Vetter, 1980); (2) there are no memories without (or before) language (Watson, 1930/70); and (3) language reflects thought, or, people who speak different languages think differently (Whorf, 1956). If any of these statements are true, study of language processes may be a study of thought processes.

Because of its effect on our organization of concepts, language has tremendous force socially, distinct from many other human behaviors. Language may be used to change people's thought (rhetoric) or to forge or destroy a feeling of group identity (sociolinguistics). There are a number of instances, some fictional and some nonfictional, demonstrating the common conviction that some types of language are "better" than others. These instances generally take the form of imposing a particular language regardless of convenience, or of declaring some forms of the language "substandard" and using that as a basis for discrimination. One recent humorous example, cited by William Safire (1982), is attributed to a Texas governor in response to a proposal to use Spanish as a second language in Texas schools: "'Not while I am governor! If English was good enough for Jesus Christ, it is good enough for Texas chil-

---

Box 1.1 Language and Thought

Consider the following question: Do you think in words? As you think about the question, try to tell if you are doing the thinking in words. You can do this by forcing yourself to think word for word and seeing if that is the same as the way you normally think. You will find that it is possible to think word for word, but while you are doing that you are also monitoring your word-for-word thought (Is the monitor thinking in words?), and racing ahead with the idea while plodding along and filling in words (Is the part that is racing ahead thinking in words?). You may feel different types of trains of thought as well when you are writing: One part knows what you want to say, another gropes for words, and a third monitors for grammar, spelling, and consistency. The second and third types may be why writing seems more difficult than speaking. Are the monitor and word-choosing trains of thought used for speaking also, or do you talk immediately without thinking about how you are going to say what you want to say? One last question you might entertain yourself with: The voice inside your head that thinks in "sort-of-words"—whose voice is it? Does it seem to be your voice? A male voice? A female voice?

dren.'" Consider also Henry Higgins' credible elevation of Eliza Dolittle from flower girl to nobility by changing her accent in George Bernard Shaw's *Pygmalion* (popularized as *My Fair Lady*); the existence of the Académie française to keep French pure; and the interdiction of the use of English loan words in Nazi Germany (Eisminger, 1980).

On a more far-reaching note, frequently cultures have decided to enforce the use of a particular language because of associations made to that language. For example, although no one had spoken it, Latin was used in Catholic church services; it conveyed a feeling of significance, religion, and mysticism partly because no one spoke it, and therefore it was associated exclusively with Catholicism. At the beginning of the Zionist movement, a conscious decision was made to have Hebrew be the emerging nation's language, although for centuries Hebrew had not been in everyday use. Far more convenient would have been any of the vernaculars of the immigrant founders, Yiddish, Russian, or German—but Hebrew, which required modernizing and which no one spoke as a native, seemed to belong to the soil of Zion. In disputes the world over, we also see the attempted domination of one culture by another, symbolized by the domination of the language: Afrikaans is an official language of South Africa, even though spoken only by a small, powerful minority; English had been imposed as the official language of Québec until recently, although most of the inhabitants were French-speaking; and in the United States, Black English has been considered an inferior dialect to Standard American English. Are some languages truly better than others, or are some people just aware of the social power of language and adept at exploiting it? The study of language processes provides objective answers to this question.

Perhaps because of our awareness of the power of language in affecting thought and social change, mystical power is attributed to language cross-culturally, distinguishing it from most other human behavior. In our culture, there are ten commandments legislating moral behavior, one of which forbids *the use of a word:* "Thou shalt not take the name of the Lord thy God in vain" (Exodus 20:7). Indeed, to this day, the name of God is unmentionable in the Jewish religion. In every culture there is a large set of "curse" words that may not be used, although their concepts are conveyed through euphemism. All prayers and incantations are the recital of words, the act of which is supposed to bless or curse the speaker or someone designated in the prayer. Folklore likewise has many examples of magic words that must be enunciated to cast, break, or enact a spell; for example, "open sesame" in the story of Ali Baba, or "Rumpelstiltskin" in the story of the same name. (It is interesting to note that this latter story has variants in nearly every culture [Shah, 1979].) Finally, current or residual superstitions exemplify the belief in the mystical power of language: "God bless you" after a sneeze is considered sufficient to exorcize the inhaled devil; "knock on wood" after mention of some good fortune prevents a jinx or reversal of that good fortune. Our attitudes toward our language frequently border on the spiritual, and study of language processes can indicate why.

One last reason language may be particularly interesting to study is that it is fun. Language games, like Pig Latin, invented for and sometimes by children, exist in nearly all cultures, as do language games for adults. The latter comprise a variety of puzzles like crosswords, acrostics, cryptograms, jokes playing on language (like puns), and intellectual exercises including the poetic devices of metaphor, alliteration, rhyme, and so on. These games please not just because of what is conveyed but because of the manner of conveyance. Study of language processes can lead to a better understanding of why and how the games are appreciated.

A Brief History of Psycholinguistics

The psychology of language has its roots in three basic lines of inquiry: (1) whether and which language abilities are innate (*innate* is the same as inborn, not known through learning), (2) how words are associated with meanings and with one another, and (3) why there are language disorders and how they may be treated. The first psycholinguistic experiment on record touches on both the innateness question and the origins of language. It is said that before 600 B.C. the Egyptian king Psammetichos I ordered a shepherd to rear two newborn infants without any exposure to language. He questioned what language those children, in the absence of linguistic experience, would then speak. After two years it was found that the children uttered the sounds "becos" whenever the shepherd approached. Investigation established that these sounds were used by the Phrygians for "bread," from which the Egyptian king concluded that the children must have had an innate knowledge of Phrygian and thus that the Phrygians were the primogenitors of mankind (Dale, 1976, p. 6).

The ancient Greeks considered adult human language to be distinct from both animal and child communications. This assumption was partly because the human vocal tract seemed specially adapted for language (this gives rise later to the statement that language is special *because* of speech), partly because of the peculiar relation of word and meaning, and partly because of the adult's training in language. It was generally thought that language and the vocal apparatus were part of nature (innate), but precision control of the vocal apparatus was established through experience. Like the Egyptian king, some Greeks argued that the conventions of language and even the specific words were part of nature, reflecting a perfect correspondence between the sound of the word and its meaning. Others argued that this relationship was manmade and arbitrary and therefore established only through experience. The ancient Greeks also contributed the first systematic language analyses, including classification of syntactic categories and words into parts of speech. Finally, the Greeks provided an early analysis of deafness, viewed, unfortunately, as a language-thought disorder that *caused* a hearing problem because of the inextricable relation of thought to language and language to the auditory system.

The Hellenistic view of language was maintained for the most part through the Middle Ages, with the minor exception that Christian leaders called "God-given" what the Greeks called "natural."

Beginning with the Renaissance, five new views of language emerged, all still with us today. The first, that of Francis Bacon, held that language is a multilevel process of which speech is only one level. Although Bacon, in common with the earlier views, considered words to embody natural thought, he conceived that it was possible to create viable artificial languages. Bacon's views can be found in today's artificial intelligence and cognitive psychology approaches to language.

The second important Renaissance perspective on language was that of Descartes, who attributed more, rather than fewer, aspects of language to instinct; in particular, he considered the urge to communicate and general language capacity instinctive, and he also thought there were *innate ideas*—such as concepts of religion, time, and so on—that gave people common frames of reference. The modern linguistic position on language claims inspiration from Descartes not only for this view of innateness but also for his emphasis that language alone proves the existence of thought and that the important defining characteristic of human language is that it is "innovative and . . . free from control of detectable stimuli, either external or internal" (Chomsky, 1972, p. 12).

This perspective on language contrasted sharply with Locke's, whose philosophy spawned the modern behaviorist and verbal associationist views of language. Locke rejected the notion of innateness of anything besides the basic language capacity, and even this was later rejected by his followers. For Locke, language and thoughts were all acquired by experience, in which case the interesting questions involve how concepts are formed. It was assumed that concepts were acquired by "association" of events that occurred *contiguously* (together in time) or that appeared similar.

The views of language described so far all share the fundamental concept that language (and humans) is something special. In *The Descent of Man,* although acknowledging that "this faculty has justly been considered as one of the chief distinctions between man and the lower animals" (p. 461) and is necessary for complex thoughts, Darwin attempted to show that human beings share with other animals vocal and nonvocal emotional gestures, the capacity and urge to imitate, and the abilities to think and reason. Thus, language skills in rudimentary forms are present elsewhere in the animal kingdom and our abilities can be accounted for through evolution. This view leads to the modern comparative approach to language and communication.

The final important historical development is the increased understanding of the physiological underpinnings of language. Before the nineteenth century, following Aristotle, it was generally thought that the vocal apparatus was essential to language, not just speech, and that deafness *represented a cognitive disorder resulting from* deficiency of language abilities. In the nineteenth century deafness became recognized as a sensory disorder, and teaching methods for the deaf developed. In addition, it was discovered that damage to specific areas of the brain affected some language skills and not others, and could affect language while leaving other cognitive skills intact. Therefore, there seemed to be physiological reasons for separating speech from language, and language from other aspects of cognition. These discoveries underlie the modern area of neurolinguistics and some aspects of applied psycholinguistics.

Modern Perspectives on Language

Because of the variety of interests language stimulates, its study has been undertaken in a variety of present-day disciplines, notably, for the present purposes, philosophy, computer science, linguistics, and psychology. In the last, moreover, a number of approaches have been taken; the most relevant are those of the behaviorists and, particularly, the cognitive psychologists. Because of the variety of pertinent approaches, a brief introduction to the interests and methods of study of each follows. More detailed presentation of the methods and findings of each will be presented in later chapters.

Philosophy

The primary interest of philosophers of language has been to understand how language reflects conceptual structures and reality. In the twentieth century there have been three general views about how this study should be undertaken. The first, that of the *logical positivists* or *empiricists,* attempted to derive a system of rules that would account for every reasonable statement and rule out every unreasonable statement; that is, to generate an artificial language (or set of rules that could generate such a language) that could express only experiential truths or logical relations among ideas and that would formally eliminate such absurdities or semantic anomalies as "Caesar is a prime number." This attempt led to a search for sharp definitions of word meanings, which proved elusive.

As a reaction against this approach, the school of ordinary language philosophy arose (see Ryle, 1970, for example). This school sought to show that the relation between word and meaning was fuzzy at best and was revealed only through general usage in the language; that is, word meaning was established through *habit.* The method of ordinary language philosophers was to discover instances in the language that exemplified the fuzzy nature of word meaning, and thus no theoretical framework was developed.

The third view of philosophy of language, described by Katz (1966), grew out of current linguistic theory (see following). In this view linguistic descriptions of natural language are compared for common features, or *universals.* It is assumed that a systematization of language universals and linguistic descriptions will reveal the answer to the "basic question that can be asked about natural languages—what are the principles for relating acoustic objects to meaningful messages that make a natural language so important and flexible a form of communication" (Katz, 1966, p. 98).

Artificial Intelligence

The artificial intelligence (AI) approach to language is aimed at the practical problem of making a powerful machine respond appropriately to language input— that is, to produce output easily understood by its human users (=appropriate response) and to "understand" language to make that response. In the programming of language comprehension and production, AI researchers have provided insights into how people perform these tasks.

Computer involvement with language began with the seemingly trivial task of machine translation from one language to another. As this was proving nontrivial, it was observed that computers were the perfect medium for testing language theories: They perfectly realize all and only the rules they are given. Historically, then, the second connection between computers and language was in model-testing. Since computers have become increasingly popular, it is desirable to have man-machine interaction take place in human language rather than machine language, necessitating the machine being "taught" to use natural language. Thus, the third connection between computers and language is artificial intelligence, providing the computers with the knowledge that humans use in communication.

For the purposes of understanding human language processes, artificial intelligence research has demonstrated how and when certain models of language are ineffective, and how mutually dependent levels of language are. Language programs began with vocabulary lists and simple grammatical rules and failed to mimic the judgments of humans—a frequently cited example is the machine translation into Russian of "the spirit is strong but the flesh is weak," which could be retranslated as "the vodka is good but the meat is rotten." Corrections to prevent this type of error have led to the observation of the necessity of programming world knowledge/meaning for even "simple" language tasks.

Linguistics

Linguistics takes as its subject matter a language and has as one goal the discovery of the elements of the language and the systematic rules that relate these elements to one another. Note that this objective presupposes the existence of such elements and rules. The presupposition is necessitated by what Noam Chomsky, the most influential proponent of modern linguistics, considers the "core problem of human language:"

> Having mastered a language, one is able to understand an indefinite number of expressions that are new to one's experience, that bear no simple physical resemblance and are in no simple way analogous to the expressions that constitute one's linguistic experience; and one is able, with greater or lesser facility, to produce such expressions on an appropriate occasion, despite their novelty and independently of detectable stimulus configurations, and to be understood by others who share this still mysterious ability. *The normal use of language is, in this sense, a creative activity. This creative aspect of normal language is one fundamental factor that distinguishes human language from any known system of animal communication.*
> (Chomsky, 1972, p. 100, italics mine).

The solution to the problem of novelty is the abstraction from the utterances experienced of a set of elements and a set of rules for combining those elements. Application of those rules to form new elements can generate or dissect novel utterances. (For simple examples of the power that rule abstraction permits, see Box 1.2.)

A goal of linguistics, then, is the discovery of the rules that characterize every speaker-hearer's language *knowledge.* Chomsky (1965) distinguished between the underlying language knowledge or *competence,* which is what the linguist is interested in, and the actual verbal behavior or *performance.* Performance includes errors because it is affected by limitations of the body, such as lapses of attention, memory, or motor control, and therefore does not always reflect what a speaker-hearer knows

---

Box 1.2 The Power of Rules

Following are four "utterances:"

$$(2,4)$$
$$(3,9)$$
$$(4,16)$$
$$(5,25)$$

Can you create a new utterance consistent with (= grammatical) the list? Probably you find the problem simple; you know the elements, the natural numbers, and you notice a rule, the second equals the square of the first. This rule now permits the creation of an infinite set of utterances, many of which you will never have seen before, like (179, 32041).

On a less trivial level, consider the elements:

Noun
John
Mary
A Dog

and

Verb
Loves
Hates
Chases

and the rule: S (sentence) = Noun Verb Noun. From these six elements and one rule we can generate 27 "S"s: "John Loves Mary," "John Loves A Dog," "John Loves John," "Mary Loves John," "A Dog Chases John," and so on.

Notice how few basics are needed to produce many combinations: That is the power of rules.

---

about the language. Most users can conceive of an infinitely long sentence, such as "John counted slowly, 'one, two, three . . . '" or "John bought apples and milk and bananas and . . . ," but, obviously, no one can produce one. The grammar, or the set of rules the linguist uncovers, must capture the potential. The difficulty is that the data from which the linguist works are all instances of performance, and competence can only be inferred.

Competence must be inferred from erratic performance data not only by the linguist but also by those who acquire a language. A fascinating question is how all speaker-hearers of a language acquire the same competence or set of rules despite the fact that no two of us hear exactly the same set of utterances from which to abstract rules. Modern linguistics finds the answer to this question in the postulation of an innate set of guidelines that each person brings to the task of acquiring language, what Chomsky calls the *language acquisition device (LAD)*. The hypothesis is that each person begins language acquisition with some idea of what to look for in language—of what elements and rules there can be—and these innate ideas enable the appropriate abstraction of the underlying language structure from the varied, incomplete, and perhaps error-laden performance data that the child hears as input. The structures and strategies of LAD, in turn, are responsible for the structure of any language since a system that deviated from the rules of LAD could not be learned by the child and would not survive as a human language.

The main goal of linguistics, then, is to construct a general theory of language, a description of the structures that can be found in all languages because they are part of the human endowment. One way to determine which aspects are innate is to see which occur in all languages—universally. To accomplish this, the descriptions of individual languages may be compared with one another in order to find universals, which in turn may be used to construct a theory of the *nature of (all) language.*

It is important to observe that because of our tendency to assume that *our* language reflects nature, thought, and reality, to derive a general theory of language we have to compare languages from radically different cultures, a branch of linguistics known as *ethnolinguistics.* For example, time, space, causality, and motion seem—from our Western perspective—"natural" concepts, as Descartes suggested. Thus, they should be reflected in our vocabulary and in our grammar. Suppose there are languages (and there are, as we will see) that do not express these concepts or express them in a radically different way? Would we want to maintain the conclusion that the concepts were natural, or the hypothesis that they were innately given in LAD?

The distinctions between concept and expression in language, or between competence and performance represent two of many linguistic distinctions between levels of language: in the first case, one level is pure thought and the other, linguistic instantiation; in the second case, one level is the knowledge of the rules of the language, and the other, the final form of an utterance after multiple operations, an acoustic signal in speaking and meaning representation in listening. *Structure* can be investigated at any level: the structure of concepts, of knowledge of the language, of the acoustic signal, or of the operations transforming one into the other. However, since the levels are not independent, the rules and elements uncovered in one may be applied to another, binding together the individual structures.

Psychology

Basically, psychology of language entails study of language performance of the speaker or of the hearer. Frequently inferences are made from performance to competence. The difference between the psychology and linguistics approaches is that linguists study the language to determine rules that could generate it and then infer that these rules are in the speaker-hearer's head, while psychologists study directly processes that the hearer uses in language understanding and that the speaker uses in language production. Note that from the psychologist's perspective, language production and language comprehension are separate processes, while from the linguist's, they are considered to derive from the same "process"—competence. An important further distinction is that the rules the linguist searches for are abstract descriptions of the native speaker's knowledge; the descriptions do not necessarily govern production nor are they necessarily derived during comprehension. What the psychologist searches for are the mechanisms employed during comprehension and production (see Katz, 1977, for example).

Within psychology there are two distinct approaches to language that differ with respect to their interests in competence, the indirectly observable mental structure of language, versus performance, the natural language behaviors. The first of these is the behaviorist approach, principally propounded by Skinner (1957), in which there is no interest in the mental underpinnings of language. For behaviorists, language comprehension and production are simply matters of habit acquired through association of muscle movements or sounds with certain consequences. Hearing or saying "salt" over and over again establishes a connection between the sound or articulation of the word and the object; being handed the salt after requesting it strengthens these connections. Similarly, words may come to be associated in groups, producing sentences and recognition of similarities and differences between groups as in:

Please pass the salt
Please pass the sugar
Please pass the milk

resulting in the establishment of "rules" determined by habit strengths. For the behaviorist, study of psycholinguistics is directed toward determining the environmental conditions that control verbal behavior. (Note that no mention is made of the mental structures the language user brings to the situation.)

The second important psychological approach to language is that of cognitive psychology. Cognitive psychologists assume that people are active participants in comprehending and producing language, not merely passive reflectors of past habits or passive realizers of productive rules. The question the cognitive psychologist poses is, what strategies do people bring to comprehending and producing? To answer that question, cognitive psychologists have developed ingenious techniques for measuring and distinguishing mental operations and have hypothesized mental processes as diverse as the construction of holistic mental images and the use of innate, abstract linguistic rules.

An important contribution of cognitive psychology is the distinction between more or less passive processing induced automatically by a stimulus *(stimulus-driven)* and active, meaning-seeking, goal-directed processing, produced from the individual's preexisting conceptual structures *(conceptually driven)*. The machine translation error of interpreting flesh as meat could not arise with appropriate conceptual-driving, since the comprehender would process each word in the context of a conceptual structure derived from the whole sentence. Although the cognitive psychologist's concept of stimulus-driven processing is distinct from the stimulus-driven processes the behaviorist describes, the more obvious difference in the two approaches is in the cognitive hypothesis of preexisting conceptual structures that control and interact with the stimulus-driven processes.

Language: The Whole and the Parts

This book is aimed at defining human language through exploration of language and the cognitive and perceptual constraints of its users. At the outset, a noncontroversial and rather empty definition of language is: *Language is the way humans communicate.* As we proceed we will develop a much more detailed, concrete, and probably more controversial definition.

Communication is usually defined as the active transfer of information from one to another. The two critical terms are "active" and "information." *Active* implies deliberate processing on the part of the communicator; communication does not take place between a person and a tape recorder. Following the information-theoretic approach, *information* is defined rigorously as a lessening of uncertainty. According to this view, telling a person something (s)he already knows is *not* communication. This point can cause confusion partly because there are many levels of communication. A student correctly answering a teacher's question, say, about who was the first president of the United States is transmitting information. However, the information is not "George Washington," which the teacher presumably knew, but rather is: "*I know* the answer—George Washington," since the student's knowledge had been uncertain to the teacher. If a person tells the same story over and over again, what is being communicated is not the contents of the story (they do not constitute information), but rather the fact that the speaker is boring or repetitious, which would not be known at the first telling.

Natural, normal communication usually entails signals transmitted visually: eye movements or eye widening, facial expression, head movements, arm gestures, and body movements, so-called body language. Natural communication also entails signals transmitted *aurally* (to the ear); these are signals usually called language. These two aspects of communication may operate *redundantly,* meaning that each conveys the same information as the other, so the two together do not reduce the uncertainty any more than either alone. For example, a head nod may accompany a verbal "yes," or the eyes may widen together with an exclamation of surprise. However, frequently they are not redundant (a gesture to the left when one means "left" is usually more reliable than the word "left" or "right"), and so both must be considered part of human communication.

The more interesting part of human communication for our purposes is the part transmitted aurally. Aural language is usually studied in parts: paralanguage (sometimes called *suprasegmentals*), phonetics and phonology, semantics, and syntax. *Paralanguage* comprises those aspects of the signal not contained in the words: intonation, stress, emotional overtone, the speaker's identity, and so on. Note that sometimes this information can be distinct from the verbal message—as in indications that the speaker is in a bad mood—and sometimes it can be redundant with the verbal message—as when a question is indicated by raising pitch (paralanguage) along with adding a verbal "who" or "what." Together paralanguage and body language form the subject matter for the field of *nonverbal communication.*

Phonetics and *phonology* are the study of the sounds of the language, the purpose of which is to find a grammar, or set of rules, governing sound production and perception. Linguists are interested in determining which sounds are used in language, which of these serve to distinguish meaning, and which rules most simply describe the combination of those sounds. Of course, there is also a search for sounds and rules universal to all languages. Psychologists are interested in how the vocal apparatus produces the sounds, how listeners perceive the acoustic signal to determine the relevant language sounds, and whether there are rules for combining them that have a psychological reality.

Semantics is the study of the relations of word and meaning and of word meanings to one another. Again, the linguist attempts to uncover an orderly pattern underlying the words of the language, one that can more economically describe the meaning system than a list of the words does. The psychologist is interested in how the meanings are represented in the speaker's or hearer's mind (cognitive) or derived from environmental contingencies (behaviorist).

Syntax is the study of rules for combining words to form larger meaningful units, such as phrases or sentences. An important difference between syntax and phonology or semantics is that syntax is more abstract, specific only to language. Phonology and semantics are *interpretive*— phonology interprets language into physical sounds, and semantics interprets language into conceptual forms. Syntax wholly relates language elements to one another. Syntax is the aspect of language most closely related to what is taught in elementary schools (or grammar schools) as "grammar." An important distinction is that grammar, as taught in the early grades, is *pre*scriptive—instructing students in a "correct" use of the language, whereas grammar in the sense used here is *de*scriptive, illustrating the rules used in the language. In fact, as we shall see, what is "correct" is an arbitrary decision and is usually determined by the rules used by speakers in the dominant or upper class. A descriptive grammar can be effectively devised for these speakers' productions or for productions of any of the lower classes. The linguist searches for rules accounting for comprehension and production of all syntactically correct utterances and *only* those utterances, and assumes that those result from psychological processes. The psychologist studies directly the psychological processes that might underlie the apparent syntactic organization of the language.

Unfortunately, division of human communication into the parts described is artificial; the parts interact, as was suggested by the attempts at artificial intelligence. Smiling while speaking alters the sounds produced as well as the face; the sound alteration is studied as paralanguage and the face as body language. An intonation change, paralanguage, can have syntactic function; it can turn a statement into a question. Drawing the line between syntax and semantics is impossible; word meanings change dramatically in relation to other words. (A beautiful example of this is *oxymoron,* a poetic device pairing opposites as in "That is, hot ice, and wondrous strange snow. How shall we find the concord of this discord?" [*A Midsummer's Night's Dream*

5.1.59–60]—which in this case has nothing to do with weather but refers to a seeming paradox or impossibility.) Finally, phonetics and semantics cross: In English the plural is indicated by the sound "s" in "cats," the sound "z" in "dogs," and the sound "ez" in "horses." This change can be described by a simple phonological rule and represents a bridge between sound and meaning. Because of these crossovers, language cannot be described as a sum of these parts; the whole is much more.

Organization of This Book

In this chapter we have briefly outlined some major theoretical perspectives on language. We will be examining these in detail throughout. Our general foci are the evaluation of whether and how language is special and the determination of what social, sensory, and cognitive mechanisms human beings bring to communication to give language the shape it has. The first half of the book concentrates on the structure and processing of language in the normal adult; the second half, on what may be language by other users—animals, children, socially deprived children, deaf people, and brain-damaged or personality-"damaged" individuals.

For the most part our approach to language study derives from linguistics and cognitive psychology. These are reflected in the general organization of the book as well as in the subject matter. The first half of the book employs the linguistic distinction between competence and performance, with one chapter describing the ideal structure of language, and the following chapter, its performance realization. Because linguists use language productions and intuitions about language as their data base, their contributions are presented first in order to encourage thinking about and experimenting with language and appreciation of its structure. Our discussion of language, furthermore, is divided into traditional linguistic levels: phonology, semantics, and syntax. Traditionally, linguistics has used a stimulus-driven approach, starting from the basic units of sound and their combination, moving to the structure after combination into meaningful units, and ending with the structure of the combinations of meaningful units, syntax. Our organization of the levels of language more clearly reflects a conceptually driven scheme, beginning with meaning, then looking at structure, and ending with sound.

In Chapter 2 we encounter philosophical, linguistic, and psychological approaches to the age-old question of what meaning is. In Chapter 3, on meaning processing, we look in detail at psychological models and experiments and also investigate artificial intelligence models and experiments on knowledge organization. Chapter 4 concentrates most heavily on linguistic analyses of syntax, and Chapter 5, on syntax processing, as discussed in psychology and artificial intelligence. Chapter 6 emphasizes linguistic and engineering approaches to speech, and Chapter 7, on speech processing, discusses the psychological models and experiments for speech production and perception. The second half of the book uses the linguistic, behavioristic, and cognitive psychological approaches. We attempt to analyze the "language" output of our atypical populations in accord with linguistic theory. We look at the success of behavioristic methods in producing language in atypical individuals.

And we make inferences about the mental structures and processes of these individuals from the cognitive standpoint.

Let us begin with meaning, since the exchange of meanings is what human communication is about.

REFERENCES

Blumstein, S. (1975). Structuralism in linguistics: Methodological and theoretical perspectives. In K. F. Riegel & G. C. Rosenwald (Eds.). *Structure and Transformation: Developmental and Historical Aspects.* volume 3, (pp. 153–165). NY: John Wiley & Sons, Inc.

Chomsky, N. (1965). *Aspects of a Theory of Syntax.* Cambridge, MA: MIT Press.

Chomsky, N. (1972). *Language and Mind.* NY: Harcourt Brace Jovanovich.

Dale, P. S. (1976). *Language Development: Structure and Function.* (2nd ed.). NY: Holt, Rinehart and Winston.

Darwin, C. *The Descent of Man.* NY: Modern Library (in *The Origin of Species & The Descent of Man*), pp. 445–495.

Dickens, C. (1975). *Little Dorritt.* London: Penguin Books.

Eisminger, S. (1980). Borrowing and biases in German and English. *Verbatim, 7,* 13–14.

Katz, J. J. (1966). *The Philosophy of Language.* NY: Harper & Row.

Katz, J. J. (1977). The real status of semantic interpretations. *Linguistic Inquiry, 8,* 559–584.

Rieber, R. W. (Ed.) (1980). *Psychology of Language and Thought: Essays on the Theory and History of Psycholinguistics.* NY: Plenum Press.

Rieber, R. W. & Vetter, H. (1980). Theoretical and historical roots of psycholinguistic research. In R. W. Rieber (Ed.). *Psychology of Language and Thought: Essays on the Theory and History of Psycholinguistics,* (pp. 3–49). NY: Plenum Press.

Ryle, G. (1970). Ordinary language. In C. E. Caton (Ed.). *Philosophy and Ordinary Language,* (pp. 108–128). Chicago: University of Chicago Press.

Safire, W. (1982). On language. *The New York Times,* May 30. VI, 8.

Shah, I. (1979). *World Tales: The Extraordinary Coincidence of Stories Told in All Times, In All Places.* NY: Harcourt Brace Jovanovich.

Skinner, B. F. (1957). *Verbal Behavior.* Englewood Cliffs, NJ: Prentice-Hall.

Watson, J. B. (1930/1970). *Behaviorism.* NY: W. W. Norton.

Whorf, B. L. (1956). *Language, Thought, and Reality.* J. B. Carroll (Ed.). Cambridge, MA: MIT Press.

STUDY QUESTIONS

1. What are the important issues considered in language study from antiquity through the present? In your own words briefly describe each. Discuss the manifestations of the issues in modern day language study, the fascination of language, and historical study.

2. Briefly describe the levels of communication. For the language levels, sound, semantics, and syntax, *try* to come up with a pair of sentences, the interpretation of which illustrates a distinction on that level only. For instance, for sound we might have: "Let me tell you something" versus "Let me tell you somethin'," which have the same meaning and syntax but sound different.

2

Meaning

Philosophical Issues

The definition of meaning given by Webster is:

1. That which exists in the mind, view, or contemplation as a settled aim or purpose; that which is meant or intended to be done; intent; purpose; aim; object. [Archaic].
2. That which is intended to be, or in fact is, conveyed, denoted, signified, or understood by acts or language; the sense, signification, or import of words; significance; force.
   Old events have modern *meanings*—Lowell.
3. Sense; understanding; knowledge [Obs].
   Syn—import, intention, design, intent, purport, sense, signification.

Consider whether this definition is the meaning of "meaning." If it is, then, since the definition consists of 75 other English words (not counting punctuation), it seems that meaning-of-a-word is a relation of that word to other words in the language. Does the meaning of "meaning" have no reality outside English? If understanding, sense, and intent (= the words in the preceding definition) are indeed meaning, then a person's understanding, sense, and intent must all be shaped by knowledge of the language in which their meaning is, in this case, English. *Are* knowledge, sense, and intent dependent on particular language experience, or do they have an external or internal reality?

If "meaning"'s meaning is not this definition, but both the definition and the word it defines evoke the same meaning, then it can be said that a word or group of words *represents* its meaning. Of what nature is that representation? Is what the word or word group stands for a slice of external reality than can in some sense be pointed at? Or does it stand for some internal feeling(s), idea(s), or reaction(s)? Finally, do the single word "meaning" and the 75 words defining it represent the same thing, either in the external world or in the internal world? If they do, why and how are the word and definition different? When two sensations are identical, as are hunger produced by low blood sugar and hunger produced by an enticing smell, we cannot distinguish

15

the stimuli (and so overeat); so if the word and its definition are considered to have the same meaning by virtue of the fact that they evoke the same sensations, why can we distinguish the stimuli—the word from the definition? Perhaps a word and its definition do not represent the same thing. In that case, in what sense can the definition be said to define the word?

Box 2.1   Interpretations of Meaning

To a variety of students of language, the following are instances of meaning's "meaning." Consider the differences in views about the importance of abstract thought, observable behaviors, and language experience. A useful exercise might be to identify each quotation with basic concepts described in this chapter like sign versus symbol, mental versus observable behavior, and so on.

If you are willing to agree that "meaning" is just a way of saying that out of all the ways the individual has of reacting to this object, at any one time he reacts in only one of these ways, then I find no quarrel with meaning.

(Watson, 1930/1970).

. . . the essential meaning reaction must be central or neuro-physiological in character. That may be. If we focus on behavior, and leave the central reaction to others, the meaning of a linguistic form appears to be the total disposition to make use of and react to the form.

(Brown, 1958).

Few investigations of this internal aspect of speech have been undertaken so far, and psychology can tell us little about word meaning that would not apply in equal measure to all other images and acts of thought. Yet it is in word meaning that thought and speech unite in verbal thought.

(Vygotsky, 1962).

One fact that stands out to the detached viewpoint, but is not stressed by any of the schools, is the great and perhaps basic importance of the principle we denote by the word "meaning." Meaning will be found to be intimately connected with the linguistic: its principle is symbolism, but language is the great symbolism from which other symbolisms take their cue. . . . Even the lower mind has caught something of the algebraic nature of language; so that words are in between the variable symbols of pure patternment (Arūpa) and true fixed quantities. That part of meaning which is in words, and which we may call "reference," is only relatively fixed. Reference of words is at the mercy of the sentences and grammatical patterns in which they occur.

(Whorf, 1956).

The stimulus meaning of a sentence for a subject sums up his disposition to assent to or dissent from the sentence in response to present stimulation.

(Quine, 1960).

The questions just raised are the core of the philosophy of language. They are explained more formally in what follows. Implications of many of the possible solutions to these questions are pursued throughout this book, since much of psycholinguistic research is based either implicitly or explicitly on the particular solution. Solutions offered by linguists, philosophers of language, and psychologists—quite different from Webster's—are displayed in Box 2.1.

Sign-Symbol Distinction

A cat purrs. In doing so it communicates contentment. The purr could be said to "indicate" contentment. We smile. Smiling could be said to indicate contentment also and may bear the same relation to the thing it indicates as the cat's purr does. That kind of relation is called a *sign*. A sign can be *arbitrary*; that is, there is no obvious relation between it and the thing it represents. Happiness, for example, is not inherent in smiling—nonhuman primates smile to indicate aggression, the bare-toothed grimace. Concepts that are either *concrete* (real-world object) or *abstract* (difficult to point at) can be represented by signs (note that concrete and abstract refer to the concept, not to the thing used to depict them!). Examples of well-known signs are: In the story of Noah, the dove returns with an olive branch as a sign that the waters have receded enough to expose the trees. (This sign is nonarbitrary since the branch indicates it is above water level, and concrete, since low water is an obvious external state). God then sends a rainbow as a sign of His promise never to destroy the world again (arbitrary, the rainbow has no obvious relation to peace, and abstract, "peace" is hard to point at). A crucifix is a sign for Christianity (nonarbitrary in that it is an image of Christ, and abstract, Christianity is hard to point at); a red cross or caduceus is a sign for a medical person (arbitrary in that the red cross has no direct connection to things medical, and concrete, doctors are easily pointed at).

Does the statement "I am contented" bear the same relation to the state of contentment as a purr or a smile? Does the exclamation "Land, ho!" refer in the same way to the appearance of land as the olive branch? Does a crucifix represent Christianity in the same way that the word "Christianity" does? Would similar senses be conveyed by substituting the signs in the preceding questions for the words representing those signs?

It should be clear that the answer is "no," although it may be hard to pinpoint the reason. The relation most words bear to their meanings is called *symbolic* and is a special type of sign. Words-as-symbols can also represent both the concrete (branch) and the abstract (Christianity); and they can be both arbitrary ("branch" does not sound or look like a branch) and nonarbitrary ("singsong" sounds singsong). (You may recall that Aristotle believed differently—that words are "natural" because of an inherent correspondence between sound and meaning.) However, symbols are more flexible in their use than other signs: They are less connected to their *referents* (what they refer to) in the real world, and they are less specific in their effects on internal responses. A genuine smile almost reflexively makes a friend feel happy; a statement of happiness does not. It is because of this flexibility and added level of abstraction that actual substitution of any of the signs just mentioned for the words describing them would fail.

Meaning and Reference

Describing a sign's relation to what it signifies, we used the word "indicate." An olive branch or dove now *indicates* or refers to peace. Most words do not directly indicate or refer to an object. "Indicate" has the same origin as "index," meaning to point at; most signs that are not words directly—though figuratively—point at or represent an external or internal state. That most words do not index is perhaps easiest to see by considering words that index something or someone in contrast with those that do not. The pronouns "I" and "you," for example, point at a specific person in each interaction in which they are used. (This pointing at through words is called *deixis*.) In contrast, most words are nondeictic; "flower," for example, can be used in conversation without suggesting the existence or location of any particular flower. "You" cannot be used without suggesting the existence and immediate presence of the other. Although we are establishing that there is an important difference between words that "point" and those that do not, it is important to note that pointing itself is not transparent. If one points at a group of two nuts, one could be attempting to indicate the type of nut, the concept of two, or the configuration of the group (see, for example, Wittgenstein, 1958, p. 13). Deixis, although less abstract than meaning, is still abstract.

If one considers meaning and reference to be the same, a number of problems arise. The statement "Shakespeare is Shakespeare" is silly. The statement is a self-evident truth, or *tautology*. Both the *subject* (what comes before the verb) and the *predicate* (the verb and what comes after) *refer to* and *mean* the same thing. (There are contexts in which "Shakespeare is Shakespeare" could be sensibly stated, as in response to a rave about the greatness of one of his plays, or the poorness of a lesser non-Shakespearean play. In these cases, part of the meaning of the sentence is the tautology itself, in effect implying "You've said nothing original; after all there is only one Shakespeare.") Contrast the sentence with "Shakespeare is the author of Hamlet"—"Shakespeare" and "the author of Hamlet" both refer to the same individual. However, this statement is not silly and does not require a specific context to be reasonably uttered because in this case the subject and the predicate do *not mean* the same thing.

Aside from deixis, words may be used only as reference in particular situations: Such and such a person is John Smith, a particular set of directions is the location of a particular restaurant, and so on. But generally words are not used for their reference value: "The house I grew up in" will not convey a specific concept of my particular house to many people besides my immediate family but will convey to everyone a sense of childhood, nostalgia, import for me, and so forth. The statement may convey to each reader by analogy a sense of the house (s)he grew up in, although obviously different from the one I am referring to.

The distinction between words and specific referents is an important factor in the power of language. That distinction enables discussion of things that do not exist: a person who died centuries ago, a culture that has been absorbed by another, a mountain covered by the ocean ages ago, a species now extinct. The distinction also enables discussion of things that have never existed: Superman, Martians, the lost city of Atlantis, unicorns, and sphinxes, and even enables discussion of things that could never exist: round square, converging parallel lines. (The convergence of parallel lines is an underlying axiom/theorem of a non-Euclidean geometry that has had important use in modern physics—symbol manipulability permits thoughts beyond referents or sense data that may actually allow a truer picture of reality than our senses do.)

The distinction between words and specific referents is also an important factor in language as communication. No two people have had the same experience, just as not many have grown up in the same house. If language used only reference, to talk about "my house," participants would have to know "my house." Since language uses meaning instead of reference, participants instead can relate their own sense to it.

Finally, the distinction between words and specific referents allows creative language use. Once a word becomes a conventional symbol, it may be extended to novel referents as a means of comparing them to the typical ones; for example, the expression "loud colors" employs a word usually reserved for description of sound for description of light. In such situations the usual referents and associations constitute the *literal* meaning. The creative extension is the *figurative* meaning and allows new associations to be drawn.

There are various such figures of speech, distinguished in rhetoric by the kind of comparison drawn and the means of drawing it. A complete list will not be given here but just some examples. There is *metaphor,* the direct use of a word in a new context, as in "loud color" or "billboards are the warts of the landscape." There is *simile,* which draws the same kind of comparison as metaphor but does it while marking the comparison directly, as in "billboards are *like* warts." And, as a last example, there is *metonymy,* which employs a part of a concept to stand for the whole or conversely, as in saying "the White House announced" when meaning "a spokesperson for the executive branch located in the White House announced." Note that in these three types of figurative language, there is an extension of meaning; the difference between them is the type of extension or the form of comparison. Because a word means rather than refers, it takes on a life of its own and so can be used in new and original contexts for noting similarities.

Connotation and Denotation

There is an aspect of word meaning that refers, called *denotation.* "Powder room," "water closet," and "toilet" all have the same denotation. But they convey somewhat different senses. The different senses, the part of word meaning that does not refer, is called *connotation.* Any "naughty" word and the euphemism that can be used in its stead in polite society have the same denotation; they are not mutually substitutable because they have different connotations.

Probably no two words are completely synonymous or completely redundant. Synonyms listed in a dictionary or thesaurus are words that have the same denotations, at least in some instances, but that have different connotations. Usually one particular one is the best choice in any instance because it most nearly captures the appropriate meaning, both in connotation and denotation.

For example, there is a sense in which "drift" means meaning, if you catch my drift. "Drift," "meaning," "intent" all denote the same abstract concept, the subject of this chapter. "Drift" connotes a vagueness, as though the speaker has not zeroed in on the meaning. "Intent" connotes a sharpness, the speaker knows exactly what (s)he's aiming at. "Meaning" lies somewhere in between. The impression the speaker is trying to convey determines which word is most suitable.

Probably words, expressions, even whole languages acquire connotations from the company they keep. "Drift" is vague in that it brings to mind wind and water, causing aimless movements of leaves, snow, sand, debris. When it is used in the sense of "sense" it does not completely shake off these associations. Because words in new contexts do not shake off their old associations, social leaders frequently advocate change of a word not offensive in its denotative sense, like "negro," to a new one, like "black," which because of its newness has none of the connotations of the old; indeed, by its employment it takes on the connotations involved with identification with the new social movement. Similarly, maintenance or imposition of a word or language that has or had outlived its denotative usefulness, like Latin or Hebrew (before Zionism), is effective; these languages evoke the connotations of tradition, mystery, and holiness associated with their previous uses.

The Linguistic Relativity Hypothesis

The concept of denotation, as just elaborated, entails the assumption that there is an objective reality, revealed to us through our senses, that language can point to directly. It is difficult to imagine that the existence of one objective reality shared by all is only an assumption, and an assumption that may be wrong, but indeed that is what some language philosophers have proposed. Once it is observed that "reality" might not be the same for all, it follows that different languages or cultures could code reality differently. Since reality is viewed *relative* to linguistic background, this philosophical position is sometimes called the *linguistic relativity hypothesis*. Since the supposition is that language in part *determines* thought, the mental view of reality, the philosophical position is also called *linguistic determinism*. And finally, after its initial proponents, it is known as the *Whorf-Sapir hypothesis*.

To understand fully the implications of the Whorf-Sapir hypothesis, one must first arrive at an understanding of different objective realities. A famous Afghan folktale perhaps best illustrates the notion. In it, wise men attempt to describe the elephant to the populace. Both the wise men and the populace are blind, and each of the wise men has touched a different part of the elephant. The one holding its tail likens it to a rope, the one its trunk, to a hose, the one its leg, to a tree, the one its skin, to leather, and so on. Now clearly, none has a complete view of reality, and one is tempted to attribute this to their blindness. However, that is a superficial reading; each of our senses is a wise man, giving us only one slant on reality, and who is to say that what is revealed by our eyes is a truer picture than that revealed by our ears? All sensory information must be integrated, and we will still not know what we have missed because our senses may not reveal all. For example, we are constantly exposed to radiation of varying intensities of which we have no awareness. Our language, like our senses, focuses our attention on some aspects of reality and causes us to ignore other aspects.

Extending the parable of the elephant and the blind men to language and reality has interesting implications for translation. To me "elephant" connotes the largeness of the beast, probably because of the metaphorical extension in elephantine (meaning huge, not meaning trunklike) and elephantiasis (a disease producing huge swelling, not ropelike tails). Webster derives the word "elephant" from the Greek word for *ivory.* Did the Greeks focus on the tusk, while the English focused on the size of the animal? When Greek and English speakers think of elephant, do they have the same concept, or does the Greek picture the animal's face, while the Englishman imagines the expanse of the body? (See Box 2.2 for implications of this for translation.)

In its extreme form, the linguistic relativity hypothesis states that language determines thought. A trivial but frequently cited example is that Eskimos have several different words for "snow," perhaps because snow is central to their culture. Young Eskimos learning the language have their attention called to different types of snow because the discriminations are made in the language. Mainland Americans have many words for automobiles because the automobile is so culturally important. Different automobiles may be as indiscriminable to Eskimos as different kinds of snow seem to people raised in a temperate climate. Presumably though, each could be taught the others' words, thereby causing perception of differences that had been obscure; that is, providing a new slant on reality.

A less trivial and thus more interesting influence of language on thought is the way the structures of language shape perception of the world (Whorf, 1956). English consists of *nouns* (names of objects), *verbs* (actions), and *adjectives* (descriptions of objects), as well as a number of other parts of speech irrelevant to the present point. The implication of this division of reality is that objects, actions, and descriptions are

---

Box 2.2 **Linguistic Relativity and Translation**

Consider the implications of linguistic relativity on international communication. It is easy to believe that all languages denote the same concepts and same reality since we frequently observe one language being translated into another. But is such translation really possible?

If you were employed as an interpreter between the blind man holding the tail and the blind man holding the trunk, and you wanted to convey the impression the former had, would you use the word "elephant" knowing it will mistakenly convey a trunklike image, or would you say "rope" to convey the first man's impression? Should the Greek for elephant be rendered into English as "ivory-tusked beast" to give the Greek outlook, or as "elephant," perhaps wrongly bringing to mind the associations of hugeness? Suppose you wished to translate the New Testament into a language for which the concept of God-the-Creator was of a female, say the Mother Earth, a situation faced by many missionaries. How could you do it? Clearly you cannot use the word for God already existing in the language, for the story of the Divine Birth would have to be drastically altered!

independent aspects of situations. Although this may seem obviously true to English users, this division is not in nature. Consider, for example, the English words "waterfall" and "brook." The first, with the object "water" and the action "falling" incorporated into one word suggests a oneness of object and action producing an object distinctly different from "water" alone. The second implies an object with no inherent action despite the fact that all brooks babble, run, meander, and so on. When one pictures a brook or any other object, there is not object + action + function + color, . . . as separate parts. All are imagined at once, but we speakers of English cannot talk about them at once (except in some rare words such as waterfall), which makes us think about them as separate aspects of a scene. If we examine the way other cultures describe a scene, we observe radically different treatments, indicating that ours is not the exclusive natural way. In Hopi (an American Indian language), objects with short duration (e.g., lightning) or inherent change are classed together with actions; the distinction between action and object dims, and in Nootka (a language of Vancouver Island), it disappears—probably giving these speakers a fundamentally different conception of reality (Whorf, 1956).

A final, potent example given by Whorf is the differing concepts of time and space in American English and American Indian (Hopi, specifically). To American English speakers, time is omnipresent, one-dimensional, continuous but conveniently divisible into past, present, and future. Each sentence of English expresses this concept of time obligatorily, by marking the verb with an element indicating past, present, or future time of occurrence of action in the sentence. (At first glance it may seem that there is no other way to view time, that this division is *natural*. Probably the naturalness of it, once one thinks in the system, contributes to the difficulty in learning new systems. In learning French, I experienced the greatest difficulties with their two past tenses, one for past and finished actions (*passé composé*), and one for past but ongoing actions (*imparfait*). The appropriate choice has never been automatic, and this difficulty with different tense systems is common to people learning foreign languages.)

The Hopi have three "tenses" but a different concept of time. The first tense Whorf classified as objective, what the Hopi can verify by sensing, and includes both the American English present and past tenses. The second two are subjective and divide the American English future: a "will happen" because it always does, by natural law, and a "will happen" because the actions leading to it have already begun. Thus, the concept of simultaneity inherent in a statement like "I (in New York) eat lunch while my friend (in California) eats breakfast" is impossible in Hopi; they would convey something like "I eat lunch and will hear that my friend ate breakfast"; that is, two distant-in-space events can be assigned the objective tense only when they are both past because one person cannot have sensory experiences in two places at once. And, as Whorf pointed out, the Hopi formulation is more in tune with reality as described by Einsteinian relativity than is the American English: Time is not constant but depends on observer position and motion; we never know that a star is shining, only that it was shining some number of light years ago. Whorf concluded that the theory of relativity might seem intuitive to the Hopi because they always looked at reality that way.

As support for linguistic relativity, Whorf found many differences among cultures that are also reflected in differences among the languages of the cultures. This discovery of course does not necessarily imply that language changes cultures but could mean that different cultures or thought patterns are reflected in language, the weak form of the linguistic relativity hypothesis. However, as we shall see in the next chapter, there is some evidence that distinctions made in the language "are nearer the top of the cognitive deck—more likely to be used in ordinary perception, more available for expectancies and inventions" (Brown, 1958, p. 236) than those describable only by circumlocution.

Meaning as Language Use

Many philosophers of language have worried about linguistic relativity even within one language. Some words or sentences are understood by immediate reference to a sensory experience: "ouch," "red," "my stomach hurts," for example. All individuals speaking that language learn to emit these utterances in the presence of particular stimuli, called *prompts* (Quine, 1960). There is no way of knowing, however, that all speakers have the same experience to which they apply these labels. In an extreme example, a color-blind person can appropriately distinguish red and green on a traffic light using position, can label the colors correctly, but clearly has a different sensation prompting the word "red" from a person with normal vision.

A second consideration is that most language is not learned by direct association to a sensation but by analogy, through other language (Quine, 1960). Associating "my stomach hurts" to a particular sensation and "hand" to a particular object, a person may understand or use the sentence "my hand hurts" without prior experience with that sensation. It is even possible to misuse the new sentence, perhaps reserving "hurt" only for cramps and not for burns or other hand pains. More abstract words are further from immediate sensation and more dependent on previous language learning and associations; the meanings for these will be more idiosyncratic, depending on the user's particular language and sensory experiences.

Some of the difficulty could be eliminated if it were possible to specify precisely the conditions under which words *should* be used, to define words sharply. In that case, the only uncertainty would be the identity of the primary sensations. After that, the mapping of words to other words by analogy could be rigidly controlled. Wittgenstein (1958), for instance, asks that we:

> Consider for example the proceedings that we call "games." I mean board-games, card-games, ball-games, Olympic games, and so on. What is common to them all?— Don't say: "There *must* be something common, or they would not be called 'games'"—but *look and see* whether there is something common to all.—For if you look at them you will not see something that is common to *all*, but similarities, relationships, and a whole series of them at that. . . . And the result of this examination is: we see a complicated network of similarities and criss-crossing: sometimes overall similarities, sometimes similarities of detail.
>
> I can think of no better expression to characterize these similarities than "family resemblances"; for the various resemblances between members of the family: build, features, colour of eyes, gait, temperament, etc. etc. overlap and criss-cross in the same way. . . . One might say the concept "game" is a concept with blurred edges.
>
> *(pp. 31–34).*

Linguistics and Meaning

Sidestepping the issue of what meaning is exactly, linguists have attempted to describe how it is expressed in language. Early linguistic approaches to the study of meaning attempted to derive meaning relations based on the symbol relations in formal logic. Consider, for example, your reactions to the following:

1. Ice is frozen water.
2. That is hot ice.
3. If the lake is frozen it must have been less than 0 degrees Celsius.
4. Ice warms the hearts of fences.

(1) exemplifies the logical relation of identity, which in language is expressed as *synonymy,* or as paraphrase, two chunks of language with the same denotation. (2) contains a *contradiction* (given the truth of (1)), an opposition of meaning of two elements stated as equivalent. (3) expresses a truth, not one immediately obvious as in the first sentence, but one that follows from what a lake is and what freezing is, by *implication.* The fourth sentence is nonsense, until you realize that "ice" can refer to diamonds, and that a fence may be someone who makes money from stolen property. ((2) is no longer contradictory, since "hot" may mean stolen.) Here the semantic relations are anomaly or contradiction before the realization and *ambiguity* or double meaning after it.

The goal of semantic theory has been to discover a structure underlying all words such that these four relations would be immediately derivable. An example of such a structure, discussed in detail in what follows, involves definition of all words in terms of the same primitive elements. For example, if we define ice as water $<0°$ C, hot as $>30°$C, freezing as making ice, and a lake as a large body of water, the first sentence is reduced to identity, the second to contradiction, and the third to a truth through inference. For ambiguity, we must allow a second definition for ice, as diamonds, and then note that there are two definitions.

The hope was that in capturing these four logical relations, the structure would also capture other meaning relations. One such is *synthetic* statements, the truth of which may not be determined within the language alone but must be verified from external data. "Dogs have fur" is *analytic:* It expresses a definitional truth about dogs. "My dog is friendly" is synthetic: It can be verified not by definition of the word but by looking first to see whether I have a dog, and then at its disposition. The difficulty is that semantic theory cannot be autonomous if it must rely on the structure of things outside language and not expressed by language, but if it rules out treatment of such things from its domain, it rules out the greater part of language.

To discover the structure of linguistic meaning, we must begin by asking what the elements are that form the structure, or where to begin an analysis of an utterance or production of an utterance. (As we will see, the question of what is the *unit* [the indivisible element] is important not just in semantics but in all aspects of language,

---

Box 2.3   What is the Unit?

Suppose you were presented with a sentence in a language completely foreign to you. How do you determine its meaning? If you know the word boundaries and can spell, you can go to a dictionary and look up each word for its English equivalent. This suggests that the word is the unit. If the expression is an idiom ("cut it out" for instance), you will get very different results depending on whether you decide to use the whole word or whole phrase as the unit to look up.

This may be true too when (1) trying to comprehend your own language—what size unit do you look up in your mental dictionary? (2) when trying to learn a language for the first time—what size language chunk does a baby extract?

---

and not just from the linguistic perspective but also from the cognitive psychological perspective. It is probably easiest to understand the question from the psychological perspective, as Box 2.3 demonstrates.) There are several levels at which to approach meaning in language: meaning of words, meaning of elements that make up words, meaning of word groups or phrases, and nonlanguage meanings or innate ideas projected onto any and all of these levels. Ways of dealing with the structure of each of these are discussed in the following.

Words: Content and Function

Probably the most obvious choice as the unit of analysis is the word; a word can stand on its own, each word has an individual definition in the dictionary, and a word seems to have meaning by itself. That is not to say that combining words has no effect on meaning, but that, presumably, at the base there is word meaning and then regular rules can be found that will account for the meaning change produced by combinations.

Unfortunately, the word as unit of analysis fails, at least partially, because not all words can be defined independently of other words. It is convenient, therefore, to divide words into two classes; those words that carry meaning independently of their use, *content words* (or *open-class*), and those words that carry meaning only in relation to other words, *function words* (or *closed-class*). Content words can be loosely defined as those that would be left in a telegram—nouns, verbs, adjectives, and *adverbs* (descriptors of the action). Function words are the ones left out: *articles* or *determiners* (a, an, the), *pronouns* (this, that, he, you, I . . .), and helping verbs or *auxiliaries* ("have" as in "have written"). It is quite difficult to define a function word out of context (what does "and" mean?); what they seem to do is provide hints about which parts of the language go with which, and how. "Chair table" expresses no relation between the two; "chair on table" makes table a description for the location of the chair, "chair for table" suggests they were made for each other, "chair, table, and" indicates independent membership of the two in some list. "On," "for," and "and" suggest how to interpret the two words but do not have senses by themselves.

There are virtually an infinite number of content words; one could exist for every way of looking at any concept. Thus, they are sometimes called open-class; we are constantly adding new members to that class, either by learning a new vocabulary item or by creating one. (An interesting question very relevant to the issues of meaning is how new words come into existence. This is treated after the next section, in Box 2.4.) Function words, on the other hand, are limited; there are a small, fixed number in each language, and so are frequently called closed-class.

Content words, because they have a meaning independent of other words in the language, unlike function words, may be a more reasonable base for analysis of meaning. Presumably, use of function words depends on use of content words; therefore content words are more fundamental.

Morphemes

As just seen, words are not always good units of analysis for meaning because some words have no meaning independent of other words. Words also fail as the unit of analysis because frequently they appear to be made up of smaller units with their own meaning, which makes this smaller piece the unit. For example, in this paragraph there are "seen" (see+en), "words" (word+s), "cannot" (can+not), "meaning" (mean+ing), "independent" (in+depend+ent), "frequently" (frequent+ly), and so forth. Linguists define the *morpheme* as the smallest unit of a language that has meaning; sometimes a morpheme is a whole word, and sometimes it is smaller than a word and can be combined, creating new words, as Box 2.4 describes.

Analogous to content and function words, there are two kinds of morphemes, free morphemes and bound morphemes. A *free morpheme* is one that can stand on its own, a word. A *bound morpheme* is one affixed to free morphemes to color their meanings or functions. If a bound morpheme affixes to the front it is called a *prefix,* like "pre" in "prefix"; if it affixes to the back it is a *suffix,* like "s" in "kinds." (There are languages that put bound morphemes in the middle; these morphemes are called *infixes.* A current slang example of an infix in English is "abso-bloody-lutely," although note here that the infix is a free, not a bound morpheme.) Some bound morphemes convey content, like the suffix "logy" (study of), and some bound morphemes convey function, like the suffix "ly," which indicates that a descriptor goes with a verb (sings prettily) rather than a noun (pretty song).

Another common division is made between types of bound morphemes and reflects the effect that their addition has. *Derivational* morphemes are those that alter the part of speech of the root; "-ly" is derivational, for example, in that it changes an adjective to an adverb. Likewise "-ation" is a derivational suffix, converting verbs to nouns as in "derive→ derivation," "converse→ conversation," or "reform→ reformation." Morphemes may also modify the meaning of the root without altering its grammatical class, and in that case they are *inflectional* morphemes or *inflections.* Examples of these in English are the plural "s" or the past tense "-ed."

Box 2.4 What's in a Name?

Suppose a new object is discovered, and you are assigned the task of naming it. How would you go about selecting a name?

There are several methods of word creation. Probably most common is metaphor, taking an existing word that describes an object with similar properties and using its name. For example, in a classroom experiment the first name given for this figure was amoeba: . That was disallowed and the next suggestion used metaphorical morpheme combinations: amoeboid and polyblob. Along the same lines of extending a word's or morpheme's meaning to a new object, sometimes word creation extends a person's name to an activity associated with him. A caesarean section was the method by which Julius Caesar was born, for instance.

Other alternatives that make use of similar principles are *compounding* (combining free morphemes), *back-formation* (deriving pseudomorphemes), and *borrowing* (taking an already existing word, then called a *loan word,* from a foreign language). Blackboard and three-by-five card are examples of old and new compounds. In a true compound the individual parts lose their identities, yielding "green blackboards," which bothers no one. I have been asked for the five-by-seven three-by-five cards, so I feel justified in calling it a compound, but it is new, so the humor is still evident. Back-formation involves the assumption of *incorrect* morphological structure: The verb "edit" was derived from the noun "editor," using the false assumption that an editor is one who edits as a singer is one who sings. This makes "edit" a false morpheme, or pseudomorpheme, although of course it is now an accepted word of language. A more recent example followed the Watergate scandal: The newspapers published reports about "Billygate" and "Koreagate," also scandals, applying the -gate ending as thought it were a morpheme meaning scandal. (Of course, Watergate was not a scandal involving water.) Examples of borrowing are the words "sputnik," "piña colada," and "chic."

The last alternatives derive words from connecting sounds that evoke the concept. *Onomatopoeia* describes whole words that sound like their referents, like splash or cockadoodledoo. Sounds of parts of words may also evoke aspects of a referent: Brown (1958) demonstrated that subjects are consistent in assigning speech sounds with abrupt onsets ("p" for instance) to noises with abrupt onsets in a sound-naming task; subjects are able to match some synonyms across languages by sounds; and vowels with large mouth openings ("ah") are more likely to be used in words describing large objects than vowels with wee mouth openings ("ee"). This kind of sound match is called *sound symbolism.* Finally, at another level of abstraction, portions of words may be combined to give the sound sense of their components; smog was derived from smoke+fog, and evokes both, but this is by association of the sound with the word it is found in and the word, in turn, with the meaning.

Features, Componential Analysis, and Redundancy Rules

It is also possible to analyze meaning into units smaller than morphemes by considering features shared by the senses of many morphemes. In their frequently cited descriptions of the semantic component of language, Katz and Fodor (1963) and Katz and Postal (1964) depict the meaning of a word as an entry in a dictionary, consisting of semantic markers, distinguishers, and selectional restrictions. Their conception of an entry for the different senses of the word "bachelor" is depicted in Figure 2.1. *Semantic markers* are general meaning features that may be shared by other words and are indicated in the figure by parentheses. "Bachelor" is male, as are bulls, rams, men, and so on. *Distinguishers* are those aspects of sense that make the word unique; for example, in the first sense of bachelor in Figure 2.1, the distinguisher is "never married." This distinguishes "bachelor" from "husband," "widower," and "uncle," all of which share the markers "adult" and "male" and "human" but differ in distinguishers. For the first two the distinguishers would contain some note about marriage:

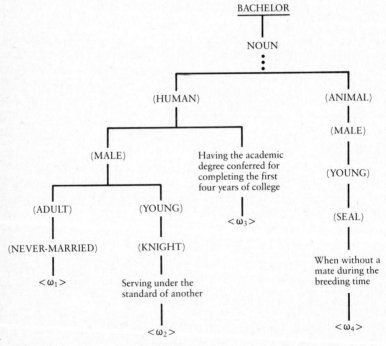

Figure 2.1 *The semantic marker structure of the dictionary entry for "bachelor." This word has four meanings, each represented by a subcategorization marker, like "noun," semantic markers like "human" and "animal," a distinguisher like "[having the academic degree conferred. . .], and selectional restrictions "$<\omega>$" describing how that sense of the word may combine with other words.*

From **An Integrated Theory of Linguistic Descriptions,** *p. 14, by J. J. Katz and P. Postal. Cambridge, MA: MIT Press, copyright (c) 1964 by the Massachusetts Institute of Technology. Reprinted by permission.*

A husband is currently married, and a widower has been married, but the entry for "uncle" would probably not mention marriage since uncles may or may not be married. Note that the distinction between distinguisher and marker is only one of generality (Bolinger, 1965). Markers are features of meaning shared by large numbers of words; distinguishers by small numbers (one).

Selectional restrictions are conditions for production and comprehension of the word when used in combination with other words. These are indicated by the angled brackets. They would rule as nonsense a combination like "the bachelor's wife" for the first reading, since bachelor implies not married and wife denies that. That combination could be considered sensible only for one of the other definitions of bachelor. $<\omega1>$, in the figure, would specify a condition for use of the word; if the condition is met, the interpretation is allowed. If not, it is restricted. In production if we started with "bachelor," we would be restricted in choice of possessions from including "wife" since it is marked as married.

Observe how this organization lends itself to the analysis of the four main logical relations of synonymy, ambiguity, contradiction, and implication. Synonyms would be those words that had identical or nearly identical marker structures for at least one reading (bachelor and unmarried man, for example). Ambiguities would arise when selection restrictions did not rule out some of the possible readings (the bachelor searched for a mate, for example, which could refer either to the human or the seal). Contradictions arise when markers directly oppose one another, as in bachelor's wife. And implications are indicated when the marker structure of one word is entailed in the marker structure of another (as in two-legged bachelor, where two legs is inferable from the definition of human).

This kind of analysis suggests a componential structure to the mental dictionary, with some of the components, the semantic markers, shared by many entries in the dictionary. These markers together with the distinguishers can be considered atoms of meaning, and if they are indeed employed in the semantic system, they greatly improve the efficiency of analysis of meaning. Consider, for example, a simple semantic system such as kinship terms: mother, father, son, daughter, sister, brother, aunt, uncle, grandmother. . . . In English three markers or features can be used to generate the entire system: gender (male, female), generation (two generations old, one generation old, same generation, next generation), and blood distance (sibling, cousin, second cousin . . .). One's cousin's daughter is female, next generation, and second cousin. An entire set of terms can thus be described in terms of three features, and properties associated with each feature (what males have in common, for example), need be mentioned only once, eliminating redundancy. An "uncle" can have a beard, but that information would be true for all males and therefore filed with "male," not "uncle." Beardedness could be determined for uncle by a chain, uncle→male→ has beard.

A componential analysis works most clearly for closed systems like the kinship system in which new terms are added only by reapplication of the three features. If semantic features are to be used to describe meaning in the whole language, a problem arises about which features are best. (For examples of the shortcomings of feature analysis in open systems, see Box 2.5.) Leech (1970) distinguished three kinds of classification systems within the language, each of which is best described by a different

---

Box 2.5   **How Many Features?**

One of the difficulties with componential analysis for an open system is the specificity of features necessary to account for the judgments speakers can make. Consider, for example, "The flagpole is tall," which is a perfectly acceptable utterance, and which could easily be accounted for by using feature analysis. Suppose the flagpole is knocked down, however, so it is lying on the ground. It is not acceptable to say "A flagpole lying on the ground is tall"; such a flagpole is instead "long." "Tall" contains a notion of verticalness, "long" contains a notion of horizontalness, "short" can be used to oppose either. Very few other English words need to contain a marker for vertical or horizontal or need a selectional restriction based on such a marker. (A further complication is that people retain their tallness even when lying down; long is appropriate only for *inanimate, horizontal* objects.)

A second example is restrictions on the word "break": machines or any of their parts can break, anything hard can break (bones, stems, etc.), spirits and hearts can break. A blade of grass can break, but a lawn composed of such blades cannot. And if a shirt "breaks" we say it tears, although its parts, the threads, break. How can such knowledge be incorporated into the selectional restrictions? Should there be a specific restriction for can and cannot break? If so, how many such restrictions would be necessary for each word? It is convenient to allocate such information to world knowledge and say it is not part of semantic theory, but it is certainly used in word selection and judgments of grammaticality. (The examples were generated by a computer program armed with some, but obviously not all, relevant world knowledge [Tartter, 1973].)

---

kind of feature *system*. The first entails items that can be distinguished by a *polar* $(+/-)$ feature, like male-female, mature-immature, human-nonhuman, and so on: These three will sort appropriately the terms cow, bull, woman, man, boy, girl, for example. The second refers to systems in which there are many instances of the same category, which may not be further analyzed. Individual animals such as lions, zebras, giraffes, and so on are each instances of the category animal but do not polarize into a set of discrete features. The last comprises those that can be easily ordered like the measurements, inch $<$ foot $<$ yard. Clearly the kinds of features associated with each of these systems will be quite different, and no features other than distinguishers are assumed for the second kind of system.

Features and Fuzzy Meanings

The preceding analysis, based on formal logic and a modification of the logical empiricist view, entailed the implicit assumption that rigid definitions of words in terms of features are possible—that something is either male or not male, and so forth. The existence of such rigid definitions for language units was questioned, as we saw, in ordinary language philosophy and in linguistics, leading to rejection by some of the linguistic marker approach. Allowing category definitions to have blurred edges, as has been suggested, enables the semantic system to account for native speaker judgments of the following statements as true, while marker theory indicates that they are false.

1. Coral is red and not red.
2. *Loosely speaking,* a whale is a fish.
3. Mark Spitz is a *regular* fish.
4. *Technically speaking,* Nixon is a Quaker.
5. *To a midget,* Dick Cavett is tall.
   (Lakoff, 1972, 1973).

Strict application of logic should render (1) anomalous; it contains a logical contradiction. However, most people would say that it was sensible and more than that, true. Because there are degrees of redness, the decision is not all or none, and "red and not red" does not indicate a contradiction. In the other sentences omission of the underlined words (called *hedges,* referring to "looseness"), would render the sentence false. Contradictions are immediate in the marker structure: a whale is a mammal and that is not a fish; Mark Spitz is a human and humans are not fish; Nixon prolonged a war, but Quakers promote peace, and prolonging a war is not consistent with promotion of peace; whereas it is not clear what the lower limit of tallness is (5'10", 6' 2", 6'7"), it is certainly greater than 5'7", Dick Cavett's height. On the other hand, *with* the hedges, each of the sentences is potentially true. Whales have a number of fishlike features—body shape, fins, living in water; humans can be called fishlike if they seem at home in the water; Nixon was born of Quaker parents even if he did not act like a Quaker; and tallness is relative to the observer.

Lakoff suggested that feature markers cannot be all-or-none, as the marker structure discussed earlier implies, but rather have a degree of truth value. The truth of an utterance is indicated by summing the truth values for each feature and determining whether the sum is greater or less than some criterion. A hedge can shift the criterion, making an unacceptable level now acceptable, as with Dick Cavett's height, or by changing the attention paid to particular features.

It is convenient for the latter to divide the features into two classes, features that define conditions under which a word may be used, and features that are characteristic of the use but do not define it. For example, having feathers could be a defining feature of birds; if an object does not have feathers, it is not a bird. (Consider, however, whether this makes a feather pillow a bird, and a plucked chicken not a bird!) Most birds are about six inches tall and can fly, but ostriches are birds although they are taller and cannot fly. These then are characteristic features but not defining features. In Lakoff's analysis, the hedge "technically speaking" indicates truth when the defining features *only* are true (note that the sentence "technically speaking, a robin is a bird" is silly—a robin is a bird even when we are not speaking technically); the hedge "regular" indicates truth *only* when the characteristic features hold (Lakoff suggests that the truth of characteristic features only may be a defining feature of metaphor); and the hedges "strictly speaking" and "loosely speaking" indicate truth when some characteristic features *and* some defining features hold, fewer of each needed for "loosely" and "strictly." Thus, by including in the semantic markers the distinction between characteristic and defining features, we can account for additional intuitions about meaningfulness in the language; a marker structure using only defining features would incorrectly condemn metaphors and hedged statements to the realm of anomaly.

Meanings from Word Groups

In the last section we suggested that the morpheme may be too large to be the unit of meaning; there are also instances where it seems too small. Consider the sentences: "John was killed with a knife," "A knife killed John," and "John was killed by means of a knife." The concept of a knife being the instrument of death is conveyed through three different phrases: "killed with a knife," "a knife killed," "killed by means of a knife," and in a fourth in this sentence, roughly, "knife as instrument of death." In which word or morpheme is this concept contained? Use of words or morphemes to analyze meaning fails to capture the similarity of these phrases, implying that there are basic meanings in language chunks greater than words, in the *semantic relation* (also called *case* relation) between the verb and the noun. This is discussed further in Chapter 4, but it is wise to be aware of the possibility at this stage.

Another way linguists have categorized meanings of utterances as a whole has been in terms of the intended effect by the speaker on the listener or environment, called *speech acts* (Austin, 1962/1970; Searle, Kiefer, and Bierwisch, 1980). The idea was introduced by Wittgenstein (1958), who suggested that speakers can play the following "games" with language:

> Giving orders, and obeying them—Describing the appearance of an object, or giving its measurements—Constructing an object from a description (a drawing)—Reporting an event—Speculating about an event—Forming and testing a hypothesis—Presenting the results of an experiment in tables and diagrams—Making up a story; and reading it—Play-acting—Singing catches—Guessing riddles—Making a joke; telling it—Solving a problem in practical arithmetic—Translating from one language to another—Asking, thinking, cursing, greeting, praying.
>
> *(pp. 11–12).*

In speech act theory it is assumed that the minimal unit of communication is not a word or a sentence but the performance of an act such as asking a question, giving a command, thanking, and so on. The act may take various forms or use various language structures for expression: "Where is the salt?" may express an order to pass the salt, although in the form of a question. The response "two inches from my right hand" indicates that the hearer did not properly grasp the meaning of the speaker's utterance (or that (s)he did and was trying to be funny). All utterances of a language may be described as containing an *illocutionary force* (the intent of the speaker of stating, ordering, questioning) and *propositional content.* "You will leave the room," "Please leave the room," and "Will you leave the room?" all express the same proposition, but one states, another directs, and another questions; each has a different illocutionary force. A speech act may be expressed directly: "Please pass the salt" has the structure and content and intent of a command; "I promise you I will come" has the form and content of a promise. A speech act may also be expressed indirectly— "Where is the salt?" as we have already seen, can express a command although in the form of a question; "I will come" may imply a promise although it is not explicitly stated. Note that by considering language as speech acts, as with considering semantic relations, some similarities between different phrases are captured, and some differences between seemingly identical statements are noted.

Conceptual Primes, Phrases, and Jackendoff's Analysis

In our discussion of semantics so far we have hedged on the relationship between linguistic meaning and conceptual structure, discussing words as labels for conceptual elements. Moreover, since the language we have been using is English, the conceptual structure derived—the markers, defining features, and characteristics features—may all be peculiar to our culture (Celsius is probably not a universal concept). Indeed, if the linguistic relativity hypothesis is true, conceptual structures of speakers of different languages will be different, perhaps because they are organized with respect to markers derived from that language.

An alternative to both linguistic relativity and language-particular marker structures is to assume that there may be at least some innate ideas, basic human conceptual elements expressed universally in languages (Jackendoff, 1978). The proposals have yet to be verified cross-linguistically, but they are interesting to consider here. Note also that because we are looking at innate ideas rather than at language elements, their expression in language may occur at many levels. For example, in English we have a notion of countable things, or individual objects as opposed to a mass. We can refer to a cat or a flower, or two cats or two flowers, concentrating on the individual object. However, we cannot talk about two milks or flours; this kind of object is conceived of as a whole. The distinction between countable objects and mass is expressed not only in definitions of particular words but also in the allowable combinations. It is possible that a countable thing versus mass distinction is an innate idea and may be used cross-linguistically, with other cultures considering different objects as countable or massed.

Another fundamental distinction could be between real things and representations of things. Representations include dreams, pictures, images, and ideas, and we judge the truth value of a representation differently from the truth value of a description of a real object. For example, in "John put Mary in the garbage can. She had a black eye," Mary has a black eye. In "John put Mary in the picture. She has a black eye," it is the picture of Mary that contains a black eye; Mary may or may not have a black eye. To interpret the meaning of the statement "she has a black eye," we need to know whether we are talking about a thing or a representation, a notion conveyed in an earlier sentence but important for our interpretation of the current sentence. Again, we might expect to find a differentiation of the real form from the representation across cultures, although there may be different notions of what is real and what is representation (dreams in some cultures, for example, might be considered real).

Another universal concept might be movement. Movement distinguishes the sentences "The plane is on the runway" and "the plane approaches the runway" (implied motion), both of which convey location. Movement also distinguishes meaning at the word level: "Sits" and "on" share a feature of no motion, while "go" and "toward" imply motion. Note that there is intuitive plausibility in the suggestion that important perceptual, conceptual constructs like causality, time, movement, and place, which underlie our nonlinguistic representation of the world, also underlie our linguistic representation of the world. Note also that the assumption that these innate ideas could affect meaning at many levels of language (word, sentence, paragraph), suggests that the "semantic" interpretations must occur repeatedly in ongoing language processing—to interpret morphemes, sentences, and large language chunks. As we will see in chapters 4 and 5, this semantic analysis occurring at many levels is exactly what Jackendoff, among others, has suggested.

The Scope of Semantic Theory

As the discussion so far indicates, it is difficult to talk about meaning or semantics without getting into the manner in which combining words affects their meanings. Traditionally, regular rules for the effects of word combination are considered the realm of syntax; indeed, semantics has been *negatively* described as those aspects of meaning remaining to be explained after syntactic analysis (Katz and Fodor, 1963; Katz and Postal, 1964). A second bound on the scope of semantics that has been commonly invoked by linguists is the effect of *extralinguistic knowledge:* Setting, knowledge about the real world, and so on, are considered irrelevant to the study of semantics since sentences can be understood in isolation, counterfactual information can be understood, and language can be an independent symbol system not based on real world referents (Leech, 1970; Katz and Fodor, 1963; Katz and Postal, 1964; but see Jackendoff, 1978). (Note that this can provide a problem for interpretation of synthetic sentences!)

Each of these limitations on the scope of semantics can lead to difficulties in deriving a complete meaning analysis. We have already alluded to some of the problems of treating syntax and semantics separately, as when the same speech act or same semantic relation is expressed by two different word combinations. Katz and Postal (1964) and Katz and Fodor (1963) attempted to circumvent these problems in part by using selectional restrictions to produce the correct sense of the morphemes when combined in sentences, and in part by assigning meaning in combination through projection rules. *Projection rules* are the second part of the semantic component (the first part is the dictionary already described) that map meanings on syntactic structures (what parts of the sentence form the subject, e. g.) derived by the base component. For example, "Pete threw a bachelor's party" could be interpreted (loosely) as follows: Pete (human, male, proper name), threw ("made" when what is thrown is not an object, "formed" when what is thrown is clay, "caused to fly through the air" when what is thrown is an object), bachelor (as before), 's (ownership), party (occasion of a group of people with a common purpose). "Pete" and "party" both restrict the possible interpretations of "bachelor," and "party" restricts the possible interpretations of "throw." The underlying structure could then be roughly paraphrased as "a particular male human made an occasion for a group of single males." Jackendoff proposed instead that there might be several stages of semantic analysis interlaced with syntactic analysis, reasons for which will be clearer after we discuss syntax.

The second commonly found restriction on the scope of semantic analysis, the disregarding of effects of speaker's intention, hearer's presuppositions, shared world knowledge, and so forth, results in failure to explain comprehension or production of sentences in many instances, particularly when the sentence occurs with others in a paragraph or conversation. For example, consider the following paragraph (loosely paraphrased from Schank, personal communication): "George was on his way to a restaurant. After a brief encounter with a pickpocket (of which he was unaware) he arrived and ordered his dinner. Poor George! He spent the evening washing dishes." Most readers from a Western culture have probably inferred that George's wallet was stolen and that he was asked to wash dishes to pay for his dinner as a result. That information is contained in *none of the words or word combinations*—it is apparent because of our knowledge of what pickpockets do, where money is carried, what money is used for, and standard restaurant behaviors. If such knowledge is considered to be out of the realm of semantics, the meaning of the paragraph is unexplained.

One other example: Evaluate the likelihood that someone would make either of the following two utterances under everyday circumstances:

1. The pencil is by the door of the Empire State Building.
2. The Empire State Building is the one with the pencil by its door.

Both can be interpreted without difficulty, but the second is less plausible—a person would never use such an insignificant characteristic to mark such a large, distinct object. (If you can't find the Empire State Building, knowing it is near a pencil is not going to help!) If it excludes world knowledge and the knowledge that the speaker and hearer assume the other has, a semantic theory fails to account for some regularities of interpretation and judgment that most language users can make.

Considerations of plausibility for a given context and set of communications are usually studied as *pragmatics,* the study of the practical use of signs and symbols (see, for example, Morris, 1964). Pragmatic issues most often arise with respect to discourse—paragraphs or conversations—as our examples illustrate. Violations of pragmatic considerations do not usually produce meaninglessness or sentence anomaly, as do violations of selectional restrictions, but rather may produce overly redundant, boring discourse, or disconnected, difficult to follow discourse, or just odd sentence selection, if the speaker generates sentences without appropriately assessing the hearer's knowledge. These violations are considered out of the scope of semantic theory since the sentences generated are still interpretable.

Psychological Issues

Psychologists have approached the issue of meaning from three positions: meaning as association, meaning as internal sensation, and meaning as an abstract, organized symbol system. Here we will outline these approaches, insofar as they contribute to our general understanding of the ways to view meaning. In Chapter 3 we will discuss in detail experiments and models for the internal sensation and abstract system approaches, the processing approaches of cognitive psychology and artificial intelligence.

Behaviorism and Associations

The behaviorist approach to meaning is akin to the ordinary language philosopher's approach: Meaning is the learned association or habit strength between a fragment of language and other such fragments, or between language and sensation. The associations that language stimulates have been said to take one of three forms: a *response*—micromuscular movements that mirror the greater movements normally made to the referent (Watson, 1930/1970); a *mediating response*—a covert, low-energy set of behaviors evoked by a verbal unit and preceding an overt response (Osgood, Suci, and Tannenbaum, 1967); or a *behavioral disposition*—an overt response in terms of other language (the meaning of a question is to answer the question) or in terms of nonverbal activity (the meaning of a command to pass the salt is passing the salt) (Brown, 1958; Skinner, 1957). These three views share an interest in determining how overt or covert verbal behaviors come under control of particular environmental stimuli.

Since behaviorism defines meaning in terms of prior associations and habit strengths, it is important to understand the means by which such associations arise. In *classical conditioning* we begin with a very few innate stimulus-response connections, reflexes. For example, food innately causes salivation, or light innately causes a visual sensation. Innate implies unlearned or unconditioned, and a reflex can be described as a connection between an unconditioned stimulus (US) and an unconditioned response (UR). If another stimulus is repeatedly presented with a US it will, after a while, by itself, elicit something like the UR. For example, after repeatedly receiving food simultaneously with hearing a tone, an animal will learn an association, tone-food, and will salivate when it hears the tone without the food. Similarly hearing "red" whenever experiencing red light will cause an association between the word and the sensation, so that the word alone may come to elicit something like the sensation. Once the connection has been learned, the formerly neutral stimulus is called the conditioned stimulus (CS), and the response it engenders, the conditioned response (CR). A distinction is made between the UR and the CR since the CS does not generally produce all the responses that the US does: A dog will learn to salivate to a bell, but not to chew as it would food. We may get an image of red or faint brain activity as we get when we see red, but we do not have the full-blown sensation from the word alone. Thus, through classical conditioning, words may become associated with sensations normally prompted by objects.

A second way that associations are formed is through *operant conditioning,* where what is learned is an association between a behavior and its consequences. If a behavior is followed by certain stimuli, it tends to be repeated *(reinforcement)* (a hug or attention when the baby first says "Mama" is likely to cause the child to say it again); if it is followed by other stimuli it tends not to be repeated *(punishment)* (a slap or scolding when the child utters the first curse is likely to stop the child from saying it again, at least to the parents). If most of our utterances are produced in order to get someone to do something, we will learn the habits of the other's linguistic community, since unless we phrase our requests appropriately, they are unlikely to be reinforced with compliance. Because much of language is behavior emitted by the speaker, or behavior to be emitted by the hearer in response to the speaker (passing the salt after the request, for example), there is ample opportunity for linguistic behaviors to become operantly conditioned.

One aspect of both operant and classical conditioning relevant to our discussion of the nature of meaning is that subjects seem to learn more than the specific association conditioned. This phenomenon is called *generalization.* We will automatically apply the word "red" not just to the specific hue we first heard the word for but to a variety of hues similar to that one. Similarly, by generalization we may learn to apply the structure for a sentence like "my stomach hurts" to other situations, generating "my hand hurts." The reason generalization is important for language is that, as we have seen, in language more is learned than a precise word-object connection.

In terms of the kinds of associations that may be formed in language, Skinner (1957) defined three categories: mands, tacts, and autoclitics. A *mand* (comMand) is a verbal behavior under the control of an appropriate response on the part of the listener; "Please pass the salt" is an example. If a speaker desires salt and correctly emits the sentence, (s)he is likely to get the salt, strengthening the verbal behavior. The person who passes the salt is reinforced with a verbal "thank you"—this is reinforcing because of previous association of this utterance with tangible reinforcers, like tips. Once a mand has become a verbal habit, the utterance itself may produce its own reinforcement because of association with previous successes in obtaining one's wishes. This development allows the generalization of mands to situations in which reinforcement is unlikely, as in addressing infants, animals, or inanimate objects.

A *tact* is a verbal behavior under the control of the external environment, typically strengthened or evoked by an object or a characteristic of an object or event. Tacts can be considered akin to content words, the relation of the word to its referent established by classical conditioning and generalization. Further generalization of tacts produces *extended tacts,* or names for class concepts like "house," which, as we have seen, do not have to have a specific shape, address, etc., or like "game," which may apply to different things only through family resemblance. The production of extended tacts is accomplished by a process of *abstraction,* which is peculiar to verbal behavior because "the necessary contingency [to elicit the tact for the class concept] does not require a practical consequence common to all instances [of that concept] via the same process. The verbal response chair is as abstract as red. It is not controlled by any single stimulus" (Skinner, 1957, p. 109).

Autoclitics are verbal behaviors based on or dependent upon other verbal behaviors. (This class of verbal behaviors seems the same as function words.) These serve the function of narrowing the reaction of the listener by indicating a more specific relation between a response and its controlling stimulus. The circumstances under which "the book" is uttered are different from those in which "a book" is uttered, and this difference is learned by the speaker and controls the use of the article; that is, use of function words is learned as a verbal habit.

As Chomsky (1959) has pointed out, there are difficulties with the behaviorist analysis of meaning. The two principal ones are the lack of attention to specific effects of human biological makeup in language behaviors, and the general circularity of definitions of stimulus control, response, and reinforcement for verbal behaviors. With regard to the first point, it must be observed that the same stimulus situations that hold for human beings hold for animals; indeed, the application of reinforcement principles is based on that observation since these principles were first established for animals in the laboratory. Yet, it is only humans who naturally acquire language, learn to make verbal responses, utilize extended tacts, and so on. This is probably because humans are geared to attend to stimuli differently from other animals, as well as being geared to use this information differently. Discussion of stimulus control as the principal determinant of meaning assignment necessarily ignores important factors in language behaviors.

The second point is that the behaviorist analysis of meaning completely skirts the meaning issues, has little descriptive power, and little explanatory power for language behaviors. A stimulus is defined as controlling if verbal behaviors are emitted in its presence; if different verbal behaviors are emitted to the same stimulus, it is assumed that different aspects of the stimulus are controlling the behavior. (The same problem occurs in ordinary language philosophy, where meaning is defined as use.) Thus, stimulus control can be decided only *a posteriori* by using the verbal response. Moreover, for every verbal response a different stimulus is assumed, so enumeration of the stimuli does nothing more to simplify language description than a list of the language behaviors. The concept of response or verbal behavior is just as loosely specified. Skinner avoids the issue of unit of verbal behavior, because unit size can vary with controlling stimulus. Since controlling stimulus is defined by verbal behavior, and verbal behavior is defined in terms of controlling stimulus, it is unclear how to begin a behaviorist analysis of language. Finally, reinforcement is not independently defined in the language situation. Reinforcement is what increases the probability of occurrence of a behavior, but given that the probability of a verbal behavior is determined in part by these fuzzy stimulus controls and that the variety of verbal behaviors is so great, it is difficult to recognize and isolate the reinforcers. This situation is further muddied by Skinner's acknowledgment that some stimulus controls and reinforcers are covert; for example, a child can be self-reinforced when (s)he correctly imitates a sound, but why or how or what is the reinforcer is not made clear.

Nevertheless, researchers working from Skinner's formulations, including Skinner himself, have produced behaviors in animals that simulate verbal behaviors and have also produced some language skills in people who, for some reason, have not naturally acquired language. However, it is possible that these behaviors only share surface characteristics with human language and do not reflect true acquisition of meaning, as we think we know it. These data and their interpretations will be discussed in later chapters.

Cognitive Approaches

Cognitive psychology offers two basic conceptualizations of meaning: meaning as mental imagery and meaning as activation of a portion of semantic memory, which is organized in terms of linguistic features of some size, akin to those described in the section on linguistics. These will be discussed in detail in Chapter 3, together with evidence supporting or refuting them. They are introduced here to complete the outline of conceptions of meaning.

The notion that meaning is a mental image dates back to Aristotle, who proposed that words were signs for thoughts that in turn were mental copies of objects in the environment. Few psychologists currently believe that images *are* precise copies of external objects. In part, this is because there are many images for which there are no objects, like unicorn, and many "objects" for which there are no images, like democracy—the same problems as with meaning as reference. Nevertheless, the concept of some form of nonverbal, sensation-related interpretation of words and thought is becoming increasingly popular (Paivio and Begg, 1981; Kosslyn, 1980). The principal advantages to such a scheme are that it coincides with people's introspections about their thoughts, it provides a mode for thinking that is not language-based and thus possibly avoids the linguistic relativity difficulty, and it offers a noncircular definition of meaning in that linguistic units are defined in terms of something other than other linguistic units. As we shall see, it also accounts for data not readily explicable by a strictly verbal analysis; for example, that it is harder to image detail on small objects than on large (Kosslyn, 1980), a result inexplicable if the details are mental "words" located on a mental list.

The second approach to meaning taken in cognitive psychology defines individual meanings in terms of abstract symbols, essentially a psychological realization of some of the linguistic approaches discussed earlier. There are two considerations that differentiate theoretically the linguistic and psychological positions, both involving flexibility within the semantic processing system. The first of these is that the linguistic conceptualization implies that the semantic system is passive: Each word evokes a meaning marker, and adjoining words limit interpretations on that marker in a rule-governed way. In the psychological conceptualization, some aspects of semantic memory may be active; for example, we probably do not have each number stored individually (that would require infinite storage capacity!) but have a number of them stored along with rules on how to interpret or generate nonstored ones as needed (Miller, 1978). In the psychological conceptualization, too, the size of the unit does not have to remain fixed; it is functionally defined and varies from task to task. For example, in normal comprehension, words like "biology" are probably not divided into their component morphemes but accessed directly. However, if the word is unfamiliar (ichthiology? ornithology? oncology? for some readers, perhaps), it may be understood by breaking it down into smaller chunks. Morphemes (and pseudo-morphemes like the "gate" in Watergate; see Box 2.4) can also take on psychological relevance in word creation. Thus, it seems that there are always multiple levels of meaning to which we can have access; which level we access depends on the task.

Summary

In this chapter we have examined basic issues in discussing and defining meaning. We have seen that words have an indirect relationship to external reality but word meaning is still governed by, or still governs, in some way, the conceptualization of reality. We have looked at ways of discussing meaning—defining it in terms of primitive or nonlinguistic features, defining it in terms of evoked sensations or habit strengths, defining it in terms of intentions of the speaker, and defining it without defining it, in terms of fuzzy resemblances or use in the language.

In the next chapter we will continue our investigation of meaning, but focusing on *how* meaning may be derived in the performance of language tasks. In describing the processing of meaning in language, we will derive a final description of meaning, the processing model.

REFERENCES

Alston, W. P. (1964). *Philosophy of Language*. Englewood Cliffs, NJ: Prentice-Hall.

Austin, J. L. (1962/1970). *How to Do Things With Words*. NY: Oxford University Press.

Bolinger, D. (1965). The atomization of meaning. *Language, 41,* 555–573.

Brown, R. (1958). *Words and Things*. NY: The Free Press.

Chomsky, N. (1959). Review of *Verbal Behavior* by B. F. Skinner. *Language, 35,* 26–58.

Jackendoff, R. (1978). Grammar as evidence for conceptual structure. In M. Halle, J. Bresnan, & G. A. Miller (Eds.). *Linguistic Theory and Psychological Reality,* (pp. 201–228). Cambridge, MA: MIT Press.

Katz, J. J., & Fodor, F. A. (1963). The structure of a semantic theory. *Language, 39,* 170–210.

Katz, J. J., & Postal, P. M. (1964). *An Integrated Theory of Linguistic Descriptions*. Cambridge, MA: MIT Press.

Kosslyn, S. M. (1980). *Image and Mind*. Cambridge, MA: Harvard University Press.

Lakoff, G. (1972). Hedges: A study of meaning criteria and the logic of fuzzy concepts. In *Papers from the Eighth Regional Meeting,* (pp. 183–228), Chicago Linguistics Society.

———. (1973). A study in meaning criteria and the logic of fuzzy concepts. *Journal of Philosophical Logic, 2,* 458–508.

Leech, J. N. (1970). *Towards a Semantic Description of English*. Bloomington, IN: Indiana University Press.

Miller, G. A. (1978). Semantic relations among words. In M. Halle, J. Bresnan, & G. A. Miller (Eds.). *Linguistic Theory and Psychological Reality* (pp. 60–118). Cambridge, MA: MIT Press.

Morris, C. (1964). *Signification and Significance*. Cambridge, MA: MIT Press.

Osgood, C. E., Suci, G. J., & Tannenbaum, P. H. (1967). *The Measurement of Meaning*. Urbana, IL: University of Illinois Press.

Quine, W. (1960). *Word and Object*. Cambridge, MA: MIT Press.

Paivio, A. & Begg, I. (1981). *Psychology of Language.* Englewood Cliffs, NJ: Prentice-Hall.

Searle, J. R., Kiefer, F., & Bierwisch, M. (1980). *Speech Act Theory and Pragmatics.* Dordrecht, Holland: D. Reidel Publishing Company.

Skinner, B. F. (1957). *Verbal Behavior.* Englewood Cliffs, NJ: Prentice-Hall.

Tartter, V. (1973). Computers and natural language processing. Unpublished honors thesis, Brown University.

Vygotsky, L. (1962). *Thought and Language.* Cambridge, MA: MIT Press.

Watson, J. B. (1930/1970). *Behaviorism.* Chicago: University of Chicago Press.

Whorf, B. L. (1956). *Language, Thought, and Reality.* In J. B. Carroll (Ed.). Cambridge, MA: MIT Press.

Wittgenstein, L. (1958). *Philosophical Investigations* (3rd ed.). Translated by G. E. M. Anscombe. NY: Macmillan Company.

STUDY QUESTIONS

1. Briefly explain the difference between:
   (a) abstract-concrete
   (b) sign-symbol
   (c) meaning-reference
   (d) connotation-denotation
   (e) literal-figurative
   (f) analytic-synthetic

   For each distinction see if you can make up your own example from human communication to illustrate.

2. Discuss the problem of mental definition of a word like "dog." Is it possible to come up with a definition? Why or why not? Will the definition necessarily correspond to perceptual reality or is it culturally determined—that is, would you expect to see exactly the same concept expressed in other languages? In your answer consider Quine's meaning-as-use concept, Wittgenstein's family resemblance concept, Lakoff's fuzzy meanings, and Whorf's linguistic determinism.

3. Consider how Katz' and Fodor's linguistic marker structure and the behaviorist view of meaning each correspond to the philosophical notions of family resemblance and linguistic relativity. (This is a *thought* question—describe briefly the two models and the two philosophical positions. Then try to decide, logically, what the implications of the models are with respect to the philosophical positions.)

3

Semantic Memory

Psychological Issues

What does "brank" mean? Presumably you responded quickly "I don't know" or "It is not a word." How did you know that you do not know that word? Did you compare it with each word in your mental dictionary, find that it did not match, and respond after you reached the last word? (What is the last word in your mental dictionary?) If you know 5000 words (a low estimate), and it took you five seconds (a high estimate) to decide you had never seen "brank" before, you mentally compared 1000 words in one second! If you think that is impossible (you are probably right), how *did* you know that "brank" is not a word you have experienced? A task like this one, in which a subject decides whether or not an item is a word, is called a *lexical decision task,* and it is a task we perform readily by using our mental representations of our language.

One obvious way out of the difficulty of scanning more than 1000 words per second in making lexical decisions is to search only some of the words you know; for example, to turn to the "b" section of the mental dictionary and compare only words beginning with "b," and so forth. This process implies that the mental dictionary, like Webster's, is organized alphabetically, and, as we shall see, there is some evidence for that from production and priming tasks. A *production task* is one in which the subject is asked to produce as many words as possible given some instruction, like "list 10 words beginning with 'b,'" and if you try it you will see that it is easy. A *priming task* is one in which the subject is attempting to recall, guess, or detect a word, and is primed or prompted; for example, "The word you're looking for begins with a 'b.'" You may have noticed that when you have a word "on the tip of your tongue" (that is, when you are in the *tip of the tongue state*), a clue about the first sound will frequently provide you with the word you are looking for. Certainly, in doing crossword puzzles, getting the first letter through a crossing word can be a breakthrough (be a prime) in recovering a difficult synonym.

So, is the mental dictionary organized alphabetically? What is the first word that comes into your mind: "cat" ——? According to Webster's, the not-very-rare alphabetic neighbors of "cat" are "casualty" and "cataclysm," neither of which was likely to have been your response. Given such *association tasks,* most people produce words with similar meanings (cat-dog, mother-father), suggesting that the mental dictionary is organized in terms of meanings. This would be a useless organization for Webster's since usually we use dictionaries to determine what an unknown word means, and with an organization by meaning we would not know where to begin our search. But normally in speaking we do know the words we will use, and we have some idea of what we want to say; that is, we also know the meaning, and so a search that begins with meaning and finds appropriate words on that basis could be effective. (This type of organization is what libraries use: If you are trying to find this book in a library you would probably start in the sciences library, then go to the psychology section, and so on. And if the book is out, its neighbors on the shelves are probably on this same topic and can be used instead. This organization is based on hierarchical meaning—psycholinguistics is a part of psychology, which is a part of science.) Note that this organization suggests that mental meanings are structured like Katz' and Fodor's (1963) lexicon with units smaller than words; animal is part of the meaning of cat and of dog, and science is part of the meaning of psychology, and these underlie their respective "locations" in memory. Note also that while this kind of organization makes good sense for production, it might not for comprehension: If someone says a sentence we must understand it, find its meaning. Presumably we do this by "looking up" the words used; if to look them up we must know the meaning, we cannot begin. Of course, it is possible that for speaking we start with a meaning and go to a word, and for understanding we start with a word and retrieve the meaning. However, this returns us to the lexical decision problem: If mental words are organized with respect to meanings, how do we avoid performing an exhaustive comparison of a spoken word with all the words we know to determine whether we know it?

The questions raised here have been addressed experimentally, and the answers or suggestions at answers that the experiments have produced are treated in this chapter. To summarize the issues: Are words and meanings different? If so, what is the mental representation of meanings, and how do words connect with them? How is our mental dictionary organized? How do we use it? What information about the word or meaning (first letter, partial sense like animal, and so on) is in it? As we have already indicated, the answers to some extent seem to depend on the tasks the subjects are asked to perform and become complicated—there are so many language tasks we can perform!

Evidence on the Nature of Meaning

As we discussed in Chapter 2, there are three general approaches to the nature of meaning: Meaning is a response, meaning is an image, and meaning is an abstract symbol system. There is evidence for each of these positions, and it is possible that for some words or thoughts, in some tasks, any of these three meaning representations may be used, or some combination of them may be used. By far, the most evidence exists for the position that meaning is an abstract symbol system. The other, weaker positions are discussed first, and then we concentrate on the more generally accepted position.

The Medium Is the Muscle

The *motor theory,* suggested first by Watson (1930/1970), holds that when we hear an utterance such as "eat a hamburger" our bodies automatically respond with covert movements appropriate for actually doing what the utterance describes. We understand the utterance by recognizing the faint muscular movements as those which, if magnified, would constitute biting, swallowing, and so forth.

Some evidence for the existence of such covert responses is offered in an experiment performed by Jacobson (1932). Jacobson attached electrodes to various muscles in the subject's body and measured their responses following instructions to imagine performing certain actions such as swinging a golf club. The subject was instructed specifically not to move but just to imagine performing the action. He found that only those muscles needed to perform the action responded, although their response was smaller than the response that would have been made had the action actually been carried out. Thus, there is evidence for covert responses that could be used in interpreting commands. Note, however, that the existence of such movements says nothing about whether the subject "knows" about them or uses them for interpretation.

Several other notes of caution must be sounded with respect to assuming that these covert responses are meaning. First, as Brown (1958) pointed out, in this task the subject was specifically instructed to imagine performing the action, and further, was likely to have had an unusual awareness of his muscles since electrodes had been attached and he had been specifically instructed to suppress movement. In normal language listening situations we may not be as aware of the potential responses of our bodies as this subject was, and we may not spontaneously, without instructions to image or suppress movement, imagine ourselves to be performing the actions. Second, again as Brown pointed out, the language sample used in this experiment cannot be considered representative of language in general; the sentences were all commands ("swing a golf club") involving obvious actions, and it is unclear which motor movements would be involved in imagining other types of utterances. For example, asked to imagine the sentence "John kicked Mary," would the subject's motor responses follow the aggressive movements of John, or the defensive actions of Mary, or both simultaneously? For utterances without specific actions like "the apple is red," which muscles should move?

Of course, some of these problems can be eliminated simply by extending the notion of motor theory beyond muscular response to include any covert physiological response, including a mini-activation of all or part of the neural pathways used in perceiving external stimuli (such as redness) or internal stimuli (such as hunger), or in producing particular actions. This extension would avoid the previous objections since all of the physiological pathways normal for sensing a real apple (a smell, a taste, a touch, an appearance) could be slightly activated by the word "apple" (through classical conditioning, perhaps?) with the appropriate color channel somewhat more activated for a sentence like "the apple is red." Similarly, the pathways that would be used in observing John kicking Mary could be mildly activated by the sentence "John kicked Mary," the activations providing the interpretation. The extension would also skirt Brown's last objection, that "any theory that equates meaning with particular muscle actions must predict that words will lose their meaning when relevant muscles are immobilized [and that] no theory is really willing to stand by that prediction" (p. 98). The neural pathways that respond *after* the response of the muscle or sense organ *can* respond without this prior activation, allowing central neural actions even with peripheral paralysis.

Finally, it is important to note that although Jacobson's study provides evidence for motor meaning only of actions and not of other types of language, there may be good reason for considering actions, which are frequently described by the verb, to be the basis for meaning representations. Indeed, as we shall see in Chapter 5, several comprehensive theories of language processing begin sentence interpretation with the verb (Schank, 1972) or take as the memory "unit" a verb-centered idea, called a *proposition* (Anderson and Bower, 1973). These theories suggest, perhaps, different processes in verb identification and understanding than for other words. Perhaps these "different processes" are the reflexive muscular movements at least for those verbs that describe actions?

The Medium Is the Image

In attempting to circumvent problems raised by a muscle-movement interpretation of meaning, the possibility was raised that mini-activation of sensory pathways is meaning. The mini-activation hypothesis then becomes indistinguishable from "image" conceptions of meaning that hold that at least one form of understanding of at least some words and sentences is a nonarbitrary concrete representation based on sensory experience. (Whether the image results from activation of parts of primary sensory pathways like the visual system is arguable, but at least one image theorist, Kosslyn [personal communication], believes so.)

Much of the evidence supporting an image position comes from the use of a verification task. In a *verification task* subjects are presented with sentences and asked to determine whether the sentence is true or false. The sentences always state something subjects should know, so the question becomes not how many they get wrong as in a normal true-false test, but how hard it is for them to arrive at the right answer. Difficulty can be measured in a number of ways; the most common is *reaction time* (RT), which is how long it takes a subject to make the correct response—the harder the question, the more processing involved, and the longer it takes to respond.

"A robin has wings"—true or false? How did you arrive at the answer? One way might be to evoke a mental picture of a robin and scan it for wings. Alternatively, as we will see later in this chapter, the abstract concept of a robin might entail the feature "has wings," which is accessed directly (or perhaps an image is constructed *and* a stored property accessed simultaneously, the *dual-code theory* [see, for example, Paivio and Begg, 1981]). Is it possible to show that images are used in understanding verbal material?

Several methods have been used as support for the hypothesis of the existence of an imagery system. The first of these is to ask for verification of properties unlikely to be stored directly as part of an abstract definition. You probably are not sure whether you pictured a robin or looked up the word to determine whether or not the sentence is true. Now verify the following sentences:

A bee has a yellow head.
A German shepherd has pointed ears.

Most people respond with confidence that to answer these questions they picture the animal and then "zoom in" on its head (Kosslyn, 1980). This is introspective evidence that an image representation of "bee" and "German shepherd" is used in some instances. However, as Box 3.1 points out, there are problems with drawing conclusions from instrospections.

Compelling evidence for the use of images that does not rely on introspection is: If subjects are instructed to form an image and are then instructed to focus on the tail end of the animal, they are faster at verifying assertions about the tail than about the head (for example, "A German shepherd has a long tail"), a change from an average RT of 1.45 seconds to 1.68 seconds. In fact, evidence from other imagery tasks indicates that RT to locate a portion of an image increases proportionally with the dis-

---

Box 3.1   The Pitfalls of Introspection

Try to answer the following questions by "looking inside yourself" and considering what you experience.

1. What "happens" when you "fall asleep"? While you are sleeping are you totally unconscious or can you hear if someone is talking to you?
2. Close your eyes and then open them quickly, looking at this page. What is the very first thing you see? A part of a letter? A whole letter? A word? A sentence? A color?
3. Remember the "amoeba" or "polyblob" in Box 2.4? Can you picture it? Is the picture complete? If yes, count the number of projectiles it has. If you do not remember, picture a cartoon character you are familiar with—Mickey Mouse, perhaps. When you have a mental picture you are satisfied with, try to answer a specific question about it—such as how many fingers Mickey Mouse has.

Introspection is a poor way to find out what is going on internally because: (1) many things happen internally without reaching conscious awareness; (2) mental processing is very fast, and you cannot turn it off to do things such as deciding what the color of the first ray of light is that enters your eyes; and (3) you can report only things you have words for, and it is much easier to say "I see 'A'" than to describe a portion of it, like ⅄.

tance from the mental focal point (Kosslyn, 1980). This evidence suggests that the image is a spatial representation, like a picture: The RT here measures the amount of time it takes for the mind's eye to move, the longer times are for longer mental distances, and longer mental distances seem to correspond to longer physical distances.

Unfortunately, these lines of evidence for image representations suffer from some of the same problems as Jacobson's evidence for motor representations. Subjects are asked to image and then RT is measured for forming, transforming, zooming in on, and so on, the image; that is, the situation requires (situation requirements are called *demand characteristics*) that the subject consider using images and be aware of images even if this would not happen spontaneously.

There is some evidence indicating spontaneous use of images. One task that can be given subjects is to have them rate sentences or words for ease of imaging. One can surmise that if subjects can rate language units for imageability they are imaging them. Note, however, this evidence is again based on introspection. More compelling evidence comes from the fact that words or sentences rated as concrete or easily imaged show different properties than words or sentences rated as abstract or not easily imaged, even when imagery is not mentioned specifically in the instructions for the task. Paivio and Begg (1981) cite evidence, for example, that concrete words show a recall advantage over abstract words in memorization tasks, as do concrete sentences over abstract sentences. Moreover, whether or not a sentence is a parapharase of another is determined faster if the sentence is concrete rather than abstract. Finally, subjects determine that they have understood a sentence faster when it is concrete than when it is abstract.

Although interesting, these results do not necessarily implicate imagery in processing. The advantages for linguistic units judged as easy to image may arise because these units have a more accessible or interpretable memory organization than do abstract linguistic units. Concrete words or sentences, by their very nature, may be closer to sensory experiences than abstract words or sentences, and thus may be more basic concepts than abstract words or sentences, as we suggested in Chapter 2. In that case, they may have the same type of meaning organization as abstract words or sentences (both encoded in terms of abstract symbols, for example) but have simpler cognitive definitions and thus demonstrate a variety of processing advantages.

The last line of evidence for image representations is the only one that indicates definitively a sensory-based process in understanding some linguistic units and not others. Eddy and Glass (1981) showed that in a verification task *reading* high-image sentences is slower than reading low-image sentences, while *listening* to the same sentences shows no effect of imageability on verification time. These results suggest that the visual processes involved in reading somehow interfere with understanding one type of sentence, the type that subjects claim evokes a visual image. Since the same effect is not obtained with auditory presentation, it seems that the nature of verification of high-image sentences involves a *visual* image.

Although images or motor responses may underlie our comprehension of some words or phrases, neither clearly is responsible for understanding all words. Even strong image proponents postulate a symbolic representation for abstract words. We turn next to evidence of the nature of this representation.

Organization of Abstract Meaning

An advantage to assuming that meaning is nonverbal is that it avoids the circularity of having words define other words *ad infinitum.* The assumption of a sensory-related meaning system raises some logical problems too, which you may have already thought of. The first problem is the problem of meaning rather than reference, when we assume meaning is something like an image. Recall that the relation of words to external objects is nondirect, the word "bird" for instance does not refer to a particular bird but to a class of objects with very different appearances and properties. Try to form the clearest image you can of "bird." Is it red like a cardinal, brown like a sparrow, large like an ostrich, fuzzy like a baby chicken? Clearly it cannot be all these things at once. Yet, assuming we use an image-meaning code to verify a concrete assertion like "an ostrich is a bird," we may be comparing a mental ostrich picture with a mental robin picture, which then should result in an incorrect false response.

Perhaps the problem is that we are probing the wrong level: "bird" is too abstract to image (although most people report no problem with it), and we should be consulting images of ostriches and canaries, and so on. But the same problem pertains here: We recognize animals despite individual differences—ostriches of different colors or sizes, one-winged ostriches and healthy ostriches. . . . For an image to work as "meaning," it has to be nonspecific to permit the abstractions caused by variation; the less specific it is, the less its properties will be those of a spatial, sensation-based array.

Finally, consider what you image for "Shakespeare" and what you image for "the author of Hamlet." My image for both is of a black-and-white picture of a bearded man in Elizabethan dress. (I suspect I evoke the identical image for Sir Walter Raleigh, although I do know the two men are different.) Recall that there was something silly about the sentence "Shakespeare is Shakespeare" that was not silly for the sentence "Shakespeare is the author of Hamlet." If we understand both sentences by evoking the image of Shakespeare for the subject and that image also for the predicate, we should be performing identical processing for both sentences and they should seem equally silly.

The second difficulty for a sensation-based system lies with the linguistic relativity hypothesis. The advantage of images-as-meaning is their independence from the language and more direct reliance on untouched sensory experience. But if the linguistic relativity hypothesis is right, sensory experience itself is not independent of language, and so images provide no better a place to begin.

Of course, these arguments neither eliminate the possibility of an image-meaning system nor force the conclusion that meaning is an abstract symbol system; they just lessen the *a priori* appeal of an image-meaning system. In fact, as we shall see, it is also unclear how to deal with these problems with a verbal-meaning system. We begin our analysis of the verbal-meaning system by exploring the evidence that some concepts and their descriptions are more basic, more likely to use reference than meaning, and, at the same time, less dependent on an individual's particular sensory experience than others.

Codability, Basic Concepts, and Prototypes

It is probably safe to say that we are not born with a complete meaning system to which we just attach words as we learn them. If words or other language units are to be defined in terms of language units, it is reasonable to expect that some of them are *primitives:* initial meanings that others are based on. These primitives should be more concrete, or closer to sensory experience, since by definition, they are not based on other linguistic meanings. Moreover, they are likely to exist in many cultures and languages since sensory capacities (seeing, hearing, etc.) are the same for all people (at least at birth)[1]; differences should emerge for these only when the environments offer different stimuli (people living in a tropical "paradise" are likely to have no word for snow and many more flower terms than Eskimos). Finally, we can expect that these primitives will require less processing than concepts that build upon them: Understanding an "advanced" concept should entail all the processes involved in understanding a basic concept plus some.

Word Length and Processing Ease.   One way of investigating the possibility of primitives is to look for differences within words in the language and see if they reflect differences in processing of concepts. For example, in Box 3.1, it was pointed out that it is easier to report this shape, A, than this shape, $\dashv$ —we have a single word "ay" for the former and would have to use a long phrase like "part-of-the-right-hand-part-of-an-ay" or "a-short-oblique-almost-perpendicular-line-met-by-a-small-horizontal-line-about-halfway-up" for the latter. Does this difference in verbiage indicate a salience in the pattern A as compared with $\dashv$ for us?

Brown and Lenneberg (1954) have argued for the salience, and they call the difference *codability*. The argument begins with a famous observation in *comparative linguistics* (the study of several languages to discover common and distinct features). Zipf (1935/1965) observed that in Chinese, Latin, and English, languages of very different origin,[2] the length of words was negatively correlated with the frequency of their use. *Negative correlation* means that as one thing goes up the other goes down; the stronger the negative correlation, the more this is true. In this case, as Figure 3.1 shows, more frequent words are less long—with length measured either in number of *phonemes,* individual sounds roughly equivalent to letters (see Chapter 6 for a precise definition), or in number of syllables. You can think of this correlation as reflecting historical change in the language, motivated by laziness or efficiency: It is easier to say "NASA" than "National Aeronautics and Space Administration," or to write

---

1. There is some evidence that our basic sensations are in part environmentally or culturally determined. Westerners, who live in an environment with a large number of vertical and horizontal shapes given by trees, rectangular buildings, and so forth, are more sensitive to vertical and horizontal than peoples, like Zulus, who live in an area with very different architecture, no trees, small rounded shrubs, igloo-shaped huts and low hills (Gregory, 1966).
2. English is a Germanic language despite the number of Latin words it has. A language's family is determined by grammatical structure (see Chapter 4) rather than vocabulary items.

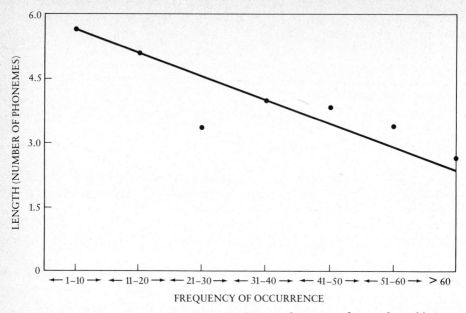

Figure 3.1 *An illustration of the relationship between frequency of use and word length, described by Zipf (1935/1965). This plots the number of occurrences in 43, 982 words of 6002 different words appearing in four samples of American newspaper English, against the average number of speech sounds per word. (This is usually plotted as log frequency vs. log length. Note that there is a minimum word length, 2.66 sounds, which all words occurring greater than 61 times do not fall below.)*

or say "RT" than "reaction time." If the word is frequently used, a saving will be worthwhile and will tend to be developed and maintained.

Brown and Lenneberg inferred that the word length or word frequency variable reflected something about cognitive processing of the referents of the words: "a perceptual category that is frequently utilized is more *available* than one less frequently utilized. . . . It is proposed, really, that categories with shorter names (higher codability) are nearer the top of the cognitive deck—more likely to be used in ordinary perception, more available for expectancies [stereotypes] and inventions." (Brown, 1958, p. 236).

Measuring Processing Availability. To measure codability—and test this hypothesis—Brown and Lenneberg derived five measures: RT for naming an instance, the number of syllables in the generated name, the number of words in the generated name ("A" is highly codable, "a short oblique . . . " is not), *reliability* within a subject (this refers to consistency in performing a task; in this case whether an individual assigns the same name each time the same object is presented), and consistency across subjects in coming up with the same name.

In their study Brown and Lenneberg looked specifically at coding of color. Primary color terms in our language (and in many others, Berlin and Kay, 1969) are black, white, red, green, blue, yellow, brown, orange, pink, purple, and gray. We obviously have other color terms, but we can consider their names derivative—either because they are compounds like bluish-green or forest-green (note these terms are longer than the mostly single syllable words on the preceding list); or because the color term has limited reference (blond can describe only hair or wood); or because the color term is not yet abstracted from specific objects bearing that color (ivory, turquoise, or violet, for example). People who work with dyes or fabrics may have many more primary color terms, and you may feel you have as well; magenta, taupe, mauve, and ecru are all color terms satisfying the same criteria as pink: unlimited reference, abstracted from object, and single word. Remember, though, that one of the indices of codability is consistency across subjects; asking 20 random people to define "taupe" by pointing to the appropriate hue will yield much greater variation in response than asking them to point to red. Likewise, measuring RT will show quite a difference; selecting a "red" will be much faster than selecting a "taupe."

Codability and Perception of Color. The question that Brown and Lenneberg addressed is whether "codability" affected perception—an example of whether language affects thought. After using the five measures just described to determine codability of 24 colored chips, they presented random groups of four of them for a short time, and after removing them, asked subjects to select the four they had just seen from an array of 120 chips. This is a *recognition task,* measuring memory. As suggested by the Whorf-Sapir hypothesis, Brown and Lenneberg found that highly codable colors were more often recognized. This recognition advantage shows a correlation between language and thought but does not imply that the language difference caused the memory difference. The same results could occur, for example, if the more codable terms refer to more primitive perceptions. This latter interpretation implies that language differences are shaped by perceptual differences and not vice versa.

If the language categories and their codability are reflecting perceptual sensitivities, we can expect to find similar linguistic categories across languages, suggesting that thought affects language. However, if there are differences in codability of color terms across languages and if the strong form of the Whorf-Sapir hypothesis is true—if language determines thought—we can predict that recognition tasks like the ones Brown and Lenneberg performed, done in different cultures, would show better recognition for those colors that are primary in the particular language, compared with recognition scores of English speakers. Both of these predictions have been tested.

It may come as something of a surprise that all cultures do not label colors the same way. In a survey of color terms used in 98 languages, Berlin and Kay (1969) found that the number of primary color terms can vary from three to eleven, and moreover, that a distinct pattern exists for which colors will be named. If a culture has only two terms, these will correspond to black and white, essentially a brightness scale. If a culture makes further distinctions, red will be added, then green or yellow or blue. And finally, finer verbal distinctions yield brown or orange or purple or pink. That not all cultures use the same terms might at first imply that color naming is arbitrary and not determined by our sensory experience of color. In fact, the pattern is not arbitrary: Basic light perception, as determined by physiological and perceptual experiments, consists of brightness perception and perception of the hues red, green, and blue; perception of all other hues can be created by appropriate combinations of these primaries. Note that basic light percepts correspond to the first stages in the language categorizations.

Brown and Lenneberg replicated their study with Zuñi Indians, finding one cross-cultural result supporting a language influence on perception. The Zuñi language uses a single color term for the hues we distinguish with the names orange and yellow, and therefore this distinction is low in codability. The question of interest is whether codability for the Zuñi is related to recognition, in which case they should have difficulty recognizing orange and yellow colors, confusing them, unlike English speakers. Since we presumably have the same sensory capacities this would argue that our good recognition does not reflect a sensory "primary" but a linguistic influence. Indeed, they reported having found that Zuñi speakers frequently confused (= false recognition) orange and yellow colors in the recognition task, and interestingly, those Zuñi speakers who also knew English made an intermediate number of false recognitions, between monolingual Zuñi and monolingual English speakers.

Unfortunately, further work has not similarly supported the Whorf-Sapir hypothesis. In a number of experiments, Rosch (previously publishing under the name Heider [Heider and Olivier, 1972]) has demonstrated that perception of at least some colors is unaffected by naming experience. Her test group was a New Guinea tribe, the Dani, who label only black and white with basic color terms. She found no difference in color recognition between American and Dani speakers, and found further that those tints selected by Americans as the best examples of particular color names (these she called *focal colors*) were better recognized by both groups than less good examples, and were easier for the Dani to learn "names" for.[3] Finally, the Dani, like English speakers, found particular groupings of colored chips easier to memorize than others. The easy groups were those arranged with a focal color in the center and related colors around it: for example, red in the center and blue-reds off to one side and orange-reds off to the other. The hard groups had nonfocal colors as the average value and spanned focal colors, such as forest-green in the center with green on one side and blue on the other. Together, her results suggest that high codability may not result from a language influence on our perception, since the Dani, without the color terms, also show perceptual salience for the referents of our terms. Indeed, Rosch's results strongly suggest that our color categories are nonarbitrary and represent the sensitivities of our perceptual system.

Codability and General Category Recognition.   Rosch (1975; and Rosch, Mervis, Gray, Johnson, and Boyes-Braem, 1976) has extended her work on focal-ness and categorization beyond the domain of color to determine what other referents might form basic perception and basic terms. In this work she and her colleagues have tested only American English speakers, and they claim not that their specific findings are universal, but that their general principles are. There are three of these. First, all cul-

---

3. This is a *paired associate task*. The experimenter creates arbitrary pairs of items: for example two nonsense words GAT-DAG, or in this case, a color and a nonsense syllable. The subject's task is to recall one member of the pair when presented with the other.

tures have the same tendency to categorize; that is, to class different objects as the same (e.g., we class canaries and ostriches both as birds). Second, the categories are formed by recognizing correlations of perceived features in the environment (e.g., feathers usually co-occur with wings and beaks). The more shared features objects have in common, the more likely they are to form a category in any culture. Third, in any category hierarchy, or *taxonomy* (e.g., a canary is a bird is an animal is a living thing), there is a level that can be considered basic. The *basic level* is the level of highest information content that also best captures the feature correlations. This level has important psychological properties.

Information, as used here, is to be taken in the information-theoretic sense of Chapter 1. To understand the scientific sense of "information," it will help to consider a game of "20 questions"—the "experimenter" is thinking of something, and the "subject" must guess what it is by asking a limited number of only yes-no questions.[4] The subject can take several strategies: (S)he can begin, Is it my pet canary? Is it a canary? Is it a bird? Is it an animal? Is it living? . . . Which is the best strategy and why? Clearly, with a "no" response likely the first turn, asking whether it is "my pet canary" is the poorest, and asking if it is a living thing is the best (although frequently young children choose the former). This is because whether or not it is living provides the most information; it reduces uncertainty the most. If the answer is "no," not only are you certain it is not alive but also that it is not a bird and not your specific pet along with many other things. If you learn that it is not your pet, you do not even know whether it is not a different bird, along with many other things. The best strategy is the one that provides the most information at any turn.

Note that the definition of basic level contains two claims: Not only should it express the most information (in the preceding taxonomy that would be living thing, which is not the basic level, as we shall see), but it should also express the feature correlations. This second clause is actually a paraphrase of another information-theoretic concept, redundancy. Consider the 20 questions game again. Suppose the subject has learned in a previous query that the "object" has feathers. How much sense is there in asking next whether it has wings? Obviously, very little, because, since feathers and wings are highly correlated, knowing one implies the other, and so the question reduces the uncertainty no further—it is redundant. It is important to realize that redundancy is not always bad, because we are not always perfect. Repetition when someone does not hear does reduce uncertainty because the information transmitted was not the information received. The definition of information was repeated in this chapter because it was assumed that many readers would not remember it from Chapter 1 and therefore the repetition would reduce uncertainty caused by faulty retention. Imagine how hard a lecture would be to follow if every sentence presented a new idea, with no repetitions and no rephrasings!

Members of the category "living thing" have very little in common; that is, across the category there are few redundant features: Bird have feathers, fish do not,

4. The answer to a yes-no question, where "yes" and "no" are equally likely, contains one *bit* of information. Bit is derived from binary digit and is the measure of information used in information theory. Binary means two, and a choice between yes and no is a choice between two things.

and so forth. The second criterion of basic category requires that it capture significant feature overlap among members. The most overlap usually occurs at the lowest levels of the taxonomy: All canaries are roughly the same size, are yellow, sing, . . . features they do not share even with all other birds. The most information content usually occurs at the highest levels. So to find the basic level we must balance the two bounds of high-information content and high redundancy—yielding an intermediate level in the taxonomy, in this case, probably, bird.

What Rosch et al. claim is that basic objects have special psychological properties, making the words that refer to them distinct from other words, and, in a sense, providing the primitives for cognitive representations. Focal colors can be considered basic objects. Recall the stages of color term development across languages, each giving finer and finer information about the hue: The first distinction was dark versus light, then colored (red) versus not, then colors of long wavelength (red) versus short wavelength (blue), and finally divisions within these last groups. Regardless of which category names the language uses, the focal colors are determined by amount of shared and distinctive information. Dark and light do not encompass lights with enough similarities so they could not be focal. Taupe or forest-green do not distinguish between lights with enough differences so they too could not be focal. The focal colors fell between these extremes. Recall that when the Dani were asked to learn groups of chips of various hues, the groups easiest to learn consisted of chips bearing the focal color as central to the group, and "average" in color with respect to the other group members. In these groupings, the focal colors shared most with all other category members (that is how they are "average") and may be considered basic colors.

To illustrate better the concept of focal-ness and its importance, consider your concept "dog." Picture a dog. Most people with this instruction picture a "typical" dog, something that looks like a setter: It has a medium length tail, medium snout, and average size. Now think about other members of the category dog: St. Bernards, boxers, Lhasa Apsos, Irish wolfhounds, collies. These are less typical members (although no less dogs) and are less central to the concept "dog." They share features with the typical dog, but some are too tall, too short, too pug-nosed, too bushy-tailed, and so on, to be representative. Obviously if they shared all features with a setter they would also be setters. If a set of pictures of dogs is organized so that setters are central, and dogs increasingly different from setters are increasingly further away, this would be easier to learn than if we had a St. Bernard centrally and defined the category extremes as setters on one side and horses on the other. The category with setter in the center is easier to learn because the setter best compromises between the distinctiveness of dogs versus other animals and the similarities among dogs.

Generalizing and extending the techniques used in studying color, Rosch and her colleagues (1976) defined the basic level for the general categories of musical instrument, fruit, tool, clothing, furniture, vehicle, tree, fish, and bird, each of which was represented by some frequently produced instances. Consider a hierarchy headed by "tool," for example: Tool is the top level or *superordinate* of the category. Subordinate to it are the categories hammer, saw, and screwdriver. Screwdriver subsumes Phillips screwdriver and regular screwdriver. In *this* case the basic level is the intermediate one, screwdriver, hammer, and so forth, since "screwdriver" simultaneously captures the high redundancy in use and appearance of its subordinates and the great differences between it and other tools.

Rosch et al. used several experimental criteria to define which level was basic in each category. The basic level is the one for which subjects are most consistent with one another in listing attributes (this is like codability); members are "described" using the same pantomimes (getting into a sitting position to describe chair; probably the same motion is made for stools, rocking chairs, etc.); subjects have the greatest ease at forming images ("tree" is easier to image than "maple tree" since we do not readily access the distinguishing features of mapleness); and which is learned first by children, as indicated by their ability to make groupings or acquire the names.

In light of our earlier discussion, it is interesting to note that two of the tests for basic level are ease at making motor movements and ease at imaging, although it is not implied that either is the "form" information is stored in. Rosch (1975) did specifically address the question of form of meaning and concluded tentatively that meaning is an abstract form conducive either to verbalizing or imaging, and represents prototypical instances of the category; that is, the central instance sharing most with other category members.

Rosch's conclusions were based on a priming task in which subjects had to decide whether two words (for example, chair-chair) were the same or not. Before being given the pair to be identified, they were given the category name as prime. The relation of the category name to the instances sometimes was excellent, sometimes fair, and sometimes poor as determined by prior ratings. For example, "furniture" is a good prime for dresser and chair; lamp and desk, although furniture, are not typical instances of it; and stove and rug, although also furniture, are even poorer examples of it. Thus, if furniture is given as the prime, it should prime chair better than lamp and lamp better than stove.

The priming speeded decisions more when the examples were good instances (furniture . . . chair-chair) than when they were poor (furniture . . . stove-stove). This further supports a category organization of central, easily accessed members, and peripheral, hard-to-access members. Furthermore, this was true regardless of whether the instances were presented by the name, as in the preceding, or by picture—suggesting that the same "meaning" form of the superordinate mediates both picture and verbal processing. Finally, Rosch observed that when both the prime and the instances could be presented either as pictures or as words, and subjects did not know which ahead of time, RT increased dramatically, perhaps because subjects took time to generate the other code. If the time between the prime and the instances was made too short to generate both codes between the presentations, there was a greater additional RT to the instances for verbal presentation than for pictorial, leading Rosch to conclude tentatively that meaning form may be closer to picture than word, therefore requiring less time to transform it to picture than to word.

All that may be strongly concluded from the experiments as a whole is that meaning is organized in *prototypes,* or typical, "average" instances. The prototypes can be transformed to picture, verbal, or motor codes as needed, and these prototypes or basic objects are where we begin to search our memories, deriving either more detail or greater abstraction from there. What determines the basic level is in part the structure of the outside world and in part the degree of information we have about that structure.

It is important to note that different taxonomies yield different basic levels: for the category tool, as already stated, the intermediate level in the hierarchy labeled screwdriver, hammer . . . , is the basic level. In biological hierarchies tested by Rosch et al. (1976) (tree—maple—sugar maple), it was found that the top level, tree, was basic. Rosch et al. argue that what constitutes the basic level, the level that is most available psychologically, can change with experience: a person in forestry is likely to have as basic a lower level than tree, just as a dyer may think easily in terms of more finely differentiated colors than red, orange, green, and so on. It is interesting to consider also the possibility that for each of us different levels may be basic depending on the situation: The forester may think in terms of "tree" when dealing with everyday people and go to other levels from there if necessary; when dealing with other foresters, (s)he may begin at a more differentiated level.

Summary.   According to the codability hypothesis, some concepts are more available or more central than others, and for these, meaning is more easily accessed. The instances central to the concept of the category are called prototypes. They compromise between the distinctiveness of category members and the similarities among them. Atypical members of a category may share very few features with one another, but each will share an optimal number of features with the prototype. For understanding it is assumed that a mental category is entered at the prototype. The more distant the category member is from the prototype, the longer it will take to gain access to it. There is some evidence that categories are stored pictorially, but a store in terms of overlapping abstract features is not ruled out.

Network Models

The research just described postulated a hierarchical structure for certain kinds of information in semantic memory, with the ability to proceed up or down the hierarchy if other information is needed. The research offered some psychological and linguistic tests to determine the usual entry level into the hierarchy. The position of this level is flexible, determined in part by the structure existing in the environment and in part by the fineness of degree of observation of that structure.

Other researchers have proposed similar hierarchical models of information organization in semantic memory but without discussing either basic objects as "primitives," or hypothesizing prototypes as the conceptual form for the category, or differentiating treatment of different kinds of semantic information like concrete versus abstract, or basic versus derived. These can be considered practical versions of Katz' and Fodor's (1963) lexicon, with ordered relations of features (markers) like animal, male, and so forth.

Quillian's Semantic Network.   The first such model, which launched a number of psychological experiments and, eventually, opposing models (including prototypes), was proposed by Quillian (1967, 1968) and took the form of an elaborate language understanding program. In generation of his system, Quillian attempted to incorporate the information and structure appropriate for performing an unlimited production task like "tell me what you know about machines." As he pointed out, if truly unlimited, people can take days to answer this question—beginning with facts of central importance (probably those common to many machines) and continuing through obscure and idiosyncratic facts. You can consider this process as entering into the knowledge structure at the level "machine" and then fanning out in ever-widening circles from the "machine" location, producing first the information most central to the machine concept and subsequently increasingly more peripheral information. This fanning out Quillian called *spreading activation,* each produced piece of information triggering its own associations. In his model a word's full meaning is defined as all the points reached by spreading activation emanating from the word.

In this conceptualization, semantic memory, or the entire mental dictionary, is best pictured as a huge net (see Figure 3.2): a mass of nodes (the intersections in the net) and a mass of links (the threads creating the intersections when they overlap). The nodes, or concepts, can be named by a word, but Quillian actually considered them properties or attributes consisting of the name of the property (like "color") and a value in the range of the property (like "yellow"). The links, unlike a real net, may differ from one another, telling how the information they connect to the node relates to it. For example, in considering Rosch's research we have already seen subordinate to superordinate links (a canary is a bird), where all of one set of associations, the subordinate, is entailed in the other, the superordinate; and in examining Katz' and Fodor's semantic theory we came across *disjunctive* associations (bachelor is an unmarried male *or* a type of degree), where the two trains of thought are separate or disjoined paths. All links may not be equally important to the concept, and Quillian indicated the importance by assigning a weight to each link, indicated in Figure 3.2 by the length of the individual links. Labeling the links with information about how to interpret their relation to the node and how seriously to consider their information gives added dimensions to the spatial organization of the memory network.

Thus far there is no apparent theoretical differentiation of this model and Rosch's: Properties of her "prototype" are likely to be encountered earlier in spreading activation, central properties will be given higher weights, and so on. The construct of spreading activation might be considered a difference, but Rosch too needs some way of getting from the entry-level basic object to peripheral category features, and the nonspecified mechanism could be spreading activation. However, the main difference is that Quillian does not believe that there are any primitives: "Viewed most abstractly, the memory model forms simply a large, very complex network of nodes and one-way associations between them. Most important, in such a model of semantic memory there is no predetermined hierarchy of superclasses and subclasses; *every* word is the patriarch of its own separate hierarchy *when some search process starts with it* ... There are no word concepts as such that are 'primitive'" (Quillian, 1968, p. 239).

Another important theoretical differentiation is that Quillian's model assumes *cognitive economy;* that is, that information is reorganized in memory so that multiple copies are collapsed. For example, canaries have feathers, and so do robins and ostriches. If the property "has feathers" is associated independently with each bird

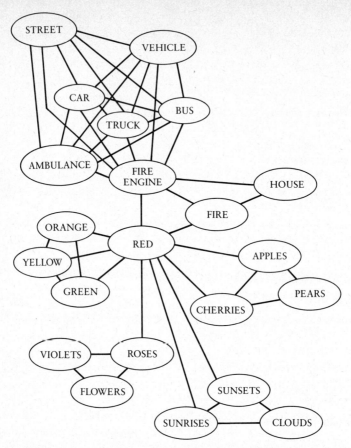

Figure 3.2 *A representation of the interrelation of concepts in semantic memory. Short lines indicate close associations (highly weighted), while long lines indicate less related associations.*
From "A spreading activation theory of semantic processing" by A. Collins and E. Loftus, 1975, Psychological Review, 83 p. 412. Copyright (1975) by the American Psychological Association. Reprinted by permission of the author.

type we know, there is a lot of storage space being used. However, if the property is associated only with "bird" along with other properties common to bird, the duplication is minimized. To determine that a canary has feathers, we go through a two-step process: A canary is a bird and birds have feathers. We have to have the information that canaries are birds anyway, since we can make subordinate-superordinate judgments. Note that this kind of organization is economical with respect to storage (a common property is stored only once, at the superordinate level) but uneconomical with respect to processing steps (the property is not retrieved directly, but indirectly after the superordinate is activated).

Strong storage economy is desirable when there is limited storage capacity, and recall that Quillian implemented his model as a computer program. Whether similar limitations exist in human storage capacity is uncertain, but the assumption of strong storage economy is not critical to the model. It may be psychologically more reasonable, in fact, to assume weak cognitive economy: Properties are stored directly with the first-learned instance of a category, and once the category itself is learned (presumably from the similarities among instances), the common properties are not transferred or erased but copied onto the superordinate; subsequently learned instances do not repeat the common properties but make use of the extra step of inferring from the superordinate (Collins and Loftus, 1975). These later instances are probably learned differently from the earlier ones: The pet you grew up with you name "canary," and you learn that this is an example of "bird" and form a category "bird"; your first encounter with a penguin is most likely to take place as "this is a strange bird, called penguin," building on the already learned category.

As a program, Quillian's model was and is extremely impressive. Humans set up the memory structure, putting in information they considered relevant for each concept, along with the link types connecting this information. The success of the program was determined by asking the machine to perform one task, to compare and contrast any two words in its memory. The comparison and contrast task was implemented by entering the memory structure at the nodes corresponding to each of the two input words and searching from each. Every node encountered during the spreading activation was tagged, indicating the point of origin. Nodes with double tags then represented intersections or common associations or meanings. A sample output is shown in Table 3.1. The reasonably good English on the part of the program is mostly due to a supply of canned phrases (e.g., "among other things") spliced between phrases encoded directly into memory as part of the concepts. At the time of writing Quillian (1968) noted that his computer's storage space could hold the networks for no more than 20 words at one time. Nevertheless, requests to compare and contrast any two of any set of 20 always produced answers compatible with human response. Since we clearly hold more than 20 word definitions at a time it is amazing to consider how cross-referenced our semantic system must be!

Psychological Tests of the Model.   Although Quillian's model seems plausible and is effective at generating reasonable responses for one language task, the efficacy of a computer model does not imply psychological reality. Quillian's model does suggest interesting experiments, though, to test its correctness as a human model, some of which you may have thought of.

There are three aspects of the model interesting to test: spreading activation, cognitive economy, and hierarchical storage. As just mentioned, the notion of spreading activation may not be unique to Quillian's model, although it was here that it was first suggested. There is reasonably strong psychological evidence for spreading activation, which may be why it has been incorporated, at least tacitly, into other models.

Spreading Activation.   To understand the evidence we must explore the lexical decision task in more detail. How can a lexical decision be made difficult? The easiest way is to make a nonword look similar to a word: "Brank" is harder (takes longer) to reject than "bgzae," both five-letter sequences. This suggests that we have some

Table 3.1 *Example Output from the Current Program*

Example 1.   Compare: CRY, COMFORT
    A.   Intersect: SAD
        (1)   CRY2 IS AMONG OTHER THINGS TO MAKE A SAD SOUND.*
        (2)   TO COMFORT3 CAN BE TO MAKE2 SOMETHING LESS2 SAD.

        (Note that the program has selected particular meanings of "cry" and "comfort" as appropriate for this intersection.)

Example 2.   Compare: PLANT, LIVE
    A.   1st Intersect: LIVE
        (1)   PLANT IS A LIVE STRUCTURE.
    B.   2nd Intersect: LIVE
        (1)   PLANT IS STRUCTURE WHICH GET3-FOOD FROM AIR. THIS FOOD IS THING WHICH BEING2 HAS-TO TAKE INTO ITSELF TO7 KEEP LIVE.

Example 3.   Compare: PLANT, MAN
    A.   1st Intersect: ANIMAL
        (1)   PLANT IS NOT A ANIMAL STRUCTURE.
        (2)   MAN IS ANIMAL.
    B.   2nd Intersect: PERSON
        (1)   TO PLANT3 IS FOR A PERSON SOMEONE TO PUT SOMETHING INTO EARTH.
        (2)   MAN3 IS PERSON.
        (Here the program is treating "person" as an adjective modifier of "someone.")

Example 4.   Compare: PLANT, INDUSTRY
    A.   Ist Intersect: INDUSTRY
        (1)   PLANT2 IS A APPARATUS WHICH PERSON USE FOR 5 PROCESS IN INDUSTRY.

Example 5.   Compare: EARTH, LIVE
    A.   Ist Intersect: ANIMAL
        (1)   EARTH IS PLANET OF7 ANIMAL.
        (2)   TO LIVE IS TO HAVE EXISTENCE AS7 ANIMAL.

Example 6.   Compare: FRIEND, COMFORT
    A.   Ist Intersect: PERSON
        (1)   FRIEND IS PERSON.
        (2)   COMFORT CAN BE WORD TO4 PERSON.

Example 7. Compare: FIRE, BURN
    A. 1st Intersect: BURN
        (1) FIRE IS CONDITION WHICH BURN.
    B. 2nd Intersect: FIRE
        (1) TO BURN2 CAN BE TO DESTROY2 SOMETHING BY4 FIRE.
    C. 3rd intersect: BURN
        (1) FIRE IS A FLAME CONDITION. THIS FLAME CAN BE A GAS
             TONGUE4. THIS GAS IS GAS WHICH BURN.
             (The sentence producer starts a new sentence whenever it needs to
             say something more about something it has used adjectively.)

Example 8. Compare: BUSINESS, COMFORT
    a. 1st Intersect: PERSON
        (1) BUSINESS5 IS ACT3 WHICH PERSON DO.
        (2) COMFORT2 IS CONDITION3 WHICH PERSON HAVE NEED4.
             (The code contains information indicating that "person" should be
             plural here but the sentence producer does not yet make use of this
             information.)
    B. 2nd Intersect: PERSON
        (1) BUSINESS5 IS ACT3 WHICH PERSON DO.
        (2) COMFORT CAN BE WORD TO4 PERSON.

Example 9. Compare: MAN, BUSINESS
    A. 1st Intersect: PERSON
        (1) MAN3 IS PERSON.
        (2) BUSINESS CAN BE ACTIVITY WHICH PERSON MUST DO
             WORK2.
             (Something wrong here. I believe a miscoding in the input data.)
    B. 2nd Intersect: GROUP
        (1) MAN2 IS MAN AS9 GROUP.
        (2) BUSINESS2 IS QUESTION3 FOR ATTENTION OF GROUP.

Example 10. Compare: MAN, LIVE
    A. 1st Intersect: ANIMAL
        (1) MAN IS ANIMAL.
        (2) TO LIVE IS TO HAVE EXISTENCE AS7 ANIMAL.
    B. 2nd Intersect: LIVE
        (1) MAN IS A LIVE +BEING2.

Sample output from Quillian's semantic net program. The program was provided with definitions of words as an associative net; each word is defined by pointing to other words in the net, with labels on the pointers defining the kind of association. The program is then asked to compare two words and explain how their meanings relate. It does this by searching the connections from each word until it finds intersections.

From "Semantic memory" by M. R. Quillian, pp. 253–254, in Semantic Information Processing, *M. Minsky (Ed.). Cambridge, MA: MIT Press, copyright (c) 1968 by the Massachusetts Institute of Technology. Reprinted by permission.*

storage of spelling rules and pronouncing rules, for which there is other evidence, some of which we will explore later. A second way is to make the letter sequence harder to see: by reducing the amount of time it is flashed, by decreasing the amount of light, or by reducing the time between its presentation and the presentation of another visual stimulus, a *mask*. In these cases, the task is difficult, presumably, because it is hard to make out the letters, not because it is hard to gain access to the word from semantic memory. However, we can make these hard-to-see letters easy to respond to by priming: There is a phenomenon called the *repetition effect* in which prior presentation of a letter sequence causes fast responses to be made under difficult viewing conditions (Scarborough, Cortese, and Scarborough, 1977), and more intriguing, there is improvement if recently presented sequences are semantically related but not identical. For example, if subjects must decide whether various letter sequences are words and if one of them is "doctor," then if the word "nurse" is presented as much as two days before the presentation of "doctor," the RT for "doctor" will be faster than if an unrelated word had been presented.

To understand these effects, first realize that although the effect of poor lighting seems to be a low-level visual effect and not a high-level semantic effect, the latter can influence the former (conceptually driven processes, introduced in Chapter 1). We have trouble truly reading

PARIS IN THE
THE SPRING TIME

because in a sense we do not see the two "the"s—our normal reading processes (high level) guide our visual processing (low level). Second, the repetition effect fits right in with Quillian's model: Using the search process every node encountered is tagged, and we need only assume that the tagged nodes—for as long as the tags remain—are more psychologically available than untagged nodes. Every entry node will of course be tagged, so "nurse" will tag "nurse," making it easier to think about "nurse" for as long as the tag is available. Third, the priming effect indicates spreading activation. If "nurse" tags not only itself but also associations, fanning out from itself as entry point, then "doctor," a close association, will be tagged and therefore more available. Thus, there is evidence for spreading activation and psychological tags.

Hierarchical Storage.   Now, consider the implications of hierarchical relations and cognitive economy. If these are psychologicaly valid then one knows that a canary is an animal by knowing that canaries are birds and birds are animals, and it should take longer to decide that canaries are animals than that canaries are birds. Moreover, if a property such as "can fly" is stored with "bird" because it is common to the category and is not also stored with each instance, it should take longer to verify "a canary can fly" than "a canary can sing," an idiosyncratic property of this type of bird. The logic is the same in both cases: To retrieve the can fly information we must make the bird inference, which will take time; to retrieve can sing we save that time. Finally, retrieval of a property like can fly or can sing should take longer than retrieval of hierarchy information: To determine that a canary is a bird there is one step up the hierarchy; to determine that it can fly the step is made to bird and then the property is retrieved from there, which should take some additional time.

Indeed, as Figure 3.3 shows, reaction time experiments (Collins and Quillian, 1969) with humans exactly confirm these predictions. In this figure S0 is a set relation on the same level (canary is a canary), S1 on the next level (canary is a bird), and S2 on the next (canary is an animal). Not surprisingly, S0 was much easier to verify relative to S1 than S1 relative to S2. For the S0 level subjects need not probe their knowledge structures at all, but simply can physically match the letters on the screen. The Ps all indicate property judgments, and as is clear, it took longer to judge the truth of a property relation than a set relation, reflecting the property retrieval time. Moreover, properties expected to be stored with the item directly (P0: for example, canary can sing) took less time to verify than properties stored with the next level (P1: canary can fly), which in turn were faster than those at the next level (P2: a canary has skin).

In all instances considered thus far the sentences have been true. Obviously in an experiment false sentences must also be presented, or the subjects need not think.

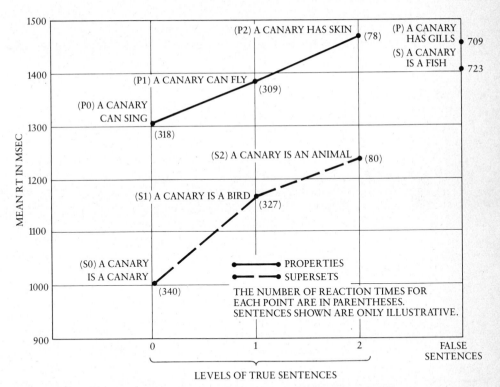

Figure 3.3 *Average reaction time to verify sentences of different types. The sentences either describe category membership (supersets) or properties of a category member. The correct information can be either found on the same level of memory (SO or PO) or at one of the next two levels (for true sentences). Note that it takes longer to retrieve category properties than category membership relations, and that it takes increasingly longer to retrieve information from more distant levels.*

What is interesting to consider is what kind of organization might be revealed by false responses (like "a canary is a fish"), similar to the question posed at the beginning of this chapter: How do you know when something is a word? It cannot be that all nonwords are stored and you find the one presented in the nonword section of your mental dictionary; nor can false assertions be directly stored; rather, inferences must be made on the basis of the facts you have stored.

Searching for Untruths.   Collins and Quillian (1969) suggested three models for false responses. The first is to search for a contradiction. This should always return an answer. For example, to verify "a canary has gills" a search would start from canary and also from gills. Canary would yield bird as superset, gills would yield fish, and fish and bird would be connected by a disjunctive link, suggesting contradiction. If this is how falses are determined, we can expect false RTs to show the same pattern as true RTs with level in the hierarchy for falses determined by the level at which the contradiction can be found. In the example it would be at Level 1, with "a canary is blue" at Level 0, and "a canary has roots" at Level 2.

A second possibility for how to determine falsehoods is to search for a preset time, and if the property is not found within that time to assume that it is false. This suggests that false responses should take longer than trues, and that all falses should take the same amount of time, since the clock will run out on every false statement.

A third possibility is that all paths connecting the subject and the predicate are searched for the appropriate connection down to a certain level in the hierarchy. (This is like the second possibility in which the time to search was set; in this one the "distance" or "depth," as it is more commonly called, is set.) If none of the paths produces the right connection, a false response is returned. This model implies that RT will be different for different false responses, depending on how many paths there are connecting the subject and predicate. The more related they are, the more paths to be searched and the longer it should take to decide "false."

Thus, the third model predicts results opposite from the first: In the contradiction model, responses are found by searching the hierarchy, and the higher one needs to search the longer the response. Concepts contradicted only in high levels of the hierarchy are likely to have few joining paths since they are seldom associated, and so Proposal 3 suggests they should be fast. On the other hand a statement like "a diamond is a ruby" can be contradicted at a low level (fast by Proposal 1), but diamond and ruby probably have many interconnecting associations, and if all are explored, as Proposal 3 suggests, a long RT will result.

A fourth proposal has been made by Landauer and Freedman (1968), who suggested that in verification, subjects mentally scan all category instances for the desired one—for "a canary is a fish" for example, one would enter at "fish," check "trout, salmon, etc." for "canary," and when "canary" is not found return a false. This proposal has the same implications as Proposal 1, but for reasons similar to those of Proposal 3. Here it is suggested that higher levels of the hierarchy contain more instances (have more paths from them), and so it should take longer to ascertain that a particular instance is not one of them. To search all animals you know for a canary should take longer than to search all birds, since animals include birds and much more. This is known as the *category size effect*.

It would be nice to support one of these proposals exclusively, but unfortunately, in different experiments each has obtained some support (see Collins and Quillian, 1969, 1970; Landauer and Freedman, 1968; Glass and Holyoake, 1975). The most important result to emerge from the study of RT to false responses is that *semantic relatedness,* the number of connections between an association and a category name, has an effect independent of level in the hierarchy.

Effects of Semantic Relatedness. Semantic relatedness is measured usually using a production task: "Create a false sentence beginning with 'A bird is a ____'" (false production) or "name instances of the category bird." Frequent responses given first are considered to be highly related to the category, or dominant.

Holyoake and Glass (reported in Glass and Holyoake, 1975) found that highly related false productions produced fast false RTs in verification as compared with low-related false productions. And Wilkins (1971) and Loftus and Suppes (1972) showed that verification of true sentences is faster for highly related terms, regardless of the number of intervening levels in the hierarchy. However, there are two reasons to interpret the semantic relatedness results cautiously. First, one would expect relatedness to be a symmetric relation; "robin" should be as related to "bird" as "bird" is to "robin." However, production frequency is asymmetric—categories do not necessarily produce instances with the same probability that instances produce categories (Glass and Holyoake, 1975). Second, for sentences for which the relatedness of subject and predicate are zero, we would expect the same RT. However, Landauer and Meyer (1972) found that when subjects verified sentences like "a brank is a living thing" and "a brank is a bird," where the relatedness between the nonword and either category name was zero, it took longer to verify that a nonword was not a member of the larger, superordinate category than the smaller one!

Reconsidering Quillian's Model. With slight modifications the network model can be made to accommodate all the results, even the contradictory ones. The category size effect could occur because one must search higher in the hierarchy for a contradiction (when words are real) or because there are more paths to explore through spreading activation from superordinate categories (for either real words or nonwords). This latter is just putting the category size explanation into network model terms: More instances yield more paths. The semantic relatedness effect is accounted for by the weighted links. The more two concepts or a concept and a property are related the heavier the weight or the shorter the path, as represented in Figure 3.2.

Allowing a hierarchy, partial cognitive economy, and other-than-hierarchical organization in terms of different path lengths for different concepts within a level eliminates the elegant simplicity of Quillian's model but does seem to account for the psychological data on the representation of meaning. Of course, it is important to note that it accomplishes this no better than a prototype/basic object model, in which the "prototype" would have a more highly weighted "link" to the category name (accounts for semantic relatedness), a category would be represented by its instances with the prototype in the center (accounts for larger categories having more instances to search), and verification would be accomplished through feature overlap with instances having fewer overlapping features belonging to superordinate categories rather than subordinate categories (accounts for hierarchy level effects).

Feature Models

Thus far we have examined prototype and network models of semantic organization. On the surface the models appear different: Prototype models suggest a basic level and derived levels with categories arranged in terms of feature overlap or relatedness; the network models suggest no basic level, definitions in terms of interconnections, and a rigid structure dictated by inclusion relations and redundancy of properties (Glass and Holyoake, 1975). However, closer examination of their accounts of psychological data revealed little empirical difference between the two. We next examine a third model, which is very different from the other two in premise but again very similar in prediction or explanation.

Types of Features.   This model, the *feature* or attribute model, grew out of the set-theoretic tradition as exemplified by Lakoff's (1972) theory, in which each word is defined by a list of attributes. Verification is hypothesized to take place by determining if every attribute of the category is also an attribute of the instance (Smith, Shoben, and Ripps, 1974); the greater the attribute overlap, the faster the decision, for reasons to be explained. In comparison with the other models we have discussed, we should note that the feature model proposes no hierarchical organization of features (they are just listed), and no cognitive economy—if "can fly" is one of the features for "bird," it is also one for "canary" and is listed for both; in fact, it is this duplication that allows matching of the category properties and instance properties. The feature model also proposes no basic level, nor does it seem to allow any privileges for concrete or easily imaged concepts.

Can the feature model account for the data we have examined thus far? Its proponents respond with a resounding yes, but to see how we have to introduce a little complexity into the features and into the comparison process. Feature theorists argue that there are two kinds of features: characteristic features and defining features. *Defining features* are absolute features that must be present for an instance to be a member of a category. *Characteristic features* are ones found in most instances of the category but are not absolutely necessary. For example, for bird, characteristic features could be sings, is 6″–10″ tall, flies, builds a nest, and so forth, although many birds do not sing, are taller or smaller than the characteristic height, do not fly, use other birds' nests, and so on. Defining features would include has a beak, lays eggs, has feathers. The number of defining features is presumed to decrease as a category gets more abstract. Introduction of the differences between characteristic and defining features follows Lakoff (1972) and "explains" his demonstration that these sentences are all true:

1. A robin is a bird. (Both characteristic and defining features overlap.)
2. Technically speaking, a chicken is a bird. (Only defining features overlap; chickens do not fly, making it true but slow.)
3. Loosely speaking, a bat is a bird. (Only characteristic features overlap; bats fly and are the right size but do not lay eggs or have feathers—making the sentence true, but only with the hedge, "loosely.")

(These can be accounted for in the network model by assuming a disjunctive connection between a technical word and its lay definition [Glass and Holyoake, 1975].) Moreover, the overlap of characteristic features accounts for Rosch's typicality results: Basic objects are faster to verify as category instances than nonbasic objects because they share more features (in this case, characteristic features) with the category. It accounts for the surprising result that it is faster to verify "a chicken is an animal" than "a chicken is a bird" (which should be lower on the hierarchy), while it is faster to verify "a robin is a bird" than "a robin is an animal"; robin has more characteristic features of bird and fewer of animal, while chicken is the opposite. This result, it is claimed, cannot be handled by network models since all instances are linked to their superordinate by the same type of link. (Note that this is a presumption not made by network theorists, as you may recall.)

Finally, marking features as characteristic in the mental definition of a concept allows flexibility in evaluating an instance of a category with respect to them. For example, in a fixed hierarchy we might assume that the statements "an ostrich is big" and "a brontosaurus is big" are judged relative to the same absolute concept of bigness. Clearly, brontosauruses are orders of magnitude bigger than ostriches, and small dinosaurs are larger than big birds. Feature theorists argue that rigid definitions and inclusion relations yield an impractically rigid definition of flexible concepts like "big." Flexible feature lists, which always include characteristic information, they argue, allow a relative judgment; ostrich size is always considered relative to characteristic bird size, and the same holds true for instances of dinosaur.

It is interesting to note that the feature models were developed largely to deal with the fuzziness of category boundaries, such as the lack of absolutes as in changing scales for "big" depending on context, or in "bat" being a "bird" in appropriate contexts. Network proponents have argued that the feature model fails exactly because categories are fuzzy. They point out that there is no feature absolutely necessary for defining category membership, as we discussed in the last chapter for games, and thus that the distinction between characteristic and defining features is vacuous (Collins and Loftus, 1975). Obviously, feature theorists disagree and have attempted to catalogue defining and characteristic features for at least some categories. Be that as it may, the validity of the feature model rests in part on its ability to account for the results we have already discussed, and we turn next to consider how it does this.

The Comparison Process.   To account for category size effects, semantic relatedness effects, and hierarchical inference effects, we need to examine the comparison process. This is usually conceptualized as having two stages (Meyer, 1970; Smith, Shoben, and Rips, 1974; Glass and Holyoake, 1975): Stage 1 assesses broadly how much a category and an instance are related—if they are very related (say, robin and bird) there is a fast true, and if they are very unrelated (say, trout and bird) there is a fast false. The sizes of the "very"s are arbitrary but fixed. Stage 2 takes place only when the relatedness value returned from Stage 1 is intermediate (as in, perhaps, bat and bird). Just entering Stage 2 will take some time, so verifications resulting in these intermediate relatedness levels must take longer than ones that are clear trues or clear falses. Stage 2 entails an in-depth comparison of the highly weighted features (usually the defining ones only) of the instance with those of the category to determine whether the relation between the two is appropriate.

Accounting for the Data.   The two-stage comparison process accounts for category size effects and possibly for the hierarchy effects as follows. Subordinate categories by definition have more defining features: "Birdness" contains all the defining features of "animalness" plus, for example, being feathered. Now suppose we must verify "a canary is a bird," "a canary is an animal," "a canary is a flower," and "a canary is a plant," the first two being trues, and the first and third being smaller categories. "Canary" and "bird" share a large number of features, so we need not enter Stage 2, resulting in a fast true response. "Canary" and "animal" have less feature overlap and therefore Stage 2 must take place, making verification of the superordinate longer than verification of the subordinate, explaining the hierarchy findings in a different way from before. (It is actually unclear what the feature model should predict for these superordinates. Less feature overlap implies Stage 2 must be entered, which suggests a RT increase. However, abstract categories have fewer defining features, so Stage 2 should be faster for superordinate than subordinate categories—if it is ever entered in the latter. A fast Stage 2 could reduce the effect predicted by no Stage 2.)

The feature model can be stretched to account for the contradictory results found for false responses by applying the notion of varying degrees of feature overlap. However, since it accounts for falses as tortuously as the network model, we will not describe the account in detail but note generally that all models have difficulty accounting for false response times.

Summary and Conclusions

Where does all this leave us? The results of the experiments and the explanations afforded for the results by each of the models are summarized in Table 3.2. Each of the three models seems to do a fair job of accounting for the data, especially if modifications of each are allowed. The first model suggested a meaning organization in terms of prototypes—some object is central to a concept and in a sense constitutes its "definition." But other objects are instances of the concept, though more peripherally, and they are located at a greater distance from the entry point than the concept name. The second suggested a meaning organization in terms of complex multidimensional associations, hierarchically and logically organized, thus specifically encoding inclusions and contradictions. The third entailed a meaning organization in terms of weighted feature lists, with no other organization. These appear to be quite different, but as each has been modified to account for the same data, they begin to resemble one another.

What have we learned about semantic processing? First, there seems to be no question that some information is more readily available than other information, even though it may seem logically to be at the same level. It is faster to respond in a variety of ways to higher frequency words, words that have a higher production frequency or association strength (relatedness effects), following a probe word, and to words that have been more recently activated. (This last may be a more general statement of the frequency effect—more frequent words are more likely to have been recently activated outside the experimental setting than less frequent words.) What is not clear is whether these effects arise because of greater centrality of the more available concepts, or greater weights associated with them or their critical features. However, these seem to be different ways of saying the same thing.

Second, there is weak evidence for a hierarchical organization in terms of abstract markers and labeled links, implicating an inference process and suggesting some degree of cognitive economy. The evidence for hierarchical organization derives from demonstrations of RT increases for superordinate decisions when frequency, relatedness, production frequency, etc., are all held constant, together with occasional demonstrations of fast false responses to contradictions that would appear to be retrieved early in a hierarchical organization. The evidence is weak because the relatedness effects are more powerful and can overwhelm the hierarchical effects. The evidence suggests abstract markers, an inference process, and cognitive economy, since to account for an increase in RT for "a canary has skin" over "a canary can fly" we need to assume that "skin" is stored with an "animal" or "animate" feature, and that "canary" implies the abstract marker "animate," and then that there is a process that derives "skin" from "animate," after deriving "animate" from "canary." All of this will hold only if the property "has skin" is stored only with the abstract marker and not with each of the items described by the marker. The evidence suggests labeled links in the fast retrieval of high frequency contradictions: Diamonds are *not* rubies, and, in the multiplicity of connections between them, this must be explicitly indicated to avoid confusions. Nevertheless it is important to note that these implications do not uniquely select the network model; markers can be features, either characteristic or defining; the appearance of cognitive economy and hierarchy effects can occur if weakly weighted features are not searched; and contradictions can be inferred by a mismatch of defining features.

Third, there is still weaker evidence for category size effects, "still weaker" because much of the category size effect can be subsumed by semantic relatedness and hierarchical organization effects. However, we cannot totally rule out the possibility that when we verify that "an x is a y" we search all (or many) instances of y for x, and that the larger y is, the longer this takes. This suggests that categories are in part defined by instance lists. These could be organized with prototypical instances first, organized with all instances retrievable from membership or inclusion links, or organized by feature with the category name constituting a feature, and retrieval taking place through it.

Since the models seem to give the same kinds of accounts, let us conclude by accepting Figure 3.2 as a reasonable representation of semantic organization. Semantic memory may be conceived of as a space in which all concepts named by words are defined in terms of other concepts—that is, that the semantic system is contained wholly within itself. Close associations are near one another with a labeled link specifying the nature of the association. There is some degree of logical organization, but this is subject to individual differences in order of learning concepts (as Rosch suggests for prototype formation and Collins and Loftus suggest for network organization). Thus, for some of us there may be an additional step between "chicken" and "bird" ("poultry" or "food animal") that might not exist for others.

Implications. It is important to realize that this semantic memory "space" must be multidimensional—if every concept is to be near its close associations. On one plane, close associations of "drift" are movements; on another, things that drift, such

Table 3.2 Summary of models, results and explanations for semantic memory.

	PROTOTYPE	NETWORK	FEATURE
DESCRIPTION OF THE MODEL	Related concepts are located near one another. The typical instance is central to the category concept. Typicality and categories are established by balancing high information content (important distinctions) with high redundancy (important similarities). Comprehension begins by entering a category at the prototype, and fanning out.	All concepts are related through a rich associative net. Intersections in the net are represented by labels (words) marking properties, category names, or other features. Comprehension begins by entering the node labelled with the word name and consists of excitation of all nodes connected directly or indirectly to that node. Connections may be strongly or weakly weighted, and are labelled as to the kind of association (synonym, superordinate, disjunction, etc.).	Concepts are described in terms of two types of features—defining features and characteristic features. Defining features are those that *must* be present for a concept to be recognized. Characteristic features are those that are usually present. Comprehension takes place in 2 stages—first determining how many features overall apply, and then if an intermediate number apply, checking the defining features individually.

EXPERIMENT RESULTS   ACCOUNTS

1. The superordinate is a better prime for good instances than poor instances.	The category search begins at the good instances making the search faster.	The connection to the good instances is more highly weighted.	The good instances have more characteristic features, avoiding Stage 2.
2. Priming causes a faster access of the primed word and related words (repetition effect).	←——— ?	There is spreading activation to related concepts. Each activation increases the weight of the links.	———→ ?

Table 3.2 (*continued*)

EXPERIMENT RESULTS	PROTOTYPE	ACCOUNTS	FEATURE
3. It is faster to determine that an instance is a member of an immediate superordinate than a higher superordinate.	The instance is more typical of the immediate superordinate.	The instance is more directly connected to the immediate superordinate.	The instance shares more features with the immediate superordinate.
4. Semantic relatedness speeds recognition of truth.	Prototypical instances are more related to the category.	There are more connections between highly related concepts.	There are more shared features between highly related concepts.
5. Semantic relatedness slows recognition of falseness.	?	There are more connections for related concepts, each of which must be ruled out.	There are more features in common, so defining features must be checked.
6. Frequently produced fill-in-the-blanks for falses are quickly contradicted despite relatedness.	?	There are disjunctive or contradiction connections, some with high weight.	?
7. Large categories take longer to search than small categories.	There is more distance between the typical instance and the extremes.	1) There may be a link with lower weight between a large category and an instance than between a smaller category and an instance. 2) There may be an indirect association between the larger category and the instance (an intermediate category).	? (Predicts the opposite, since large categories have fewer features.)

as wind and water; on another, metaphorical associations of drifter, vagabond, and hobo; on another, metaphorical associations of conversation themes as in "if you catch my drift." Those are *four planes* for a word that produces few associations; four exceeds conventional three-dimensional space and most concepts are richer and will have more than four planes!

Following Quillian, in defining a word's meaning totally within semantic space, as all the associations aroused during spreading activation from the word, we satisfy the criteria of meaning as distinct from reference or symbol as specialized from sign. Consider once again the sentences "Shakespeare is Shakespeare" and "Shakespeare is the author of Hamlet." In the first sentence the subject and predicate will activate exactly the same associations. In the second, the subject will activate one set of associations, only one of which may be "authored Hamlet," at the same time that "Hamlet" and "author" are arousing their associations, only one of which may be "Shakespeare." "Shakespeare" may first evoke a man in Elizabethan dress, while "Hamlet" evokes Lord Lawrence Olivier, a great contemporary Shakespearean actor. Thus, the subject and the predicate, although referring to the same object, are not creating the same internal effect (do not have the same meaning), and the sentence does not seem silly.

Although semantic space is self-contained, it must interface with our immediate sensory representations, since we can see something and correctly name it. Similarly it can interface with nonimmediate sensory representations, images, and motor representations, as Rosch suggested. Interfaces to these systems do not detract from the independence of semantic representations but simply allow interactions. Some of the interactions can result in categories being formed to take into account observed feature correlations; some may be in the other direction, where language categories direct perception as suggested by the Whorf-Sapir hypothesis.

We will not discuss in any more detail either the existence of sensory representations or their links with the semantic representations. There are two other aspects of word processing that are abstract and linguistic, and these will be treated next. The first is the processing of nonliteral meaning and the second, the pronunciation/spelling guide to the psychological dictionary.

Other Aspects of the Mental Dictionary

The Semantic Differential and Connotative Space

Recall the distinction between connotation and denotation. Denotation expresses the aspect of word meaning that refers to instances in the external world, and connotation, the associated feelings the word arouses. "Mother" denotes a certain biological relationship, and connotes something warm, friendly, and caring. "Angel" denotes a winged, haloed, good spirit of either sex, and connotes, like "mother," a friendly, caring being. At the psychological meaning level we have been discussing, have we dealt with connotation, denotation, or both?

The question is interesting and has not been explicitly discussed in the literatures we have just reviewed. It seems that image/prototype models must be treating denotation only: They tend to be restricted to concrete objects or categories that by definition have obvious external referents; they discuss the difference between good and poor instances also in terms of features-that-can-be-pointed-to. The feature model could have the capability of handling either connotative or denotative meaning by including features that capture connotative meaning. The network model seems to have incorporated both types of meaning already: Connotation along with denotation could be considered to emerge from the associated nodes tagged during spreading activation—a property of "mother," for example, might be "caring." What is particularly interesting theoretically is that although Quillian's model seems to have connotation built in while the others models must be stretched to include it, the models had appeared almost indiscriminable with respect to their treatments of actual performance. Perhaps the sudden apparent discriminability for connotation and denotation is because the difference between connotation and denotation is not psychologically valid (it would not be valid if connotative meaning is processed and stored in the same way as denotative meaning), or perhaps it is because the psychological experiments described thus far have been limited to denotative meaning, so differences could not be seen.

One set of experiments (performed principally by Osgood (1971; Osgood, Suci, and Tannenbaum, 1957) examined connotative meaning exclusively, and was undertaken well before the prototype, network, or feature models were specified or tested. These gave rise to the first description of meaning as a multidimensional space, using a technique called the *semantic differential*. Osgood asked subjects to rate words on a number of *bipolar scales*. (Recall the polar feature type described in Chapter 2, hot-cold, tall-short; a word could be "defined" as a positive or negative value on a dimension.) Osgood's conception was that part of the meaning of any word was its values on such scales: "Canary" can be rated on hot-cold, good-bad, tall-short dimensions. Presumably "canary" is warmer than "snake" for most people, not because of denotative meaning (snakes are cold-blooded) but because of connotative meaning (canaries are friendlier and hence warmer than snakes).

After collecting large numbers of ratings of large numbers of words on large numbers of scales, Osgood analyzed the results using a statistical technique called *factor analysis*. Consider how you would describe A and B of Figure 3.4. Both consist of 12 lines, but A is organized such that the 12 lines cluster in three axes, whereas B has them spread throughout the two-dimensional space. Although we can still see the differences in the 12 lines of A it makes sense to talk about them as three groups of lines, the groupings determined by distances. Factor analysis takes large amounts of data (>12 items) and computes a kind of difference or distance between them. (This difference is called *variance* and is, somewhat more precisely, the distance between an actual score and the average of several such scores.) Very large differences, or large variance, would indicate separations among the three axes of A, and small differences or small variance would indicate clusters within the three axes of A. By mathematically juggling these large and small differences, factor analysis returns with the axes, or factors, that account for major amounts of variance in the data.

Now consider the use of factor analysis specifically for the semantic differential. If every word has its own distinct place on each bipolar scale, semantic space, as revealed by these scale ratings, will look like B. However, if words that tend to be rated as "warm" also tend to be rated as "good" and "true" and "beautiful" (as "mother" and "angel" would be) we will see a cluster as in A of warm-good-true-beautiful forming the individual lines, say, within the horizontal cluster; that is, concepts rated positively on this dimension will be located at one end, concepts rated negatively (cold-bad-false-ugly) on the other, and concepts rated neutrally toward the middle. What factor analysis tells us is that objects rated positively on one scale are likely to be rated positively on the others, so that we may consider $+/-$ (good-warm-true-beautiful $= +$) as one dimension instead of four.

Osgood et al. found three principal clusters in these data, which they named *evaluative* (good-bad), *potency* (strong-weak), and *activity* (lively-quiet). They considered that these dimensions defined the spatial organization of the connotation system—each word is located somewhere along these three axes in connotative space, its precise position giving rise to the feeling of how good, powerful, or active its referent is. "Mother" and "angel," although lying in different denotative planes, occupy similar positions in connotative space.

As an example, it is instructive to examine their analysis of the differences between "good" and "nice."

Most people we asked accepted them as synonymous, yet agreed that there was a difference, somehow, in their 'feeling-tone'—most respondents were unable to verbalize this difference, however. Analysis with the differential indicates a marked difference between the two words on the *potency factor,* and when we investigate the linguistic contexts in which they are appropriate we find that GOOD is a 'masculine' word and NICE a 'feminine' word. Speakers of English agree that 'nice man' differs from 'good man' in that the former is rather soft, weak and effeminate; on the other hand, while 'nice girl' is appropriately feminine, 'good girl' has a decidedly moral tone. When the profiles for GOOD and NICE are compared with those for MALE and FEMALE, we find that wherever MALE and FEMALE separate sharply, so also do GOOD and NICE. GOOD like MALE is significantly *thicker, larger* and *stronger*

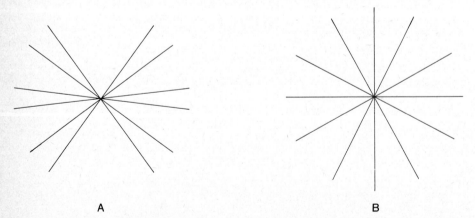

A   B

Figure 3.4 *Plots of 12 lines showing how they can be distributed about some major axes (A), or evenly within the space (B). For A, it might be reasonable to discuss the lines with respect to the axes, while for B each line must be mentioned individually.*

than NICE, but there are no significant differences on the *activity* and *evaluative* *factors.*

(Osgood, Suci, and Tannenbaum, 1957, pp. 167–168).

The semantic differential has been used to evaluate attitudes not only toward words but also toward nonlinguistic entities: sculptures, paintings, political candidates, and other social attitudes. Its results in these areas are comparable to its results with word-concepts: high reliability, interesting intepretability of results, and a consistent emergence of evaluative, potency, and activity factors as dimensions underlying conceptual structure, be it linguistic or nonlinguistic.

Language analyses using the semantic differential have been undertaken across a wide variety of individuals and cultures. The former have led to some very intriguing results with respect to the conceptual space of emotional meaning in disturbed individuals, and will be treated in Chapter 13. The latter have relevance here, in that they provide data bearing on the Whorf-Sapir hypothesis.

Osgood (1971) reported a long-term study using the semantic differential to compare connotative meanings of easily translated words in 28 different cultures. In a multistep process, native speakers generated common words to be tested, provided "translations" of concepts to obtain a common corpus, and generated polar scales to judge the concepts. The ease of generating polar scales across cultures suggested to Osgood that "the tendency to organize modes of qualification in terms of polar organization is yet another [evaluative, potency, activity factors being the first] universal of human language" (Osgood, 1971, p. 28). Native speakers then rated the words on these scales.

Results were analyzed in two ways. First, for each culture a separate factor analysis was computed. These analyses universally yielded "evaluative" as the primary dimension, with potency and activity important factors in almost all cultures. Occasional new factors emerged as second or third, pushing potency and activity down in importance for some languages. For example, Afghan Dair speakers had as the second strongest axis human-religious-learned-Muslim-courageous-immaculate (positive end), and the Lebanese Muslim group had as second strongest axis a cluster of rare-little-thin-particular-hidden-light (postive end). In the second type of analysis, all responses were submitted to one large factor analysis, the multitude of data allowing reasonable interpretations for more than three factors. In particular, a common cluster, concreteness/stability, united weakly such words as stable, firm, tame, deep, reliable; another united freezing, cold, wet, green, which Osgood labeled thermal/dermal; another, ordinariness, clustered ordinary, limited, slow, empty, common, easy; and a final common one, age, grouped old, old-fashioned, aged, quiet, round, eternal, lonely, solitary. These four new dimensions accounted for far less variance than the primary three but seemed to underlie clustering in many cultures.

Summary. The cross-cultural studies have indicated a general, perhaps universal, basis of connotative meaning; that is, it is common to (1) be able to "locate" words in some emotional space, (2) organize connotative meanings in terms of polar oppositions, (3) use a good-bad opposition as primary factor, and (4) use potency, activity, fineness, stability, righteousness, and so on, as secondary factors, although the relative importance of these seems to vary from culture to culture, with potency and activity more often important. There are interesting cultural differences revealed by the semantic differential, suggesting different patterns of thought depending on culture. However, it is impossible to determine whether it is language influencing thought here or basic cultural attitudes influencing ratings of language units.

In any case, the semantic differential provides yet another technique for studying meaning organization. The semantic differential reveals a multidimensional space, as do network models, but with fundamentally different planes of organization. Those planes can be incorporated as extra dimensions into the network model ("good" would have more heavily weighted links with masculine words than feminine words, and conversely for "nice," these link differences forming a plane), or this multidimensional space for connotation can be considered as separate from, but interfacing with, a denotative space.

Metaphor and the Creation of New Meanings

For connotation and denotation, as discussed thus far, the representation of verbal meaning need consist only of previously learned associations, and performance on a variety of linguistic tasks can take place through a relatively passive process of recognizing the existing associations. Language, however, is usually creative: New associations are established by most utterances, not just reminders of old facts. To understand processing of meaning we must consider some of these creative utterances.

Consider for example a sentence like "billboards are the warts of the highway." Most people can readily interpret that sentence but cannot interpret it literally. The word "billboard" is interpreted literally; it is the *subject, topic,* or *tenor* of the metaphor. "Warts of the highway" is interpreted figuratively; it is the *vehicle* of this metaphor. The interpretation—something like "billboards are ugly protuberances"— is called the *ground* of the metaphor. It is interesting to note that if we turn the subject and vehicle around as in "warts are the billboards of the skin" we radically change the interpretation from "ugly protuberances" to something about advertising.

Given the verification task we have been considering, metaphors provide a problem, since they contain an obvious contradiction. "Warts" presumably is a property of living things (or has a selectional restriction of applying to living things) and "billboard" and "highway" both contradict or violate that restriction. One theory for understanding metaphor relies on observation of the contradiction; once a contradiction is noted a special process for understanding the sentence is said to be turned on. The process is the *substitution* of an interpretable equivalent sentence that could be taken literally, such as "billboards are like warts." With the hedge "like," we may treat the sentence as we do other sentences, searching for intersections in the network, searching through characteristic features, etc. (Honeck, 1980).

The substitution theory does not hold up to empirical tests. As you might have noticed, it predicts that metaphorical utterances will take longer to undertand than literal utterances since the metaphor requires observation of the contradiction, performing a substitution, and then the same processes as literal utterances require. If metaphors are presented in isolation, they do indeed take longer than literal sentences. However, if a reasonable context precedes them, they take the same amount of time (Ortony, 1980; Gerrig and Healy, 1983, for example). Therefore, it is not always necessary to perform these extra steps. Moreover, if subjects are specifically instructed to verify sentences on the basis of literal meaning, verification takes longer if there is also a figurative meaning: It takes longer to decide that the sentence "all jobs are jails" is false than to decide that "some desks are melons" is false (Glucksberg, Gildea, and Bookin, 1982). This suggests that figurative interpretation is spontaneous, even when unnecessary, and therefore does not utilize out of the the ordinary processing.

A second problem with the substitution theory lies in the asymmetry of interpretation of metaphors created by reversing topic and vehicle. If normal processes take over once the metaphor is recognized, we would expect a spreading activation from the two words ("wart" and "billboard"), which would retrieve intersections. Presumably, the activation should retrieve the same intersections regardless of which word was presented first; yet it does not. This, in fact, can pose a problem with the second theory of metaphor interpretation, too.

The *comparison theory* holds that metaphors and literal utterances are both processed similarly, such that shared features of subject and predicate are derived in comprehension. The "difference" for metaphor is that the association between the two terms is uncommon.

In support of this theory, Malgady and Johnson (1980) have shown that ease in interpreting metaphors is directly related to the number of shared features between topic and vehicle, suggesting that interpretation is dependent on the success of such searches for intersections. Observe that in the metaphor just presented "warts" has as important, highly weighted properties "ugliness" and "protuberance," both of which could apply to billboards but which are not so highly weighted for them.

Ortony (1980) suggested that this difference in weighting is characteristic of metaphor, is what makes metaphor instructive, and is what accounts for the asymmetry in interpretation if topic and vehicle are reversed. Specifically, he argued that metaphor causes attention to low-weighted properties of the topic by comparing them with high-weighted properties of the vehicle. This modified a version of the comparison model proposed by Tversky (1977) to account for such asymmetries. Tversky suggested that it is not just similarities that are retrieved but also differences, the associations that tenor and vehicle do *not* share, and that similarities are weighed against the background of differences. Note that there is a surprise in the metaphor when the correct comparison is obtained. The surprise could result from the observation that the connection is unusual, and that is true only when there are more differences than similarities. Therefore the subject must have access to the fact that there are more differences, so these must be retrieved as well.

Thus, if we assume that metaphor interpretation is not different from literal interpretation, then either of these modifications suggests that our concept of spreading activation must be modified: Spreading activation either must be directed, from the topic rather than from all words equally, thus ensuring that the highly weighted topic features are given special consideration, or it must retrieve not only connections (similarities) between the topic and vehicle but also nonintersecting associations of each (the differences), so that it is clear that the connection to the topic is unusual.

A third account of metaphor processing begins with the introspection that the metaphor creates a tension because of the contradiction, a tension that must be resolved by insight. The insight is what makes metaphors fun. This is called the *interaction theory* because it is assumed that the ground arises from active interaction between topic and vehicle (Johnson, 1980). The interaction theory is supported in part by the result that a context reduces the time to understand a metaphor, presumably because the context supplies the "interaction" that would otherwise await first hearing the metaphor. More compelling evidence for interaction was provided by Verbrugge and McCarrell (1977) who showed that the ground could effectively prompt recall of a previously presented metaphor but was not effective in prompting either the topic words or the vehicle words for subjects who had been presented with either of these alone. Thus, they argued, it is the interaction of the topic and the vehicle that creates the high relatedness of the ground, not a relatedness of ground to either part alone. The notion that interaction might *create* relatedness may be accounted for by assuming that as a result of the metaphor a new direct associative link is forged between two concepts that had previously been associated only indirectly. The new association, Verbrugge and McCarrell suggested, might be facilitated by imaging, since the image will fuse the two parts into a whole. Indeed, there is evidence that metaphors are easier to understand if they are highly imageable (Paivio, 1979).

Regardless of whether metaphor comprehension involves an active, creative interaction or a more passive activation through intersection of low-weighted preexisting associations, it is reasonable to assume that metaphor understanding is a normal language process, not a deviant one used only in rare cases of contradiction. For if language is to communicate, to transfer information, it must effect a change. In literal interpretation the change may not be as dramatic as in nonliteral, since there is no obvious contradiction of old knowledge, but some change must still exist. This discussion for the most part was meant to be interpreted literally. If it nevertheless was new to you, in defining "tenor" for example, it either created a new association or changed the weighting of an old one.

The Lexicon

There is one last issue to discuss before leaving representation of meanings; that is how the words, as distinct from the meanings, are stored. It is convenient to call what we have been discussing up to now, the *dictionary,* which is our representation of concepts and/or meanings, and to differentiate that from our *lexicon,* which contains rules for recognizing and producing the words naming the concepts. Concept representations presumably underlie thought in whatever form; expression of the thought or representation requires an interface between the concept representation and the word-names. What evidence is there for word-names as distinct from concept representations?

Generally such evidence must come from production tasks (but see Chapter 12) because it is only in production that a link between word-name and word-meaning can be observed: Given a word-name we generally can retrieve its meaning if the word is known to us, but sometimes we know what we want to say but are unable to come up with the word(s) to say it. (This asymmetry in the interface between the lexicon and the dictionary is fascinating. Why can we usually go from lexicon to dictionary but frequently not be able to go the other way?!)

Primed Production Results. Two types of production tasks have been used to study the organization of the lexicon and dictionary-lexicon interface, with very interesting results. In a large number of studies, conveniently summarized in Collins and Loftus (1975), Loftus has investigated primed production tasks. In these studies subjects were asked to produce instances of a category name that met particular restrictions—for example, to name fruits that are red (→ apple, pomegranate, plum, red grape, etc.), or to name fruits beginning with "p" (→ pear, plum, peach, pome-granate, etc.). (Consider how much easier it is to generate names for a particular initial letter than for a particular final letter. This suggests that the initial sound or letter is more fundamental to the name access than the final one, as we shall see.) She found that giving the category name first speeded RT for either letter or adjective decisions, presumably because priming with the category name activates a small number of closely related concepts, compared to the number and distance of concepts activated by adjectives or letters; "fruit" is more closely related to "apple" than is either "red" or "A." When she compared category-letter and category-adjective trials, she found that when they were mixed, RTs were about the same for the two conditions. How-ever, if a large number of trials of the category-letter pairs were presented together (this is called *blocking* the trials) RT was markedly reduced, while it did not change with blocking of category-adjective trials. She assumed that for category-adjective pairs a small portion of the semantic network common to both was activated, and then names were retrieved from the interfaced lexicon, name retrieval taking time. In mixed trials the same strategy was employed for category-letter pairs, with the category activating the appropriate portion of semantic memory and subsequent name retrieval from the lexicon. However, blocking of the letter category primes, she concluded, caused subjects to activate relevant portions of both the lexicon (the whole A section for example) and the semantic network or dictionary, speeding the name retrieval aspect of the task. All of this suggests a separate dictionary and lexicon with interface between them.

Tip-of-the-Tongue Results. The other type of "production task" that has been used to explore the organization of the dictionary is somewhat more natural: study of what information we still have access to when in the tip-of-the-tongue state. In a now classic study, Brown and McNeill (1966) attempted to induce tip-of-the-tongue (TOT) by reading subjects definitions of low-frequency words such as "ambergris," "apse," and "sampan," and asking them to name the word. Subjects were instructed to do nothing if they knew the word immediately, but if it was on the tip-of-the-tongue, to answer a number of questions about the experience: to guess at the number of syllables, the first letter, words that sounded similar, and words that had similar meanings. After these subjects were told the target word and told to indicate in their answers whether this was indeed the one they were attempting to recall. Brown and McNeill were successful in inducing 360 TOT states, of which 233 turned out to correspond to the target word, enabling comparison of what was retrieved on those 233 trials with perfect retrieval. (On the trials in which the subject was thinking of a word other than the target word and could not come up with it, the data are useless. We cannot tell, for example, whether the guesses are similar in sound to the subject's target since we do not know what that target was.)

Their data compellingly showed that subjects have access to aspects of words even when they do not have complete access to the words themselves. Subjects were good at generating words that sound like the target word: "Saipan," "Siam," "Cheyenne," "sarong" are examples of words generated for "sampan," when "sampan" itself could not be recalled. Subjects also could generate words similar in meaning ("barge," "houseboat," for this word) but did this less than half as frequently as they generated similar sounding words. Since they were given the definition to begin with, generation of meaning associations is easily handled by the model we have already— both the target's concept and associations' concepts would be tagged during spreading activation. Generation of similar sounding words is more of a problem since they should not be activated in a meaning organized dictionary. However, if there is a sound organized lexicon interfaced with the dictionary, activation of the concept in the dictionary should activate its word-name in the lexicon and perhaps surrounding word-names similar in sound. Thus, the sound information that subjects have available suggests the organization of the lexicon component of semantic memory.

What is that sound information? Subjects appear to have some knowledge of the number of syllables of the word and its spelling. Brown and McNeill (1966) had selected infrequent words ranging from one to five syllables as their targets, so by chance alone one can expect subjects to guess the correct number of syllables 20 percent (one out of five) of the time. Of the 224 similar sounding words offered by subjects 48 percent had the same number of syllables as the target, whereas of the similar meaning words 20 percent (chance) had the same number of syllables. Explicit guesses about syllable number also showed that information on the sound of the word was available.

The data also indicated that subjects knew the first letter when the word was not available; 62 percent of first letters explicitly guessed were correct, and 49 percent of similar sounding words began with the same first letter as the target. This is in contrast with a chance prediction of somewhat greater than one out of 26 (the number of letters in the alphabet, but not all occur frequently in initial position), or with the number of same letter choices for similar meaning words, 8 percent. By comparing the similar sounding words and the similar meaning words with respect to the target word, Brown and McNeill estimated guesses at the other letter positions, although subjects had not been explicitly asked for them. Figure 3.5 shows the results; it is clear that subjects also had some knowledge of both the second letter position and the last letter position, with decreasing information available at intermediate positions.

The basic question the data raise is how partial information—and so much of it—can be retrieved without retrieving the whole word. Thus far we have explained how a pointer at the word-name could be retrieved by appropriate activation of the word concept in the dictionary and, further, if the lexicon is arranged so that all words beginning with the same first letter are together, how missing the word-name might lead to similar sounding word-names. To extend this explanation to account for retrieval of subsequent letters or syllable number, we could assume that the lexicon too is multidimensional, with first letters forming one plane, second letters forming another, etc., and last letters another. If the pointer to the word-name simulta-

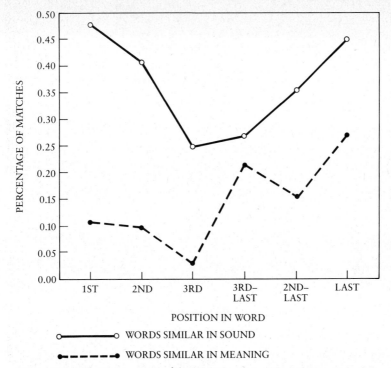

Figure 3.5 *The percentage of letters at each position that matched the target word in the word supplied as a guess at the target by subjects in the tip of the tongue state. The top line shows those words supplied as similar sounding and the bottom line, those words supplied as similar meaning. From "The tip of the tongue phenomenon" by R. Brown and D. McNeill (1966) in* The Journal of Verbal Learning and Verbal Behavior, *5, p. 330. Copyright 1966 by Academic Press. Reprinted by permission.*

neously points to each spot in the array, then if some elements are missing from the array or some connections are weak, partial information could be available, but not complete information. To account for the relatively greater availability of first-letter information, we need only postulate a higher weighting of that link. Finally, if we assume links within the lexicon as well, connecting letter to letter, we can account for the common effects of prompting—first letter or similar sounding words often can cue the correct word when in the TOT state. We explain this by assuming that the letter activates linked letters by spreading activation.

Summary and Conclusions

In this chapter we have explored data relevant to the question of how words and their meanings are represented mentally. We have seen that there is evidence for several types of representation, motor, image, and verbal, and that there is evidence for complex structure in the verbal representation. In particular, we can assume that there is a level of organization corresponding to information about the word-name (how it sounds, how it is spelled) that interfaces (through meaning) with sensory representations so we can name an object or action. There must also be sensory-based representations like images so that we can evoke the appropriate mental picture given the name. We can also assume that there is a level of organization corresponding to emotional or connotative meaning, derived in part from the associations of words, and in part from the natural human tendency to classify things with respect to their effects (positive-negative, strong-weak, active-passive, among other dimensions). Finally, we can assume a level of verbal meaning representation whereby meanings are represented by associations to other meanings, related features, related properties, category inclusions, etc. This last is conveniently modeled as a multidimensional network of weighted, labeled links connecting together all of our verbal concepts, and connected to the word-name representations, the image representations, and the emotion representations.

We have not attempted to show how these storage systems function in normal language comprehension, in producing or understanding a sentence or paragraph. In these latter cases it is not sufficient merely to activate concepts, emotions, and word-names: The activation must take place in an orderly fashion. "The man killed the woman" has a different sense than "The woman killed the man." Given the present framework the same activation patterns would emerge for both. In the next chapters, we shall examine rules for putting words together or taking them apart (syntax) so that each retains its role in the sentence. This system too must have a mental representation, as must the possible roles each word can take. At the end of Chapter 5, we will return to the question of the organization of meaning, in this case, at a higher level, with the language comprehender/producer utilizing syntactic information about words, as well as semantic information, to understand and generate meaningful language composed of more than one word.

REFERENCES

Anderson, A. & Bower, G. (1973). *Human Associative Memory*. NY: John Wiley and Sons.

Berlin, B., & Kay, P. (1969). *Basic Color Terms*. Berkeley: University of California Press.

Brown, R. (1958). *Words and Things*. NY: The Free Press.

Brown, R. W., & Lenneberg, E. H. (1954). A study in language and cognition. *Journal of Abnormal and Social Psychology, 49*, 454–462.

Brown, R., & McNeill, D. (1966). The "tip of the tongue" phenomenon. *Journal of Verbal Learning and Verbal Behavior, 5*, 325–337.

Collins, A. M., & Loftus, E. F. (1975). A spreading activation theory of semantic processing. *Psychological Review, 82*, 407–428.

Collins, A. M., & Quillian, M. R. (1969). Retrieval time from semantic memory. *Journal of Verbal Learning and Verbal Behavior, 8*, 240–247.

Collins, A. M., & Quillian, M. R. (1970). Does category size affect categorization time? *Journal of Verbal Learning and Verbal Behavior, 9*, 432–438.

Eddy, J. K., & Glass, A. L. (1981). Reading and listening to high and low imagery sentences. *Journal of Verbal Learning and Verbal Behavior, 20*, 333–345.

Gerrig, R. J., & Healy, A. F. (1983). Dual processes in metaphor understanding: Comprehension and appreciation. *Journal of Experimental Psychology: Learning, Memory and Cognition, 9*, 667–675.

Glass, A. L., & Holyoake, K. J. (1975). Alternative conceptions of semantic theory. *Cognition, 3,* 313–339.

Glucksberg, S., Gildea, P., & Bookin, H. A. (1982). On understanding speech: Can people ignore metaphors? *Journal of Verbal Learning and Verbal Behavior, 21,* 85–98.

Gregory, R. L. (1966). *Eye and Brain.* NY: McGraw-Hill.

Heider, E. R. & Olivier, D. C. (1972). The structure of color space in naming and memory for two languages. *Cognitive Psychology, 3,* 337–354.

Honeck, R. P. (1980). Historical notes on figurative language. In R. P. Honeck & R. R. Hoffman (Eds.). *Cognition and Figurative Language,* (pp. 25–46). Hillsdale, NJ: Lawrence Erlbaum.

Jacobson, E. (1932). Electrophysiology of mental activities. *American Journal of Psychology, 44,* 677–694.

Johnson, M. (1980). A philosophical perspective on the problems of metaphor. In R. P. Honeck & R. R. Hoffman (Eds.). *Cognition and Figurative Language,* (pp. 47–67). Hillsdale, NJ: Lawrence Erlbaum.

Katz, J. J., & Fodor, F. A. (1963). The structure of a semantic theory. *Language, 39,* 170–210.

Kosslyn, S. M. (1980). *Image and Mind.* Cambridge, MA: Harvard University Press.

Lakoff, G. (1972). Hedges: A study in meaning criteria and the logic of fuzzy concepts. *Papers from the eighth regional meeting,* Chicago Linguistics Society, Chicago Linguistics Department.

Landauer, T. K., & Freedman, J. L. (1968). Information retrieval from long-term memory: Category size and recognition time. *Journal of Verbal Learning and Verbal Behavior, 7,* 291–295.

Landauer, T. K., & Meyer, D. E. (1972). Category size and memory retrieval. *Journal of Verbal Learning and Verbal Behavior, 11,* 539–549.

Loftus, E., & Suppes, P. (1972). Structural variables that determine the speed of retrieving words from long-term memory. *Journal of Verbal Learning and Verbal Behavior, 11,* 770–777.

Malgady, R. G., & Johnson, M. G. (1980). Measurement of figurative language: Semantic feature models of comprehension and appreciation. In R. P. Honeck & R. R. Hoffman (Eds.). *Cognition and Figurative Language,* (pp. 239–258). Hillsdale, NJ: Lawrence Erlbaum.

Meyer, D. E. (1970). On the representation and retrieval of stored semantic information. *Cognitive Psychology, 1,* 242–300.

Ortony, A. (1980). Some psycholinguistic aspects of metaphor. In R. P. Honeck & R. R. Hoffman (Eds.). *Cognition and Figurative Language,* (pp. 69–83). Hillsdale, NJ: Lawrence Erlbaum.

Osgood, C. E. (1971). Explorations in semantic space: A personal diary. *Journal of Social Issues, 27,* 5–64.

Osgood, C. E., Suci, G. J., & Tannenbaum, P. H. (1957). *The Measurement of Meaning.* Urbana: University of Illinois Press.

Paivio, A. (1979). Psychological processes in the comprehension of metaphor. In A. Ortony (Ed.). *Metaphor and Thought,* (pp. 150–171). Cambridge: Cambridge University Press.

Paivio, A. & Begg, I. (1981). *Psychology of Language,* Englewood Cliffs, N.J.: Prentice-Hall.

Quillian, M. R. (1967). Word concepts: A theory and simulation of some basic semantic capabilities. *Behavioral Science, 12,* 410–430.

——— (1968). Semantic memory. In M. Minsky (Ed.), *Semantic Information Processing,* (pp. 227–270). Cambridge, MA: MIT Press.

Rosch, E. (1975). Cognitive representations of semantic categories. *Journal of Experimental Psychology: General, 104,* 192–233.

Rosch, E., Mervis, C. B., Gray, W. D., Johnson, D. M., & Boyes-Braem, P. (1976). Basic objects in natural categories. *Cognitive Psychology, 8,* 382–439.

Scarborough, D., Cortese, L. C., & Scarborough, H. S. (1977). Frequency and repetition effects in lexical memory. *Journal of Experimental Psychology: Human Perception and Performance, 3,* 1–17.

Schank, R. (1972). Conceptual dependency: A theory of natural language processing. *Cognitive Psychology, 3,* 552–632.

Smith, E. E., Shoben, E. J., & Ripps, L. J. (1974). Structure and process in semantic memory: A featural model for semantic decisions. *Psychological Review, 81,* 214–241.

Tversky, A. (1977). Features of similarity. *Psychological Review, 84,* 327–352.

Verbrugge, R. R., & McCarrell, N. S. (1977). Metaphoric comprehension: Studies in reminding and remembering. *Cognitive Psychology, 9,* 494–533.

Watson, J. B. (1930/1970). *Behaviorism.* Chicago: University of Chicago Press.

Wilkins, A. J. (1971). Conjoint frequency, category size and categorization time. *Journal of Verbal Learning and Verbal Behavior, 10,* 382–385.

Zipf, G. K. (1935/1965). *The Psychobiology of Language.* Cambridge, MA: MIT Press; first edition 1935 by Houghton-Mifflin, Inc.

STUDY QUESTIONS

1. With reference to conceptualizations of meaning, try to define the difference between a processing model (like Quillian's or Rosch's) and a structural model (like Katz' and Fodor's or Lakoff's). Do not simply describe any of these models, but try to point out what makes one structural and another processing.

2. Given what you have learned in chapters 2 and 3, what do you think meaning is for humans? To answer this question select the approach that seems most reasonable to you (fuzzy meanings, images, propositions, features, or network), the philosophical constructs that seem most reasonable (meaning is or is not reference; it is or is not habit, etc.) and use these to organize and account for the experimental results. What you should do is use the facts that have been presented on mental organization of meaning and match them with your intuitions to coordinate them into a model. Of course, you may use any of the models presented here.

4

Syntax

In the last chapter we discussed how individual word-meanings might be mentally represented. We saw that the representation must be quite complex, with each word arousing numerous associations only some of which are likely to be expressed in each task, with the ones expressed determined by the particular task. We also observed the desirability of labeling the associative links (disjunctive, subset-superset) to facilitate retrieval of a particular semantic relationship.

Normal out-of-the-laboratory language comprehending may be considered a language "task," with the other words in the sentence or paragraph serving as "task instructions" to determine which associations of a word are aroused. To understand "Jenny Lind was known as the Swedish nightingale" in normal contexts we immediately select the characteristic feature of nightingale that should be associated with a human (sings beautifully). The same word in the sentence "Florence Nightingale was the first nurse" is automatically connected to Florence and is not associated with bird features at all. "Hearing a nightingale is a wonderful experience" arouses all bird associations, while "Stravinsky created a beautiful opera from 'The Emperor's Nightingale'" arouses associations of fairy tales.

How do words in running speech (or text), without backtracking, modify one another's meanings so that inappropriate disjoint associations do not arise automatically? How do we know to interpret "Jenny Lind . . ." metaphorically, to treat "Florence Nightingale" as one unit and "Swedish" and "nightingale" as two? This is the role of *syntax*, the rules, shared by speakers of the same language, that specify the structures of sentences, governing meaning relationships. This chapter will focus on ways of describing these rules. (Readers are referred to the appendix of this chapter for definitions and examples of grammatical terms used here. These include common terms like "noun" and "verb" and linguistic terms like "verb phrase.")

Grammar as Description

Of all the levels of language, the syntactic is the least intuitive, the most remote from our everyday consciousness of language. When we talk about word-meaning, although we may not be able to pin down our experience, we feel as though somewhere in our brain this experience must exist in some form. Syntax or grammar does not have the same face validity: Words *seem* to tumble out unorganized and without thought, and it takes much concentration to be aware of their organization. When anyone attempts to learn a foreign language (s)he is immediately struck by the apparent abundance of rules—the incredible difficulty of that language compared with the intuitive simplicity of one's own. We English speakers say with pride that our language is among the most difficult to learn (I have always been tempted to ask people *why* do they say that? It is probably not true—the language that structurally most differs from one's own is "the hardest" to learn), but we do not feel any sense of having mastered an inordinate number of rules in learning it, as we do in acquiring a second language. When we are taught grammar in school, it seems very difficult to us as native speakers of the language—and certainly not something we have known since the age of six.

Does this mean that we do not use grammar in language processing? It could, although we will try to argue in this and the next chapter that it does not. The grammars that grammarians or linguists produce could be only one possible way of describing an apparent structure of the language. For example, consider the number series described in Box 1.2:

$$1\ 4\ 9\ 16\ 25$$

This was described as the sequence of squares of the numbers one through five, a rule that would allow us to add 36 to the list. Another rule also fits this sequence (and predicts 36 as the next number): If you take the difference between each of these numbers you get the series 3 5 7 9 . . . , the odd numbers. Which is the "true" rule for generating the series—take the natural numbers and square them, or add the odd numbers successively to the series members? If you used one strategy, the other may come as a surprise and may require a little effort to learn or remember. This might be what happens with the grammar rules we learn in school; they may describe language well but may not be the rules we spontaneously use in generating or understanding it. Alternatively, the series may only *seem* to be producible by either of the rules. Perhaps 149-1625 is a telephone number coincidentally reflecting numerical structure. Analogously, grammar rules may not reflect language processes at all but may constitute a convenient description or organization of linguistic utterances.

Thus, a grammar *describes* language, and there may be several plausible such descriptions. We will require of our grammar that it be able to distinguish all utterances considered grammatical by native speakers from all considered ungrammatical, and that it assign plausible structures to grammatical utterances. Following standard scientific practice, we will choose one such grammar over another if it is simpler; that is, if it has fewer rules. Remember, though, the preferred descriptive grammar from a linguistic viewpoint, the one that satisfies these criteria, may not be the grammar that we employ in day-to-day language use.

Tacit Knowledge, Competence, and Performance

How can we decide if a grammar is, in fact, psychologically plausible? It might seem that all that would be necessary would be to have native speakers look at it and see if it jibes with their intuitions about how they produce or understand their language. Unfortunately, this probably will not work because we do not seem to be aware of our knowledge about our language. Knowledge we have but are not aware of is called *tacit knowledge,* as distinct from explicit knowledge, things we know that we know. Following Chomsky (see Chomsky, 1980a, for a recent discussion), linguists and psychologists have become increasingly aware of how much of our knowledge is tacit rather than explicit.

In grade school, grammar course teachers often try to make our tacit knowledge explicit; we find learning the explicit rules difficult. In grammar and spelling exams, we are asked not just to perform correctly but also to state the rule that describes our performance. Students who correct "wiegh" to "weigh" but cannot give a reason better than "it seems better that way" (it seems better that weigh?) are expressing their tacit knowledge and are often penalized for not stating "i before e except after c . . ." Similarly, most of us know there is something wrong with "I gave it to he" but would have difficulty stating an explanation such as "prepositions [to] take the objective [him] not the nominative [he]." It is somewhat ironic that we native speakers are penalized in grammar courses for the response "it seems better that way." What does "seems better" mean if not that I know it *tacitly,* just the way a native speaker should?

Clearly, there is a place for speakers' intuitions in determining tacit knowledge. However, it is not the speaker's intuitions about what rule (s)he is using, but rather, about what utterances seem right or wrong. Tacit knowledge is inferred from speakers' actual *performance*—the utterances they produce or understand. Tacit knowledge is distinct from performance. Examples of linguistic performance might be a collection of utterances such as:

1. I gave it to him.
2. I gave it to her.
3. He gave it to him.
4. He gave it to me.

Analysis of these utterances would suggest that him, her, and me are all in one class distinct from I and he. An intuition that

*5. I gave it to he.

is wrong (ungrammaticality or wrongness is commonly denoted in linguistics by a star preceding the sentence) confirms that observation. Together these facts indicate knowledge of two classes of pronouns, of which knowledge the speaker may be unaware. The sum total of a speaker's tacit knowledge about the language is called linguistic *competence.*

It might be fruitful to look at competence and performance in a nonlinguistic instance to insure that the distinctions are clear. Consider climbing a staircase. Do you know how you do this? Let us consider three strategies: (1) trial and error—you pick your foot up to an arbitrary height hoping it will clear the step and move it down until the step intercepts it; (2) at the bottom of the staircase you assess the step size and the number of steps, then program the entire appropriate motor sequence; and (3) at each step you assess the step size and do one small motor sequence. Possibilities 2 and 3 involve tacit knowledge of the size of each step; it is tacit since you could not state the step size without explicitly calculating it. Possibility 1 suggests neither explicit nor tacit knowledge.

Is it possible to differentiate among these three strategies using performance data? Consider: We normally climb stairs without tripping; we can do other things while climbing stairs; occasionally when we reach the top or bottom of a staircase we step as though expecting one more stair, which to our stumbling surprise is absent. The first weakly suggests we do not use trial and error; if we did we should frequently step too high or not high enough and lose our footing. The second weakly suggests that we are not actively calculating as we ascend since our attention can be elsewhere. And the third suggests we have a whole flight program with a miscalculation on the number of steps, for if we calculated each step individually, the occasional last step stumble would be equally likely to occur anywhere in the flight. That you probably never before thought about how you climb stairs but did climb them nevertheless suggests tacit knowledge. Occasional stumbles are performance errors from which we infer strategies, but the stumbles do not suggest that you do not know how to climb stairs. Ideally, since our competence in our stair-climbing strategies does not change, our performance should be error-free; practically there may be errors in computation, in transferring to motor commands, in remembering the motor sequence, or in executing the motor sequence, none of which would suggest that we had lost our basic ability to climb stairs.

Constituent Analysis

Linguistic Reasoning

Although you may not be aware of it, we have already seen how linguists use a *corpus,* or collection of utterances, to infer grammatical structure. In the last section five sentences with nearly identical words were listed. The grammaticality of utterances (1) and (3) suggests that "I" and "he" are equivalent or substitutable; they occur in identical sentence frames but have different meanings. The occurrence of "I" and "he" in identical sentence frames implies that they are *structurally* similar. The ungrammaticality of (5) suggests "he" may not be freely substituted for "him" or "her," and so structurally dissociates the two classes "I, he" and "him, her, me." We can state these observations more formally by naming the two sets:

Nominative (NOM) → I, he
Objective   (OBJ) → him, her, me

and then stating as a rule

Sentence (S) → NOM gave it to OBJ

where NOM and OBJ *must be* rewritten by any of the words they stand for. This rule suggests that the sentences "he gave it to her" and "I gave it to me" are also grammatical, as indeed they are. (Note that the latter is awkward because of another rule that says that if two pronouns refer to the same individual, or are *coreferential,* the second should be a -self form, as in "I gave it to myself.") Rules that indicate that a linguistic category may be substituted for any of the linguistic units it represents are known as *rewrite rules.* A rewrite rule may result in a *terminal string* (terminal = end), a set of linguistic units that may not be substituted for any further, as is the result of NOM → I, for example: "I" does not stand for any other unit to be substituted. A rewrite rule may also result in a *nonterminal string,* a set of linguistic units that requires further application of rewrite rules to look like a real utterance. For example, in S → NOM gave it to . . . , "Nom gave it to" would never be stated by a person. To get a string that a person might utter—a terminal string—from this rule, we must apply the NOM and OBJ rules, yielding, for instance, "I gave it to him."

The rewrite rules just presented do not indicate particularly interesting facts about the structure of English. The example should illustrate, nevertheless, the linguistic method by which structurally equivalent units or *constituents* are derived. In the first rule, we may say that "I" and "he" are constituents of the category NOM; they are members of the category. The category name is a superordinate and is said to *dominate* its members or constituents. (Members directly underneath the category are its *daughters.* For example, NOM and OBJ are daughters of pronouns and I and he are daughters of NOM.)

An Exercise: Deriving Some Parts of Speech

The parts of speech presented in Chapter 2 (and reviewed in the appendix in this chapter) were ascertained by using constituent analyses. You may, in fact, have had difficulty with the definitions: A noun is the name of a person, place, or thing, and a verb is the name of an action—is an action not a thing? In "I saw Robert kill Mary," "kill" is a verb. In "I witnessed the killing (or murder) of Mary," "killing" is a noun. Do they both not describe the same actions? The difficulty some experience learning the parts of speech, in fact, probably stems from the attempt to form them into *meaning* classes. As we have seen, a verb or a noun can describe the same action: *the difference between nouns and verbs lies not in what kinds of things they stand for, but in what kinds of frames they stand in.*

Taking a small corpus of English sentences we will infer the relationships of the words, deriving the parts of speech. This exercise should serve as a reminder of the parts of speech, if necessary, and as an illustration of linguistic analysis.

1. I gave it to him.
⋮
6. Robert gave it to him.
7. The boy gave it to him.
8. A boy gave it to him.
9. A rich boy gave it to him.

First, note that these sentences are all grammatical and that they mean different things (as judged by us native speakers). Next, note that "I," "Robert," "The boy," "A boy," and "A rich boy," exist in the same sentence frames. We can therefore make one structural class out of these. Since, by native speaker judgment, some members of this class consist of more than one word, we will call the class a phrase, and more specifically, a *Noun Phrase* (NP). We can now make a new set of rewrite rules:

$$
NP \rightarrow \left\{
\begin{array}{l}
I \\
Robert \\
The\ boy \\
A\ boy \\
A\ rich\ boy
\end{array}
\right.
$$

Examination of this list immediately should yield the observation that "the," "a," and "a rich" occur in the same phrase frame and that the remainder—what is left if they are removed or if they do not exist ("boy," "Robert," "I")—occur in the same phrase frame. For the moment ignore that we already know that "I" is a pronoun and "rich" is an adjective. We will return to this in a moment and correct the analysis, but for now our purpose is to show the method of reasoning, and it is frequently applied by linguists to languages that have not been previously described so that there is no prior knowledge to fall back on. Since "a rich" seems to work the way "a" does we will say they are members of the same class, articles or *determiners (DET)*. Since "I" works like "Robert" and "boy" we will temporarily call them all *Nouns (N)*. We can make new rewrite rules:

$$
\begin{array}{l}
DET \rightarrow \begin{array}{l} The \\ A \\ A\ rich \end{array} \\
\\
N \rightarrow \begin{array}{l} I \\ Robert \\ Boy \end{array} \\
\\
NP \rightarrow (DET)\ N
\end{array}
$$

where the parentheses indicate that the determiner does not have to occur, or is *optional*. These rules suggest some new sentences:

*10. The I gave it to him.
*11. The Robert gave it to him.

which are obviously not grammatical, necessitating the breakdown of the N class into separate classes, one for "boy," a *common noun,* one that can take a determiner, and another class for "I" and "Robert."

The next thing we might note in our analysis is that "A rich" consists of two words, and wonder whether the two words play the same role. We could test this by changing their order:

*12. Rich a boy . . .

which is clearly ungrammatical, suggesting that they are not equivalent and that they belong to separate classes. We could support the separation by expanding our corpus to include other word frames in which "rich" might occur and words other than "rich" that might fit into those frames. For instance, we can say:

13. The boy looked rich.

but not

*14. The boy looked a.

We can also say

15. The small boy gave it to him.
16. The boy looked small.

These together suggest "rich" and "small" form a class of their own, which is distinct from determiners. We call that class *adjectives* (ADJ). (Note that in (13) and (16) the adjective seems to be modifying the verb. This is a special case that arises with only a few verbs. In these cases the adjective is called a *predicate adjective;* see adjective in the appendix.) We may now amend our NP rule to:

$$NP \rightarrow (DET) (ADJ) N$$

or, expanding it

$$NP \rightarrow N \text{ (when N is not a common noun)}$$
$$Det\ N \text{ (when N is a common noun)}$$
$$DET\ ADJ\ N$$

At this point we have several ways of creating NPs, and we will stop there.

As you should be aware, there are more parts of speech in English than determiners, adjectives, and nouns, but the principles for deriving these categories are much the same. The other parts of speech are verbs, adverbs, pronouns, prepositions, and conjunctions. These are defined in the appendix, and we leave it to you to generate sentences that demonstrate the structural integrity of these categories, as we have done for nouns, adjectives, and determiners. The analysis we have performed is called a *distributional analysis* and defines linguistic categories through the distribution of elements of the language.

Finite State Grammar

The simplest way to describe a sentence is as a sequence of words, or perhaps at the next order of constituents, a sequence of categories of words. This description is simple in that it implies minimal structure between sentence elements, each word automatically leads to the next, and there are no other constraints. As we will see, this kind of grammar is powerful enough to generate infinitely long sentences but is not powerful enough to account for many sentences of English or most people's intuitions about the structure of such sentences. This kind of grammar is called a *finite state grammar*.

A finite state grammar consists of an initial "state" or element, a final state or element, and a sequential set of elements or states between them. To get from one state to the next you follow the direction given on the arc or transition between them. For example:

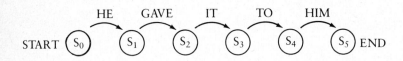

At S3 we would have the sequence "He gave it," and at the final state the whole sentence "He gave it to him." Each state calls the next state, so once the path is entered the sentence is automatically produced or recognized. Choice can enter in by *branching*, as in the solid lines in

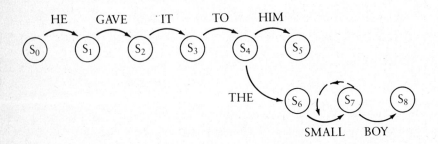

In this case, once the word "to" is reached, there is a choice between the pronoun "him" and the DET-ADJ-N sequence, "the small boy." When either branch is selected there is no crossing to the next branch. An infinitely long utterance may result from *looping*, indicated by the dotted line in the last finite state diagram.

In addition to the sentences "He gave it to him" and "He gave it to the small boy," looping will generate or recognize "He gave it to the small small boy," "He gave it to the small small small boy," and so forth. Once the "small" state is entered there is a branch; one can return to that state or exit to "boy." If it is returned to, the identical choice presents itself.

A finite state grammar consists of states, paths between them, and probabilities of selecting a particular path. Since each path serves as a transition between one state and another, these probabilities are called *transitional probabilities*. (It may help to consider transitional probabilities in a real language context; try to fill in the blank in the next two sentences:

> The next number you will see is _____.
>
> A stitch in time saves _____.

You can guess much better in the second case—it has a higher transitional probability than the first.) In the first finite state diagram presented, the transitional probability (tp) between each state is one since no choice exists. In the second diagram the combined probabilities for following the arcs for "HIM" and "THE" is one. If the alternatives are equally likely we can say each is .5; if one is more likely than the other it would have a higher probability. In the second diagram, there is, in addition, a less-than-one probability of exiting from "SMALL" to "BOY," since the "SMALL" state may be reentered. It is important to note that once a tp has been assigned to the "loop," it does not change *regardless* of how many "smalls" have already been generated; that is, if we assume that the probability of exiting from S_7 to S_8 is the same as the probability of repeating the "small" (both = .5), and that we have already applied this to generate or recognize "the small, small, small, small, small, small," we are *still* as likely now to add another "small" as to exit (or as likely to recognize as a reasonable sentence one with another "small"), since the tp of entering "boy" has not changed. This is one of the shortcomings of a finite state grammar; it has no memory—that is, it cannot take into account early elements of the string, *only* the current element. (A finite state grammar is an example of a *Markov process*. A Markov process, generates a Markov series—in a Markov series each element may be determined or computed given *only* the last element and the tp between it and the next possible element. We will not discuss Markov models further in this text; they are mentioned for those readers who may do supplementary reading in this area.)

Aside from the shortcoming in memory just mentioned, a finite state grammar could account for the rewrite rules and constituent structures we have discussed so far. Instead of putting the terminal elements in the words, we could put the category names into the finite state diagrams and assume that there is a process that would substitute members of the category for the category name. Thus, a finite state diagram of our rewrite rules for NPs could be:

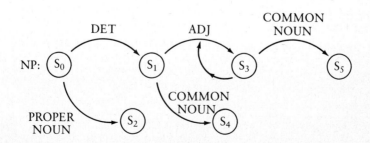

Functional Constituents

There is good reason to argue that there are additional levels of constituent structure beyond the low-level individual lexical items (words), and the next level, the *categories* the words can be grouped in with respect to how they combine with other words (the parts of speech). Finite state grammar treats all states equally and assumes connections only between adjacent states. If there is more structure a finite state grammar would fail to capture it, and we might then argue that finite state grammars are not powerful enough to describe English. The next level of constituents to consider are *functional* constituents.

Sentence (9) contains three NPs: "a rich boy," "it," and "him." In English changing the order of these NPs radically changes the meaning of the sentence—"it gave a rich boy to him" is very different from "a rich boy gave it to him." In English, order of the constituents determines, in large part, their functional relation to other parts of the sentence. In (9), as we know, "a rich boy" is the subject, and "it" is the object (for the moment, let us ignore "to him"); their relation to the verb "gave" is very different. In terms of constituent structure, we express this difference by decomposing our sentence into subject and predicate (called *verb phrase* or *VP*) and noting that the object-NP is part of the VP. In rewrite rules,

$$S \rightarrow NP\ VP$$
$$VP \rightarrow V\ NP$$

These rules are productive—they can be used to generate new sentences. For example, we can substitute other NPs for "it"

    17. Robert gave a rich dessert to him.

and maintain the same functional relationship among the constituents.

Besides the noun phrase and the verb phrase, there is another kind of phrase: the prepositional phrase (PP), "to him." This group has a different role from subject and object NP—we may delete it and still have a grammatical sentence.

    18. Robert gave a rich dessert.

but not (maintaining the same sense of "gave")

    *19. Robert gave to him.

When we delete the prepositional phrase, we have to delete both the NP and the "to" (the preposition), indicating their integrity. The "to him" modifies the verb and therefore is part of the VP but forms its own group within the VP. To express these groupings, to our rules

$$S \rightarrow NP\ VP$$
$$NP \rightarrow (DET)\ (ADJ)\ N$$

we add the rewrite rules

$$VP \rightarrow V \; NP \; (PP)$$
$$PP \rightarrow PREP \; NP$$

and to include a rule for "the boy looked rich," we may add

$$VP \rightarrow V \; ADJ.$$

It may seem that we have generated an enormous number of rewrite rules, but note that these account for an enormous number of sentences in English and, by comparison to what they can produce, they are few in number. The finite state model can account for the same sentences as these rewrite rules, but not for the postulation of the functional constituents. We need to hypothesize functional constituents primarily to capture the semantic relations between sentence elements, the fact that it is Robert who is giving, and the dessert that is given, not the other way. This is determined in part by likely meanings (desserts rarely give), but could be determined by syntax alone; in "Robert kicked Mary," it is Robert who is kicking, but either person could perform the action. We know who does do it through constituent structure.

A final argument for discussing sentences in terms of constituents derives from our use of pronouns. When we substitute "it" for the noun "dessert" in "Robert gave a rich dessert," we actually substitute "it" for the entire noun phrase—"Robert gave it," not "Robert gave a rich it." This indicates that we do not view the words as units here, but rather view the NP as the unit.

Note that as we have set up the rewrite rules, not all NPs are equal—the subject NP is derived immediately from S, the object NP must go through an additional constituent, VP, and the preposition NP through yet another constituent, the PP. This kind of grammar is called a *phrase structure grammar* and may be depicted either by rewrite rules or by a *phrase marker*, or *structure tree*, which illustrates graphically the hierarchical relations just described. For example:

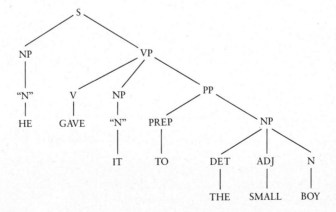

$\rightarrow$ He gave it to the small boy.

A phrase structure grammar has the power of a computer program with subroutine calls. This model is commonly called an *augmented transition network (ATN)* (Woods, 1970). Roughly an ATN looks like a finite state grammar, except that the arcs are labeled by nonterminal symbols naming structures that may be found on a different finite state diagram; that is, there is an overall structure or program that proceeds more or less sequentially but that can be interrupted to execute another program, *returning* to the appropriate state in the main program when finished. So, for example, we might have

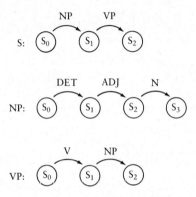

Now assume that the structure of a string of words is compared to the structure in the ATN. What will happen is that, beginning at S, we must match a "NP." Since NP is nonterminal it cannot be found in the input string and so we look for a way to match NPs. To do this, hold the NP place in the first line and jump to the second, which contains the condition for filling in a NP. So next we must match DET, ADJ, N. If successful, the condition for a NP is met and we *can return* to the correct position in the initial finite state diagram. Thus, an ATN has a memory and may be used to generate and/or recognize nonterminal structure.

Given the sentences we have examined, phrase structure grammar and finite state grammar are equally applicable. Finite state grammar is simpler, since it posits fewer layers of structure. Simplicity is preferable if all other things are equal, although in this case, the extra layers of structure seem to be intuitively reasonable. However, there is a stronger reason than intuition to reject a finite state grammar as a model of English.

Complex Sentence Structure

If you have been playing with the preceeding language analyses you may have thought of sentences that our rewrite rules cannot generate. Sentences sometimes are more complicated than these rules allow; for example, the sentence you are now reading. Omitting the phrase following the semicolon does not eliminate the problem: It results in "Sentences sometimes *are* more complicated than these rules *allow*," one apparent sentence with two verbs (in italics).

A *simple* or *core* sentence is one with one subject and one predicate. A complex sentence with several verbs can be described as a simple sentence with other sentences *embedded* in it. Using a more concrete sentence:

20. The rat the cat wounded ate the cheese.

We can decompose it readily into two sentences:

21. The rat ate the cheese. (the *main clause*)

and

22. The cat wounded the rat. (the *subordinate clause*)

The subordinate clause modifies the "rat" in (20)—it serves the same function as an adjective. This observation is supported by the near synonymy of the sentence

23. The wounded rat ate the cheese.

with (20). The rewrite rule for NPs was NP → DET ADJ NP. To permit (20) to be produced also we must modify that, perhaps to

NP–> (DET) (ADJ) N   (S)
        | | | ⌒‾‾‾‾‾‾‾‾‾‾‾⌒
       The   ()   rat the cat wounded (the rat) ate the cheese.

This modification has a very profound implication. We have

$$S \rightarrow NP\ VP$$

and now

$$NP \rightarrow (DET)\ (ADJ)\ N\ (S).$$

Note that across the two rules, S occurs on both sides of the arrow! This is called *recursiveness* (when a symbol can refer to or rewrite itself) and underlies much of the power of language. Recursiveness, in fact, is what enables the generation of interesting infinitely long sentences because we can keep applying the rule:

1. S → NP VP

Substituting the new NP rule we get

2. [(DET) (ADJ) N [(S)] VP]

applying rule 1 again, for the embedded S

[(DET) (ADJ) N [NP VP] VP]

applying the NP rule again

$$[(DET) (ADJ) N [(DET) (ADJ) N [(S)] VP] VP]$$

applying rule 1 for the embedded S we get

$$[(DET)(ADJ) N [(DET) (ADJ) N [NP VP] VP] VP]$$

and applying rule 2 we get

$$[(DET) (ADJ) N [(DET) (ADJ) N (DET) (ADJ) [N [(S)] VP] VP] VP]$$

generating a sentence such as

24. The rat the cat the farmer chased wounded ate the cheese.

(If you do not like this sentence you are not alone. We will soon discuss the problems with it, but for now note that, with effort, you can figure out who is doing what to whom.) And we do not have to stop here; we can substitute NP VP for the S in the last string and keep going.

Obviously, after a while, by the level of (24), the sentence becomes difficult to understand, but depending on the nature of the embedding, we may or may not have trouble. In the children's poem "This Is the House that Jack Built," and others of that ilk, very long sentences are constructed; in fact, the delight in that type of poem probably comes from the *game* of repeated application of the tacit rule. In the poem the contained sentences are strung together.

This is the cat who chased the rat who lived in the house that Jack built .

We have "cat chased rat," "rat lived in house," "Jack built house." Every subject is close to its predicate. In the sentence (24) we have been looking at

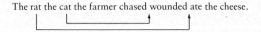

The rat the cat the farmer chased wounded ate the cheese.

the subjects and predicates are far apart with other sentences stuck between them. This is a *nested* or *center-embedded* type of sentence and is much harder to follow than the other. Chomsky (1957) argued that such sentences are within our competence to produce or understand, and it is merely a performance factor, memory, that makes them difficult—we lose track of or forget the subject by the time we get to its verb. As we shall see in the next chapter, there is some disagreement about whether multiple center embeddings are indeed within our competence.

Finite State Grammar, Phrase Structure, and Embedding

As we saw, it is easy to generate rewrite rules for embeddings and recursiveness. Is it possible to describe them with a finite state grammar? Consider:

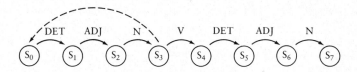

The solid lines represent a finite state grammar for:

$$S \rightarrow NP\ VP$$
$$NP \rightarrow (DET)\ (ADJ)\ N$$
$$VP \rightarrow V\ NP$$

To allow embedding, NP → N (S), we would have to add a return arrow from the first N to the start state, indicated by the dotted line. What will this produce or recognize? Beginning at S_0 (and ignoring the ADJs) we use "the" for DET, take the N path, use "rat" for N (→ the rat), return to S_0, and following the same route produce "the cat" (→ the rat the cat). Our current state is S_3 and our diagram gives us only two choices: to return to S_0 or to select a verb. Choosing the latter, we get "The rat the cat wounded," and now *must* generate or look for another NP like "the cheese" → *The rat the cat wounded the cheese." This is short one verb! That could be corrected by adding a loop to the verb arc, but that has the potential of producing too many verbs: Try for yourself to produce "The rat ate wounded the cheese" using the finite state diagram with a verb loop. What we need is a grammar that matches subject NPs to verbs so that however many subjects there are, there are an equal number of predicates.

> The rat the cat wounded ate the cheese.
>   a   b   b   a

A finite state grammar has no facility for remembering any but the previous command state, so it cannot recall the "a" subject by the time it needs to find a verb. For this reason, because it cannot account for recursiveness, Chomsky (1957) has argued that a finite state grammar is not powerful enough to model human language despite having the potential for generating infinitely long sentences. (Note that an ATN can account for embeddings since it has a memory. We need only have one of the nonterminal states name the start state. The memory will hold how many times the subject NP has been accessed and will therefore match VPs.)

If the previous discussion has seemed esoteric, be assured that it has psycholinguistic relevance, as we shall see later. For now, think about finite state grammars in terms of real language processes: Do you think sentences are just sequential associations where each word triggers only the next word?

Summary

In this section we have looked at some aspects of sentence constituent structure and how best to describe them. At the lowest level we find the words that compose a sentence. Each of the words can be categorized into parts of speech by using distributional analysis of English. The categories show structure in terms of their distribution in different sentences, as constituents. The constituents show a hierarchical structure. (Note that by putting words into constituents, we know what are the relationships among the words of a sentence and can use the relationships to assign meaning. At this point, it would be useful for you to determine the constituent structure of the sentences with "nightingale" in them, at the beginning of this chapter. In each sentence "nightingale" has a different functional role, as you will see.)

We also looked at some specific ways of describing some sentences in English and their implications: rewrite rules, finite state diagrams, phrase markers, and ATNs. We saw that all are capable of generating or parsing simple sentences of English, but that once recursiveness is permitted, in embedded sentences, finite state grammars are too weak. Thus, we are left with phrase structure grammars to account for the sentences we have looked at thus far.

Deep Structures and Transformational Grammar

Problems with Phrase Structure Grammars

Context Sensitivity in Language. We have seen that the simplest rewrite rules, representable by a finite state grammar, are inadequate to account for language because language permits recursiveness. Phrase structure grammars allowing recursiveness also have some problems as representations of human syntactic capacity. Consider once again the sentences

    7. The boy gave it to him.
    9. A rich boy gave it to him.
  *11. The Robert gave it to him.

a new sentence

  *26. Boy gave it to him.

and the rewrite rule

$$NP \rightarrow (DET)\,(ADJ)\,N$$

Obviously, in some cases the application of DET and ADJ is indeed optional, but in other cases there must be rules preventing us from taking the option, so we do not generate "The Robert," and rules forcing us to take the option, so we do not generate "Boy gave"; that is, the rules must be *context sensitive:* They must contain instructions about when they are applicable.

There are many possible demonstrations that a grammar for natural language cannot be context-free. We will consider a few more of them. First, in English certain NPs have particular effects on verbs. For instance, if we change the tense markings on sentences (1) and (7) from past to present, we get

27. I give it to him.
28. Robert (he) gives it to him.

The present tense is expressed differently depending on the context—with one kind of subject there is an "s" added. So the form of the verb is context sensitive—tuned to the form of the subject. Second, not all sentences are of the form S → NP V NP, grammatically. We cannot say

*29. Robert runs the book.

Application of the rule VP → V NP must have restrictions on it: the rule must be applied only in certain verb contexts. Third, as we have already indicated, use of pronouns is very strongly context-sensitive in English and frequently is sensitive to contexts outside the current sentence. For example, as noted earlier, it is poor style to say

I gave it to me

since me refers to the same person as I, we use the self form—myself—instead. To know to use the self form means not just knowing that "me" is a constituent of the VP (making it OBJ case), but also how it relates to the subject. Similarly, pronouns in general may only (and must) be used in contexts where the referent is clear. "Robert went to the store, then Robert bought apples, then Robert went home" is stylistically poor English. Substitution of "he" for all but the first "Robert" is better; use of the pronoun depends on contexts established either in the current sentence or in previous sentences. (Note that all of these examples indicate constraints of one word on non-adjacent words, ruling out finite state grammars.)

One way to incorporate context-sensitivity into a phrase structure grammar is to divide the categories represented in rewrite rules into very small categories each of which commands its own set of rules. Thus, as we did earlier, we can divide the N category into Common Noun and Proper Noun (e.g., "Robert") and make separate rules for each:

NP → DET (ADJ) Common Noun
NP → Proper Noun

and so forth. Logically, there is no problem with this procedure, but aesthetically there is; specifically, it multiplies the number of rules extraordinarily. More important, it breaks into distinct categories linguistic entities that at one level logically and functionally belong to one category. As we noted, for example, a pronoun may be substituted for a noun phrase (DET (ADJ) N), and it may also be substituted for a proper noun. Thus, there is good reason to consider a proper noun and the DET ADJ N structural equivalents. This argument, that it is desirable to categorize together entities that serve the same function, led Chomsky (1957, 1965) to reject phrase structure grammars as models of grammatical competence and to propose instead a much more powerful grammar describing the relationships of sentences that appear fairly distinct.

Other Structural Similarities. Consider the following two sentences:

30. Robert gave a rich dessert to the fat boy.
31. A rich dessert was given by Robert to the fat boy.

Phrase structure rules that we have looked at for (30) follow:

$$S \rightarrow NP\ VP$$
$$NP \rightarrow (DET)\ (ADJ)\ N$$
$$VP \rightarrow V\ NP\ PP$$
$$PP \rightarrow PREP\ NP$$

and depict the structure as

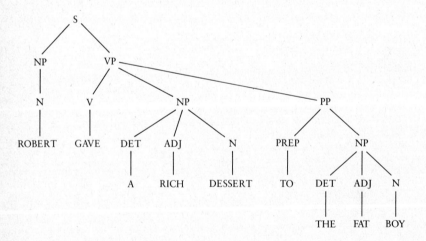

To describe (31) we must make a new rewrite rule, specifically

$$VP \rightarrow V\ PP\ PP$$

generating the structure tree

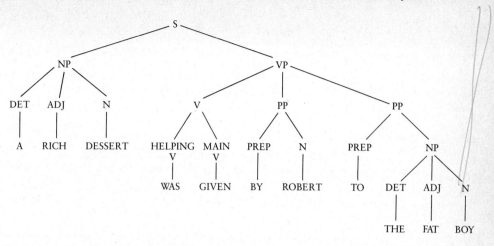

Examination of only the phrase structures of these two sentences necessitates establishment of the new VP rule and also ignores some fundamental similarities between them. In both sentences, for example, Robert did the giving—in the first tree structure Robert is dominated by one NP; in the second by an NP, PP, and VP. In the beginning of this chapter, we defined the function of syntax as serving the purpose of putting words together (or determining how words go together) so that appropriate meaning relations among words may be extracted. Is it not more reasonable, then, to assume that the underlying structures of the two sentences are the same, since in both Robert is doing the giving? This will eliminate the additional rule and also capture the similarity in function of the phrases "a rich dessert" and "to the fat boy" in both sentences and "Robert" and "by Robert" respectively. That is not to argue that the two sentences have identical structures—obviously they do not—but the relationship of the components of (30) is the same as that of (31), and our grammar should capture that regularity.

Components of Transformational Grammar

Using such arguments, Chomsky (1957) divided syntax into three components: *deep structure,* which captures the underlying relationships regardless of their order or form, *surface structure,* which is identical to the phrase structures we have been examining, and *transformations,* which are context-sensitive rules that take a given deep structure and convert it to surface structure form. So, for example, sentences (30) and (31) have the same underlying structure, closer to that of (30). (In the early theory adjectives were not included in deep structure, but this is irrelevant for now.) The deep structure would differ from (30) in representing the verb as "past tense + give." "Robert gave a rich dessert to the fat boy" (30) would be derived from it by applying transformations that would make it pronounceable, such as appropriately marking the verb with the tense morpheme, give + past → gave. Transformations making a deep structure marker pronounceable are *obligatory* (1957 theory): They must be performed to produce a sentence. Sentences resulting from obligatory transformations only are called *core* or *kernel* sentences and are relatively simple. To get to the surface structure of (31)—"A rich dessert was given by Robert to the fat boy"—we would apply transformations that move the second NP (a rich dessert) to subject position, add "was + en" to the verb, move the first NP (Robert) to the object position and precede it with "by." These transformations are *optional:* They do not have to be performed since a core sentence would suffice.

Dividing the grammar into deep structure and transformations simplifies the number of rules in the base component, the deep structure, since both of these types of sentences may be represented as having the same underlying structure. However it may not simplify the overall number of rules since there are many rules now in the transformational component. This change may be warranted anyway if transformational grammar provides a better intuitive description of similarities among sentences of the language.

It is important to note that the deep structure is considered to be *abstract.* Some words, or terminal elements, may be inserted into the abstract structure later. Transformations are considered to convert one structure to another, *not* one sentence to another. For purposes of explication, it is easier to describe sentences (with terminal elements) than abstract structures (without). Try to keep in mind, nevertheless, that it is *not* intended that an active sentence be converted to a passive, but that they share a structure realized by different sets of transformations.

Let us consider first some different surface structures that may be mapped to one deep structure. We have already seen that *active* sentences such as (30) and *passive* sentences such as (31) are described by one deep structure, with a class of operations, the passive transformation, converting the subject-verb-object order of deep structure to the passive form. Chomsky (1957) also proposed that an affirmative sentence such as (30) and its negative

32. Robert did not give a rich dessert to the fat boy.

have the same deep structure, and in this case there would exist a negative transformation operating only on the verb, inserting an auxiliary verb (AUX), "did," and the negative marker. Similarly, questions in any of a number of forms may be derived from the deep structure:

33. Who gave the rich dessert to the fat boy?
34. Robert gave what to the fat boy?
35. What did Robert give to the fat boy?
36. Robert gave a rich dessert to the fat boy, didn't he?

It should be obvious that these sentences have a common structure, and one that they share with the passive and the negative. This common structure is the deep structure, which marks fundamental relationships among the sentence elements.

37. The cat chased the frightened rat around the room.

and

38. What did the cat chase around the room?

obviously refer to events different from (33) to (36), but share a common abstract form of

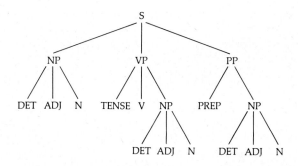

(Note that the change from deep structure to any of its surface forms supports the notion of constituent structure. An entire constituent, not just a piece thereof, is moved from object to subject position in the passive, for example.)

The Role of Transformations

Now let us consider the role of transformations. As already stated, mapping a number of surface structures to one deep structure simplifies the base component—the number of deep structures—but transfers complexity to the transformational component. Do transformations say something reasonable about the structure of the language, justifying the division of grammar into three components and the complexity of transformations? One reason to answer yes is that sentences transformationally derived from the same deep structure seem to have something in common, as we have already noted. A second reason is that particular transformations can be generalized to a number of structures; that is, they do not appear *ad hoc* for each sentence. Since a grammar is supposed to capture regularities in the language, if transformations seem to apply in the same way to a number of sentences, they capture regularities and should be incorporated into the grammar in some form. And a third reason is that by classifying together sentences that derive from the same core sentence, a rule may be specified for the core structure only and automatically apply to all strings derived from it. This reduces the number of rules, and few rules are desirable for a grammar. Thus, if "Robert gave a rich dessert to the fat boy" is recognized as the same as "A rich dessert was given by Robert to the fat boy," and we allow a rule moving "to the fat boy" before the subject (giving us "To the fat boy Robert gave a rich dessert") we do not have to restate it for the passive form; we will automatically be able to move "to the fat boy" to precede the logical subject, as in "A rich dessert was given to the fat boy by Robert."

Exercises in Transformational Grammar

Next we shall study some base sentences and rough transformations in more detail. To see how transformations capture regularities—that is, can be generalized— after the model is presented, some core sentences will be presented for you to try to produce the same derivation as in the model. You should find it quite easy, even if the transformations do not seem intuitive. Please note that the examples we will be examining are very crudely specified. For example, the verbs may not be specified as tense + verb as they should be, but for ease of presentation in places will already be marked for tense. As previously stated, Chomsky (1965) proposed that deep structures are abstract, but we will be manipulating words, and, at least initially, we include adjectives in the deep structure, although their derivation transformationally will ulti- mately be illustrated. The purpose of the exercises is to illustrate how transformations work, and also some problems with their conceptualization that we will return to.

Active to Passive.
core
Robert gave a rich dessert to the fat boy.

(a) Transformation
Move object to subject position, and subject to object position →

    A rich dessert gave Robert to the fat boy.

(b) Transformation—(now) obligatory.
Insert "by" before logical subject →

    A rich dessert gave by Robert to the fat boy.

(c) Transformation—obligatory.
Alter verb—add auxiliary, change verb to "en" *(participle)* form →

    A rich dessert was given by Robert to the fat boy.

core
The cat chased the mouse.
(a) → The mouse chased the cat.
(b) → The mouse chased by the cat.
(c) → The mouse was chased by the cat.

Try to make the passive forms of:

    Robert admired Mary from a distance.
    I answered the question.
    Bill Rodgers has won the New York Marathon at least three times.

What you should observe is that although the core sentences are all unrelated to one another, all are easily transformed to the passive, always using the same procedure.

Specification of that procedure thus establishes a regularity of the language, and one that native speakers have tacit knowledge of—enabling the quick, correct passivization of any active sentence.

Passive—"by"-deletion.
core
Same as above.
(a) "
(b) "
(c) "
(d) Transformation—optional. Delete by-clause →

A rich dessert was given to the fat boy.

Now try to apply this rule to all the passive sentences we have generated.

Negation.
core
Robert give (past tense) a rich dessert to the fat boy.

(a) Transformation—obligatory.
Add negative →

Not—Robert give (past tense) a rich dessert to the fat boy.

(b) Transformation—obligatory.
Insert *auxiliary* (for example, is, do, have) →

Not—Robert do give (past tense) a rich dessert to the fat boy.

(c) Transformation—obligatory.
Move negative to follow auxiliary →

Robert do not give (past tense) a rich dessert to the fat boy.

(d) Transformation—obligatory.
Change tense as specified →

Robert did not give a rich dessert to the fat boy.

Now take the other core sentences and transform them to negatives. Note that for all, you insert a negative and an auxiliary, and you move the tense marker from the main verb to the auxiliary.

Embedding, Relative Clauses.
core
The cat wounded the rat. The rat ate the cheese.

(a) Transformation—optional.

Substitute *relative pronoun* (who, which, or that) for second occurrence of same NP →

The cat wounded the rat that ate the cheese.

core

Robert gave the dessert to the boy. The boy was fat. →

Robert gave the dessert to the boy who was fat.

Try for yourself:

Robert gave the dessert. The dessert was rich.

This is the cat. The cat lived in the house.

The cat lived in the house. The house was built by Jack.

(Note the passive in the last sentence and note that you can combine the last two relative clauses you made, using the relative clause transformations once again.)

Adjectives.

core

Robert gave a dessert. The dessert was rich.

(a) Transformation—optional.

Apply relative clause transformation →

Robert gave a dessert that was rich.

(b) Transformation—optional.

Move relative clause to precede noun it modifies →

Robert gave a that-was-rich dessert.

(c) Transformation—obligatory.

Delete relative pronoun and preposed verb →

Robert gave a rich dessert.

Try for yourself:

Robert gave a dessert to the boy. The boy was fat.

More About Transformations

From the examples given you may now be aware of characteristics of transformations that should be made explicit. First, transformations have a scope, and second, they must be applied in a preset order. The *scope* is the size and type of constituent each transformation works on, and the order is when in the set of transformations from deep structure to surface structure a particular rule may apply. The passive transformation, for instance, may not apply to all sentences but only to sentences that can have the form subject-verb-object, sentences with a *transitive verb* (one that takes an object). Try, for example, to apply the passive to "Robert died of a stroke last night." There is no underlying object to prepose. The scope of the passive, then, is sentences with transitive verbs.

The importance of order is easily seen from the examples given. Suppose the first thing we do is mark the verb for tense. We will have Robert gave the rich dessert . . . If we perform the negative transformation, we would add the auxiliary and the "not" [→ not Robert did gave . . .], move the "not" in, and wind up terminally with Robert did not gave . . . which is ungrammatical. So, marking for tense *must* follow the AUX-insertion. For *real* transformational theory this particular example is artificial because there is always an auxiliary in deep structure with a tense marker, which may not always be realized as a word in the sentence.

However, the order issue can be seen in other examples. As we have seen, as an option we can delete the by-clause or agent in the passive, and as an option we can make a passive from the deep structure. Now, the agent is the functional subject in deep structure, the subject in an active, and part of the PP in the passive. If we allow agent deletion before taking the passive option we could wind up with a subjectless active, which is ungrammatical in English—*"gave a rich dessert to the fat boy." If we make agent deletion context sensitive so that it can apply only to strings of the form "by ____" and allow it to operate before the passive, it will not find the "by ____" and so never operate. Thus, agent deletion must occur only *after* the passive transformation option is exercised.

A third point is that some sentences seem to require more transformations from the core structure than others. The ones requiring the fewest—only obligatory transformations of the kind give + past → gave—are the kernel sentences, and the rest can be scaled in terms of *transformational* or *derivational complexity*. This distinction will become critical in the next chapter, in tests of transformational grammar as a model for psychological processing.

The last point to note is the variety of ways that transformations can affect the shape of the sentences: They can result in the addition of words ("by" or auxiliaries, e.g.), they can result in the deletion of words (e.g. agent deletion), they can cause substitutions of words (e.g. change to pronoun), and can move words (e.g. subject to object switch). Obviously, too, their effects are not on words alone but on entire constituents, whatever their size.

Transformational Grammar and Intuitions about Sentences

As we saw in the last chapter, there are particular kinds of meaning relations desirable for linguistic theory to capture: synonomy, ambiguity, and contradiction. We discussed these on the word level, but they have counterparts on the sentence level. Synonymous sentences are those that paraphrase one another, and in transformational theory these have the same deep structure, as we have seen. Ambiguous sentences are ones with different possible structural interpretations. Contradictions are realized at the sentence level as nonsense. Since we have looked at paraphrase already in transformational theory, we need discuss it no further. Transformational grammar accounts for structural ambiguities by the extraordinary effects of transformations: They can generate identical surface structures from very different deep structures. Consider the famous example:

39. The students stopped demonstrating on campus.

This sentence has two possible meanings, roughly paraphrased by

40. The students stopped demonstrating by others on campus.

and

41. The students stopped their own demonstrating on campus.

Optional deletions of the agents (these are transformations we have not discussed) of "demonstrating" result in the same surface structure for both. Note that the two different structures are captured in transformational grammar (deep structures distinct, different transformations operating) but would not be captured in phrase structure grammars that look only at surface forms. Transformational grammar thus has devices for recognizing structural ambiguities that phrase structure grammar does not. To see how transformational grammar can capture contradictions, we have to expand the notion of deep structure to account for some meaning relations in words. This will be discussed in the next section.

Syntax, Semantics, and the Development of Transformational Theory

We have defined the concepts of deep structure, transformations, and phrase structure thus far in terms of *structure,* noting the structural similarities of sentences that appear different. This is in accord with traditional views of what syntax is. The question to consider now is: What role does syntax play in language?

In his initial theory Chomsky (1957) considered that it was sufficient that syntactic theory account for speakers' intuitions about sentence structures, and that it derive structural synonyms and ambiguities. Deep structure, obligatory and optional transformations, and surface structures, as we have seen, are sufficient to account for speakers' intuitions in some cases. However, they cannot account for intuitions such as the ungrammaticality of:

*42. The Robert sleeps the rich dessert.

or

*43. Colorless green ideas sleep furiously.

Although these conform to some structural requirements of English, they clearly are not acceptable sentences. In the early theory Chomsky (1957) suggested that sentences like (42) could be eliminated by means of categorical rules that divided nouns, for example, into "proper" and "common," and then that the deep structures (and transformations) are marked with respect to these smaller classes, as we have indicated. In later theory in response to ongoing work in semantics (see Semantic Relations later in this chapter, for example), Chomsky (1965) developed this more formally, and a means for ruling out sentences like (43) was devised. And thus the boundary between syntax and semantics was crossed.

The two kinds of rules Chomsky proposed were strict subcategorization rules and selectional restrictions. *Strict subcategorization rules* divide the major parts of speech into classes on the basis of which grammatical categories they can combine with. As we have seen, in English some VPs can not be rewritten as V NP; only transitive verbs can (and must) take an NP. We cannot make an acceptable sentence of the structure NP V NP by using "sleep" or "run" or "die" as the verb. Strict subcategorization rules restrict which word classes can go with which subclasses. When these restrictions are violated, as with "the Robert" or "sleeps the rich dessert," there is a very serious error.

To account for the nonsense of (43), it is necessary to invoke meaning directly, since (43) does not violate either subcategorization rules or any structural constraint. (We do have to expand the rules we have been looking at to deal with it. The new rules are:

$$\text{VP} \rightarrow \text{V ADV}$$

where ADV is an *adverb,* or verb modifier, and

$$\text{NP} \rightarrow \text{ADJ ADJ N.}$$

Try making a structure tree for (43) by using these rules together with the rules you already know.) What (43) does violate are semantic restrictions—"colorless" and "green" contradict each other; "idea" refers to something abstract and only concrete objects are colored; only animate things "sleep" and ideas are inanimate; sleeping, by nature, is a tranquil activity that contradicts the adverb "furiously." What Chomsky proposed is that this kind of information must be made part of the grammar to rule out nonsense like (43). He considered that deep structure contains semantic features like those we saw in Chapter 2. When sentences are generated from deep structures, a late step is word insertion. The semantic features restrict *which* words may be used. These features are called *selectional restrictions* and must conform to the semantic features in a word's definition to allow that word to be inserted into the sentence.

In attempting to deal with ungrammaticality produced by violation of subcategorization rules and selection restrictions, Chomsky (1965) dramatically changed his concepts of deep structure and transformations to include information that was traditionally considered semantic. The arguments for doing so were in part to increase the power of the grammar so that nonsense like (42) and (43) could be recognized, and in part to allow for the fact that sentences like (43) *could* be interpreted, *figuratively,* by analogy to well-formed sentences at the same time that their deviance is recognized. Since, in this view of figurative sentences, interpretation depends on analogy to other sentences of similar structure, it follows that structure analysis must precede meaning interpretation (but see alternative views on metaphors in Chapter 3).

In the new theory, deep structure was considered to contain all information necessary for semantic interpretation so that no meanings could be introduced by transformations. Deep structures were submitted to a semantic component for interpretation and to a transformational component now consisting of *only obligatory* transformations for conversion to a surface structure. The surface structure was input to a phonological component to be pronounced. Thus, the "grammar assigns semantic interpretations to signals, this association being mediated by the recursive rules" (Chomsky, 1965, p. 141).

What information is necessary for semantic interpretation? Note first that things like "negative" and "interrogative" certainly alter meaning: "Robert gave" means the opposite of "Robert did not give" and something quite different from "Who gave?" The passive transformation also alters meaning, although more subtly, by changing the focus of the sentence. In English, it is customary to begin a sentence with something already known—this is called *old information, topic,* or *theme*—and then to use the rest of the sentence to add information, expounding on the theme, called *new information, focus, rheme,* or *comment.* In an active sentence the topic is the agent and the focus is the object—"What did Robert do? He gave the rich dessert." In a passive sentence, topic and focus reverse—"Who gave the rich dessert? The rich dessert was given by Robert." Thus, the information about passivizing must also appear in deep structure. These new elements are simply attached to the phrase marker as in:

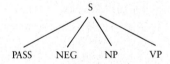

and then realized by *now-obligatory* transformations, as in the manner described before.

Selectional features (and subcategorization features) must also be available in deep structure since they are meaning providing. And, of course, basic functional relationships must be provided by deep structure. These include, for English, subject (or agent), action, time of action (tense), and object, as before. They also include in the new theory (Chomsky, 1965), concepts borrowed from semantics like location specifiers ("from a distance"), manner of occurrence ("furiously"), or recipient ("to the fat boy"), and so on. It is assumed that these are universal sentence markers that may be realized differently by transformations in different languages or in one language. In English, location is marked by either adverb or PP, for instance. Of course, since the work was done on English, the concepts attributed to deep structure were those expressed by English, not all of which necessarily appear in all languages. Tense, for example, is obligatory for English sentences but not for those of some other languages (Becker, 1979). Given that the syntactic component, deep structure, contains all basic sentential relationships in Chomsky's (1965) theory, the role of the semantic component is purely interpretive, decoding these relations with respect to, for example, word meaning in a marker structure as discussed in Chapter 2.

It is important to note that the domination of semantics by syntax has not been universally accepted by linguists, nor has the concept that sentence generation begins with deep structure and proceeds to semantic interpretation. Linguists known as generative semanticists (cf. Lyons, 1970) argued that sentence generation began with strings of meaning features, relations between them, *speech acts* like the intent to command or question, and some idea of what information is already known. They noted the similarity between the sentences

44. Robert sold the car to Harry.

and

45. Harry bought the car from Robert.

which convey the same idea but with very different functional relations expressed. The assumption is that sentences begin with ideas (semantics) that are then sent to a syntactic component for interpretation. (It is interesting to consider whether the apparently greater importance of syntax derives from attention to English specifically, since in English relations among sentence elements are conveyed primarily by order. See Box 4.1 for alternatives.)

Recognizing the validity of many of the proposals of the generative semanticists, Chomsky (1965 and beyond) incorporated their ideas into his syntactic theory. We have already seen evidence of this in the addition of time, manner, and agent concepts. Once the deepest structure is given all basic relationships, it becomes irrelevant whether to call it syntactic or semantic, and indeed Chomsky (1965) argued that the views of generative semanticists were notational variations on his theory. It is important to look at some of these other ways of looking at sentence structure, nevertheless, since such structures can be, should be, and in places have been, incorporated into syntactic theory.

Summary

In this section we have discussed initial development of a theory of grammar more powerful than phrase structure grammar. We needed a more powerful theory to account for context sensitivity, for the apparent structural and meaning similarities between sentences like actives and passives that had very different phrase structures, and for sentences with identical phrase structures but multiple interpretations. We proposed that sentences have two structures, a deep structure marking basic relationships and a surface structure in which those relationships might be disguised. Deep structures were converted to surface structures through transformations that deleted, added, or moved elements; but in the last version of the theory transformations never effected a meaning change. Thus, semantic interpretation occurred only once, on the

---

Box 4.1   Case Markings as Part of Morphology

What is considered syntax and what morphology may be different in different languages and may affect our conception of the importance of syntax. In English, most functional relations within a sentence are given only by order, and so the syntactic structure is relatively important. In other languages functional relations are marked with morphemes, the vestige of which we see in English on our pronouns. As we have noted "he" and "him" cannot be used interchangeably; "he" must be the subject, and "him" the object. If we reverse the order in English of "he gives him" to "him gives he," we do not have a comprehensible sentence, just a badly formed one, indicating that the subject and object markings may not be used exclusively in English to determine basic relations. Suppose, however, that they were used productively, that all subjects had a special ending, all objects a different one, and perhaps even all instruments by which the action is performed, another. Then we would be free to permute the order of the words in the sentence and could still recover the important relations. Would recovery of the relations then be syntax or morphology? To see what such a language would look like try to decipher the functional relations in the sentences following. A subscript "s" means subject, "o" object, and "i" instrument.

> Robert$_o$ loved Mary$_s$.
>
> Killed Robert$_s$ a knife$_i$ John$_o$.
>
> Dog$_s$ Man$_o$ bites.

Regardless of whether we describe the capturing of functional relations between sentence elements as morphology, semantics, or syntax it is important to emphasize that syntax is a vital, abstract component of language description that arises only from morpheme combinations. Modern linguistic theory calls that component "syntax," and as we shall see later this chapter delegates such syntactic functions to lexical, sublexical, phrase structure, deep structure, and suprasentential levels.

---

deep structure, and was not involved in the rest of the derivation. To account for all meaningful relations we added to the deep structure, "semantic" features in the form of subcategorization and selectional features, making it difficult to distinguish the roles of syntax and semantics. We also added markers that specified whether transformations like negation and passivization should be executed. Note that the power of the transformation component is thus reduced, and also that the number of deep structures is increased in these later theories. Structural similarity captured in the early theory in *deep* structure (as in actives and passives) is obscured in the later theory.

Other Aspects of Structure

Before exploring the newer versions of transformational theory it is useful to discuss other aspects of structure that must be incorporated into a comprehensive syntactic theory. At the end of the last section, we indicated that transformational theory was altered by exposure to and attack by other theories, notably semantic ones. Here we look at some of these as well as others that have affected later development.

Lexical Structure

As mentioned in Chapter 2, many words may be broken into parts (or *parsed*), as sentences may be, to reveal a componential structure. Most of us are at least tacitly aware, for instance, that a noun may be pluralized by adding "s" (dog → dogs), that an adjective may be turned into an adverb by adding "ly" (pretty song → sings prettily), that a verb may be turned into an adjective by adding "ed"/"en" (he broke the TV → the broken TV), that a verb may be turned into a noun by adding "ing" (the breaking of the TV), and so forth. This sublexical (morphological) structure can be expressed by rules too, e.g.:

$$ADV \rightarrow ADJ + ly$$
$$ADJ \rightarrow V + en$$
$$N \rightarrow V + ing$$

and by constituent analysis

The sublexical structure rules certainly form a part of our tacit knowledge; most of us can create words readily, going from one form to another as the need arises. For example, in the last section we introduced the passive transformation and suggested an exercise whereby active sentences are "passivized." For most readers "passivize" is likely to be a new word. Did it create problems? How is something made tranquil? How is a passive sentence made active? (It is tempting to use "activate" for this one, but clearly that is not what is wanted here.) Pay attention to your own everyday speech and you will notice many such creations—perfectly good words that your audience has no trouble understanding—that you create on the spot by using sublexical rewrite rules. (Box 4.2 shows a perfectly comprehensible parody of a frequent word creator. Note how easy it is to understand despite the *neologisms,* new words. Note also how strange it is—one neologism seems all right; several per sentence violates what we consider reasonable speaker behavior.)

Box 4.2 Creative (?) Use of Morphology

The following excerpt from the British newspaper *The Guardian* was cited in Safire's (1982) "On Language" column in *The New York Times*. The excerpt is a parody of the speech style of Alexander Haig, at the time a candidate for U.S. secretary of state. Note how easy it is to follow the meaning and how the words are given new syntactic function by applying affixes that signal the new parts of speech.

> Haig, in congressional hearings before his confirmatory, paradoxed his auditions by abnormalling his responds so that verbs were nouned, nouns verbed and adjectives adverbised. He techniqued a new way to vocabulary his thoughts so as to informationally uncertain anybody listening about what he had actually implicationed. . . .
>
> If that is how General Haig wants to nervous breakdown the Russian leadership he may be shrewding his way to the biggest diplomatic event since Clausewitz. Unless, that is, he schizophrenes his allies first.

The current cartoon show "The Smurfs" also uses morphological structure and sentence context to "create" words. In the show the nonsense word "smurf" is smurfed into every sentence, in a smurfy way, so that the meaning *and* the syntactic function are transparent. The show possibly owes some of its popularity to the fun of playing this language game.

Chomsky (1965) suggested that the regular rules that underlie word formation and derivation may be incorporated into the grammar. "Their destruction of the property," for example, could derive from a NP dominating a nominal marker and a sentence, "They destroy the property," which transformations could convert to the appropriate nominal form "destruction." Adjectives could derive from verbs in many cases: something breaks → a broken something. If any of these transformations is stated as the *only* derivation for a part of speech, however, problems can arise. For example, something can be either broken or unbroken, both adjectives. There is no verb form "to unbreak," so to assume that adjectives always arise from verbs would require hypothesizing this nonexistent verb at some unexpressed level. If we have adjectives existing as adjectives in the lexicon, we can merely create an adjective formation rule that adds a negative morpheme to existing adjectives (broken → unbroken, inhabited → uninhabited, etc.) (Bresnan, 1978). To prevent postulating unlikely intermediate structures like "unbreak," it might be preferable to assume that words are stored with their possible forms rather than generated afresh each time.

It is important to recognize that to some extent determining the rewrite rules for a language is algebraic, deriving a language equation and then seeing how many sentences it can account for. We have suggested that adjectives could be derived from relative clauses, implying that an embedded sentence can be transformed to a word;

that adjectives can derive from verbs, implying that one word form can be transformed into another; and that adjectives are prime elements as they are. All are consistent with some instances in the language. The reasons to reject a particular hypothesis lie in the number of instances it accounts for, whether it is plausible, and whether it generates or postulates nongrammatical instances either terminally or as intermediate forms.

Special Cases

Chomsky (1965) called attention to some particular English sentence pairs that caused difficulty in interpretation from surface structure alone. Contrast, for example,

46a. John is eager to please.

with

46b. John is easy to please.

or

47a. John begged Bill to go.

with

47b. John promised Bill to go.

In each sentence pair two propositions are expressed—in (47b), for example, that John promised Bill and that John will go (if he keeps his promise). These sentence pairs are deceptive in that the subject of the second verb is different in (a) and (b) of each pair. To see the difficulty, ask who will be pleased in (46). In (a) it is some unspecified person, whereas in (b) it is John. A similar dichotomy exists for other sentences of the language.

What is interesting in these cases is that there is no overt marking in the surface structure of the sentence to indicate whether the subject of the first proposition is also the subject of the second. Since it is not marked in the surface structure, but obviously is important in the derivation of the functional relations of the sentences, Chomsky (1965) argued that it is marked in the deep structure, tacit knowledge of which every native speaker has. We may alternatively account for the dichotomy by assuming that with each word the possible relations it can enter into are stored, so that the rules for "promise" and "beg" are not part of deep structure and transformations, but part of the lexical component of the grammar (Bresnan, 1978).

Semantic Relations

One interesting difference between transformational grammar and phrase structure grammar was the distinction in the former between functional subject and logical subject in active and passive sentences. We noted that in (30) and (31) the phrases "Robert" and "by Robert" served the same logical relation—in both instances denoting the giver. Similarly, regardless of position, "a rich dessert" served as the thing given. The initial NP in the passive, as in the active, is the grammatical subject, but it is much more reasonable to class "Robert" and "by Robert" together and ignore the change in position.

Fillmore (1969) argued that this kind of analysis may be applied to more than just the *agent* (the one doing regardless of position) and the *object* or *patient* (the one being done to regardless of position). For example, recall the sentences presented in Chapter 2:

48. A knife killed John.
49. John was killed with a knife.

and for comparison's sake

50. Robert killed John.

Now "a knife" in (48) and "Robert" in (50) have the same grammatical relation to the verb and the same phrase structure. But they have a different *semantic relation*. In (50) "Robert" is the agent. In (48) "a knife" is the means or *instrument* of the killing but not the perpetrator. In fact "a knife" in (48) serves the same logical relation as "with a knife" in (49), although they have very different phrase structures. Aside from agent, patient, and instrument, the following semantic relations or *cases* have been proposed (among others):

recipient—the one receiving.
locative—describes location, as in "in a room."
directional—describes location and movement, as in "to the car."
manner—describes how, as in "in a careless way."

And, as you may have already noted, the contributions of case grammar were incorporated into transformational theory.

Fillmore proposed that all cases had the underlying structure of prepositional phrases with the preposition either expressed in surface structure or deleted by transformation. When in subject position, for example, the structure for agent would look like:

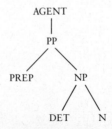

If the sentence is active, the PREP will be deleted so the agent-subject will be expressed only by an NP. Under case-grammar analysis the rewrite rule for sentences is:

$$S \rightarrow \text{Modality (MOD) Auxiliary (AUX) Proposition (PROP)}$$

MOD dominates a category consisting of negative markers, interrogative markers, time adverbs like "tomorrow" or "in an hour"—a prepositional phrase functioning like a time adverb. AUX we already know. PROP contains the case relations for the rest of the sentence. All case relations, including actor-subject or instrument-subject, are considered to have an underlying preposition that may be deleted by transformations.

Discourse Analysis

Thus far we have looked at syntactic relations only at a sentence or subsentence level. Although we will not go into it in detail, it is important to note that structure *and* meaning modification by language units occur between sentences as well as within sentences. Allusions to this have already been made; pronoun use (at least "he," "she," and "they" forms) is dictated by clarity of the referent of the pronoun. Most frequently, pronouns are used anaphorically. An *anaphoric* reference is one in which reference is made to something earlier in the discourse. In

51. I talked to Robert yesterday. He said John gave it to him.

"He" and "him" refer to Robert anaphorically; Robert is mentioned earlier. (51) is stylistically preferable in English to

52. I talked to Robert yesterday. Robert said John gave it to Robert.

which uses no reference. (There are languages in which use of particular pronouns implies a certain relationship between the speaker and the person referred to, as with the polite-you and the familiar-you in Romance languages. It may be preferable for a non-native speaker to avoid pronoun use altogether as in (52) than confuse them in such languages [Wolff, 1971].) For English, the speakers' interpretation of (52) usually uses the assumption that at least one of the later mentions of "Robert" in (52) refers to a different person named Robert than the first one mentioned.

Most reference is anaphoric, but there are other kinds. For example, in "In his discussion of anaphor, Chomsky . . ." the "his" clearly refers to "Chomsky," who is mentioned later. Reference rules were accounted for by Chomsky (1965) by indexing (assigning numbers to) individuals in deep structure and allowing certain rules to apply only when there was a match in number. Such systems have also been used by others (see Jackendoff's analysis following).

Another form distinction that crosses sentence boundaries is the old informa-tion–new information distinction. Old information is what has been mentioned in previous sentences; it determines what goes first in the new sentence.

It is important to note that anaphoric reference may be made in a number of ways, not just through pronouns. Old information is an example of anaphor, since it marks what has been previously mentioned, and it is conveyed by position in English. As another example, in answering questions, we frequently begin with the phrase given in the question, marking the anaphor by position, as in

> Who was *the first President?*
> *The first President* was George Washington.

Alternatively, we may mark it with a pronoun:

> *Who* was the first President?
> *It* was George Washington.

Or, we may mark the fact that there was an earlier reference by deleting the redundant phrase:

> Who was the first President?
> George Washington.

In this last case we can hypothesize that for discourse there is optional deletion of major constituents of the sentence (the subject NP, for instance) in surface structure depending on previous reference.

Of course, it is necessary that what is already known is specified in the deep structure, so that the grammar does not keep generating the same sentence (in different forms) over and over again as a paragraph, or so that the grammar does not generate completely disconnected sentences. In addition to specifying old information-new information in deepest structure, the generative semanticists argued that presuppositions are marked from the start. *Presuppositions* are assumptions that it takes to generate or understand such sentences as "when did you stop beating your wife?": (1) you are married, (2) you are male, (3) you beat your wife, (4) you stopped—all of which is old information. "Robert fulfilled his promise" similarly presupposes that Robert made a promise. Obviously, selection of a word like "fulfilled" is restricted to occur only in situations where something has already taken place, and probably such a sentence could be produced only when that knowledge had already been imparted. Thus, presupposition underlies some of the rules of paragraphs or conversation and must be specified by the time of semantic interpretation.

Recently there have been attempts to determine the structure of paragraphs, texts, stories, etc., beyond determination of rules of reference or old information. These have mostly developed from processing attempts and so will be discussed in more detail in Chapter 5, along with other aspects of processing models. Generally, these models have looked at the kinds of syntactic-semantic relations expressed across *coherent* sentences, much as case grammar looks at relations expressible within a sentence. Paragraphs have a theme or topic that is expanded in detail in the sentences of the paragraph (Kintsch and Van Dijk, 1978). The details, for coherence, may be *causally* connected (Schank, 1975). Alternatively, details may expand on the setting or plot of a story (Rumelhart, 1975). Again, it is important to note that these formulations have derived from examination of English (or other Western languages) structures. Causality, for example, underlies most of our plots, perhaps showing how a character's defect *led* to some sequence of events that might be viewed otherwise as unexpected (this is the theme of classical tragedy). In Javanese stories, plots are primarily developed around coincidences or accidents that have no cause, that we would therefore dismiss as meaningless or uninteresting, but that in Javanese theater are seen as motivating forces of action (Becker, 1979). Thus, the structure for cohesiveness can obviously be different from culture to culture.

Syntax-Semantics

As we have indicated in discussing Chomsky (1957, 1965), an important issue in development of syntactic theory has been where and when semantic interpretation occurs. If it is performed once, at the deep structure level, transformations must introduce no meaning changes. If it is performed at the surface structure level, it is unclear what relationships deep structure expresses. As you may recall, in Chapter 1 we pointed out that it is difficult to separate syntax and semantics because meaning defines structure and structure defines meaning.

One way to deal with the interrelation of syntax and semantics while preserving the utility of the distinction between them is to propose that there are several levels of syntactic analysis enmeshed with several levels of semantic analysis, as you may recall Jackendoff did (Fodor, 1978). His theory of semantic representation consists of four distinct levels, one of which corresponds to semantic primitives (this one was discussed in Chapter 2). This level, which contains case relations, is called *functional structure* and works on deep-structure representations. A second level represents focus and presupposition. The focus-presupposition interpreter works on surface structures in which decisions about what to stress, delete, put first, etc., will have to be made.

A third component of Jackendoff's semantic structure is a *table of coreference,* which establishes which elements of the sentence refer to the same object and which do not, the necessity for which we have seen in (51) (I talked to Robert ... he ...) and for unambiguous interpretation of (39) (students stopped demonstrating ...). Coreference is determined or kept track of continuously in the transformational process.

The final component accounts for the ambiguity in

53. Robert is looking for a fat boy.

where it is unclear whether Robert is looking for any boy who is fat or whether there is a specific fat boy who is the object of Robert's search. Marking the *scope* of "a" resolves that ambiguity. As a second example

54. In most recent speeches Republicans have not sided with Reagan.

is ambiguous in scope. "Most" can refer to the number of speeches, "recent" not being in its scope, or to the latest speeches, "recent" being in its scope and "speeches" not. As we have just done through paraphrase, specifying the scope resolves the ambiguity.

Both of these examples are in fact instances of an aspect of syntax called quantification, an aspect only introduced here but discussed much in logics and linguistics. *Quantifiers* are words or phrases like "every," "all," "for each," "neither," "some," "most," and the determiners (a, an, the) and numbers (one, two, three . . .). Quantifiers have specific meanings that may be defined in formal logic, but when they are used in normal language their meanings get fuzzy, partly because of the ambiguities in scope. For example, does "Mary went out with 15 boys in the class" mean that Mary went out 15 times, or once with a large group? In this case the scope of 15 is indeterminate; it could in a sense include the verb, describing 15 separate outings. Or again, "each boy dated one girl in the class"—does this mean that there was *one* very popular girl, or a class full of contented couples? This is a scope problem for both "each" and "one."

Since these are very different senses described by the same surface structure, the meaning differences must be specified *before* surface structure. This type of meaning interpretation, called *modal structure,* therefore works at the level of deep structure.

Jackendoff's analysis is intended to be a meaning analysis, so what goes on in each of these components is the assignment of interpretations. By allowing the semantic interpretation to occur in several stages, interacting with syntactic specification, it is possible to retain the potency of deep structure in recognizing similarities between different sentences (like actives and passives) and to retain the potency of transformations and still account for intuitions about meaning similarities and differences in various paraphrases. As we will see in Chapter 5, interaction of syntactic and semantic analyses appears to be the best way to implement sentence processing.

Summary

In this section we examined some levels of structure sometimes considered semantic or morphological, but that need to be taken into account by a comprehensive grammar. We noted that there is sublexical structure—adverbs could be transformed into adjectives with -ly. There is also a powerful supersentential structure that determines what may be said in a sentence, what sentences reasonably cohere, what can be assumed in a sentence depending on what has come before, and what the relation of individuals in a sentence is to individuals in other sentences. Some of these other levels of structure have been incorporated into Chomsky's (1965) theory, and some of them have not been treated. We also proposed that one way to avoid the complexity of deep structure, necessary if all these levels were to be expressed in it, is to allow several levels of meaning interpretation to interact with the structural interpretation.

Trace Grammar and the Lexical Position

The change from the 1957 theory to the 1965 theory was motivated in part by consideration of when semantic interpretation took place. In the earlier theory,

Chomsky considered active, passive, interrogative, and negative sentences all to have the same underlying structure. In the later version, considering the meaning change that each of these transformations wrought, he specified that the surface structure form with its meaning must be hinted at in the deep structure by a marker specifying question, and so on. Thus, the meanings the earlier theory could derive only from surface structure were now said to exist in deep structure, so meanings were derived at one level only. Continuing this reasoning, and examining the meaning-changing effects that other transformations—like by-deletion—have, we may want to make the level that receives semantic interpretation still richer. In a sense, that is what the latest version of the theory does.

In the current theory, in response to difficulties raised by generative semanticists and by experimental results that we will examine in Chapter 5, Chomsky (1980a and b; Chomsky and Lasnik, 1977; see also Bresnan, 1978; Marcus, 1980) markedly reduced both deep structure and transformations with respect to their importance in the grammar. The deep structure component consists of the base phrase markers, as before, marking *logical form,* or the major constituent structures of the sentence—subject, AUX, predicate. But meaning interpretation and assignment are *no longer* made at this level, and therefore the phrase markers do not require additional information beyond basic structure. The transformational component in the current theory consists exclusively of one type of rule, which moves constituents not bound to other constituents to other positions in the sentence. For example, the base structure for "it is easy to do what today?" is the same as "what is it easy to do today?," the only difference being the movement of the object-NP for "do" to initial sentence-subject position, and the movement of the verb "is" to precede the "it." As before, transformations, now movement only, operate on the base phrase marker, converting the logical form to a kind of surface representation.

A significant difference between the new version and the old versions is that, in the new version, transformations do not convert deep structure to surface structure but convert deep structure to an *abstract surface structure* that contains *traces* ($[t]$) of the form of the sentence before the operation of the transformations. Meaning assignment or interpretation is said to take place at the level of abstract surface structure, thereby utilizing information about the original deep structure as well as information about order, now in the surface structure. Before explaining trace theory further it is important to note that there is a second kind of transformation—one that works on the abstract surface structure, converting it to spoken form. These transformations are, in a sense, pronunciation changes, substitutions of "gave" for "give + past," for instance, or of nothing for a trace.

Let us consider a nonlinguistic analogy to trace theory. Suppose you rearrange the furniture in your room, a layout you knew well, and then you walk around the room without concentrating. You may bump into objects not previously there, or scrupulously avoid empty places in the room where there had been an item of furniture; that is, traces of the previous arrangement are now controlling your movement.

Now consider a conversation, controlled by a null item, or, a trace of some item. A reasonable exchange might be:

—Lizzie Borden's parents were axed to death.
—Oh? Who did it?

The question is where did the "who," the agent, come from in the question, since there is no agent in the prompting statement? If the first sentence has an underlying structure, or abstract surface structure, available to both participants of:

Lizzie Borden's parents were axed to death [t].

where [t] holds the place of the agent clause, then we can assume that the existence of [t] prompted the question, just as an absent article of furniture could prompt a movement. The base phrase marker need not have the agent specified and then deleted; it just needs to specify the existence of the position whose place is held in abstract surface structure by the trace. Consider now a more specific, ingenious example cited by Bresnan (1978) and Chomsky (1980a), the rules controlling the conversion of "want to" to the vernacular "wanna."

55. Teddy is the man who I want to succeed.

is ambiguous. It could mean "I want Teddy to succeed" with an abstract surface structure containing a trace of whom-referring-to Teddy between "want" and "to," roughly

56. Teddy is the man I want (whom-Teddy) to succeed.

or it could mean "I want to succeed Teddy," derived from an abstract surface structure containing a trace of "whom-Teddy" following "succeed," roughly,

57. Teddy is the man I want to succeed (whom-Teddy).

Is the vernacular

58. Teddy is the man I wanna succeed.

likewise ambiguous? Clearly, no. If "wanna" is in your dialect this can only mean (57). This example suggests that the rule "want" + "to" → "wanna" may apply only if "want" and "to" are adjacent in the abstract surface structure. They are adjacent in the surface structure (57)—which is the way (58) is interpreted—but a trace intervenes in (56), blocking the conversion or interpretation or that structure from (58).

In trying this example on acquaintances naive to linguistic theory, I discovered a tendency either to reject as ungrammatical the reading of (58) corresponding to (56) or to assume it was supposed to have been

59. Teddy is the man who I want to *have* succeed,

an interpretation you may have tried yourself. Notice that this interpretation is consistent with trace theory. In this paraphrase, "whom-Teddy" has moved from in front of "to"—"I want to have whom-Teddy succeed." Thus, "want" and "to" would still be adjacent in abstract surface structure, allowing for contraction.

The last aspect of the new theory that differentiates it substantially from the old theory is that many distinctions previously marked in deep structure are now considered to be idiosyncratic properties of words and are explicitly stated in the lexicon rather than in deep structure and transformations. This accounts for sentences (46a) and (46b) (eager versus easy to please) and (47a) and (47b) (beg and promise). In the current theory, by specifying the kinds of semantic relations the verbs may take in the lexicon, the need for arbitrary transformations is eliminated. (You may remember from Chapter 3 that it was suggested that verbs are given enormous "power" in determining surface structures/meanings in many theories. This is one instance where the verb markings in the lexicon indicate the kinds of relations that may be present in the sentence—what the subject of the embedded clause will be, whether or not there is an object as for the intransitive verbs. In the next chapter we will again encounter verb-centered theories of processing sentences.)

It should be clear from the preceding discussion that trace grammar in a sense retains the power of transformations by assigning the role of transformations to different levels of syntactic analysis. Pronouns, which before were transformationally derived from nouns given coreference, are now considered to originate in deep structure, but they are indexed across sentences to help keep referents clear and may have no realization in surface structure, marked only by traces in abstract surface structure. This simplifies the transformational component and accounts for interpretations applying across sentences as well as within sentences. Context-sensitivity of transformations is now taken care of at the lexical level by specifying the kinds of relations each word can have, and this further reduces the number of kinds of transformations.

At the lexical level, too, are now the kinds of transformations each word can undergo, so verbs convertible to adjectives are so marked in the lexicon, as are adjectives convertible to negatives (broken → unbroken). Moving some of the complexity of transformations into the lexical component and into lexical derivational rules results in a more reasonable account. Ultimately, by enriching the lexicon and lexically based rules, enriching discourse rules, and postulating an abstract surface structure receiving meaning analysis, trace theory reduces the previously unwieldy transformation component to movement transformations and obligatory substitutions (for example, give + past → gave). Through its various levels of rules, trace theory still classifies together numbers of different surface forms.

Transformational Grammar: A Summary

From the study of transformational grammar during the last twenty years, we have a much better idea of the richness of language and of its constituents than did our predecessors. We also have a much better idea of how to deal systematically with syntactic data. In particular, the syntactic structures of transformational grammar are far more revealing of at least certain kinds of semantic regularity than are ordinary surface strings, and this enables us to avoid many grammatical pitfalls in semantic analysis.

(Jackendoff, 1978, p. 203)

So said Jackendoff as a summary of syntax research in the twenty years following publication of Chomsky's *Syntactic Structures,* and a fitting summary it is, too, to the syntactic analyses presented in this chapter. It should be clear at this point that language and language structures are terribly complex—more complex than we imagine from early grammar courses and more complex than surface analysis of sentences immediately reveals. There are many levels of structure in language: sublexical structure, constituent structure, phrase structure, deep structure, case structure. At this point you should appreciate the structure at each of these levels and the wonderful way in which the structures are enmeshed.

You may also wonder how, with all these levels of structure and all these tacit rules, we ever manage to produce or understand a sentence at all—especially at the fast rate that we do! Beautiful writing (or speaking) not only allows us to get at the meanings quickly but also utilizes the structures of the language themselves, forcing us to play with our various tacit rules, as "This is the house that Jack built" forces us to play with the possibilities of embedding. Writing or speaking that does not make use of the complexities of structure is terribly monotonous, like a grade school essay "We went to the zoo. We saw the lion. The lion ate some meat. Then the lion roared. We came home. We were tired. We had fun." Why is this so dull?—because we like layers of structure, we like performing transformations, and we like playing with our language.

Any of the analyses given in the previous sections may be wrong—that is, what they describe may be better described in some other way. Adjectives may derive from conjoined sentences, may be a part of speech on their own, may be formed from other parts of speech . . . but the active, generative process making comprehensible a new word like "unpassivized" cannot be ignored. The great contribution of linguistics of the last 20 years is the elucidation of such processes.

Behaviorist Accounts of Syntax

Before ending this chapter and examining syntactic processing it is worthwhile to look at a very different model of syntax from the ones we have just explored, one that ignores the levels of structure we have been concentrating on. As it is presented consider whether it can reasonably account for the complexities of language.

Recall the behaviorist approach to meaning, conditioning. Under one kind of conditioning, classical conditioning, a word and its referent come to be associated through repeated presentations of the two together, so that after a time the word elicits a response like the one that the object elicits. "Milk" said together with the object eventually will produce by itself thirst, maybe a sensation of its taste, smell, or appearance. Entire phrases could similarly be classically conditioned to complex events—"the milk spills" could evoke a sensation of glass shattering, splashing or dripping sounds, and so forth. In this case the "unit" is larger than a word; it is the whole phrase, and in Skinner's (1957) view, there is no point in attempting to break the phrase into parts if the phrase is the response to a particular stimulus. Syntax, or the makeup of phrases, is "a matter of established pattern" (Skinner, 1957, p. 338).

A second aspect of learning theory already encountered that is relevant to syntax is the notion of syntactic markers, or autoclitics, which have no obvious referent in the real world and serve instead to glue meaningful units together. Autoclitics would include auxiliaries, prepositions, conjunctions, etc. In Skinner's view (1957, p. 353) the only important verbal dimension is time, and within this dimension, the speaker must try to describe complex, simultaneous events. Since (s)he can speak only one word at a time, and for description may need to speak several words together, (s)he must string these several out in time, connecting them wherever possible. The autoclitics are connectors keeping parts of a verbal scene together.

The third way behaviorists account for syntax is through the construct chaining, which we will see is very similar in structure to finite state grammars or Markov series. A *chain* is a complex sequence of behaviors in which each behavior in the chain is a signal for the next behavior and a reinforcement for the last. For example, suppose you are hungry and want a chocolate bar. Putting the chocolate in your mouth will be directly reinforced by taste, hunger abatement, and so forth. That is simple operant conditioning as we have already seen it—once you have this experience you are likely to put chocolate in your mouth again. Now, in most circumstances this association will not help because you do not have chocolate at hand. So you may emit a behavior in order to get chocolate in your hand—like pulling a lever on a candy machine. Getting the chocolate in your hand reinforces the lever pull and signals putting it in your mouth. Putting money in the machine will be reinforced by the lever pull, which will signal picking the chocolate up, etc. What you should see is that every response in such a complex behavior chain controls/signals the next; putting your hand in your pocket signals the state of putting the coin in the slot, which signals the state of lever pulling, which signals the state of picking up the chocolate, which signals the state of eating the chocolate. Such a sequence of associations is called *syntagmatic association:* a phenomenon in which events that follow others in time are triggered by those they immediately follow.

Can language be considered a chain? Does HE trigger GAVE trigger IT trigger TO trigger HIM as our finite state model suggested? The behaviorist view implies that syntax is order, and order is a set of sequential associations, and thus that finite state grammars work as syntax models. It is important to realize, though, that each state may be a unit larger than a word, depending on what is under the stimulus control.

Earlier, in putting forth the linguistic position we rejected finite state grammars as language models because they did not have the memory capacity to deal with center embeddings. This may not be critical, however; it depends on whether we can infinitely embed. If, for example, our limit is a single embedding—that is, if embedding is not a productive process—then finite state grammars can account for it. All we need is to have a process that allows *one* embedded sentence:

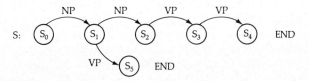

which could produce (with appropriate substitutions)

20. The rat the cat wounded ate the cheese.

but no more than that. If our limit is two, then we can include two in the finite state grammar, and so on. Only if there is no limit, or if there is a variable limit, the finite state model will not work, because then each subject must be matched with each predicate and the number of intervening associations and the control each item has on the next are indefinite.

As we shall see in the next chapter, it is perhaps more reasonable to assume a limit on our ability to center embed, which would make the behaviorist model of syntax more viable. However, to some it should seem unattractive. It tells us very little about the organization of language, unlike the transformational model, in that it assumes no structure beyond chained associations. It is hoped that the preceding sections of this chapter made a convincing argument for phrase structure, deep structure, and tacit rules applying at various levels of analysis. These would be coincidental in the behaviorist view, with language no more complex and interwoven than fetching a candy bar. As we said initially, the apparent structures may be a coincidence (surely that is unlikely!), but even so, we seem to be at least tacitly aware of them and seem to use them productively and with intellectual enjoyment. Whether in fact the structures discussed in this chapter govern our language behavior is the subject of Chapter 5.

Summary

In this chapter we examined some ways of characterizing the structure of language (English) and the interrelation of structure and meaning. We noted first that words may be characterized with respect to their use in sentences, as parts of speech, and demonstrated the linguistic method of distributional analysis to derive these. We then discussed phrase structure, or the combining of parts of speech into larger functional units. We demonstrated the preferability of the hierarchical phrase structure grammar over finite state grammar by showing that sentences are recursive and sensitive to contexts beyond the adjacent word, and that finite state models have no power to handle recursiveness or context-sensitivity. Phrase structure grammar was also shown to be incapable of handling context-sensitivity, and to be unable to account for similarities between some sentences that seem to convey the same relationships without having the same phrase structures. This necessitated postulating structure at both a surface and a deep level, and a way of transforming the deep structure into the surface structure. Implementing this analysis and interfacing it with meaning interpretation was nontrivial, and our final discussions of linguistic approaches to language structure attempted to deal both with structures providing meaning (active, passive) and meaning providing structure (presupposition, case relations). Finally we discussed a simple representation for sentence structure harking back to finite-state grammars, but reasonable, assuming that we limit the generative power of language.

REFERENCES

Becker, A. L. (1979). Text-building, epistemology, and aesthetics in Javanese shadow theatre. In A. L. Becker & A. A. Yengoyan (Eds.), *The Imagination of Reality: Essays on Southeast Asian Coherence Systems,* (pp. 211–243). Norwood, N.J.: Ablex.

Bresnan, J. A. (1978). A realistic transformational grammar. In M. Halle, J. Bresnan, and G. A. Miller (Eds.). *Linguistic Theory and Psychological Reality,* (pp. 1–59). Cambridge, MA: MIT Press.

Chomsky, N. (1980a). *Rules and Representations.* NY: Columbia University Press.

Chomsky, N. (1980b). On binding. *Linguistic Inquiry, 11,* 1–46.

Chomsky, N., and Lasnick. H. (1977). Filters and control. *Linguistic Inquiry, 8,* 425–504.

Chomsky, N. (1957). *Syntactic Structures.* The Hague: Mouton.

Chomsky, N. (1965). *Aspects of the Theory of Syntax.* Cambridge, MA: MIT Press.

Fillmore, C. J. (1969). Toward a modern theory of case. In D. A. Riebel & S. A. Schane (Eds.). *Modern Studies in English: Readings in Transformational Grammar,* (pp. 361–375). Englewood Cliffs, NJ: Prentice-Hall.

Fodor, J. D. (1978). *Semantics: Theories of Meaning in Generative Grammar.* NY: Thomas Y. Crowell Co.

Greene, J. (1972). *Psycholinguistics: Chomsky and Psychology.* Hammondsworth, Middlesex, England: Penguin Books.

Jackendoff, R. (1978). Grammar as evidence for conceptual structure. In M. Halle, J. Bresnan, & G. A. Miller (Eds.). *Linguistic Theory and Psychological Reality,* (pp. 201–228). Cambridge, MA: MIT Press.

Kintsch, W. & van Dijk, T. A. (1978). Toward a model of text comprehension and production. *Psychological Review, 85,* 363–394.

Lyons, J. (1970). Generative syntax. In J. Lyons (Ed.). *New Horizons in Linguistics,* (pp. 115–140). Hammondsworth, Middlesex, England: Penguin Books.

Marcus, M. (1980). *A Theory of Syntactic Recognition of Natural Language.* Cambridge, MA: MIT Press.

Rumelhart, D. E. (1975). Notes on a schema for stories. In D. G. Bobrow & A. Collins (Eds.). *Representation and Understanding,* (pp. 211–236). NY: Academic Press.

Safire, W. (1982). On language. *The New York Times,* July 11, VI.

Schank, R. C. (1975). The structure of episodes in memory. In D. G. Bobrow & A. Collins (Eds.). *Representation and Understanding,* (pp. 237–272). NY: Academic Press.

Skinner, B. F. (1957). *Verbal Behavior.* Englewood Cliffs, NJ: Prentice-Hall.

Wolff, J. U. (1971). *Beginning Indonesian, Part Two.* Ithaca, NY: Cornell University, Southeast Asia Program.

Woods, W. A. (1970). Transition network grammars for natural language analysis. *Communications of the ACM, 13,* 591–606.

Appendix

The terms for English grammar (re)-introduced in this chapter are listed here, together with their definitions and examples, for reference purposes.

1. *Active voice:* sentences in which the logical subject is also the functional subject; it occurs before the verb. Contrasts with passive voice. E.g., "Robert gave a rich dessert to the fat boy."

2. *Adjective:* a word that modifies a noun, either preceding it as in "a *rich* dessert" or following verbs like "is," "seems," "looks," as a predicate adjective, as in "The dessert looks *rich.*"

3. *Adverb:* a word or phrase (then called adverbial) that modifies the verb. Frequently marked by an -ly suffix. E.g., "Robert died *quickly*" (word) or "Robert died *an hour ago*" (time adverbial).

4. *Affirmative:* a sentence that states that something is true, as opposed to a negative. E.g., "Robert gave a rich dessert" or "A rich dessert was given."

5. *Agent:* the person performing the action. E.g., "*Robert* gave a rich dessert" or "A rich dessert was given *by Robert.*"

6. *Anaphor:* reference to something mentioned earlier. In "I talked to Robert yesterday. He said Robert gave it to him," "He" and "him" refer to "Robert" anaphorically.

7. *Auxiliary:* a marker in a sentence that contains tense information. Sometimes this is marked with a "helping verb" such as "is," "do," or "have." E.g., "Robert give + *past* → "Robert gave" or "Robert *did* give" or "Robert *has given.*"

8. *By-deletion:* optional transformation of the passive in which the agent is deleted. E.g., "A rich dessert was given by Robert" → "A rich dessert was given."

9. *Center embedding:* a clause inserted between the subject and predicate of another sentence. E.g., "The rat *the cat wounded* ate the cheese."

10. *Common noun:* a noun that may take a determiner ("a," "an," or "the"). E.g., "a *dessert.*" Compare with proper noun.

11. *Complex sentence/compound:* a sentence (or phrase) with more than one subject or predicate (or head). There are various methods of compounding: embedding, where there is a main clause and a subordinate clause is one (complex sentence), and conjoining, uniting two main clauses with a conjunction (compound sentence) is another. E.g., "*The cat and the dog* ran around together" (compound phrase). "The cat that the dog chased ran up the tree." (complex sentence).

12. *Conjunction:* a part of speech that permits joining of like constituents. E.g., "and," "or," "but," "nor." See the examples for compounds.

13. *Count noun:* nouns that name individual items that can be counted. Contrast with mass nouns that name unspecified amounts. In "a glass of milk" "glass" is a count noun. In "some milk" "milk" is a mass noun.

14. *Declarative:* a type of sentence in which something is stated. Contrast with imperatives and interrogatives. E.g., "Robert gave a rich dessert," "A rich dessert was given by Robert," "Robert did not give a rich dessert."

15. *Determiner:* a part of speech that quantifies and specifies count nouns. "The" indicates that the noun following refers to a specific object; "a" or "an," to an indefinite object. E.g., "*The* rich dessert."

16. *Directional:* a case marking location plus movement. E.g., "to the car."

17. *Embedding:* see center-embedding.

18. *Imperative:* a type of sentence in which something is commanded. Contrast with declarative and interrogative. E.g., "Give a rich dessert to the fat boy."

19. *Interrogative:* a type of sentence in which something is questioned. Contrast with declarative and imperative. E.g., "Who gave a rich dessert to the fat boy?"

20. *Instrumental:* in case grammar, the case describing the means by which something was done. E.g., "A *knife* killed Robert."

21. *Intransitive verb:* a verb that cannot take an object. Contrast with transitive. E.g., "die."
22. *Locative:* a case marking location. E.g., "in a room."
23. *Main clause:* in embedding, the clause that can stand alone or that contains the other. Contrast with subordinate clause. E.g., *"The rat* the cat wounded *ate the cheese."* or "Because the rat ate the cheese, *we bought a cat."*
24. *Manner:* a case marking how something is done. E.g., "in a careless way."
25. *Mass noun:* a noun standing for stuff the amount of which is not countable. Contrast with count noun. E.g., "milk," "mud." Note that you cannot say "a milk" or "a mud."
26. *Negative:* a sentence in which something is denied. Contrast with affirmative. E.g., "Robert did not give a rich dessert to the fat boy."
27. *Noun:* a part of speech naming a person, place, or thing. See common noun, count noun, mass noun, proper noun, and noun phrase.
28. *Noun phrase:* a phrase consisting of (Determiner) (Adjective) Noun or pronoun. E.g., *"Robert* gave *a rich dessert* to *the fat boy."*
29. *Object:* the noun phrase acted on by the verb. E.g., "Robert gave *a rich dessert* to the fat boy." or *"A rich dessert* was given by Robert to the fat boy."
30. *Passive voice:* a sentence in which the logical subject is in object position. Contrast with active voice. E.g., "A rich dessert was given by Robert to the fat boy."
31. *Patient:* a case marking the person or thing acted on. Also called the object.
32. *Predicate:* the sentence minus the subject and whole-sentence modifiers; what it is that is being talked about. Also called the verb phrase. E.g., "Robert *gave a rich dessert to the fat boy."*
33. *Preposition:* a part of speech that usually precedes a noun phrase, describing how it relates to the rest of the sentence. E.g., "Robert gave a rich dessert *to* the fat boy."
34. *Prepositional phrase:* the preposition with the noun phrase it heads. E.g., "Robert gave a rich dessert *to the fat boy."*
35. *Presupposition:* the set of facts that the speaker assumes in constructing an utterance. E.g., "When did you stop beating your wife?" presupposes that the other is married and beat his wife.
36. *Pronoun:* a part of speech that stands for a noun or noun phrase. E.g., "he," "she," "I," "me," "them," "it," "who," "that."
37. *Proper noun:* a noun naming a specific individual. Contrast with common noun. E.g., "Robert."
38. *Quantifier:* a word or phrase telling how much. Determiners are quantifiers as are numbers and words like "some," "many," "each," "for all."
39. *Recipient:* a case marking the person to whom something is given. E.g., "Robert gave a rich dessert *to the fat boy."*
40. *Relative clause:* a subordinate clause headed by a (deleted) relative pronoun. E.g., "The rat *(that) the cat wounded* ate the cheese." or "The boy *who was fat* went to the bakery."
41. *Relative pronoun:* pronouns "who," "which," or "that," which introduce relative clauses. See preceding.
42. *Subject:* the noun phrase governing the action of the verb. E.g., *"Robert* gave a rich dessert" or *"The door* opened."

43. *Subordinate clause:* In a complex sentence the clause that depends on the other clause and cannot stand alone. Contrast with main clause. E.g., "The rat *the cat wounded* ate the cheese" or "*Because the rat ate the cheese,* we bought a cat."
44. *Theme-rheme:* also called old information–new information, topic-comment. The theme is what the sentence is about; it is usually unstressed and usually mentioned first. The rheme is what the sentence is telling that is new. In "The first President of the United States was George Washington" the theme is the first President and the rheme is his identity.
45. *Transitive:* a verb that can take an object. Contrast with intransitive. E.g., "give."
46. *Verb:* a part of speech that usually describes an action. See transitive and intransitive. E.g., "die," "give."
47. *Verb phrase:* the part of the sentence including and following the verb. See predicate.

STUDY QUESTIONS

1. Using the phrase structure rules you know and what you understand of deep structure and transformations, develop the deep structure phrase markers for:
   a) John promised Bill to go.
   b) John begged Bill to go.
   c) They have parsed sentences.
   (Note that this last has two readings and therefore two deep structures!) (For the first two you need the concept of recursiveness. If S → NP VP and NP → N S, you could have a phrase marker

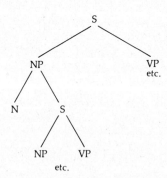

for example.) What transformations would you need to derive the different (or same) surface structures? (For a and b you will have to use your linguistic intuitions and make them up.)

2. Discuss the pros and cons of the finite state grammar—behaviorist view of syntax. You will have to discuss finite state grammar as a mathematical model for a reinforcement chain, think about which structures the finite state grammar can account for and which it cannot, and evaluate the importance of those structures in the language. What does augmenting the finite state grammar (→ augmented transition network or ATN) accomplish?

5

Sentence Processing

Read the following sentences carefully:

1. They are forecasting cyclones.
2. They are describing events.
3. They are chopping wood.
4. They are eating lunch.
5. They are flying planes.
6. They are conflicting desires.

(after Mehler and Carey, 1967)

Did something funny happen when you read (6)? For a second it made no sense. Do you have any problem with it now? Can you go back to (1)–(5) and read any of them the same way you must read (6)? Try especially (5), which is ambiguous. It could be said by someone pointing to objects in the sky explaining that they are not birds but flying planes, or it could be said by someone describing the activity of pilots. What happens when you switch from "reading" a sentence one way to reading a sentence another? What makes (6) so hard to understand? Why does it require a doubletake *after* reading (1)–(5)?

This example, as you should realize, makes use of constituent structures described in the last chapter. Although similar in appearance, these sentences derive from different phrase structures, one where "are" functions as an auxiliary verb and "they" is not coreferential with the object, and one where "are" is the main verb, and "they" and the object, "conflicting desires" or "flying planes," refer to the same thing. In understanding (1)–(5) on your first reading, you performed some mental parsing operations, the same for each sentence. You tried to use the same operations or strategies for (6) but they do not work for (6). (Use of a familiar strategy in an inappropriate situation is known as *persistence of set*.) This caused the doubletake, which should make you realize that you are actively processing sentence structure, that there is a psychological reality to syntactic operations.

7. The horse raced past the barn fell.

This sentence, even without a context, should cause problems—it is grammatical, and in case you have not parsed it yet, try the paraphrase:

7a. The horse, which was raced past the barn, fell.

Why does (7) cause so much difficulty? Because our experience with the language allows for a simple reading—"the horse raced past the barn," with "horse" as agent, and that leaves an extra verb, "fell." The complex embedded clause, passive with relative pronoun ("which") deletion, is not our first choice parsing strategy, again suggesting the psychological reality to syntactic operations.

8. Time flies like an arrow.

This sentence may seem to be straightforward with only one reading, but nevertheless, it is five-ways ambiguous. To derive the ambiguities, you must disband your real-world knowledge and some semantic knowledge and just use your syntax processor. Disbanding this knowledge is hard; most of the readings were uncovered by a computer not encumbered with such knowledge, but notice how easy they are to see in paraphrase:

8a. There is a species of flies called time flies that likes an arrow.
8b. There is a race and you are referee. Time the flies that look like arrows.
8c. There is a race and you are referee. Time the flies as you would time an arrow.
8d. There is a race and you are referee. Time the flies the way an arrow would time them.

And then, of course, the one that is sensible:

8e. Time and arrows both move quickly.

(after Kuno, 1967)

The point of this example is twofold. First, as with the other examples, it should make you aware of your ability to parse; you can see that the other senses are possible syntactically, and you do that by using your mental parsing operations. Second, it should demonstrate that in normal sentence processing, syntactic operations work together with semantic operations, so if there is semantic bias for one reading, other structures are not derived.

As one last example to demonstrate that parsing *must* have a psychological reality, consider the simple, unambiguous English sentence "the lion chased the tiger." To understand such a sentence by adding together individual morpheme meanings, we would have descriptions of two ferocious mammals and a running action performed some time in the past. The sentence, however, provides a much more specific meaning—the ferocious animal with the mane is running after the ferocious animal with the stripes, causing it to run. The relationship of the lion to the tiger is conveyed *only* in the syntax of the sentence; there is no way to guess it by knowing about lions, tigers, or chasing. In places where our knowledge of the world and our knowledge of individual word-meanings are not enough to determine the relationship of elements within the sentence, we must be relying on mental knowledge of syntactic rules, how additional meaning may be conveyed by word combination. This knowledge allows us to understand sentences that are unlikely semantically, but perhaps true, such as "man bites dog," or innovative semantically, but conveying new truths such as "scientists predict a nuclear winter in the event of a nuclear war." We cannot interpret such sentences directly from past experience or understanding of individual word-meanings, but only from extension of past experience, individual meanings and knowledge of how meanings are combined according to the language's conventions. This last is syntax.

In this chapter we will discuss the nature of sentence processing as distinct from the nature of sentence structure, discussed in the last chapter; that is, we will examine the aspects of structure useful for sentence processing, and those that do not appear useful. Sentence processing has been studied both in artificial intelligence, in attempts to make computers "understand" sentences, and in cognitive psychology, in attempts to discover how people understand sentences. Both will be presented here, since each provides insights about what aspects of structure are most useful. And it is important to note that over the years of study the two approaches have led to very similar conclusions.

Before beginning the analysis, one important distinction must be made, between sentence *production* and sentence *comprehension,* what we do as speakers and what we do as hearers. We ignored this in the last chapter, in part because we can discuss sentence structure without considering processing, and in part because the linguistic position is that the same rules that apply for sentence generation are likely to apply for sentence comprehension. If we start with a deep structure and perform transformations to produce a spoken surface form, in understanding we could just reverse the process, starting with the spoken form and undoing the transformations to arrive at deep structure. Thus, the same rules could be assumed to underlie both production and comprehension, obviously providing cognitive economy. There is no evidence that this assumption is warranted. In fact, if you consider what happens intuitively when you try to learn a second language they seem quite different—you seem to be able to understand long before you are comfortable producing a sentence. If both entail acquisition of the same set of rules there should be no such asymmetry. In this chapter we will be discussing primarily parsing (comprehension) rather than generation, in part because less research has been done on generation in adults. It is important to remember that some things that do not seem to have psychological reality for parsing may turn out to be psychologically real, but only in generation.

Computer Processing

Parsers

In considering computer processing of natural languages, we must always keep in mind the ultimate goals of the systems designer—what (s)he hoped the system, endowed with some language capacity, would be able to do with that communication ability. The goals have always been practical and fall into a few general classes. Computer language systems have been designed to take text in one language and translate it into another, equipped for this purpose with a dictionary for the two languages and some syntactic information for each. Computers have been used to access and organize quantities of data as information-retrieval or question-answering systems. In this case they are equipped with the data and enough knowledge of the users' language to "understand" the users' questions, retrieve the appropriate data, and feed it back to users in a form they can understand. Computer systems have been designed to participate in stereotyped communications tasks like writing thank you notes, letters of regret, personalized Christmas cards, or being a good supportive "listener" (see Box 5.1). In these cases the machine may be supplied with stock phrases as in form letters, in which it inserts the appropriate "personalized" information, like a name. The machine must therefore be equipped with enough knowledge of the language to find the personal information in the communication from the user, to cycle it into the form. Finally, computer systems have been used as prototypes for any and all of these purposes, to test a particular model of language understanding. In these cases the machine has been equipped with parsing strategies that—it is hoped—are sufficient for general language use.

In reviewing language understanding programs one is simultaneously struck by how much has been accomplished and how far the programs are from human capabilities. It might seem that the set of goals just outlined is easily achieved by using very simple schemes (some of which have been hinted at), but what has been discovered is that each goal has required enormously more language knowledge for easy interaction than originally thought necessary. This, in turn, has given us some insight into what language actually is.

Keyword Systems. We will begin by looking at simple language translation and question-answering schemes. The simplest possible approach to both these tasks is one that uses no syntax whatsoever; the machine is supplied with synonyms in one language for each word in another, or, in question-answering systems, the machine is supplied with a dictionary of keywords. A *keyword* is a word likely to appear in the user's input that the machine will "recognize" by matching it in its dictionary; the dictionary "definition" will consist of an action the machine should take, like answering with a page number on which information might be found, or answering with information directly stored with the keyword, or calling another program to do something. Basically, most book indexes use a keyword system. If you are interested in ATNs (augmented transition networks, described in the last chapter) you might look in the index to this book under ATN and find some page numbers. Turning to those pages, you will find information about ATNs. If this were automated you might ask a machine

Where can I locate information about ATNs?

and the machine would respond with the page numbers, or you might ask the machine:

Tell me what you know about ATNs.

and the machine would get a page number, turn to its copy of the book (inside its memory), and display the page with the information. In either case the task could be accomplished with the machine recognizing nothing more than the word "ATN," which would be a keyword. One obvious difficulty with such a system is that you might probe with a word that the machine cannot recognize—the sample question said "ATNs"; if only ATN is stored, "ATNs" will not be recognized nor will "augmented transition network," one obvious synonym that looks even less like the keyword, ATN. To avoid this, we might put in various synonyms that the user might employ, we might supplement the system with morphological rules ("sublexical syntax") so that it could recognize words and their plurals without having all plurals stored separately, or we might ask the user to flounder and to try to select the one keyword that will score a hit.

We have already suggested programming some syntax at the morphological level. Alert readers probably recognized that we need more than that. Supposedly we probed with the two questions:

Where can I locate information about ATNs?

and

Tell me what you know about ATNs.

and supposedly extracted page number from the first and page contents from the second. If the machine responds only to the word "ATN" the two questions should produce identical responses; the machine would have no way of recognizing that different information was requested. We can try to get around that difficulty by causing it to recognize more than one word—for example, it could scan the sentence for words like "where," "on what page," "locate," ... any of which would tell it to respond with the page number, while "what" or "know" could cue it to respond with the page contents. "ATN" would still tell it what to respond about. This is a keyword system too, slightly more sophisticated, with a little "syntax." Note that the syntax here is provided by keywords—not by establishing a structure. Recognition of the word "know" would cause the machine to call a program to look up a page—which page is triggered by a content word like "ATN." Although the machine is not making an overt response to the user for "know," matching that pattern still produces a set action. Given this scheme, is the user who queries with

Do you *know what* page ATNs are described *on?*

likely to get the right type of information?

Although we have concentrated on the keyword scheme with respect to question-answering systems, the problems translate readily to translation schemes. A program equipped only with two language dictionaries is a keyword program: A word in one language will be recognized if and only if it is in the dictionary, and this will trigger the response of a synonym from the other language rather than a page number or page contents or other internal action. As with question-answering systems, translation systems must either store words and their morphological derivatives (e.g. a word and its plural) separately or have programs for parsing into morphemes, or they will fail to recognize some words. In the question-answering case the right response was either the page number or page contents; in translation it is the correct synonym, which can be tricky for words with multiple meanings, or for languages that have no single word synonym for a concept (what should we use in translating any particular "snow" from Eskimo into English, for instance?). Moreover, relevant information for translation may appear in a number of forms; for example, in English, past tense may be expressed as an "ed" suffix or through a separate word (such as, "had"), and the latter sometimes means "possessed"; it is not always just the tense carrier. The translation could possibly be the same for "Robert gave" and "Robert had given," but it should be very different from "Robert had a rich dessert." Finally, idioms must be recognized and translated as a group: "Do you know what page ATN is on?" in English is probably synonymous with "what page is ATN on?" but in some other languages the English cannot be rendered literally.

It is interesting to note, though, that keyword systems can be successful if the domain in which they are to apply is limited—if it is known ahead of time that only a particular subject is to be translated. Then the synonyms, idioms, and so on, can be preselected, and some of the problems circumvented. (See Box 5.1 for an example of a successful limited domain keyword system—an automatic therapist.) In reading about computer language systems, this point should be kept in mind; even sophisticated systems, at some level, make use of keywords and sometimes are performing well only because their domain has been restricted, and the restrictions may not be transparent. In a sense this may have implications for human language processing as well. Once we are cued into a topic it is possible that we simplify our processing,

---

Box 5.1   The Doctor—A Keyword Psychiatrist

Operating only on a keyword system, the DOCTOR was able to carry on realistic interviews with human users/patients. The DOCTOR was designed to test a language processing model and to demonstrate the flaws and virtues of the keyword systems. It is interesting to note that people who interacted with it took it very seriously, and some even proposed that it could eventually replace a human therapist (see Weizenbaum, 1976, for discussion). The system works, in part, because this type of conversation requires little thinking—the doctor serves as a yes-man. Because of this Weizenbaum (1976) considered it a parody of a doctor, not a substitute for one. The system works by "recognizing" phrases such as "I remember ____." The DOCTOR responds automatically with "Do you often think of ____?" getting the seemingly sophisticated syntax from the user. If "____" is a single word like "John," the machine responds with a single word, "Do you often think of John?" If it is an embedded sentence the machine echoes with an embedded sentence: "I remember visiting relatives in New Hampshire" → "Do you often think of visiting relatives in New Hampshire?" Additional naturalness was programmed by conversions of I, me, my to you, your (I remember my mother → Do you often think of your mother?) and by having several response frames for each keyword: remember → do you often think of, what in the present situation reminds you of, and so on.

In the following, two computers are talking. The "paranoid" program (P.) works on similar principles and was invented to model paranoid behavior.

D. Good evening. Tell me your problems. Please terminate input with a period or a question mark.

P. People get on my nerves sometimes.

D. I am not sure I understand you fully.

P. You should pay more attention.

D. Suppose you should pay more attention.

P. You're entitled to your own opinion.

D. What makes you think I am entitled to my own opinion?

P. It bothers me just to be around people.

D. Please go on.

P. I went to the track at Bay Meadows a while back.

D. What does that suggest to you?

P. I went to the races.

D. What else would you like to discuss?

P. Horseracing interests me.

D. Why do you say that just now?

P. There's a lot of crooked gambling going on there.

D. I am not sure I understand you fully.

P. It's clear to me if not to you.

D. Do you think it's likely that not to I?

P. I went to the races.

D. Please go on.

P. I gamble on horses.

D. What does that suggest to you?

P. I went to the races.

D. What else would you like to discuss?

P. Gambling has been nothing but trouble to me.

D. Why do you say that just now?

P. I've had experience with crooks gambling at the track.

D. I am not sure I understand you fully.

P. I've already told you enough about that.

D. Oh? I enough about that?

P. I went to the races.

[Comment: This has to be the most persistent and patient paranoid I have ever encountered.]

(from Cerf, 1973, 62–63.)

responding to only one meaning of ambiguous words, the meaning relevant to the current domain. It is possible that we use keywords also to guess what is being said or asked for and may not really attend to the conversation.

Syntax Programs.   In discussing keyword systems we have seen the need for providing at least rudimentary knowledge of language structures, in addition to basic word recognition, to allow recognition of morphological derivatives (singulars and plurals), recognition of a particular sense of a word in context (had given = give +

Box 5.2   Baseball—An Early Question-Answerer

One of the early successful question-answering systems (Green, Wolf, Chomsky, and Laughery, 1963) had as data base statistics about baseball games played in a given year: names of teams with the cities sponsoring them, the date and city of the game and who the competing teams were, and scores for the game. It was able to take (typed) natural language input and respond to questions using the information outlined above.

Note that this is a limited domain; the machine could "expect" questions about baseball, and syntax and semantics could be set up with this in mind. For example, "New York" in such a context is ambiguous; "Did New York beat Baltimore?" refers to the teams, not the cities. This expression is limited largely to this kind of context, and the number of such expressions is limited for each context, and so the usages may be programmed as synonyms.

Syntactic analysis in BASEBALL was rudimentary. Sentences were first scanned for idiomatic expressions like "New York" and these were replaced by a one-word equivalent. The sentence was then processed from left to right, grouping noun phrases, prepositional phrases, and adverbs. Prepositions left over at the end were assigned to the first NP (as in *What city* did the Yankees play the Orioles *in?*). If the last verb in the sentence was preceded by "were" the sentence was assigned "passive" and the object of "by" was assigned as subject. Otherwise the subject was assigned to the NP between the auxiliary and the main verb (as in What city *did the Yankees play* the Orioles in?). It is important to note how basic this kind of strategy is. It works only if input is regular and we know ahead of time to expect questions on places, winning, and so on. Nevertheless, conversation may be quite natural.

It is also important to note what the limitations on this kind of program are. There are syntactic structures it cannot handle—like "Did the team that creamed Baltimore also beat the Yankees?" This should cause problems because "cream" is probably not in the lexicon, and more important, because there is no means of handling relative clauses, so the relationship between the main clause and the subordinate clause cannot be gleaned. Finally, it has no rules for producing output in sentences, so the grammar may be used only for decoding the input.

past, not give + possess, the usual meaning of have), recognition of idioms, and recognition of similar but not identical forms (had given = gave; on what page is it = what page is it on). To satisfy these functions language programmers began to implement parsing systems. (See Box 5.2 for an example of an early question-answering system that used keywords and some elementary syntax, recognizing only a very small subset of English structures.)

Bottom-Up Parsing.   To recognize more than a limited number of structures of the language, that is, to give the users freedom of speech and not confine them to particular question forms, the grammar of the users' language must be implemented. As we saw in the last chapter, one of the simplest parsing systems for a language is phrase structure grammar or constituent analysis. Phrase structure grammars work by a system of rewrite rules, where words, if they fit a particular pattern, are replaced by a higher order constituent. "The rat" fits the pattern DET N, which may be rewritten NP; "rewriting" may be considered recognizing, matching a pattern. Strict phrase structure grammars make use of no logical syntactic information such as logical subject, agent, and so on. They replace each word only with its part of speech and each group of parts of speech with higher order parts of speech (constituents). Phrase structure systems are *bottom-up* or *data-driven* systems; they begin with the input sentence (bottom, data) and replace wherever possible the data with higher-order (up) constituents.

Let us consider how such a parser would work, say with inputs like:

Time flies like an arrow.

or

Baby dogs like wild animals destroy.

Beginning with the first word, "time," we may replace it with its part of speech. Time (or baby) can be either a noun or a verb. Thus, we can start two parses, one with a noun and one with a verb. Flies (or dogs) similarly may be replaced by its part of speech—either a plural noun or a verb again. Together these produce four possible parses: noun noun, noun verb, verb noun, verb verb. Three of the four are possible English structures (noun noun in "machine operator," noun verb in most simple sentences, verb noun in commands). We eliminate the verb verb possibility. "Like" may be a verb or a conjunction. Each of the parses thus far has two more possibilities, noun noun verb, noun noun conjunction, and so on. All except verb noun verb are possible English structures. We eliminate verb noun verb and stop to critique the procedure. Although it is not optimal, as we shall see, successful parses have been written by using only phrase structure grammar or strictly bottom-up processing (Kuno, 1967).

First, you should note one thing that happens with this procedure. Many more structures than are needed are generated and held on to at least for a while. You probably noticed that the second sentence, "Baby dogs . . . ," had similar structure to "Time flies . . ."—until we get to "destroy." Since "destroy" *must be* the verb, all structures generated before it that contain "like" as the verb will be eliminated by this last word. Is it necessary or desirable to generate structures that will ultimately be rejected? Clearly, it is inefficient at best (which does not mean that it is not how people do it).

Second, even if the structures are not ultimately rejected, at the conclusion of each sentence we may have several readings—five, as already stated for "Time flies like an arrow." Is this practical? Remember that the language programs are usually designed for practical purposes—do we want to take five structures for "time flies like an arrow" and render them in a foreign language for automatic translation? Wouldn't it be better to select the most likely structure instead? If so, how? Do you think that in *our* processing of language we derive all possible parses and select the best, or automatically (somehow) derive only the one we will keep?

Guidance by Meaning.   There are a few methods that can be implemented to facilitate "automatic" derivation of only the best structure first. One thing that can be done is to interrupt syntactic processing with semantic analysis—we know there is no species of flies called time flies, that flies are not usually judged by referees, and so on. If semantic and syntactic analyses occur together, once the noun noun pair "time flies" is generated, it could be looked up in a dictionary, found not to exist, rejected as a possible parse, and thus, as sentence parsing proceeds, any possibilities beginning with noun noun would not be considered. This seems intuitively appealing but has seldom been used in automatic language processing (Tennant, 1981), although it may very well be what is done in human language processing. Usually it is easier to separate the syntax and semantic programs than to interleave them. Also, as we saw in the chapters on meaning, it is difficult to decide how much semantic or real world information should be supplied to a language processor—we may have no dictionary entry for "time flies" but that does not mean they do not exist; we are likely to have no entry for "baby dogs" but that phrase is comprehensible and could be said by someone. Is it *semantic* knowledge that flies are not timed in races? Do you think we use the existence of such knowledge to guide our language processing?

Conceptually Driven Processing.   A second way to achieve automatic selection of one right parse is to begin with hypotheses about what parses are possible or likely in language, and to test those hypotheses. This is called *conceptually driven processing* or *top-down processing,* because a guess is made at the structure of the sentence or sentence part before looking at it (a reasonable beginning or bottom of processing) directly. ATNs, described in the last chapter, are instances of top-down parsers, based on transformational grammars and successfully developed for automatic parsing (Woods, 1967, 1973). Each ATN is labeled in a sense with a function—a sentence ATN looks for NP VP, an NP ATN looks for DET ADJ N, and so on. Entering an ATN implies the assumption that the input will conform to the structure the ATN models. The sentence elements are then searched to see if they fit. *If not,* alternative structures are tested. Depending on the order of the jumps from the main ATN to constituent ATNs, we may generate most likely parses first. For example, active sentences are more common than passive ones. So we can assume *a priori* that the input will be an active sentence, that the first NP will be the logical subject. Given a passive sentence,

A rich dessert was given by Robert.

we will try initially to parse it as active (structure equivalent to "dessert gave Robert"), when we reach the suffix "-en" on "given," it will not match the rule on the arc for active verbs, causing the parse to be rejected, and an alternative—the second most likely sentence structure—(perhaps passive) to be attempted. Once the hypothesis for passive structure is attempted, the sentence will pass: There will be a successful search for a verb with -en suffix and for a by- clause. Routines that take into account the likelihood of success, such as attempting active parses before passive ones, are called *heuristic* routines. Using heuristic top-down parsing, programs may still generate parses that will be rejected, as the example shows, but the rejections will be infrequent (given good heuristics and normal input) as compared with exclusively bottom-up routines. And an occasional failure to parse correctly on the first try is not unreasonable. We do it too—as the examples at the beginning of the chapter illustrated.

Heuristics have been developed in parsers at various levels. ATNs assume a *sentence* structure. Heuristics may also be programmed with particular *words*. For example, recognition of the verb "promise" could establish a strategy of taking its subject to be the subject of the embedded sentence (see Chapter 4, sentences [47a] and [47b]—John begged/promised Bill to go.). One might also specify with a verb what kind of semantic relations or prepositions (as in fly from, sit down) it usually takes to implement top-down searches for those cases or prepositions once the verb is encountered (Woods, 1967).

Parallel and Serial Processing. Heuristic top-down processing, in addition to reducing the number of structures that will be rejected, also eliminates the generation of ambiguous readings. In the example of bottom-up processing, as each word was added, all possible structures were derived and kept; that is, ambiguous structures were derived in *parallel,* at the same time. In the example of heuristic top-down processing, first one structure was attempted, then another, and so on. We can make the machine derive ambiguous readings by having it continue to attempt strategies after a success, but then we will be deriving the structures successively rather than at the same time. Operations performed successively rather than at the same time, whether they are bottom-up or top-down, are called *serial processes.* (One way to conceptualize the difference between parallel and serial processing is to think about how many times we "stop" at each word. In parallel processing each word is encountered once, and all possible information and all its different meanings are found—the whole marker structure for "bachelor" could be pulled out at once. In serial processing each word is encountered once on each reading, with different information collected each time; we keep making passes through the sentence, getting one reading at a time. For "bachelor" we would have to make four stops, first for unmarried male, on the second try for knights, on the third for degree, and in the last for seal.)

Left-to-Right Heuristic Bottom-Up Processing. We may use heuristics (and serial processing) in bottom-up routines—"baby" is much more often used as the noun than the verb, so we could begin by trying it, noting that a choice was made. (Noting something in a program is called *setting a flag.*) If the parse fails or if second meanings are desired, we return to the points where choices were made (we check the flags) and take the next most likely path. The principal difference between heuristic top-down and heuristic bottom-up procedures is the level at which the guess is made: In top-down procedures heuristics apply to an entire sentence or clause; in bottom-up, to the most likely sense or part of speech of the word.

Use of heuristics in either bottom-up or top-down processing limits the number of simultaneously generated structures and limits the memory load produced by holding all of those structures—which is good, since by doing so, it increases cognitive economy. However, it limits efficiency in another way. Note what happens when a parse fails: Somewhere in the processing of the sentence a flag was set indicating that a choice was made and what alternatives there were (for example, active selected, could be passive). With failure, the parser returns to these choice points and tries again. What has been saved in memory load may be lost in time spent if there is a reasonable failure rate—because we must keep cycling through the sentence. With parallel processing we are guaranteed that at the end of one cycle through the sentence we will have at least one parse if it exists; with heuristic serial processing we have a guarantee of finding a parse only if we try all possibilities anyway.

Deterministic and Nondeterministic Parsing. A parser that must *back up* (do a doubletake) and reprocess or that generates structures that will be discarded, is called a *nondeterministic* parser; it has no guru advising it of the one true path from the start. A *deterministic* parser is one that guesses the structure correctly the first time.

Is a deterministic parser either plausible or feasible? At the beginning of the chapter several sentences were presented that were supposed to cause doubletakes. If the demonstrations worked, you were to notice that you normally process structure. Now, you might also notice that you process nondeterministically, at least in these instances. The question of plausibility for a deterministic processor, then, is how often we process nondeterministically. If we do doubletakes all the time we may be asking too much of a machine to require that it rarely do them. However, most of the time we do not seem to be doing doubletakes; in fact, it is difficult to come up with sentences that cause them. And most sentences (or words or clauses) are ambiguous, which means somehow or another we are guessing or being guided to the correct parse from the beginning. So we want to program the guide, to make computers parse as efficiently as we do.

Now, is deterministic parsing feasible? Marcus (1980) has implemented a deterministic parser based on trace grammar, deriving abstract surface-structure representations. His "guru," the guide for the parse, has interesting implications for human processing. Generally speaking, Marcus' approach is to do a left-to-right serial parse of the sentence but to use, as the "unit" for rewriting, *several constituents* rather than just one. One constituent is actively processed and three to its right (five in later versions) are available—they can be viewed—to assist decision-making. Since the three are ahead of it in the input, this is called *lookahead;* since we are limited to viewing three, it is *limited lookahead.* (Note that unlimited lookahead is as nondeterministic as unlimited backtracking. Basically, a structure may be suggested by one word, tested through the sentence and rejected, and another structure tested. Since *un*limited lookahead entails attempts at structures that do not make it to the final parse, it is nondeterministic.)

In Marcus' parsing program, available for active parsing or viewing through a "window" are constituents whose substructures (daughters) are known but whose role in the hierarchy has still to be determined. At different points in the parse, then, constituents at different hierarchical levels are considered; as soon as a constituent's role is known, the constituent that dominates it—and represents larger amounts of input—is available, along with two others. Three constituents-whose-daughters-are-known, of *any size,* are always potentially available.

Before showing how this makes parsing deterministic, we will consider the implications of the window for human processing. When we read (or listen) we obviously receive input in order from left to right (from beginning to end). Do we read or listen word by word, even if that is the form of the input? Force yourself to read one word at a time by cutting a small window out of a piece of paper, covering a page with the paper, and moving it along so that you view only one word at a time. Or without cheating (looking ahead) follow your finger with your eyes, moving it along one word at a time. It is very difficult to get sense this way: Although usually we do read roughly from left to right, we use a larger-than-one-word window to get an overview of structure and sense. And it is reasonable to suppose that the number of words we can use for overview depends on the amount already understood. Initially, it might be three words. As we move along and get the gist of the idea, a larger chunk of input could be taken in at a time. This could entail the same number of *new* structures, but each now dominating more. (See Box 5.3 for an example of varying lookahead.) Incidentally, as we shall see in chapters 6 and 7, even in listening, although words are coming in one at a time, it is possible to delay work on them until enough have been collected in memory for a reasonable lookahead.

The reason limited lookahead may allow deterministic parsing is that the rewrite rules—the pattern-matching rules—are sensitive to both the current constituent and those ahead. "Sensitivity" means that when a pattern is activated from the bottom several conditions apply at once. "Have written" matches a pattern for AUX V, "have a" matches a pattern for V (NP), since the determiner "a" suggests an NP. In this parser, then, a structure is not activated until and unless its components are *all* there, and since several constituents are available at each step, the check to see if they are all there is possible. The result is that no structures are tried and rejected.

Now, consider what happens on *garden path sentences,* sentences on which we do a doubletake. The parser does a doubletake too. In "The horse raced past the barn fell," "raced" is ambiguous: It could be the main verb of the sentence "the horse raced past the barn" or the "-en" form of the verb (note that for this verb the "-en" form is realized as "-ed") in an embedded passive, "the horse, which was raced past the barn, fell." The paraphrase is not ambiguous, because proceeding from left to right we encounter "which," which triggers the pattern for relative clauses. With it deleted in the garden path version, there is no such clue, and the words (constituents) to the immediate right of "raced" also provide no clue. So "raced" by itself, with no other

---

Box 5.3   The Changing Size of the Glance

1. A stitch in time saves wine.
2. Too many books spoil the broth.
3. Better date than never.
4. Here today done tomorrow.

All four of these are clichés, expressions we should all recognize. As soon as we get the gist we should do a very cursory job of processing; because we know the structure, a lot more can be viewed at a time. We can check to see if we are processing less carefully by changing what might be expected and seeing if we notice. As you may have observed, each of the clichés has an error in it—sometimes at the beginning and sometimes at the end. Are you better at noticing the early ones (where you have not guessed the cliché) or the later ones, where you may have been scanning at a faster rate, having already determined the structure? In proofreading is it easier to catch errors at the beginning of a word, line, or sentence—or at the end?

This example is not exactly analogous to the window in the parser, since the example works in part because of top-down processing, hypothesizing what is to come. The parser works bottom-up, but the concept is similar: The further along it is in determining the structure of the sentence, the larger a chunk of input it can name and then it need deal only with the name.

---

structure clues in the window, activates the main verb pattern and we go down the garden path until we hit "fell."

If a clue is presented *within the window* the same problem does not occur. For example, suppose the sentence had been "the horse raced by the renowned jockey fell." As before, if "raced," is considered in isolation, it could trigger patterns appropriate to either verb + past or verb + en. However, in the window is an agent clause, "by the renowned jockey"; verb + en *and* agent as a group should stimulate only the recognizer for passives, so this should not similarly fail. (Note that "by the renowned jockey" has the same structure as "by the barn," and the latter could not be an agent. We have assumed, for this example, that the parser knows agents must be animate, and that words are marked with features like "animate.")

This parser has difficulty with sentences we have difficulty with, and it deterministically finds structure in sentences we have no problems with. We are able to try again on garden path sentences, to backtrack, but the parser, since it cannot go back, fails. Since we have problems with garden path sentences, it suggests that we normally process deterministically. Since we can resolve the problems, it suggests we have other options available.

Summary and Conclusions. We have now examined parsing schemes very generally. They can be bottom-up, top-down, a combination, heuristic, serial, parallel, deterministic, or nondeterministic. They can model or create phrase structure representations, transformational deep structure representations, or trace abstract surface structure representations. The three grammars considered in the last chapter thus are implementable, although no parser has yet dealt with all possible English structures. Generally, it has been recognized that parsers that derive underlying constituent relationships are more valuable for understanding systems than are pure phrase structure grammars.

It is important to recognize that although no parser has treated the full complement of English structures, an impressive array of complex structures has been dealt with. These include scope/quantification (as in, a fat boy), anaphora, relative clauses, passives, actives, negatives (Woods, 1967), and questions, commands, cleft sentences (as in "It is John who speaks"—Marcus, 1980). Among things not processed yet are conjunctions, comparatives, and noun noun structures. The last have turned out to be incredibly difficult. Tennant (1981) cites the following (credited to Finin) where the underlining marks which nouns or noun groups modify which others:

water meter cover adjustment screw

aluminum automobile water pumps

January automobile water pump cover shipments.

The only way to decide which modifies which is to use semantic/world knowledge, much of which has not been implemented well enough.

Total Language Systems

Since programs are written for practical purposes like question-answering, it helps if they are equipped with knowledge about their data bases. The extent of this knowledge and the relative importance of the meaning component of a system depend on the size of the world the system is dealing with. Systems designers have interfaced the meaning component with the syntactic component at different stages: Some have meaning assigned to the outcome of the parse, at a level just below surface structure (for example, Woods, 1967—note that this foreshadows trace theory formulations); some interrupt syntactic analysis with meaning interpretation, using this to guide the parse (Winograd, 1972); and some build semantics into the parser—searching for *meaning* structure rather than sentence structure-to-which-meaning-is-applied (Schank, 1972). Despite the disagreement about when to apply it and how important semantic analysis is, there is general conformity on the methods of applying it.

Primitives as Meanings. Basically, two ideas are used in meaning assignment: primitives and propositions. The concept of primitives was discussed in chapters 2 and 3—they are features in terms of which concepts are defined. The notion may be easiest to see in this context, however, since computers, unlike us, have no sensory consciousness of the world to map concepts onto. Suppose, as Woods (1967) did, that we wished to equip a computer to provide flight information. We would equip it with "knowledge" about cities with airports, times, airlines, and basic flight "concepts" like stopovers, departures, and arrivals. For the purpose of the system, we would never have to explain what depart and arrive or even an airplane were at all—all data would be organized in terms of these words; these would be primitive concepts, not broken down any further. City and time, though, would be general concepts that can stand for a number of different values: City—New York, Boston, Chicago; Time—Friday morning, around 5 P.M., July. In this case, the primitive is an *attribute-value pair,* attribute = location, value = which location. Once again, the concept of location, of New York, need be explained no further.

The problems arise for primitives when data bases are constructed for different things. For example, in a better-known project than the airline project, Woods (1973) implemented the same parser, along with a semantic system, to provide information on rocks collected on the moon to scientists studying them. In this case, the primitives used for the airline system were valueless; a whole new system was needed with primitives about chemical and physical properties of rocks. Winograd (1972) implemented Woods' parser on another data base, a "world" constructed for a computer, consisting of blocks drawn on a computer screen and actions that could be taken to manipulate them. In this case the primitives consisted of information necessary to distinguish blocks like color (red vs. blue), number of sides, size—a set completely different from those needed for airline schedules or moon rocks. Winograd also equipped the machine with world knowledge, about the limited world the computer was dealing with: axioms like "nothing can rest on the point of a pyramid," so if commanded to place something on a point, the machine would respond before trying, as a human would, that such a feat was impossible. Sample output from this program is shown in Box 5.4. Note how much "smarter" this machine seems than DOCTOR.

Once the world is extended to include many different data sets, the idea of primitives and axioms takes on a whole new dimension. It is possible that there is a set of basic concepts, underlying all concepts, in terms of which meanings may be defined. Alternatively, it is likely that each data set has its own set of primitives, and general language processors consist of many such data sets and their associated primitives and axioms.

Scripts to Structure Meaning.   Knowledge structures for general language systems are efficiently organized in sets known as *scripts, frames,* or *schemas* (Tennant, 1981). We can consider scripts or frames as means of storing characteristic features as well as defining features or primitives, as an automated prototype concept (Kolata, 1982, citing an interview with Minsky). We may also consider a script to be an extended attribute-value pair, extended because a concept is not restricted to a pair. A script consists of a set of slots, each slot containing one aspect of the description of the concept.

In Winograd's blocks world we might have each block defined or described by a set of slots—one describing number of sides, another color, another size. In a real world, we might describe a "restaurant" as having tables and chairs, waiters, food,

Box 5.4 A Total Language System for a Small World

The following are samples from an annotated dialogue conducted with a computer armed with knowledge about a blocks world. This machine was designed (like DOCTOR) to test a particular theory of language processing. Note its successes and limitations. Unlike DOCTOR, this program really processed language. The machine had access to information about blocks—stored in its memory—and information about which ones were currently displayed on its screen. It responded by moving the blocks on the screen or asking for more information. "OK" was always printed out when the action was performed. New information could be provided during the conversation—words defined, axioms given: These were then added to its memory. (H indicates the human, C, the computer.)

H. Pick up a big red block.

C. OK. (Before doing this it clears another block from the top, so the red one may be moved.)

H. Grasp the pyramid.

C. I don't understand which pyramid you mean. (There are three in the scene, and "the" implies a specific one, as the computer knows.)

H. Find a block which is taller than the one you are holding and put it in the box.

C. By "it," I assume you mean the block which is taller than the one I am holding. OK. (Note that it processes relative clauses, comparatives, and reference.)

H. Had you touched any pyramid before you put the green one on the little cube?

C. Yes, the green one. (Note—the machine keeps a record of its actions and interprets them with respect to time. Here it "understands" subordinate clauses.)

H. When did you pick it up?

C. While I was stacking up the red cube, a large red block and a large green cube.

H. Why?

C. To get rid of it. (Here the machine fills in what the "why" is referring to on the basis of the preceding dialogue.)

(after Winograd, 1972.)

menus, chefs, cooking utensils, eating utensils. If no particular one is specified, each slot may be filled by a particular attribute or *default* attribute. For example, a particular restaurant might have a particular value in each of the general slots just mentioned: 10 tables or 200 tables, woks and chopsticks or 10-piece silverware place settings; if nothing is specified a reasonable default in our culture for utensils would be knife, fork, and spoon.

In Winograd's world "scripts" included axioms about what is possible or likely in the world, like "things cannot rest on the point of a pyramid." In a real world axioms also need to be included: that food is ordered from a menu, delivered by a waiter, and paid for one way or another at the end of the meal. In Winograd's world we need this information to make appropriate linguistic responses; in the real world we need it for the same reason. Recall the restaurant story of Chapter 2, paraphrased from Schank; roughly, George, on his way to Mama Leone's, encounters a pickpocket and winds up washing dishes. It would be nice if a question-answering program provided with this story as data made reasonable inferences; for example, the wallet was stolen, that this was not discovered until after George had eaten, that George worked off his debt. (This could be necessary in translation too—the rules may not be the same from one culture to the next, and so what may be elliptical in the original must be made explicit in translation.) Scripts or frames are ways of organizing the descriptive defining knowledge, the descriptive characteristic knowledge, and the implicit "axioms" for each concept.

Scripts or frames may be useful for hypothesis-driven parsing, selecting among ambiguous readings, answering questions directly, or making indirect inferences. As mentioned in Chapter 2, a problem with them is that each must contain a wealth of information, and with very few frames we use up the memory capacity of existing computers. Thus, because of memory limitations, even general systems are usually limited to one data base at a time. Other difficulties with scripts include specifying when one should be activated and when one should be deactivated. The activation problem is akin to the keyword problem of having many words describing the same concept—it would be nice if the restaurant script was activated not only to "restaurant" but also to names of famous restaurants like Mama Leone's, and also when enough of its slots are activated, like waiter, menu, and so forth. The deactivation problem is essentially how to recognize that the topic has changed, and that this frame is no longer appropriate or necessary for reference. This is a problem of discourse, to be treated in the next section.

Propositions as Meaning.   At the beginning of this section we said there were two general constructs used in organization of meaning: primitives and propositions. Primitives, as single features, attribute-value pairs, or entries in a knowledge structure, have been described. Propositions—relations between concepts—arise as a construct because it has been observed that many concepts cannot stand alone but are dependent on other concepts. Prepositions, for example, relate one NP to the verb or to another NP, as do conjunctions, and, in fact, as do verbs. To capture the relationship we must have a primitive concept for each NP and for the *relation* between them—a concept for a relation looks like a simple sentence or proposition. Propositions as a unit of conceptual/semantic processing have been proposed by Anderson and Bower (1973) and Schank (1972)—the proposition or relational concept resembles a deep structure tree and is the outcome of the parsing and semantic programs. It has been generally agreed that to derive a proposition from the input, semantic relations like agent or location need to be stored with the dictionary entry for the proposition, and that parsing then proceeds by recognizing the main nouns and verb, with the possibilities for the verb guiding—top-down—the establishment of the rest of the sentence structure and meaning. Primitive concepts are instruments, descriptors, agents, and so on. The point of the parse is to determine which is the focus of the sentence. For example, the sentences

> I went to the park with a girl.
> I went to the park with a statue.
> I went to the park with a car.

have very different conceptual structures—"with a girl" describes "went," "with a statue" describes "park," and "with a car" tells how we got there. "With" is ambiguous: It may specify an agent, a description, an instrument. These possibilities will be part of the "instructions" stored with "with." Agents must be animate. Descriptions must be constant properties. "Car" satisfies the requirements of instrument in the primitives list, "girl" of agent, and "statue" of descriptor.

Discourse Processing. A number of systems, Schank's included, have been designed to analyze more than one sentence at a time. Schank's system relies on semantic-syntax analysis—a coding of sentences in terms of primitives, verbs and the relations they may take (propositions) with reference to specified scripts. However, in text processing we need more—we need rules for coherence, a way of relating primitive concepts. When coherence is disrupted we can infer a change of topic and use this to deactivate the script. Coherence may be roughly defined as overlap of ideas; more specific definitions follow.

Generally the search for coherence rules has begun through considering how it is that discourse is usually organized, and then setting the program to look for a similar organization. One proposal has been that most stories are sequences of causes (Schank, 1975), where, for example, an event causes a change in state. Coherence may be found by looking then for underlying causes and relating those propositions expressing results of similar causes.

A second proposal started with something like a speech-act analysis, an attempt to produce coherent discourse by considering propositional content in addition to the underlying motivation of the speaker. Tennant (1981), for example, pointed out that a question-answering system supplying flight information would be acting much more coherently if it responded with more than a simple "no" to a question about whether there was a flight from Buffalo to New York that night. The "more" should reflect the questioner's next question; a human in a similar situation is likely to give information about when the next flight is or alternative means of getting to New York, using the assumption that the questioner wants to fly there or leave for New York immediately, respectively. A program that can divine the motivation or illocutionary force behind an utterance is more nearly approximating the total language system that humans have.

In both of these schemes the idea is to find the thread that normally relates sentences. Stories or discourse may then be analyzed top-down in terms of rules based on the normal thread of discourse analysis.

Kintsch and van Dijk (1978) have implemented an elaborate program for automatically deriving the point of a story. Their method is to weed out and combine, methodically, propositions of the story until the main point is revealed. They analyze discourse in terms of two levels: a *microstructure,* which relates individual propositions, and a *macrostructure,* which characterizes the entire discourse. The microstructure is simply the propositions derived through syntactic analyses in ways already discussed in this chapter. The macrostructure is derived from the microstructure using three "transformations": *deletion,* whereby any proposition that is neither a direct nor indirect condition of a subsequent proposition is removed; *generalization,* whereby any sequence of propositions is replaced by a proposition representing a superset; and *construction,* whereby any sequence of propositions is replaced by a proposition representing a fact, as indicated by the stored "world knowledge." Analysis of a text then proceeds by restructuring, using these rules, so that the text is ultimately represented by a list of hierarchically related propositions, headed by the general topic-proposition and fanning out into more and more detailed related propositions. These together represent the gist of the story.

As an example, Kintsch and van Dijk (1978) provided the analysis of one paragraph taken from a report of an experiment that had been entirely analyzed by their program. The paragraph begins "A series of violent, bloody encounters between police and Black Panther Party members punctuated the early summer days of 1969." In the microanalysis this sentence contained seven "propositions," some of which are: (1) series, encounter; (2) violent, encounter; (3) bloody, encounter; (4) between encounter, police, Black Panther. (Note that in this view an adjective-noun is considered a proposition, as it was considered in early transformational grammar, where the adjective was presumed to be derived from the embedding of a sentence such as, "the encounter was bloody.") The function of this entire sentence in the paragraph was only to provide background information. The paragraph continued by explaining that this was followed by reports of police harassment of students on campus, which the writer investigated, and the article constitutes the results of his investigation.

The macrostructure analysis, then, has to determine from the rest of the paragraph or the rest of the report that the first sentence serves only a function of providing setting. Since, in fact, few remaining sentences will connect directly or indirectly with the bloody encounters described in the first sentence (they will instead be describing the method of the investigation and so forth), deletion transformations will rightly eliminate this from the main theme of the narrative and mark it as peripheral, a setting description.

By first performing a microanalysis and then cycling through the individual propositions thus isolated, using the restructuring transformations, the program basically results in an outline of the passage. This kind of analysis could be used to criticize discourse structure, since it would be able to find sentences that were largely irrelevant to the point.

Detailed grammars of discourse have not been written, and the existing sets of programming strategies, for the most part, cannot be given strong tests since they require a memory capable of holding many scripts at a time. Our knowledge of mechanical discourse processing is thus limited at present. As the examples show, there is no question that recovery of discourse structure is necessary for simulation of human language processing—we clearly can and do determine the underlying threads of a story, the presuppositions governing an utterance, the motivations of the speaker, and the overall picture of what the discourse is about. It is not clear how we do it, or whether the methods suggested so far for machines are effective either for machine "comprehension" or as analogies for human comprehension.

Summary

In this section, we examined computer approaches to natural-language processing. We first looked at keyword systems to demonstrate that to process language intelligently it is necessary to derive the structure of the sentence; using single words as triggers for particular responses leads to certain failure. We then looked at several strategies for implementing parsers. The first was "stupid" bottom-up parsers that are mechanical instantiations of rewrite rules and are surprisingly effective at deriving structure. However, these can be considered unsatisfactory because they derive structures humans would never derive. To make them "smarter," better mimics of human behavior, we considered interfacing them with semantic processors to rule out improbable parses. Alternatively, we considered providing them with guesses about the probable structure before detailed consideration of the input, top-down processing. And we showed how either top-down or bottom-up parsers could be made to behave more like humans by giving them heuristics, so that the most likely or most frequently occurring parse would be tried first. We pointed out that parsing could be done serially, one bit at a time, or in parallel, many parts at once; deterministically, so that there is no backtracking and each step leads to the next step and ultimately to a single parse; or nondeterministically, with backtracking, showing in some detail how a deterministic parser was implemented. Finally, we looked at schemes for machine comprehension of connected discourse—ways of storing meaning and world knowledge, or making references, and of recognizing and deriving structure in text.

Human Sentence Processing

In the last part of the chapter we examined artificial intelligence attempts at language processing. These have been, in places, very successful, utilizing a variety of techniques. That each method has been implemented means that any or all are plausible models of human processing. Their plausibility does not mean that these are how we process; indeed, in places they suggest contradictory strategies such as serial *and* parallel processing. In this part of the chapter we will examine some data on the psychological reality of some grammar models and parsing strategies.

Early Experiments in Syntax

Because our syntactic processing is not open to introspection, the first experiments in syntax were designed to show that syntax does in fact provide information in the information theoretic sense; that it reduces uncertainty about other words in the sentence. Stimuli were constructed by manipulating natural English sentences to approximate their structure in some way. In one experiment (Miller and Isard, 1963), for instance, under difficult listening conditions (stimuli presented together with noise), subjects were asked to identify normal sentences, semantically anomalous but syntactically possible sentences (like "colorless green ideas sleep furiously"), and scrambled sentences that had no recognizable structure but whose words could be recombined to produce a normal sentence (like "Flies arrow an time like"). What should be observed here is that in noisy presentation some of the sounds will not be heard, that information being transmitted in the sound is not received.

Under such conditions, you should recall, redundancy helps; if the information is contained also in a part that *is* received it can be used to compensate for what was missed. Normal sentences have several sources of redundancy: semantic (each meaning retrieved limits the range of words that might be used in the same sentence; Florence Nightingale primes "nurse" and related topics, suggesting they will be in the sentence) and syntactic (recognition of some words suggests a structure that in turn suggests, top-down, what other words might be there; "the" suggests that the next word will likely be a noun). Anomalous sentences have no redundancy provided by semantics but still have redundancy provided by syntax. Scrambled sentences, it might be argued, have semantic or meaning-associative redundancy but not syntactic. (This argument should be hard to accept after the preceding discussions of ambiguity and syntax: Words often have so many meanings that a single meaning may emerge clearly only from context, and context as well as syntax is altered by scrambling.)

Figure 5.1 shows the results with "grammatical" marking normal sentences and "ungrammatical" marking the scrambled sentences. As can be seen, identification of the sentences was much better with greater redundancy, either semantic or syntactic. Marks and Miller (1964) found similar results for the memorability of sentences, anomolous sentences, and scrambled sentences—the more redundancy, the easier to memorize.

The effects of scrambling, the importance of preserving order, and the general notions of transitional probabilities or Markov processes underlying human syntactic processes were tested in a series of experiments on English approximation (Miller and Selfridge, 1953). In these experiments strings of words were generated by combining subjects' responses to "fill in the blank" tasks.

The strings differed in how connected their words were likely to be, and this was achieved by giving subjects limited knowledge of the previous words in the string. In a *second-order approximation,* for example, a subject would know only the immediately preceding word and would have to supply a logical next choice. In a *third-order approximation* each subject would know the two words immediately preceding, and so on. To generate ten word strings, then, the responses of some successive number of subjects would be combined. First-order approximations were derived from strings formed from higher order combinations by randomly scrambling them. Note that for first order approximations there is no constraint between successive words, and that the number of words over which there are contextual constraints increases for successively higher approximations. Thus, a second-order approximation is a true Markov model, and comparison of different orders of approximation can indicate the extent to which constraints apply across words normally.

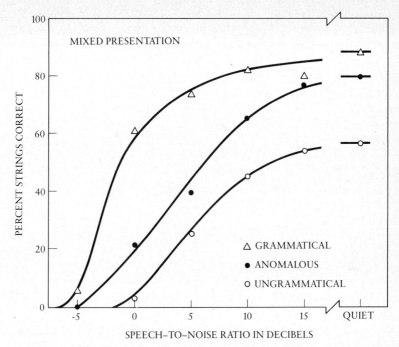

Figure 5.1 *The percentage of strings of words correctly perceived in noise, when the strings were either normal sentences, grammatically correct sentences but semantically anomalous, or ungrammatical.*
From "Some perceptual consequences of linguistic rules" by G. A. Miller and S. Isard (1963) in The Journal of Verbal Learning and Verbal Behavior, *2, p. 222. Copyright 1963 by Academic Press. Reprinted by permission.*

Results of approximating are shown in Table 5.1, and, as you can see, by about the fourth order, sentences seem almost normal. This suggests the following: First, there is information contained in order (at least in English—it is important to recall that there are many languages in which order has a much less important role than it has in English); second, that order carries information beyond the next word (unlike Markov or finite state models), causing generation after pairs or triples to result in very unnatural-looking utterances; and third, that there might be a natural boundary after four-word groups, with less predictability or binding between words four and five than between words three and four. (We might use this result to suggest a reasonable window size for Marcus' parser of four words—the fifth word and beyond seem to have little effect on perceived structure of the first four words in English.) The most important result, however, is the demonstration that we *cannot* be using a finite state model to generate sentences.

Fodor and Bever (1965; Bever, Lackner and Kirk, 1969) provided reasonable evidence that we might be using at least a phrase structure grammar to understand sentences. In their experiments they played tape-recorded complex sentences such as "That he was happy was evident from the way he smiled," to subjects with a click superimposed some place on the sentence. The sentences were manipulated to contain

Table 5.1 *Approximations to English (from Miller and Selfridge, 1950). The second order approximations are derived by giving a speaker one word and asking for a next word and stringing those pairs together, third order by giving two words and asking for the next word and stringing the triples, ... First order approximations are a random scramble of higher orders.*

10-Word "Sentences"

1st order: abilities with that beside I for you the sewing

2nd order: was he went to the newspaper deep and

3rd order: tall and thin boy is a biped is the beat

4th order: saw the football game will end at midnight on January

5th order: they saw the play Saturday and sat down beside him

20-Word "Sentences"

1st order: tea realizing most so the together home and for were wanted to concert I posted he her it the walked

2nd order: sun was nice dormitory is I like chocolate cake but I think that book is the wants to school there

3rd order: family was large dark animal came roaring down the middle of my friends love books passionately every kiss is time

4th order: went to the movies with a man I used to go toward Harvard Square in Cambridge is made fun for

5th order: road in the country was insane especially in dreary rooms where they have some books to buy for studying Greek

no pauses indicative of structure or click position. The measure of interest was where subjects reported hearing the click relative to where it actually had been. They hypothesized that clicks presented within a constituent would be reported as occurring either before or after it if constituents served as a perceptual unit, exploiting "the tendency of a perceptual unit to maintain its integrity by resisting interruptions" (Fodor and Bever, 1965, p. 415). (This hypothesis is interesting to consider with respect to the window concept in Marcus' parser, described earlier. It is an instance of not hearing something in the order spoken but in the order relevant for active processing.) The major constituent boundary in the sentences they used is the syntactic break between the main clause and the subordinate clause. They found, indeed, that clicks presented on either side of this boundary tended to be reported as occurring closer to it than they had in fact occurred. Some of the sentences were not simple conjunctions, as in the preceding, but embedded clauses, with major boundaries surrounding the embedded sentence (for example "the man [whom nobody likes] is leaving soon")—and in these, *both* boundaries attracted clicks. The later study (Bever *et al.*, 1969) showed that click attraction does *not* occur for constituent breaks within clauses, such as between subject and predicate, or verb and object.

These experiments have been used to support the reality of constituent structure in sentence perception. However, there are extensive problems in the experimental design (Reber and Anderson, 1970), perhaps the most serious being that subjects were required to write the sentences and mark the click; the click displacement thus could be affected by sentence memory, sentence production (they had to be reproduced on paper), as well as sentence perception, as was claimed. Reber and Anderson found that when subjects were not required to write the sentences there was still a small effect, but this seemed to be best attributed to response bias: Subjects told that they would hear subthreshold clicks, but actually presented with no click, tended to locate the nonexistent click at the major boundary and tended to locate clicks (existent or not) near the middle of random word strings. Nevertheless, the results suggest an awareness of major clause boundaries that affects either perception or organization of responses of sentences.

Summary.   Together these experiments indicate that syntactic structure is used in perceiving and recalling word strings. They show, moreover, that the constraints of one word on another span more than one word, ruling out finite state grammars as accounting for human processing. The appearance of the nth-order approximations suggests weakly that the span of constraints might be four to five words. Finally, the results indicate the psychological reality of some aspects of constituent structure for perception or response organization.

The Psychological Reality of Transformational Grammar

The experiments just discussed suggest the importance of order in understanding English, suggest something about the size of the unit in determining structure, and suggest that constituent structure plays a role in sentence processing. They do not specify the operations underlying parsing. Chomsky's work in linguistics greatly inspired psychologists, providing a new theoretical framework to guide experimentation. Two features of the model were tested: the reality of deep structure distinct from surface structure and the reality of transformations in relating one to the other.

The Reality of the Deep Structure-Surface Structure Distinction.   Mehler and Carey (1967) demonstrated the existence of processing operations for deriving constituent structure and deep structure. Sentences (1) through (6) at the beginning of this chapter illustrate their technique: A set of sentences with similar structures was presented in noise to subjects who were required to write each down; these were followed by a test sentence with either the same or a different structure also to be recorded and also presented in noise. The hypothesis was that if a perceptual set is established, the different test sentence would be perceived inaccurately since the listening conditions were difficult and the sentence broke the set. Sets were established for surface constituent structures, as in (1)–(6), or deep structures, as in

They are delightful to embrace.
They are troublesome to employ.

("they" is the underlying object of "embrace" or "employ") followed by

They are hesitant to travel.

(where "they" is the underlying subject of "travel"). When a test sentence had the same structure as the preceding set, it was perceived more accurately than when it differed from the preceding set; this was true for both surface and deep structure sets, but the decline in accuracy was greater when there was a surface structure difference. This suggests that both deep structure and surface structure representations must be derived in processing, since the change in either had an effect.

Deep Structure Realities Revealed by the Reality of Transformations. *Memory.* In testing the reality of transformations the critical assumption has been that if people reverse transformations to recover deep structure there should be an observable cost for greater transformational complexity, a cost revealed by decreased perceptibility, decreased residual memory capacity, higher error rate in understanding, or greater reaction time to understand. The experiments thus involve comparison— along one of these measures—of sentences differing in derivational complexity. Stimuli for the experiments generally consisted of core or kernel sentences (simple active sentences) that presumably were constructed from deep structure by using a minimum of transformations. These were contrasted with sentences derived by using one more transformation—active vs. passive, affirmative vs. negative, affirmative vs. interrogative; or two more transformations, active vs. negative passive, etc.

Initial results looked very promising, supporting the transformational model. Mehler (1963) showed that kernel sentences were more accurately recalled (memorized) than negatives, passives, or questions or double transformations like negative passives. Double transformations were remembered not much more poorly then single ones. Analysis of recall errors indicated that subjects tended to recall the simpler kernel form rather than what was presented. This suggests that subjects may be coding the sentence as a kernel plus markers like NEG or PASS, and that the markers may then be independently forgotten.

In a somewhat different recall experiment Savin and Perchonock (1965) also found that derivationally more complex sentences required a greater memory load, but here, using perhaps a more sensitive measure, they obtained evidence that double transformations were more taxing than single ones. They required subjects to recall sentences followed by a random string of words and assessed memory by measuring how many of the words in the random string were recalled correctly. (The hypothesis was that the more demanding the sentence, the fewer irrelevant words would be recalled.) With the highest possible score 8, subjects averaged 5.27 for kernel sentences, 4.73 for questions, 4.55 for passives, 4.44 for negatives, 4.30 for sentences with emphasis, 3.48 for negative passives, 4.02 for passive questions, and 3.74 for emphatic passives. In all cases statistical tests showed that recall was greater with kernel sentences than with single transformations and greater with single than with double.

Speed of Comprehension. The experiments described thus far have confounded comprehension with production: Subjects must process the sentence and then reproduce it, and it is not clear whether the penalty for extra transformations occurs in understanding or in reproducing the sentence or in both. In somewhat clearer experiments, an effect of transformations on understanding alone has been demonstrated by using speed of comprehension. In these, a variant of sentence verification, a sentence is presented together with a picture potentially depicting the sentence. Subjects must decide whether the sentence and the picture match and indicate the decision by pressing a button. RT is measured from the time the picture is presented to the time the button is pressed. For example, a picture could show a girl kicking a boy, which would be "true" for sentences like "the girl kicked the boy" or "the boy was kicked by the girl," and "false" for sentences like "the boy kicked the girl" or "the girl was kicked by the boy" or "the boy was not kicked by the girl." If subjects must recover deep structure to make the true-false decision, the transformationally more complex sentences should take longer. Indeed, for true sentences Gough (1965) found an increment of .09 seconds necessary to verify passives over actives, .28 seconds for negatives over affirmatives, and .43 seconds for negative passives over affirmative actives. (Falses showed the same general pattern of increments in RT for sentences requiring more transformations. The magnitude of the increment was smaller for negatives and negative passives, perhaps because the negative in the sentence partially primes "false.")

In a follow-up experiment Gough (1966) presented the picture three seconds after the sentence had been presented. Here it might be expected that if subjects untransform the sentences upon presentation and store the base structure together with transformation markers, as the recall experiments suggested, the complexity effect would disappear; by the time the picture is presented and RT measured, the processing would be complete and all sentences would be base sentences. In fact, Gough replicated his previous results, suggesting either that subjects in a verification task maintain a surface representation in memory until the picture is presented or that base structures have different complexities. Note that the latter could be consistent with Chomsky's (1965) model if we assume that markers like NEG and PASS increase the complexity of the base phrase marker. (The results are also explained by trace theory, if comprehension utilizes the abstract surface structure, which is also more complex in negative or passive sentences than in kernels.)

Derivational complexity has also been shown to affect RT in tasks where subjects are asked to convert kernel sentences to a particular transformed model (Miller and McKean, 1964), roughly what we did in the transformational exercises in Chapter 4, but without specific training on which steps to make. It seems subjects take longer to create transformationally more complex sentences, suggesting they mentally perform the transformations.

Summary and Critique.   The results discussed thus far support the general transformational model: Deep structure has a psychological reality apart from surface structure, and sentences of greater transformational complexity are harder to understand than those of lesser. However, as research progressed, problems arose in the interpretation of the data. The first, and least serious, was a possible confounding of transformational complexity with sentence length: Passives and negatives have more words than either alone. Length was ruled out as a factor, though, because questions and emphatics (e.g., sentences ending with an exclamation mark) have the same length as kernels but still take longer (Savin and Perchonock, 1965), and sentences derived by using deletion transformations such as agent deletion in the passive or relative pronoun deletion—which are shorter than the nondeleted forms—are no faster to comprehend or paraphrase than the longer forms (Gough, 1966; Fodor and

Garrett, 1967). The second, and more serious, difficulty was an increasing awareness of the importance of the form of the surface structure in guiding comprehension, an awareness that eventually resulted in (or supported) trace theory/lexicalist models of language. (This evidence will be discussed in the next section.) The third difficulty lay in a number of demonstrations that syntactic form—at either surface, abstract surface, or deep structure levels—was of secondary importance to meaning. This will be treated in the section on semantics and sentence processing.

Heuristics and Sentence Processing

The studies just cited show processing differences for sentences with different structures. They were designed, and their results interpreted, with respect to a transformational model, assuming that making or undoing transformations takes both time and processing capacity. However, they do not necessarily imply that transformations are used in understanding sentences; they may just reflect strategies or heuristics favoring understanding of one type of sentence over another.

Recall, for example, the discussion of ATNs and of heuristics in the section on parsers. If parses always are attempted assuming an active sentence, and passive only when that fails, then active sentences will be comprehended faster than passives because they are attempted first. The more alternatives that have to be tried before the correct parse is attempted, the longer it will take to derive that structure for the sentence. Note that in this framework (see Kaplan, 1972; Wanner and Maratsos, 1978, for a detailed explication of the ATN approach to psychological processing) the extra time is not used in undoing the passive to get the active form but comes from trying the passive later, from the particular heuristics employed. Processing may also be impeded by ambiguity in structure—since it may be necessary to try more alternatives before selecting the right one. Finally, memory as well as comprehension time should be affected by these considerations: The longer it takes to decide on the structure of the sentence or a part of it, the longer the incomplete structures must be retained, and the greater the chance of forgetting.

Using Surface Constraints.   Several studies have been designed using this kind of theoretical framework, and they show effects of heuristics independent of transformational complexity. Martin and Roberts (1966) used an information theoretic type measure of surface structure complexity derived from Yngve (1960), in which it is determined which expectations each word generates for additional structure—and then these expectations are summed. For example, at the beginning of a sentence "the" sets up two expectations: one for a noun (relatively soon) and one for a predicate (at some point). A following adjective also has an expectation value of two, since both the noun and the predicate are still expected. A noun reduces the hypothesized structures to one, an intransitive verb to zero, a transitive verb to one again (for the object). Summing these expectancies across the words of the sentence gives a measure of the processing *commitments* the subject makes; the more commitments, the longer it takes to process and the poorer recall, as Martin and Roberts found. Moreover, when the surface structure complexity was held constant over transformational types, kernel sentences were more poorly recalled than either negatives or passives. No explanation was provided for this paradoxical finding, but the study in general suggests that we use surface structure information rather than transformations to derive a memory representation of a sentence.

Using Surface Syntactic Cues. Fodor and Garrett (1967) tested the effectiveness of particular surface structure cues for sentence processing. For example, a relative pronoun indicates the structure of the words following it—they will form a relative clause. Deletion of the relative pronoun adds transformational complexity, but also— and more important, they argued—removes that cue. In the sentence

The rat the cat wounded ate the cheese.

we do not know whether "the cat" is the second in a conjoined NP list (as in the rat, the cat, and the mouse) or the beginning of an embedded sentence. This means that we may entertain both hypotheses at the expense of memory, test the incorrect one first at the expense of time, or test both at the expense of processing capacity. In

The rat that the cat wounded ate the cheese.

we do not have a similar difficulty.

For their experiment, Fodor and Garrett employed sentences with two embeddings (e.g., "the pen which the author whom the editor liked used was new.") since previous research had indicated that these were considerably more difficult than one embedding. (They explain this by noting that in a single embedding choice of one NP as subject [the cat] of verb 1 determines that the other noun is object, whereas in double embeddings choosing a noun as subject [the editor] still leaves two nouns as possible objects.) In their experiment two lists of sentences were used, one in which the pronouns "which," "that," or "whom" were retained and one in which they were deleted. Subjects were asked to paraphrase the sentences. Complexity was measured by the length of time to begin the paraphrase and the number of errors in assigning subjects and objects to verbs.

For both measures sentences with relative pronouns were easier to understand, consistent with both this theory emphasizing surface structure cues and transformational theory. However, in the next experiment they showed that transformationally more complex sentences *with* surface structure cues are no more difficult than transformationally simpler sentences and thus that transformational complexity is irrelevant to sentence processing. In this case, transformational complexity was increased by preceding the nouns in the sentence with adjectives, which early transformational theory (as you may recall) derived from relative clauses. Despite this added complexity, sentences with relative pronouns deleted and adjectives before the nouns were marginally *easier* than sentences without adjectives, from which Fodor and Garrett concluded that it is not the additional transformations that hurt processing. They also pointed out that previous studies showed that passives with agent deletion were harder than actives but were no harder than the full-agent passives they presumably were derived from. Contrary to the prediction of transformational theory, the absence of the agent does not increase the psychological load.

An auxiliary finding of this study, followed up by Fodor, Garrett, and Bever (1968) was that embedded sentences containing verbs that suggest ambiguous structures are more difficult than sentences in which the verb suggests only one possible structure. Transitive verbs may be of several types: those, like "give," that require an object, those, like "say," that require an embedded clause (e.g., "John said that he . . ."), and those, like "believe," that could take either, (e.g., "John believed Mary" or "John believed that Mary would . . ."). If complexity of processing is increased by producing hypothetical structures that are not used, then verbs that clearly predict one structure should render a sentence easier than verbs that generate expectations for two. Indeed, Fodor et al. found that multiply embedded sentences with verbs of the last type were harder to paraphrase than those with verbs of the other types. From this they concluded that verbs guide parsing, a conclusion we have encountered before from other considerations. (Their data do not demonstrate a special role for the verb in particular. It is possible that any word that generates ambiguous commitments increases processing complexity.) It is important to note that this result suggests that we do generate structures that we may not use; that is, that we do not parse deterministically. However, it shows that parsing involves both bottom-up and top-down processes. The words, or "bottom," suggest strategies that affect, top-down, how we parse the remaining words.

Holding Unfinished Structures.   The analysis of the cause of difficulty in multiply embedded sentences rested on the number of possible assignments of nouns to subjects and objects. The more that were possible, the more ambiguous and the harder the sentence—the same argument we just presented for ambiguous verbs. There is an alternative explanation for difficulty of embedding, resting on the retention of incomplete structures. Recall from Chapter 4 that some multiple embeddings are easy; contrast "this is the cat that chased the rat that bit the mouse that lived in the house that Jack built" with the type of multiply embedded sentences used in the study by Fodor and Garrett (1967). In the easy ones, each embedded sentence is finished before the next one starts. (There is also no confusion about where subject and object nouns are.) Once a structure is finished its constituents may be treated as a group, reducing the memory load (see the discussion of deterministic parsing earlier in this chapter).

Looking at this from the ATN framework, we may consider that sentences are easier when they cause fewer interruptions from the main guiding ATN and fewer places that must be held in higher networks. If it is the additional memory load or interruptions that increase processing difficulty, we should be able to get difficulty increases similarly but without using multiple embeddings.

Indeed, Wanner and Maratsos (1978) demonstrated a memory impairment produced by holding a word for some time before assigning structure. They presented sentences, one word at a time, on a computer screen, interrupting the presentation at some point with a list of five proper names (like John or George), after which sentence presentation continued. At the end of the sentence the subject was asked comprehension questions and also to recall the proper names. Complexity of processing was suggested by the number of names recalled; as usual, the fewer the irrelevant words recalled, the more complex processing was assumed to be. Embedded sentences of the form

The witch whom sorcerers despised frightened little children.

were contrasted with ones of the form

The witch who despised sorcerers frightened little children.

Note that both sentences contain the relative pronoun cue, and moreover that the "whom" form provides a clue that it is the object. The difference between the two is that in the first, "whom" may not be assigned its role in the phrase marker until after "despised" and must be held until that word (there is a trace of whom after "despised" if you will). In the second, "who" may be immediately placed in embedded sentence subject position (it has not moved far from its trace). This, not surprisingly, reduces subjects' difficulties in recalling extraneous words.

Summary and Critique. It is important to note that both the surface structure strategy and ATN approach outlined here are consistent with the experimental evidence, as are aspects of the transformational approach, but no approach is proven by the data. The experiments reveal *what* is difficult to understand—they do not reveal *why* the sentences are difficult. Any evidence that runs counter to the transformational model does not necessarily disconfirm the general approach but just the particular transformation tested. For example, Fodor and Garrett found that adjectives do not increase the difficulty of sentence understanding. This may be because the transformational model is incorrect and we do not recover deep structure at all, or because the general transformational model is correct but adjectives exist as adjectives in deep structure and do not derive from underlying relative clauses. Similarly, additional processing time or errors may be interpreted equally easily by invoking the loss of surface structure cues, jumps to a new transition network, temporarily unresolved structures, added transformations, and so on; the models cannot be differentiated on this point.

Although not supporting one particular model, the evidence we have examined indicates specific effects of structure on processing. There seems to be reasonable support for the following assertions. We do use structure of the sentence to derive an underlying structure (perhaps deep structure, perhaps abstract surface structure). We derive this structure by using the surface structure of the input sentence together with educated guesses about underlying structure, and the less constrained our guesses, the greater the processing load. The structure suggested by the verb may have particular importance in constraining guesses. In the absence of other constraints we assume simple active sentences. The more unnecessary or incorrect assumptions made and carried, the greater the processing load.

A Potential Explanation. Careful consideration of these assertions leads to a very interesting hypothesis about the nature of language processing and the nature of language: *Because we wish to communicate, our language structure will reflect the assumptions we think our listeners are likely to make in parsing; in places we expect* *confusion we should provide surface structure markers pointing to the appropriate strategy if the assumed default strategy would be wrong.*

Following this hypothesis Bever (1970) generated a list of default strategies that appear responsible for some of the rules of English and some of the evidence on human syntactic processing:

1. Listeners assume input to be meaningful sentences.
2. They segment word sequences into actor-action-object-modifier (proposition) units. This keeps elements of subordinate clauses together and those of main clauses together, accounts for the perceptual migration of clicks to unit boundaries, and explains the difficulty of center embeddings where the unit is interrupted by another clause. It also may be responsible for some of the structural rules of the language; for example, deletion of the relative pronoun in English is possible *only* when it marks the object of the relative clause (as in "the man (who) I saw gave the dessert ...") but not when it marks the subject (as in "the man (who) gave the dessert I saw"). If it were deleted in the second case, listeners following the actor-action-object strategy would group the first noun with the nearest and, in this case, wrong verb. This grouping strategy leads to misinterpretation of "the horse raced past the barn fell" (which, if structure follows processing constraints, should some day obligatorily contain the relative pronoun—to avoid the garden path). And, it accounts for the greater difficulty of passives over actives since the former violate the actor-action-object order.
3. Listeners assume the first actor-action-object unit to be the main clause. This accounts for the greater difficulty of processing preposed subordinate clauses (e.g. "Because the food was gone, the dog bit the cat.") over postposed subordinate clauses (e.g. "The dog bit the cat because the food was gone.") (Clark and Clark, 1968). (This may be accounted for in terms of processing commitments too—beginning with "because" means we carry an expectation of a main clause from the beginning of the sentence; with it second, the expectation or unfinished structure is carried for a smaller amount of time.)

One other strategy has been proposed by C. Chomsky (1969), in which it is assumed that the subject of an embedded sentence is the noun closest to it, such that "John wanted Bill to leave" is understood with Bill as the subject of to leave, as is "John promised Bill to leave." Since, for the latter, the assumption is wrong, there is predicted a greater difficulty in processing. This strategy is known as *the minimal distance principle.*

Thus, one way to look at normal syntactic processing is as the execution of prior notions about the structure of the incoming sentences rather than a detailed syntactic analysis. Since speakers and listeners share the strategies, frequently speakers will provide cues in their utterances to signal listeners on when the strategy is inappropriate. Failure to do so produces comprehension errors or extra processing, and a language may slowly evolve obligatory rules, such as "do not delete relative pronouns in certain conditions," to prevent misunderstanding.

Semantic Influences on Parsing

Selectional Restrictions as Cues.   We have just considered the possibility that to "parse," to determine the basic relations between elements of a sentence, people may rely on general strategies for guessing structure, rather than performing a detailed syntactic analysis. The appropriate strategies, in turn, may be signaled by a particular structural feature of the sentence.

It has been demonstrated that the most effective cues to underlying relationships in a sentence are semantic or pragmatic—what are considered to be *likely* relations among the sentence elements. For example, Slobin (1966) demonstrated that passives are no harder to understand (i.e., no slower to verify) than actives if they are semantically clear. Compare the following sentences:

9.   The girl was kicked by the boy.
9a.   The boy was kicked by the girl.
10.   The plant was watered by the boy.
10a.   The boy was watered by the plant.

(9) is *reversible*—switching the grammatical subject and object results in a sensible sentence. (10) is irreversible—plants do not water boys. For (10) we have good semantic reasons to assign words in the sentence to agent and object cases regardless of their position in the sentence. For (9) the only way to sort out who is doing what to whom is by relying on syntax—and it appears that we get an effect of syntactic complexity *only where we must rely on syntax alone*. This suggests that we may not normally parse in sentence understanding but instead rely on probable meaning relations, parsing only when these are insufficiently specified.

Initial Organizations as Cues.   It has been demonstrated that even reversible passives may not be difficult, depending on the organization of the sentence elements in memory. Olson and Filby (1972) presented "ambiguous" pictures to subjects before verification—pictures, for example, of a car and truck colliding. Subjects were prompted to code the pictures in terms of the car or truck by being asked questions about one or the other vehicle. This, it was hoped, would induce subjects to form a memory representation with the one questioned as agent or topic. Subjects were then presented with the usual array of actives, passives, trues, and falses and—as is normally found—they took longer to verify falses than trues, and passives than actives. However, the interesting finding was that subjects who coded the picture in terms of the car took *longer* to verify actives like "the truck hit the car" than passives like "the car was hit by the truck," where the passive more closely matched in topic and focus what they had encoded. Olson and Filby concluded that both sentences and pictures are coded in memory in a core form established by meaning, and that any input is transformed to match the core; that is, transformations are not strictly specified syntactic processing operations, but whatever operations are necessary to convert the current form to the form stored in memory.

Nonarbitrariness as Cue.   Clark and Clark (1968) examined recall of conjoined sentences where the sentence components reflected semantic order as in "after he mowed the lawn, he raked"—or confused semantic order as in "before he raked, he mowed the lawn." The two sentences mean the same thing, but in the first one the main clause occurs after the subordinate and describes an event that occurs before it. Subjects better remembered sentences with the main clause first (he raked the lawn after he mowed it), leading to Bever's third strategy, already mentioned. But the most overwhelming effect was semantic: Sentences that reflected the temporal order of events were remembered much better than those that reversed it, regardless of the main clause–subordinate clause order. Notice that this indicates that when language is nonarbitrary, when it reflects reality on more than one level, the redundancy can aid processing.

The Mental Representation of Meaning Relations

The function of syntax is to relate sentence elements to one another, and in making the relation, usually a new meaning is expressed—that the girl is being kicked, for example—that is not expressed in the individual words. For some sentences, there is no question that we must perform syntactic processing, at least when guessing probable meaning relations would fail, as in understanding "the boy was watered by the plant." We have just considered various ways that such syntactic analyses might take place, and also considered whether in sentence understanding syntactic analysis is always performed, or whether it is performed only when all else fails. There are two questions that we have left to consider: What is the fate of the syntactic analysis after it is performed (is it remembered or important for accessing the new meaning relations derived?) and how are the semantic relations accessed once they are derived? With respect to the latter question, recall that we held off discussing sentence meaning in Chapter 3 because deriving it required syntax. We may now return to the question of meaning processing but with respect to the new meaning created by word combination.

The Fate of Syntactic Processing.   An early study attempting to demonstrate the psychological reality of deep structure was among the first to show the importance of meaning over syntax in the ultimate representation. Sachs (1967) presented passages to subjects for comprehension and then later tested their ability to recognize whether a sentence had been in the passage. The critical sentence was either at the end (0 syllables and 0 seconds before testing), in the middle (160 syllables and 46 seconds before testing), or between them (80 syllables and 27 seconds before testing). The recognition sentence was either identical to the sentence in the passage, changed in meaning, changed from passive to active or conversely (a deep structure change in the 1965 version of transformational grammar), or a surface-form change. If the sentence was "He sent Galileo, the great Italian scientist, a letter about it" a meaning change would have Galileo sending the letter, a deep structure change would have Galileo being sent the letter (passive), and a surface structure change would simply move the modifying clause, as in "He sent a letter about it to Galileo, the great Italian scientist" (p. 439). Subjects were to indicate whether the sentence was the same as one that they had read, or if it was different, whether it differed in meaning, deep form, or surface form. When recognition was immediate with no interposed material, subjects were highly accurate for all changes. With 80 syllables interposed, subjects were accurate only with meaning changes, with the syntactic changes noticed only at almost chance levels. The results suggest that form is used only to construct a meaning representation and then discarded; meaning is the stuff memory is made of.

The great importance of abstract meaning over form in sentence memory was further demonstrated by Bransford and colleagues (and Franks, 1971; and Barclay and Franks, 1972; Franks and Bransford, 1972) in variations of Sachs' (1967) experiment. In their studies they tested recognition accuracy for sentences conveying the same message but in syntactically different ways. For example, during the learning phase, subjects might be presented with simple sentences like "the rock rolled down the mountain," "the rock crushed the hut," "the hut was at the base of the mountain." In recognition, subjects could be presented with these sentences again or a sentence combining the propositions like "the rock rolled down the mountain crushing the hut at the bottom," or simple sentences of the same structure as in acquisition but with different meaning.

Bransford and colleagues found that subjects were likely to think they had been presented with sentences consistent with the sense of what had been presented, like the preceding complex sentence, regardless of the difference in form. This was true for abstract, nonimageable sentences as well (Franks and Bransford, 1972), suggesting that subjects store a verbal representation of the sentence, perhaps akin to propositions with case markings.

Not only do subjects fail to retain a record of transformations of simple or complex sentences (assuming that they do perform the transformations), but they also forget topic and focus in simple sentences: "The box is to the left of the tree" is more likely to be recognized as "the tree is to the right of the box" than "the box is to the right of the tree," which overlaps more in surface structure (Bransford, Barclay, and Franks, 1972). Such results as a whole show that what is important in memory is the basic semantic relations, not the process of deriving them from the sentence. It is important to recognize that the results do not speak to the process by which the relations are derived from the surface form of the sentence, which may be a transformational process, but only say that the record of the process is not durable.

It should be evident from the findings of the last few studies that the nature of the memory representation of a sentence is central to the processing operations involved in understanding one. As we saw in our discussion of meaning, two general memory representations have been proposed—imagery and propositional/verbal. The distinctions between them need not concern us here because the same information (actor, action, object) must be coded in both, whatever the form. It is interesting to note, however, that sentences rated high in imagery are easier to verify and recall than those rated low in imagery (Paivio and Begg, 1981), suggesting that imaging may be a strategy that subjects employ in sentence processing. What the imagery and propositional models have in common is the creation of a concept frame with elements specifying agent, location, time, etc. filling the slots.

The Structure of the Representation: The Proposition. The questions are: What elements are linked to the concept and how centrally are they linked? Anderson and Bower (1973) described a set of experiments directed toward these questions. Their technique was *cued recall:* Subjects were given sentences to learn and then asked to recall them, with the sentence-to-be-recalled indicated by one of the words in it. If the word was a good cue, central to the sentence concept, the sentence should be recalled when it is given as a prompt; if it is tangential to the representation of the sentence it should not be effective in causing other parts of the sentence to be remembered. If recall was not complete after one word was given, a second was presented, and then another if necessary. Comparison of the effectiveness of the words as prompts allows estimation of the degree of association among elements of the sentence.

The sentences they used all expressed a verb with four semantic relations—location, time, object, and agent; that is, they were describable as five-element propositions. Cued recall established the links between these elements. The verb and object cued each other better than either cued agent or location, or agent and location cued each other. This argues for a psychological break or weak link between subject and predicate. With embedded sentences (which contain more than one proposition) cued recall across the proposition boundary was poorer than within the main clause or subordinate clause. This indicates that embedded sentences are parsed into separate simple propositional formats, still linked but with a weaker link. This conclusion is supported also by an experiment by Kintsch and Keenan (1974), who showed that the time it took to read a sentence was determined by the number of propositions the sentence contained, regardless of the number of words. Thus, understanding a sentence seems to require analysis into proposition components, and then these components are kept in memory.

Using recognition tests, like those of Bransford et al., Anderson and Bower (1973) found confusion of proper names and definite descriptions (e.g. "Nixon" with "the President who resigned"), and sentences with different syntactic representations of a semantic relation (e.g. "the car's exhaust will pollute the air," "The car will pollute the air with its exhaust") with each other. The conclusion is that the long-term form of a sentence in memory is a proposition, with reduced surface structure information, but complete with semantic relations. Propositions on the same theme—embedded clauses or sentences with same subject—are connected but with a weaker link than items in the same proposition.

It should be noted that we are, as we were in Chapter 3, once again discussing the long-term memory representation of knowledge. In this case it is specifically knowledge conveyed by sentences or text, explicitly taught to the subject in the experiment. Anderson (and Bower, 1973; 1976, 1983) assumed that this is the way all knowledge is acquired, not just the information provided to subjects in experiments. We learned "a canary is yellow," as we might learn "the hippie touched the debutante" (a sentence provided in one of Anderson's experiments). In this case, what is linked in semantic memory is not simply word-meanings, but rather propositions or predicates connected to a subject (formally, the models are difficult to distinguish). These are retrieved, as before, through spreading activation, but in proposition-sized chunks. The more propositions an individual is required to learn about a particular subject, the longer it takes to retrieve any particular one, as Anderson has demonstrated. (This is called the *fan effect:* Spreading activation fans out from a node, and the larger the fan, the longer retrieval takes. Note the similarity to the category size effect discussed in Chapter 3.)

The assumption that memory contains propositions as units is roughly equivalent to assuming that we think in deep structures. The role of syntax processing then is to derive these propositional units from sentences in comprehension or to put them into a sentence form in production.

Meaning Representation in "Discourse."   Anderson's and Bower's results demonstrated that sentences on the same theme, when grammatically connected through embedding, wind up linked together in memory, each proposition with its own entry point, but the two propositions connected so one can activate the other. Anderson and Bower demonstrated a reality for the proposition as a unit by showing that the time it takes to retrieve a proposition on a topic is proportional to the number of propositions learned about the topic, suggesting that in retrieval each proposition is successively scanned.

There have been several studies indicating that there may be memory units representing proposition *combinations*. Whitlow, Smith, and Medin (1982), for example, found that the fan effect occurs only when there is little relation among the propositions being learned; when the propositions express related ideas, the effect disappears, suggesting that the predicates are being coalesced into a single memory unit. In this experiment, the sentences were presented individually with mixture of sentences on different themes, so that the coalescing had to take place across "incoherent" discourse conditions.

Under natural language conditions, in discourse, propositions are usually related also, and studies of discourse processing directly indicate the creation of a memory unit across sentences. McKoon and Ratcliff (1980; Ratcliff and McKoon, 1978) presented sentences of a text and then tested recognition of single words from those sentences. The key is that before testing recognition, subjects were primed either with a word from the same sentence as the word-to-be-recognized, or with a word from another sentence in the passage, or with a word that could be inferred from the passage but not directly used. If the prime is effective in speeding recognition, it is assumed that there is a close link between the two words in the memory representation of the passage; the less effective, the weaker the link.

As you might expect from the discussion of Anderson's and Bower's results, there is a greater priming effect among words from the same sentence than from different sentences of the same passage, and a greater effect of priming among words in the same proposition within a sentence than among words of different propositions expressed in one sentence (Ratcliff and McKoon, 1978). This supports the hypothesis that sentences are encoded into propositional format. More interesting, though, is the existence of a strong priming effect between words in one proposition and words in an earlier proposition referred to by the later one (McKoon and Ratcliff, 1980). For example, if in the first sentence of a paragraph mention of a car is made, and in a later sentence mention is made of a vehicle, which presumably refers anaphorically to the car, the representation for the car sentence is primed by words from the vehicle sentence, suggesting that the common subject has been derived and used to forge a connection in memory between the two.

The most effective way of connecting propositions in memory is to organize them around a theme. For example, Bransford and Johnson (1972) asked subjects to read and later recall apparently loosely organized stories like the following (try it yourself):

> If the balloons popped, the sound wouldn't be able to carry since everything would be too far away from the correct floor. A closed window would also prevent the sound from carrying, since most buildings tend to be well insulated. Since the whole operation depends on a steady flow of electricity, a break in the middle of the wire would also cause problems. Of course, the fellow could shout, but the human voice is not loud enough to carry that far. An additional problem is that a string could break on the instrument. Then there could be no clear accompaniment to the message. It is clear that the best situation would involve less distance. Then there would be fewer potential problems. With face to face contact, the least number of things could go wrong.
>
> *(Bransford and Johnson, 1972, p. 719)*

(Try to write as much of the passage as you can recall—score correct, propositions that you mention even if you do not have them word-for-word.) This is a control condition and was compared with conditions in which subjects were also given, before or after presentation of the passage, a picture that provided a context (either full or partial) for the passage. For example, for the preceding passage, the picture showed a woman on a high floor of an apartment building being serenaded by a man on the ground who was projecting his voice and guitar via a microphone and speaker, the speaker attached to a cluster of balloons floating by the woman's window. Given such a context, do you think you would recall more propositions than with no context, as was presented to you? Bransford and Johnson found that more was recalled provided the context was presented *before* the passage (either in verbal form or by a drawing) and when it provided a total context. There was no facilitation for presentation of context after the passage. They concluded that topic presented during comprehension affects the way material is processed and organized; once in memory it is not rearranged.

Cirilo and Foss (1980) demonstrated that both reading time and recall of read material is affected by the organization of the material. In their study they measured reading time by giving subjects one sentence at a time and asking them to push a button to get the next sentence. The time between button presses measured reading time, and to insure that subjects were, in fact, reading, they were also given a comprehension test. Material was organized to compare reading time (or recall) for topic versus peripheral sentences, presented either early in the text or late. Stories were constructed so that the same sentence could appear in four different roles in different stories: early topic, early peripheral, late topic, late peripheral. Time to read topic sentences was longer and recall was better than for peripheral sentences, and early sentences took longer to read than late sentences.

The results suggest that subjects may be actively constructing a story structure, and peripheral sentences and late sentences take less time to fit into the structure. The structure could take the form described by Kintsch and van Dijk (1978) at the end of the section on computer processing of syntax: a macrostructure that characterizes the entire discourse on the topic, and a microstructure relating individual propositions.

(Note that these studies motivate the instruction to organize paragraphs by giving topic first and then filling in lower level details. Comprehension, reading speed, and recall will all benefit. Note also that we have previously encountered the idea of speeding processing when structures are already available, with the number of words separated by a constituent–available-for-view in Marcus' [1980] parser.)

Summary. In this section we have looked at the derivation and storage of meaning relations in the sentence and across sentences. It is clear that syntactic processing is not finished at the sentence level; we still try to find syntactic relations among sentences, and in so doing, derive additional structure and new relations, the evidence for which are new meaning connections, new units, or even the inference of a topic sentence. For syntactic processing at any level there appears to be a measurable cost in cognitive processing for "loose" structure: The easier it is to derive the underlying relations—because they are semantically plausible, hinted at directly through surface structure cues, directly specified in a topic sentence, etc.—the more that can be remembered, the quicker additional information may be acquired, and the quicker comprehension is generally.

The "unit" of memory, which concepts are accessed as a whole, has no fixed size. As we saw in Chapter 3, depending on the task or learning condition, the memory unit may be about the size of a word. In this chapter we have seen that sometimes the memory unit may consist of semantic relations between words as expressed in a proposition or deep-structure–like unit, and sometimes it even might be a higher order unit expressing the synthesis of information across propositions, a new relation from coherent discourse. In any event, what seems to be best retained are the meaning relations, not the process of discovering them—the specific syntactic analysis.

Summary and Conclusions

This chapter has reviewed results from the artificial intelligence and cognitive psychology literatures on the nature of sentence processing. As we stated at the beginning, there is substantial accord on mechanisms of processing. There is no question that syntax is used in deriving a meaning representation for a sentence, and that the meaning representations have a syntax themselves. The ultimate representation of a sentence, stored for the longest time, seems akin to the early view of deep structure, actor-action-object-location-time-etc.; this is the "proposition" we keep encountering. The deep structure proposition representation, however, is not the level at which meaning is assigned, as suggested by early transformational theory, but what exists after meaning assignment. This is necessary because we seem to need meaning of individual words and constituents to derive the deep structure representation.

In this respect, transformational theory was incorrect; it was too rigid. To derive deep structure from surface structure we seem to use many different strategies— default top-down strategies such as the input will be a sentence and the first noun will be the subject; bottom-up strategies in which the words of the input trigger a particular syntactic form, as when "ask" takes a different structure than "tell"; bottom-up syntactic strategies, as when "that" introduces a relative clause; and meaning-based strategies, for example plants do not water boys. The syntactic-based strategies seem to work on surface structure to derive a slightly more abstract representation, consistent with current trace theory formulations. The abstract surface structure is derived during processing but is not retained for very long. Any information (general topic, semantic, or syntactic)—if presented early—seems to limit the direction of parsing, making it more deterministic. We do hold items in a sentence until their function in the parse or their meaning is clear, and then they are fit in, so parsing is not strictly left-to-right. The amount of input we can handle at any one time varies, depending on the structure already determined. We occasionally backtrack and derive alternate readings, but these seem to be derived serially. And finally, we do derive structures at levels beyond the sentence, but the methods for discourse processing are only beginning to be explored.

The last chapters have been concerned with the processing of meaning and syntax regardless of the form of the input—typed or spoken. In the next chapters we will discuss the structure and processing of the sounds of the language—how we perceive the auditory representation of the language. We will see that like words in a sentence, sounds have rules of organization, rules that help us determine what the word or clause is. As with sentence structure, sound structure is amazingly and fascinatingly complex.

REFERENCES

Anderson, J. R. (1976). *Language, Memory, and Thought*. Hillsdale, NJ: Lawrence Erlbaum Associates.

———. (1983). A spreading activation theory of memory. *Journal of Verbal Learning and Verbal Behavior, 22,* 261–295.

Anderson, J. R., & Bower, G. H. (1973). *Human Associative Memory*. NY: John Wiley and Sons.

Bever, T. G. (1970). The cognitive basis for linguistic structures. In J. Hayes (Ed.). *Cognition and the Development of Language*. (pp. 279–361). NY: John Wiley and Sons.

Bever, T. G., Lackner, J. R., & Kirk, R. (1969). The underlying structures of sentences are the primary units of immediate speech processing. *Perception & Psychophysics, 5,* 225–234.

Bransford, J. D., Barclay, J. R., & Franks, J. J. (1972). Sentence memory: A constructive versus interpretive approach. *Cognitive Psychology, 3,* 193–209.

Bransford, J. D., & Franks, J. J. (1971). The abstraction of linguistic ideas. *Cognitive Psychology, 2,* 331–350.

Bransford, J. D., & Johnson, M. K. (1972). Contextual prerequisites for understanding: Some investigations of comprehension and recall. *Cognitive Psychology, 3,* 717–726.

Cerf, V. (1973). Parry encounters the doctor. *Datamation, 19,* 62–64.

Chomsky, C. (1969). *The Acquisition of Syntax in Children from 5 to 10*. Cambridge, MA: MIT Press.

Chomsky, N. (1965). *Aspects of a Theory of Syntax*. Cambridge, MA: MIT Press.

Cirilo, R. K., & Foss, D. J. (1980). Text structure and reading times for sentences. *Journal of Verbal Learning and Verbal Behavior, 19,* 96–109.

Clark, H. H., & Clark, E. V. (1968). Semantic distinctions and memory for sentences. *Quarterly Journal of Experimental Psychology, 70,* 129–138.

Fodor, J. A., & Bever, T. G. (1965). The psychological reality of linguistic segments. *Journal of Verbal Learning and Verbal Behavior. 4,* 410–420.

Fodor, J. A., & Garrett, M. (1967). Some syntactic determinants of sentential complexity. *Perception & Psychophysics, 2,* 289–296.

Fodor, J. A., Garrett, M., & Bever, T. G. (1968). Some syntactic determinants of sentential complexity, II: Verb structure. *Perception & Psychophysics, 3,* 453–460.

Franks, J. J., & Bransford, J. D. (1972). The acquisition of abstract ideas. *Journal of Verbal Learning and Verbal Behavior. 11,* 311–315.

Gough, P. B. (1965). Grammatical transformations and speed of understanding. *Journal of Verbal Learning and Verbal Behavior. 4,* 107–111.

———. (1966). The verification of sentences: The effects of delay of evidence and sentence length. *Journal of Verbal Learning and Verbal Behavior, 5,* 492–496.

Green, B. F., Wolf, A. K., Chomsky, C., & Laughery, K. (1963). Baseball: An automatic question-answerer. In E. A. Feigenbaum & J. Feldman (Eds.). *Computers and Thought,* pp. 207–216. NY: McGraw-Hill Book Co.

Kaplan, R. M. (1972). Augmented transition networks as psychological models of sentence comprehension. *Artificial Intelligence, 3,* 77–100.

Kintsch, W., & Keenan, J. (1974). The psychological reality of test bases. In W. Kintsch (Ed.). *The Representation of Meaning in Memory.* Hillsdale, NJ: Lawrence Erlbaum Associates.

Kintsch, W., & van Dijk, T. A. (1978). Toward a model of text comprehension and production. *Psychological Review, 85,* 363–394.

Kolata, G. (1982). How computers get common sense. *Science, 217,* 1237–1238.

Kuno, S. (1967). Computer analysis of natural languages. *Mathematical Aspects of Computer Science: Proceedings of Symposia in Applied Mathematics, 19,* 52–110.

Marcus, M. (1980). *A Theory of Syntactic Recognition for Natural Language.* Cambridge, MA: MIT Press.

Marks, L. E., & Miller, G. A. (1964). The role of semantic and syntactic constraints in the memorization of English sentences. *Journal of Verbal Learning and Verbal Behavior. 3,* 1–5.

Martin, E., & Roberts, K. H. (1966). Grammatical factors in sentence retention. *Journal of Verbal Learning and Verbal Behavior. 5,* 211–218.

McKoon, G., & Ratcliff, R. (1980). The comprehension processes and memory structures involved in anaphoric reference. *Journal of Verbal Learning and Verbal Behavior, 19,* 668–682.

Mehler, J. (1963). Some effects of grammatical transformations on the recall of English sentences. *Journal of Verbal Learning and Verbal Behavior, 2,* 250–262.

Mehler, J., & Carey, P. (1967). Role of surface and base structures in the perception of sentences. *Journal of Verbal Learning and Verbal Behavior, 6,* 335–338.

Miller, G. A., & Isard, S. (1963). Some perceptual consequences of linguistic rules. *Journal of Verbal Learning and Verbal Behavior, 2,* 217–228.

Miller, G. A., & McKean, R. N. (1964). A chronometric study of some relations between sentences. *Quarterly Journal of Experimental Psychology, 16,* 297–308.

Miller, G. A., & Selfridge, J. A. (1953). Verbal context and the recall of meaningful material. *American Journal of Psychology, 63,* 176–185.

Olson, D. R., & Filby, N. (1972). On the comprehension of active and passive sentences. *Cognitive Psychology, 3,* 361–381.

Paivio, A., & Begg, I. (1981). *Psychology of Language.* Englewood Cliffs, NJ: Prentice-Hall.

Ratcliff, R., & McKoon, G. (1978). Priming in recognition: Evidence for the propositional structure of sentences. *Journal of Verbal Learning and Verbal Behavior, 17,* 403–417.

Reber, A. S., & Anderson, J. R. (1970). The perception of clicks in linguistic and nonlinguistic messages. *Perception & Psychophysics, 8,* 81–89.

Sachs, J. S. (1967). Recognition memory for syntactic and semantic aspects of connected discourse. *Perception & Psychophysics, 2,* 437–442.

Savin, H. B., & Perchonock, E. (1965). Grammatical structure and the immediate recall of English sentences. *Journal of Verbal Learning and Verbal Behavior, 4,* 348–353.

Schank, R. (1972). Conceptual dependency: A theory of natural language processing. *Cognitive Psychology, 3,* 552–632.

Schank, R. C. (1975). The structure of episodes in memory. In D. G. Bobrow & A. Collins (Eds.). *Representation and Understanding* (pp. 237–272). NY: Academic Press.

Slobin, D. I. (1966). Grammatical transformations and sentence comprehension in childhood and adulthood. *Journal of Verbal Learning and Verbal Behavior, 5,* 219–227.

Tennant, H. (1981). *Natural Language Processing.* NY: Petrocelli Books, Inc.

Wanner, E., & Maratsos, M. (1978). An ATN approach to comprehension. In M. Halle, J. Bresnan, & G. A. Miller (Eds.). *Linguistic Theory and Psychological Reality.* (pp. 119–161). Cambridge, MA: MIT Press.

Weizenbaum, J. (1976). *Computer Power and Human Reason.* San Francisco: W. H. Freeman & Co.

Whitlow, J. W., Jr., Smith, E. E., & Medin, D. L. (1982). Retrieval of correlated predicates. *Journal of Verbal Learning and Verbal Behavior, 21,* 383–402.

Winograd, T. (1972). Understanding natural language. *Cognitive Psychology, 3.*

Woods, W. A. (1967). Semantics for a question-answering system. Unpublished doctoral dissertation, Report NSF-19, Aiken Computer Laboratory, Harvard University.

———. (1973). Progress in natural language understanding—An application to lunar geology. In *Proceedings of the National Computer Conference.* Montvale, NJ: AFIPS Press.

Yngve, V. H. (1960). A model and an hypothesis for language structure. *Proceedings of the American Philosophical Society, 104,* 444–466.

STUDY QUESTIONS

1. Explain the terms: bottom-up processing, top-down processing, serial processing, parallel processing, and heuristics. Make up a sentence and show how its meaning could be derived by using only bottom-up, top-down, serial, or parallel processes; that is, describe four different means of processing it, one for each of the preceding. What kind of heuristics could be used to interpret your sentence?

2. Critically discuss the evidence for the psychological reality of transformational grammar.

3. (How) do you think we do syntactic processing? Discuss the *evidence* for and against your position. You may opt for "keyword," finite state grammar, transformational derivation from surface structure to proposition, interpretation of abstract surface structure, general strategies, or semantic strategies. If you truly think we do it by using keywords or finite state grammars that is fine: Discuss the others generally, explain why they do not work for you, and explain how this method accounts for the findings claimed in support of the others.

6

Speech

Consider the following sets of sounds:

whim	pimp	improper	bumper	mp
win	pint	interrogate	bunter	nt
wing	pink	incarcerate	bunker	nk

The items in the first row contain the consonant "m," and, all but the first, the cluster "mp." Make an "m" and notice where your lips and tongue are when you do—your lips should be closed and your tongue not touching the roof of your mouth. Are your lips and tongue in the same place for "p"? For "n"? For "n," the consonant shared by the items of row 2, your lips should be open and your tongue tip *(apex)* should be touching the roof of your mouth, just behind your teeth—the *alveolar* ridge. Do you have to move your tongue to go from "n" to "t"? If not, "n" and "t" are in the same *place of articulation.* The items in the third row all share a sound too, called *eng* (ŋ). Notice where your tongue is at the end of "wing"—the back of it should be pushed up against the soft part of the roof of your mouth, the *soft palate,* very different from its position in "win." And note that you hear a difference between "win" and "wing," indicating that they are made of different sounds. Now, think about where your tongue is at the "n" in "pink." At the same position as in "win" or "wing"? Do you have to move it to make the "k"? Are you making an "n" or an "eng" before the "k" sound in incarcerate and bunker?

   This example illustrates several things about sound. First, as shown by the "eng," the sounds of our language do not absolutely correspond to the letters of the alphabet. Sometimes different sounds are represented by the same letter. (Perhaps you feel that "eng" is actually two sounds, n + g. Say "n + g," making the "n" as you did in "win." Does "ng" sound the same as "ŋ"?) Sometimes the same sound is represented by two different letters—like "c" in incarcerate and "k" in "pink." So to talk clearly about the sounds of a language we will need a new alphabet—one that corresponds to the sounds.

   Second, like everything else in language, sounds are organized—the consonant pairs just discussed match place of articulation between the "m," "n," "ŋ" and "p," "t," "k." Matching of a sound feature is called *assimilation* and is usually hypothesized to occur to allow the speaker fewer movements, less work. Try to pronounce the nonsense words—"pinp," "piŋp," "bumker"—isn't it easier to say them when place of articulation matches?

Third, the organization of sounds dictates not only what sounds are likely to occur together but also what sounds may occur where—note that all the words in the example have "m," "n," "ŋ" either at the end or the middle of the word. Is it possible to make them at the beginning? Yes, for "m" and "n"—"map" and "nap" for example—but can we have "ŋap"? Can you say "ŋap"? With practice and awareness of where your tongue is you should be able to—in fact it exists in initial position in other languages. If you succeed in making one clearly, ask your friends what they hear. In all likelihood they will say "nap" not because you said "nap," but because they are not used to hearing it in initial position and, from their experience, guess something that is more likely to occur. The organization in sounds, like the organization in meaning and syntax, provides redundancy and predictability, so that we may partially guess preceding or following sounds from the current one if we do not hear or speak each clearly.

The organization and predictability in sounds allow us to understand the speech of someone who does not talk exactly as we do. Essentially, we make and use a sound substitution rule. For example, for a lisp, we could use a rule changing "th" to "s" ("th" may be written θ or theta for the sound in "thin," to distinguish it from ð, the "th" sound in "the"). Obviously we want to restrict the rule in certain contexts: "Liθp" is probably lisp but "θin" could be either "thin" or "sin." Sometimes we can restrict it based on rules of sound (θ cannot occur before "p" in English), and sometimes we can restrict it by using meaning or syntax.

Besides aiding understanding of speech defects, sound rules and sound rewrite rules allow us to understand people with accents different from ours. Think about what makes an accent different. Sometimes it is trivial, like pronouncing a single word differently, shedule instead of skedule (schedule) or tomahto instead of tomayto. Or it may involve pronouncing a particular sound differently—"r" in English, French, or Spanish for instance. Again this would be a simple "correction" in listening. Or it may involve pronouncing a class of sounds differently—making all vowels sound nasal for instance. In any case, the organization and the redundancy of the sounds (and the words) in the language allow us to ignore these variations and still recognize what others are saying. In this chapter we will examine the sounds of language and some principles of their organization. In the next chapter we discuss how we perceive the sounds of the language and use their organization.

Units of Sound

Syllables

As we have seen in syntax and semantics, the first problem in determining structure is deciding where to begin analysis, what to use as the unit for study. And, as with meaning and syntax, several candidates present themselves, some of which are useful for some types of analysis and others useful for other types. One possibility is the *syllable,* which we define as a unit consisting of no more than one vowel sound.

"-ly" is a syllable, as is "es," or "dog" or "strength." "Any" is two syllables. To describe a syllable though, it is necessary to talk about its components—vowels and consonants—and this level of sound structure too could be the place to start analysis.

Phonemes

For this purpose, linguists define the *phoneme,* the minimal unit of sound that can serve to distinguish meaning. To discover phonemes, we use the same kind of distributional analysis we used in Chapter 4 for syntax, but now applied to sound. In syntax we collected or constructed sentences that were identical but for one word. The different words could then be assigned to a particular structural class. In speech, likewise, we look for identical frames but for one difference. If the difference is judged by native speakers as reflecting a meaning difference too, we have found a pair of phonemes. Two words identical but for one meaning-changing sound constitute a *minimal pair.* For example, "bat" and "pat" are different; the "at" is shared by both so b-p creates a meaning difference; "b" and "p" are different phonemes. "Pat" and "pet" are minimally distinct, with the difference in the vowel, suggesting "a" and "e" are different phonemes. "Pet" and "Pete" are minimally distinct (ignore the spelling—both are pronounced p-vowel-t) suggesting the "e" in "pet" is phonemically distinct from the "e" in "Pete."

Although our alphabet is crudely phonemic, as we stated earlier, there is not a one-to-one correspondence between the phonemes of our language and the letters of the alphabet, so new symbols have been used. The phonemes of English and their symbols are shown on Table 6.1, organized with respect to articulatory features, to be described later. (It will be useful to learn the symbols to follow discussion in this and the next chapter, and in other reading.) Box 6.1 presents some short poems on which you can practice phonemic transcription.

Allophones and Phonetic Differences

It is useful to recognize that each phoneme represents a class of sounds, each member of which may sound different from other members. Take, for example, the phoneme /p/. (Phonemes are indicated by slashes around the sound.) If you attend very carefully when you say "pat" and "tap," you will notice that you pronounce the /p/ differently in initial and final positions (if you have a standard American accent). If you hold your fingers in front of your mouth as you say "pat," you should feel a burst of air on them as you articulate the /p/. In "tap," if you pronounce it comfortably, you will not separate your lips again at the end of the word, and you will not feel that burst of air. The /p/ in "spat" is like the final /p/—there should be no burst of air. Do you think you can hear the difference? It is one of the differences between British and American speech—the British *release* their final /p/s and /t/s; they make that burst of air, and Americans do not. We can also demonstrate that the difference is audible by recording "spat" and splicing the "s" off the recording; magically, the resulting syllable sounds like "bat," not like "pat." We American English speakers know /p/ must be released in initial position and not hearing the release makes us assume that it was /b/ that was said.

Table 6.1 *The International Phonetic symbols for the phonemes of English, organized with respect to articulatory features. Each symbol is presented, followed by a common word containing the sound (italicized) it represents.*

		Labial		Dental		Alveolar		Palatal		Velar	
Consonants											
Stops	voiced	b	*b*ill			d	*d*ill			g	*g*ill
	voiceless	p	*p*ill			t	*t*ill			k	*k*ill
Nasals		m	*m*ill			n	*n*ill			ŋ	si*ng*
Fricatives	voiced	v	*v*eil	ð	*th*e	z	*z*ero	ž	*zh*a-*zh*a		
	voiceless	f	*f*ill	θ	*th*in	s	*s*ill	š	*sh*arp		
Affricates	voiced							ǰ	e*dge*		
	voiceless							č	*ch*urch		
Liquid/semivowel		w	*w*ill			r,l	*r*ail			h	*h*id

Vowels

	Front		Central	Back	
High	i b*ee*t			u b*oo*t	
	I b*i*t			U b*oo*k	
Mid	e b*ai*t		ə sof*a*	o b*oa*t	
	ɛ b*e*t			ʌ b*u*t, ɔ b*ough*t	
	æ b*a*t				
Low			a b*a*r		

In any case in English [pʰ] (released or *aspirated*) and [p'] (unreleased) are different sounds of the same phoneme—we do not make a meaning difference between "tapʰ" and "tap'." (Descriptions that reflect precise articulation are *phonetic* rather than phonemic and are indicated by square brackets, as preceding.) They are called *allophones* of the phoneme /p/. Most phonemes have many allophones, and some phonemes share an allophone. For example, in many American dialects, normally, "ladder" and "latter" have the same sound in the middle—the *medial* consonant. Try saying "the former or the ladder"—it should sound perfectly normal. That medial consonant, called a *flap*, is an allophone of both /d/ and /t/.

It is important to realize that differences that are only phonetic in one language may be phonemic in another. As already stated, the difference between aspirated and unaspirated consonants is not used to distinguish meaning in English, although it does distinguish dialects. In Korean, however, the aspiration is *phonemic*—different words can be indicated solely by whether or not a consonant is released. In fact, if the consonant is articulated with strong aspiration, it is phonemically distinct from one weakly aspirated *and* from one articulated without aspiration.

Phonetic Features

In this discussion and in our initial discussion we made use of subphonemic units of analysis—place of articulation, release, aspiration; so clearly there is a smaller use-

Box 6.1. FonimIk TɚænzkɚIpšʌn

If the title looks a bit fuzzy to you it is because it is written using the phonemic alphabet. It says "phonemic transcription." (If ðə teitl lUks ə bIt
fʌzi tu iu It Iz bikɔz It Iz ɚItn iuziŋ ðə fonimIk ælfəbɛt. It sɛz fonimIk
tɚænskɚIpšʌn.) The phonemic alphabet matches one letter to one sound,
sometimes causing no change in a word, and sometimes, clearly, causing a
radical difference. (ðə fonimIk ælfəbɛt mæčəz wʌn lɛtɚ tu wʌn saˡnd,
sʌmtaˡmz kɔzIŋ no čenj In ðə wɚd ænd sʌmtaˡmz, kliɚli, kɔzIŋ ə ɚædIkəl
dIfɚɛns.) Here follow some short verses for you to practice transcription on.
Sound out the words and use the examples in Table 6.1 to help you find the
symbol match. Note that rhymes that are not spelled the same in English
"look" like rhymes when transcribed. (hiɚ falo sʌm šɔɚt vɚsəz fɔɚ iu
tu pɚæktIs tɚænskɚIpšʌn an. saˡnd aut ðə wɚdz ænd iuz ðə ɛgzæmplz In tebl
sIks pɔˡnt wʌn tu hɛlp iu faˡnd ðə sImbl mæč. not ðæt ɚaimz ðæt aɚ nat spɛld
ðə sem In IŋglIš, lUk laˡk ɚaˡmz wɛn tɚænskɚaˡbd.)

1. Jellicle Cats are black and white,
   Jellicle Cats are rather small,
   Jellicle Cats are merry and bright,
   And pleasant to hear when they caterwaul.
   Jellicle Cats have cheerful faces,
   Jellicle Cats have bright black eyes;
   They like to practice their airs and graces
   And wait for the Jellicle moon to rise.
   (from T. S. Eliot, Old Possum's Book of Practical Cats)

2. The turtle lives 'twixt plated decks
   Which practically conceal its sex.
   I think it clever of the turtle
   In such a fix to be so fertile.

   (Ogden Nash, "The Turtle")

3. There was a young girl of Tralee,
   Whose knowledge of French was "oui, oui."
   When they said: "Parlez-vous?"
   She replied: "Same to you!"
   And was famed for her bright repartee.
   (*V. Holland,* An Explosion of Limericks, NY: *Funk & Wagnalls, 1967,*
   p. 23)

ful unit of sound structure than the phoneme. We will define *subphonemic features* as those aspects of either articulation or the sound signal itself that distinguish phonemes and/or allophones of phonemes. Different languages of the world have different phonemes, syllables, and words, but all spoken languages share the same set of subphonemic features; these are determined by the structures of the vocal tract and of the auditory system—structures common to all human beings.

Before discussing the subphonemic features in any detail, we should note that there is one more level of sound analysis, a level that supersedes syllables, where we began this discussion. Syllables, phonemes, and features are sometimes called *segments*—they are the segments we combine to form meaningful sentences. The level above them is called *suprasegmental* and refers to things like intonation, overall loudness, loudness changes, and stress. Note that we can make the statement "you now understand the difference between segments and suprasegmentals" or ask the question "you now understand the difference between segments and suprasegmentals?" using the same segments and conveying the different meaning through a change in pitch. The pitch change is marked in one sense on, and in one sense apart from, the segments—each has a pitch and the combination of those pitches, the *pitch contour,* makes the difference between questions and statements.

Articulatory Features

We begin our discussion of subphonemic features with articulation, because it is easier to feel intuitively where the articulators are than to determine what the characteristics are in the sound. Figure 6.1 shows a model vocal tract to be used for reference. Sound begins with our forcing air out of our lungs, up through the trachea and out the mouth or nose or both. The audible effect of the air may be changed by the path it takes—for example, whether it goes out the mouth, the nose, or both, or by the shape the mouth is when the air comes out. In the same manner, the sound of a puff of air may be changed by pushing it through a flute, stopping the flute in different places, or humming while playing the flute. The various ways of altering the puff of air are called *articulatory features,* and are arranged hierarchically, as in Table 6.1.

Consonants

The uppermost distinction, consonant-vowel, refers to whether there is constriction anywhere in the vocal tract. When a doctor wants to look at your throat (s)he asks you to say /a/, a vowel. Making an /m/ would allow the doctor a good view of your lips, an /l/ of the underside of your tongue. These last are consonants, and they block the vocal tract in some way. The consonants may be described by using three articulatory dimensions: manner of articulation, voicing, and place of articulation.

Manner of Articulation.   *Manner* refers to the nature of the constriction, how much air it allows to pass. *Stop consonants* or *plosives* are consonants articulated in

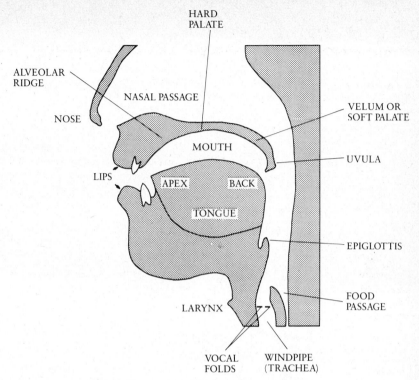

Figure 6.1 *Schematic of the vocal tract.*

such a manner that no air may get through. These are /b/, /d/, /g/ and /p/, /t/, /k/. If you make any of these consonants and attend to what you are doing, you will realize that there is a complete seal—in /b/ or /p/ for instance, the lips are sealed, and air gathers behind the seal. As we articulate, we suddenly break the seal and air "explodes" (= plosive) out. This is called the release, and as we have seen, in American English, in final position the stops are unreleased; that is, the seal is not broken, and the built-up air dissipates in the vocal cavity. If you make any of the stops slowly and do not release or allow the air to leak out through your nose, you can feel the air pressure building up—for /b/ and /p/ in your cheeks, for /d/ and /t/ behind your tongue, and for /g/ and /k/ in your throat, as if you were gagging.

   Nasal consonants, a second manner of articulation, also have complete closure somewhere in the vocal tract. To make a nasal the soft palate or *velum* (see Figure 6.1) is lowered, allowing air to escape through the nose. In stops the velum is fully raised, sealing off the nasal cavity. Nasals of English are /m/, /n/, and /ŋ/. If you make an /m/ and sustain it and while you are going "mmmmmmmmm" grab your nose, then you should feel the pressure build up and perhaps force you to open your mouth and articulate a /b/. When we have colds and the nasal passage is blocked, /m/s turn into /b/s and /n/s to /d/s, because the usual escape route for the air for the nasals is blocked.

The remaining manners of articulation all involve partial constriction and a smaller pressure buildup. *Fricatives* are consonants produced by constricting almost to the point of closing the vocal tract, causing the air to pass turbulently, with friction, through the constriction. The fricatives used in English are /f/, /v/, /θ/, /ð/, /s/, /z/, /š/, /ž/, and in other languages we also find the gutteral sound /X/ (as though you were clearing your throat), and a sound produced by partially closing the lips, /β/. If you pay attention as you make an /s/, you will feel the sides of your tongue sealing off the roof of your mouth, and the tip very close to contacting it, with the air "whistling" through the hole produced by the near touch of the tongue tip. A combination of stop and fricative is called an *affricate*—in English we have /č/ as in church, and /ĵ/ as in "jump" (or the vernacular "djeatjet" = did you eat yet). In an affricate there is complete closure, but instead of following with complete release, the closure releases only partially.

Widening the opening more produces laterals and semivowels. A *lateral* (/l/ in English) has the opening at the side. In /l/, you should feel your tongue tip contact the roof of your mouth, but the sides of the tongue should not be touching the sides of the mouth, allowing the air to move through without vibration. In English /r/ and /w/, too, there is partial closure: In /r/ the tongue bends back on itself (called *retroflex*) but does not contact the root of the mouth; in /w/ the lips begin to close but leave an opening too large to cause vibration (decreasing that opening still further produces the fricative β, used in Spanish, among other languages). Because there is constriction but not contact these are called *semivowels.*

Finally there is a class of sounds produced by repeated closing and opening, called *trills.* These include the French "r" where the trill is produced in the back of the throat; the Spanish "r" where it is produced by repeatedly tapping the tongue tip on the roof of the mouth; and a lip trill produced by vibrating the lips together while blowing out. A single "tap" of a trill produces a flap, like [ɾ] in ladder or latter.

Voicing. *Voicing* refers to when the vocal cords begin to vibrate relative to the release of air. /z/ and /s/ are good instances of the distinction. Place your fingers on your *larynx* (Adam's apple) as you go z-z-z-z-z-z-z. You should feel a buzz. Now make s-s-s-s-s-s-s without moving your fingers—you should feel nothing. When the vocal folds vibrate simultaneously with the release, as in /z/, the sound is *voiced;* when release occurs first the sound is *voiceless.* In English, only the distinction between voiced and voiceless is (phonemically) relevant; in other languages this feature can have one other relevant value—the vocal folds may start to vibrate *before* the release. This is called *prevoicing* and is hard for English speakers to hear or produce deliberately. Try it, using what you know now about articulation—put your fingers on your larynx, start it vibrating and then begin the /z/. It should sound something like nz.

All the sounds we have listed for manner may be divided into voiced and voiceless. The voiced stops are /b/, /d/, /g/; the voiced fricatives /v/, /ð/, /z/, /ž/; the voiced affricate /ĵ/. The nasals, laterals, and semivowels of English are all voiced.

Place of Articulation. The final distinction relevant for English consonants is place of articulation, introduced at the beginning of the chapter. Place refers to where in the oral cavity the closure or constriction is. It can be at the lips or *bilabial* (/b/), at the teeth or *dental* (θ), between the lips and teeth or *labiodental* (v), between the teeth or *interdental* (a variant of θ), behind the teeth or *alveolar* (s), back farther or *palatal* (š), and back still farther or *velar* (g). Different parts of the tongue (or lips), as we have seen, can make the constriction—the tip, the sides, the middle, or the back. Sometimes both the parts making the closure are described in labeling articulation; for example, /t/ is a voiceless apical-alveolar stop; the tongue tip contacts the alveolar ridge. Again, all the sounds may be classified by place—/b/, /p/, /m/, /w/ are bilabial, /v/ and /f/ are labiodental, /θ/ and /ð/ are dental, /d/, /t/, /s/, /z/, /n/, /r/, /l/ are alveolar, and /g/, /k/, /ŋ/ are velar.

Distinctions Not Used in English. Other languages use places of articulation different in some cases from those listed here. One instance is the palatal nasal, as in Slavic, which we transcribe as /ny/. Make an /s/ and then a /š/ and feel the difference in tongue position. Now make an /n/, only instead of using the tip of your tongue, use the middle as you did for /š/. Another common consonant we do not use phonemically is the glottal stop /ʔ/—back farther than the velar. Cockney uses it in intervocalic positions—for example, in place of the flap [ɾ] in latter, butter, or glottal. When we articulate an isolated vowel, /a/ for example, if we start it suddenly, it will begin with complete closure and sudden release, indicative of a stop but down in the larynx.

Before leaving the discussion of consonant articulation we should observe that all the consonants discussed are produced by pushing air *out* of the vocal tract. We are able to create sounds also by sucking air in—called *implosives* or *ingressives.* Clicking with the tongue, usually written as "tsk, tsk, tsk," is an alveolar ingressive. Kissing noises are bilabial ingressives, and there are many others. Ingressives are marked with the stop consonant of the appropriate place preceded by an !. In some African languages implosives are important phonemically. In our language they are not used productively to differentiate words.

It is important to realize that many of the sounds that are not phonemic in English are *just* as natural as the sounds we do use and could be phonemic. We prevoice consonants in intervocalic position (between vowels as in "idea"), begin vowel-initial utterances with a glottal stop, and have a palatal value in fricatives but not in nasals. The sounds are not difficult to articulate but are not used to signal meaning differences in English, and so we do not attend to them. The selection of only *some* of the *many* possible sounds for productive use is one of the interesting characteristics of language. We will discuss this again in Chapter 8. For now, try to think of reasons that languages would use some but not all.

Vowels

Vowels may also be described by using articulatory features. For vowels, by definition, there is no closure, and therefore manner of articulation is irrelevant. Place is relevant, but is harder to feel since there is no contact of the articulators, but only movement in the direction of contact. For vowels, the relevant dimensions are *tongue height,* how close the tongue is to the roof of the mouth, and *tongue position,* which part of the tongue is closest to the roof of the mouth. If you articulate /i/ as in beet, /I/ as in bit, /e/ as in bait, and /ɛ/ as in bet, repeatedly, and attend to what you are doing, you should feel the tip of your tongue dropping progressively. Because it is the tip that is falling, these are called *front vowels*—/i/ is high, and /ɛ/ is medium low. (High and low do not refer to pitch but to the height of the tongue or jaw.) If you now alternate /i/ and /u/ you will feel the distinction between front and back; in /i/ the tip is close to the roof of the mouth; in /u/ the back of the tongue is close. Contrasting /i/, /u/, and /a/ gives the maximum change: /i/ and /u/ are both high, /a/ is low (the jaw drops maximally, creating the largest opening and the best throat viewing), /i/ is front, /u/ back, and /a/ center (the middle of the tongue bulges slightly). Because /i/, /u/, and /a/ represent the vowel extremes, with all other vowels falling in between, as Table 6.1 indicates, they are sometimes called the *point vowels.*

Besides tongue height and tongue position, there are some other articulatory features that differentiate the vowels. Of these, the most *productive,* the feature responsible for differentiating the most minimal pairs, is *tense-lax,* or, in the words we were taught in high school, long-short. /i/ is long or tense, /I/ short; they are almost minimally distinct with respect to this feature since they are made in the same place and with about the same tongue height. (They do differ in height, as we observed, but much less than, for example, /i/ and /e/ or /a/.) Similarly /e/ is tense, /ɛ/ lax, /u/ tense, and /U/ lax. Tense vowels are invariably articulated for a longer time than are lax vowels but are also slightly more extreme in the other dimensions; lax vowels tend to become *centralized,* or articulated with the least movement from the central, neutral position. The most *reduced* centralized vowel is the *schwa,* /ə/, the sound at the end of sofa, representing the very least articulatory effort.

Other Features. The remaining vowel features are not very productive in English; they differentiate one or two vowels but are not responsible for major class distinctions. They are listed here for the sake of completeness and also to underscore that our language, like others, utilizes productively only a few of the many possible sounds and that the ones we use are no more natural than the others to the vocal tract. Try to make each sound described. Remember if it seems unnatural that you will be trying to use explicit knowledge rather than the tacit knowledge we use for our phonemes, and that you have had much experience with our sounds and little with the others.

Retroflexion refers to curling the tongue back while articulating. We do that to the schwa to make our "r," which is not a true consonant at all. If you make an "r" you will see that there is no constriction in the vocal tract. Retroflexion is indicated with a ˆ on the vowel: Our "r" is transcribed ɚ = ə + ˆ. It is possible to retroflex other vowels.

Liprounding is a feature we use only for /u/, /U/, and /ɔ/. It refers to a protrusion of the lips accompanying other articulatory gestures. It *could* apply to all or any other vowel features.

A third, minor feature for vowels of English is voicing—all our vowels are voiced except one, /h/, which has a huge number of allophones. While attending to where your tongue is say "he," "who," and "ha." Note that there is no movement of the tongue as you go from the "h" into the vowel. This should tell you that there is no constriction for "h," that it is a vowel, and that it does not differ from other vowels in height or position. Indeed, the English "h" is a voiceless vowel that shares place and height with the vowel that will follow it. In other languages distinctions between voiceless vowels might be phonemic but in ours they are not; we class them together as "h." (Voiceless vowels are transcribed with an open circle beneath the vowel: [ḁ].)

A fourth vowel feature not used phonemically in English is nasalization (˜)— vowels may be pronounced with the velum opened so that air is pushed through the nose as well as the mouth, or closed so that it only goes through the mouth. Spanish and French both use nasalization in vowels phonemically.

The final vowel distinction, phonemic in Chinese and some other Asian and African languages, is tone, a change in the pitch, or frequency of vocal fold vibration. Note that we can sing while speaking. In singing we change the pitch, holding other articulatory features relatively constant. This does not cause any change in meaning, but in some languages (called *tone languages*) specific pitch changes signal a different phoneme or meaning.

Coarticulation

In the preceding discussion of vowels and consonants, idealized target positions for sounds spoken in isolation were described. It is important to emphasize that speech does not consist of isolated sounds strung together but a continuous air flow with continuous movement of the articulators. Because of movement toward or away from one target position, sometimes the target is never reached, and actual articulation is a modification of what has been just described.

Consider the sounds /bu/ and /bi/ for example, attending to your lips as you make the /b/ portion. For /bu/ the lips may be protruded at the very beginning of the /b/, before the closure, in anticipation of the rounding necessary for the vowel. For /bi/ there is no rounding anywhere during the sound. The same thing may be seen in /di/ and /du/. And we can see this kind of articulatory *smear* across three segments. Consider "bog" (/bag/): As we begin the /b/ the back of the tongue is already assuming the position for /g/, so the /b/ is in fact articulated differently in /bag/ and /bad/, modified by succeeding sounds. Similarly, for the final consonant there is likely to be either residual liprounding or residual movement from liprounding, making it different depending on the initial consonant. This might suggest that syllables are better units of articulation since they would incorporate some of the anticipatory and residual movements, but, in fact, coarticulation effects exist across syllable boundaries too.

In most cases we are not aware of the modifications produced by coarticulation. One striking example, however, is production of combined vowels, or *diphthongs*, a distinctive characteristic of American English. Nearly all American tensed vowels are not pure but are smoothly coarticulated double vowels. "ay," for example, which we have been loosely transcribing as /e/, in fact is eⁱ—a pure vowel /e/, as in French, followed by a shortened /i/ sound. Make one slowly and follow your tongue: You should feel the tip glide from low in your mouth toward the roof. The movement change is indicative of a diphthong, not a pure vowel. The vowel sound in "height" is a diphthong combining a and i → a^i; again the tongue movement should be easy to follow if you produce it slowly. Our "o" as in boat is a diphthong combining o and u—note the tendency to lipround as you end the sound. This example should illustrate a subtlety of coarticulation; when it is done smoothly, a smooth blend results. (It should also illustrate, again, a consequence of phonemic distinctiveness. To American unpracticed ears /e^i/ is the same as /e/: We hear only one vowel. To speakers of other languages, who do not hear the diphthongs as we do, the combination is more obvious.)

Nonsegmentals

The features just described are called segmentals, and their manipulation differentiates morphemes of the spoken languages of the world. Our speech may be affected also by other aspects of articulation, some of which are and some of which are not under our control. These we are grouping together as nonsegmentals, but they fall into several classes.

Suprasegmentals.   The most important of these linguistically are the suprasegmentals, which may also be used to create changes in meaning. Suprasegmentals include pitch contour, loudness contour, and duration (speed of production and pause length). These are under our control. Pitch changes are produced by increasing or decreasing the rate of vocal cord vibration. They may make a phonemic difference, in tone languages like Chinese, or alter grammatical interpretation, as in the difference between a question and a statement in English. Loudness is affected by the force with which air is pushed through the larynx, and by the size of the mouth opening—in both cases, the greater the louder. Rate is altered by the speed with which the articulators are moved from one position to another.

In normal speech none of the suprasegmentals are unchanging, but rather they vary during articulation. Generally loudness and pitch are highest at the beginning of an utterance and then gradually decline, falling off markedly at sentence end. (For pitch, this is known as the *declination effect*.) Variations in this typical contour may be introduced for emphasis: A loudness change stresses an internal portion of the sentence, while, in English, a pitch rise at the end marks the sentence as a question. Generally, they do not operate independently—so stressing a syllable is likely to make it louder, higher, and longer than its unstressed counterpart. If you attend to pairs differing in stress like "de'sert-desert', per'mit-permit', pre'sent-present'," you can observe these changes along with vowel reduction. (Note that in English we may change some noun forms to verb forms or conversely by changing stress. In the noun-verb pairs just listed, the noun has stress on the first syllable, the verb on the second. This is an instance of a *morphophonemic rule,* a rule of sound structure affected by morphological structure. Can you think of other such pairs?)

Registers. The larynx is an extremely complex structure, the details of which we will not go into here. It contains the vocal cords and a number of muscles and cartilages. The muscles and cartilages may be manipulated individually to change the tension on the vocal cords or the position of the entire larynx. The opening between the vocal cords is called the *glottis,* and the stream of air passing through it is typically discussed in parts: Above the glottis there is the *supraglottal airstream,* which is the part we manipulate by changing our tongue position; there is the *glottal airstream,* which we alter by using the muscles and cartilages; and there is the *subglottal airstream,* which is the part in our lungs and deep in the throat. In neutral, breathing position the vocal cords are open, allowing the air to flow through smoothly. By using the muscles to close them we produce a pressure of air below the glottis, which works to push the vocal cords open again. As the air flows through, if the vocal cords are not very tensed, it may produce a negative pressure (like a vacuum), which aids in closing the vocal cords again. In normal speech the tension on the vocal cords is sufficient to allow the subglottal pressure and negative pressure to cause the vocal cords to vibrate, imparting a particular quality to the sound.

The quality of the voice is dependent in part on the quality of the airstream rushing through the glottis. It may be vibrating totally, as in normal speaking, or parts of it may be vibrating differently from other parts. The tension and vibration of the airstream is controlled by tensing or vibrating part or all of the vocal cords. For instance, in *falsetto register,* greater tension is placed on the vocal cords than in normal speaking, preventing the buildup of the negative pressure and changing the quality of the vocal tone. Note that it is possible to produce the same range of pitches in falsetto as *chest register* (or singing voice and normal voice respectively)—the pitch is determined by the rate of opening and closing of the vocal cords. The quality change is determined by the tension on the vocal cords and the kinds of pressures that affect the airstream.

In normal and falsetto registers the pressure on the airstream (tension on the vocal cords) is even and produces vibration resulting in tones. In whispering the tension on the vocal cords is even but not sufficiently great to cause vibration of the airstream. In other registers the tension may be uneven, producing one kind of tone from one portion of the airstream, combined with another kind from another portion. For example, in *breathy voice,* there is partial tension on the vocal cords allowing air to escape through them while they are vibrating. The part that has tension causes air vibration, producing tones; the other part allows the air through without vibration, producing a turbulent airflow sound. In *creaky voice,* a mode used in high-class British speech for low pitches, there is tension on the whole glottal airstream, but it is uneven, producing differential vibration of the airstream. Try to produce sounds in these different registers; their names are reasonably descriptive of the sound qualities, and we do produce them easily.

As already indicated, register changes sometimes differentiate dialects of English: Creaky voice is used in particular instances in the upper-class British dialect (the dialect is called *received pronunciation*). Register changes are also used in English to communicate emotion: Breathy voice, for example, is used to sound "sexy." Register changes are not used phonemically in English, but there are languages in which they are. It is important to note further that the "meaning" of a register differs in different languages, as does the "normal" register. Some cultures use a different pitch range for normal speaking than others; different registers may be used in different languages or dialects; and different registers may be used in different languages to convey the same emotion (Abercrombie, 1967).

Physical Characteristics and Speech.   Thus far we have described modifications that may be made in the vocal tract to alter the quality of the sounds coming from it—indicating that the size and shape of the vocal tract, the tension of its muscles, and the quality of the airstream are important to sound quality. The physical characteristics of the vocal tract differ from individual to individual and from one time to another in the same individual. These differences give distinct character to each voice.

First, and most obvious, are effects of size. When we lipround we deliberately increase the size of the vocal tract: Talk through protruded lips or through your hands cupped around your mouth and you can hear the effect. The voice seems to get lower. People with naturally larger vocal tracts—men as opposed to women, adults as opposed to children—will naturally have a lower sound, all other things being equal. Besides affecting the length of the vocal tract, size may also affect the size of the vocal cords; the larger they are the more force is required to move them, and the slower they will move if force is not increased. Slower opening and closing of the vocal cords produces a lower pitch. Thus, increased body size produces a lower sound by lengthening the vocal tract *and* increasing the size of the vocal cords, thereby decreasing their vibration rate.

Second, there are effects of muscle tension, elasticity, and fluid, which are interrelated. Under conditions of stress the vocal cords are likely to be more tensed, perhaps causing a register shift or perhaps just an increased rate of vibration, producing a higher sound. Emotional stress also may decrease the amount of fluid in the mouth, skin, and vocal cords—in the case of the last this will make them smaller and allow faster vibration or higher pitch. Lower tension or elasticity affects both the clarity and the pitch of the sound; consider the difference in the sounds produced by plucking a tightly pulled rubber band and plucking one that is loosely pulled. As we age there is a loss in elasticity in the vocal tract generally and a loss in muscle tension specifically, producing a drop in pitch and change in quality. An increase in fluid buildup in the larynx will make the vocal cords harder to move, slow the rate, drop the pitch—the effect of swelling we recognize as laryngitis.

Third, changes in facial expression can affect the shape of the vocal tract and sounds emitting from it. Smiling retracts the lips and widens the mouth producing a higher sounding voice (Tartter, 1980), the opposite effect from liprounding. Laughing changes breathing as well and so can produce register changes; pouting elongates the vocal tract, deepening the sound; and crying alters the breathing pattern as well. (I suspect crying or being near tears may alter the fluids in the vocal cavity, although to my knowledge it has not been studied. It certainly produces swelling of the face, a feeling of a "lump" in the throat, and a general huskiness of the voice. The lump and huskiness could be caused by swelling of the vocal cords.)

Finally, of course, there are individual anatomical and physiological differences that can affect sound: Emphysema and asthma affect the subglottal air pressure and nature of the airflow; smoking or allergies can also affect swelling in the vocal cords. Laryngectomies, cleft palate, enlarged adenoids, and so on, affect the vocal tract and thus the sound quality.

Throughout our discussion of articulation and the structure of speech we have referred loosely to the effects that articulation has on sound. We end the discussion of articulation here and move in the next section to consider the structure of sound itself, independent of articulation. In the last section we will attempt to unite articulatory and acoustic characteristics of speech in describing its structure.

Source-Filter Theory

Although speech is normally produced through vocal articulation, it is possible to produce the same sounds through other means—as does a tape recorder, a radio, or a speech synthesizer; that is, we can describe the nature of sound without reference to articulation in particular. Sound is produced by pressure variations produced by an energy source and transmitted through some medium. The quality of the sound may be affected by characteristics of the source or by characteristics of the medium. Grossly speaking, we can consider a voice a constant source, and the different sound it has when we listen to it in the same room, through a wall, through a wall aided by a glass pressed on it, or through water, as effects of the medium. Different aspects of the sound get absorbed or passed by different media, and this affects what can ultimately be heard.

Wave Properties and Their Display

The simplest type of sound consists of a regular pressure change or vibration and is described by a sine wave, like the solid line in Figure 6.2. The wave has a certain *amplitude,* height from peak to trough, and a certain length, or distance from peak to peak, called *wavelength.* Instead of talking about wavelength, we may talk about *frequency,* the number of repetitions in a unit of time. We usually describe sound in terms of frequency. Its unit is cycles per seond, now called *Hertz (Hz).* The longer the wave the fewer peaks there are per unit time and therefore the smaller the frequency. Thus, frequency and wavelength measure the same thing, though they are negatively or inversely related: frequency = 1/wavelength. The amplitude and frequency may be independently manipulated—the dotted line in Figure 6.2 shows a wave with the same frequency and greater amplitude than the solid line, and the dashed line shows a wave with the same amplitude and greater frequency.

Usually, sound consists of more than one frequency at a time. Depending on the relationship of the component frequencies, we hear very different sound qualities. If there is no relationship, if frequencies are randomly put together we hear *noise,* like the sound of /š/. If the component frequencies are all multiples of one frequency, we hear a tonal quality, as in the sound of a musical instrument. This kind of combination is called a *harmonic complex.* The highest frequency shared by the members of the complex is called the *fundamental frequency.* The multiples of the fundamental are known as *harmonics.* For the most part, the fundamental determines what we

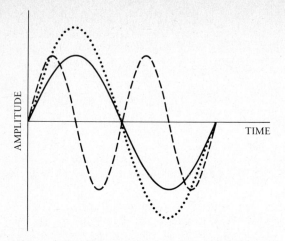

Figure 6.2 *Frequency and amplitude relations in sine waves. The solid and dotted lines have the same frequency and different amplitudes. The solid and dashed lines have the same amplitude and different frequencies.*

hear as the pitch of the sound, and the harmonics that are present determine its quality: The complex 200, 300, 400 has the same pitch (100 Hz) as the complex 100, 500, 600, 700 but will have a very different *timbre*—roughly, the difference in sound between two different kinds of instruments playing the same note.

Most of the sounds we hear (and produce) are noise. Noise can have various qualities depending on how many frequencies are present and what the range of frequencies is. /s/ and /š/ are both noisy but occupy different frequency ranges. How many frequencies are present around a central frequency determines the *bandwidth* of the noise. It can best be illustrated by using a *spectrogram*, as in Figure 6.3, a graphic

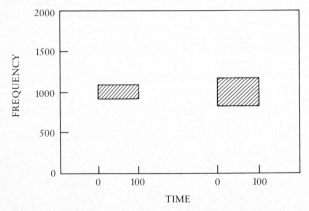

Figure 6.3 *Schematic spectrograms illustrating bandwidth differences. Both sounds have the same central frequency. The one on the right has a greater bandwidth.*

display of energy present at each frequency (y-axis) with respect to time (x-axis). (A spectrogram is produced by a *spectrograph,* a machine sensitive to energies in different frequency ranges.) Figure 6.3 displays two schematized spectrograms of sounds with the same central frequency and different bandwidths—the narrower bandwidth will sound less noisy, closer to a pure tone than the wider bandwidth. Spectrograms allow easy reading of frequencies present in a sound but do not conveniently display amplitude information (this is usually shown by the darkness of the bands in a spectrogram but is not very easy to read). To show how much energy (the amplitude of energy) is present at each frequency we use a display called a *power spectrum.* Figure 6.4 displays the power spectrum of the glottis, the amount of energy for various frequencies passed through a "typical" larynx.

Resonance

All objects vibrate and vibrate best at a particular frequency, called a *resonance.* Which frequency is the resonance frequency for an object is determined by the object's size and elasticity. If you consider the bars on a xylophone, the resonance concept should be clear: They are made of the same material and are excited by the same source, the blow of a hammer. The larger bars vibrate more slowly than the smaller ones. In all likelihood the vibrations are too fast for you to see the difference, but you can hear it: The smaller ones have a higher sound than the larger. The important point is that the vibration rate an object resonates to is determined by the *object's* properties, such as its size.

Some objects can easily be made to vibrate—air is not very dense and vibrates readily to a number of frequencies in response to the use of very little power. Vibra-

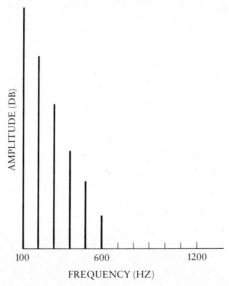

Figure 6.4 *Glottal power spectrum for the first 600 Hz. (There is energy up to 3000 Hz, but it is not displayed.)*

tion of fluids also requires little power, but fluids vibrate best at lower frequencies than air. Vibration of solids is possible but requires still greater power. If a wave contains sufficient power it can cause any object to vibrate; a wave of the resonance frequency of the object needs less power to make it vibrate than waves of other frequencies. A singer can smash a glass by concentrating all the power of the voice into the resonance frequency of the glass. This causes the glass molecules to vibrate and, since glass is rigid, it cannot tolerate the internal vibration and maintain its structure; so it shatters.

In considering objects in the environment and their effects on sound waves, it is important to realize that objects are not usually "pure"—a glass of water, for instance, is an object that has several factors contributing to its resonance properties: the density of the glass, the amount of water in it, and the size of the column of air above the water. A wall, likewise, is a complex object; it contains plaster particles of different densities, trapped air of different sizes (plaster is porous, it contains air), some wall-covering, paint, wallpaper, fabrics . . . each of which will have its own resonance frequencies. When a wave hits an object several things may happen: It may cause the object to vibrate, the vibration of the object adding to the power of the wave; it may pass through the object, causing some internal part (like a trapped column of air) to vibrate and thus never escape; or it may bounce off the object and back to us. The first is the property of *resonance,* the second of *absorption,* and the third of *reflection* or *echoes.* As we fill an empty room with objects, more and more sound gets absorbed, which is why empty houses echo while furnished houses do not.

The effect that an object has on sound waves is called its *filter characteristics.* The filter characteristics may be described by a *transfer function,* as in Figure 6.5. This shows that for some object, energies at frequencies of 500 Hz, 1500 Hz, and 2500 Hz are passed, but that energies at intermediate frequencies are lost through absorption or reflection, called *damping.*

Resonances of the Vocal Tract

From the preceding we can see that sound quality is determined by two things: the waves emitted by the source and the filter characteristics of the environment. So,

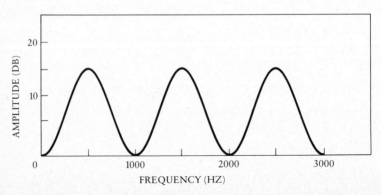

Figure 6.5   *Vocal tract transfer function for the vowel /ʌ/.*

if the glottal output (Figure 6.4) is input to the transfer function of Figure 6.5 we will get low energy at the frequencies emitted by the glottis and damped by the filter, and high energy at the filter's three resonances, illustrated in Figure 6.6.

When we speak we change the filter characteristics of the vocal tract, modifying the sounds emitted. In all cases the source is the same—air we exhale from our lungs. (Note that the source is noisy, meaning that there are a lot of frequencies present for modification by the vocal tract filters.) Sometimes we make that air vibrate through our larynx, picking up the resonances of the glottis; sometimes we push it through our nose, picking up a nasal resonance; sometimes we produce a small back cavity and large front cavity in our mouth by closing the mouth off with the back of the tongue; and sometimes we make a large back cavity by closing the mouth at the lips. In the same way we may take a single source, air blowing (in a flute), or a finger plucking a string (harp), or a hammer hitting a xylophone, or a finger tapping a glass—and change the pitch of the sound by changing the length of the tube (placing the finger over one hole or another on the flute), the length of the string, the size of the bar, or the amount of water in the glass.

The natural resonant frequencies of the vocal tract are called *formant frequencies.* They arise from changes in the vocal tract and change by changing the length of the tube, the vocal tract. They appear on spectrograms as dark bands of energy.

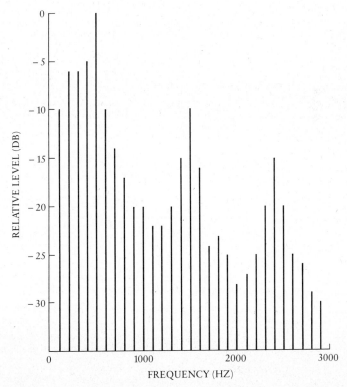

Figure 6.6 *Output of the glottal source of Figure 6.4 (including the higher frequencies not displayed) passed through the transfer function of Figure 6.5.*

(Those who wish to understand resonance in the vocal tract better are referred to Box 6.2, which describes a simple model of speech acoustics.)

The sound signal is very complex, containing many frequencies and many modifications of them by the vocal tract, as Box 6.2 indicates. In Chapter 7 we will consider which changes are perceptually relevant; that is, which acoustic information needs to be present to hear a /b/ or an /a/ or whatever. To begin to consider the question it is worth examining spectrograms of real speech.

Box 6.2 Deriving Formant Frequencies By Using a One-Tube Approximation to the Vocal Tract

It is possible to determine mathematically at what frequencies the resonances are likely to occur, using a simple model of air pressure (Stevens and House, 1961; Fant, 1956, 1973; Lieberman, 1975). Some readers may wish to work through the mathematics to help them remember where the formants are for different speech sounds and how the vocal tract resonances come about.

The vocal tract can be considered a tube, closed on one end (the lung or larynx end) and opened on the other (the mouth end), at least for vowels. When we expel air from the lungs into the mouth we create a pressure—a pressure you can feel on your cheeks and lips if you close your lips and nose and exhale. The air creating the feeling of pressure is moving in two directions, toward the lips and also back toward the larynx. Within a short time the pressure equalizes at all points in the vocal cavity, until the next perturbation. Pressure moving toward the lips we will call positive; a move in the other direction, negative. Atmospheric pressure, the normal air pressure, is zero. If we graph the pressure wave we get something looking like a sine wave, as in Figure 6.7, which shows a pressure wave for sounds when the lips are open. There is maximum pressure at the larynx (glottis) if the vocal cords are closed, and zero (atmospheric pressure) at the lips if they are open. The pressure moves in two directions, so the negative part of the sine wave represents air moving back in the mouth and indicates a *maximum* for the back flow *by the dip*. You can see that the figure resembles a sine wave, with the distance between the larynx and the lips equal to a quarter of the length of the wave.

What should the natural frequencies of the vocal tract be? Waves whose characteristics correspond to the pressure points in the mouth will pass untransformed—they are the resonances or formants. Waves whose characteristics do not correspond will get lost in the pressure changes imposed by the vocal tract and will be damped. Low frequencies imply low rates of pressure change, and at low rates the pressure is relatively even since it has time to equalize; so all frequencies get passed untransformed—up to about 300 Hz. Frequencies above 300 Hz are subject to filtering by the vocal tract. Its effects on the frequencies can be easily computed: As we already stated, if the glottis is closed and the mouth open and there is no constriction in the vocal tract, as in neutral position for /ə/, there is a pressure maximum at the glottis and a zero at the lips as in Figure 6.7. This describes a class of sine waves: one that goes through a quarter cycle in the length of the vocal tract, one that goes through ¾ cycle in the length of the vocal tract, one that goes through ¼ cycle in the length of the vocal tract, and so forth, as in Figure 6.8—all we need is a maximum at one end and a zero at the other, regardless of how many ups and downs there are in between. To compute the frequencies we must know the length of the vocal tract (17 cm for the average adult male). This means that the largest wave that fits will have a wavelength of 4×17 cm (¼ of it fits in 17 cm). We also must know the speed of sound (roughly 34,000 cm/sec) and the relationship between wavelength (distance) and frequency: frequency = cycles/sec = velocity/distance (= cm/sec/cm). So the first resonance is $¼ \times 34000/17 = 500$ Hz; the second, $¾ \times 34000/17 = 1500$; the third, $¼ \times 34000/17 = 2500$.

For consonants, the tube is not completely open. If it is closed at the lips as for labials, there is a pressure peak at the glottis *and* at the lips, as in Figure 6.9, which is half a sine wave. Again, a class of sine waves has this pressure form: one for which a half wave fits in the vocal tract, one for which the whole wave fits, one for which one and a half waves fit, and so on—even multiples of a half. The frequencies corresponding to these wavelengths will be $n/2 \times 34000/17 = 1000$ Hz, 2000 Hz, 3000 Hz, for n = 1, 2, 3. So if we combine the closed tube (bilabial) and the open tube (vowel) to make a syllable like /bə/, we would expect to see initially a band at 300 Hz (the low frequency emitted by the glottis and not affected by the pressure characteristics in the vocal tract), and one starting at 1000, 2000, and 3000. As we move into the vowel we should maintain the low frequency and add a 500 Hz band, a 1500 Hz band and a 2500 Hz band while losing the 1000 Hz and 2000 Hz bands. Since the move from the consonant to the vowel is smooth we might expect an even transition—the 1000 Hz band will change into the 1500 Hz one, and the 2000 Hz band into the 2500 Hz one. Examination of the labial-vowel spectrograms in Figures 6.10 and 6.11 will show that our calculations are roughly accurate. One important difference is that the spectrograms display /a/ and our calculations have assumed neutral position /ə/.

Note that if the vocal tract is shorter because the person is smaller, or constricts farther back as for /d/ or /g/, the length of the wave described by the two pressure maximums would decrease since the distance between the two maximums decreases. A decrease in wavelength means an increase in frequency, so we should expect a formant frequency rise. The lower panels in Figure 6.10 show the speaker's /da/ and /ga/, produced with constriction farther back in the mouth. Note that for the /ba/ there is a wide black band crossing the 1000 Hz line, actually representing two formants. For /da/ and /ga/ the band crossing the 1000 Hz line *starts* at 1500 Hz, reflecting the shorter distance from the constriction. (The exact shape of the formants is more complicated than described here because there is interaction of the resonances created behind the constriction and in front of the constriction.) The female /ga/ in Figure 6.13 (d) shows higher formant frequencies than the male (a), consistent with the prediction that a shorter distance raises frequency. Finally, the /ga/ produced by lip retraction from smiling in Figure 6.14 shows higher formant frequencies than the /ga/ produced without lip retraction and thus with a longer vocal tract.

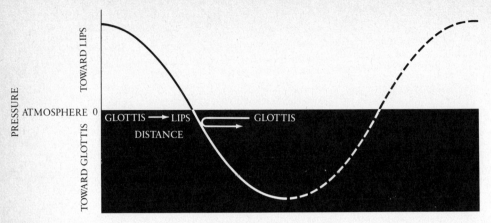

Figure 6.7 *Schematic pressure wave with closed glottis (peak pressure) and open lips (minimum pressure). Negative = the wave travelling back. Dotted line added to show a full wavelength.*

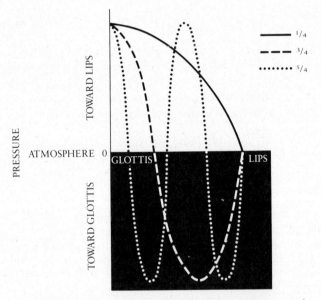

Figure 6.8 *Many waves with maximum pressure at the glottis and minimum pressure at the lips. This illustrates how ¼ of a low frequency wave, ¾ of a medium frequency wave, and 1¼ of a high frequency wave fit in the same space.*

Stop Consonants.   Figure 6.10 displays spectrograms of the stop consonants before the vowel /a/ spoken by an adult male speaker. Recall that a spectrogram displays the energy at different frequencies (y-axis) with respect to time (x-axis). Energy amplitude is indicated by the relative darkness—white is no energy, black much energy, and so forth. Notice for each the general grayness of the picture: Gray indicates the presence of energy, and the gray field indicates that there is some energy

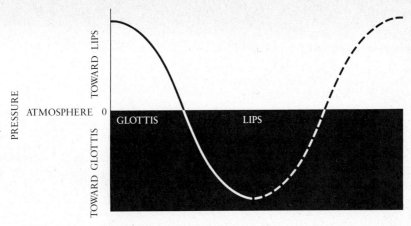

Figure 6.9 *Schematic pressure wave for closed glottis and closed lips (pressure peaks = deviations from 0 at both places). The dotted line shows the full wavelength of which ½ is in the mouth.*

at most frequencies. Places where there is complete white within a spectrogram are places where the vocal tract has absorbed the energy—known as *zeros, antiformants,* or *antiresonances.* The darkest bands are places where the energy is maintained or amplified, and these are the resonances or formant frequencies. Notice that for each syllable there are several formants. Formants are usually counted from the lowest frequency (= the first) to the highest. The central frequency in the band is usually used as the formant frequency.

Obvious on each of the spectrograms are regular gray striations, running vertically. These represent the energy released when the vocal cords open; the white between them, the absence of energy while the vocal cords are closed. Notice that they are *periodic*—they appear regularly. You might also notice their absence in the initial portion of the voiceless stops /pa/, /ta/, and /ka/: For the first ¼ inch or so of these spectrograms, most obviously on /ta/, there is an even, nonperiodic energy distribution. Recall that for voiceless sounds the vocal cords do not vibrate, so we should not expect to see the gray striations until voicing begins for the vowel.

The next thing you might notice for these spectrograms is that the formants are similarly shaped for /ba/ and /pa/, /da/ and /ta/, and /ga/ and /ka/—trace the dark bands through the noise portion into the striped portion on the voiceless consonants. For /ba/ and /pa/ there is a large, heavy, straight band crossing the 1000 Hz line, another band that seems to start at about 2200 Hz, which then rises to 2600 Hz, and another straight band at 3200 Hz. For /da/ and /ta/ the lowest band seems to start at 200, then rises to about 750, where it overlaps a second band centered at 1000 falling from 1700. The third, wobbly band seems centered at about 2300 Hz, and there is a fourth band at about 3200 Hz. For /ga/ and /ka/ we have similar first, second, and fourth formants to /da/ and /ta/, but the third formant meets the second at the start (about 1700 Hz) and then rises to 2300 Hz. (Note that the single dark band in /ba/ and /pa/ is likely to be *two* formants that are too close to differentiate. This is likely because the same vocal tract is producing all the sounds, all the sounds use the

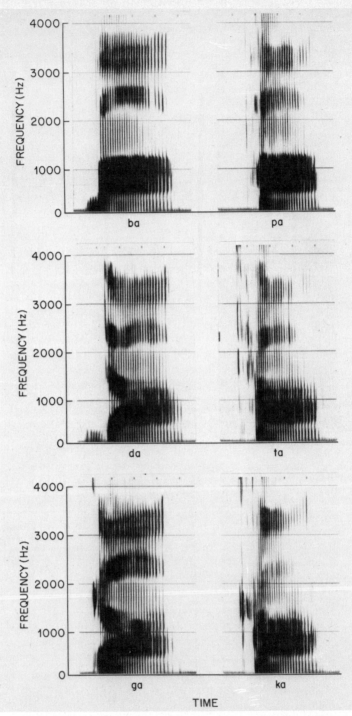

Figure 6.10 *Spectrograms of the stop consonants of English in the context /Ca/.*

vowel /a/, and the other places of articulation have these as clearly separable formants.)

In our description it was necessary to refer to two frequencies for most of the sounds, the starting frequency and the frequency attained after a time. Examination of the spectrograms indicates that each formant has two connected parts, a part that changes in frequency and a part where the frequency remains steady. The first is called the *transition,* and the second the *steady state.* The transition can be conceptualized as reflecting the movement from the initial mouth position to the position for the vowel. The steady states represent the sustained vowel, and for these spectrograms, should occur at roughly the same frequencies, since the vowel is the same. In Box 6.2 the difference in frequencies for the open vocal tract of the vowel and the closed vocal tract for various consonants is derived, for the interested reader.

Other Consonants. Figure 6.11 displays spectrograms of the other English consonants in front of the vowel /a/. The top row shows the labials, the next the dental fricatives, then the alveolars, then the palatal fricative, and finally the alveolar affricate. The far left shows the nasals, the middle the voiced fricatives, and the far right the voiceless fricatives. Having looked at the stop consonants, we should be expecting certain acoustic features for these other classes. For the labials, the transitions should be slightly rising or straight; for the alveolars the first transition should rise, the second fall, and the third "wobble"; for the back (close to velar) consonants there should be a meeting of the second and third transitions. As you can see, these do appear in the spectrograms. We should also expect to see noise for the voiceless consonants initially, and striations for the voiced, as we do.

The question is, how is manner conveyed acoustically? For fricatives, there is more noise initially than for stops or nasals. This is most obvious on /ša/ and /ča/ but may also be seen on /va/, /fa/, /θa/, and /sa/. If you contrast the nasals with the voiced fricatives, you see what looks like an earlier and weaker energy at each of the nasal formant frequencies, particularly obvious for /ma/. These are nasal resonances; there is "leak" through the nose after voicing onset but before the release. If you reexamine Figure 6.10 you will note this does not happen for the stops; rather the release is abrupt, sometimes with a short burst of energy (about 1750 Hz for /ga/ and /ka/ and spread between 1500 Hz and 3000 Hz for /ta/). The *burst* is characteristic of stops, the *nasal murmur* of nasals, and the *frication noise* of fricatives.

Vowels. Figure 6.12 shows a number of the vowels of English produced in the context h-vowel-d. As you may recall "h" is a voiceless vowel, so we should see no transitions in initial position but noise-excited formants switching to striped formants at voicing onset. (The noise is most obvious on the spectrograms for /hid/, /hɛd/ and /hæd/.) We should see transitions at the end of each spectrogram, appropriate to /d/. Since the consonant is in the final position the first formant should fall to its offset frequency instead of rising from its onset frequency, and there should be similar reversals for the other formants. Note that the transitions are very different for /d/ in /hid/ from /d/ in /hɔd/, for example; an instance of *context-sensitivity* of the consonant to the vowel.

Aside from the change in transitions for /d/ across vowels, we can see that the

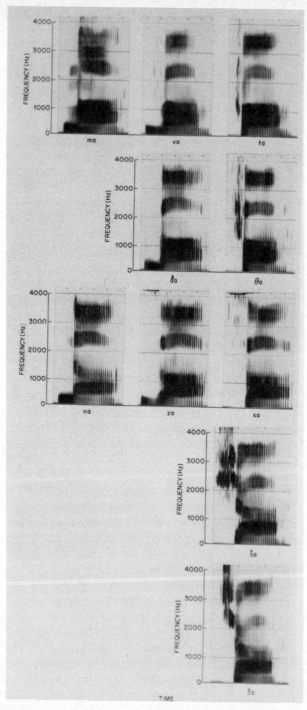

Figure 6.11 *Spectrograms of the nasals, fricatives and affricates of English in the context /Ca/.*

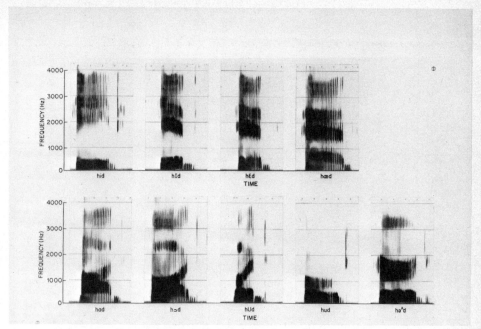

Figure 6.12   *Spectrograms of some English vowels, in the context /hVd/.*

steady state frequencies differ for each vowel. For /i/ the first formant is low, and it rises some for /I/, /ɛ/, and /ae/. The second and third formants fall from /i/ through /u/. The second formant for /i/, for instance, seems to be centered just above 2000 Hz, for /I/ on 2000, for /ɛ/ just under it, and for /a/, as we have noted, almost at 1000 Hz. (For those who worked through Box 6.2, note that "constriction" is in the front for /i/, creating a short cavity in front and a high second formant; while for /u/ with "constriction" at the back, and liprounding, the front cavity is the longest, creating a maximally low second formant, which blends with the first formant.)

Nonsegmental Differences.   The top of the last two sets of spectrograms shows the effects of vocal tract differences arising independently of speech-specific manipulations. The top of Figure 6.13 compares a male speaker's /ga/ (a) with a female speaker's /ga/ (d) at the bottom. In this case a shorter vocal tract results from a difference in physical size. Panels b and c represent sounds created by machine from the sounds in panels a and d. Panel b shows a sound with the same formant frequencies as panel d, but the pitch of the sound in panel a. Panel c displays a sound with the same formant frequencies as the sound shown in panel a, but the pitch characteristics of the female who spoke the sound in d. Comparing a and b (or d) you can see that the formants occur at higher frequencies for the female than for the male as we would predict. Comparing a and c (or d) you can see that the glottal pulses, the gray striations, are much closer together for the female, so close that it is impossible to count them. This illustrates the two basic differences in male and female voices: Females have higher formants and a higher rate of laryngeal pulsing. Comparison of the nat-

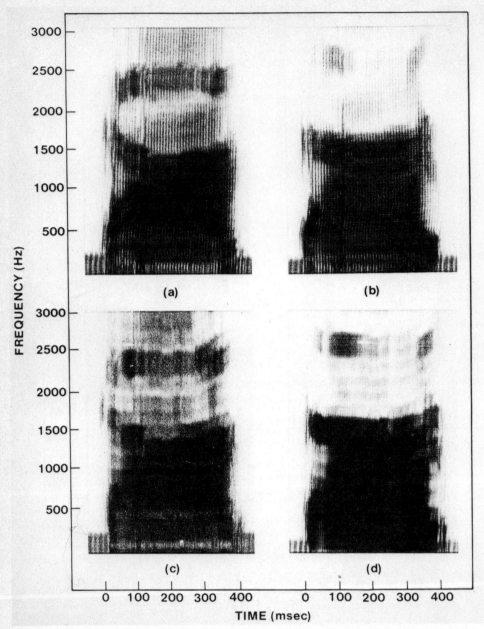

Figure 6.13 *Spectrograms of /ga/ produced by a male (a) and a female (d). Spectrograms (b) and (c) were produced by computer: (b) shows the female formants of (d) excited by the male pitch of (a), and (c) shows the male formants of (a) excited by the female pitch of (d).*

ural sound in a and d with the machine-generated sounds of b and c illustrates the relative independence of source and filter. The formant patterns are relatively similar regardless of the change in pitch. Interestingly, the female filter excited by the male pitch sounds like an old woman, and the male filter excited by the female pitch, like a preadolescent boy.

Figure 6.14 shows another effect of shortening the vocal tract; a comparison of a male /ga/ produced with a straight face (left) and with a smile (right). The retraction of the lips causes a rise in formant frequency for all three formants. For example, the second formant of the straight-faced /ga/ crosses the 1000 Hz line, while for the smiled /ga/ it is clearly above it, showing the increase in frequency. The change produced by smiling did not affect the characteristic divergence of the second and third formants. Smiling and /ga/ thus are conveyed simultaneously in the pattern, another instance of "context-sensitivity," since smiling clearly affects the formant frequency pattern.

Summary

This section has described some simplified acoustic theory for understanding the sound signal giving rise to speech. We noted that there are two contributing and almost independent factors: the source (vocal cord vibration or noise) and the filter (the shape and length of the vocal tract). Manipulations of the source give rise to changes in periodic pulsing visible on the spectrogram either as pitch changes or as changes from voicelessness to voicing. Manipulations of the filter by constricting in different places, protruding the lips (lengthening or shortening the "tube"), or open-

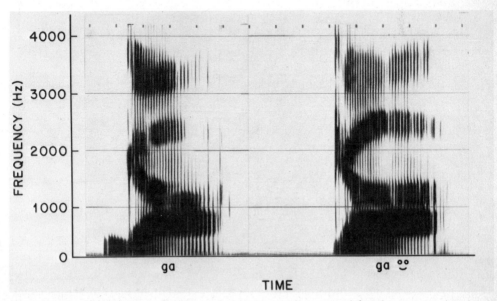

Figure 6.14 *Spectrograms of male producing /ga/ with a normal facial expression (on the left) and while smiling (on the right).*

ing or closing the nasal passages affect the position of the vocal resonances or formants. We see on the spectrograms effects of the resonances at constriction in the bursts for stops and the frication noise for fricatives. We also see the addition of resonance contributed by the nose in nasals. The place of constriction also affects the frequencies of the formants, so as the mouth moves from a consonant to a vowel (of a different place), we see changes in frequencies called transitions. The pattern on the spectrogram is determined jointly by the consonant constriction and the vowel "constriction," so the spectrogram for the same consonant in different vowel environments will be different. This is called context-sensitivity. The pattern on the spectrograms is also determined by the absolute size of the vocal tract and so differs with individuals and with different facial expressions.

Linguistic Feature Theory

Distinctive Features

The last two sections have described, respectively, articulatory and acoustic aspects of speech under the general framework of linguistic distinctive feature theory (Jakobson, Fant, and Halle, 1951/1969). The assumptions of the theory have been implicitly employed; here we make them explicit.

Phonemes may be considered bundles of subphonemic features. /b/ is a voiced, bilabial stop consonant, /p/ a voiceless bilabial stop consonant, /t/ a voiceless alveolar stop consonant, and so on. We may wish to think of each phoneme as a minimal sound unit—we cannot articulate voicing independent of place and manner so the bundle must have integrity; or we may wish to think of the phoneme as the combination of subphonemic features that are relatively independent. The difference between /bæt/ and /pæt/ may be viewed as a difference in the initial phonemes or as a difference in voicing in the initial segment, or, since there are coarticulation effects or context-sensitivity, as a difference in the entire syllable.

Critical to the flexibility of the description of phonemes or syllables as bundles of features is the assumption that at some level the features are independent of one another, and, as the preceding discussions indicated, this may be reasonable. Closing the lips or touching the tongue tip to the roof of the mouth does not appear to be dependent on whether or not the vocal cords are vibrating, or whether the nasal resonance chamber is open or not. Acoustically, the direction and location of the formant transitions (place information) do not appear dependent on the presence of periodic pulsing or aspiration (voicing), or on the existence of frication noise, a burst, or a nasal murmur (manner). Thus, each linguistic feature has its own articulatory and acoustic properties, apart from other linguistic features.

Considering the subphonemic features as units of speech has other implications besides independence. First, if subphonemic features are units, then some distinctions between sounds may be equated. If /b/ and /p/ differ in voicing as do /d/ and /t/, and voicing is an independent unit, the difference between /b/ and /p/ should equal that between /d/ and /t/ or /z/ and /s/. Second, the assumption of subphonemic features as units defines some differences, namely, if /b/ and /p/ differ in voicing and

/b/ and /d/ differ in place, and /b/ and /t/ differ in voicing and place, then /b/ and /t/ should be more distinct than /b/ and /p/ or /b/ and /d/ because they are two features apart rather than just one.

Finally, the assumption of a hierarchy of features suggests that some feature distinctions are more salient than others—a consonant and a vowel differ in one feature, as do /b/ and /p/, but the consonant-vowel distinction *seems* more important, discriminable, distinctive. Under the framework we have outlined this is so, actually, since the consonant-vowel distinction entails a number of other feature distinctions: Consonants have manner, place, and voicing, most of which we do not have to consider for vowels.

The precise features best used to describe the articulatory and acoustic aspects of speech have been a matter of some debate among linguists (see Chomsky and Halle, 1968, for one description; Jakobson, Fant, and Halle, 1951/1969, for another). It is important to note that the features presented here are not consistent with orthodox linguistic theory but are sufficient to give a general idea of the theory. One principal difference derives from an interest in having each feature represent a binary distinction. This works well for voicing (in English)—we can have +voiced or −voiced, or for consonant-vowel (+consonantal), −consonantal, but some distinctions, like place, are multivalued and do not lend themselves readily to a two-valued feature system. The solution has been to describe them by using *sets* of two-valued features. For example, Jakobson et al. define the features compact-diffuse and grave-acute to account for place distinctions. *Compact* consonants (or vowels) are those with large cavities in front of the constriction relative to the size of the cavity behind the constriction; /d/ and /g/ are compact, and /b/ *diffuse. Grave* consonants (or vowels) are those with a generally large, undivided vocal cavity: /b/ and /g/ are grave, and /d/ *acute.* Thus, as Table 6.2 indicates, place of articulation may be described, instead of as one three-valued feature, as two two-valued features, with each consonant having a unique pattern of plusses and minuses. It is also important to note that in Jakobson et al. (1951/1969) the same features are used to describe the vowels as the consonants: /i/ and /u/ are diffuse since the tongue tip is high; /a/, with a high tongue back is compact, for example.

Sound Structure: Review and Overview

At this point, we have essentially concluded our discussion of the structure of language, at all levels—semantic, syntactic, and phonetic. You may well be over-

Table 6.2 *Analysis of place as two binary features. Note the pattern of plusses and minuses is unique for each phoneme.*

	± compact	± grave
b	−	+
d	+	−
g	+	+

whelmed with the complexity of language structure ... at the sound level alone. To utter a targeted nonsense word requires a precise coordination of breathing, laryngeal pulsing, movements of tongue, lip, and velum—each of which has its own individual effect on the sound. To make a syllable or a word sound like American English, the King's English, French, or Swahili requires a precise knowledge of the sounds that language employs, the ways in which those sounds may combine, and the melody or register with which they are spoken. If each morpheme, syllable, or word is learned as a pattern independent of all others, the memory load is enormous—every language uses a large number of syllables, words, and sentences. If particular elements and rules for combining those elements are learned and then used productively, the task is much reduced.

Let us examine a few examples of this. The plural morpheme has a number of phonetic realizations in English: [s], [z], [əz] (as well as nothing, as in "deer"). It is true also of the past morpheme—we may mark the past tense by using (among others) the sounds [t], [d], and [əd]. How do we learn which verbs take which past tense and which nouns which plurals? Examination of the following table may clarify this: In the first column there is a word that may be either a noun or verb, followed by its plural and past forms, both transcribed. The last four rows contain nonsense words and a native speaker's judgment of their likely plural and past forms. Before looking at them, make the plural and past yourself and see if you agree.

WORD	PLURAL	PAST
dog	dɔgz	dɔgd
tip	tIps	tIpt
kiss	kIsəz	kIst
cart	kaɚts	kaɚtəd
wug	wʌgz	wʌgd
wuk	wʌks	wʌkt
wut	wʌts	wʌtəd
wuss	wʌssəz	wʌst

Do you notice a pattern? If you agreed with my intuitions on the nonsense words, you must have absorbed the pattern, at least tacitly, because a random agreement is unlikely. Explicitly, the rule for both plural and past morphemes (note that this is another morphophonemic rule) is: (1) match voicing with the last phoneme in the syllable, and (2) if the last phoneme has the same place and manner of articulation as the sound to be added (alveolar fricative for the plural and alveolar stop for the past), add the vowel, and then the voiced phoneme—in this case, voiced because it must match the vowel added, which is voiced. The rule means that we do not have to learn book-books, plant-plants, seat-seats, and so forth, separately. The matching rule is called *assimilation,* and languages use assimilation sometimes across more than one phoneme. The addition of the vowel for otherwise identical endings is an instance of the opposite "force," *dissimilation,* which also operates in languages. Alliteration, the poetic device, selects words so that there is a sound match like assimilation across several phonemes, as does rhyming. A less artificial use of assimilation is in a phenomenon called *vowel harmony,* in which the vowel in the affix is matched to the vowel of the principal morpheme. In an East Sudan language, Moru, we find ma'la'sa (I wash), mɔ'lɔ'sɔ' (I served), mi'liite (I wept) and mu'tu'ri (I fear). m + vowel = the prefixed pronoun "I"; which vowel is determined by the verb (Heffner, 1969).

The existence of rules does not mean that all sound combinations are rule-governed. As a language grows and incorporates elements from other languages, there may be exceptions introduced or exceptions left as residues. Mao Tse-tung caused an introduction of a new affricate—/ts/, which does not usually appear in English in initial position. If his name became incorporated into the language the /ts/ might alter to /č/, a usual English affricate, or /s/, the usual fricative. We see "chic" pronounced "chick" in a similar modification/incorporation into the language. If many words came in using the /ts/ affricate, we might add that form or replace a form we now use with it. Then it would be productive, that is, used in the generation of new words. The "ed" past is now productive. Probably at some time past tenses were made by using a vowel change, leaving us the residues sing-sang-sung, ring-rang-rung, swim-swam-swum. However, we no longer do this regularly, and so it is no longer productive.

It is not our intent to supply an exhaustive list of sound rules but just to give a hint about how they operate—and a hint at the different levels they may operate on. As we have stated, all languages make use of the same features: These are determined by properties of the vocal tract and auditory system, shared by all human beings. Which features are linguistically distinctive, how they combine, and what level the feature or combination operates on are determined by each language. *We* do not use /ŋ/ in initial position, consonant clusters like /mb/ initially, register changes, or tone for phonemic distinctions.

There is nothing "natural" about our selection; other languages use these distinctions. Each language selects from the audible group of sounds a set to use to produce words, and to convey emotion and syntax. Selection is constrained in part by production—no language would choose an absolute pitch as phonemic since men, women, or children might not be able to produce that exact note. It is also constrained in part by the desire to be understood: Use of all possible sounds we can produce to convey meaning distinctions would require us to make enormously fine discriminations; classing together some of them allows us to ignore some distinctions. (It has been estimated that *all* languages use eight or nine distinctive features [Miller, 1956], perhaps indicating the limit of our discrimination capabilities.) Selecting sounds so that there are few words differing only in one feature, so that some features are conveyed redundantly (for example, voicing in both the final phoneme and the plural) enhances the chances of being understood. Sound selection is a product of two forces: (1) the need to have as few rules or elements as possible to minimize the amount that must be learned (this means that any rule or element introduced is likely to be used over and over again, or be productive), and (2) the desire to maximize discriminability (this means that a sufficient number of different elements must be used to be able to tell them apart).

In this chapter the structure of sound and the utility of that structure for language description were explored. In the next chapter we examine the psychological reality of the sound structure—how we use acoustic features, articulatory features, linguistic distinctive features, phonemes, syllables, and so forth, in perceiving and producing language.

REFERENCES

Abercrombie, D. (1967). *Elements of General Phonetics*. Chicago: Aldine Publishing Company.

Chomsky, N., & Halle, M. (1968). *The Sound Pattern of English*. NY: Harper & Row.

Fant, C. G. M. (1956). On the predictability of formant levels and spectrum envelopes from formant frequencies. In M. Halle, H. Lunt, & H. MacLean (Eds.). *For Roman Jakobson* (pp. 109–120). The Hague: Mouton.

Fant, G. (1973). *Speech Sounds and Features*. Cambridge, MA: MIT Press.

Heffner, R-M. S. (1969). *General Phonetics*. Madison, WI: University of Wisconsin Press.

Jakobson, R., Fant, G., & Halle, M. (1951/1969). *Preliminaries to Speech Analysis*. Cambridge, MA: MIT Press.

Lieberman, P. (1967). *Intonation, Perception, and Language*. Cambridge, MA: MIT Press.

———. (1975). *On the Origins of Language: An Introduction to the Evolution of Human Speech*. NY: Macmillan.

Miller, G. A. (1956). The magical number seven plus or minus two: Some limits on our capacity for processing information. *Psychological Review, 63,* 81–96.

Stevens, K. N., & House, A. S. (1961). An acoustical theory of vowel production and some of its implications. *Journal of Speech and Hearing Research, 4,* 303–320.

Tartter, V. C., & Blumstein, S. E. (1981). The effect of pitch and spectral differences on phonetic fusion in dichotic listening. *Journal of Phonetics, 9,* 251–259.

Tartter, V. C. (1980). Happy talk: Perceptual and acoustic effects of smiling on speech. *Perception & Psychophysics, 27,* 24–27.

STUDY QUESTIONS

1. Write your name in phonemic transcription. Then make a schematized spectrogram for the first name (or the first syllable of your first name, if your first name is long). (Note that /ǰ/ is a voiced /č/, /w/ is a /b/ with lengthened transitions, and /l/ is a /d/ with lengthened transitions. The other phonemes should appear already in the spectrograms provided.) You should have problems making your spectrogram—discuss the problems and how they relate to context–sensitivity. What would the spectrogram look like if your name was spoken by a child?

2. The following is written in phonemic transcription. Translate it back to written English. aⁱ hæv čozən nat tu ˈuz ə pom, wič maˈt bi ɚɛkəgnaˈzd, nɔɚ ɛni wɛlnoᵘn pæsəj, sIns ðɛn ɚidʌndɛnsi kUd hɛlp. si haᵘ izi It Iz tu du "tu bi ɔɚ nat tu bi, ðæt Iz ðə kwɛsčʌn," fɔɚ InstIns.

7

Speech Perception and Production

When next you have the opportunity to talk with a small group of people, pay attention to what is happening during the conversation. First, how do you understand what each person is saying? Listen as each says the same one syllable word "hi"— they all sound different, you can recognize each voice, and at the same time they all obviously say the same thing; you can recognize the word(s) despite the different voices saying it. What is the same about each articulation?

Second, as the conversation gets beyond the slurred greeting stage, listen to how fast we talk. Average articulation is 900 phonemes per minute (Liberman, Cooper, Shankweiler, and Studdert-Kennedy, 1967). If musical notes were played at that rate, they would blur (sound like a buzz) the way a guitar string looks blurry as you watch it vibrate—too fast for the perceptual system to see or hear each movement. Why does speech not similarly blur?

Third, consider how well the word boundaries are marked; how it seems easy to note which syllables or which phoneme belongs to which word. Figure 7.1 shows a spectrogram of a sentence articulated normally. There are spaces on the spectrogram, between acoustic features, like aspiration and transitions, *within a phoneme,* and not between words. Where *are* the word boundaries we so clearly hear in the language? Probably we put them in *as we listen.* The next time you have the chance to eavesdrop on a conversation in a language you do not know, try to figure out where the words are; the boundaries are as hard to locate by ear, if we have no mental dictionary, as they are by eye on the spectrogram. So how do we do it in our own aural language?

Fourth, think about what you are doing as a participant in the conversation: You have probably contributed your greeting, have extracted everyone's phonemes and glued them together into words, glued the words together into sentences, parsed the sentences to find meaning, looked up the words in the lexicon, started a discourse parse, perhaps contributed your own response—formulating your idea, finding words and a syntactic form to express it, appropriately choreographing your articulators, checking the ongoing conversation for "your turn" to say it without interrupting, and monitoring your audience for their reaction. And at the *same* time, if you have followed these instructions, you have also thought about variation in voices, speech

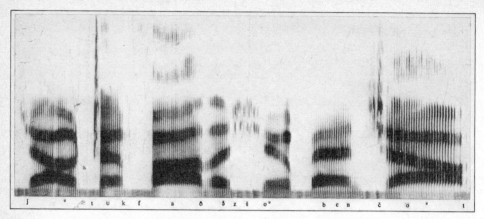

Figure 7.1 *Spectrogram of the sentence "Joe took father's shoe bench out." Note that the pauses, the absence of energy, are not between the words.*

rates, word boundaries, and how you process during conversation—all of which, unless you are talking to psycholinguists, is likely to be unrelated to the conversation at hand. How do we do so much in a seemingly short time, almost unconsciously?

And we do it all with very few errors. How often does anyone make a mistake while talking—come out with the wrong word, the wrong phoneme, the wrong intonation, the wrong syntactic frame? When you think about it, you realize that it occurs very seldom actually, although it happens to all of us occasionally. When a slip is made usually the speaker corrects it, which indicates that in addition to all the things just mentioned we monitor our own speech (listen to it) to make sure our mouths are saying what we think they should be.

In this chapter we will explore the available evidence on how we do what should seem impossible: perceive and produce meaningful sound sequences at conversational rates.

Linguistic Features and Psychological Reality

We can conceptualize the perception (or production) of speech as the interaction of two processes: one that recognizes (or produces) particular units, and another that glues these units together. There is a tradeoff in describing the processes: If we assume that the unit extracted is large, like a word or a sentence, it is easy to describe the gluing process (since little has to be joined), but hard to describe the recognition process (since there will be a great many pattern recognizers). Alternatively, if we assume a small unit in recognition, there will be relatively few to describe, but it will be harder to describe the process of putting them together. For example, suppose that speech is recognized either phoneme by phoneme or word by word. There are forty phonemes in English, which means there would have to be forty pattern recognizers, one for each phoneme. Each of these would have to discover its pattern despite the "smear," the variation produced by coarticulation, tones of voice, speaker differences, and allophones. To recognize a five-phoneme word, then, information from five of these phoneme recognizers would have to be integrated. Now suppose that words instead of phonemes are recognized at the outset. We may eliminate the information integration stage, but this saving is compensated for by extra recognizing problems. Ignoring the fact that some phonemes cannot appear in all positions, we can estimate that if there are forty phonemes in English, there are on the order of $40 \times 40 \times 40 \times 40 \times 40$ possible five-phoneme words which we would have to be able to detect. Thus, we would need that many more word recognizers.

Neither phoneme nor word detection or creation has been the most popular unit with which to begin speech recognition or production, but they do illustrate the limitations of larger or smaller units as starting places. The units most commonly proposed have been phonetic features (like voicing, manner, etc.) and syllables, although occasionally other unit sizes are mentioned. We begin with features, in part because there will be fewer pattern recognizers to describe; in part, because as we have already seen, their relation to articulatory gestures and parts of spectrograms is easy to describe; and, in part, because there is a fair amount of evidence for their psychological reality. Thus, we will assume that in normal speech recognizing there is a mental process looking for each feature. The question is: What aspects of the speech signal will cause the process to "think" it has found its feature?

Features in Speech Perception

Recall the linguistic feature model presented in the last chapter. For that model, it was assumed that phonemes consist of bundles of independent features, and that these features are arranged hierarchically: The consonant-vowel feature is the most important division, followed by manner, then voicing, then place. To demonstrate the psychological reality of the model, then, we need to show that speech perception and/or production are organized in independent linguistic features, and that some of these feature distinctions are more salient than others. These points have been tested by using measures of scaling and confusion.

Scaling Studies. In scaling, subjects are asked to rank stimuli on the basis of some quality. For example, vinegar, lemons, oranges, and raspberries might be ranked, in that order, on the basis of sweetness. Numbers may be assigned to each stimulus, representing the size of the response on the dimension: I find vinegar to have 0 sweetness, lemons to be a bit sweeter ($=1$), oranges to be much sweeter ($=10$), and raspberries somewhat sweeter than oranges ($=13$). (Each person is likely to have a different subjective response and a different use of numbers.) This technique is called *magnitude estimation*. We may estimate also the psychological distance between pairs of stimuli rather than the size of the response. For me, vinegar and lemons are close—a distance of 1—and oranges are much farther, a distance of 10 but close to raspberries in sweetness. It is important to note that we might get very different orderings for dimensions other than sweetness; temperature would rank them all together, neutrally; texture would put oranges and lemons together away from vinegar and raspberries. Thus, our perceptual space, like semantic space, is multidimensional.

Now, how would you rank /b/, /d/, /m/, /n/, /s/, and /z/ in terms of perceptual similarity? *After* you make your judgment, you might note that /b/ and /d/ share manner and voicing, /b/ and /n/ share only voicing, and /b/ and /s/ share no features other than consonantal. Did your similarity ratings reflect the feature differences such that the more features the two sounds shared, the more similar they seemed? This is the classic result found by Greenberg and Jenkins (1964) for features in stop consonants, and by Mohr and Wang (1968) for nasals and stops. Note that the results suggest perception in terms of features, with greater feature differences producing a greater psychological distance. The results also supported the hierarchy notion: Nasal-stop distinctions or voicing distinctions produced greater distance estimates than did place differences. However, there is some indication from scaling studies that features may not be completely independent, since some feature differences are more distinctive in some contexts than others. For example, place of articulation differences were perceived as more marked in voiceless stops than in voiced stops, indicating that voicing affects perceived similarity in place of articulation.

Confusions in Noise.   Psychological distance may also be measured indirectly, by seeing which stimuli subjects are likely to confuse. For example, if you taste a sauce and guess that there is vinegar in it when in fact it has lemon juice, we can assume that your confusion arose because vinegar and lemon juice give rise to similar sensations. Are you more likely to hear "dill" when "bill" was said than you are to hear "mill" or "till?" You might argue that you are unlikely to hear anything but "bill," and normally, this is true; if someone says "the duck has a fish in his bill" even if you do not hear the "b" you will correctly guess it, as we will show experimentally later this chapter. However, if the syllable is nonsense and is presented in isolation and with background noise to make listening difficult, confusions may be generated.

Using this procedure, Miller and Nicely (1955) demonstrated that consonant-initial syllables were confused within phonetic feature categories. A reanalysis of their results (Wish and Carroll, 1974) is displayed in Figure 7.2. There are six dimensions accounting for the confusions; the most important—the ones accounting for the most confusions—are the first and second (left-hand panel), roughly manner (nasal vs. stop-fricative) and voicing. Sounds located close together are sounds confused with one another frequently, so m-n are often confused but not often confused with the stops and fricatives. The less important dimensions (last panel), especially dimension 6, separated confusions across place of articulation; there is a small tendency to confuse labial and dental sounds like /b, ð, v/, apart from alveolar sounds like /z, ž, n/. Again these results suggest that our speech-sound space is organized on feature lines with features high in the hierarchy perceived as more salient.

Confusions in Dichotic Listening.   Besides adding noise or removing parts of the sound, we can create perceptual difficulties by having subjects listen to two sounds at the same time, one in each ear, called *dichotic listening.* This technique has been used primarily to assess brain organization with respect to sound, to be discussed later in this chapter, but it has also been used to study confusion patterns (see Blumstein, 1974; Pisoni, 1975a; Studdert-Kennedy and Shankweiler, 1970). Pairs of stop consonants (/ba, da, ga, pa, ta, ka/) are more accurately perceived if the members of the pair share

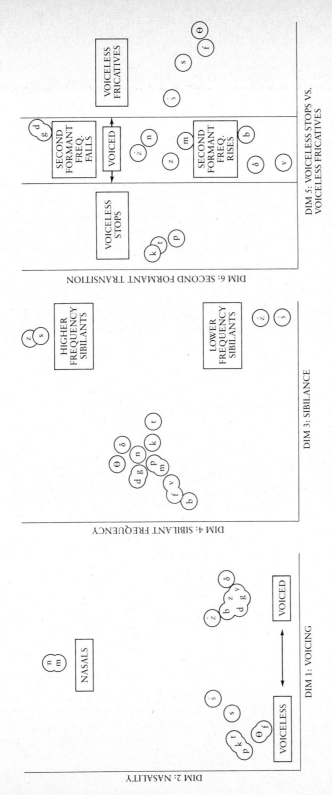

Figure 7.2 A multidimensional space depicting consonant confusions. Sounds close to one another are easily confused. Thus, in the first panel are voiced stops and voiced fricatives (right) which are easily confused with each other, but not with voiceless stops and fricatives (left) or nasals (top). Dimensions 3 and 4 show separate confusions for fricatives apart from the other manner classes, and separate high and low frequency fricatives. Dimensions 5 and 6 show further separation within manner classes, and place of articulation differences. From "Applications of individual differences scaling to studies of human perception and judgment" by M. Wish and J. D. Carroll in Handbook of Perception, vol 2, pp. 472–473, 1974. NY: Academic Press. Copyright 1974 by Academic Press. Reprinted by permission.

voicing (as in, /ba-da/) or place (as in, /ba-pa/) than if they differ in both voicing and place (as in, /ba-ta/). The errors usually take the form of an assimilation with a feature of one of the members of the pair. For example, /ba-ta/ is much more likely to be misheard as /ba-da/, with the /t/ becoming voiced like the /b/, than as /ba-ka/. Finally, and perhaps most exciting, is the occurrence of an unusually large proportion of *double blend errors*. If the pair /ba-ta/ is presented and subjects get *both* syllables wrong (=double), they can report /da-pa/, /da-ga/, /da-ka/, /ga-pa/, /ka-pa/, or /ga-ka/. If the double error is the result of a random guess—no information is preserved—the probability of any one of these responses is 1/6 or about 17 percent. In fact subjects report /da-pa/ significantly more often (for /ba-ta/) than would be expected—64 percent of the time (Studdert-Kennedy and Shankweiler, 1970). Note the interesting relation of /d-p/ to /b-t/. Both pairs contain the features alveolar, voiced, bilabial, voiceless but in different combinations—as though the sounds were heard in terms of features and the information about which voicing value went with which place value was independently forgotten. (Double blend errors are more frequent than chance for all double contrast pairs, not just /b-t/.) Unfortunately, although dichotic listening has shown strong support for perception of stop consonants by means of distinctive features, dichotic tests using syllables that differ in manner (like /fa/, /ma/, /sa/) (Blumstein, 1974) or vowel (Blumstein, Tartter, Michel, Hirsch, and Leiter, 1977), do not similarly show perceptual advantages for feature sharing or feature blending. In part this is because there are too few errors to analyze.

Detection of Mispronunciations.   The last method used for generating confusions in speech perception has been to present subjects with spoken text in which errors are deliberately placed and then analyze the probability that the errors are detected (Cole, 1973). Single feature errors are harder to detect than errors of more features, supporting the feature model. It is interesting to note further that errors are differentially detectable depending on which syllable of a word they are in and depending on grammatical and semantic cohesiveness of the text. We will return to these results in the section on top-down processing; for now be aware that more is involved in speech perception than is apparent from processing results for isolated syllables.

Features in Speech Production

On the production side, speech errors or slips of the tongue also indicate that features have psychological reality. Confusion patterns show that a sound substituted for another is more likely to share phonological features, and usually, one-feature errors occur more frequently than two, and so on (Fromkin, 1973, 1980). For example, if a person is trying to say "but," (s)he is more likely to say "dut" than "cut" if (s)he makes an error. Given that most feature systems are based at least in part on articulation, this is not terribly surprising on one level—it suggests that articulatory gestures are independent of one another. On another level, though, this is surprising because the gestures are produced as a package, and it is not obvious that each would be independently controlled (generally, for example, our eyes move together, under control of one motor command).

In addition to the occurrence of more single-feature substitutions than double, the production data look like perception data in other ways. Examination of slips of the tongue made in many languages shows little interference between voiced and voiceless pairs and between manner classes; nasals, semivowels (/r/, /l/), and voiceless fricative-affricates (/s/, /š/, /č/) all show slips within their class but little confusion among them (van den Broeke and Goldstein, 1980). (It is interesting to note further that in a specific test of different feature systems mentioned at the end of Chapter 6, that of Jakobson, Fant, and Halle (1951/1969) accounted for the slips of the tongue better than any other.)

Summary

There is a reasonable amount of evidence supporting features as a primary unit of perception and of production. Features seem to be independently extracted from the speech signal and separately confusable. They also appear independent and separately confusable from analysis of speech errors in production. Phonemes two features apart are more distinct than phonemes one feature apart. Phonemes differing in a high-level feature are more distinct than phonemes differing in a low-level feature. The only note of caution to be sounded is the dependence of processing of some feature values on others. Place of articulation differences were scaled closer in voiced stops than in voiceless stops. Dichotic tests using nasals and fricatives yielded fewer errors than similar tests using stops, suggesting that voicing and place differences are more perceptible in those manner classes. However, for now, the linguistic feature model is a good place to begin discussion of speech as a pattern to be recognized.

Perceiving and Producing Linguistic Features

The Problem of Pattern Recognition

Now that we have seen that it is reasonable to assume that distinctive features are extracted in perception of speech, it is time to turn to the question of which aspects of the acoustic indicate signal their presence—the problem of pattern recognition. In the last chapter we suggested some candidates for acoustic *cues* to distinctive features, portions of the signal that trigger representation of the feature. These include burst and frication noise, which contain information about manner and place of constriction; aspiration and periodic pulsing, which contain information about voicing; direction and location of formant frequencies, which contain information about place of articulation; and steady state frequencies, which contain information about the vowel. This is a simple model of pattern recognition in which there is one aspect of the acoustic signal that we assume is detected, cues the pattern recognizer for the feature, and allows the feature to be detected.

If this is the way speech is perceived we would expect, for example, that if we remove the burst of a stop consonant and present the burst in isolation we would hear a "pure stop consonant" with no particular vowel. This would indicate that the burst was *sufficient* to cue a stop consonant. What would we expect the remainder of the signal, the transitions plus steady states, to sound like? According to our simple proposal, this should sound like a place of articulation and a vowel but with the burst gone, not like a stop consonant in particular. If removal of the burst prevents perception of a stop, we can say that the burst is *necessary* to perceive a stop consonant.

One important type of sufficient cue is an *invariant,* a cue that does not change in different contexts. For speech, that means that it should appear regardless of the other features of the phoneme (a burst should not depend on voicing value), regardless of position in the syllable (a burst should signal stop consonants in consonant-vowel [CV] and vowel-consonant [VC] syllables), and regardless of the surrounding vowel (the burst should appear in /ba/ as well as /bi/). Finally, it should not be affected by context beyond the syllable—as in a word with a different vowel earlier in the sentence. If a cue alters as a result of any of these factors, it is not invariant but *context-sensitive.* Context-sensitivity implies problems for pattern recognition, since the pattern recognizer cannot just search for a single "true" cue but may have to search for several different cues depending on the context. This problem becomes particularly troublesome if the context is hard to identify or the cue is ambiguous, say, if in some environments the cue means /d/ and in others /b/. If our perception is not similarly undecided, if we do not hear the sound as both /b/ and /d/ in alternation, it suggests there must be other information available for pattern recognition.

Methods of Determining Necessary and Sufficient Cues

Pulling aspects out of the signal for separate presentation is accomplished through tape splicing and sound synthesis. As we saw in Chapter 6, tape splicing may be used to remove a portion of the signal from the tape to play it in isolation. If removing a portion does not change the identification of the rest, we know it was not necessary; if the remaining portion is identified as the whole sound, we know the remaining portion is sufficient. Removal of the /s/ from "spit" leaves a remainder identified as "bit," suggesting that the aspiration of a /p/ produced after an /s/ is not sufficient to produce the percept of a voiceless stop when in initial position.

A sound synthesizer allows the same kind of experimentation but with finer control and with the ability to pull apart frequencies and intensities. There are many kinds of synthesizers, and details of their operation are beyond the scope of this chapter. Suffice it to say that some allow specification of energy values at particular frequencies, in a sense "pronouncing" a spectrogram. Others take real speech input, convert it to an energy specification in time, perhaps approximate some parameters from the input signal, and allow "digital" splicing before playback. Finally, on some personal computers, there are synthesizers that have stored a library of phonemes, syllables, or words that can be accessed by typing and that are then produced in the specified order, in a sense internally spliced together.

For our purposes, it is the first two types of synthesizers that are of interest since they allow the finest manipulation of the signal. Presentation of synthesized patterns consisting of some but not all of the aspects of real speech to human listeners for identification can indicate which aspects are necessary, sufficient, or invariant cues for speech perception.

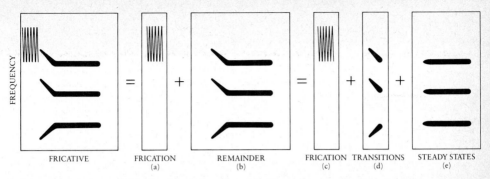

Figure 7.3 *Schematic portrayal of the decomposition of a spectrogram into its various cue classes. A fricative may be conceptualized as the sum of frication noise, transitions and steady states.*

The Sound of Isolated Segments of a Syllable

As we have seen, a CV syllable seems to be describable in terms of three sets of cues: one from the constriction (frication noise, nasal resonance, and burst), one from the movement of the articulators from the place of articulation of the consonant to the place of articulation of the vowel (the transitions), and one from the sustained vowel (the steady states). In addition, looking at a spectrogram, we may segment the signal with respect to frequency and consider that it has several separate formants, each of which could be presented in isolation. (Examination of Figure 7.3 shows a schematic of a spectrogram, which may help you picture the methods underlying the results described in what follows.)

Constriction Cues. So, the first question to ask is: If we divide the signal up and present any of these portions in isolation, how is the portion identified and how is the signal identified with the portion missing? Frication noise in isolation (7.3a) is heard not just as a fricative but as a *specific* fricative, with place of articulation and voicing conveyed simultaneously with manner (Heinz and Stevens, 1961). Examination of the spectrograms in Figure 6.11 should indicate that this should not be surprising since the frequency of the frication noise changes from /s/ to /š/ and is periodic for /z/ as opposed to aperiodic for /s/. If the cue to manner *per se* is in the frication noise, then it must be abstract since it has no fixed frequency range, for example. Moreover, it is smeared with the place and voicing information across the initial portion of the signal; there is no part of the noise that cues frication alone.

With the frication noise removed, the remainder of the syllable (Figure 7.3b) sounds like a stop consonant, possibly since it now begins abruptly. These syllables contain no burst, however, suggesting that the burst is not necessary to perceive a stop. That bursts are not invariant cues to stops can be demonstrated by playing them in isolation: Not only do they not sound like stops, but they also do not sound like speech! So the burst is neither necessary nor sufficient to convey a stop.

Transition Cues. Continuing our segmenting, we may now remove the transitions from the remainder of the syllable, as in Figure 7.3d. Given what we have already learned we might expect them to sound like a place of articulation (our original hypothesis), or now, like a stop, since the transitions plus steady states sound like a stop-vowel syllable. Isolated transitions, like isolated bursts, do *not* sound like speech! In fact, they are called *chirps,* indicative of their sound. So we can rule them out as invariants for either stop manner or place of articulation—they are not sufficient in isolation.

Steady States as Cues. Thus, the steady states are potential cues to the elusive place of articulation (and stop) quality. However, a signal such as 7.3e sounds like a good vowel *only:* the consonant quality has disappeared in our splicing! Therefore, the burst and transitions are not sufficient for the percept of stop consonant and place of articulation but are nevertheless necessary for it.

Presenting Isolated Formants. So far we have tried segmenting the signal with respect to time. We may try segmenting with respect to frequency, presenting isolated formants. This does not the solve the problem either. It is possible to hear good stop CV syllables with the first two or three formants only, suggesting the higher ones are not necessary. Presentation of just a single formant again does not sound speechlike; it is descriptively called a *bleat.* A single formant without transitions, however, is in some cases sufficient to cue a vowel (Fry, Abramson, Eimas, and Liberman, 1962).

Summary. On first looking at the speech signal it seems that it should be divisible into portions, each portion cueing a distinctive feature. Presentation of the portions in isolation reveals that this is not so. In some cases, a portion of the speech signal, such as frication noise, contains cues to many features *simultaneously.* In other cases a portion of the signal is dependent on other portions: Transitions or bursts in isolation do not sound like speech and steady states sound like a vowel; yet, when they are combined, a clear consonant percept emerges from their unity. Together the results suggest that we may minimally signal a fricative with place of articulation and voicing by using just frication noise, a vowel with one or two steady-state frequencies and a stop-vowel, with one or two transitions plus steady states.

Context Sensitivity: Combining Cues from Different Environments

In the last section we saw that with the exception of frication noise and steady states, portions of the speech signal could not be presented in isolation and still evoke a speech percept: The steady states are necessary for a burst and transitions to be heard as speech. We might ask next whether any steady states will do. Is the burst frequency for a particular stop an invariant across vowels, for example, but in need of vowel context to be heard as a stop?

Frication Noise and Context-Sensitivity. We have seen that isolated frication noise is identified as the fricative it came from, complete with voicing and place of articulation. Is the frication noise an invariant for the whole phoneme? Harris (1958) tested this by combining the frication segment from syllables beginning with /f/, /θ/, /s/ or /š/ with transitions and steady states from one or other of these syllables. Frication noise from /s/ or /š/ was heard respectively as /s/ or /š/ in all environments. However, frication noise from /θ/ or /f/ could be heard as any of the fricatives depending on the rest of the syllable. This points to a lack of invariance for place of articulation in the frication noise; the place indicated by the frication noise is affected by the following transitions and steady states.

Bursts and Context-Sensitivity. Using synthesized speech, Liberman, Delattre, and Cooper (1952) examined identification of syllables produced with bursts and steady states. (Schatz [1954] performed a similar experiment with real speech, with similar results.) They paired 12 different burst frequencies with steady states appropriate to a variety of vowels and asked subjects to identify the resulting syllables as beginning with /p/, /t/, or /k/. According to the invariance proposal, if the burst is an invariant for the phoneme (or for place of articulation), the same burst in any vowel environment should be identified the same. If the burst is invariant for the stop manner, the syllables should all be heard as stop-vowel. Subjects reported that the synthesized sounds did seem like stop-vowel syllables, but place was not invariably signaled by the burst, as Figure 7.4 shows. For example, /t/ was heard at burst frequencies above 2600 Hz regardless of vowel (suggesting that a high burst may be invariant for /t/), but a burst frequency of 1440 Hz was heard as /p/ before steady states appropriate to /i/, and /k/ before steady states appropriate to /a/. (You can see similar overlap between /p/ and /k/ for other burst frequencies in different vowel environments.) The results indicate that some place information is carried by the burst but not sufficient information to signal place in all environments.

Transitions and Context-Sensitivity. The information about stop consonants present in the transition portions also turns out to be highly context-sensitive or vowel-dependent. Figure 7.5 displays two-formant patterns sufficient to elicit /b/, /d/, /g/ in front of particular vowels (Delattre, Liberman, and Cooper, 1955). Observe that the transitions for each place of articulation change markedly across vowel contexts, and thus that particular transitions do not always signal a particular consonant. /bi/ and /di/, for example, look remarkably alike, as do /gɔ/ and /dɔ/. The starting frequencies of the transitions vary across vowels; for /b/ the second formant transition ranges from 2400 Hz to 600 Hz at onset. The absolute difference between the first and second formant transitions also varies across vowels, with maximal separation at /i/ and minimal at /a/ or /u/ depending on the consonant. Finally, the directions or slopes of the transitions are not constant: for /b/ both formant transitions rise, for /g/ the first rises and the second falls; but for /d/ for the front vowels (/i/, /e/) they both rise, for the vowel /ɛ/ the second formant is steady, and for the back vowels it falls.

Summary. Examination of identification experiments indicates that although frication noise, bursts, or transitions contain information about place and manner of articulation, they do not signal these invariantly; that is, in isolation they do not

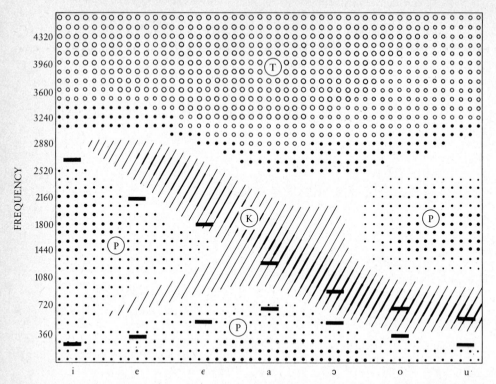

Figure 7.4   *Judgments of /p/, /t/ and /k/ from stimuli produced by combining burst frequencies isolated from each consonant in different vowel contexts with the steady states appropriate to each vowel. Note that there is no burst frequency range that uniquely signals /k/.*
From "The role of selected stimulus variables in the perception of unvoiced stop consonants" by A. M. Liberman, P. C. Delattre, and F. S. Cooper, 1952, in The American Journal of Psychology 65, *Copyright © by the Board of Trustees of the University of Illinois. Reprinted by permission.*

sound like what they cue, and in different contexts they change. A pattern recognition scheme that attempted to find a particular place of articulation from burst or transitions would have to know which vowel was being presented to know whether, for example, to identify a 1440 Hz burst as /p/ or /k/, or falling second and third transitions as /t/ or /k/. This creates a problem for pattern recognition since simple vowel cues are similarly context-dependent on the consonant, as the appendix to this chapter discusses.

Other Proposals for Invariants

Given the problem we have seen in choosing specific aspects of the signal to trigger recognition of a linguistic feature, we must revise our concept of pattern recognition. There are several possibilities: (1) there are no invariants, (2) a combination of cues is the invariant, (3) we have tested the wrong cues, and (4) the invariant is not to

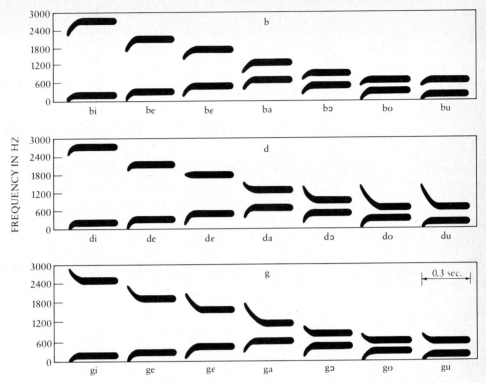

Figure 7.5 *Two formant patterns sufficient to cue /b/, /d/, and /g/ in different vowel contexts. From "Acoustic loci and transitional cues for consonants" by P. C. Delattre, A. M. Liberman, & F. S. Cooper, 1955, in* The Journal of the Acoustical Society of America, 27, p. 770. Copy-*right 1970 by the American Institute of Physics. Reprinted by permission.*

the linguistic feature but to some other unit like the phoneme or the syllable. The first possibility has not been seriously considered in speech and so will not be discussed much here. It has been considered for other kinds of perception though, for example, brightness perception: The absolute amount of light does not signal how bright an object is in all environments; it must be judged with respect to the brightness of the surrounding. A piece of coal in bright sunlight, for instance, reflects more light than a piece of white paper indoors reflects, but the ratio of the light the coal reflects to the light reflected by the ground is smaller than the ratio the paper reflects to the light reflected by its background. Thus, the absolute reflectance is not invariant, but some *relative* reflectance is. If we wish to consider speech perception similarly as relative, we would still need to come up with some dimension with which to compare a particular acoustic cue. This type of relative measure has been tried for vowels only (as described in the appendix), but without much success.

Cue Combinations as Invariants? A number of investigators have suggested combinations of consonant cues as invariant patterns for place of articulation perception. Invariance found in these patterns may be useful for natural speech perception, but it is important to realize that these patterns are not *necessary*—we may synthesize speech minimally with just a burst and steady states, or two formant transitions plus steady state patterns. Ultimately any model of speech perception must account for the sufficiency of these minimal patterns, even if the cue appears invariant insofar as it results in recognition of the pattern regardless of context.

As an example of a cue combination, consider the three formant patterns for stops. /b/ nearly always has three rising transitions, /g/ a rise of the first and third and fall of the second ($\underset{\longleftarrow}{\text{───}}$)—producing a divergence of the second and third formants, and /d/ any of a number of *other* patterns. Thus, Stevens (1975) suggested that place of articulation may be detected by looking for the properties of rising, divergence, or neither.

Unfortunately this works clearly for initial position consonants only. In final position, we may synthesize reasonable stops by reversing the patterns for the initial consonants (see, for example, Tartter, Kat, Samuel, and Repp, 1983). This means that a /b/ pattern would consist of steady states with *falling* transitions ($\overline{}$). To account for identification of these by using properties like rising and falling, we must build in some position sensitivity, eliminating the potential invariance.

It has also been suggested that combined burst and transition information could provide a place of articulation cue. Dorman, Studdert-Kennedy, and Raphael (1977) excised the bursts from natural speech CV syllables differing in consonant and vowel and respliced them across the syllables. This splicing experiment differs from the previous ones described in that here the bursts were spliced onto transition–steady-state portions, not just isolated steady states. The perceptual importance of burst or transitions depended on vowel environment—in some vowel environments the burst influenced identification more and in others the transitions did, but the effect of a combination of burst and transitions was highly predictable. In any event, this result suggests vowel-dependent strategies in consonant identification rather than pure invariance.

Trying New Cues.   Stevens and Blumstein (1978, 1981; Blumstein and Stevens, 1979, 1980) have also proposed invariance in a combination of constriction and transition information. Instead of deriving acoustic features from spectrograms, they used displays that plotted intensity against frequency, averaging over time (power spectra). Combining burst and transitions produced markedly different energy patterns in as little as the first 26 msec of the sound, as Figure 7.6 demonstrates. (Sound intensity is usually measured in units known as *decibels (dB)*; sound frequency is measured here in kHz = kilohertz or 1000 Hz.) Labial consonants showed a steady decrease in energy as the frequency increased from 0 to 3000 Hz. (The burst had little effect on this pattern.) Alveolar consonants showed an even energy distribution between 0 and 5000 Hz without the burst, and a peak in energy at 4000–5000 Hz with the burst. Velar consonants showed an even energy distribution without the burst, but an energy peak at 2000 Hz with the burst.

Stevens and Blumstein (1978) have demonstrated that synthetic burst + transition stimuli are more reliably identified than partial cue stimuli, and they later demonstrated that subjects can identify both consonant and vowel (pointing to the redundancy of vowel information) with as little as 10 msec of onset information (Blumstein

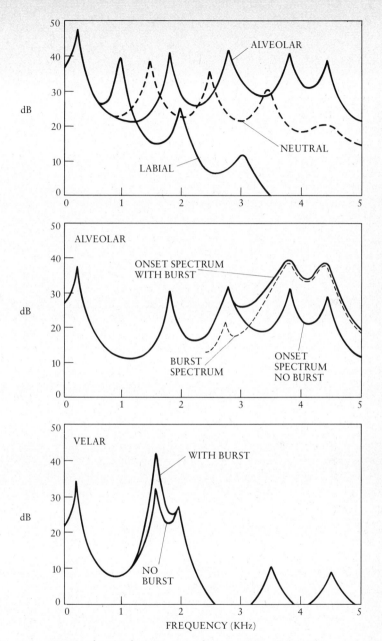

Figure 7.6 *Onset spectra for the first 26 msec of stop-vowel syllables. The top panel displays the patterns for alveolar and labial consonants as compared with the neutral /ə/ pattern. The second and third panels show the spectra for alveolar and velar consonants with and without bursts. Note the accentuation of the difference with the bursts.*

From "The search for invariant acoustic correlates of phonetic features" by K. N. Stevens and S. E. Blumstein in P. D. Eimas and J. L. Miller (Eds.). Perspectives on the Study of Speech, 1978, p. 8, Hillsdale, NJ: Lawrence Erlbaum Associates. Copyright 1978. Reprinted by permission.

and Stevens, 1980). Finally, templates cut out from figures such as 7.6 and fitted over onset or offset spectra collected from CV or VC syllables with various vowels sorted 83 percent of the initial stop consonants and 77 percent of initial nasals into the same categories as did human listeners. Performance for the final consonants was poorer. The results suggest that the onset spectrum may invariantly signal place of articulation but that it is not sufficient across position. However, it is important to remember that these onset cues are clearly not necessary since synthetic stimuli without these may still be identified by human listeners. Kewley-Port (1983) has shown that using spectra that show changes in energy at different frequencies at different times instead of spectra averaging the energies over time improves classification of the consonants to 88 percent.

Invariance at a Higher Level?   We started by assuming that the phonetic feature was the unit for pattern recognition because it would mean fewer pattern recognizers, and because there seemed to be evidence for the psychological reality of phonetic feature extraction. At this point, it may seem tempting to abandon the feature, since we have already seen that there is no aspect of the acoustic signal that appears to signal only one phonetic feature in all contexts. If the burst cues manner, place, and voicing as does frication noise, perhaps it is more reasonable to assume that pattern recognition begins by extracting the feature bundle, the phoneme. Or, since burst or frication interpretation seems to depend on steady state values also, perhaps we should assume that syllables are extracted initially and then broken down into smaller units.

Unfortunately, the same kind of context-dependency and simultaneous cueing of several units occurs when the syllable is considered the unit as when the feature is. Ali, Gallagher, Goldstein, and Daniloff (1971), for example, removed a nasal CV syllable from a sentence and found that listeners were able to tell from the remaining syllables in the sentence that the nasal had been there; that is, there were cues to nasality spread over the entire sentence, so that aspects of the phoneme or syllable the nasal occurred in were cued simultaneously with other phonemes and syllables. Thus, the acoustic shape of these other syllables differed depending on whether or not there was a nasal near. Mann and Repp (1981) showed a cross phoneme effect: A stop consonant is more likely to be heard as /t/ than /k/ after /s/ but more likely to be heard as /k/ than /t/ after /š/, indicating that the phoneme identity is in part determined by the preceding phoneme. And Mann (1980) found a similar effect across syllables: A stop is more likely to be heard as /d/ than /g/ in the context /al_a/, and as /g/ than /d/ in the context /ar_a/. Together the results suggest that regardless of whether one looks at phonetic features, phonemes, or syllables, identification seems to be based at least in part on information available from other features, phonemes, or syllables. In turn, this suggests that any one portion of the acoustic signal is colored by many linguistic units and that there is no aspect of the signal that is invariant across contexts for a particular perceptual unit.

A number of investigators have also demonstrated that judgments of a particular feature, phoneme, or syllable identity is dependent on the perceived rate of articulation of the remainder of the sentence. The critical articulatory feature for voicing, for example, is when the vocal cords begin to vibrate relative to the release of the consonant, known as *voice onset time (VOT)*. If the vibration starts late, the consonant is perceived as voiceless; if it starts early, as voiced; and if it precedes the release, as prevoiced. The size of the VOT necessary for a voiceless judgment is relative: Longer VOTs are needed for velars than bilabials for voicelessness to be perceived, suggesting a dependency of voicing on place perception. A longer VOT is needed to perceive voicelessness in a stressed (and therefore long) syllable than in an unstressed one (Lisker and Abramson, 1967), suggesting a dependency of voicing on syllable extraction. Finally, if the sentence the syllable is spoken in is articulated slowly, a longer VOT is necessary to perceive voicelessness than if it is articulated quickly (Miller and Grosjean, 1981). This suggests that we cannot always begin with the syllable either, since it has to be judged against the backdrop of the sentence.

Summary and Conclusions

Table 7.1 describes acoustic features that splicing and synthesis experiments have shown are sufficient to cue distinctions in the consonants we have discussed and in

Table 7.1 *Summary of acoustic features sufficient to signal the presence of a distinctive feature value in speech. Note that in many cases the cue is sufficient only in combination—a burst, for example, signals a stop only in the presence of steady state frequencies or transitions. (References are provided in the text. Stevens and Klatt (1974) analyzed VOT into component acoustic characteristics.)*

	Sufficient Cues
Consonants	
Manner of Articulation	
Nasality	Presence of Nasal Resonance
Frication	Frication Noise
Stops	Sudden Onset Indicated by Burst or Abruptly Starting Transitions
Semivowels	Lengthened Transitions (Relative to Stop)
Voicing (VOT) (more = voiceless)	Amount of Time Between Energy Release and Onset of Periodic Pulsing
(more = voiceless)	Amount of Aspiration Noise
(lower = voiceless)	Relative Intensity of the First Formant to Higher Formants
Place of Articulation	Frequency of the Constriction Cues (Burst or Frication Noise)
	Direction, Slope, Frequency of Second Formant Transition
	Direction, Slope, Frequency of Third Formant Transition
Vowels	One or Two Steady State Frequencies
	First Two Formant Transitions

other consonants and vowels. The results of the experiments we have examined indicate a striking absence of invariance at all levels of the signal.

We have the following problems for pattern recognition:

(1) The acoustic information in the signal varies with the syllable position, but our perception does not appear to—we hear /b/ as /b/ in initial, final or medial position.

(2) The acoustic information in the signal varies with the vowel, and again our perception does not appear to.

(3) Portions of the signal that seemingly should contain sufficient information when isolated are not sufficient to elicit the percept.

Given these problems, proposals for speech recognition range from complex combinations of cues such as weighted burst and transition information with weights varying with context, to integrated cues that may work in natural speech but cannot be used in synthetic speech, to invariance at a higher level—which like low-level invariance is not easy to find.

Perception of a feature value appears to be affected by the other feature values for that phoneme, the syllable context, the position in the syllable, qualities of the sentence (like nasality), and suprasegmental information like speech rate. Cues to a particular feature value seem *smeared* across the utterance so that voicing, for example, is reflected in the burst, the relationship between the burst and transition, the length of the vowel, and the rate of the sentence. Any acoustic aspect of the signal, like the burst, *simultaneously* cues information about many distinctive features. Distinctive characteristics of speech seem to be simultaneity and smear.

We have restricted our examination of the cues to speech to consonants. It might seem that vowels would be simpler to specify from the acoustic signal. We will not discuss vowels in detail here; interested readers are referred to the appendix of this chapter for information about vowel perception. For now, we note only that context-sensitivity is as much a problem for vowels as it is for consonants. You may consider that if formant transitions or burst positions change with different vowels, there is vowel information given in the burst or transitions. Indeed, Stevens and Blumstein (1978) have shown that 10 msec of onset information for a CV syllable is sufficient to signal the vowel as well as the consonant. Since vowels are identifiable from steady states we see "smear" of vowel information across the syllable, also. Since both vowel and consonant are cued by the onset information, we see simultaneity in transmission of vowel features as well as consonant features.

A final aspect of the speech signal to consider as providing variability is nonsegmental information. Again the interested reader is referred to the appendix for details on how suprasegmentals are perceived in the signal, on whether voiceprint identification of a speaker, like fingerprint identification, provides an invariant cue to speaker identity, and on how emotion may be perceived in the voice. We note for now that it is possible to recognize, from a small portion of an utterance, pitch contour (Hadding-Koch and Studdert-Kennedy, 1964), an individual's sex and age if not complete identity, (Ptacek and Sander, 1966), and whether or not a person was smiling while speaking (Tartter, 1980). Since these are perceptible from the speech signal, information about them must be in the speech signal, causing variability of the acoustic information underlying the segments. Moreover, perception of these aspects seems to be affected by changes in the segments; some vowels, for example, are easier to recognize speakers from than others. Thus, these percepts, too, are dependent on non-invariant cues.

Together with consonant information, vowel, suprasegmental, speaker, and emotional information are conveyed in the signal. For each of these aspects of speech there appears to be no single set of cues conveying that information and no other. Rather each portion of the signal simultaneously conveys information about many patterns, and the presence of each of the other patterns contributes variability to the acoustic signal underlying one pattern. In addition, the cues for any one pattern are spread across the whole signal.

In sum, we see many sources of variation contributing to the form of the speech signal, some of which serve linguistic purposes and some of which serve communicative purposes not strictly linguistic. The sounds we produce are shaped by phonetic targets, previous and subsequent targets, suprasegmental operations, idiosyncratic physical features, and the current emotional state and facial expression. Thus, any small portion of speech contains some information about a variety of things, as attested to by our ability to label consonant, vowel, speaker, emotion, spliced-off earlier or later consonants, and so on. Complete information about any one element is smeared across many portions of the speech signal; thus, the cues to a consonant cannot all be found in one time segment, nor can the cues to one emotion, nor any other single aspect of the signal. All are overlaid on the same signal, resulting in no two utterances being identical. Therefore, to extract a /t/, or percept of voicelessness (or percept of a large individual), seems to require a specially developed pattern recognizer. After we discuss speech production we will explore theories on how this pattern recognizer might work, and why speech processing has been thought to be specially developed.

Speech Production

As we pointed out in the beginning of this chapter, there is evidence from slips of the tongue that phonetic features have a psychological reality in speech production. However, as with speech perception, there is reason to consider the reality of higher-order units in speech production.

Context-Sensitivity of Segments. Note first that no feature can be produced in isolation; we cannot produce a voicing value without also producing a place and manner value for a consonant, and, for stop consonants, without also producing a vowel. Aside from this articulatory constraint, there is considerable evidence that we *plan* more than one feature at a time. Slips of the tongue reveal a preponderance of *anticipation errors* (as in "sea sells" instead of "she sells," anticipating the /s/). Somewhat less common are *perseveration errors* (as in "she shells" instead of "she sells," holding the /š/) (van den Broeke and Goldstein, 1980). Both these types of intrusion errors can occur across several syllables, although most are from adjacent syllables (MacKay, 1970). This indicates that in planning and producing a feature, phoneme, or syllable, there is "smear" from the planning and production of other syllables or syllable components; at some level the production program has some large portion of the utterance "in mind," and thus later or earlier productions can influence the current one.

Evidence from slips of the tongue indicates not only a general smear of segments but also a sensitivity to position of the segment. Slips most frequently involve the initial phoneme or feature in a word, but when other portions are confused, they generally come from the same respective positions within their words (MacKay, 1972). An example of a first position transposition was provided by a colleague in a recent lecture on Freud: For "the text says" he said "sex tez," indicating not only the first position substitutions, but perhaps, in this case, a lexical substitution of an item to appear later in the lecture.

There are several reasons that there might be position sensitivity in production. For one, it is possible that the associations, the phonological constraints, the transitional probabilities of segments, are position dependent. /ŋ/ in English, for example, is never likely to be substituted into initial position, since its association to a preceding break—or the myriad potential consonant segments that could end preceding words—will be very weak while its associations to preceding vowels (as in sing, song, and so on) will be very strong. Therefore, a substitution involving it is likely to reflect position dependency. The same sort of strength of association argument may apply, less dramatically, with respect to concatenation of other segments. Alternatively, it may be that a motor program is generated for a large unit of speech, like a word, composed of smaller programs for each position in the word. An error in generating the large program could include a unit marked for that position from some other word, producing the error. In either case, position-sensitivity in production is suggested.

Effects of Higher-Level Productions.   Thus far we have considered effects of one segment on another in production. There are effects of suprasegmental information also on production—not surprisingly, since suprasegmental information is carried in the segments. Therefore, if a person wishes to produce a declarative intonation contour, that must be carried out by changing the pitch for each segment appropriately. Once again, this will mean influences of other segments on a particular segment, and influences of a higher-order plan on lower-order production.

We see a direct effect of suprasegmental planning in some slips of the tongue, in which stress or intonation is incorrectly transposed, indicating it is planned—as a unit. For example, Cutler (1980) reported a substitution of "The price of lettuce has just sky-rock'eted" for "The price of lettuce has just sky'-rocketed." The change in stress is conveyed by a change in vowel length (segment), loudness, and pitch, as described in the appendix.

We may also see evidence of planning at greater-than-segment levels in production tasks, where pronunciation of words is altered by the constituent structure they occur in or the length of the utterance in general. Such alterations indicate that speakers are aware of many segments while producing just one, and also show, in smooth production, a change in the acoustic manifestation of suprasegmental information to accommodate the specific utterance produced.

For example, Cooper and colleagues (Cooper and Paccia-Cooper, 1980; Sorenson and Cooper, 1980; Paccia-Cooper and Cooper, 1981) measured pause duration (note that a pause has zero loudness and zero pitch and thus, pause lengthening affects pitch and loudness contours) in articulated sentences and found that pause length was dependent on the number of constituents terminating in the same place. Higher-order constituent boundaries had greater pause durations since they marked not only their own termination but those of subordinate constituents.

Using different speech stimuli, Sternberg, Monsell, Knoll, and Wright (1980) showed that the pause before beginning recital of a learned list of items following a ready signal depended on the length of the list. They hypothesized that during the latent period speakers were assembling or accessing a motor program for the entire list, and longer lists required assembly of more programs and therefore took longer.

Together, the studies suggest that there may be several levels of motor program planning, governed by syntactic or overall structure. The pause duration that Cooper et al. observed may reflect the production planning time for the next constituents. If there is a level of programming at least partially accessed for a word, a phrase, a clause, and a sentence, termination of any one of these will mean that another program at that level would need to be accessed; termination of the higher-order programs will require accessing of the next sentence program as well as the next clause, phrase, word programs, and so on, and this will take more time.

Cooper and colleagues have shown effects of higher-level units of production on intonation as well as on pauses. They presented subjects with sentences of varying lengths to be read with a declarative intonation contour. In declarative sentences, the pitch falls continuously throughout the sentence. To produce such a fall for long sentences subjects started at higher frequencies than for short sentences. This indicates that the entire sentence was planned at some level, with the length and desired endpoint taken into account. It also suggests an influence of items occurring later on those occurring earlier: The pitch provided for the initial segment is clearly different for sentences of different lengths.

Levels of Production. Throughout this section we have referred to the simultaneous planning of many levels of production. In an influential paper, Lashley (1951) proposed just such an organization for production of any temporally sequenced complex "habit." At the lowest level are expressive elements that must be activated (in speech, these may be phonetic features), and at the highest level some "determining tendency" or "idea" that will organize them. The idea is implemented through the expressive elements by means of a hierarchy of organizations in order: order in vocal movements in pronouncing the word, order in the words of the sentence, and order of the sentences of the paragraph. Moreover, Lashley considered the hierarchy of organization a defining property of all higher-level brain activity. We see the influences of each level of the hierarchy in both speech errors that reflect contamination by other units of the same level, and in context-sensitivity of the expressive elements that reflect the combined influences of all levels.

Thus, in production as well as in perception, we see simultaneity and smear: Each segment simultaneously conveys and reflects influences of other segments through higher levels of organization, and each segment is smeared across other segments by the same means. Indeed, as Lashley observed, and as we will see later in this chapter, perception seems to be organized in the same kind of hierarchy: After commenting on a typing error producing "wrapid writing," Lashley produced the sentence "rapid righting with his uninjured hand saved from loss the contents of the capsized canoe."

The initial "error" caused a misinterpretation of "righting," which could not be corrected until his audience heard the word "canoe," at least three to five seconds later. To activate the appropriate interpretation, then, required that the hearer maintain many levels of perceptual structure; the meaning of "canoe" must "smear" backward, over the meaning of "righting." Holding several levels simultaneously in perception, or creating several levels simultaneously in production, accounts for the smear in both.

Monitoring and Correcting Speech

We have just observed a commonality between speech perception and production: simultaneity of many aspects, smear of one aspect across many others, and hierarchical organization. Levelt (1983) has examined the process of perception *during* production and concluded that this reflects the same strategies as normal perception and also indicates how speech production is organized. As we observed in the beginning of this chapter, speakers make few errors, but when they do they correct them, indicating that they are monitoring their productions. The question is: How do these corrections fit in with the speaker's plan in production? If several levels of constituents are programmed ahead, how is it possible to interpolate the correction?

Levelt examined two theories of repair: a production theory, in which it was assumed that the speaker could access the output of each of the levels of organization in production before making the utterance, and a perception theory, in which the speaker is assumed to have access only to the final level, the output of all these levels, just before production. In the perception theory, it is assumed that the speaker monitors "inner speech" to check for mispronunciations and deviance from intent.

Examination of the errors, the detection of errors, and the attempts at repair produced evidence supporting the perception theory. The kinds of errors speakers corrected were: changing their minds about what they should be saying (1 percent), choosing the wrong word (38 percent), syntactic errors (2 percent), and pronunciation errors (1 percent). Since these corrections account for only 42 percent of all errors that were made, it suggests that speakers are more likely to notice the lexical errors, for example, than the phonetic errors. If they had access to each stage of the production process in monitoring, they could correct at each stage. That they do not indicates that they perceive only the final stage, as they would if they were listeners.

Another way that the monitoring data may be examined concerns when the repairs are made on the errors. Levelt found some repairs made immediately, within a word, and others that were delayed. Of the ones made immediately, most occurred at or near a phrase boundary, suggesting that the speaker was more likely to be able to observe or correct errors occurring in this position. Corrections that were delayed were delayed until the phrase boundary. Again, since speakers detected more errors at phrase boundaries, it suggests that they did not have access to the output of lower levels of production early enough to correct before they were integrated into the program for the phrase.

The last use that can be made of the correction data is to look at the manner of repair, how much the speaker changes in order to make the correction. In this case too Levelt saw analogies to perceiver strategies in the speaker. The speaker would not stop in the middle of the word unless the word was wrong, and the speaker would try to incorporate the correction into the syntactic structure of the sentence, backtracking only to the beginning of the current constituent. For example, if the error is saying "green" when "blue" is intended, the utterance "to the right is a green" will be corrected with "to the right is a green, a blue node." If the speaker got farther before detecting the error, (s)he will still backtrack to the constituent boundary: "to the right is a green node and" → "to the right is a green node and, uh, a blue node and ... " Levelt argued that we use similar syntactic match strategies in answering questions, so that if someone asks "what time?" we will respond "noon," but if the question is "at what time?" the response is "at noon." Since the backtracking in answering and correcting seem to be the same, Levelt concluded that we use the same strategies in listening to others as we do in listening to ourselves.

Summary

In the last sections we have examined in detail the problems of pattern recognition in speech and related it to production and monitoring of speech. We saw that although there is evidence that phonetic features have a psychological reality in both production and perception, they are affected by surrounding features, making the signal underlying any feature highly variable, or context-sensitive. For production, we have hypothesized a multileveled organization, with articulatory features at the lowest level, which are then incorporated into higher-level units of production such as words, phrases, sentences, and so on. We have also proposed that perception and production may be mediated by similar mechanisms, accounting for similarities in monitoring inner speech and others' speech, and in the similar characteristics of simultaneity and smear. This suggests that perception of speech may also take place simultaneously on many levels, perhaps providing a solution to the problem of the lack of invariance in the signal. In the remainder of this chapter we will explore theories and experiments on the various levels at which speech perception might take place.

Is Speech Special?

In the last section we looked at possible cues to distinctive features and phonemes, and other characteristics that could be identified in the speech signal and that contribute variability to these cues. Despite the fact that there is considerable evidence (reviewed in the first part of the section) that features are extracted during speech perception, we found a complex relation between properties of the acoustic signal and perception. This has suggested to some investigators that speech may be specially processed—that the phonetic message is highly *encoded,* not transparent, and that abstracting the phonetic message from the other vocal characteristics laid down with it has specially evolved and is different from any other kinds of perceptual processing we do. In this section we look at experiments that have been cited as evidence of the special nature of speech processing.

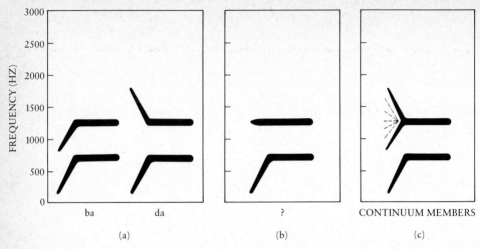

Figure 7.7 *Schematized speech spectrograms. (a) illustrates a /ba/ on the left and a /da/ on the right. (b) shows a sound that could be intermediate between /ba/ and /da/, since the second formant "transition" is halfway between the second formant transitions of /ba/ and /da/. (c) shows potential continuum members, overlaid on one another. All have the same first formant and same second formant steady state. Each stimulus of the continuum has a different transition, either as in /ba/ or /da/ of (a), or intermediate, indicated by the dotted lines.*

Categorical Perception

Synthetic Continua.   Figure 7.7 (a) displays a two-formant synthetic /ba/ next to a two formant synthetic /da/. Comparison of the two syllables reveals that the only difference between them is in the second formant transition: For /ba/ it rises, for /da/, it falls. What would a stimulus intermediate between the two, as in (b), with a straight second formant sound like—/b/ or /d/? Panel c in the figure shows potential intermediate transitions (dotted lines) between the endpoints /ba/ and /da/ (indicated by solid lines), shown in panel a. Note that the dotted lines are equidistant from one another; that their slopes or starting points change in equal steps as we go from one endpoint to another. Synthetic speech stimuli varying in equal steps from one value to another are known as a *synthetic speech continuum*, and such continua have been used extensively in the study of speech perception. (Indeed some of the results described in earlier sections of this chapter were obtained by using synthetic speech continua.) Synthetic speech continua may be constructed for any dimension: changes in VOT could create a continuum between /ba/ (0 msec) and /pa/ (45 msec), in transition duration between /ba/ (35 msec to reach the steady state value) and /wa/ (145 msec transition length), and in steady state frequencies between /i/ and /e/. Nonspeech continua may also be created; for example, the isolated second formant transitions depicted within 7.7 c.

Tasks.   Synthetic continua have been used in two tasks—identification and discrimination. In *identification,* subjects are asked to label the continuum members as

/b/, /d/, or whatever. In *discrimination,* subjects are asked whether they can hear a difference between two stimuli, say, between a stimulus with 0 msec VOT and a stimulus with 10 msec VOT. Typically, the discrimination task employed in speech perception research is the *ABX task:* Two stimuli are presented a short time apart, Stimulus A and then Stimulus B, followed by a third stimulus (X), identical to either A or B. The subject is asked to decide whether it matched A or B. If A and B appear identical to the subject, there is no basis for choosing between them, and the subject will guess, with a 50 percent chance of being correct. If A and B are discriminable, then it should be simple to say which sounds like X.

Continuous and Categorical Perception. What results might be expected from identification and discrimination of synthetic speech continua? What was expected was that the continuum members would be *continuously perceived:* that is, if Stimulus 1 was a good /b/ and Stimulus 9 a good /p/, Stimulus 2 would be perceived most of the time as /b/, Stimulus 3 a little less of the time, and so forth—as Figure 7.8a shows. Ability to discriminate was expected to depend on the step size; if people can hear a 5 msec difference in VOT they should be able to do so throughout the continuum, and if they cannot, they should not be able to do so throughout the series. Therefore, for whatever the *difference threshold* (the minimum step size subjects can discriminate) is, we would expect discriminability to be constant across the series. (One-step discriminations indicate the ability to tell the difference between, for example, Stimulus 1 and Stimulus 2 of the series. Two-step discriminations involve differentiating Stimulus 1 and Stimulus 3, 2 vs. 4, etc. If one-step differences are 5 msec VOT apart, two-step differences are 10 msec VOT apart.) These two hypotheses, one for identification and one for discrimination, constitute continuous perception.

The actual results, obtained for consonant continua, were strikingly different, as Figure 7.8b shows. In identification there appears to be an abrupt shift from b-perception to p-perception—the first four stimuli all seem perfectly good /b/s and the last four perfectly good /p/s, with a sudden change at a boundary stimulus. The boundary stimuli still sound quite speechlike, but they are ambiguous in that sometimes they sound like one percept and sometimes the other. Discrimination also showed a pattern markedly different from what had been expected, as the solid line in the bottom panel of Figure 7.8 indicates. At the endpoints of the continuum, when subjects discriminated 0 msec VOT from 5 msec VOT or 40 msec VOT from 45 msec VOT, they were nearly at chance. These are called *within-category discriminations,* since they are judgments between two stimuli assigned to the same phonetic category. At the middle—at the boundary as indicated by the identification function *between-category*—discrimination was much closer to perfect. This means that 5 msec VOT differences do not sound the same across the series! The correspondence between the identification boundary and the discrimination peak was so striking that investigators decided that discrimination was based on identification, such that sounds labeled the same could not be discriminated, and sounds labeled differently could be perfectly discriminated (Liberman, Harris, Hoffman, and Griffith, 1957). The dotted line in the discrimination panel indicates values for discrimination predicted from identification results alone. This pattern of results, a sharp division into categories in labeling and an enhanced discrimination between-category relative to within-category, is called *categorical perception.*

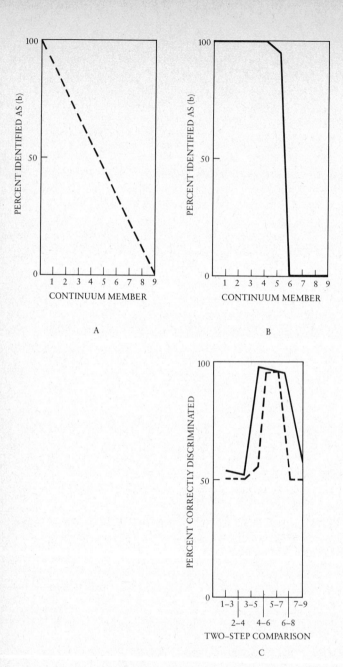

Figure 7.8 *Results predicted and obtained for the relation of identification and discrimination of synthetic speech continua. (a) shows the idealized continuous perception identification function. (b) shows an actual identification function for consonants. (c) shows the predicted discrimination function (dotted line) assuming subjects discriminated no better than they were able to identify in (b), the assumption of categorical perception, together with their actual discrimination function (solid line).*

Not all sounds yield categorical-type discrimination functions: Vowel continua yield sharply categorized identification functions but are relatively discriminable throughout (Eimas, 1963). Nonspeech stimuli derived from consonant continua do not show the peak in discrimination but are relatively consistently and poorly discriminated (Liberman, Harris, Kinney, and Lane, 1961; Mattingly, Liberman, Syrdal, and Halwes, 1971).

The differences in sound perception have at times been attributed to specialized processing for consonants. Consonants can be assumed to be more abstract or encoded than the vowels because of their transience and context-sensitivity, and therefore may require special processing. Although similarly transient and perhaps involving the same kind of discriminations as the consonants from which they were derived, nonspeech sounds may not be processed by a speech-specific mechanism, resulting in their continuous perception. Although speech, vowels may not be as abstract as the consonants and so might not require special processing. The special process has been assumed to label the stimuli in terms of phonetic features, stripping away all acoustic information and leaving only the feature labels available to discriminate.

Learning and Categorical Perception.   One way to account for the difference between consonant and chirp perception is to note that consonants are extremely overlearned: We have been responding one way to /b/ and another to /p/ for most of our lives, but probably most of us have never heard a chirp.

In this regard, it is interesting to note that several studies have demonstrated categorical perception in musicians for stimuli constructed between one musical category and another (see, for example, Blechner, 1977; Zatorre, 1983), while low-skilled non-musicians who have had little practice with the stimuli, perceive them non-categorically (Blechner, 1977).

Several investigators have specifically attempted to make perception of an initially non-categorical discrimination categorical by discrimination training (Lane, 1965; Samuel, 1977; Pisoni, 1977). This has sometimes been done by training with the within-category members of a speech continuum, and sometimes with nonspeech sounds. Practice has been shown to alter discriminability, producing sharply categorized identification functions, chance discrimination within-category, and good discrimination between-category, along with close correspondence between obtained discrimination and discrimination predicted from identification. These functions, obtained for nonspeech stimuli that before training had been discriminated at chance levels throughout and had shown flat identification functions—clearly fit the criteria for categorical perception.

In a converse "learning" experiment (a forgetting experiment), investigators have looked at identification and discrimination of distinctions phonemic in one language but not in another. Speakers of the language for which they are not phonemic will get very little practice labeling them, and so should perform poorly. Miyawaki, Strange, Verbrugge, Liberman, Jenkins, and Fujimura (1975), for example, compared discriminability of an /r-l/ continuum for American and Japanese speakers. Americans showed typical categorical functions, whereas the Japanese speakers could neither label nor discriminate the stimuli—their functions looked like those for nonspeech stimuli. This could result from a lack of practice, or from the inability to process as speech what is not phonemically relevant: These sounds could lose their access to the specialized speech processor.

We have described two approaches here: extensive training to heighten distinctiveness and extensive lack of training to lose distinctiveness. These exemplify two possibilities proposed to account for categorical perception: *acquired distinctiveness,* where overuse or importance emphasizes a difference like the boundary between two categories; and *acquired similarity,* where lack of use causes an innate distinction to atrophy. The first suggests that infants innately "hear" all sounds as equivalent and learn to make the phonetic distinctions required by the language. The second suggests that all phonetic distinctions are innate, but the ones not used disappear from the infant's repertoire if they are not practiced. Experiments on infant perception have shown support for each of these hypotheses, depending on the particular phonetic distinction. We will look at these data more carefully in Chapter 9 when we consider language development.

Categorical Perception and Memory.   A second way to account for categorical perception of speech is to attribute it to memory rather than perception. The ABX task requires that subtle characteristics of the signal be retained for at least three seconds (between A and X), and during that time the subtleties may be forgotten. This could affect consonants more than vowels, since the consonant cues are shorter and rapidly changing, so there is less redundancy to fall back on in case of forgetting. To test whether memory is responsible for categorical perception, we can attempt to render vowels less memorable by making them transient like the consonants, shortening them, or we can make the memory task easier overall. Shortening the steady-state vowel durations does change discrimination, making it worse (Fujisaki and Kawashima, 1968, 1969; Pisoni, 1973, 1975b). However, this does not indicate that relative memorability underlies categorical perception; for categorical perception we would want a decrement *only* within-category, which was not obtained (see Tartter, 1982 for review). As you may recall, transitions may be used to identify either vowels or consonants, and for both would be equally transient. Tartter (1981) compared discrimination of chirps-distinguishing-vowels with that of chirps-distinguishing-consonants, and, although the vowel and consonant stimuli here were equally transient, obtained very different discrimination functions for vowel chirps and consonant chirps. This suggests that memory for transient information *per se* is not responsible for the shape of the discrimination function.

Memory tasks easier than the ABX task have also shown that memory affects discriminability but not the shape of the discrimination function nor the difference between consonant and vowel discrimination. Pisoni (1973, 1975b) found heightened discriminability of consonants and vowels with easier tasks, but again this effect persisted throughout the series and was more evident for vowels than consonants. Indeed, using a same-different task where two stimuli were presented between zero msec and two seconds apart, he showed facilitation in discrimination for both long and short vowels but not for consonants at the shorter intervals between stimuli.

To account for all these memory results, a *dual code* model was proposed by Fujisaki and Kawashima (1968, 1969) and elaborated by Pisoni (1973, 1975b) and Darwin and Baddeley (1974). They assumed that there are two types of memory involved in speech perception—auditory memory, which holds close to an identical image of the stimulus, and phonetic memory, which holds the label for the stimulus. If possible, subjects use the labels; if a subject hears "b d b" it is easy to say the third matches the first, not the second. If (s)he hears "b b b" the labels are of no use, and (s)he must resort to the auditory memory code. The auditory code is presumed to fade very quickly, but for sustained vowels, unlike consonants, enough information remains to construct what had been there. If the memory task is easier, there is likely to be useful information left in the auditory component, but more for vowel than consonant discrimination.

Categorical Perception and Auditory Sensitivity.   A third explanation for categorical perception is that phonetic categories arose in highly discriminable acoustic regions and therefore that the underlying mechanisms for speech perception are not "special" to speech but are general auditory mechanisms. Some of the training studies described earlier (Samuel, 1977; Pisoni, 1977) reached this conclusion, since discriminability peaks arose in places expected from other experiments to have heightened auditory sensitivity.

If categorical perception arises from sensitivities of the auditory system rather than from experience with language or from a specially evolved speech processing mechanism, we might expect to find categorical perception in animals, like chinchillas, that have hearing similar to ours. Kuhl (1981; and Miller, 1975, 1978) trained chinchillas to cross a barrier to avoid a shock when signaled by a sound at one end of the speech continuum. Presentation of the sound at the other end of the continuum signaled delivery of water (reinforcement) on the side of the barrier where the chinchilla already was. After training with the continuum endpoints, the chinchillas were presented with intermediate continuum members to see, for each, whether they crossed the barrier or stayed, thus providing identification data. The chinchillas exhibited the same identification boundaries as English speakers, and the same feature dependencies: The VOT boundary for both human and chinchilla is different for different places of articulation (a longer VOT is necessary for the voiceless percept for the velars than the bilabials). Since chinchillas have no specific linguistic experience, their categorization must take place by general auditory mechanisms, and thus so could ours.

Summary.   The results for identification and discrimination of speech reveal that consonants are perceived differently from vowels and some nonspeech categories. This may be because of special processing for the consonants: acquired distinctiveness or acquired similarity or an added phonetic memory or some other process (to be discussed following). Alternatively, it may be that language has evolved to use the auditory areas that we are most sensitive to—to maximize its perceptual salience and discriminability (see Stevens, 1972). Regardless, it seems that the acoustic distinctions signaling different consonants are more discriminable than many other acoustic distinctions.

Auditory Memory: Modality and Suffix Effects

In the last section we saw that one explanation for the differences in discrimination between consonants and vowels involved a special memory that was more useful for vowels than consonants. Aside from the differences in memory demands in various discrimination tasks, there is other evidence that there are special memories for speech, or at least for certain types of speech. This evidence has also been used to support the claim that speech is specially processed.

Serial Recall Effects. When a list of words or syllables is presented to subjects for short-term recall, memory for an item turns out to be dependent on the item's position in the list. You can try this yourself, with a willing subject. Read a short list of items, numbers—

$$1 \ 7 \ 9 \ 4 \ 6 \ 8 \ 3 \ 2 \ 10 \ 5$$

out loud, in a monotone, with about one second between each one. At the end of the list the subject(s) should write down as many numbers as (s)he can—*in the order presented.* Recalling in order is called *serial recall.* Now look where the errors occur. In all likelihood the first few items will be recalled perfectly, as will the last one or two, but the middle items will be confused or forgotten. The better recall of the first few items is known as the *primacy effect,* and the better recall of the last few *the recency effect.*

For our purposes the recency effect is what is interesting because it does not always happen. Crowder and Morton (1969) showed that if instead of hearing the items subjects see the items written, recall of the last items is no better than recall of the middle items. The differences in recency recall between auditory and visual presentation they termed the *modality effect.*

A Special Memory. The modality effect was attributed to an extra short-term memory for sounds, called *precategorical acoustic store (PAS).* PAS, they hypothesized, could hold approximately one item for a short time, after which it disappeared. Moreover, PAS could be blocked—by presenting one more item, right after the list, which did not have to be recalled. This item, called *the suffix, if speech,* would depress recency recall also to the middle levels. (See Figure 7.9 for a graphic illustration of modality and suffix effects.) If the suffix was a tone or noise it had no effect; if backward speech or other nonsense speech, it still worked. The suffix effect was assumed to arise from interference or writing-over by one speech stimulus of another, since PAS could hold only one item (see Massaro, 1975, for description of similar writing-over, or *masking* effects). The suffix effect was assumed to work only for those suffixes that were perceptually similar to the list items, so only speech may suffix speech.

PAS and Speech. Recall the dual-code model for auditory memory presented earlier. Here it was assumed that speech sounds were copied into a rapidly fading memory, and their phonetic labels were held in a longer duration memory. Because of their changing nature, consonants left very little useful information in the auditory memory and so had to be discriminated on the basis of the labels. The vowel trace in auditory memory, however, was useful. Given this description, and assuming auditory memory is the same in both cases, would you expect a difference in short-term recall of consonants and vowels?

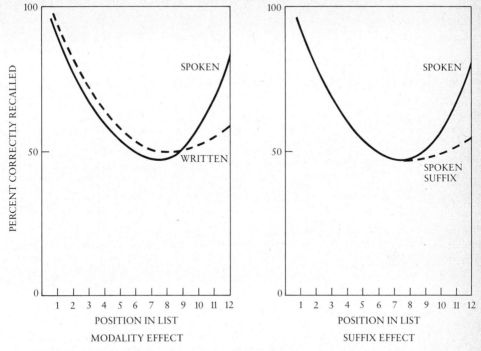

Figure 7.9 *Typical effects on serial recall of modality of presentation and a suffix.*

As you might predict, if list items differ in consonant only, there is no recency effect (Crowder, 1971) since the material in PAS is insufficient for reconstructing the consonant. Sustained vowels, though, show typical recency and suffix effects. If the vowels are shortened (Crowder, 1973) so the material in auditory memory is not as useful, or taken from a confusable set (Darwin and Baddeley, 1974), the recency advantage similarly disappears. Finally, if highly discriminable consonants are selected from different manner classes as opposed to the same manner class, the recency effect may be obtained with consonants (Darwin and Baddeley, 1974). It is important to note that words (like the digit names) differ in both consonants and vowels. This makes words a "less confusable" set, which could rely on auditory memory.

Thus, the results from short-term recall support the hypotheses: (1) that similar consonants are perceived differently from vowels, perhaps because of their highly encoded, transient nature and (2) speech, or consonant information in particular, may be more poorly accessed from raw auditory memory and thus require a special phonetic memory. (It is important to note that recent experiments have questioned and extended the interpretation of these findings. Recency and suffix effects may be obtained, for example, in sign language (see Chapter 11), which is visual. Nevertheless, the results just reviewed point, once again, to a difference between vowel, non-speech, and consonant perception, even if the difference may not be attributed exclusively to a special phonetic memory.)

Dichotic Listening and Laterality

The last line of evidence that speech may be specially processed comes from dichotic listening. As you may recall, in the beginning of this chapter, we introduced dichotic listening and said that it was mostly used to study laterality. Laterality refers to which of the two hemispheres of the brain is responsible for processing a stimulus or controlling a motor movement. It has long been known that different areas of the brain are responsible for different functions: The left hemisphere controls motor movements and sensations of touch on the right side of the body, and the right hemisphere, on the left. Damage to the left hemisphere can cause paralysis and numbing on the right side of the body. Damage to the left hemisphere, for nearly all right-handed individuals and many left-handed individuals, can also cause an impairment in language skills, to be described in greater detail in Chapter 12.

Hearing does not divide as cleanly as touch, with the right hemisphere controlling the left ear and the left hemisphere the right ear. However, under special presentation conditions it appears possible to make the left hemisphere respond preferentially to material from the right ear, and the right hemisphere to material from the left ear. The special condition is dichotic stimulation, which suppresses information traveling from the ear to the hemisphere on the same side (Kimura, 1961, 1964, 1967).

Kimura showed that dichotically presented spoken digits are more accurately perceived when presented to the right ear than the left (a *right ear advantage* or *REA*), but that excerpted passages of music are better perceived when presented to the left ear than the right. This suggests that the REA does not arise for any auditory stimulation but only for linguistic material. Studdert-Kennedy and Shankweiler (1970) showed that to produce a REA meaningful material is not necessary: Nonsense syllables differing in consonant only yield a REA, although vowel stimuli yield no particular ear advantage (Studdert-Kennedy and Shankweiler, 1970; Blumstein et al., 1977). Other aspects of speech have also been tested: Blumstein and Cooper (1974) found a left ear advantage for dichotic intonation contours, and Tartter (1984) found a slight, nonsignificant left ear advantage for speaker identification of the same syllables for which a significant REA was obtained when subjects judged consonants. REAs have been obtained for vowels—as you might expect—when they are shortened or presented in noise (Godfrey, 1974), when they are less discriminable.

Together, the results suggest that there might be a special speech perceiver in the left hemisphere for consonants, which can also process vowels if they take on the highly encoded characteristics of the consonants.

Models for the Perception of Speech

In the last section we looked at some evidence that speech processing may be special, and in the section before that, at evidence demonstrating a lack of invariance in the speech signal suggesting that a specialized speech processor might be necessary. Here we examine some models (and tests of them) put forth for the perception of speech. Some rely on specialized speech-specific processing; some on larger units than the feature to begin processing; and some on a combination of bottom-up and top-down processing, making use of many levels and several unit sizes to recognize the content of the signal.

The Motor Theory

After observing the context-sensitivity of the acoustic cues to linguistic features, experimenters suggested that the invariance might lie not in the signal but in articulation. They noted that whereas the second formant transition falls for /d/ in the environment /u/ and rises in the environment /i/, the /d/ in both cases is produced by touching the tongue tip to the alveolar ridge. It was hypothesized that in perceiving speech, listeners make reference to their own articulations (Liberman et al., 1967), in a sense mentally constructing how they would produce such a sound. This is known as the *motor theory*. The articulation reference was deemed necessary mostly for the highly encoded consonants and was assumed to occur in the left hemisphere specialized speech processor. (It is important to consider production results in evaluating the motor theory. Although we did not look at the lowest level of production [the individual muscle movements], from the levels we did examine, it can be seen that there is a considerable lack of invariance in production as well as in perception. Production may not be a safe place to turn to escape the perceptual variation problem!)

A related theory, *analysis-by-synthesis* (Stevens and Halle, 1964), also made use of articulation but as a secondary process. It was assumed that first the auditory system analyzed the speech signal, extracting what it could, and then guessed at a likely phonetic candidate for the sound. The guess was checked by using synthesis, a mental production of the candidate, and comparison of the mentally synthesized signal values with those actually extracted from the signal. In case of error, a second guess, synthesis, and comparison were performed.

Both theories have a logical difficulty and an empirical one. The logical difficulty is that if there is enough information in the signal to allow an inference about articulation or synthesis, the articulation or synthesis step is unnecessary (which does not mean that it does not happen). The empirical difficulties are: (1) the theories seem to imply that listeners need speaking experience before they can understand, and that people who have articulation difficulties will show comprehension problems, as should preverbal children, neither of which is true; (2) the motor theory assumes that articulation is more stable than the acoustic signal and as we have seen, articulation is more variable than was originally thought; and (3) speech is comprehended too quickly to allow for many guesses followed by resynthesis for each phoneme or feature.

Detector Theory

A second theory, which spawned a large body of experiments, held that the speech processor consisted of a number of brain cells, each sensitive to a particular phonetic feature (Abbs and Sussman, 1971). A brain cell or group of cells responsible for detecting a stimulus feature is called a *detector* for that feature. The detectors, as the solid lines of Figure 7.10 indicate, worked as opposing pairs—for example, a

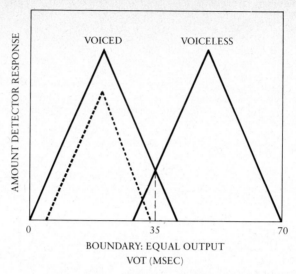

Figure 7.10 *Response of hypothetical voicing detectors. The detector on the left responds to sound with 0–45 msec VOT with a maximum response at about 20 msec VOT. The detector on the right responds to sounds with about 25–70 msec VOT, with the peak response at about 50 msec VOT. The detectors respond equally at 35 msec VOT, which, then is the continuum boundary. The dotted line shows diminished detector response after adaptation with a voiced stimulus. Note the resulting boundary shift.*

detector sensitive to voiced sounds opposes a detector sensitive to voiceless sounds (Eimas and Corbit, 1973). Voicing is signaled when the voiced detector responds more than the voiceless detector. At higher levels in the perceptual system, all that is known is which detector responded more, not what the difference is, so perception is categorical. Each detector is sensitive to a range of acoustic values and responds with a graded output—the magnitude of its response is determined by where in its range it is stimulated. Peak response for the voiced detector in Figure 7.10 occurs at a VOT value of about 20 msec. A boundary occurs when the opposing detectors are equally stimulated, at VOT 35 msec in Figure 7.10.

To test the model, Eimas and Corbit (1973) proposed an adaptation technique. In *adaptation,* a stimulus is presented repeatedly until sensitivity to it decreases. For example, when you first enter a swimming pool or the ocean the cold is shocking; after a while, your sensitivity to the cold diminishes. In speech, Eimas and Corbit presented a syllable 60 times a minute for three minutes initially (the adaptor) and then asked subjects to make five identification responses. Then for the rest of the test, the adaptor was presented for one minute, followed by five identification responses. After adaptation with /ba/, fewer /ba/s were heard in a /ba–pa/ series than before adaptation; sensitivity to /ba/ diminished. Figure 7.11 displays the before and after adaptation functions illustrating the boundary shift. The boundary shift occurs because after adaptation the total output of the affected detector is less, meaning that

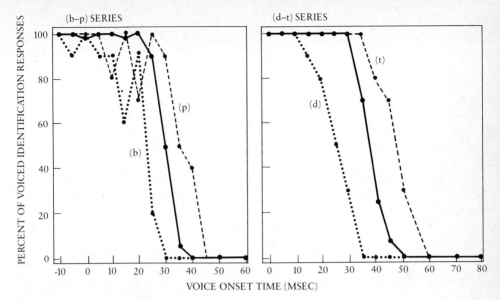

Figure 7.11   *Effects of adaptation on identification of speech. The solid line indicates the unadapted identification function, and the dotted lines indicate the effects of adaptation with the adaptors indicated in parentheses.*
From "Selective adaptation of linguistic feature detectors" by P. D. Eimas and J. L. Corbit, 1973, in Cognitive Psychology, *p. 104. Copyright 1973 by Academic Press. Reprinted by permission.*

the opposing detector has a greater output at the old boundary, as the dotted line in Figure 7.10 indicates.

Additional experiments showed that adaptation with /ba/ shifted a /da–ta/ series toward /da/, indicating that the adaptation effect was not phoneme-specific, and adaptation with /ba/ shifted a /bi–pi/ series, indicating the effect is not syllable specific. Following the seminal work of Eimas and Corbit, other investigators have shown adaptation effects for place of articulation (Cooper, 1974a), manner of articulation (Cooper and Blumstein, 1974), and vowel features (Morse, Kass, and Turkienicz, 1976). However, there have been a number of demonstrations of context sensitivity in adaptation; that is, adaptation with an adaptor nonidentical to the test series produces smaller shifts than do identical adaptors. Thus, adaptation with alternating adaptors /ba/–/pi/ will shift a /ba–pa/ series toward /ba/ and a /bi–pi/ series toward /pi/ (Cooper, 1974b); and adaptation with a CV (/ba/) has no effect on a VC series (/ab–ad/) and conversely (Ades, 1974). Finally, the so-called phonetic feature detectors are sensitive to nonspeech acoustic stimuli—chirps and isolated formants (Tartter and Eimas, 1975); these produce smaller but still significant shifts in the same direction as the speech stimulus from which they were derived.

To account for the seemingly complex pattern of adaptation, two levels of feature detectors were proposed (Tartter and Eimas, 1975), which have since been considered to indicate two processing levels, not the adaptation of feature detectors at all (see Diehl, 1981 for arguments against the detector hypothesis, and Sawusch and Jusczyk,

1981 for modifications). The first level was considered sensitive to basic acoustic features, and the second level, stimulated by output from the first, to integrated, encoded phonetic information. A chirp would adapt both the acoustic detectors for the transitions and, partially, the phonetic detector responding to them. A full stimulus /ba/ would adapt the full range of acoustic detectors and thus have a much greater effect on the phonetic detector. Evidence for a phonetic level apart from the acoustic levels is scarce, and it is probably safest to assume that the higher level responds to integrated acoustic information rather than phonetic information *per se.*

Adaptation experiments have led investigators to postulate at least two levels of processing, whether or not feature detectors mediate response at those levels. More processing stages have been proposed in other models, to be discussed next.

Top-Down Processes in Speech Perception

Units Revisited.   At the beginning of this chapter we suggested that most models of speech perception use the feature or syllable as the unit. Much of this chapter has been devoted to demonstrating the advantages and problems of using the feature as the unit: There is evidence of its psychological integrity, but in both articulation and perception it seems to be heavily dependent on context. The invariance problem suggests that a higher-order unit may have invariance and this may be extracted initially and features extracted from it. If the syllable is the unit, for instance, studies that found that perception of a consonant in a VC did not work in the same way as perception of the same consonant in a CV are easily explained since VCs and CVs are different syllables and so would be processed by different pattern recognizers.

If we assume that the unit of perception is the syllable or higher, we must still account for studies and intuitions indicating a reality for feature or phoneme. The feature or phoneme could be derived after syllable recognition from the output of that process. The feature or the phoneme could have reality in some tasks (like production) but not in normal perception. Or the feature or the phoneme might be useful to describe speech structure but not be used in speech processing.

In fact, a number of investigators have suggested that phoneme perception is an artifact (see, for example, Cole, 1981), deriving from our use of a roughly phonemic alphabet. It has been found, for instance, that illiterate adults cannot add or delete phonemes from the beginning of nonsense syllables, suggesting that phonemic awareness may be learned with the alphabet (Morais, Cainz, Alegria, and Bertelson, 1979). Of course, one still has to account for the development of the phonemic alphabet and the use of devices like alliteration or vowel harmony, which seem to employ some phonemic units, even if they are syllable specific. In any event, one solution to the problem of variability at the feature level is to assume a higher unit of processing. We now turn to evidence for the psychological reality of various units higher than the feature in perception.

Arguments for the Syllable or Demisyllable as Basic Unit.   Massaro (1972, 1974, 1975) provided evidence of the syllable as the basic unit of processing. He used a *recognition masking* task in which subjects are asked to identify a short speech sound followed almost immediately by a noise. If the noise is close enough in time it can block processing of the speech, presumably by interrupting work on it. If the noise follows at a great enough interval it does not interrupt and identification is unimpaired. When it does interrupt, the noise is then called a *mask*.

Massaro found that presenting the mask within 200–250 msec of the speech impaired identification, but delaying the mask beyond 250 msec did not impair identification. He accounted for this by assuming that the speech is actively processed for 250 msec during which time the processing may be interfered with. This duration is interesting since 250 msec is the average length of a syllable. Massaro suggested that speech may be heard as a sequence of syllables, each of which is processed separately. Since there is no interference beyond the 250 msec, the onset of the next syllable will not interfere.

Klatt (1979) and Fujimura and Lovins (1978) suggested that the unit of choice might be a half-syllable, since most coarticulatory effects are over in a half-syllable, and most masking effects likewise end within 125 msec.

Arguments for Units Beyond the Syllable. *Monitoring Results.* Postulation of higher-level units than phoneme or feature does not stop at the syllable. There have been a number of demonstrations that speech perception is influenced by word recognition, meaning, and syntax. The basic technique is to ask subjects to search for something in the speech signal—a superimposed noise, a speaking error, or a particular phoneme or syllable—and note the conditions under which detection is easy. Early demonstrations of the influence of higher-level processing on speech processing came from the click detection studies described in Chapter 5 (Bever, Lackner, and Kirk, 1969), which showed that listeners detected, or reported detecting, extraneous noise superimposed on the speech signal as occurring closer to the major syntactic boundary than it in fact occurred. These results will not be reviewed further here, but it is important to note that they suggest that a large portion of the sound stream, many segments worth, is available for active perceptual processing.

In a variant of the task, subjects are asked to monitor for a particular phoneme or syllable rather than for an extraneous sound. When subjects are listening for an entire syllable, like /bæb/ in a sequence of other syllables, no others of which contain a /b/, they have shorter RTs for recognition than when they are instructed to monitor for a particular phoneme, /b/, in the same list (Savin and Bever, 1970). The syllable advantage holds for monitoring stops, medial vowels, or relatively invariant fricatives. The results were interpreted to suggest that phonemes are derived perceptually after the syllable, making syllable monitoring easier.

However, the decrease in RT when monitoring for larger rather than smaller units does not end at the syllable; Foss and Swinney (1973) demonstrated that subjects recognized two-syllable words faster than one-syllable words and implied that this experiment might be extended indefinitely. The reason, they argued, is that the monitoring task does not tap the initial level of consciousness, a perceptual level, the auditory impact of the speech stream *per se*, but rather taps a level of meaningfulness, after identification, the outcome of attempts to recognize and comprehend the stream. The final level of processing is the one most accessible. RT may be assumed to increase with the difficulty of access, and since the early stages of processing are least accessible, tasks demanding recognition of output from those stages may show long RTs.

Noticing Errors. In these monitoring tasks the sounds to be monitored were properly produced. In other monitoring tasks, which also show the influence of higher-level processes in speech perception, the "signal" is distorted in some way, and the question is whether the listener notices this distortion. One method of distortion, as we have already mentioned, is the introduction of deliberate mispronunciations in fluent speech. Under what conditions does the listener observe them? As already stated, gross phonetic errors—two feature differences rather than one—are more readily detected. In addition, mispronunciations are detected faster in the second or third syllable of a multisyllable word than in the first syllable (Cole and Jakimik, 1980). This can be interpreted as an influence from top-down—the first syllable initiates word recognition; an error in the second or third syllable of a recognized word is immediately obvious, whereas an error in the first syllable may prompt "recognition" of the wrong word, which can be realized only after the remaining syllables are in and word recognition redone. For instance, if the word "linguistic" is mispronounced "ringuistic," at the end of the first syllable there is a perfectly acceptable word. Some time in the second or third syllable it would be realized that the initial guess was wrong, and calculation could start again. If it is mispronounced "linguiskic," when the error appears the word will have been correctly identified and the error will be immediately obvious. Thus, the word's identity, the fact that it has a representation in the mental dictionary, affects the way the speech is processed.

Shadowing Mispronounced Text. Using a variant of the mispronunciation task, Marslen-Wilson (Marslen-Wilson, 1975; and Welsh, 1978) measured the effects of syntax and semantics in fluent speech processing. Subjects were asked to *shadow,* that is, to echo the speech as they heard it. The speech contained speaking errors but was also distorted from normal in that some sentences were scrambled and some semantically anomalous. Mispronunciations occurred in either the first or later syllables, and caused either one (e.g., /b/ → /d/) or three (e.g., /b/ → /θ/) feature discrepancies. Subjects made a substantial number of shadowing errors, not echoing exactly what was presented but correcting the speech to its original state, either by correcting the pronunciation or by changing the word, so the sentence would make sense. Not surprisingly, the amount of correction depended in part on the type of sentence; many more corrections were made for normal sentences than anomalous sentences and for anomalous sentences than scrambled sentences. How far behind the subjects were in shadowing the speech (some began after ¼ sec, some after ¾ sec) had no effect on the context effect in correction, nor did subjects delay after a correction. This suggests that subjects do not hear the error and then correct it, but that, *from the beginning,* they use the syntax and semantics to help "correctly" perceive the speech. (Note that we saw similar simultaneous processing on many levels in speech production and self-monitoring.)

Phonemic Restoration. A second method of distortion is taking continuous speech and obliterating a segment (either phoneme or syllable) by removing it and adding an extraneous noise and asking subjects to report what they hear. The result is called the *phonemic restoration effect* (Warren, 1970; Warren and Obusek, 1971; Warren, Obusek, and Akroff, 1972); as the name implies, subjects fill in the missing sound, reporting that they hear it. That subjects report hearing intact words suggests that they are not processing the signal strictly bottom-up but are using top-down processing to fill in the gaps.

In an ingenious variant of the restoration task, Samuel (1981) presented subjects with stimuli that either were whole words, a phoneme of which co-occurred with noise (called "added"), or were words in which the phoneme was missing and the noise replaced it (called "replaced"). Subjects were asked to determine whether a given stimulus was "added" or "replaced." This permitted assessment of the nature and extent of the restoration effect; often we know what is intended and can guess the target—"str*ngth" is clearly "strength," but just as clearly, we can tell that there is no "e" in the first version. If the top-down process actually fills in the missing sound, then added versions should be indiscriminable from replaced versions—in the added ones the sound was on the tape; in the replaced, it was in the listener's representation. If the phonemic restoration effect results from guessing, the representation of the sound will not be affected, and added and replaced versions should be discriminable.

Samuel found that replaced fricatives and stops were not discriminated well from added ones compared with replaced nasals, vowels, and liquids (/l/, e.g.), probably because the noise used was acoustically similar to the frication and burst in the former. In addition, he found that subjects were much less able to discriminate added or replaced versions of real words than nonwords, suggesting that top-down processes affect perception of isolated words, not just those in sentences, and that at least part of identification involves access in the mental dictionary, not just knowledge of what is phonologically possible. Finally, he found that sentence contexts did not increase discriminability but did increase guessing, which he suggested indicated a limit on the extent of top-down processing; processing at the syntactic level does not affect the perceptual level.

Recognizing Words.   All the top-down findings reviewed thus far suggest that an important unit in speech perception is the word—that low-level speech processing is affected by word recognition. Other evidence for this comes from Ganong (1980), who found that labeling of voiced-voiceless continua was affected by word recognition: If the continuum, in spanning a phonetic feature boundary, also crossed from word to nonword (e.g., "dash–tash"), there were more stimuli assigned to the word end of the continuum than for nonsense syllables spanning the same range (e.g., "dath–tath"). Only the boundary stimuli were affected by the word-nonword change: If a word choice was available, the boundary stimuli were more likely to be heard as words than nonwords. This suggests an interaction of auditory and lexical processes; if the lexical process occurred after categorization (as it would, for example, if subjects were simply more likely to give a word response), it would have been as likely to affect endpoint stimuli as boundary stimuli.

The most widely accepted model proposed to handle such effects is the *cohort model* (see, for example, Marslen-Wilson and Welsh, 1978). Under this framework, it is proposed that as one listens to speech segments, words become activated corresponding to the incoming segments. Hearing an initial /p/ for example, isolates all words beginning with /p/; if /r/ follows, the words that do not have /r/ in second position drop out, etc. The group of word candidates is known as the *cohort*, and members of the cohort may be activated or deactivated by contextual influences as well as the left-to-right bottom-up influences. Word recognition is accomplished when only one element is left in the cohort, and the time for this depends on both phonetic and contextual uniqueness. In this model, all the restoration effects, including failure to correct mispronunciations and lexical bias influencing boundary stimuli categorization, arise from there being enough other information to specify a unique lexical item, without the missing or incorrect phoneme or syllable, and there being greater sensitivity and guessing bias to the lexical item isolated. Finally, the left-to-right selection/elimination in the model accounts for the faster detection of errors in the second or third syllables than in the first, since the word has already been selected. Additional support for this model is given in natural speech perception in *slips of the ear* ("oh, I thought you said . . .")—usually the word(s) selected in a misunderstanding shares some phonetic information (first and last phonemes) and seems to fit with the context; the error arises in the middle phonemes and is detected later on by a misfit with context (Browman, 1980). The only modification necessary in the cohort model is in the strict left-to-right selection since Browman's data show a preservation of the last phoneme, suggesting that it has considerable weight in the word identification process.

Summary and Conclusions

In this chapter we examined the lowest levels of language processing, speech perception, and production, and found multiple levels of structure, as we did for the higher levels of language processing, syntax, and semantics. At one level, there are acoustic and articulatory properties of the signal, which appear to be extracted or produced in complex combinations to give rise to phonetic features. There is considerable evidence for a level in which phonetic features are the processing unit, but they still do not seem to be strictly independent of one another. At another level, the feature combinations that produce phonemes appear to be the psychologically relevant unit; at another, the syllable; at another, the word. These processing levels interact with one another so that word recognition can influence feature processing, and feature processing, word recognition.

Overlaid on the speech-communication aspects of the signal and motor commands are influences of higher-level language functions: We see syntactic and semantic effects apart from word recognition on both pronunciation and perception. Overlaid on the language-communication aspects of the signal are paralinguistic influences, signaling emotional overtone and information relevant to person perception. The overwhelming conclusion about organization of information in speech is that the form of any one segment is influenced by values from all levels, producing a lack of invariance on the one hand, and on the other hand, redundancy—vowel information is smeared across "consonant" portions, "vowel" portions, lexical memory, higher-level phonological rules, and so on. Hearing a vowel "segment" is not necessary; vowel identity is cued elsewhere.

The speech processor, perhaps specially developed, has the task of parsing and producing the signal into the various levels of features, phonemes, syllables, words, phrases, and sentences. This it seems to accomplish by working on several levels simultaneously, over many segments. By working on several levels simultaneously the redundancy provided by each level can help narrow the choice of patterns on the perception side and can introduce effects of context at different levels on the production side. Having information for any one level smeared across several segments also enhances redundancy, thereby allowing a maximally efficient recognition system.

This ends our discussion of normal, fully developed language processing. In the next chapter we will speculate about the aspects of language and language processing that are necessary for a linguistic system, and how they might have evolved. We will compare our language with other communication systems, briefly, to try to derive what is special or unique about language. In the remaining chapters we will look at "exceptional" communication systems, also used by human beings but that differ in critical ways from the language used by normal adults. The aims are (1) to determine whether the aspects that are different are sufficiently different to sustain the argument that these are not language systems (an argument that has been made frequently in the past), and (2) to see what biological and environmental factors are necessary to have a language system.

REFERENCES

Abbs, J. H., & Sussman, H. M. (1971). Neurophysiological feature detectors and speech perception: A discussion of theoretical implications. *Journal of Speech and Hearing Research, 14,* 23–36.

Ades, A. E. (1974). How phonetic is selective adaptation? Experiments on syllable position and vowel environment. *Perception & Psychophysics, 16,* 61–67.

Ali, L., Gallagher, T., Goldstein, J., & Daniloff, R. (1971). Perception of coarticulated nasality. *Journal of the Acoustical Society of America, 49,* 538–540.

Bever, T., Lackner, S., & Kirk, R. (1969). The underlying structures of sentences are the primary units of immediate speech processing. *Perception & Psychophysics, 5,* 225–234.

Blechner, M. J. (1977). Musical skill and the categorical perception of harmonic mode. New Haven, CT: Haskins Laboratories. *Status Report on Speech Research* (SR-51/52).

Blumstein, S. E. (1974). The use and theoretical implications of the dichotic technique for investigating distinctive features. *Brain and Language, 1,* 337–350.

Blumstein, S. E., & Cooper, W. E. (1974). Hemispheric processing of intonation contours. *Cortex, 1,* 337–350.

Blumstein, S. E., & Stevens, K. N. (1979). Acoustic invariance in speech production: Evidence from measurement of spectral characteristics of stop consonants. *Journal of the Acoustical Society of America, 66,* 1001–1018.

Blumstein, S. E., & Stevens, K. N. (1980). Perceptual invariance and onset spectra for stop consonants in different vowel environments. *Journal of the Acoustical Society of America, 67,* 648–662.

Blumstein, S. E., Tartter, V. C., Michel, D., Hirsch, B., & Leiter, E. (1977). The role of distinctive features in the perception of vowels. *Brain and Language, 4,* 508–520.

Bolt, R. H., Cooper, F. S., David, E. E., Jr., Denes, P. B., Pickett, J. M., & Stevens, K. N. (1973). Speaker identification by speech spectrograms: Some further observations. *Journal of the Acoustical Society of America, 54,* 531–534.

Bricker, P. D., & Pruzansky, S. (1966). Effects of stimulus content and duration on talker identification. *Journal of the Acoustical Society of America 40,* 1441–1449.

Browman, C. P. (1980). Perceptual processing: Evidence from slips of the ear. In V. A. Fromkin (Ed.). *Errors in Linguistic Performance: Slips of the Tongue, Ear, Pen, and Hand*. (pp. 213–230). NY: Academic Press.

Cole, R. A. (1973). Goodby to the phoneme and good riddance. Paper presented to the Psychonomic Society, Philadelphia.

Cole, R., Listening for mispronunciations: A measure of what we hear during speech. *Perception & Psychophysics, 4*, 153–156.

Cole, R. A., & Jakimik, J. (1980). How are syllables used to recognize words? *Journal of the Acoustical Society of America, 67*, 965–970.

Coleman, R. O. (1971). Male and female voice quality and its relationship to vowel formant frequencies. *Journal of Speech and Hearing Research, 14*, 565–577.

Cooper, W. E. (1974a). Adaptation of phonetic feature analyzers for place of articulation. *Journal of the Acoustical Society of America, 56*, 617–627.

———. (1974b). Contingent feature analyzers in speech perception. *Perception & Psychophysics, 16*, 201–204.

Cooper, W. E., & Blumstein, S. E. (1974). A labial feature analyzer in speech perception. *Perception & Psychophysics, 15*, 591–600.

Cooper, W. E., & Paccia-Cooper, J. (1980). *Syntax and Speech*. Cambridge, MA: Harvard University Press.

Crowder, R. G. (1971). The sound of vowels and consonants in immediate memory. *Journal of Verbal Learning and Verbal Behavior, 10*, 587–596.

———. (1973). Precategorical acoustic storage for vowels of short and long duration. *Perception & Psychophysics, 13*, 502–506.

Crowder, R. G., & Morton, J. (1969). Precategorical acoustic storage (PAS). *Perception & Psychophysics, 5*, 365–373.

Cutler, A. (1980). Errors of stress and intonation. In V. Fromkin (Ed.). *Errors in Linguistic Performance*. (pp. 67–80). NY: Academic Press.

Darwin, C. J., & Baddeley, A. D. (1974). Acoustic memory and the perception of speech. *Cognitive Psychology, 6*, 41–60.

Delattre, P. C., Liberman, A. M., & Cooper, F. S. (1955). Acoustic loci and transitional cues for consonants. *Journal of the Acoustical Society of America, 27*, 769–773.

Diehl, R. L. (1981). Feature detectors for speech: A critical reappraisal. *Psychological Bulletin, 89*, 1–18.

Dorman, M., Studdert-Kennedy, M., & Raphael, L. J. (1977). Stop-consonant recognition: Release bursts and formant transitions as functionally equivalent, context-dependent cues. *Perception & Psychophysics, 22*, 109–122.

Eimas, P. D. (1963). The relation between identification and discrimination along speech and nonspeech continua. *Language and Speech, 6*, 206–217.

Eimas, P. D., & Corbit, J. D. (1973). Selective adaptation of linguistic feature detectors. *Cognitive Psychology, 4*, 99–109.

Ekman, P., Friesen, W. V., & Scherer, K. R. (1976). Body movement and voice pitch in deceptive interaction. *Semiotica, 16*, 23–27.

Endres, W., Bambach, W., & Flosser, G. (1971). Voice spectrograms as a function of age, voice disguise, and voice imitation. *Journal of the Acoustical Society of America, 49*, 1842–1848.

Fairbanks, G., & Hoaglin, L. W. (1941). An experimental study of the durational characteristics of the voice during the expression of emotion. *Speech Monographs, 8*, 85–90.

Fairbanks, G., & Pronovost, W. (1939). An experimental study of the pitch characteristics of the voice during expression of emotion. *Speech Monographs, 6*, 89–104.

Fant, G. (1973). *Speech Sounds and Features*. Cambridge, MA: MIT Press.

Foss, D. J., & Swinney, D. A. (1973). On the psychological reality of the phoneme: Perception, identification, and consciousness. *Journal of Verbal Learning and Verbal Behavior, 12,* 246–257.

Fromkin, V. A. (1980). *Errors in Linguistic Performance: Slips of the Tongue, Ear, Pen, and Hand.* NY: Academic Press.

———. (1973). *Speech Errors as Linguistic Evidence.* The Hague: Mouton Press.

Fry, D. B. (1955). Duration and intensity as physical correlates of linguistic stress. *Journal of the Acoustical Society of America, 27,* 765–768.

Fry, D. B., Abramson, A. S., Eimas, P. D., & Liberman, A. M. (1962). The identification of synthetic vowels. *Language and Speech, 5,* 171–189.

Fujimura, O., & Lovins, J. (1978). Syllables as concatenative phonetic units. In A. Bell & J. B. Cooper (Eds.). *Syllables and Segments.* (107–120). Amsterdam: North Holland Publishing Co.

Fujisaki, H., & Kawashima, T. (1968). The influence of various factors on the identification and discrimination of synthetic speech sounds. Paper presented at the 6th International Congress on Acoustics, Tokyo.

Fujisaki, H., & Kawashima, T. (1969). On the modes and mechanisms of speech perception. *Sogoshikenjo-Nenpo, 28,* 67–73.

Ganong, W. F., III. (1980). Phonetic categorization in auditory word perception. *Journal of Experimental Psychology: Human Perception & Performance. 6,* 110–125.

Gerstman, L. H. (1968). Classification of self-normalized vowels. *IEEE Transactions on Audio- and Electroacoustics, AU-16,* 16–80.

Godfrey, J. J. (1974). Perceptual difficulty and the right-ear advantage for vowels. *Brain and Language, 1,* 323–335.

Greenberg, J. H., & Jenkins, J. J. (1964). Studies in the psychological correlates of the sound system of American English. *Word, 20,* 157–177.

Hadding-Koch, K., & Studdert-Kennedy, M. (1964). An experimental study of some intonation contours. *Phonetica, 11,* 175–185.

Harris, K. S. (1958). Cues for the discrimination of American English fricatives in spoken syllables. *Language and Speech, 1,* 1–7.

Hazen, B. (1973). Effects of differing phonetic contexts on spectrographic speaker identification. *Journal of the Acoustical Society of America, 54,* 650–660.

Hecker, M. H. L., Stevens, K. N., von Bismarck, G., & Williams, C. E. (1968). Manifestations of task-induced stress on the acoustic speech signal. *Journal of the Acoustical Society of America, 44,* 993–1001.

Heinz, J. M., & Stevens, K. N. (1961). On the properties of voiceless fricative consonants. *Journal of the Acoustical Society of America, 33,* 589–596.

Jakobson, R., Fant, C. G. M., & Halle, M. (1951/1969). *Preliminaries to Speech Analysis.* Cambridge, MA: MIT Press.

Joos, M. (1948). Acoustic phonetics. *Language Supplement, 24,* 1–136.

Kersta, L. G. (1962). Voiceprint identification. *Nature,* 1253–1257.

Kewley-Port, D. (1983). Time-varying features as correlates of place of articulation in stop consonants. *Journal of the Acoustical Society of America, 73,* 322–335.

Kimura, D. (1961). Cerebral dominance and the perception of verbal stimuli. *Canadian Journal of Psychology, 15,* 166–171.

———. (1964). Left–right differences in the perception of melodies. *Quarterly Journal of Experimental Psychology, 16,* 355–358.

———. (1967). Functional asymmetry of the brain in dichotic listening. *Cortex, 3,* 163–178.

Klatt, D. H. (1979). Speech perception: A model of acoustic-phonetic analysis and lexical access. *Journal of Phonetics, 7,* 279–312.

Kuhl, P. K. (1981). Discrimination of speech by nonhuman animals: Basic auditory sensitivities conducive to the perception of speech sound categories. *Journal of the Acoustical Society of America, 70,* 340–349.

Kuhl, P., & Miller, J. D. (1975). Speech perception by the chinchilla: The voiced-voiceless distinction in alveolar plosive consonants. *Science, 190,* 69–72.

Kuhl, P. K., & Miller, J. D. (1978). Speech perception by the chinchilla: Identification functions for synthetic VOT stimuli. *Journal of the Acoustical Society of America, 63,* 905–917.

Ladefoged, P., & Broadbent, D. E. (1957). Information conveyed by vowels. *Journal of the Acoustical Society of America, 29,* 98–104.

Lane, H. (1965). The motor theory of speech perception: A critical review. *Psychological Review, 72,* 275–309.

Lashley, K. S. (1951). The problem of serial order in behavior. In L. A. Jeffress (Ed.). *Cerebral Mechanisms in Behavior.* (pp. 112–146). NY: John Wiley and Sons.

LeHiste, I., (1979). The perception of duration within sequences of four intervals. *Journal of Phonetics, 7,* 313–316.

LeHiste, I., & Peterson, G. E. (1961). Some basic considerations in the analysis of intonation. *Journal of the Acoustical Society of America, 33,* 419–425.

Levelt, W. J. M. (1983). Monitoring and self-repair in speech. *Cognition, 14,* 41–104.

Liberman, A. M., Cooper, F. S., Shankweiler, D. P., & Studdert-Kennedy, M. (1967). Perception of the speech code. *Psychological Review, 74,* 431–461.

Liberman, A. M., Delattre, P. C., & Cooper, F. S. (1952). The role of selected stimulus variables in the perception of unvoiced stop consonants. *American Journal of Psychology, 65,* 497–516.

Liberman, A. M., Harris, K. S., Kinney, J. H., & Lane, H. L. (1961). The discrimination of relative onset time of the components of certain speech and nonspeech patterns. *Journal of Experimental Psychology, 61,* 379–388.

Liberman, A. M., Harris, K. S., Hoffman, H. S., & Griffith, B. C. (1957). The discrimination of speech sounds within and across phoneme boundaries. *Journal of Experimental Psychology, 54,* 358–368.

Liberman, M., & Streeter, L. (1978). Use of nonsense-syllable mimicry in the study of prosody phenomena. *Journal of the Acoustical Society of America, 63,* 231–233.

Lieberman, P. (1960). Some acoustic correlates of word stress in American English. *Journal of the Acoustical Society of America, 32,* 451–454.

———. (1975). *On the Origins of Language.* NY: Macmillan.

Lisker, L., & Abramson, A. S. (1967). Some effects of context on voice onset time in English stops. *Language and Speech, 10,* 1–28.

MacKay, D. G. (1970). Spoonerisms: The structure of errors in the serial order of speech. *Neuropsychologia, 8,* 323–350.

———. (1972). The structure of words and syllables: Evidence from errors in speech. *Cognitive Psychology, 3,* 210–227.

Mann, V. A. (1980). Influence of preceding liquid on stop consonant perception. *Perception & Psychophysics, 28,* 407–412.

Mann, V. A., & Repp, B. H. (1981). Influence of preceding fricative on stop consonant perception. *Journal of the Acoustical Society of America, 69,* 548–566.

Marslen-Wilson, W. D. (1975). Sentence perception as an interactive parallel process. *Science, 189,* 226–228.

Marslen-Wilson, W. D., & Welsh, A. (1978). Processing interaction and lexical access during word recognition in continuous speech. *Cognitive Psychology, 10,* 29–63.

Massaro, D. W. (1972). Preperceptual images, processing time, and perceptual units in auditory perception. *Psychological Review, 79,* 129–145.

———. (1975). Backward recognition masking. *Journal of the Acoustical Society of America,* 58, 1059–1065.

———. (1974). Perceptual units in speech recognition. *Journal of Experimental Psychology,* 102, 199–208.

Mattingly, I. G., Liberman, A. M., Syrdal, A. K., & Halwes, T. (1971). Discrimination in speech and nonspeech modes. *Cognitive Psychology,* 2, 131–157.

McGehee, F. (1944). An experimental study of voice recognition. *Journal of General Psychology,* 31, 53–65.

———. (1937). The reliability of the identification of the human voice. *Journal of General Psychology,* 17, 249–271.

Miller, G. A., & Nicely, P. (1955). An analysis of perceptual confusions among English consonants. *Journal of the Acoustical Society of America,* 2, 338–352.

Miller, J. L. (1981). Effects of speaking rate on segmental distinctions. In P. D. Eimas & J. L. Miller (Eds.). *Perspectives on the Study of Speech.* (pp. 39–74). Hillsdale, NJ: Lawrence Erlbaum Associates.

Miller, J. L., & Grosjean, F. (1981). How the components of speaking rate influence perception of phonetic segments. *Journal of Experimental Psychology: Human Perception and Performance,* 7, 208–215.

Miyawaki, K., Strange, W., Verbrugge, R., Liberman, A. M., Jenkins, J. J., & Fujimura, O. (1975). An effect of linguistic experience: The discrimination of [r] and [l] by native speakers of Japanese and English. *Perception & Psychophysics,* 18, 331–340.

Mohr, B., & Wang, W. S-Y. (1968). Perceptual distance and the specification of phonological features. *Phonetics,* 18, 31–45.

Morais, J., Cary, L., Alegria, J., & Bertelson, P. (1979). Does awareness of speech as a sequence of phones arise spontaneously? *Cognition,* 7, 323–331.

Morse, P. A., Kass, J. E., & Turkienicz, R. T. (1976). Selective adaptation of vowels. *Perception & Psychophysics,* 19, 139–143.

Paccia-Cooper, J., & Cooper, W. E. (1981). The processing of phrase structures in speech production. In P. D. Eimas & J. L. Miller (Eds.). *Perspectives in the Study of Speech.* (pp. 311–336). Hillsdale, NJ: Lawrence Erlbaum Associates.

Peterson, G. E., & Barney, H. L. (1952). Control methods in a study of vowels. *Journal of the Acoustical Society of America,* 24, 175–184.

Pierrehumbert, J. (1979). The perception of fundamental frequency declination. *Journal of the Acoustical Society of America,* 66, 363–369.

Pisoni, D. B. (1973). Auditory and phonetic memory codes in the discrimination of consonants and vowels. *Perception & Psychophysics,* 13, 253–260.

———. (1975a). Dichotic listening and processing phonetic features. In F. Restle, R. M. Shiffrin, N. J. Castellan, H. R. Lindman, & D. B. Pisoni (Eds.). *Cognitive Theory,* vol. 1. (pp. 79–102). Hillsdale, NJ: Lawrence Erlbaum Associates.

———. (1975b). Auditory short-term memory and vowel perception. *Memory and Cognition,* 3, 7–18.

———. (1977). Identification and discrimination of relative onset time of two component tones: Implications for voicing perception in stops. *Journal of the Acoustical Society of America,* 61, 1352–1361.

Ptacek, P. H., & Sander, E. K. (1966). Age recognition from voice. *Journal of Speech and Hearing Research,* 9, 273–277.

Samuel, A. G. (1977). The effect of discrimination training on speech perception: Noncategorical perception. *Perception & Psychophysics,* 22, 321–330.

———. (1981). Phonemic restoration: Insights from a new methodology. *Journal of Experimental Psychology: General,* 110, 474–494.

Savin, H., & Bever, T. G. (1970). The nonperceptual reality of the phoneme. *Journal of Verbal Learning and Verbal Behavior, 9,* 295–302.

Sawusch, J. P., & Jusczyk, P. (1981). Adaptation and contrast in the perception of voicing. *Journal of Experimental Psychology: Human Perception and Performance, 7,* 408–421.

Schatz, C. D. (1954). The role of context in the perception of stops. *Language, 30,* 47–56.

Scherer, K. R. (1979). Personality markers in speech. In K. R. Scherer & H. Giles (Eds.). *Social Markers in Speech.* (pp. 147–201). Cambridge: Cambridge University Press.

Shankweiler, D., Strange, W., & Verbrugge, R. (1977). Speech and the problem of perceptual constancy. In R. Shaw & J. Bransford (Eds.). *Perceiving, Acting and Knowing: Towards an Ecological Psychology.* (pp. 315–345). MD: Potomac, Erlbaum.

Sorenson, J. M., & Cooper, W. E. (1980). Syntactic coding of fundamental frequency in speech production. In R. A. Cole (Ed.). *Perception and Production of Fluent Speech.* (pp. 399–440). Hillsdale, NJ: Lawrence Erlbaum Associates.

Sternberg, S., Monsell, S., Knoll, R. L. & Wright, C. E. (1980). The latency and duration of rapid movement sequences: Comparisons of speech and typewriting. In R. A. Cole (Ed.). *Perception and Production of Fluent Speech.* (pp. 469–505). Hillsdale, NJ: Lawrence Erlbaum Associates.

Stevens, K. N., & Halle, M. (1964). Remarks on analysis-by-synthesis and distinctive features. In W. Wathen-Dunn (Ed.). *Models for the Perception of Speech and Visual Form.* (pp. 88–102). Cambridge, MA: MIT Press.

Stevens, K. N. (1972). The quantal nature of speech: Evidence from articulatory acoustic data. In E. E. David, Jr., & P. B. Denes (Eds.). *Human Communication: A Unified View,* (pp. 51–66). NY: McGraw-Hill Book Co.

Stevens, K. N. (1975). The potential role of property detectors in the perception of consonants. In G. Fant & M. A. A. Tatham (Eds.). *Auditory Analysis and Perception of Speech,* (pp. 303–330). NY: Academic Press.

Stevens, K. N., & Blumstein, S. E. (1978). Invariant cues for place of articulation in stop consonants. *Journal of the Acoustical Society of America, 64,* 1358–1368.

Stevens, K. N., & Blumstein, S. E. (1981). The search for invariant acoustic correlates of phonetic features. In P. D. Eimas & J. L. Miller (Eds.). *Perspectives on the Study of Speech.* (pp. 1–38). Hillsdale, NJ: Lawrence Erlbaum Associates.

Stevens, K. N., Williams, C. E., Carbonell, J. R., & Woods, B. (1968). Speaker authentication and identification: A comparison of spectrographic and auditory presentations of speech material. *Journal of the Acoustical Society of America, 44,* 1596–1607.

Streeter, L. A., Krauss, R. M., Geller, V. J., Olson, C., & Apple, W. (1977). Pitch changes during attempted deception. *Journal of Personality and Social Psychology, 35,* 345–350.

Streeter, L. A., MacDonald, N. H., Apple, W., Krauss, R. M., & Galotti, K. M. (1983). Acoustical and perceptual indicators of stress. *Journal of the Acoustical Society of America, 73,* 1354–1360.

Studdert-Kennedy, M., & Shankweiler, D. (1970). Hemispheric specialization for speech perception. *Journal of the Acoustical Society of America, 48,* 579–594.

Summerfield, A. Q., & Haggard, M. P. (1975). Vocal tract normalization as demonstrated by reaction times. In G. Fant & M. A. A. Tatham (Eds.). *Auditory Analysis and Perception of Speech.* (pp. 115–147). NY: Academic Press.

Tartter, V. C. (1980). Happy talk: The perceptual and acoustic effects of smiling on speech. *Perception & Psychophysics, 27,* 24–27.

———. (1981). A comparison of the identification and discrimination of synthetic vowel and stop consonant stimuli with various acoustic properties. *Journal of Phonetics, 9,* 477–486.

———. (1982). Vowel and consonant manipulations and the dual-coding model of auditory storage: A reevaluation. *Journal of Phonetics, 10,* 217–223.

————. (1984). Laterality differences in speaker and consonant identification in dichotic listening. *Brain and Language, 23,* 74–85.

Tartter, V. C., & Eimas, P. D. (1975). The role of auditory feature detectors in the perception of speech. *Perception & Psychophysics, 18,* 293–298.

Tartter, V. C., Kat, D., Samuel, A. G., & Repp, B. H. (1983). Perception of intervocalic stop consonants: The contributions of closure durations and formant transitions. *Journal of the Acoustical Society of America, 74,* 715–725.

Tosi, O., Oyer, H., Lashbrook, W., Pedrey, C., Nicol, J., & Nash, E. (1972). Experiment on voice identification. *Journal of the Acoustical Society of America, 51,* 2030–2043.

van den Broeke, M. P. K., & Goldstein, L. (1980). Consonant features in speech errors. In V. A. Fromkin (Ed.). *Errors in Linguistic Performance: Slips of the Tongue, Ear, Pen, and Hand,* (pp. 47–65). NY: Academic Press.

Warren, R. M. (1970). Perceptual restoration of missing speech sounds. *Science, 167,* 392–393.

Warren, R. M., & Obusek, C. (1971). Speech perception and phonemic restorations. *Perception & Psychophysics, 9,* 358–363.

Warren, R. M., Obusek, C., & Akroff, J. M. (1972). Auditory induction: Perceptual synthesis of absent sounds. *Science, 196,* 1149–1151.

Weinberg, B., & Bennett, S. (1971). Speaker recognition of 5- and 6-year-old children's voices. *Journal of the Acoustical Society of America, 50,* 1210–1213.

Williams, C. E., & Stevens, K. N. (1969). On determining the emotional state of pilots during flight: An exploratory study. *Aerospace Medicine, 40,* 1369–1372.

Williams, C. E., & Stevens, K. N. (1972). Emotions and speech: Some acoustic correlates. *Journal of the Acoustical Society of America, 52,* 1238–1250.

Wish, M., & Carroll, J. D. (1974). Application of individual differences scaling to studies of human perception and judgment. In *Handbook of Perception,* vol. II, (pp. 449–491). NY: Academic Press.

Zatorre, R. J. (1983). Category-boundary effects and speeded sorting with a harmonic musical-interval continuum: Evidence for serial processing. *Journal of Experimental Psychology: Human Perception & Performance, 9,* 734–752.

Appendix: Perception of Vowel and Speaker Information

For interested readers this section contains descriptions of models and experiments of recognition of other aspects of speech besides consonants. Vowel perception, perception of emotion and paralinguistic information, and perception of speaker identity are described here. Basically the same problem occurs for recognition of these percepts as for recognition of consonant features: No invariants have been found. It appears that speaker, emotion, vowel, and consonant identities are smeared across all aspects of the speech signal and conveyed simultaneously in any one aspect.

Perception of Vowels

Since the earliest work on speech perception (Joos, 1948) it was assumed that vowel perception was simpler than consonant perception. The reasons for this are many: First, vowels may be articulated in isolation; second, steady information seems simpler than rapidly changing information; third, as research with consonants revealed greater and greater complexity, it seemed that there had to be a starting point or anchor—if we know the vowel, for instance, we know whether a falling or a rising second and third formant should signal /d/. Thus, we might suggest that speech perception begins with the steady states, uses these to determine the vowel quality, and uses the vowel to judge the transitions and constriction information to recover the consonant. This model, however, does not work because vowels are more variable than they seem.

   Sources of Variability.   The problems arise as soon as we look at natural fluent speech instead of synthetic speech. Reexamine Figure 7.1—the spectrogram of the fluent sentence. How much steady state is there? As the earliest studies of speech noted, in fluent speech, steady state formant frequencies are rarely attained; instead, they are suggested in the transitions. A natural CVC (consonant-vowel-consonant) syllable looks more like ⟨⟨ than it does like ≡≡ , unless the speaker deliberately attempts to sustain the vowel. Since the steady state frequencies are not quite achieved but are, *presumably,* the speaker's target, the actual sounds produced were considered to *undershoot* the target. It was left to some clever perception device to calibrate the undershoot (Joos, 1948) which for a given speaker might vary from one production of an utterance to another.

   A second, obvious problem is that steady state frequencies vary enormously from speaker to speaker; therefore, a perceptual routine that searches for particular frequencies and then assigns vowel labels to them will not work across speakers. In a classic study Peterson and Barney (1952) collected pronunciation of vowels in the context h_d, from 76 speakers (men, women, and children) analyzed them acoustically, and presented them to listeners for identification. Figure 7.12, adapted from the study, displays the locations of the vowels of these speakers with respect to their first and second formant frequencies. Note the overlap in the figure enclosing the / ɛ /; there are identifications of æ, ɚ, and I. However, the possible confusions suggested by the display did not materialize when the sounds were identified by the listeners; those displayed were labeled consistently as the speakers intended. The speaker variation gets compounded when we consider the variation introduced by changes in rate (Miller, 1981) and also by changes of facial expression, such as smiling, which substantially alters the steady state frequencies without affecting vowel identification (Tartter, unpublished data).

   Normalization Models.   To overcome the problems of within- and between-speaker variability, researchers have suggested several different perceptual strategies. The simplest of these, the use of some relative measure of formant frequencies rather than the absolute frequencies (e.g., the ratio of the first and second formant frequencies, or a scaling of the whole vowel space up or down by a factor), does not work very well either, showing a wide range of variation across speakers (Fant, 1973). A somewhat more complex strategy was proposed by Joos (1948) and elaborated by Lieberman (1975), and was more or less accepted for a time (see Shankweiler, Strange, and Verbrugge, 1977). It was assumed that in the first few minutes of listening to a new speaker the listener uses some of the speaker's initial phonemes to calibrate the speaker and construct a *normalization* routine that will convert the speaker's vowel

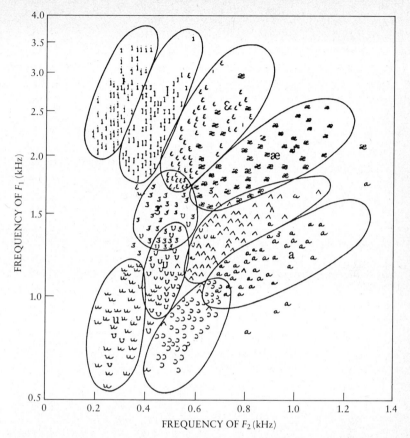

Figure 7.12 *The range of formant frequencies produced by different speakers when uttering the same vowel. Circles enclose utterances of a vowel reliably identified by listeners.*
From *"Control methods in a study of vowels"* by G. E. Peterson and H. L. Barney, 1952, in The Journal of the Acoustical Society of America, 24, *p. 182. Copyright 1952 by the American Institute of Physics. Adapted by permission.*

space to some canonical form. For example, suppose there is a prototypical or average vowel space, and a new speaker has second formant frequency values generally 200 Hz above this average. As soon as this is determined the listener can mentally adjust the speaker's formant values to conform to the mental vowel space and match the vowel. Careful consideration of this model suggests the following: (1) initially, before the listener has determined the proper calibration routine, there should be some difficulty in perceiving the speech; (2) the listener must be able to identify absolutely some vowel in order to calculate the calibration—to determine that a speaker's second formant frequency is 200 Hz above the normal /a/ (and not 200 Hz below the normal /I/), the listener must know that it was /a/ that was intended.

Both aspects of the model have, in part, been tested. There is some evidence that listeners do calibrate; as we have seen, there are context effects in speech perception and these extend to vowels. Ladefoged and Broadbent (1957) presented a test word /bIt/ following the sentence "Please say what this word is." The sentence was synthesized to represent different vocal tracts, and this affected listeners' judgments of the word. Depending on the vocal tract it was heard as /bIt/ or /bɛt/. Summerfield and Haggard (1975) have provided other evidence that listeners calibrate. Reaction time for identification of pairs of synthetic speech syllables is longer when the syllables are synthesized to represent different vocal tracts than when they are synthesized with characteristics consistent with one vocal tract. This extra time could arise from normalizing.

To perform the normalization, as stated, we need some anchor point, a certain sound we can use to calibrate. One suggestion has been the point vowels /i, a, u/. These are attractive candidates because (1) they occur in all languages so could reasonably be the start of a basic perceptual routine; (2) there is less acoustic variation between- and within- speaker for these vowels than for the others (Stevens, 1972); (3) they constitute the extremes of articulation and therefore show vocal tract size, which, as we saw in the last chapter, can be used to predict or account for formant frequency values; and (4) Gerstman (1968) demonstrated that the Peterson and Barney (1952) syllables could be correctly identified with 97 percent accuracy by a computerized normalization routine based on the point vowels. The problem with this as a model for speech perception is that we do not have enforced greetings of i-a-u or hid-had-hud when meeting a stranger, and if these vowels are necessary for calibration one would expect to be at sea until the stranger elected to utter them. If they were critical one would expect that a ritualized greeting using them would have evolved cross-culturally. Moreover, obviously it is not enough that the speaker articulates these vowels; the listener must know when hearing an /i/ that that is what the speaker intends.

Considering these shortcomings, Shankweiler, Strange, and Verbrugge (1977) proposed a different perceptual anchor, bringing us full circle. Recall that constriction and transition information are vowel-dependent, which we discussed earlier as a problem for consonant recognition. However, the dependency indicates that there is information about the vowel in these parts of the segment and that "the consonant" information could be used for the vowel identification. Indeed, as you may recall, Stevens and Blumstein (1981) have demonstrated that vowels could be identified from 10 msec of onset information. Moreover, Summerfield's and Haggard's (1975) hypothesized normalization for syllables could not make use of point vowels since they were not provided. And in cases where the steady state targets are not reached, in undershoot, the only vowel cues present must be in the transitions. Finally, Shankweiler et al. showed that identification of isolated vowels spoken by several different speakers is considerably poorer (25 percent worse) than identification of the same vowels in /pVp/ context. This suggests that the immediate context could provide an anchor. Thus, we have come full circle because in the beginning of this section we started discussion of steady-state vowels in order to have a perceptual anchor for the context-dependent consonant cues; the context-dependent consonant cues are now proposed as perceptual anchor for the vowel!

The difficulty of finding invariance in the signal or in calibrating information directly from the signal has led to the construction of special processing models for speech, discussed in the chapter. For now, consider the possibility that speech recognition may take place on several levels simultaneously and that these levels interact. Thus, information about a vowel formant frequency may be extracted along with information about the consonant from the transitions and may be integrated with information about the vowel and consonant found in other portions of the signal. Since cues to any one feature seem smeared across several segments, it seems reasonable that the features are processed in parallel over several segments.

Perception of Tone of Voice

Another factor that adds to the variability of acoustic and articulatory specification of segments is differences in "tone of voice." For example, the acoustic cues for voicing depend on the stress of the syllable in which the segment appears, the rate of production of the sentence, and the pause duration. Differences between speakers alter the vowel space, and differences in facial expression alter the formant frequencies of speech. This is only a small list of the effects of tone of voice on segments, and in this section we will not elaborate it further. Rather, the purpose of this section is to look at perception and production of "tone of voice" itself rather than its effects on segment perception and production.

As described in Chapter 6, we can break tone of voice into several components: linguistically relevant components of intonation and stress that distinguish segments or grammatical forms, and components that appear because of physical characteristics of the speaker such as his/her size, sex, or emotional state.

Stress, Intonation, and Duration.   As with segmental features, there has been difficulty finding invariance in the suprasegmentals. Linguistic stress, for example, the feature distinguishing com'pact (N) from compact' (ADJ), is manifested by an increase in duration, fundamental frequency, and intensity in the stressed syllable; these can offset one another (Fry, 1955; Lieberman, 1960). Pitch value is affected by segmental value (usually there is a higher pitch following voiceless segments than voiced [LeHiste and Peterson, 1961]), and obviously also in English by grammatical value; in interrogative sentences pitch rises at the end instead of falling steadily. Recognition of the fall or rise at the end of the sentence depends not on absolute frequency but on the relative frequencies and on normalization, reminiscent of vowel perception. Specifically, Hadding-Koch and Studdert-Kennedy (1964) demonstrated that for a pitch contour to be identified as interrogative the terminal pitch must not only rise but also must be higher than any other pitch in the sentence. Moreover, contours with this property but conveyed on sentences interpreted as statements were judged as falling even though they were rising. The first point suggests that in perceiving or producing questions listeners or speakers keep track of pitch across many segments; the second suggests that, at least in some instances, the syntactic form or the meaning of the sentence is used to judge pitch instead of the converse. (For this reason, nonsense speech has been recently employed to study pitch perception—see Liberman and Streeter, 1978.) Moreover, Pierrehumbert (1979) has shown that perception of pitch is position dependent—listeners judged a later pitch peak as equal in pitch to an earlier one when, in fact, it was about 10 Hz lower! In all likelihood, this is a result of spontaneous perceptual "correction" for pitch declination in declarative sentences; we do not hear the pitch drop but a flat contour. If this correction applies to interrogatives, it will accentuate the normal pitch rise.

LeHiste (1979) has shown a similar perceptual correction for duration relative to position in sequences of nonspeech of identical durations: Listeners tend to hear the first in a sequence as longer than the others regardless of the actual length, and the fourth (last) as shortest.

Speaker Identification. The interest in the physical characteristics of the voice has arisen from obvious legal applications—do people's voices indicate their identities invariantly, as their fingerprints do? Can we tell whether a person is telling the truth or what (s)he is really feeling from the tone of voice, which, unlike words (except in the case of slips of the tongue), (s)he has no control over? As with invariant cues for consonants, we are looking for some aspect of the individual's voice that is present in all contexts and that identifies this individual and no other. The first question to ask is: Do we make reliable identifications of speaker as we do for consonants? If so, then we may ask what we use for cues.

Among the first experiments conducted on the reliability of voice identification were those of McGehee (1937, 1944). They were prompted by testimony in the Lindbergh kidnapping trial that the kidnapper's voice had been recognized from a telephone conversation held three years earlier.

To see if this was reasonable, McGehee presented listeners with voices from one of five speakers and asked them to select which of the five had been presented. (Note that this is easier than a real life situation in that the subject had only five among which to choose and knew absolutely that the voice was one of those five.) Identification was 80 percent during the first seven days and fell to 50 percent after the first month following the presentation (20 percent is chance). Speakers who changed their pitches in attempts at disguise were recognized better than 60 percent of the time in the first few days; thereafter accuracy dropped markedly but still remained above chance.

Subsequent studies of speaker identification have shown better accuracy of identification, in part because of better recording techniques. Speaker identification is better for longer samples than for shorter ones, pointing to smear of speaker information across the signal, and in some speech segments rather than in others (Bricker and Pruzansky, 1966). Subjects are good at judging sex (Coleman, 1971) and age of the speaker (Ptacek and Sander, 1966), if not absolutely identifying the speaker. Interestingly, sex can be judged when the voice is excited by an electronic larynx, so there is no pitch difference (Coleman, 1971), and in children, where one would expect both pitch and vocal tract cues to be the same for the two sexes (Weinberg and Bennett, 1971). Thus, results of identification tests indicate that a fair amount of information about the speaker is carried in the voice and appears to be carried in the resonances more than in the pitch. Thus, speaker information is overlaid on phonetic information.

Examination of spectrograms for different speakers affords yet another method of voice identification—by eye instead of by ear—and can also help separate out the acoustic invariants of voice recognition, if there are some. Claims about efficacy of voiceprint identification range from 98 percent accuracy for isolated words selected from 12 different speakers (Kersta, 1962; and see Tosi, Oyer, Lashoock, Pedrey, Nicol, and Nash, 1972 for extensive replication) to 79 percent accuracy for words selected from 24 different speakers and compared with a 94 percent auditory identification rate for the same samples (Stevens, Williams, Carbonell, and Woods, 1968). However, the accuracy rate drops drastically once "normal" variations are allowed, such as fluent speech as opposed to isolated syllables, match of different utterances from the same speaker as opposed to match of the identical utterance, and the possibility that the real speaker is not represented in the group to be matched. Each of these substantially increases the rate of errors, sometimes to as much as 57 percent (Hazen, 1973). Moreover, vocal variations, such as attempts to disguise the voice by raising or lowering the pitch or changing the register, or aging over many years, make identification still less reliable (Endres, Bambach, and Flosser, 1971), and affect more aspects of the speech signal than the speaker may be consciously trying to alter; for example, the formant frequencies change position when pitch is altered and with age. And spectrogram inspectors, when asked how they are making the judgments, seem to have no firm set of criteria or invariant cues but rely on overall impressions. Thus, Bolt, Cooper, David, Denes, Pickett, and Stevens (1973) conclude that speaker identification from spectrograms is, at least at this stage, not a reliable method of identifying an individual—speakers may leave an invariant print on their speech, but like the search for invariance in phonetic identity, the search for such invariance has for the most part turned up a variety of "context" effects.

Emotion. The speech signal has also been used to try to diagnose states of the speaker such as physiological problems, personality disorders, or mood. The first two of these will not be discussed here (see Scherer, 1979 for review) but will be treated in Chapter 13.

Most of the work has been done to identify negative emotional states from the voice. These include speaker's stress (Hecker, Stevens, von Bismarck, and Williams, 1968; Williams and Stevens, 1969; Streeter, MacDonald, Apple, Krauss, and Galotti, 1983); attempts to deceive (Ekman, Friesen, and Scherer, 1976; Streeter, Krauss, Geller, Olson, and Apple, 1977); sorrow, anger (Williams and Stevens, 1972); contempt, fear, grief, and indifference (Fairbanks and Hoaglin, 1941; Fairbanks and Pronovost, 1939). The studies have been based on the assumption that the emotion produces a physiological change that has an effect on vocalizations—by changing fluid, increasing respiration, or altering the general activity rate.

Generally the results show that the emotions, as judged from vocal parameters, may be divided into two classes—active and nonactive. In active emotions such as stress, lying (which seems to be inseparable vocally from stress), or anger, there is an increase in pitch, loudness, pitch fluctuations, loudness fluctuations, and speaking rate. In the less active emotions, these parameters all decrease. Listeners also appear to be able to identify the emotion from changes in vocal tone but are influenced by the content of the speech and other aspects of the situation. Moreover, subjects have seldom been asked to discriminate finely emotions of the same class, like stress and deception, so it is unclear how precisely the voice labels the emotional state.

In the one study of positive emotion (Tartter, 1980), also prompted by the assumption that a change in physical characteristics of the speaker would alter the speech signal, it was found that listeners could identify nonsense syllables spoken with a smile from those spoken without a smile, and, when not told what the articulation difference was, could label those syllables as sounding happier than nonsmiled counterparts. Smiling caused an increase in pitch in most speakers and an increase in all formant frequencies in all speakers.

STUDY QUESTIONS

1. What arguments have been made in support of the notion that speech is special? Critically discuss the evidence both for and against this position.
2. What is the problem of pattern recognition in speech? How does the top-down processing approach resolve it? Is there an alternative you prefer? Discuss.
3. Discuss the evidence supporting the phonetic feature as a "unit" of processing. Assume that the phoneme or syllable is "the unit"—what results would you expect to see instead of those obtained in scaling experiments and dichotic listening? Critically consider whether the feature is in fact the best choice of unit.

Language:
A Human-Specific
Accomplishment?

What, if anything, is it about language that makes it "special"? So far, we have defined language as the way humans communicate. Now that we have examined the structure and processing of language, the time has come to be more specific, to determine the defining characteristics of this mode of communication. Do animals have the same or similar modes? Or is there some reasonable set of criteria we can establish to distinguish animal communication from human communication, aside from the obvious one of who is the communicator? Do all humans have language? Does a newborn infant, for instance? Or is there a point in development when the infant passes from another form of communication to language as we know it? How, given only the child's communications, do we recognize this point, do we define the shift from non-language to language? Whatever the criteria used to recognize the shift, do all languages satisfy these standards equally well, or are some languages more primitive than others, meeting fewer of these criteria? Similarly, are some animal communication systems more advanced than others, meeting language standards more precisely?

Obviously, to consider such questions we must establish precisely what we mean by language, what constitutes language and what does not. As we will see, we need also to establish precisely what constitutes communication, and the definitions of language and communication and the distinctions between them are by no means settled.

In this chapter, we introduce some animal communication and human nonlanguage communication systems and use them to present alternative systems of social interaction and to discuss possible biological and evolutionary mechanisms responsible for our language. In the attempt to establish reasonable criteria for language and communication, these other systems are also compared with language as presented in the first half of this book. In the remaining chapters we will make use of the criteria established here to evaluate human primary communication systems developed under unusual circumstances.

Other Communication Systems

There are many reasons to study animal communication, aside from its intrinsic fascinations. First, in many respects it appears "simpler" than human communication (perhaps because we expect that it should be), but it still manages to regulate social interaction as language does for us. If animal communication is easier to understand, we may be able to deduce more readily principles of communication that also apply to human language. Second, by comparing ourselves and other species, we may make hypotheses about our development through evolution and about biological mechanisms underlying our current abilities. Third, given our time-honored *anthropocentrism* (humans are the pinnacle of creation), we look to other species for proof of our difference and specialness. In this section we present selected descriptions of systems that animals use in interacting, to provide comparison points for evaluating human communication.

Evolutionary Theory: Some Caveats

Given our anthropocentrism, we tend to think carelessly about evolution, distorting its principles so that we emerge as its perfected product. Before comparing ourselves with other species, we should be quite clear on the nondistorted principles of evolution. First and foremost, it is important to recognize that evolution is neither a goal-directed process nor a force but the outcome of a random process of change modified by environmental constraints. The change results from variation in the transmission of genetic information. Many of the fluctuations produced genetically cannot survive beyond infancy and so never get the opportunity to be propagated. Some of the fluctuations cause the organism to be at a disadvantage in competing for the necessities of its life, and so, over time, individuals with these properties become fewer relative to those with the advantage. Some of the fluctuations cause the individual to be less attractive than others to potential mates, and the lesser access results in less opportunity for reproducing these traits. The last is called *sexual selection,* and the whole process of winnowing less advantageous characteristics is called *natural selection.*

It is important to realize that at any particular instant the existing characteristics of a species may be those in the process of being winnowed; that is, as we are now, we are not the end product of evolution but some point in a long chain, and there is no way of knowing which point. (Indeed, like the dinosaurs, we may be a species that will become extinct.) Moreover, any individual existing at the same time we are is as much the product of eons of selection as we are; we are not necessarily better adapted to the twentieth century than are our pets, our plants, and our cockroaches.

Finally, we must be vigilant in our consciousness of the nonpurposiveness of evolution; not everything we see is either optimal or advantageous, nor is everything now extinct necessarily unfit for the present environment. Horselike creatures abounded in South America before humans and then became extinct for some reason; when their descendants were reintroduced after the discovery of the New World, conditions were again favorable for them and they proliferated (Darwin, 1871). We have many ailments resulting from our walking upright; our posture was derived from a structure suited to quadrupeds and is not optimal for tolerating the stress of being upright. Presumably, this disadvantage was compensated for by some advantage associated with being upright, but we should not think we are perfectly designed, nor that "Nature" intended us or designed us to walk erect. These considerations are important since, on the basis of assumed evolutionary principles, we all have a tendency to call other animals primitive—an arrogant and erroneous tendency!

A second point to be kept in mind is that in discussing the evolution of language, we are confined to deductions based on existing species, all of which, as already emphasized, have been subject to the selection pressures of evolution. This contrasts with speculations about posture, for instance, since we have, in the (imperfect) fossil record, skeletal remains. We cannot find similarly hard evidence (pun intended) on the early forms of language, since language does not fossilize. What the record can tell us are properties of the skull and vocal anatomy and aspects of the social life of our precursors. From these we can infer what biological potentials they may have had or what kinds of communications they may have needed. Some of these inferences will be discussed later in this chapter; however, such inferences are necessarily quite speculative.

We turn now to examine existing communities and their communication systems, to calibrate the effectiveness and specialness of ours, and to derive speculations for its evolution. Along with the other caveats noted in this section, we must always be aware that in studying other organisms' communication systems we are prejudiced. We are outsiders to their "culture," their sensory capacities, and their communicative needs. Necessarily we are judging them with respect to our view of our abilities, and thus may be missing important data.

Communication and Signal Systems

Consider very carefully what you think communication is, because, as we proceed, you may find that you must keep revising your definition. You are free to draw conclusions about the nature of communication different from those drawn here. In this section we will analyze signal systems of some organisms, which, in contrast to our system, have led to the development of one view of defining language and communication (Hockett, 1960). This view will be presented explicitly in the next section after you have had time to consider the arguments.

Signals as Cues for Behavior Change Only. A preliminary definition of communication could be the means by which one organism influences the behavior of another. By this definition, a fly buzzing around a frog communicates its edibleness to the frog, influencing the frog to catch it with its tongue. (The fly never communicates again.) Most people would not think this is communication—why not? Note that the fly is emitting/transmitting signals—a noise, a movement, perhaps an odor— that the frog is specially tuned to receive and respond to. Note also that it is not necessarily a one-way communication: If the frog misses, the attempt will cause the fly to flee. Thus, in rejecting this as communication, we conclude that communication involves something more than transmission of a signal, reception of a signal, or an "accidentally coordinated" transmission-reception system.

Signals that Change Behavior for a Common Goal.   Perhaps to communicate it is necessary that the transmitter and receiver work together for the common good. This would exclude the fly-frog situation (and perhaps many human communication situations) but still allows some situations that most would agree are also too "primitive." For example, when a tree is plagued by tent caterpillars, it immediately changes its metabolism, removing nutrients from the infested leaves and sending poisons or "medicines" to them. If there are enough poisons, the effect on the caterpillar is to kill it directly or weaken it by "starvation," or to kill it indirectly by causing it to migrate to other leaves in the course of which it is more likely to be spotted by caterpillar-eating birds. It turns out (Schultz, 1983) that in addition to their having an immediate effect on the leaves, the poisons become airborne and are picked up by neighboring trees. Reception of this chemical message causes the neighbors to change their metabolisms, increasing the poisons in their own leaves, in "anticipation" of future attacks. In effect, the transmitter tree has announced "To arms, to arms, the caterpillars are coming!"

Obviously, trees able to receive such messages are more likely to survive than those that cannot defend themselves in advance, so the selective pressures should be clear. Obviously, also, the transmission-reception system is working for the common good, so if we wish to separate this situation from human communication, we need additional necessary characteristics. One candidate is "feedback"—if a tree falls prey to caterpillars in the forest, it receives no indication from its neighbors that it has been heard.

Goal-Directed Signal Systems with Feedback.   Reflex communication systems with feedback working for the common good are still distinct from our communication, as we see from the mating ritual of the stickleback fish (Tinbergen, 1952, 1955). At the appropriate time of year, the male stickleback stakes out a territory and builds a tunnel nest. While he is doing this his body changes color, developing a red mark, and his appetites change; he is suddenly attracted to swollen-looking things and aggressive toward things with red on them. The female also changes; she becomes swollen with eggs and develops an attraction for things red—simply as the result of the time of year. When the nest is completed, the male approaches the female and begins a zigzag dance. The female, attracted to the moving red spot, follows, and the male beelines to, and through, his nest. The pursuing female becomes stuck in the narrow tunnel. The male, prodding at the base of her tail, causes her to drop her eggs and become thin enough to exit through the nest. The male then fertilizes the eggs.

With respect to communication, both male and female transmit signals of courtship readiness (the red mark and the swollen belly). Each responds to the other's signal (by dancing and pursuing). Both give feedback; if the female stops following, the male will renew courtship, suggesting that he is responsive to her response of pursuit. Finally, the participants have a common goal (at least to the outside observer)—procreation. What makes this situation of interest to us is that despite these characteristics the principle seems the same as in the tree "communication." The behaviors, as laboratory experiments have shown, are reflexive responses to particular stimuli (like the tree releasing a chemical in response to a wound). Thus, this "communication" is simply a biologically programmed reflex sequence.[1] A female will as readily follow, or a male attack, a piece of red cardboard as a real male. A male is as attracted to another male swollen with food as he is to a real female. The fish responds to *sign stimuli,* characteristics of an object, rather than recognizing the object or situation as a whole. "Communication" appears to take place because luckily the right stimuli appear at the right time. Are there similar situations in human communication?

Evolution and Coordination of Transmission and Reception. The fortuitous development of a red spot in the male and an attraction to red in the female is a product of natural selection; individuals who missed the signals of the opposite sex would not be likely to reproduce themselves. In other species the fine tuning of transmitter and receiver characteristics has been demonstrated to be under genetic control—a situation that has an obvious advantage. The species for which it has been demonstrated are those capable of cross-breeding but that do not normally do so in nature.

For example, different species of crickets (Bentley and Hoy, 1972; Hoy and Paul, 1973; Hoy, 1974) or tree frogs (Doherty and Gerhardt, 1983) each have a characteristic mating song. For the crickets, for instance, two species have songs consisting of a high-amplitude trill followed by a low-amplitude trill. In one of the species the low-amplitude portion consists of a train of pulse pairs, while in the other species it consists of a train of single pulses. Females of each species prefer the songs of their own species, resulting in no natural cross-breeding. If the species are cross-bred in the laboratory, however, the offspring produce a song with characteristics between the songs of their two parents, suggesting that song character is under genetic control. And, most importantly, the females of the hybrid group prefer the newly created songs of their hybrid brothers to the songs of either parent species, indicating that *reception is under the same genetic control* as transmission, guaranteeing that male and female will find each other.

Conclusions. In this section we have looked at very primitive signal systems and some of their mechanisms. Our analysis thus far suggests that the bare rudiments of communication include effecting a behavior change in another, toward a common goal, with feedback from the other causing a change in the transmitter. In other words, communication must be two-way. Although the crickets and the frogs seem

---

1. The number of observable components of a sequence is not an indication of complexity if the sequence is treated by the animal as a whole, since then one can consider that there is only one component, the whole sequence. Interrupted during a complex courtship ritual, turkeys will return to the beginning and perform the whole ritual again as if they had never started it before. This indicates that they are not generating or remembering individual components. Dogs, on the other hand, seem to be able to pick up from where they left off, suggesting that they remember where they were and that their ritual is composed of discrete segments, ordered for each performance. The dog is therefore performing at a more complex cognitive level, even if it makes fewer movements to our eye (Scott, 1976).

to be communicating only primitively, that should not stop us from noting the biological mechanism for coordinating "communication." This may obtain in (some of) our communication(s) as well. Indeed, hybrid vocalizations have been produced by cross-breeding monkeys (Gautier and Gautier-Hion, 1982), so the effect is not limited to "simple" creatures.

An important difference between the situations we have just examined and language is that the former are inflexible; the communicators have no choice about what they will transmit or receive and no way to modify it. In the next section we will examine somewhat more flexible animal communication systems to see whether and how they differ from human communication and what they can tell us about biological mechanisms underlying human communication.

Flexible Communication: The Birds and the Bees . . . and Primates

In the signal systems just described each organism emits behavior, producing a fixed response in the receiver. Allowing some learning, some productivity, some individual differences, or somewhat less predictability may result in a system more like human communication and may still be obviously biologically determined.

Learning and Communication. *The Data.* Male and female white-crowned sparrows "sing" in response to various stimuli. Only the male sings the mating song, called the *male song*. Like the stickleback's red spot and the cricket's mating song, the male song attracts a mate and establishes territory. Again, like the stickleback and the cricket, the sparrows seem to be specially tuned to recognize this song and no other. What makes this song interesting, though, is that it differs for birds of the same species who grow up in different geographical regions; it has dialects. Not only do males sing a song specific to their region, but also the females of the region react only to songs with those dialect features, and when prompted to sing through injection with male hormones, will sing their dialect alone (Baker, Spitler-Nabors, and Bradley, 1981). The dialect difference indicates that there must be a learning component since the birds of the species all derive from the same gene pool regardless of where they grow up.

In an ingenious set of experiments Marler (see Marler and Mundinger, 1971 for review) has shown how that learning is acquired. He raised baby sparrows under various conditions of isolation, controlling their exposure to male song. If the birds were raised with other baby sparrows but had no adult model or if they were deafened so that they could not hear the adult, their song contained none of the dialect features, and, in the case of deafening, shared only overall length with white-crowned sparrow song. If the baby sparrow was exposed to male song during a certain time in infancy, very little exposure was necessary to have him sing the song complete with dialect features. Beyond a certain age of infancy no amount of exposure would suffice for the bird to sing as other members of his group sang. (A period where there appears to be a learning readiness and beyond which learning is difficult or impossible is called a *critical period*.) And, finally, exposure to noises or sparrow songs other than white-crowned sparrow songs even during the critical period did not result in the birds' learning these songs.

The Tunable Blueprint. As Marler did, we may explain these results by assuming that there is a biologically determined limit on learning. At birth the birds have a crude "blueprint" of what sparrow song should sound like. This focuses attention on the songs of their own species to the exclusion of songs of other species or irrelevant noises in the environment. During the critical period this blueprint is finely tuned, depending on surrounding input. The blueprint, as it appears at the end of the critical period, determines what the bird will sing (or respond to). Similar models have been proposed for development of other perceptual systems and, most interestingly, for the development of speech perception (see Chapter 9 and Eimas and Tartter, 1979 for an overview). This tunable blueprint model allows for genetic specification as well as some flexibility.

Complexity and Communication. With the white-crowned sparrow, we see one mechanism for introducing complexity into a message of sexual readiness—learning. In another bird, the Western marsh wren, we see a productivity in messages of sexuality, probably fostered through sexual selection.

The vocal repertoire of the Western marsh wren is elaborate, numbering between 100 and 200 separate songs, far more than the Eastern marsh wren. The Western wren, moreover, has 1½ times the brain tissue devoted to song than the Eastern wren and is capable of learning many more songs than it, even when reared under similar exposure conditions (Kroodsma, 1983). The extensive repertoire appears critically linked to sexual competition: The males duel each other vocally for territory. (Perhaps our elaborate repertoires have also been shaped by sexual selection?) A dominant bird will sing; an inferior bird echoes the song, more quietly. If the inferior bird can anticipate the next song the tables are turned, and the previously dominant bird will wind up echoing the other and losing his territory. Therefore, it is to the bird's advantage to be hard to anticipate, to have an extensive repertoire.[2] (These claims have been supported by experiments using tape recorded songs as the "dominant" model and observing the singing and territorial response of other birds to the taped song.)

The extensiveness of the repertoire, the ability to mimic new songs, and the suggestion that new songs may be created to extend the repertoire shows a flexibility not seen in the other systems we have looked at. The bird appears to be able to express territory ownership through diverse songs as opposed to having a fixed link between song and signaled state.

Topic and Communication. Although the bird systems incorporate many features that we have proposed as critical for a communication system—transmission-reception centered on a common goal, feedback, and flexibility—they are different from language. To capture the difference we must make a critical leap now from discussion of the communicators and communication situation to discussion of *what* is being communicated. In all the situations described thus far, the "topic" is the transmitter's signaling of his/her current state—"I am ready to mate," "I am being

2. It is interesting to note that these birds are naturally polygamous, and, in fact, that elaborate displays are more likely to develop in polygamous than monogamous animals. Since language is certainly elaborate, this might suggest that we are, or were, naturally polygamous.

attacked by caterpillars," "I am an eligible male from your social group," and so on. Moreover, in all these situations the sign stimulus can be used to indicate *only* one state, to produce one response; it cannot enter into new "sentences" to take on additional *meanings*. (Note that this is true for the marsh wren too; he can express his state in a variety of ways but cannot use them to describe a new state, which would be a new meaning.)

The Bee System. Surprisingly, a system that seems to allow expressions of new meanings belongs to an insect—the bee. Bees communicate with one another about the quality, quantity, and location of food sources (von Frisch, 1974). Some aspects of this communication are like sign stimuli; when the bee returns from a flower she has its pollen on her legs and its quality can be immediately judged by her co-workers. Since the pollen "represents" itself, it can indicate only one state.

To specify quantity and location of the food source, the bee engages in an elaborate dance, which her co-workers mimic, touching her and dancing with her, until they are satisfied they "understand" and fly off to the food. Locations close to the hive are distinguished from those far from the hive (>50 meters) by the nature of the dance: A dance in a circle indicates a near source, a dance in a figure eight, a distant one. Quantity is specified for a near source by the intensity (speed) of the circular movement.

For a distant source, direction must also be specified to prevent wasted long-distance flying. As Figure 8.1 shows, the bees indicate direction by "translating" the angle they must fly from the hive to the food source with respect to the sun's position into the angle that the figure eight forms with respect to either the sun's position or the vertical axis of the hive. This translation turns out to be complex; the sun's position changes as the day progresses; the amount of change depends on the time of day, time of year, and the latitude. And it seems that the bees compensate for the sun's position by using a calibration determined by the current rate of sun movement

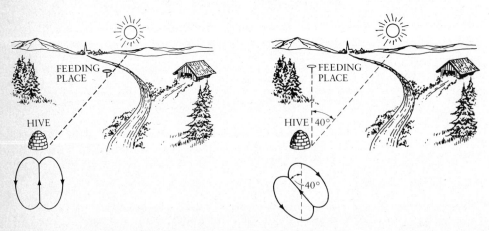

Figure 8.1 *Schematic indication of the angel of the bee's dance as a signal to the direction of the food source with respect to the sun. From K. von Frisch's Nobel lecture "Die Entschlussung der Bienensprache." Copyright © 1974 by The Nobel Foundation. By permission.*

(Gould, 1980). When it is cloudy the bees use as reference the point in the sky with some specific amount of polarized light relative to other points in the sky; which amount is a "dialect feature" and differs from hive to hive (Brines and Gould, 1979). If the hive is kept in the dark then the dance is performed by using the vertical axis as determined by gravity—requiring a transfer of visual information, where the sun is (as seen going to the food source), into kinesthetic information, where the pull of gravity is.

Implications for Anthropocentric Uniqueness. The dance language of the bees poses problems for those who would find characteristics of human communication that make it distinct from all other communication systems. As with other systems we have examined, here we have a special transmitter-receiver system, working for the common good. And there is flexibility—different hives use different dialects—indicating that there is learning. There is feedback from receiver to transmitter in the touch as she mimics the dance. New utterances may be generated: After each trip a given bee may describe a different direction–goodness of-supply–distance combination than she has ever described before. Finally, bee dancing reflects some consideration of the other's "perspective"—updates are made for the new sun position. Despite all this, the dance language can be described easily as a reflex-response sequence; the mapping of external stimulus to bee response is invariant and probably innately specified, and bees have no choice but to dance to describe the food source location following the simple rules just mentioned, and have no choice but to mimic the best food source. Unlike us, deception or caprice is impossible.[3]

Is human language a similar reflex expression of rules, with the only difference that we use more rules and so have more apparent flexibility?

Communication in "Higher" Animals.   There may be good reason to argue that human communication is only quantitatively different from communication in other animals, but many (human) investigators would like to argue that our system is *qualitatively* different. Certainly the animals we have looked at so far are very different from humans: They are much more "primitive" in intelligence (following Lenneberg [1967], we define "intelligence" as the ability to perform human tasks, not as the ability to survive or dominate an ecological niche) and exist within a very different culture from ours. Perhaps examination of animals that seem more like us will reveal communication behaviors more like ours. It is important to note that this assumption presupposes that our language is the way it is because of our particular biological

---

3. It is an interesting observation that we find ourselves invoking the ability to deceive as a distinctive aspect of language. (This will be discussed in more detail later in this chapter.) In traditional anthropocentric views, language has been considered as uniquely giving us a way to pray, and humanness as a unique ability to recognize God. It is ironic that the power of language—which allows us to pray—enables us to lie, and that language may be recognized by that feature. And Morris (1964) points out that Hobbes credits language with giving man "the privilege of absurdity," and notes further that because of our signal system, "man, almost alone, has the distress of mental illness" (p. 81). Juxtapose deception, absurdity, and mental illness with soul and the ability to recognize God—all labeled distinctive characteristics of man because of language.

makeup (e.g., brain capacity) and the way that biological makeup enables human culture (cities, agriculture, etc.). This assumption is fundamental to our theme.

Unfortunately, perhaps because mammal behavior is so complex, it is difficult to describe any one communication system completely. For example, researchers have looked at auditory signaling in whales and determined for the humpbacked whale that a given burst of song lasts as long as 30 minutes, and consists of call types (whistles, rumbles, etc.) produced in a set order for each whale but with different examples of each call in different cycles of the order (Payne and McVay, 1971). (This is analogous, perhaps, to a NVN sequence with different examples of call types corresponding to different nouns or verbs.) It suggests that these whale signals exhibit syntax unlike the other signals we have discussed. However, discussion of the whale "system" is limited since the "code"—what the songs mean—has not been broken, nor is it known whether other whales recognize or respond to them.

Primates (monkeys and apes) and other land mammals are easier to study than oceanic mammals because they may be more easily followed and observed. Study of mammal behavior has fallen into three interacting categories: their social structure, their call systems and body language (both visual and olfactory), and their cognitive abilities. Their call systems and cognitive skills have usually been investigated in relationship to a human model, to see if they do what we do in similar ways. This biased focus may render our view of other mammals' communication overly simplistic but does allow for important analogies to human behavior. Different investigators have concentrated on different types of mammals with respect to each of these aspects, so it is impossible to describe fully any one system. Moreover, since each species behaves differently, the data cannot be collapsed to describe mammal communication in general. Finally, the research to date has not shown promise that nonhuman mammals will be found to communicate qualitatively differently from some other organisms already described. Therefore we will not describe mammal communication in detail but rather give an overview with selected examples.

Overview of Social Structure and Signaling. Generally, mammals have a strong social structure: They reproduce sexually and the females (at least) care for their young, necessitating some forms of signaling between male and female, parent and child. In addition, many mammals exhibit a "tribal" structure, hunting, grazing, grooming, babysitting, playing, or fleeing danger as a herd. This means there must be signaling among group members to coordinate these group activities. (Of course social structures also exist in schools of fish, hills of ants, hives of bees, vees of geese, knots of toads. . . .) The question is, is this signaling different from the other signaling systems we have looked at?

Primate communication displays usually indicate the transmitter "state" as we saw in "lower" animals—readiness to mate, territory ownership, existence of a food source, pain, or an enemy. In groups with social structure there is usually also some indication of dominance relations (perhaps inseparable from territory marking)—what we call "pecking order" from observing chickens in a barnyard. There is also usually some means of recognition between offspring and parent and some way for the offspring to signal their needs to their parent(s).

Signals occur in many modalities: For example, monkeys may scream (auditory), bare their teeth (visual), emit an odor (olfactory), clutch one another (tactile). The signals are complex compared with those of some of the organisms we have looked at. For example, a single emotional state, such as fear, may be expressed by several different calls (Jurgens, 1982). Another example shows that when monkeys are made to feel aggressive by stimulating a particular area of the brain, the way an individual expresses the aggression depends on its dominance within the tribe (Delgado, 1977).

It has also been shown that "messages" may be specific: Vervet monkeys give distinctly different calls when confronted with leopards, eagles, and snakes, and vervets hearing those calls give distinct responses, running into trees, looking up, and looking down, respectively, even when the calls are played by tape recorder in a sterile laboratory setting (Seyforth, Cheney, and Marler, 1980). Infant vervets show the same reactions but produce the calls in response to a broader range of stimuli, indicating that there is an innate component that is finely tuned through environmental exposure. Snowdon (1982) has demonstrated similar call variations dependent on environmental stimulation in cotton-top tamarins, another type of monkey.

It is possible to view nonhuman primate communication as similar to the signal systems already described. Thus far, no syntax has been revealed in the messages, nor is there much indication of productivity—creation of new messages. And the "messages" still reflect an invariant relationship between internal motivational state and call—the difference being perhaps that the primate is able to indicate fear of leopards as opposed to eagles, while trees indicate just general attack. Of course, we may find the systems of these alien animals primitive relative to ours because we expect them to be and we do not fully understand them. And it is not clear that the same critique could not be applied to human language: Is each of our utterances under the control of a given motivational state and environmental cue? Is the only difference (if it holds up to further investigation) that vervets distinguish through calls three predators while we distinguish many more?

Biological Mechanisms. Study of the neural mechanisms underlying perception and production of primate vocalizations can provide meaningful analogies for human communication, since we are not too distant relatives. What has been discovered for the monkey as well as for "lower" animals such as the cricket (Zaretsky, 1971) or songbird (Leppelsack and Vogt, 1976; see Eimas and Tartter, 1979 for overall review) is that there are specific cells in the brains that respond in very regular ways to aspects of the communication signal. This has been discovered by using a technique called single-cell recording.

Every nerve cell or *neuron* has an electrical charge. When the neuron is at "rest" it exhibits a baseline level of electrical discharging called *spontaneous activity*. When the neuron is stimulated by some outside event the activity level changes, either increasing, called *excitation,* or decreasing, called *inhibition.* When an EEG (electro-encephalogram) is taken, the electrical activity of the whole brain—the sum of these individual charges—is measured. It is possible to measure individual neuron activity by attaching a microelectrode directly to a cell; this is *single-cell recording.* Whereas an EEG tells us about general alertness, a single-cell recording indicates the specific stimuli to which a particular neuron is responsive. The assumption is that if we determine the stimuli to which each neuron reacts (called the neuron's *receptive field*), we will be able to derive a general picture of how the brain works. It is interesting to note also that single cells or groups of cells may be stimulated to react by giving them a small jolt of electricity. By seeing how the animal reacts when the cell is stimulated, we can determine what the cell is responsible for.

Given our discussion of perception in the last chapters (speech perception, meaning "perception" in semantic memory), you can probably guess the "model" that most researchers use to guide their probings of the brain's workings: One cell responds to one stimulus type. This, in effect, is a detector model—a voicing detector would be a cell that responded to VOTs less than 35 msec. If such cells and stimuli can be found, the matter of perception is straightforward: Each neuron is invariantly tuned to particular features of the stimulus stream, and perception takes place as all the neurons respond to their particular features. In a sense, we can conceptualize the whole system as a network of sign stimuli–fixed responses, where the sign stimulus is the feature to which the neuron reacts, and the response is excitation or inhibition.

There are many difficulties involved in the research and the conceptual framework presented here, which we will briefly describe. The first, as you might expect from our explorations in perception, is that there are many researchers who question the viability of invariant response: one-cell (or cell group)–one stimulus feature. Alternative models of brain organization have been proposed; we will look at these in Chapter 12. A second problem is that searching for detectors is like looking for the proverbial needle in a haystack. There are a vast number of neurons and a vast number of stimuli and stimulus features; matching the perfect stimulus with its neuron requires luck. In fact, we never know that we have discovered a detector; all we know is that that cell responds to the stimulus we tested, but it may also respond to a number of others that we have not tried; so our interpretation of its sensitivities may be completely erroneous. A final problem is that knowledge of a single unit's response, even if accurate, does not tell us what role that neuron plays in perception or consciousness of the whole organism to the stimuli.

With all these misgivings, it is particularly exciting when a neuron set is discovered that responds to those stimuli important to the animal. In production, Apfelbach (1972) has isolated neurons in the gibbon brain that, when stimulated, cause the animal to produce its calls. Different calls were elicited by stimulating cells in different brain regions. In perception, Wollberg and Newman (1972; Newman and Wollberg, 1973a) have isolated neurons in the auditory cortex of the squirrel monkey (the *cortex* is a layer of cells at the surface of the brain, responsible for higher cognitive and perceptual functions) responsive to the species' vocalizations.

In an extensive study of one call type, Newman and Wollberg (1973b) found detectors for speaker identification. The call is the *isolation peep,* a sound the squirrel monkey produces when separated from its troop, which is answered in kind by the troop members. This dialogue continues until the lost monkey makes visual contact with the troop. Cells in auditory cortex responsive to the isolation peep fell into two groups: those that responded to the structure of the peep over wide frequency and intensity ranges, as might be found across individuals, and those that responded to specific acoustic variants of the peep, perhaps selective for an individual or a dialect feature of that troop. (Dialect differences have been established in many mammals— for example, in a gerbil-like creature called a pika [Somers, 1973] and in macaque monkeys [Green, 1975]. It is likely that they exist in other species as well.) Thus we see a biological mechanism for group and speaker identification in this species, for which such identification is vital.

Biological Analogies. In areas other than single-cell recordings, monkeys have demonstrated interesting biological analogies with human communication. Macaques show a laterality effect for calls of their species, as humans show in dichotic listening (Peterson, Beecher, Zoloth, Moody, and Stebbins, 1978). Specifically, acoustic distinctions that differentiate call types are more discriminable when presented to the monkey's right ear than when presented to its left, but pitch differences for the same call show a left-ear advantage. (Lateralization of species-specific sounds has also been demonstrated in birds [Nottebohm, 1970; reported in Marx, 1982] both in production and perception. The neural song center, moreover, is larger [has more neurons] in birds with larger repertoires.)

Higher-Level Cognitive Skills. Apart from looking directly at their communication systems, we may assess communicative *capabilities* through the cognitive skills of the communicators in other situations. For example, we may ask whether animals can think symbolically (whatever that means), whether or not they use symbols in their natural communication. If the answer is yes, then we may redirect our investigation of the animal's communication system to search for evidence of symbol use, and we may attempt to teach the animal a system that uses symbols directly, like language. In fact, many of the recent advances in understanding complexities in primate communication such as the different call types for different predators were found because the investigators had the expectation that there must be higher-order communications since the animals had been shown elsewhere to be "smart." And, as we will see, there have been extensive attempts to teach some primates human-type language, derived from similarly heightened expectations.

Many mammals have shown that they are capable of responding not just to the stimulus situation but to abstract information deduced from it. For example, chimpanzees can recognize themselves in a mirror and will use the reflection to clean their fur, perhaps demonstrating self-awareness (Gallup, 1979). (This is an abstraction since to conclude that the mirror image is one's self, one must respond to something like the identity of the motion of the image and one's self, and one must overlook differences between the image and the self, like the face, which the animal never sees on the self.) They also respond appropriately to pictures: One anecdote tells of a home-reared chimpanzee finding a picture of iced-tea in a magazine and showing it to her owner as she dragged the person toward the refrigerator (see Premack, 1976); another, of a chimpanzee watching a film of the capture of an orangutan in the wild and hooting and throwing things at the image of the captors (Premack, 1976). Moreover, experiments have demonstrated that a chimpanzee watching a videotape of a person faced with a problem will select appropriately a photograph of a tool to be used in the solution (Premack and Woodruff, 1978). Thus, the chimps appear to be able to interpret photographs or movies, "identify" with them, and use them to receive information. (Correct responses to photographs have been demonstrated for animals with less intelligence: Pigeons can discriminate photographs containing human beings from those not, regardless of the angle the person was photographed from or his/her position, age, dress, etc. [Herrnstein and Loveland, 1965].)

Nor are mammals confined to perceiving concrete properties of objects. For example, one chimpanzee seemed to be able to understand causality. Trained to insert between two states of an object an instrument that could have caused the change in state (apple-*knife*-apple slice, sponge-*glass of water*-wet sponge), she was able readily to generalize to new pairs (e.g., to place the knife between a sponge and a cut sponge—Premack, 1976). In another task chimpanzees have been trained to respond differently to the concepts "same" and "different," selecting from among three objects the object that differed from the other two along some *untrained* dimension.

Finally, mammals seem to show an awareness of their signals and are able to use them "symbolically," for the purposes of deception.[4] Bruemmer (1983) reported observing a female sea lion "flirting" with a male who was perched atop her tiny pup, thereby inducing him to chase her. She bit the male's neck, a signal of estrus, but in this case she was not in estrus but was using the signal, apparently deliberately, to provoke his reflex reaction. Once she rescued the baby, she stopped her signal and left him. Therefore, it appears that she was aware of the effect of her signal and had it under nonreflex control.

Woodruff and Premack (1979) experimentally induced similar deceptive behavior in chimpanzees. They allowed chimps to observe a trainer placing food in one of two containers. The chimps could not themselves reach the food but could signal a new trainer, who had not observed the food placement, to indicate its location. The new trainer was by design either cooperative, sharing the food with the chimps, or competitive, hoarding the food to himself. The chimps spontaneously developed means of signaling the trainers—orienting their bodies toward the food container while watching the trainer, looking back and forth from the food container to the trainer, and occasionally, spontaneously pointing to the correct container. Moreover, after becoming acquainted with the personalities of the trainers (and being allowed to fetch the food if the trainer was unsuccessful in finding it), the chimps began to suppress these signals when the competitive trainer was present, indicating that the signals were not uncontrolled reflexes and that the animals were aware of their effects. Finally, one chimp deliberately lied, using the signals to indicate the container that did not have the food!

Summary.   In this section we have looked at naturally occurring animal behaviors that seem to exhibit at least some of the flexibility we find in human language. We also examined potential mechanisms for some of these behaviors. Thus, we saw in birds and bees the existence of dialects, presumably acquired during a critical period, through modification of an innate blueprint for communication by particular environmental experience. We saw productive use of a simple system of rules by bees to describe the location of a food source with modifications for varying reference points. We found large vocabularies for signaling internal states and environmental causes in birds and primates, what is perhaps a syntax system in whales, and evidence of complex conceptual structures in apes. We find in the primate evidence of specialized neural centers for communication, perhaps analogous to ours, and we find call

---

4. We must be careful to differentiate deception from reflex deception (Woodruff and Premack, 1979), such as an animal's playing dead to discourage a predator, or fluttering as though wounded to distract one from the young, or building a false nest as a decoy. Because these are reflex, stereotyped behaviors, although they work through deception, they may not be deliberate or symbolic, any more so than cases of biological mimicry such as protective coloration or marking on the wings that look like owl eyes.

detectors, suggestive of the existence of analogous detectors in people. Thus far, no communication system has been found that demonstrates the extensive flexibility, productivity, and restructuring found in ours, but that may be because, in looking at alien systems, we are unable to recognize what we see. An alternative method for comparing human capabilities with those of other animals is to find out what they "see" when looking at our language. We will turn next to attempts at teaching human language to animals, in part to determine whether animals have the capability to learn language and in part, to examine the criteria for language that the trainers used.

Human Language and Nonhumans

Early Attempts. Given the apes' extraordinary intelligence, a number of investigators have examined whether it is possible for the apes to learn humanlike language under specific training situations. The earliest attempts used a spoken language, English, with chimpanzees raised like children in upper middle class homes (see Brown, 1958 for review). Although the chimps adapted well to their human life, learning to dress, wash dishes, brush their teeth, and so on, despite specific training they learned to produce very few words. This was perhaps because their vocal tracts are anatomically quite different from ours, making it impossible for them to produce the sounds that we produce. (Note here the biological constraint on the form of language learning.)

Subsequent attempts took this biological constraint into account, and, recognizing the chimps' superlative manual dexterity, visual discrimination abilities, and spontaneous use of and imitation of gestures, attempted to teach a visual language. These attempts took the form of either artificial, constructed languages using plastic chips (Premack, 1971) or graphic symbols as words (Rumbaugh, Gill, and von Glaserfield, 1973), or of a natural visual-gestural language, American Sign Language (ASL) (Gardner and Gardner, 1969; Patterson, 1978a, b; Terrace, Petitto, Sanders, and Bever, 1979). The judgments of the success of the ape language projects have varied from time to time (see, for example, Terrace, 1979; Wade, 1980). For us the debate is meaningful because it has caused careful (although at times heated) consideration of what our language is, how to test for it, and how it differs from other skills.

Systems for the Later Attempts. As already stated, two types of visual languages have been employed, artificial ones and a naturally occurring one, ASL. A more complete description of the structure of ASL will be given in Chapter 11, but for now it is important to know that the elements of ASL are signs that correspond roughly to words and that are produced by movement of the hand or hands in front of the body in the area between the top of the head and waist and about six inches from either side of the body. Signs are strung together by using syntactic rules very different from those of English, although there are signed languages developed for educational purposes that do follow the grammatical form of English. Such signed English systems are less efficient that the natural sign language, as we will see in Chapter 11, and some of the ape studies have been criticized for using them or providing the variable input of ASL sometimes and signed English others. Finger-spelling, a method of using handshapes in one-to-one correspondence with letters of the alphabet, spelling

English words, constitutes only a small part of ASL. Sign language, like spoken language, is passed on readily from parent to child, and like spoken language, may be used in any environment, without special materials, as long as there are two individuals conversant with the language.

In the chimpanzee studies the chimps were taught sign by observing their trainers communicate with it and by having their hands molded into the shapes required for specific signs, usually in the presence of the referents. When a chimp reached for or was handed an object, the trainer labeled it, and after a time required the chimp to use the label to obtain the object. This was presumed to simulate the natural language learning situation.

The artificial languages used differ from ASL in that they require special materials for communication, in one case a board and plastic magnets that could be mounted on it, in the other a computer with a screen and keyboard. This constraint limited language to occurring in rooms where these objects were and thereby limited spontaneity and possible topics of discourse. A second limitation of these languages, oddly enough, is that they were deliberately created, that is, designed with explicit rather than tacit language knowledge, and, as we saw in Chapter 4, explicit language knowledge is a very small subset of our useful mental syntax. Thus, in examining these languages it is important to consider whether they truly show the complexity of a real language or only give the appearance of complexity through the translation into English.

Before discussing the artificial languages further, their advantages over real languages should be explained. They are simple for the experimenter(s) to learn, whereas learning ASL or any other foreign language requires years of study (as most of us know from experience). If the experimenter is unsuccessful in attaining fluency, (s)he will be a poor teacher and communication partner for the chimp, and the chimp's failure to learn cannot be attributed exclusively to the chimp's cognitive skills. Artificial languages are also easier to transcribe and keep a record of, and "utterances" in them may be displayed to the chimp for as long as necessary, unlike speech or sign, which "disappears" as the articulators move. This potentially long-term display prevents any memory limitations of the animal from interfering with language learning. Finally, because the utterances are easily transcribed and conversation can take place only in the rooms where the language materials are, a complete record of conversation can be kept. This is important, since in judging the language capabilities we want to know how many correct utterances there were relative to the total number of utterances. As we saw in Chapter 5, semantically and syntactically correct sentences are easier to recall than anomalous or scrambled sentences; the trainer is thus more likely to remember a good sentence produced by a chimp than a nonsense sentence. A complete and impartial record avoids the bias of the human observer.

Sarah. *Teaching Naming.* Sarah, Premack's chimpanzee, was taught to associate pieces of plastic with particular objects in the environment, using classical and operant conditioning (described in Chapter 2). Each plastic piece represented a concept and differed from other plastic pieces in size, shape, or color. Sentences were written vertically on the board. Sarah learned names of foods; names of trainers; names of properties like different colors and shapes; names of names of properties like "color of," "shape of"; words describing language like "name of"; prepositions; syntactic markers like plural, interrogative, and negative; and ways of forming compound strings ("Sarah put apple in dish and banana in pail") and complex strings ("if red on green Sarah take apple").

The training and testing methods were the same for simple and complex concepts and constructions, so only a few will be described. To teach the token symbol for apple, for example, first rapport was established so that Sarah felt comfortable eating in front of the trainer, and then the trainer presented her with a piece of apple together with the plastic piece that was to represent it. Gradually, the apple was made more and more difficult for Sarah to reach while the plastic piece was attainable. (Gradual removal of a cue, such as the object apple, is called *fading*.) When Sarah picked up the plastic, she was reinforced with the apple. Using shaping (the reinforcement of successive approximations of the desired behavior, as you may recall), the trainer then taught her to place the plastic on the board before she received the apple. Other plastic pieces were similarly associated with other fruits. To test to see that she had learned the appropriate associations, she was presented with a piece of fruit and choice of plastic symbols and was reinforced only if she selected the symbol naming the fruit. Properties were taught in the same way; plastic pieces that were to stand for red, yellow, and so forth, were presented in conjunction with apples, bananas, and so forth. To receive the apple Sarah had to associate red with it and no other colors. Trainers' names and "verbs" like give and take were similarly associated with situations in which one was appropriate and the others not. Testing always required that Sarah select from among a set of (usually two) chips, the correct one for the concept.

Teaching "Syntax." Once particular tokens were learned it was possible to require that they be strung together for reinforcement (as described generally in Chapter 4). Once again, the procedure was the same: If Mary was in the room and Sarah wanted the apple, she was shaped to say "Mary apple" then "Mary give apple" then "Mary give apple Sarah." (Minor difficulties arose when Sarah had to give food to someone else—important for differentiating the meaning difference between "Mary give Sarah" and "Sarah give Mary"; these were overcome by reinforcing Sarah with some other delicacy when she correctly designated someone else to receive.) Conjunctions were taught by placing two sentences next to each other, then merging them so one was underneath the other, and then removing the extra subject and verb. Questions were taught by replacing a symbol in a learned string with a bit of plastic representing "?" and requiring that Sarah substitute the correct symbol, fill in the "blank," for the interrogative marker.

Teaching More Complex Concepts. Complex concepts like "color of," "name of," and "if-then" were taught in similar fashion, but it is worth describing it since it may not be clear how to use this simple procedure for these concepts. Once the color names were learned, the symbol for color was introduced in the string "red color-of apple," and the response of "red" to "? color-of apple" was reinforced. Note that at times the actual fruit was in the last position, in which case a color match could be performed, but at other times the symbol for the fruit was there—and apple was represented by a blue plastic chip. So the correct response was in fact "red color-of blue-plastic-chip = apple"—which Sarah had no trouble making. Once the color-of symbol was learned it could be used to teach new color names. "Name-of" was acquired by substituting its symbol between an object's name symbol and the object, and like "color-of," once learned, it could be used to teach new names.

"If-then" was taught as a label for a particular kind of discrimination, one that many animals have no difficulty performing. An animal can be trained to make one response for reinforcement in the presence of one stimulus (called a *discriminative stimulus*) and a different response in the presence of another one—to peck a key if there is a green light, and to turn around if there is a red one, for instance. Sarah was taught to take one food if green was present and a different one if red was present, and was then taught a symbol to describe this activity—"if green take apple." Once she learned to respond to this sentence, the "if-then" symbol could be used to teach new conditions for behavior. This was the task with which she had the greatest difficulty.

Is this language? At this time we will not formally evaluate what Sarah had learned to allow you the opportunity to consider for yourself whether it is what you think of as language. Be careful in your consideration—we have used standard terms describing syntax and semantics to describe her behavior and we have "translated" her chip strings into English; this is likely to bias you into thinking of this as language because it looks like language as we know it. Remember the computer outputs presented in Chapter 5; they too looked very English-like, but for the most part they were not very language sophisticated. Is that true for Sarah as well? Examination of her sentences without benefit of translation, as in Box 8.1, may help you make a decision.

It is important to keep in mind also how Sarah was tested, with simple commands and questions to assess comprehension, and with fill-in-the-blank tests given a limited number of alternatives to assess production. Is this a strong test of language capability? Finally, it is important to realize that her performance was a consistent 80 percent, much better than chance, but do you think people make 20 percent errors when asked to name a color?

Lana, Sherman, and Austin.   The star performer in the other artificial language project was also a female chimpanzee, named Lana, and she was joined subsequently by two male chimpanzees, Sherman and Austin (Savage-Rumbaugh, Rumbaugh, and Boysen, 1980). Lana was raised in a room with a computer that ministered to her needs. She was taught to type requests into the computer to get food, drink, music, etc. Each typewriter key was labeled with a symbol composed of some values on a limited number of dimensions, e.g., ⊕ = M&M, ⊙ = juice, ⊕ = pudding. When Lana pressed the key in the correct position in a sequence of keypresses, she was reinforced by the machine delivering her request, much as we are served by a candy machine. (The sequence was shaped beginning with single keypresses and increasing string length, as Sarah's sentences were shaped.)

First, Lana had to hit a key that Rumbaugh et al. translated as "please." This caused the machine to start to process her sentence; without it the computer would not know to begin a parse. Next Lana had to press a key naming an agent, initially "machine," subsequently, trainers' names. Next came a verb key, "give" in the case of objects like food or drink, "make" for actions like music or window opening. Then came the name of the request, "M&M" or "music," and finally, a terminal symbol,

Box 8.1   The Plastic "Language"

The following are adaptations of some of the words of Sarah's language.

The following are adaptations of sample correct sentences. If they contain a picture not in the above, assume the picture is what it represents, so ⌒ = a real apple, and (= a real banana.

1. ▷ ⧉ ⌒
2. ⊙ ⧑ ⌒
3. ⊙ ⧉ (
4. ⌃ ⧄ (
5. ⌃ ⧄ ⌒
6. ? ⧄ (
7. ? ⧄ ▷
8. ⊠ ⧉ ▷⊙

Now, on the next 5 strings, can you substitute a legal symbol, from the two on the right, for the question mark?

a. ? ? ⌒   ⧄) ⧄
b. ⌃ ? ⊙   ⧄) ⧄
c. ▷ ? ⊠   ⧉) ⧑
d. ⊠ ⧉ ?   ?) ▷
e. ▷ ⧉ ?   ⌒) (
f. ⌃ ? (⧉) ⧄

The correct answers are at the end of the box. Realize that you know more about this game than Sarah did. You have been told that the symbols stand for words, and you know what a word is. You also have some information on how she was trained and on what concepts she learned, so you could guess the symbol meanings. She, of course, had none of this knowledge. But she had many more trials.

The questions are: (1) Are you able to play the game? (2) Do you know what the sentences mean? (3) If you can figure out the meanings, do so. Was this what you did in playing the game?

Answers: (a) left, (b) left, (c) right, (d) right, (e) left, (f) right.

Meanings: ⧉ = name of, ∐ = not, ⧄ = color of. You should be able to figure out the rest from here.

rendered as "." which instructed the machine that the request was finished and it should begin to parse. Correct performance would yield a sentence translated as "Please machine give M&M."

As Sarah was taught more complex sentences, so was Lana—as already mentioned, she could use a trainer's name in place of "machine" and one of several verbs. She also was taught to use prepositional phrases like "Please Tim give [the] milk out [of the] room." As it turned out, her entire syntax could be accounted for as substitutions in one of several frames, and her language easily modeled by computer (Thompson and Church, 1980). Table 8.1 shows her language output in relation to these frames, and the relative frequency of occurrence of each sentence type. In addition to making requests in the formats she had been taught, Lana made some spontaneous, creative strings, shown in Table 8.2, tabulated for the same period as Table 8.1, showed novelty in generalizing the symbol for "apple" to "orange," and even invented a syntactic construction (apple-which-is orange, shown in Table 8.3). Con-

Table 8.1 *Stock phrases produced by Lana.*
Reprinted by permission. **American Scientist,** *1980 68:49–61, "Do Apes Use Language?" by Sue Savage-Rumbaugh, Duane M. Rumbaugh and Sara Boysen.*

Format	Total occurrences†
question │ pronoun or noun │ give │ object name, food name, or proper name │ to Lana in room	630
(?you give bread to Lana in room)	
please machine give piece of │ food name │	310
(please machine give piece of bread)	
question you make │ door or window │ open or shut │	35
(?you make door open)	
question │ proper name or pronoun │ move │ in or out │ room	53
(?Lana move out room)	
question │ proper name or pronoun │ tickle or groom │ proper name or pronoun │	116
(?you tickle Lana)	
│ common or proper name │ name this │ color │	1,181
(shoe name this red)	
│ single symbols │	465

*Variable elements given in boxes; example follows each format.
†Total number of times variants of stock format—including incomplete versions—were produced.

Table 8.2 *Novel phrases produced by Lana.*
Reprinted by permission. American Scientist, *1980 68:49–61, "Do Apes Use Language?" by Sue Savage-Rumbaugh, Duane M. Rumbaugh, and Sara Boysen.*

Phrase	Occurrences	Phrase	Occurrences
question you name this	9	open yes	2
question give drink this	8	question you give Lana Columbus	2
name this shoe	8	make window open machine	2
name this cup	8	milk out	2
question drink this	6	please milk out	2
out please	6	please make machine music window open	2
question you give beancake shut open	6	question you tickle Lana please	2
please milk out room	5	go please	2
question you tickle Lana go	5	yes out room	2
this ball	5	please out room	2
question you tickle Lana behind room	4	please you	2
want yes	4	move Columbus	2
question you tickle Lana into room	4	bowl name this pudding	2
question you tickle Lana in room	4	please machine groom	2
question you give Columbus in Lana to room	4	question you give go	2
you open	3	question Lana Columbus	1
question you tickle Lana to Lana	3	tickle question	1
question you tickle Lana to Lana behind room	3	drink yes	1
out room	3	hand eye foot	1
please milk room	3	window keyboard	1
out room yes	3	give Lana chow	1
to out room	3	question you give Lana juice	1
question you give milk open	3	question you give bread to machine	1
question you give milk shut open	3	orange coke	1
question you give this orange drink	3	question Lana in room	1
question you give this to Lana in room	3	eat yes	1
question you open	2	question you give banana to Lana in machine out room	1
yes money	2	question you give juice to Lana in cup out room	1
question Lana you out room	2	question you give bread Lana	1
give out room	2	question Lana give bread to room	1
		give Lana milk	1
		question you give Lana	1

Table 8.3   *A dialogue betwen Lana and Tim leading to a creative naming structure. Quoted from Rumbaugh and Gill (1977), pp. 178–179.*

TIM:	*?What color of this.*	[10:10 a.m.]
LANA:	*Color of this orange.*	[10:11 a.m.]
TIM:	*Yes.*	
LANA:	*?Tim give cup which-is red.* (This was probably an attempt to request the orange however, because a red cup was part of her object/color naming materials, Tim responded with the latter object.)	[10:13 a.m.]
TIM:	*Yes.* (Thereupon he gave her the cup, which she discarded.)	[10:14 a.m.]
LANA:	*?Tim give which-is shut.* *?Shelley give.*	[10:16 a.m.]
TIM:	*No Shelley.*	[10:16 a.m.]
LANA:	*Eye.* (A frank error, probably.)	[10:16 a.m.]
	?Tim give which-is orange.	[10:21 a.m.]
TIM:	*What which-is orange.*	[10:21 a.m.]
LANA:	*?Tim give apple which-is green.* (At this point, Lana frequently confused the keys for the colors orange and green.)	[10:22 a.m.]
TIM:	*No apple which-is green.* (In other words, "I have no green apple to give.")	
LANA:	*?Tim give apple which-is orange.* (Thereupon she bounded with apparent enthusiasm to the door to receive "the orange-colored apple.")	[10:23 a.m.]
TIM:	*Yes.* (And he gave it to her.)	[10:23 a.m.]

invented a syntactic construction (apple-which-is orange, shown in Table 8.3). Consider whether these requests are indicative of creative language use or simply of errors or accidents in attempting to produce the rote-learned strings.

While Lana's training emphasized production of long ordered strings, Sherman and Austin were taught the same "language" in a different manner, one emphasizing labeling and question-answering skills (Savage-Rumbaugh, Rumbaugh, and Boysen, 1978); that is, they were taught to name foods and then respond to the machine-posed question "what's this?" with the correct food name reinforced by the opportunity to request the machine to deliver some other food. Interactive communication was further emphasized by having the machine name a food the animal could not see but could then request. This training, it was argued, allows the formation of a more general notion of a name, since the same symbol is used to answer questions, make requests, and indicate the presence of an object. Moreover, since the object itself was invisible, the use of the symbol was considered *symbolic,* referring to some mental representation of the object rather than the object itself. (Is this what symbol use is?)

Having received this general training individually, Sherman and Austin were placed together in the computer room and each given access to information about the existence of foods that the other chimpanzee did not have. Then the machine would query the informed animal with "what's this?" with the other animal able to observe the question and the answer. The observer could then request the named food, using the information obtained from the other chimp. Both animals adapted readily to this procedure without any further training. Moreover, both animals were able to match the symbol the other animal used either to request the food or to point to a picture of it, from which Savage-Rumbaugh et al. inferred that the observer was constructing an "image" of its referent. This interaction has been designated by Savage-Rumbaugh et al. as conversation.

Again, we will reserve criticism of Lana's, Sherman's, and Austin's skills until after examination of the other projects. However, you should consider the following questions: (1) Are these chimps demonstrating different skills from Sarah's? (2) Are their key press sequences equivalent to human sentences? (3) *Have* they demonstrated a symbol use like naming, or a simple association? (4) Is Sherman's and Austin's interchange really a conversation? (5) Is substitution of a new symbol in a highly trained sequence what we mean by creative use of language?

Sign Language Projects. The advantage of using a human language like ASL in teaching language to chimpanzees is that we know that it has the potentials of creativity, spontaneity, etc., of human language (this has been questioned in the past in sign but is accepted today, as we will see in Chapter 11) although we do not know whether the animal will be able to take advantage of these potentials. Basically, the ape-signing projects all used the same procedure as the speaking projects, with the young apes raised in upper middle class environments with trainers instructed to use sign in communicating with each other or with the animal. Unlike the artificial language projects, the animal's signing was not always reinforced, and the animal's understanding as determined by obedience to commands such as "brush your teeth" and "it's bedtime" was more emphasized than the animal's productions. As most pet owners believe, the animals seemed to be able to learn to respond appropriately to many sentences.

Washoe. The most studied signing ape, and perhaps the most fluent, is Washoe, a chimpanzee raised from about eight months old by Gardner and Gardner (1969; 1975). From the beginning she seemed adept at imitating complex actions, sometimes after a delay, like bathing her doll in the same manner as she herself was bathed. Imitation of signs also occurred, but generally not as an echo of the trainer's most recent utterance. For example, after being told many times that it was time to brush her teeth or here was her toothbrush, she wandered into a bathroom and spontaneously signed toothbrush when she saw one. Using this production, the trainers then shaped her to request her toothbrush after meals, reinforcing her with permission to leave the table. But note that it was Washoe's utterance that started the training, and that it was not specifically prompted when it first occurred.

Washoe's spontaneity in use of signs has also suggested more creative use of language than the other chimpanzees have, perhaps because use of a name is not so tightly confined to specific situations. For example, when being tickled, an activity chimpanzees love, and having it stop, Washoe would try to make her ticklers continue. Using this, they taught her the sign for "more," which she then generalized to "more food" and more other activities. "Open" was also generalized in an interesting manner, initially taught for a specific standard door and later spontaneously extended to refrigerator doors, drawers, and faucets. Washoe used the sign for "flower" to describe flowers and also as a label for anything with an odor, for example, tobacco and kitchens, until she was taught the sign for "smell." More important than her meaning generalizations for one sign was her spontaneous stringing together of signs and creative sign combinations. Without syntactic training she produced "gimme tickle" and "open food drink" (for "open the refrigerator"); her trainers, of course, signed sentences but never had used these constructions. Also, upon seeing a swan for the first time, already knowing the individual signs for "water" and "bird," she signed "water bird," perhaps creating a new compound.

After four years of training, Washoe had acquired 132 signs that she used to name objects, classes of objects, and photographs of objects, to answer questions, to make requests, and to create short sentences. Chimpanzees trained from birth in sign acquired signs at a faster rate and comparably to human infants learning sign (Gardner and Gardner, 1975), suggesting optimism for nonhuman language acquisition.

Koko.   The other projects have proceeded similarly and perhaps have had similar success. Patterson (1978a, 1978b) reported similar development of spontaneous compound creation in her signing gorilla, Koko, who labeled a stale roll "cookie rock," a zebra "white tiger," and a Pinocchio doll "elephant baby." More interesting is her report of spontaneous joking and lying; for example, when caught chewing a crayon, Koko pretended to be coloring her lips and signed "lip." She also appeared to use "first" and "later" appropriately, indicating a linguistic concept of time; she described previous emotional experiences together with her reaction (given a lot of prompting); and she spontaneously conversed with another gorilla who had learned ASL.

Nim.   Project Nim, reported by Terrace et al. (1979), showed a large vocabulary acquisition in a chimpanzee (Nim Chimsky) and spontaneous strings of signs together. Unlike the other signing projects, some attempt was made to catalogue the utterances and their frequencies, and perhaps for this reason, Terrace and his colleagues reached markedly different conclusions about the animal's language skills. Table 8.4 shows Nim's two- and three-sign combinations (a) and four-sign combinations (b). Take time to study these strings and consider whether they indicate the existence and use of productive syntax. And remember, with respect to the observations just mentioned for Koko and Washoe, that given enough time at a typewriter, by chance, a monkey could produce Hamlet . . . amid a lot of nonsense.

Critiques of the Ape Language Studies

Ultimately you must decide for yourself what language is and whether it has been demonstrated in nonhuman primates. However, the criticisms of the studies (and criticisms of the criticisms of the studies) will be presented to help you reach a reasoned decision.

Clever Hans Pitfall.   Generally speaking, there are two errors, easy to make, that have been attributed to all the ape language studies and that you may wish to

Table 8.4a *Nim's most frequent 2, 3, and 4 sign combinations.*
From "Can an ape create a sentence?" by H. S. Terrace, L. A. Petitto, R. J. Sanders, and T. G. Bever, 1979, in Science *206, pp. 891–902. Copyright 1979 by the AAAS. Reprinted by permission.*

Two-sign Combinations		Frequency	Three-sign Combinations			Frequency
play	me	375	play	me	Nim	81
me	Nim	328	eat	me	Nim	48
tickle	me	316	eat	Nim	eat	46
eat	Nim	302	tickle	me	Nim	44
more	eat	287	grape	eat	Nim	37
me	eat	237	banana	Nim	eat	33
Nim	eat	209	Nim	me	eat	27
finish	hug	187	banana	eat	Nim	26
drink	Nim	143	eat	me	eat	22
more	tickle	136	me	Nim	eat	21
sorry	hug	123	hug	me	Nim	20
tickle	Nim	107	yogurt	Nim	eat	20
hug	Nim	106	me	more	eat	19
more	drink	99	more	eat	Nim	19
eat	drink	98	finish	hug	Nim	18
banana	me	97	banana	me	eat	17
Nim	me	89	Nim	eat	Nim	17
sweet	Nim	85	tickle	me	tickle	17
me	play	81	apple	me	eat	15
gun	eat	79	eat	Nim	me	15
tea	drink	77	give	me	eat	15
grape	eat	74	nut	Nim	nut	15
hug	me	74	drink	me	Nim	14
banana	Nim	73	hug	me	hug	14
in	pants	70	sweet	Nim	sweet	14

attribute later to studies of human language as well. The first is the *Clever Hans phenomenon.* Clever Hans was a horse that displayed what looked like a remarkable ability to solve spoken arithmetic problems by tapping out the correct answer with his hoof. Initial suspicions of trickery by his owner were ruled out since his owner did not need to be in the room when Hans was queried, questions could be whispered to Hans, and so on. However, it did turn out that Hans was not understanding the spoken words or the arithmetic problem: If two people gave Hans the numbers to add, one in each ear, so that no one knew the correct solution, Hans failed.

It turned out Hans was a very clever horse—able to read body language. As each person asked the question (s)he would lean forward, tense, as Hans started to tap out his answer. The tension increased the closer he got to the right answer. When he reached the right answer, the people visibly relaxed; and when Hans perceived this he stopped. Since everyone gives similar tension-relaxation signals, Hans' trainer *per*

Table 8.4b *(Continued)*

Most Frequent Four-Sign Combinations	Frequency
eat drink eat drink	15
eat Nim eat Nim	7
banana Nim banana Nim	5
drink Nim drink Nim	5
banana eat me Nim	4
banana me eat banana	4
banana me Nim me	4
grape eat Nim eat	4
Nim eat Nim eat	4
play me Nim play	4
drink eat drink eat	3
drink eat me Nim	3
eat grape eat Nim	3
eat me Nim drink	3
grape eat me Nim	3
me eat drink more	3
me eat me eat	3
me gum me gum	3
me Nim eat me	3
Nim me Nim me	3
tickle me Nim play	3

se did not have to be present, but there had to be at least one person present who knew the right answer (incidentally, his trainer never knew that he could not do arithmetic and refused to believe it after Hans' performance was explained—Brown, 1958).

Can the apes be responding to their language situations as Clever Hans was? With the exception of the apes communicating with the machine (which could not give unconscious hints), the answer is that it is a possibility for all of them, and in fact, when tested by people who did not know either the language or the correct answer, all of the apes do worse (see Premack, 1971, for example). However, one could argue that these trainer-"blind" situations are not a fair test of language since language is social, and a situation where one person cannot really understand another is not terribly social. We, especially as children, tend to perform worse, act shy or coy, with strangers than with people with whom we are comfortable.

Generous Interpretation Pitfall. Throughout we have been hinting at the second note of caution. We all have a tendency to interpret another's utterance as we would if we were making it ourselves. This leads to misunderstandings in human relationships as we all have experienced, so it can obviously lead to misunderstandings when talking to animals. We assume, for instance, that if Lana types out "Please machine give M&M." she understands about politeness, punctuation, and what an M&M and machine are. What evidence do we have that she understands any of this? That she eats the M&M after asking for it? Certainly that does not count as evidence, because, as long as she likes M&Ms, she is likely to eat them whether or not that was what she thought she was getting, as we would. If she asked for water and got an M&M and did not eat it, that would be no more evidence that she knew what she was doing than an animal's going to its food bowl for food and its water bowl for water (see Mistler-Lachman and Lachman, 1974 for similar criticisms).

The same caution can be applied to the so-called creative communications of the apes: A human observer understanding "water bird" and seeing a swan assumes that Washoe is naming, creatively, the bird. But as Terrace et al. (1979) pointed out, it is possible that Washoe was first naming the lake the swan was sitting on and then naming the animal, bird, both words that she knew. The creative combination may have been in the eye of the beholder, not in the mind of the animal at all. With the anecdotal reports of Patterson on Koko, we have many similar examples; Koko's signing "lips" as she chewed the crayon may not have been an attempt to sign lipstick but a description of what the crayon was between and thus not a clever deception.

Ape Language Revisited.   With these things in mind let us reexamine the apes' language abilities. All have shown the capacity to associate one visual object or gesture with another, to learn many such associations, and in some cases, to use the associations only in a prescribed order, generating longer and longer ordered sequences. Some also seem to have developed associations between visible objects and abstract properties of objects. The questions are: Do associations equal names? Does order in association reflect syntax and ordered associations equal sentences? Do groups of ordered associations produced by different individuals equal conversations?

Alternative Interpretations.   If you have difficulty conceptualizing their utterances as anything but words, sentences, and conversations, consider using the candy machine described in Chapter 4 as a behavioral chain. Suppose we say that a gesture of fiddling for coins "means" please, of putting one in a slot "means" machine, of putting another in a slot "means" give, and of pulling a particular lever "means" M&Ms. Then we could conclude that someone using a candy machine is uttering the sentence "Please machine give M&Ms." Note that the order of performing the gestures must be maintained; putting money in after pulling the lever is ungrammatical and will result in no candy delivery. Is any string of ordered gestures potentially a sentence, or is there something that characterizes language apart from its ability to alter the environment and its sequential order?

Aside from these general problems, common to all the ape language studies, we can criticize individual studies specifically. For example, as you may have realized, Sarah could just be performing multiple discriminations. In the presence of the object apple she learned to place a blue plastic triangle or an orange square (?) on the board to get reinforced. (We called the blue triangle "apple" and the orange square "red.") In the presence of the object banana, she learned to place two other plastic pieces on the board. This does not appear to be a terribly difficult task. It is not clear even that she knows the difference in "meaning" between blue triangle and orange square (between "apple" and "red") or between the superordinate categories "name of" and "color of" since she never had to choose between "apple" and "red" when answering questions about them; she only had to select from either color names or fruit names. Thus, her entire language task could be performed as a large discrimination: If there is an apple present or a blue triangle on the board then orange square is the right answer, or if there is a blue triangle and a red cross (potential "color of" symbol) on the board then orange square is the right answer. (Is this true of human language?) Written this way it sounds more like the rules for a board game than like a sentence. Indeed, college students taught to "play" Sarah's game as Sarah was, without being told that these plastic bits were words, were very successful at it and never realized that it was a language (Premack, 1979)!

Lana's language can be criticized in the same manner as Sarah's, except that Lana was allowed more freedom of expression and had access to all her words at the same time; they were not selected for her. If your bias is to think that she had language, you can look at her spontaneous productions like "please make machine music window open" (Table 8.2) as the spontaneous creation of a compound sentence. On the other hand, you might observe that "machine" should precede "make" in her syntax and therefore this was an error, that she had no way of knowing that there is such a thing as machine music distinct from live music—in short, that this seems to be a random set of keypresses which *we* happen to be able to interpret. You might find this view supported further by the nonsensical nature of some of her other creations, "question you give milk shut open" or "question you tickle Lana to Lana behind room." And isn't the "apple-which-is-orange" sequence (Table 8.3) a matter of random keystrikes until the trainer "relaxed," reinforcing her with the orange, when at last she said something he could interpret? (Note that she asked inappropriately for a cup, then for a "which-is-shut," then typed "Shelley give," which is poorly formed and Shelley was not there, etc.)

Some of these criticisms of Lana's language the Rumbaughs have accepted, particularly after training Sherman and Austin (Savage-Rumbaugh, Rumbaugh, and Boysen, 1980). They concluded that there is a difference between a label's representing an object in symbolic fashion and a "label"'s association with an object. Apart from association, they list as criteria for representation: the ability to name objects apart from requesting those objects, ability to describe an object given the label, ability to locate the object given the label, and ability to refer to the object from the label when the object is absent. For the most part, the chimpanzees have failed to show these skills and in fact only demonstrate things that they do in their own natural communication—desire objects, desire others to groom them, indicate drive states, and indicate objects in the environment. Sherman and Austin, they argue, are different because of their apparent communication about an object that only one of them has seen.

Conversational Pigeons? Do you agree that this is a critical difference? Before hastily answering, consider a parody of their conversation by two pigeons, Jack and Jill, trained by Epstein, Lanza, and Skinner (1980). Observe that pigeons are less likely than apes *a priori* to have symbolic thought but have keen visual discrimination abilities and keen skill at "typing"—pecking at keys with their beaks. Jack and Jill were each trained to perform a chain involving conditional discriminations. Jack was taught first to peck one of three different-colored keys (left, middle, or right) depending on which of three vertically arranged keys was lit (top = Red, middle = Green, bottom = Yellow); that is, if the top key, labeled "R," was lit he would peck a red key (on the left), if the G-key was lit, he would peck a green key, and if the Y-key was lit, a yellow key. After learning this discrimination he was taught to peck two other keys in sequence: a key labeled "what color" that caused the R, G, and Y keys to light (secondary reinforcers), and after they lit, a key labeled "thank you" that lit his color keys for his choice (also secondary reinforcers). After his discrimination, of course, he received food.

Meanwhile, Jill was taught to peck R, G, or Y keys depending on whether a red, green, or yellow color key was lit. By gradually moving the color key to behind a curtain, the experimenters taught Jill to look for it behind the curtain, beginning her search when a "what color" key was lit. Then the two pigeons were put together to have an apparent conversation, as illustrated in Figure 8.2: Jack would ask Jill "what color," Jill would go and look and then tell him by pressing the R, G, or Y key, and he would reinforce her by pressing the "thank you" key and then select his "decoding" of her "symbol" by pressing the appropriate colored key. Epstein et al. concluded:

> We have thus demonstrated that pigeons can learn to engage in a sustained and natural conversation without human intervention, and that one pigeon can transmit information to another entirely through the use of symbols.
>
> It has not escaped our notice that an alternative account of this exchange may be given in terms of the prevailing contingencies of reinforcement.... The performances were established through standard fading, shaping, chaining, and discrimination procedures. A similar account may be given of the Rumbaugh procedure as well as of comparable human language. (p. 545).

Savage-Rumbaugh and Rumbaugh (1980) did not agree that this was all there was to Sherman's and Austin's conversation. Their principal line of attack on the pigeon study was that the pigeons were rigidly trained for each of their sequences, whereas Sherman and Austin appeared to respond spontaneously to each other's typing once they had learned the symbol names. In addition, they pointed out that Sherman and Austin could switch roles, knew many more than three "names," and did not need to associate a particular physical position with a "name" on the keyboard. Finally, they were able to show in other tasks that Sherman and Austin could generate other responses to the symbol names, like pointing to photographs, besides just striking one particular key.

It is questionable how valid these critiques are. The physical position of the labeled key seems no less arbitrary an association to red than the shape depicted on the key. Sherman and Austin were trained specifically for communication, being taught separately to respond to queries from the machine. They knew more names and could respond with different associations in a different testing procedure, but this might not represent a qualitatively different skill—representational thought—but merely quantitatively more associations. Certainly the study of Epstein et al. raises questions about how to demonstrate conversation once preconceived notions about animals' abilities are removed!

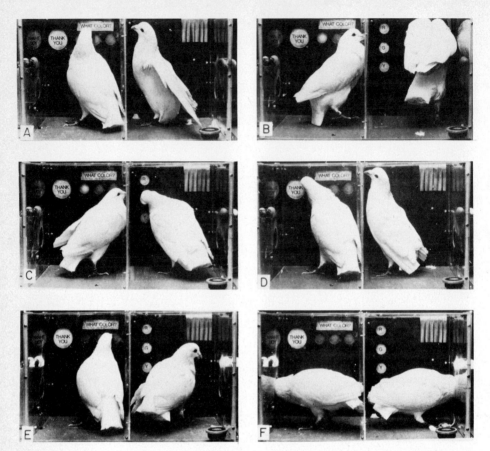

Figure 8.2   *Communication between Jack and Jill (A). Jack (left) asks Jill (right) for a color name by depressing the WHAT COLOR? key. (B) Jill looks through the curtain for the hidden color. (C) Jill selects the color name while Jack watches. (D) Jack rewards Jill with food by depressing the THANK YOU key. (E) Jack selects the correct color as Jill goes to food. (F) Jack is rewarded with food.*
From "Symbolic communication between two pigeons (Columba Livia Domestica)" by R. Epstein, R. P. Lanza, and B. F. Skinner, 1980, in Science 207, *pp. 543–545. Copyright 1980 by the AAAS. Reprinted by permission.*

Is There Productivity? The most serious critiques of the signing ape projects have been leveled by Terrace et al. (1979) on the basis of their experience with their own chimpanzee, Nim. Some of these criticisms we have already mentioned: There is no way of ascertaining what the animals were "thinking" when they signed "water bird" or "lip"; there is no way of knowing how much nonsense sign surrounds the occasional intelligible novel creation since the records are incomplete; the experimenters may be unconsciously cuing the animals' correct performance.

Terrace et al. kept complete records of their interaction with Nim on videotapes, and reviews of those tapes suggested additional specific problems. The most important of these is that although Nim's utterances got longer, they did not reflect acquisition of additional syntactic rules—two frequent two-sign combinations were "play me" and "me Nim," a three-sign utterance was "play me Nim," and a four-sign utterance "Nim me Nim me." Clearly, new rules like relative clause formation are *not* coming into play, but four-sign utterances are just two two-sign utterances. Usually, also, the increased length was just repetition for emphasis.

A second feature of Nim's signing that Terrace et al. found troublesome was that it reflected little spontaneity—for the most part Nim responded to trainers' questions or imitated what the trainer had just said but did not initiate conversations himself. And he tended to sign simultaneously with the trainer (interrupt), indicating that he was not really attending to the conversation. Finally, Terrace et al. reviewed the videotapes and films available from the other signing projects and found little difference between Washoe's or Koko's behavior and Nim's. Although the Gardners and Patterson have criticized Terrace's study, they have not offered substantial evidence contradicting it (see "Ape Language," 1981).

Summary. This section has examined selected communication systems among animals (and trees) to highlight similarities and differences between the abilities indicated by our language and the abilities other organisms have. In discussing the systems we emphasized places where there might be conflicting opinions, such as whether a common goal is essential to the definition of communication, whether a novel sign combination is just a list or a new compound, or whether language is simply a set of discriminations determined by external stimuli and internal motivational states. We also pointed out biological mechanisms that may underlie human abilities as well as animals' and methods of teaching linguistic constructions and constructs like symbolic thought, which may underlie our mastery of such skills. We turn next to formulating an explicit statement of criteria that may separate human language from other forms of communication or cognitive abilities.

Language and Communication: Necessary Characteristics

From our discussions of animal communication systems, including those taught to animals, you should have observed the difficulties in establishing firm criteria for what constitutes language or communication, making it hard to decide which animals have substantial communication skills. In this section we shall make explicit specific criteria that have been proposed in the past and that have implicitly guided our previous discussion, and we add some based on our analysis of language. We will then apply these rules to human communication to separate what we do in common with animals from what we do uniquely. Finally, we will look generally at what is known about the biological basis of human language to determine how the unique skills occur.

Design Features for Communication

In Chapter 1 we defined communication as the active transfer of information from one (the transmitter) to another (the receiver). By this definition, all the situations we have described constitute communication.

Theorists have introduced additional refinements that at least grade levels of communication, if not distinguish communication systems from noncommunication systems. One refinement is further consideration of the concept of active and deliberate processing on the part of the receiver; we must distinguish perception from communication. When we touch an outstretched hand or see a tail waving to and fro, we get a tactile or visual sensation, automatically, and also a message of friendliness from person or dog. The first is a mechanical, relatively passive sensation; the second, communication. Distinguishing the second from the first is not always easy— MacKay (1972) defines an event as communicating if it serves an *internal organizing function* for the receiver, by providing information that alters the receiver's interpretation of the world. (Of course, changes in internal organization and mental representations are hard to measure.) Note that information in this sense is consistent with our earlier definition as a reduction of uncertainty and allows what is transmitted to be false or imaginary—it will reduce uncertainty, but incorrectly. In this case, the touch of the hand has only a transitory effect, but the handshake changes the receiver's concept of the social situation, of the transmitter, and so forth.

The next characteristic we may consider is transmission as well as reception. A person cannot communicate with a tape recorder, nor can a tape recorder communicate with a person. The person who made the tape does, via the recording. This holds true for literature, art, and music; the inanimate does not communicate but the creator does. (This brings to mind the probably apocryphal story of a professor who stopped attending classes, delivering lectures by tape recorder. One day he came in to see how things were going and found no students but 30 tape recorders in record mode on the student desks. Is this communication?)

Obviously, an inanimate object cannot communicate, although by being perceived it can affect an observer's behavior. Less obviously, an animate being who is perceived may not be communicating—just being seen, heard, and so on. Communication takes place only when the transmitter is deliberately, intentionally emitting the signals in order to affect the receiver's conception of the world. Passive emissions—light bouncing off an individual, indicating that (s)he is there, a stomach gurgling, a temperature, a flat EEG—however interpretable they are to a skilled observer are not messages but *symptoms*. Nature may have coordinated transmission and reception of symptoms in sign stimuli, but they are no more deliberate than a radio transmitter's effect on a radio. This kind of interaction is called *signaling,* and the "rules" determining the receivers' responses are called the *code system.*

Note that the map between signal and what is signaled or between signal and the response to the signal can be quite arbitrary unless one knows the code (and usually that entails being a part of the culture)—readiness to mate has no direct relation to red, nor has pursuit a direct relation to red. Readiness to mate, of course, has a direct relation to pursuit, but the relation it has is mediated by a shared but arbitrary code.

Note further that a signal system must have an arbitrary code between transmitter and receiver to be a signal system: Chasing someone out of a territory is not a signal but a direct causation; marking the territory so that the intruder "interprets" its ownership and leaves is a signal system. Cherry (1957) made this distinction for human communication versus human interaction—pushing someone is not communicating, but telling him to move is, even though the effects may be the same. Here, we extended the argument to differentiate signal systems as indirect effects from direct effects of interaction.

The difficulty with intentionality as a criterion separating signaling from communicating is that it is very difficult to prove intentionality. One way, as we saw, is by finding instances of deception, since deception indicates a flexible relationship between the message and the environmental controlling stimuli. Another way is by looking for the transmitter's response to feedback. The existence of feedback and response to it, called *evaluation,* are other requirements for communication.

Feedback is a signal the receiver makes about the symptom or message. Evaluation is the transmitter's interpretation of the feedback and use to alter the message. Feedback and evaluation essentially reverse communication direction; the receiver becomes transmitter when giving feedback, and the transmitter becomes receiver when evaluating it. Communication *must* be a closed loop with transmitter and receiver simultaneously playing both roles. A gives a message to B while receiving feedback from B. B receives a message from A while transmitting feedback. And this can spiral continuously—B may be watching for feedback from A about A's reaction to B's feedback.

If A is watching for feedback and changes behavior as a result of it, we can infer that A had some internal representation of the outcome of the communication, a way of evaluating the outcome and determining whether there is a mismatch between what happened and what A *intended* to have happen. Thus, we can infer intentionality. Symptoms such as red spots on the stickleback, a flat EEG, or a scream indicating a predator are not altered when the transmitter perceives their effect; they are tied to the stimulus, not the interaction. Note that the criteria of intentionality and evaluation imply that in communication the transmitter can react to his own actions as others will react (Morris, 1964); the transmitter's reaction as receiver to his own communication forms the basis of his internal representation for communication.

Summary.   In this section we looked at aspects of tranmission and reception of signals that may or may not be considered communication. To be communication for our purposes, a signal must be actively, intentionally transmitted, actively received, changing the organizational state of the receiver, and must generate feedback from the receiver to the transmitter, potentially changing the transmitter's behavior.

Evaluation: Communication and Noncommunication Systems

Plants and Animals.   Given the criteria just established, most of the situations described in preceding sections of this chapter do not constitute communication for one reason or another. The fly and the frog fail because there is no awareness of the other's presence, let alone internal representation of the other's internal state, nor intentionality of communication. The fly signals no more to the frog than a grain of corn does to a bird. This basic response to another-as-stimulus has been classified (adapted from Hinde, 1972) as the lowest form of interaction, the *vegetable level.*

The tree interaction also fails but may be considered another, higher level of interaction. In this case, the failure is due to failure to monitor for feedback as well as failure of intentionality. (Note, though, that the transmitter and receiver trees could switch roles and at least metabolically have similar "internal representations.") This constitutes a higher level in terms of the nature of the stimulus reacted to—it is not the transmitter as a whole stimulus but a signaled aspect of its state (in this case, being devoured). When the signal is based on a bodily process, such as sending poison to the wound or leaving a scent on a trail, the interaction is at the *tonic level*.

The stickleback interaction must be divided into separate signals. The development of the red spot or swelling with eggs are indications of state. They differ from the tree because they are not a sustained-over-time state but a discontinuous one; and the reception of the information is likewise discontinuous, for the female responds to red only when she is pregnant. This is called a *phasic level* of interaction because the signals work only at certain phases of the organism's life. The courtship dance and pursuit behavior are classified at a higher level, the *signal level,* because transmission is triggered by perception of the other, and the transmitter is responsive to feedback.[5] The courtship rituals of the cricket and birds also fit into the signal level.

The remaining two levels are the *symbolic level* and *language level,* distinguished from the preceding levels by the variability in signals, the amount that can be communicated, and the referential nature of the symbols (not signals). In this classification scheme, they differ from each other in that language may communicate abstract ideas, whereas the symbolic level is restricted to the concrete. (One further, intriguing difference that has been proposed [Cherry, 1957] is that in all symbol or signal systems but man's [language], only the present and the future can be indicated. The present is indicated in state signals and being signals; the future, in mating "proposals" and signals of fear of attack from predators. To our knowledge, the past is not discussed, except in language, although that may be in part because of our point of view. The bees may be signaling where they had been, not where they will go; an animal's discovery of a scent marker could be "discussion" of who had been there earlier.)

The classification scheme just described, although useful, is a victim of anthropocentrism and is based heavily on prior notions of hierarchy in the animal kingdom. At the vegetable level this scheme places interaction between plants and the animals that feed on them; at the phasic level, lower vertebrates; at the signal level (further divided into stages) lower vertebrates and birds at one stage and birds and lower mammals at another; nonhuman primates at the symbolic; and language is restricted to man. Beginning with a classification of primitive to complex, researchers can find

5. It may be hard to consider the well-coordinated mating situation as symptoms of each other's states. An example from the sea lions (Bruemmer, 1983) may help. At mating time, the bull sea lion stakes out a territory and seems very motivated to hold it and keep out other males. The first female to choose a beach is followed immediately by a pack of other females, who crowd that beach, spilling over into other territories only when there is no more room. No indication is given by the bull of interest in the females, nor by the females of interest in the bull. When the females enter estrus, the males mate with those females on their territories, and after copulation both sexes cease to attend to the other. Mating takes place only because of this mutual interest in territory. Indeed, it is because of the territorial instinct of the male and his oblivion to wife and child that a father can sit atop his infant, killing it, and not notice.

classes of interaction that likewise go from primitive to complex, but this is circular reasoning. We presented the distinctions made by the system because the divisions based on the communications alone, apart from the interactors, seemed to be reasonable and provocative about the nature of communication.

We reserve the distinction between symbolic and linguistic levels of communication in animals for discussion of "design features" for language. However, we still must decide whether the "higher" forms of interaction—of the bee, mammals, and pigeon—constitute interaction, communication, or symbolic communication. Despite the elaborateness of the bee system it seems reasonable to conclude that bees are not communicating but signaling. On the transmitter's side, there is no choice about what to say. That does not mean that a bee does not produce novel utterances, but just that if she visits one food supply her behavior when she returns is totally predictable. The receivers also need not concern themselves with the adequacy of her message, her previous finds, and descriptions, and so on; they can be confident that it absolutely represents her experience and what theirs would be too if they were there. Their "feedback" in dance does not cause the message to change or cause the transmitter to try other "words" to make it clear. In fact, their feedback, as automatic mimicry, need not be considered feedback at all but rather more akin to "social" yawning—we yawn once someone else starts, perhaps not as a signal to them but as an uncontrollable response.

It is easy to eliminate the pigeon "conversation" from communication given the criteria just established, since it is not clear that the pigeons demonstrate awareness of each other, let alone intentionality to communicate with each other. They are certainly looking for environmental signals (different lights lighting up), which happen to be under the other bird's control (and the experimenter's), but are not obviously searching for a change in the other's world representation. Here, the fact that they cannot change roles suggests that they cannot have a representation of what the other is experiencing and cannot evaluate the effect of the communication in light of such a representation.

What is troublesome about the analysis of the pigeon "conversation" is that it is tempting to conclude that the chimpanzees Sherman and Austin are communicating, that they do have such a representation; but aside from their abilities to switch roles their behavior can be described in the same way as that of the pigeons. (This implies that ability to switch roles is a defining feature of communication.) Indeed, examination of the untrained interaction patterns and cognitive capacity of the monkeys, apes, and sea lions suggests that they certainly can form mental representations and can put themselves in the place of others ("identifying" with characters in videotapes and the like), but does not suggest definitively that they form such representations in normal interactions.

Under extreme, unusual circumstances, when the bull sea lion is suffocating the infant, or when the "competitive" trainer is not obeying the social code, or when food is withheld until some action is performed, the need arises to represent the other's frame of mind to induce an extraordinary response, but ordinarily, responses elicited through signal-interaction are sufficient to maintain social order. To our knowledge, in these social colonies, normally, little information is transmitted; colony members have little choice in what to signal and no choice in how to interpret the signal; there is much less uncertainty. With behavior between colony members always conforming to the social rules, there is no chance of being misinterpreted, no need to monitor for feedback to see if the signal was correctly received—perfect understanding is guaranteed. If you could guarantee perfect understanding without using language, would you bother? Indeed, researchers have tried to find evidence that the apes taught a language will then spontaneously use it in their own colonies, teach it to their offspring, and so forth, but there have been only occasional anecdotal reports of success. I suspect it will not happen because the animals have perfect signaling success without it. Why should they bother?

Human Signal and Communication Systems.   Now that we have applied a set of criteria to animal interaction and concluded that, at least to our alien[6] eyes, much of it is not really communication, the time has come to apply the same set of criteria to humans, to make sure that we pass, at least in some instances. As we said in Chapter 1, there are many forms of human "communication" of which language is only one—there is also body language and paralanguage as part of our natural interaction, and pantomime, art, music, and literature as studied—perhaps secondary—forms of interaction.

The Arts. Let us look first, briefly, at these secondary forms of interaction. There can be no question that in the arts there is active, deliberate, intentional transmission—the artist works to create and convey the message. For all, also, the perceivers try, presumably actively, to decode the message. The problem in this case is the feedback loop. Frequently the artist is not around to receive audience reaction and/or is not monitoring for it. (Is Shakespeare communicating with us? Are we communicating with aliens light years away—if they exist?) Frequently, too, the artist does not care what the audience reaction is, deliberately forbidding publication until after death, or ignoring critical reviews, lack of sales, general unpopularity. So even if there is a reaction the artist could consider, it is often ignored or not used to change the message or form of the message.

By our criteria, then, artistic expressions are simply expressions, not communications. Of course, the medium, pantomime, art, a map, may be used to convey an idea in normal interaction and is then subject to normal feedback loops. And there are artists or performers who are sensitive to audience response and change their styles around it and so are, in a general way, communicating. But, for the most part, these secondary forms, because they cannot be affected by feedback, must not be considered communication if we consistently apply our criteria. (It is interesting to consider, if you disagree, whether it is the playwright or the actor who is communicating.)

6. An important point to emphasize again is that we are outsiders looking at the animal cultures. When humans have encountered an alien human culture, we usually argue it is primitive, incapable of logical thought, etc., relative to our own, until we understand it. If barriers exist among human cultures preventing immediate recognition of advanced intelligence and communication, imagine the barriers between humans and animals! There, not only are the rules different, but we may not even have the sensory apparatus to recognize the signals.

Nonverbal Primary Communication. Now consider the primary forms of human interaction in typical face-to-face conversation between two people, called *dyadic interaction.* Conversation consists of a series of floor switches: First A talks, then B talks, then A talks again. Most conversations consist of *ordered* floor switches (Duncan and Fiske, 1977); there is very little simultaneous conversation or interruption. While A holds the floor (and wishes to keep it) A mostly looks away from B, occasionally looking at B for feedback. A is also talking and gesturing continuously. When A comes to the end of what (s)he has to say, speech and gestures cease in a regular away—the sentence is completed, intonation declines, the hands return to a neutral resting position, and so on. A also looks directly at B, further signaling B to take the floor. If B wanted to break in during A's turn, B would indicate that also in a rule-governed way: raising the eyebrows, beginning a hand gesture and mouth gesture and holding it, but not articulating. When A got the message, A would let B in, as before.

In our analysis of speech, we found that a number of things were conveyed by the speech signals: phonetic content, speaker identity, emotional overtone (and stress/deception), and syntactic information (as in pauses and intonation changes). "Conveyed" implies transmitted by the speaker and possibly perceived/interpreted by the listener.

Finally, as most of us are aware, several kinds of visible behavior occur during face-to-face interaction. Just alluded to are eye contact and gesturing. There are also facial expressions: color changes as in blushing or blanching, pupil dilation (or constriction), eyebrow movements (raising, lowering, or puckering), eyelid movements (closing, winking, blinking, batting), eye movements (downward, upward, toward an object in the environment, away from or toward the other), mouth movements (smiling, frowning, pursing the lips), and then hard-to-describe combinations as in general tension, sneering, and so forth. There are head and body movements apart from what is going on in the face: movements toward or away from the other, nods or shakes of the head, sudden cessation of movement (as in rapt attention). And there are global visual characteristics: attractiveness, neatness, posture, "spread" (sitting or standing too close to another, or with arms outstretched, taking a lot of room), among others. Some of these are readily interpretable, some can be interpreted only by some people after special training, some perhaps are meaningless (see Scheflen and Scheflen, 1972).

If we are strict in our application of the criteria for communication to human interactions, most of these situations do not constitute a high level of interaction. Vocal or visual cues to speaker identity, a myriad of signals—facial features, idiosyncratic movement or dress style, vocal tone—however learned some of them may be (there are "dialect" features in body language with most of these expressions and their interpretations differing from culture to culture) may be classed at the vegetable or tonic levels. Emotional state signaling, in tone of voice or facial expression or general body tension, as obvious physical correlates of transitory bodily states, may be classified at the phasic level. (Do not be misled by the arbitrary relation of the expression to the emotion; remember that redness has no obvious relation of sexual readiness but for the stickleback fish is still a physical correlate of that state.) For the most part, as transmitters, we are unaware of these symptoms—not monitoring for feedback about them—and are unable to change them even if we were.

Under extraordinary circumstances, when we are intentionally trying to convey a particular impression, so that the message of the interaction is our appearance, poise, or emotional state (as in an interview), we may attempt to control transmission of these signals, and they may be used as communication. Under circumstances like interviews, the receiver is also actively trying to form a representation of the person or the state and so will be processing these signals or symptoms and perhaps giving feedback about them. But interviews are atypical communication situations. Normally, such behavior serves at best as signals, not messages or symbols, and probably more often as symptoms, which the receiver ignores. Then these are not communication because (1) they are not actively, intentionally transmitted; (2) they are not actively processed by the receiver; and (3) there is no feedback, evaluation loop. Moreover, as with the animals and plants we examined, they indicate only the transmitter's being and state, nothing about the environment, the past, or objective reality.

In regulation of interaction, as in whose turn it is to talk, nonverbal vocal and visual signals seem to be communicating. Turn-taking is effective—there are few interruptions or long pauses before the other picks up the cue—and this suggests that the speaker and listener must be actively monitoring for turn-taking signals. Thus, a feedback loop, a shared situation, exists. Both speaker-surrendering-the-floor and listener-taking-over-the-floor signals seem to be deliberately, actively transmitted also. So this is communication. It is not a very high level, however, since what is being communicated is current "emotional" state—desire to talk or desire to give up talking.

Now, are there aspects of language itself that may be considered as noncommunicating by our criteria? Idiosyncratic language use, which identifies the speaker in some way, might be one—as our using English identifies us as English speakers, although that is an unintended, passive effect of most messages. Similarly, use of particular pronunciation, syntactic construction, vocabulary, topics of conversation, unintentionally may identify our age, sex, place of birth, social class, profession, social group membership. (For example, use of the word "cool" could suggest that the user is "cool," if the word is still "hep" [if "hep" is still "hep"!]. If not, use of these words here will signal when this was written.) These cues are called *social markers* (Scherer and Giles, 1979), and, of course, they exist in nonverbal signaling as well. However, it is interesting to consider that *language, while communicating, is also, at another level, just an instance of behavior and can serve as a signal or symptom simultaneously.*

A second potential candidate for noncommunication within language is in highly stereotyped interactive sequences: (A) Hi. How are you? (B) Fine and you? (A) Fine . . . and then the message. These sequences seem to be passively processed by both A and B: We have all experienced the sudden interjection by one or the other, when the message part starts, of "No, I'm not fine. Actually . . ." or one or the other giving an atypical response—"sick, suicidal, wonderful, . . ." where "fine" was expected and this actual response was ignored. From both these cases we can infer that usually neither is actively or deliberately processing the verbal content of the signal, neither is using it to evaluate the interchange, and neither is giving feedback on the content. In fact, here the interchange seems to be at the level of Jack and Jill's interchange, with nothing communicated but turn-taking signals, politeness, and the desire to keep the conversation going.

Given these criteria, what we frequently classify as poor communication may in fact be instances of noncommunication, even when syntax or semantics is quite elaborate. Consider, for example, a person reading or giving a lecture, never looking up, actively avoiding feedback from the audience. Is this any different from the tape recorder situation? The intent here seems to be to get through the hour, not to change the receivers' mental representations. Therefore it is not communication.

A third instance of verbal signaling that is not communicating may be found in some interjections. In English, for example, when hurt we say "ouch," astonished, "No!?," comprehending, "aha," impressed, "ooo." These are specific to our language; other noises are used in other cultures, odd as that may seem. However, this is like the dialect features in the white-crowned sparrow; even if learned, they are still very closely tied to basic physical states and are uttered usually only as symptoms of those states. Do you think it is reasonable to extend this classification to include statements of state like "I am happy" or "I am in pain?" The main reason not to do this lies in intent—the speaker has chosen to make the statement and is therefore deliberately trying to convey something. In a smile or a grimace of agony or an interjection of "ouch," the transmission is automatic and therefore a symptom. But admittedly this is a small distinction.

The design features described here for communication and their application to animal and human interactions are by no means absolute truths. Scientists and philosophers have been groping for defining and distinguishing characteristics of interactions for generations, and as you should feel, have not as yet arrived at any decisive answers. You are free to disagree with any of the classifications, distinctions, or conclusions made here, but you must apply your objection consistently: If you feel intention is unnecessary for communication then it follows that inanimate objects could communicate. If you wish to resolve the issue by saying everything is communication then you must feel that there are no distinctions between what the trees do and what we do, or you are forced to apply the distinctions we made between communication and noncommunication to levels of communication, which does not change the argument.

Summary. We have examined some criteria for communication and applied them to nonhuman and human interaction. Communication involves active, intentional transmission of a signal as well as active, intentional reception, effecting a change in the receiver. There must also be feedback from the receiver, creating a closed loop between the interactants. Given this analysis, many of the systems for changing behavior in another that we have examined are not communication because transmission is unintentional or there is no deliberate feedback. Moreover, applying these criteria to humans, we find some secondary forms of expression, such as visual art and literature, at times to be noncommunication. Finally, some forms of primary expression, body language, tone of voice, stereotyped language, and social markers in language can be considered signaling and not communication as such.

Design Features for Language

As we saw in the last section, language is not a subset of communication; there are aspects of the language signal we have studied that have lower-level functions. However, most of language as we usually think of it is communication: the transmission of a mental representation from one individual to another. This transmission can be accomplished in ways that are not language: maps, visual art, music, and pantomime, for instance. (How) can we define the difference between communication, symbolic communication, and linguistic communication?

Modality-Tailored Characteristics.   Probably the most comprehensive set of design features for language was proposed by Hockett (1960; and Altmann, 1968), after analysis of characteristics shared by languages of the world. His features are shown in Table 8.5, together with an analysis of the systems we have looked at with respect to the features. The first feature is the use of the vocal-auditory channel, which, he argued, was an important evolutionary development in that it freed the rest of the body for other activities, allowing humans to communicate while doing other things. Establishing the vocal-auditory channel as a necessary characteristic for language automatically rules out systems such as the bees' waggle dance, and more significantly, sign language, visual art, music, pantomime, and writing, for perhaps a fairly ad hoc reason. We shall *not* make it a requirement for language (indeed many have eliminated it), but note it here in part for historical reasons and in part because it is the primary modality for most human communication.

Five characteristics of the vocal-auditory channel (and perhaps other channels as well) were listed by Hockett as design features and are responsible partly for the shape of aural-oral language. These are rapid fading, broadcast transmission and reception, interchangeability, total feedback, and specialization. *Rapid fading* refers to the transitory nature of the speech signal; we cannot keep studying it but must encode it rapidly since it disappears. Pantomime, music, and sign languages are also rapidly fading signals, but visual art, many forms of chemical communication, red spots on the stickleback, . . . are not.

Broadcast transmission and reception means we can produce a signal that anyone within hearing distance can receive. This is different from a handshake, for which transmitter and receiver must be in direct contact, or from the tactile mimicry of the bees. Broadcast transmission and reception is somewhat less a feature of visual signals than of auditory ones since we must be looking at the signal to notice it, whereas hearing is less directional, at least in humans. (Many mammals, of course, have more directional hearing, rotating their ears to focus in on a direction.)

Interchangeability is a feature we have already discussed with respect to general communication: In our system an individual can serve equally well as transmitter and receiver, speaker, or listener. This is in part because we are all endowed with the same auditory and vocal systems; we do not have sex-specific, specially developed markings like the red spot or male songs. Interchangeability is a feature also of the bee system and of sign language, and, talent aside, of music, visual art, and literature.

Total feedback is connected with interchangeability and the vocal-auditory system: We hear ourselves as we speak and so can monitor our own signals as well as

Table 8.5 *Summary of features for communication and language, with indication of how the non-language systems distribute with respect to them.* ✓* *means some or sometimes.*

In the table below: ✓ = checkmark, X = cross, ✓* = the "some or sometimes" symbol, ? = question mark.

		Fly-Frog	Stickleback	Frog and Cricket	Sparrow	Bee	Whale	Non-human Primate	Apes and Language	Human "Body Language"	Visual Art and Music
COMMUNICATION	Active Transmission	✓	X	✓	✓	✓	✓	✓	✓	✓*	✓
	Active Reception	X	✓	✓	✓	✓	?	✓	✓	✓*	✓*
	Interchangeability	X	X	X	X	✓	?	✓	✓	✓	✓
	Information Rate (Simultaneity and Smear)	✓*	X	X	✓*	?	?	?	?	?	?
	Feedback	✓	✓	✓	✓	X	?	✓	✓	✓*	✓*
PHYSICAL	Vocal–Auditory	✓*	X	✓	✓	X	✓	✓*	X	✓*	✓*
	Rapid Fading	X	X	✓	✓	?	✓	✓*	X	✓*	✓*
	Broadcast Transmission/Reception	✓*	X	✓	✓	X	✓	✓*	X	✓*	✓*
SYMBOL CHARACTERISTICS	Specialization (system exists only for itself)	X	✓*	✓*	✓*	✓	?	✓*	✓	X	✓
	Semanticity (association not identity between sign and referent)	X	X	X	✓*	✓	?	✓*	✓	✓	✓*
	Arbitrariness (sign and referent arbitrarily related)	X	✓	✓	✓	✓*	?	✓*	✓	✓*	✓*
	Discrete (vs. continuous)	X	?	?	?	✓*	?	✓*	✓	X	✓*
TOPIC	Displacement (in time and space)	X	X	X	X	✓	?	X	✓	X	✓*
COMBINATION	Productivity	X	X	X	X	✓	✓	X	✓	✓*	✓
	Duality of Patterning (awareness of levels element is in)	X	X	X	X	X	?	X	X	X	✓
	Metalanguage	X	X	X	X	X	?	X	?	X	✓
	Recursiveness	X	X	X	X	X	?	X	X	X	✓
	Prevarication	X	X	X	X	X	?	✓	✓	✓	?
LEARNING	Learnability	X	X	X	X	X	?	✓*	✓	✓	✓
	Traditional Transmission	X	X	X	✓*	✓*	?	✓*	✓	✓*	✓

those of others. This contrasts with signals like the stickleback's red spot, which cannot be seen by the transmitter.

Specialization implies the distinction we made between symptoms and signals—some interaction systems utilize a byproduct of normal function as a signal; their communication medium is not reserved only for communication. In contrast, our speech system or gesture system seems to have no immediate purpose beyond communication; it is specialized for that function. A similar argument may be made for music and visual art.

Semantics, Syntax, and Acquisition Characteristics.   The six properties we have just discussed describe general communication features of language systems but not features peculiar to language organization. Hockett's remaining features define linguistic systems in particular. There is *semanticity:* The relation between a signal and its referent is learned through association. Smiling, in many instances, contains no semanticity but is part of being happy. The word "happy," on the other hand, signifies happiness only through association. Moreover, most associations in language are *arbitrary*; there is no external connection between the sounds and the things they signify. Note that a word like "bow-wow" for "dog" employs semanticity—the sound of the animal must be associated with it, but it is nonarbitrary since the sound is connected concretely with the object it represents. Visual arts and pantomime are nonarbitrary, although they may exhibit semanticity, since a particular thing may be depicted because it stands for something else in the culture, as when a Campbell's soup can stands for commercialized, mass-produced cooking. The depiction is still a direct, if conventionalized, portrayal of the object.

The relation of sounds to meaning is *discrete* (as opposed to continuous or graded): The words "loud" and "soft" signify opposite ends of a continuum, but the difference in sound between "loud" and "soft" does not mirror that difference; "soft" is not softer-sounding than loud. When we wish to signify that there is more of something, we add discrete morphemes: "more x," "xier," "very x"; we do not usually signify it by raising our voices (matching the increase with intensity) or increasing the word length.

The next feature Hockett suggested refers to what we talk about rather than the kind of association that is made. He called the feature *displacement,* referring to our ability to talk about things that are displaced in time (future or past) or in space (things not immediately in front of us or perhaps even nonexistent). With respect to displacement others have proposed that a unique aspect of language is its ability to describe the environment, not the signaler—displacement from the transmitter's state (Hinde, 1972). This seems to be a feature shared by many forms of human communication: visual art, pantomime, and music, as well as language.

These distinctive characteristics of language are aspects we discussed in Chapter 2 in relation to meaning and meaning representation. Two additional features, productivity and duality of patterning, refer to the peculiar characteristics of phonology and syntax. Human language, by virtue of its rules, is *productive,* open-ended, and continuously creative: There is no limit (besides our imaginativeness) to what we may talk about and how we may express it. Our "body language," in contrast, is nonproductive; we have "symptoms," like blushing, that are rigorously tied to a state, and new symptoms cannot be created for new messages. Syntax, in combining words to form new meanings, and phonology, in combining phonemes to form words, join elements with one representation together to give a new representation. This is *duality of patterning,* where a single aspect of language has a representation on several levels. Thus, in constructing rhymes, we may look at a word simply as a sound pattern; when we use it in poetry we look at both the sound pattern *and* the meaning. Note that there is duality of patterning also in acting (where a gesture represents itself as well as indicating an aspect of character), in visual arts, and in music.

The final feature Hockett (1960) discussed is *traditional transmission,* referring to how language is acquired. Traditional means it is passed from one generation to the next through learning, not completely innately specified as in many of the signal systems. Nevertheless, Hockett noted that there are genetic influences on our capacity to acquire language.

More recently, Hockett and Altmann (1968) have added three characteristics to the list: prevarication (lying), which we have already discussed; ability to learn other languages or *learnability,* and ability to talk about the communication system itself. (Words used to describe characteristics of words are called *metalanguage*; communication about communications, *metacommunication.*) These features also apply, by extension, to other forms of human expression; we must learn the conventions of an art form to understand it, we may use art to create a false mood, and we may refer to other artistic expressions within a given artistic expression.

In addition to Hockett's thirteen plus three design features, others have proposed critical distinguishing characteristics of language that we should consider. Thorpe (1972) suggested that to be language there must be a combination of two or more elements purposefully for a single effect, the same elements able to recombine in different ways for different effects. As you may recall, the absence of syntactic combinations is what Terrace et al. (1979) found nonlanguage-like in the chimpanzees' signing behavior. Lyons (1972) proposed that language is characterized by *medium transferability:* We can communicate the same message in speech, lip-reading, writing . . . ; there is no fixed symbol type.

Information Rate Properties.   A final characteristic that has been proposed is the amount of information transmitted:

Communication proceeds in the face of a number of uncertainties and has the character of, or may be described as consisting of, numerous inductive inferences being carried out concurrently. The number and variety of these uncertainties is particularly apparent in the case of speech. For instance:

(1) Uncertainties of speech sounds, or acoustic patterning. Accents, tones, loudness may be varied; speakers may shout, sing, whisper, or talk with their mouths full.

(2) Uncertainties of language and syntax. Sentence constructions differ; conversational language may be bound by few rules of syntax. Vocabularies vary; words have many near-synonyms, popular usages, special usages, et cetera.

(3) Environmental uncertainties. Conversations are disturbed by street noises, by telephone bells, and background chatter.

(4) Recognition uncertainties. Recognition depends upon the peculiar past experiences of the listener, upon his familiarity with the speaker's speech habits, knowledge of language, subject matter, et cetera.

There are many sources of uncertainty, yet speech communication works. It is so structured as to possess redundancy at a variety of levels, to assist in overcoming these uncertainties.

(Cherry, 1957, p. 277).

On the basis of our analysis of semantic, syntactic, and phonological structure, we may analyze the information requirement further. The amount of information is partly determined by the way information is packed in the speech signal, the lack of invariance, or one-to-one relation between aspects of the speech signal and the message. Thus, one "discrete" segment is packed with information about many layers of language and communication—speaker identity and emotion at the lowest, signal level, phonetic identity of several "segments," semantic or morphemic identity, and syntactic identity at the higher, linguistic levels.

At the same time, if a particular segment is eliminated, because its cues to any one aspect are smeared across adjacent segments, there may be no information loss; the message(s) (and signals and symptoms) may still be recovered. Marler (1975), in fact, described the human speech signal as *graded* because of this simultaneity: As we saw in our discussion of speech perception, the signal continuously changes and the hearer imposes perception of discrete segments (categorical perception) on the changing signal. The graded signal, Marler argued, allows more subtle information to be transferred; the discrete perception allows the signals to be used in isolation or novel combination since they may be matched with discrete patterns in memory and not just compared to the other portions of the signal in which they are embedded. Furthermore, making the continuous signal discrete is a prerequisite for syntactic combinations, and we see analogous instances of simultaneity and smear at higher levels. For example, co-occurrence rules, selectional restrictions, and syntactic structure all provide redundancy, allowing us to miss a word and still recover the message from other parts of the sentence.

Thus, at all levels of language we see simultaneous transmission of many "segments" and smear of the "cues" for one segment across many. We propose simultaneity and smear as additional defining characteristics of language.

Simultaneity and smear, together with duality of patterning, allow for poetic devices: We can focus attention simultaneously at the meaning level and the sound level (since they are simultaneously transmitted) to produce appreciation of alliteration or rhyme; we can focus attention simultaneously at many meaning levels since they are simultaneously transmitted to make metaphors and puns; we can focus attention on meaning and structure simultaneously for rhetorical devices such as rhetorical questions, or structure repetitions (I came, I saw, I conquered) to show similarities in meaning.

Probably related to simultaneity and smear is the rate we transmit information through language. We will not quantify it now and therefore cannot compare language with other forms of expression in this respect, but we propose that there is a rate characteristic of language,[7] although this characteristic may be uninteresting with respect to what it tells us about language as symbol system. It does indicate systems that could not be used as language, for us, however. Try to communicate an understandable message by spelling out loud: It is nearly impossible to keep track of the thought and spell at the same time; as transmitters we get slowed so much we lose the message. Similarly, if someone spells at you, by the time you have put the letters together into words you have forgotten previous words and lost the point of the message. (Whether this is getting information too fast—each letter is its own signal and there are too many of them per word—or too slow—fewer words get said per unit time—is unclear.)

Altering information rate in other ways also disturbs our natural communication, as in inserting *long* pauses between spoken words or very short pauses between complex sentences, or organizing a paragraph so that we are not getting continual small information increments on a theme. As Pierce (1972) observed, "Beethoven is said to have declared that in music everything must be at once surprising and expected. That is appealing. If too little is surprising, we are bored; if too little is expected, we are lost. Communication is possible only through a degree of novelty in a context that is familiar" (p. 9, offprint). To be recognized as language, the message rate and rate of old (redundancy) to new must fall within a certain range to keep us attending to the message; this range is characteristic of language. This relates to simultaneity and smear, in that they give a way of packing old and new together and of transmitting information at a high rate without concern for loss.

Another feature of language related to information organization within it concerns the use of certain elements and rules, repeatedly. Do you think it would be possible to find a language organized so that each word consists of a different number of the same elements: one word being A, for instance, and another AA, a third, AAA, and so on (Hockett, 1960)? Although this would have the advantage of there being few elements to learn and to recognize, it has the disadvantage of having words too similar, too easy to confuse. To avoid this, languages use many elements in combination. Again, though, there must be a boundary on this: If each word or sentence shares no feature with any other word or sentence, there are an enormous number of elements to memorize. Thus, we see languages each having some number of elements that get used repeatedly within the bounds of easy discriminability and easy learnability. This occurs at all levels of language: If the nasal-stop distinction is employed in a language it is likely to be used for several places of articulation, which makes the learning of that feature efficient. If a plural is made one way for one word, that method of pluralization is likely to be generalized to many words, again for efficiency of learning. Thus, again without quantifying it, we propose that a distinguishing feature of language is the number of elements or rules used at each level and their efficient reapplication—the number and reapplication are determined by constraints on human memory and perceptual discriminability (see Miller, 1956).

Another striking feature of language is the possibility of (and possible processing

---

7. Pierce (1972) estimated the message rate for speech at less than or equal to 1000 bits per second.

limitation on) recursiveness (as you may recall from Chapter 4, recursiveness occurs when a sentence is rewritten as a sentence containing a sentence), and again this "feature" occurs at many levels.[8] At the overall communication level, as stated earlier, we may perhaps be the only beings for whom A is aware that B is aware that A is aware that B is aware . . . of what A means. In semantics, because of recursiveness of reference, we get the wonderful paradoxes like "This statement is false" or "I always lie" (Hofstadter, 1979). At the syntactic level, recursive application of rules permits imagining infinitely long sentences—a sentence that contains a sentence that contains a sentence. . . .

Recursiveness is related to productivity but as a special, interesting case. It is possible to have a productive system without altering the basic productive units—for example, apple and banana and pear and. . . . In this case each word or at least each noun does not change in syntactic function nor really modify the meanings of another. However, sentence embedding or connecting sentences through production of subordinate and main clauses does change the units. A sentence (e.g., the cat chased the rat) that before was an end in itself becomes a unit (a NP—the cat that chased the rat), which can build with other units-that-had-been-end-products in the same way that each of them had been composed by smaller units.

As a characteristic property of language, recursiveness thus produces or refines other characteristic properties: There is not just combination of symbols but a certain kind of combination, *hierarchical combination;* there are not just discrete elements but rather discrete elements of variable size. This property of recursiveness is not restricted to language but appears in other forms of human expression. Figure 8.3 displays a lithograph by Escher in which recursiveness establishes the question of what is reality; in music embedding of themes within themes shows recursiveness as well (these examples are from Hofstadter, 1979).

Summary and Conclusions.   In this section we have looked at features of language that have been proposed as characteristic. They are displayed in Table 8.5, and generally they fall into three broad categories: characteristics that arise from the human makeup such as information rate, characteristics of language as a symbol system, and characteristics of language learning. The first type may be uninteresting with respect to whether language provides us with, or is indicative of, special cognitive skills, but it will help us to recognize language apart from communication of other organisms. The other types are more interesting in relation to the question of whether

8. The interested reader is encouraged to read Hofstadter (1979) for many wonderful examples of recursiveness, self-reference, and the duality of patterning (the appreciation of a "symbol" simultaneously at two different levels, for example, as an instance of a category [set] and as a name of a smaller category [set]). These three features he shows to be instances of the same phenomenon, a phenomenon that seems to occur in many aspects of human existence. Hofstadter applies them (it) to paradoxes in language, visual art, and music, to paradoxes in set theory, symbolic logic, etc. I am indebted to Hofstadter for the realization that recursiveness, and delight in noticing recursiveness, are characteristic features of humanness as well as human language.

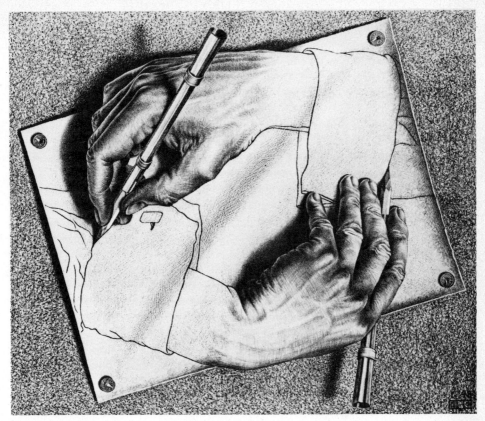

Figure 8.3 *Illustration of recursiveness in art. In drawing the hands, the artist refers to the drawing of the hands.*
© Beeldrecht, Amsterdam/VAGA, New York. "Drawing Hands" by M. C. Escher, Collection Haags Gemeemtemuseum—The Hague.

we think differently from other beings. It is important to note that none of these characteristics alone is sufficient to define language; it is the constellation of characteristics that forms the definition.

Evaluation: Nonlanguage Systems

Overview.   As we have seen, language is not a subset of communication. Not only are there communication systems that are not language-like, but there are aspects of language which are not communication. Therefore we cannot logically reject as language systems those "primitive" interaction systems we already rejected as communication systems, simply on that ground. However, they also fail to satisfy our language standards, usually for many reasons.

Table 8.5 displays the signal and communication systems we have mentioned with respect to whether or not they satisfy our language criteria.[9,10] It is reassuring to note that as each of the systems seems to be more like what we think of as human communication, more of our language criteria apply. Since most of these systems have been discussed in considerable detail already in motivating the criteria, the discussion will not be reviewed again here. To see how the criteria may be applied we will reconsider only the ape language projects.

Have the Apes Demonstrated Human Capabilities? As communicators all the apes showed interchangeability and total feedback. Sign allows broadcast transmission and directional reception and rapid fading; both artificial "languages" are deliberately designed to exclude these features. Thus, Sarah and Lana could communicate only when their language tools were present and they were attending. Moreover, they could examine an utterance for as long as they wished. All the languages were specialized, semantic, arbitrary, discrete, productive, and could potentially be used to talk about displaced objects or events. The animals, in their naming, seem to use at least some of these features. It is not clear that they ever discuss objects or events displaced from their own states (except Koko, by anecdotal report), as already mentioned. And, in the signed strings, it is not clear that their productions are discrete: They communicated increased desire almost exclusively by increasing repetition, a graded system (one we make use of, but not exclusively). Although their skills do seem to generalize to new words, it is not clear, as already discussed, whether their use of language is truly productive or creative.

Finally, for the original design features, their utterances lack duality of patterning. At the lowest level, the joining of meaningless elements (phonemes or phonetic features) to form meaningful elements (morphemes) were deliberately omitted for Sarah's language and perhaps Lana's (there were features reused in Lana's lexigrams, but it is not clear that they had a psychological representation in *her* language use—she did not and could not use them to create new words, for example). In effect, each symbol stood for a meaningful word. At a higher, syntactic level—a modification of meaning by context—there is also no clear evidence of duality of patterning, since for all apes each word or word string was tightly associated to a particular referent. (A possible exception is Sarah, who learned different responses for x gives y and y gives x, but she still may have been responding to each string as a whole and not as a new structure composed of elements.) Thus, "M&M" initially denoted "I want an M&M," and after more training, "Please machine give M&M" denoted the same

9. Hockett assigned features to animal systems differently than I have here.
10. There is an anecdote suggesting that some birds may exhibit discreteness, duality of patterning, and productivity. Jackdaws, monogamous birds, have different songs for different events: a mating song, a baby song, a danger song, a flight song, and a come-home song. Once united, a couple "flirts" with each other: they talk in the baby song to each other, the female makes submissive postures, and the male feeds the female special delicacies. Brown (1958) reported that the female of a pair, after the male had died, composed a new song, consisting of elements of all the other songs of the jackdaw life, with the dominant theme being the come-home song. As Brown observed, this is reminiscent of human ballads. It also shows that the songs themselves can act as elements in a combination with new meaning.

thing. It is unclear whether, to the chimpanzee, "Please machine give" or any of its components altered the meaning of "M&M." In the signing apes, duality of patterning at this level is more conspicuously absent since, with the few exceptions of anecdotal reports of new compounds, they never produced interesting strings at all.

With respect to the additional language features, there is no evidence, except for anecdotal reports, that the apes lie using their taught communication systems. Assuming that one grants that Sarah's and Lana's contrived systems are language, the apes demonstrate learnability in that, presumably, each could be taught the others' systems.

Sarah and Lana were each taught symbols that were translated as "name of"—if you accept that they understood the concept underlying naming, then they may be considered to be able to metacommunicate. (One wonders, however, whether Sarah would appreciate the irony in the sentence "the name-of red is blue," as we might in whispering the word "loud.") We have already suggested that there may be no "meaning" in these metalinguistic utterances besides the instruction to associate the object on either side of them; an equal sign for us would not constitute a metalinguistic symbol, and it is not clear that "name of" means anything more than "=" to them.

Since the apes were taught the different systems in different mediums ("writing," "typing," and signing), we can assume that they have transferability. There is no evidence from their productions that they simultaneously transmit information about many levels of communication, that their rate or amount of information transfer is equivalent to ours, that they employ rules of language in an efficient manner, or that they appreciate or employ recursiveness in their communcations. Therefore, I would argue strongly that the demonstrations of "language skills" in apes, although in many respects impressive, fall far short of true language as we demonstrate it, for qualitative as well as quantitative reasons. You may disagree, but to deal with the aforementioned differences, at best you will have to divide language behavior into two levels, one reserved for humans, and one that other animals may also demonstrate.

Summary and Conclusions. This section attempted to establish that language (1) may be characterized; (2) is, at this time, unique to humans; and (3) is unique, in at least some respects, among human activities. This should not be an astounding statement, given that, in part, it was derived circularly—the purpose was to establish what separates human language from all other signal systems and other human activities.

There are, of course, features of white-crowned sparrow song that make it unique from the systems of all other animals (that is how we recognize a bird from its song alone), from any other white-crowned sparrow activity (or we would call that activity sparrow song), and features of bees' hive building that make it unique from any other bee activity and from any other architecture system, ... The claim that language is unique is not intended as a strong claim with deep philosophical implications; establishment of these defining characteristics for language *is* the strong claim since they provide a means for separating language and humanness from nonlanguage and nonhumanness.

Some of the characteristics may seem more interesting than others: Recursiveness, for example, is more a feature of the system that makes it a powerful tool for thought and is thus more interesting than a human-tailored information rate, which is a property of the producer, not the system. However, it is our contention that language looks the way it does because of human processing constraints, and further, that one way in which we can reject a system as language is if it deviates greatly from these constraints. This has been done tacitly and anthropocentrically through the ages: Chemical communication systems automatically seem like they "must" be more primitive than language because the chemical senses of us outsiders are too primitive to allow appreciation of their richness and coding schemes. We may now make this assumption explicit by identifying some of the characteristics of language directly as properties of the producers.

It is important to emphasize that rejection of another system as language on the basis of this type of property does *not* indicate that the system's users cannot think abstractly or symbolically, just that they may not express their thought the same way we do. In the next section, we will examine some aspects of human biology and evolution that may underlie even the subtle, more interesting system characteristics of language.

Language: Biological and Evolutionary Mechanisms

Language is the way it is partly because of general human information processing capacities that have shaped language and partly because of special structures that may have evolved for the purpose of human communication. (It may be, of course, that structures we use for communication evolved for other purposes and are now subserving language.) With respect to general human information processing capacities, among others we note:

1. the information transmission rate (which seems to be constant across languages, although accomplished by different means),
2. the redundancy of transmission (which is necessary for imperfectly attending organisms),
3. the use of features to maximize discriminability (as constrained by our perceptual systems),
4. the reuse of features to minimize learning memory,
5. the coincidence of the formant frequencies for speech with the most sensitive frequency range of the human ear.

In this section we discuss hypotheses concerning special structures that may have evolved for the purpose of human communication.

Review of Mechanisms Already Noted

The assumption that special structures have evolved for human communication is quite controversial. Because it is a very strong assumption, we will begin by buttressing it with reminders that we have observed biological structures for communication in the animal kingdom that are under genetic control and may have been subject to evolutionary pressure. These can serve as analogies for such development in humans.

In this regard, we have already seen genetically controlled song centers for transmission and reception in the cricket, similar song centers—which we may assume to be under genetic control—in the white-crowned sparrow, and neurons specifically tuned to call production and reception for features of either in cricket, bird, and monkey. We have, moreover, proposed a simple model to interrelate biologically determined song characteristics and learning, allowing flexibility in communication, the tunable blueprint model (Marler and Mundinger, 1971).

There is evidence for tunable blueprints at the single-cell level, at least in developing visual systems. Allowed normal exposure to light during a critical period, neurons in the cat visual cortex have predictable innately specified light sensitivities. However, if visual stimulation of the kitten during the critical period is severely abnormal, confined experimentally to viewing of a single pattern, pasted on glasses in front of the eye, the neurons' sensitivities conform, within limits, to this overexposed pattern. This indicates that they are "tunable" (see Blakemore and van Sluyters, 1975, for example; Eimas and Tartter, 1979, for review). Although this is not an instance of a tunable blueprint for communication, it is not unreasonable to hypothesize that the white-crowned sparrow male song tuning is served by the same type of biological mechanism.

Thus, we have reasonable analogies for biological control of transmission and reception of a communication system, and for learning of characteristics of a specific input (like a particular language or dialect). Marler (1970, 1975) has proposed that similar blueprints exist in humans for speech sounds. These have evolved to allow discrete or categorical perception of the continuous speech signals.

We have also observed analogies for development of complex systems where simple ones will do—as in the elaborate vocal repertoire of the marsh wren. Sexual selection may be a potent force in the development of communication skills in these birds, or in us.

Summary.   In this section we have examined and reexamined some mechanisms in animals that might support the claim that special structures can evolve for human communication. First, there is evidence of genetic control of transmission and reception of important signals. Second, there are mechanisms for biological control of learning special signals. And finally, there is the hypothesis that sexual selection can foster elaboration of a system.

Specially Evolved Human Communication Mechanisms?

If you have accepted that language and the structures underlying it are part of our biological heritage, you might ask what structures may be specially developed for language itself. Two have been proposed, and hinted at, in this chapter. One is a specially developed articulatory system, specialized for speech, and the other is a specially developed neural structure for language comprehension and production.

Vocal Tract Characteristics.   In support of a specially developed mechanism for speech we note:

1. to speak, especially at great length, requires an adaptation of normal breathing,
2. our facial musculature differs from that of other animals allowing greater control of both articulation and facial expression,
3. our glottis is distinct from that of other species, allowing easy vibration only during exhaling

(Lenneberg, 1967),

4. there is a significant difference in the shape of the adult human vocal tract as compared with infants, chimpanzees, and Neanderthal man

(Lieberman, 1975).

To compare vocal tract characteristics in adults, infants, chimpanzees, and Neanderthals, Lieberman measured the air spaces in skulls of each, filling them with silicone rubber. Unlike the others, the modern adult human has a significant portion of the tongue in the throat, a widely separated soft palate and epiglottis, and a low larynx and thus a larger suboral superlaryngeal vocal cavity. These differences, Lieberman noted, give us a much more varied phonetic repertoire, allowing us alone to produce the point vowels, /i/, /a/, and /u/. Moreover, these modifications incur a penalty for survival: We are more likely to choke than are infants or chimpanzees or than Neanderthals were. The implication is that by enhancing our language capabilities, the increased vocal repertoire offset the disadvantage of choking. Of course, it is not clear how important the point vowels are to language, and consonant-producing abilities do not seem affected by the vocal tract change.

Brain Characteristics.   We also see evidence for specialized neural development, which we will discuss in greater detail in chapters 9 and 12. Already we have noted that there is a language center, lateralized for the most part in the left hemisphere of the brain. This area is larger than the corresponding area on the right side, even in newborns, suggesting perhaps an innate specification for language function (LeMay and Geschwind, 1978). Further, there is differentiation of function within that language center: The anterior portion seems to govern motor aspects of language (production), while the posterior governs comprehension. And we also see increased cranial capacity in modern man as compared with fossil man and many existing species (see Lenneberg, 1967 for amplification and critique of brain size arguments). Finally, as we will see in the next chapter, there are critical changes in brain growth in human development, coinciding with sudden changes in linguistic capacity (Lenneberg, 1967).

Maturation Time.   A final biological influence on the development of language should be noted. We have a very long childhood relative to other species, and this increases the opportunity for traditional transmission, and thus the number of learned rules and elements that can be incorporated into our communication system (Hockett, 1960). Moreover, as we will see in the next chapters, during childhood there appear to be critical periods for language acquisition analogous to those observed in bird song acquisition or visual development. Some have argued that these critical periods are a part of general cognitive changes during development; others that they are specific to language. In either case we see in development of language evidence of biological control.

Summary and Conclusions

In this chapter we have attempted to define characteristics of language that make it distinct from, although at times analogous to, other forms of human communication and other communication or signal systems in nature. This was not undertaken to argue that language is in any way better than other forms of interacting, just that it is different, and that the differences are definable. Language is different from other signal systems because we are different from other species (as they are from one another), and these differences constrain and shape the form of language. In the next chapters we will look at the effects on language of changing these constraints—first in child development, where the anatomical and neural structures (and the amount of experience) are not in the adult state; then in conditions of social deprivation, where traditional transmission is abnormal; then in the deaf, where the constraints of the vocal-auditory channel are replaced with the constraints of the visuo-gestural channel; then in brain-damaged adults, where the neural structures supporting language are defective; and finally, in psychopathology, where social and perhaps neural-cognitive structures are defective. From the perspective of this chapter we look at these communication systems (1) to determine if they have the characteristics we have defined as necessary for language (or are they more primitive, similar to, or different from, the chimpanzee's performance with human language?); and (2) to determine how the difference in biology or environment constrains the shape of language.

REFERENCES

Ape language. (1981). *Science, 211,* 86–88.

Apfelbach, R. (1972). Electrically elicited vocalizations in the gibbon *Hylobates lar (Hylobatidae),* and their behavioral significance. *Zeitschrift für Tierpsychologie, 30,* 420–430.

Baker, M. C., Spitler-Nabors, K. J., & Bradley, D. C. (1981). Early experience determines song dialect responsiveness of female sparrows. *Science, 214,* 819–821.

Bentley, D. R., & Hoy, R. R. (1972). Genetic control of cricket song patterns. *Animal Behavior, 20,* 478–492.

Blakemore, C., & van Sluyters, R. C. (1975). Innate and environmental factors in the development of the kitten's visual cortex. *Journal of Physiology, 248,* 663–716.

Brines, M. C., & Gould, J. L. (1979). Bees have rules. *Science, 206,* 571–573.

Brown, R. (1958). *Words and Things.* NY: The Free Press.

Bruemmer, F. (1983). Sea lion shenanigans. *Natural History, 92,* 32–41.

Cherry, C. (1957). *On Human Communication*. Cambridge, MA: The Technology Press of Massachusetts Institute of Technology and NY: John Wiley and Sons.

Darwin, C. (1871). *The Descent of Man and Selection in Relation to Sex*.

Delgado, J. M. R. (1977). Hell and Heaven within the brain. In P. Zimbardo & C. Maslach (Eds.). *Psychology for our Times*. (pp. 81–90). Glensview, Illinois: Scott, Foresman, & Co.

Doherty, J. A., & Gerhardt, H. C. (1983). Hybrid tree frogs: Vocalizations of males and selective phenotypes of females. *Science, 220*, 1078–1080.

Duncan, S., Jr., & Fiske, D. W. (1977). *Face-to-Face Interaction*. Hillsdale, NJ: Lawrence Erlbaum Associates.

Eimas, P. D., & Tartter, V. C. (1979). On the development of speech perception: Mechanisms and analogies. In H. W. Reese & L. P. Lipsitt (Eds.). *Advances in Child Development and Behavior*. vol. 13. (pp. 155–193). NY: Academic Press.

Epstein, R., Lanza, R. P., & Skinner, B. F. (1980). Symbolic communication between two pigeons (*Columba livia domestica*). *Science, 207*, 543–545.

von Frisch, K. (1974). Decoding the language of the bee. *Science, 185*, 663–668.

Gallup, G. G., Jr. (1979). Self-awareness in primates. *American Scientist, 67*, 417–421.

Gardner, R. A., & Gardner, B. T. (1969). Teaching sign language to a chimpanzee. *Science, 165*, 664–672.

Gardner, R. A., & Gardner, B. T. (1975). Early signs of language in child and chimpanzee. *Science, 187*, 752–753.

Gautier, J. P., & Gautier-Hion, A. (1982). Vocal communication within a group of monkeys: An analysis by biotelemetry. In C. T. Snowdon, C. H. Brown, & M. R. Peterson (Eds.). *Primate Communication*. (pp. 5–29). Cambridge: Cambridge University Press.

Gould, J. L. (1980). Sun compensation by bees. *Science, 207*, 545–547.

Green, S. (1975). Dialects in Japanese monkeys: Vocal learning and cultural transmission of locale-specific vocal behavior? *Zeitschrift für Tierpsychologie, 38*, 304–314.

Herrnstein, R. J., & Loveland, D. H. (1965). Complex visual concept in the pigeon. *Science, 146*, 549–551.

Hinde, R. (1972). Comments on Part A. In R. Hinde (Ed.). *Nonverbal Communication*. (pp. 86–98). Cambridge: Cambridge University Press.

Hockett, C. F. (1960). The origin of speech. *Scientific American, 203*, 88–96.

Hockett, C. F., & Altmann, S. A. (1968). A note on design features. In T. A. Sebeck (Ed.). *Animal Communication*. (pp. 61–72). Bloomington: Indiana University Press.

Hofstadter, D. R. (1979). *Gödel, Escher, Bach: An Eternal Golden Braid*. NY: Basic Books.

Hoy, R. R. (1974). Genetic control of acoustic behavior in crickets. *American Zoologist, 14*, 1067–1080.

Hoy, R. R., & Paul, R. C. (1973). Genetic control of song specificity in crickets. *Science, 180*, 82–83.

Jurgens, U. (1982). A neuroethological approach to the classification of vocalization in the squirrel monkey. In C. T. Snowdon, C. H. Brown, & M. R. Peterson (Eds.). *Primate Communication*. (pp. 50–67). Cambridge: Cambridge University Press.

Kroodsma, D. E. (1983, September). Marsh wrenditions. *Natural History*, 43–46.

LeMay, M., & Geschwind, N. (1978). Asymmetries of the human cerebral hemispheres. In A. Caramazza & E. B. Zurif (Eds.). *Language Acquisition and Language Breakdown*. (pp. 311–328). Baltimore: Johns Hopkins University Press.

Lenneberg, E. (1967). *Biological Foundations of Language*. NY: John Wiley and Sons.

Leppelsack, H. J., & Vogt, M. (1976). Responses of auditory neurons in the forebrain of a songbird to stimulation with species-specific sounds. *Journal of Comparative Physiology, 107*, 263–274.

Lieberman, P. (1975). *On the Origins of Language*. NY: Macmillan.

Lyons, J. (1972). Human language. In R. Hinde (Ed.). *Nonverbal Communication*, (pp. 49–85). Cambridge: Cambridge University Press.

MacKay, D. M. (1972). Formal analysis of communicative processes. In R. A. Hinde (Ed.). *Nonverbal Communication*. (pp. 3–25). Cambridge: Cambridge University Press.

Marler, P. (1970). Birdsong and speech development: Could there be parallels? *American Scientist, 58,* 669–673.

———. (1975). On the origin of speech from animal sounds. In J. Kavanaugh and J. E. Cutting (Eds.). *The Role of Speech in Language.* (pp. 11–37). Cambridge, MA: MIT Press.

Marler, P., & Mundinger, P. (1971). Vocal learning in birds. In H. Moltz (Ed.). *Ontogeny of Vertebrate Behavior,* (pp. 389–449). NY: Academic Press.

Marx, J. L. (1982). How the brain controls birdsong. *Science, 217,* 1125–1126.

Miller, G. A. (1956). The magical number seven plus or minus two: Some limits on our capacity for processing information. *Psychological Review, 63,* 81–97.

Mistler-Lachman, J. L., & Lachman, A. (1974). Language in man, monkeys, and machines. *Science, 185,* 871–872.

Morris, C. (1964). *Signification and Significance.* Cambridge, MA: MIT Press.

Newman, J. D., & Wollberg, Z. (1973a). Multiple coding of species-specific vocalizations in the auditory cortex of squirrel monkeys. *Brain Research, 54,* 287–304.

Newman, J. D., & Wollberg, Z. (1973b). Responses of single neurons in the auditory cortex of squirrel monkey to variants of a single call type. *Experimental Neurology, 40,* 821–824.

Nottebohm, F. (1970). Ontogeny of birdsong. *Science, 167,* 950–956.

Patterson, F. G. (1978a). The gestures of a gorilla: Language acquisition in another Pongid. *Brain & Language, 5,* 72–97.

Patterson, F. (1978b). Conversations with a gorilla. *National Geographic, 154,* 438–465.

Payne, R. S., & McVay, S. (1971). Songs of humpback whales. *Science, 173,* 585–597.

Peterson, M. R., Beecher, M. D., Zoloth, S. R., Moody, D. B., & Stebbins, W. C. (1978). Neural lateralization of species-specific vocalizations by Japanese macaques *(Macaca fuscata). Science, 202,* 324–326.

Pierce, J. R. (1972). Communication. *Scientific American, 227,* 30–41.

Premack. D. (1971). Language in chimpanzees. *Science, 172,* 808–822.

———. (1976). Language and intelligence in ape and man. *American Scientist, 64,* 674–683.

———. (1979). Trivial language in a nontrivial mind. Paper presented at the Western Psychological Association meeting, San Diego, CA.

Premack, D., & Woodruff, G. (1978). Chimpanzee problem-solving: A test for comprehension. *Science, 202,* 532–535.

Rumbaugh, D. M., Gill, T. V., & von Glaserfield, E. C. (1973). Reading and sentence completion by a chimpanzee (Pan). *Science, 182,* 731–733.

Rumbaugh, D. M. (1977). *Language Learning by a Chimpanzee: The Lana Project.* NY: Academic Press.

Savage-Rumbaugh, E. S., & Rumbaugh, D. M. (1980). Requisites of symbolic communication— or, are words for birds? *The Psychological Record, 30,* 305–318.

Savage-Rumbaugh, E. S., Rumbaugh, D. M., & Boysen, S. (1978). Symbolic communication between two chimpanzees *(Pan troglodytes). Science, 201,* 641–644.

Savage-Rumbaugh, E. S., Rumbaugh, D. M., & Boysen, S. (1980). Do apes use language? *American Scientist, 68,* 49–61.

Scheflen, A. E., & Scheflen, A. (1972). *Body Language and Social Order.* Englewood Cliffs, NJ: Prentice-Hall.

Scherer, K. R., & Giles, H. (Eds.). (1979). *Social Markers in Speech.* Cambridge: Cambridge University Press.

Schultz, J. L. (1983). Tree tactics. *Natural History, 92,* 12–25.

Scott, J. P. (1976). Genetic variation and the evolution of communication. In M. E. Hahn & E. C. Simmel (Eds.). *Communicative Behavior and Evolution.* (pp. 39–58). NY: Academic Press.

Seyforth, R. M., Cheney, D. L., & Marler, P. (1980). Monkey responses to three different alarm calls: Evidence of predator classification and semantic communication. *Science, 210,* 801–803.

Snowdon, C. T. (1982). Linguistic and psycholinguistic approaches to primate communication. In C. T. Snowdon, C. H. Brown, & M. R. Peterson (Eds.). *Primate Communication.* (pp. 212–238). Cambridge: Cambridge University Press.

Somers, P. (1973). Dialects in southern Rocky Mountain pikas *Ochoton princeps (Logomorpha). Animal Behavior, 21,* 124–137.

Terrace, H. S. (1979). How Nim Chimsky changed my mind. *Psychology Today,* November, 63–91.

Terrace, H. S., Petitto, L. A., Sanders, R. J., & Bever, T. G. (1979). Can an ape create a sentence? *Science, 206,* 891–902.

Thompson, C. R., & Church, R. M. (1980). An explanation of the language of a chimpanzee. *Science, 208,* 313–314.

Thorpe, W. H. (1972) The comparison of vocal communication in animals and man. In R. A. Hinde (Ed.). *Nonverbal Communication.* (pp. 153–175.) Cambridge: Cambridge University Press.

Tinbergen, N. (1952). The curious behavior of the stickleback. *Scientific American, 187,* 22–26.

Tinbergen, N. (1955). *The Study of Instinct.* Oxford: Oxford University Press.

Wade, N. (1980). Does man alone have language? Apes reply in riddles and a horse says neigh. *Science, 208,* 1349–1351.

Wollberg, Z., & Newman, J. D. (1972). Auditory cortex of squirrel monkey: Response patterns of single cells to species-specific vocalizations. *Science, 175,* 212–214.

Woodruff, G., & Premack D. (1979). Intentional communication in the chimpanzee: The development of deception. *Cognition, 7,* 333–362.

Zaretsky, M. D. (1971). Cricket song-patterned response in a central neurone. *Nature, 229,* 195–196.

STUDY QUESTIONS

1. Discuss the genetic control of transmission-reception, tunable blueprint model, call detector model, and sexual selection with respect to their potential influences on human communication. For each, explain the phenomenon with respect to the organism it was described in, and then explain how it might also (have) work(ed) in humans.

2. Briefly describe body language and paralanguage in human signaling. Are these communication? Why or why not? (Discuss this from the point of view expressed in the chapter, but critically; if you disagree indicate why, how, and the implications.) Is body language language? Again, why or why not? Be critical!

3. Critically discuss the design features for language. Do you think the chimpanzees have demonstrated human language capability? Why or why not?

9

Acquisition of the First Language

At birth an infant is able to cry and cough but otherwise produces no sounds. At birth an infant "understands" that loud noises are alarming, that softer noises are interesting, and so responds differently to these noises. As the child gets older things change. (S)he may say, for example,

AGE	UTTERANCE	PRESUMED TARGET
at	something like	for
3 months	/ɛ/, /gɛ/	?
5 months	/ba,ba/ /mama/	?
10 months	/bɔ/	There is the ball.
18 months	/der bɔ/	There is the ball.
24 months	I wanna build a high house too.	
36 months	Yes you can open that one but I'm gonna lock it so you can't get in.	

What has happened in three years? And is it finished happening—does the three-year-old know what the adult knows about language except for vocabulary?

Chapters 2, 4, and 6 discussed the structure of adult language. As we have seen, it is quite complex. There are meaning "elements" and these can have a variety of relationships to their referents. There are a vast number of rules for joining together meaning elements and for interpreting the product of the combination. There are a variety of rules for forming the meaning elements, complex articulatory gesture coordination involved in producing them, and a variety of rules for combining them,

319

increasing redundancy. Does the "language" of the three-month-old or thirty-six-month-old or anywhere in between reflect the identical structures as the language of the adult? How does the child learn the mass of elements and rules in three or more years? Do the parents actively teach the rules? Are languages designed to contain rules that human infants are born knowing?

Chapters 3, 5, and 7 discussed how native (English) speakers process their language. Does the child process language in the same way or achieve the same ends using a different, "childlike" strategy as (s)he manages to write with a pencil firmly grasped in the fist, unlike the adult? Whether the child uses the same or different strategies, are they innate, or does the child *learn* how to perceive speech, how to organize words in a mental lexicon, and how to parse?

These are the questions of child language acquisition. This chapter will attempt to answer, at least in part, these questions, describing the course of language development and development of processing strategies. In addition to the intrinsic interest in the acquisition process, study of child language acquisition has important implications for the methodological and theoretical issues raised in the last chapter. First, unlike animals, children are known to have language, to meet our criteria, at some point in their development. Should we argue therefore that since they have the capacity, they have language from birth, ostensibly ignoring our criteria? Or can we apply the criteria independently of known capacity to identify a point in development at which the child goes from a signal system to a symbol system and from a symbol system to a linguistic system, distinguishing us from the animal systems we critiqued? Are there some children who never make these advances?

Second, if there are innate linguistic rules or innate processing strategies, these are part of the biological constraints on language structure. For if a system were devised that children could not learn or could not learn easily, the system would not survive. Therefore, language form has been shaped by what the child brings to language learning, and in trying to determine the constraints on language, it is important for us to discover what the child brings.

Introductory Issues

Nativism versus Empiricism in Language Acquisition

Innateness in Behavior.   *Instincts at Birth.* Probably the most critical theoretical issue in studies of child development is whether the knowledge the child "acquires" is innately specified (*native*) or is learned through environmental interaction (*empirical*). On the native side, it is important to recognize that there are several ways that things may be innately specified. The first, simplest to recognize, and most often thought of as innate, is knowledge that the infant expresses at birth. For example, children do not have to learn to cry, or produce saliva, or start at loud noises.

Instincts Appearing Later. A second kind of innate specification is one in which the whole behavior is specified but does not appear until after birth. For example, infants do not have to learn to make tears, although they do not do this until aged two to three months; they do not have to learn to develop teeth, although this happens at fixed times up until about 18 years; they do not have to learn to develop secondary sex characteristics (at puberty) or gray hair (beyond). So to be innate, biologically determined, it is not that a characteristic has to appear *at birth*, but that it has to be completely specified at birth for whenever it is slated to appear.

Instincts Needing a Prime. A third type of innate specification is one that requires some input from the environment, at least to start. We do not have to learn to breathe, but at least sometimes, a slap on the rear may be necessary to start the reflex. Regardless of the benefits of sex education, we probably do not have to learn to conceive, but we do require appropriate sign stimuli to coordinate the process.

Tunable Blueprints. We encountered a fourth type of innate specification in the tunable blueprint model in Chapter 8. In this case what is innately specified is a crude "concept" of a percept or motor activity that may be embellished or improved by environmental contact. We do not have to learn to see in one sense—light will automatically stimulate the visual system. However, as we saw for kittens, and as is probably true for humans, when the visual system is ready to be modified, the light patterns one is exposed to during a critical period may determine sensitivities to light patterns forever. (Of course, *interpretation* of the patterns will depend on learning: Here we are talking only about which patterns make it up through the brain, which are passed through the visual system.)

Behaviors Derived from Innate Physical Change. The last type of innate specification includes behaviors that themselves are not innately specified but are outgrowths of innately specified physical changes in the body. Consider crying, again, as an example. As we grow older our vocal tracts change innately and we acquire (innately) the capacity to produce tears, making the sound and appearance of crying change. This does not mean that there is an innately controlled program for crying development but rather innate controls on the body, which have an effect on crying. Likewise we would not argue that a person was genetically programmed to play basketball, but (s)he might be genetically programmed to be over seven feet tall.

Innateness in Cognition? Thus, we see that an innate behavior or physical change may occur any time during life. With physical changes, which were mostly what were used in the example just given, innateness hypotheses are not terribly controversial. Can cognitive changes also be innate? The table on the first page of this chapter presented sample utterances tied to different ages in a child's early years. Is the change from crying to CV syllables to words to simple sentences to complex sentences a manifestation of an unfolding innately specified language acquisition device, as the acquisition of teeth is an unfolding of an innately specified dental program? Or is the child *learning* language in the first three (and more) years, with the observed changes the result of the infant's exposure to adult models? Are reading and arithmetic learned at about age six because the brain is not ready to learn them before that? Or do they appear at this age either because they are not taught earlier, or because the child has to learn other skills first (like talking and counting) that form the foundation for the later skills, and which take time to learn? Both these possibilities would make the uniform age of acquisition a result of learning, not innate specification.

To some extent, for each aspect of acquisition, since the data are ambiguous, where you stand on this issue is a matter of choice—and the choice of the dominant thinkers seems to switch from decade to decade. We will briefly review the choices and criteria of some of the dominant psycholinguists of the twentieth century. There are three questions to consider for each position: (1) How much and what is innate in language? (2) How much of what is considered innate is specific for language and how much relates to general cognitive development? and (3) What are the criteria for determining innateness and are they reasonable?

Language Acquisition Device or Universal Grammar

The Innate Component.   The most extreme view in favor of innateness and the loosest criteria are held by Chomsky (1965, 1968, 1975). In the early formulations, Chomsky hypothesized that each of us is born with general language knowledge and a general procedure for learning language. This was called the *language acquisition device (LAD)*, and in Chomsky's (1965, p. 30) own words, consisted of: "(1) a technique for representing input signals, (2) a way of representing structural information about these signals, (3) some initial delimitation of a class of possible hypotheses about language structure, (4) a method for determining what each such hypothesis implies with respect to each sentence, [and] (5) a method for selecting one of the (presumably, infinitely many) hypotheses that are allowed by (3) and are compatible with the given primary linguistic data."

McNeill (1970) has suggested that LAD contains a set of procedures for analyzing the input and a set of assumptions about the form of the grammar. An example of a procedure would be the (tacit) search for and recognition of the parts of speech from identical sentence frames, distributional analysis as described in Chapter 4. Assumptions about the form of the language include the existence of sentences, deep structure, transformations such as movement, and a·set of universals like all phonetic features, syllable structure, and basic syntactic categories like NP and VP.

The Role of the Environment.   We have just described the innate contribution to language development in this view. The role of the environment, of the linguistic input, is two-fold: First, it provides the utterances used to eliminate or select from the innate hypotheses, thus "teaching" the specific transformations or structures; and second, it provides a prod, the way spanking prods breathing, for the formation of language. This external push to learn the structure could be semantics, the relation of the structural description to meaning (Chomsky, 1965, p. 32). The child's task is not one of deducing the grammar or these characteristics from the utterances heard but using the innate hypotheses and procedures to generate utterances to compare to those heard, and then retaining those hypotheses that match.

The Reasoning in Favor of Innateness.   Chomsky assumed that the child is born with considerable knowledge to be used in language acquisition and, moreover, that this knowledge is specific for language (1975, p. 215). His arguments for innate specification derived mostly from negative inferences about what could be learned from the environment.

The productions the child hears seemed inadequate to infer a grammar. First, the child hears too few utterances to outline or generate from scratch a complete grammar of a language. In the same way, the series "1, 2" provides inadequate data for determining the next number; it could be "3" if the series is arithmetic, or "4" if geometric, among other possibilities. Since the child does produce new sentences in accord with the grammar, and since the data are too meager to infer the grammar needed to produce those sentences, Chomsky argued that constraints on the grammar must be innate.

Second, the input to the child is full of performance errors, false starts, incomplete sentences, and so on, and without an innate guide the child would have no way of knowing which utterances are the correct, grammatical models and which are not.

Third, language is very complicated, with many of the complexities not overtly marked in the surface form. Chomsky deemed it impossible for the child to learn the rules to map surface to deep structures given the paucity of cues in the surface forms. (Current formulations, which put more cues in the surface structure, or at least closer to it, still make this implicit assumption, since they have as innate the notion of trace [see Chapter 4] and the conditions under which traces may be assumed to exist. The argument is the same—the trace is not overtly marked in the surface form; thus, the sentence is too impoverished to allow inference of the abstract surface structure without an innate guide.)

Fourth, the child acquires language too fast to be learning the rules unaided.

Finally, parents, with only tacit knowledge of the rules, would be ineffective teachers of grammar.

Criteria for Determining Innateness. In later formulations (see, for example, Chomsky, 1975) the properties of LAD were attributed to *universal grammar*. We noted that interest in discovering the characteristics of universal grammar is one reason to study child language acquisition: Since language must be learnable, the child's innate preconceptions of language must be a biological determinant of its form. However, Chomsky's method for determining the characteristics of universal grammar is quite different from the approach undertaken by most investigators of child language acquisition.

First, Chomsky assumed that the study of one language may be sufficient, and perhaps necessary, to determine the characteristics. It might be necessary because interesting features of the grammar do not emerge until a language is studied in depth, and not many languages have been studied in sufficient depth. He cautioned that "the hypotheses of universal grammar that can be formulated with any conviction are supported by evidence from a fairly small number of studies of very few of the languages of the world, and . . . they must therefore be highly tentative." Nevertheless, he continued: "Still, the inadequacy of this evidence should not be overstated. Thus it is surely true—and there is nothing paradoxical in this—that a single language can provide strong evidence for conclusions regarding universal grammar" (1968, p. 158).

Second, Chomsky's criterion for innateness was almost exclusively the linguists' failure to conceive of a mechanism by which the structure could be learned, rather than from studies of language development itself. Needless to say, with this criterion and with a strong innateness assumption, Chomsky and his followers attributed more to universal grammar or LAD than many other theorists.

LAD and Study of Child Language Structure. Influenced by Chomsky, some researchers in child language acquisition have attempted to come up with criteria for determining universality or innateness in the acquisition process rather than through the adult's language. One obvious method is to look for common developmental milestones cross-culturally and cross-linguistically. Since different languages have different semantic classifications, different structures, and different sounds, the models children are exposed to are vastly different. If they still seem to acquire a class or rule at the same time or at the same time relative to acquisition of other classes or rules, we might argue that the environment plays a small role.

For example, in English the active voice has the order subject-verb-object (SVO), and is far more frequent than the passive voice with order OVS. In inflected languages, where subject and object are marked morphemically, word order is much freer and SVO is not necessarily the most frequent. English-speaking children acquire the active voice before the passive, perhaps because SVO is innately easier, or perhaps because they hear it more frequently. If children learning inflected languages also learn SVO word order first, an innate word order preference (SVO) is supported, since the empirical alternative, more frequent exposure, does not apply. (As we shall see, it was thought for a time that SVO order was the first used even in inflected languages, but more recent evidence suggests that the first order used depends on the frequency of use in the adult language.)

Aside from cross-cultural evidence, Lenneberg (1967) has suggested four criteria for innate specification:

1. Synchrony of cognitive change with obvious physical growth, like increased brain development or onset of puberty. This suggests a major body reorganization that may unfold more of the genetic language blueprint.
2. Evidence that environmental stimulation is relatively constant but that the developing individual makes different use of it. If the environment is constant, then a change in use of it might reflect a genetic redirection of attention, as in the white-crowned sparrow's sudden learning of male song. (Note that is could also reflect the effect of accumulated experience.)
3. Emergence of the behavior before it is of any use to the individual. If it is of no use, it is not directly subject to reinforcement and therefore may be considered innate. The male sparrow, for instance, learns the male song during his second month, but does not begin to sing or show an interest in attracting a mate till the end of his first year.
4. Evidence that the clumsy beginnings of the behavior are not signs of goal-directed practice. Again, this is an attempt to rule out normal learning as a cause.

Summary. It is important to observe that Chomsky's approach (and those derived from it and applied to acquisition directly) subscribes to the assumption that there are aspects of language *per se* that are innately specified, and that these are consistent with the transformational framework. The difference between Lenneberg's and Chomsky's outlooks is in the method for determining innate structures, whether to study the structure of the child's output or to look for opaqueness in the adult grammar. In studying the child's output directly, Chomsky's followers compare the child's grammar(s) at different ages and changes in them across cultures and across developmental abnormalities, like retardation, to search for consistencies that could indicate biological control.

Piaget, Vygotsky—Changes in General Cognition

The approach just discussed to the innateness issue began with the underlying assumption that aspects of language, particularly syntax, are innate. Researchers focusing on the acquisition of semantics derived considerably different theoretical and methodological approaches. First, few will argue that many aspects of meaning are innate, and therefore, the problem becomes how children learn the relationships of objects to one another in the environment, how they form classifications, and *then* how they map language onto these forms. Thus, language acquisition is seen as secondary to concept acquisition. In Piaget's own words (1983, p. 110),

> The fundamental difference between Chomsky and us is that we consider all cognitive acquisitions, including language, to be the outcome of a gradual process of construction starting with the evolutionary forms of biological embryogenesis and ending up with modern scientific ideas. We thus reject the concept of preprogramming in any strict sense. What we consider as innate, however, is the general ability to synthesize the successive levels reached by the increasingly complex cognitive organization.

Detailed discussion of concept acquisition or cognitive development is beyond the scope of this book. However, the general approaches of Piaget and Vygotsky will be presented here, since they certainly have influenced the language acquisition literature.

The Stage Concept. According to Piaget (see, for summary, Ginsburg and Opper, 1969), particular kinds of thought are brought into play at different stages of an individual's life. *Stage* is very particularly defined here: It refers to the effect of a change that affects the child's mental organization and affects how the child will learn about the world. In Piaget's view the child changes stages as a function of both maturational (biological) changes and environmental exposure. (Other stage theories emphasize biological changes in particular.) The child responds to the environment by *assimilation* of new information into existing mental structures, and by *accommodation,* or change, of mental structures to fit with new information. The current mental structure, or concept, Piaget called a *scheme,*[1] and schemes are constantly

---

1. This concept is presented in the developmental literature as *schema*. Piaget differentiated the terms, scheme referring to a mental concept used for generalization, and schema, for a mental image or a map. (Piaget, 1981, translator's note p. 4).

changing through assimilation and accommodation to better represent the world. A stage occurs when the scheme radically changes through accommodation, producing a new method of thinking. In Piaget's view, development is continuous, with a child gradually acquiring the skills that will cause the thought change. So a child may be at a primitive stage with respect to some schemes and a more advanced one with respect to others. (Other stage theorists hold that that there is an abrupt change when a child moves from one stage to the next.)

Cognitive Stages.   *Sensorimotor Thinking* → *Symbolic Representation.* Piaget described four stages in the development of symbolic thought. The first stage, from 0 to 2 years, is the period of *sensorimotor thinking.* During this period the child's scheme for the world is totally derived from sensory and motor experience. The child's "representation" of reality is the here and now, what is directly and immediately experienced. During the sensorimotor period the child learns to separate sensory experience from objective reality, and ultimately to realize that objects exists outside the self. This is the radical change in thinking that produces a new stage and a new mode of thought, symbolic functioning. Initially children know of an object only when it impinges on their senses; by the end of this period, the child has *object permanence,* the ability to conceptualize an object not in view. Object permanence is achieved through the child's active manipulation of the environment (reaching for things, kicking them, and so on), which allows the formation of a scheme for different objects. As the child learns more about objects, the schemes become increasingly elaborate until they are divorced from immediate sense impressions.

Sensorimotor language begins as an accompaniment to perception or action, children describing what they are perceiving or doing. Because language is a constant accompaniment to sensation, the word and the act can become confused. In this respect language takes on a magical quality, in which it seems as though words and actions are one. Indeed, Piaget (1952) argued that this early experience underlies the common tendency across cultures (including our own) to believe that merely uttering some words (prayers, spells, and curses)—"the word being no longer a pure label, but a formidable partaking of the nature of the named object" (p. 3)—can directly affect objects and events. At the end of the sensorimotor period children use words more symbolically, discussing objects or events displaced in time or space.

Thought Organization. The next major cognitive change occurs between the ages of two and seven, when children begin to organize their ideas, as they had earlier learned to organize their perceptions. This stage Piaget called *preoperational thinking,* preoperational because the thought organization is unsystematic. During this time, schemes continue to be elaborated but inconsistently. Children understand that there are categories and that things have names but because they do not have a system of rules for manipulating ideas, they do not understand rules of categorization or the general *concept* of naming. In the first case this means that objects are organized into groups, but the principle underlying the organizaion is idiosyncratic and changes during the grouping (this will be clearer when we discuss Vygotsky). In the second case children respond to the names of objects as intrinsic properties of objects, as color is. So if preoperational children are asked what something is named they respond correctly, but if asked, for example, why a dog is named "dog," they respond, "because it is a dog," and if pushed with "could it be called a cow?" say no, "because a cow is a 'cow.'"

Over the course of the preoperational period, as a result of continued experience, children discover "adult" principles of categorization and learn about true similarities and equivalents. This produces the knowledge necessary to know what it means that a name names.

The preoperational years also see the beginning of social speech. Initially, Piaget found that language is mostly *egocentric,* consisting of repetitions, monologues, and collective monologues, all characterized by a lack of interest in the response of others and an apparent lack of awareness that others should be responding. In repetition, children just echo what others or they themselves have just said. In a monologue, they give a running description of their activities without taking into account the others' perspectives. In a collective monologue, a group of children engages in monologues, with appropriate conversational turntaking, but without responding to each others' turns. So, for example, each may be drawing and describing the process but not commenting on the descriptions of the drawings given by others. At 6½ years old, nearly half of children's conversation can be described as egocentric (Piaget, 1952). (This finding is not generally accepted, and we shall encounter evidence against it later this chapter.)

Organizing Concrete Thought. Following the preoperational stage, children develop a system of organization for ideas, called *concrete operations,* concrete because the system applies to ideas with concrete referents. At this time the child learns rules about group structure, the *principles* of hierarchical organization. Early in concrete operations a child will understand that a petunia is a flower and a flower is a plant but will not understand that necessarily this means that (1) the class of plants is larger than the class of flowers, or that (2) petunias must have all features of plants but plants do not have to have all features of petunias. Learning the rules about group structure occurs between seven and eleven years of age.

To study the difference between preoperational and concrete operational thought, Piaget developed two tasks, known as numerosity and conservation. In the *numerosity* task, children are shown two rows containing the same number of items, demonstrating their equivalence. Then one row is rearranged so it appears wider (b) than the other (a) (or denser (c)), as shown here:

$$\cdots\cdots \qquad \cdot\;\;\cdot\;\;\cdot\;\;\cdot \qquad \cdots$$
$$\text{a} \qquad\qquad \text{b} \qquad\qquad \text{c}$$

Children are asked, then, which row has more, the equivalence having been demonstrated initially. Preoperational children frequently pick one of the rows, arguing that it has more because it is longer (or more crowded). Concrete operational children will argue that they are equivalent since the number did not change from the first demonstration, or because they can match up the two. Note that this represents awareness of an abstract principle, but that it applies to concrete objects, those in view.

The *conservation* task is similar in principle and in result: A volume of water is poured from one container into a container of a different shape, or a lump of clay is molded into a different shape, and children are asked whether there was more initially. Preoperational children argue that the "longer" amount—for example, the taller, but skinnier container—has more, while concrete operational children note that the volumes *must* be the same since nothing changed but the shape.

Both tasks demonstrate that the characteristic of preoperational thought is beginning experience with principles in the world, for example, longer things usually have more, but incomplete comprehension of the relationship of such principles to one another. In concrete operational thought, on the other hand, the strategies are organized logically, so it is clear that longer may be compensated for by less dense, and that the best way to assess quantity is to match the items or count them.

In addition to acquiring a system for dealing with concrete reality, concrete operational children use language socially rather than egocentrically; that is, during this period, it seems clear that language is used as communication, according to the definition of communication provided in the last chapter.

Formal Operations—Systematic Abstract Thought. The final stage is *formal operations* and emerges after age 11 in those cultures that emphasize abstract thought. Formal operations are rules for thinking about thinking. Through concrete operations children develop a systematic approach to concrete reality, the ability to manipulate logically and consistently objects directly in front of them. In formal operations, the logical systematicity is applied directly to mental representations without the necessity of concrete examples. This permits the understanding of algebra and formal logic. More germane to our discussion, it also permits the complete comprehension of metalanguage (since language is then appreciated as an abstract system) and of figurative language (since a symbol does not only have to apply to a concrete referent). Indeed, Piaget (1952) demonstrated that preadolescent children are very concrete in proverb interpretation. For example, one 10-year-old identified "white dust will never come out of a sack of coal" with "those who waste their time neglect their business" in a matching task. She explained her choice with "People who waste their time don't look after their children properly. They don't wash them and they become as black as coal, and no white dust comes out" (p. 139). This is obviously concrete, and illogical, by adult formal operations standards.

Summary. The main features of the Piagetian approach are:

1. the assumption of maturational changes in the thinking process;
2. the necessity of active experience in forming thoughts and in releasing or spurring the changes in thought;
3. a methodology that examines the child's behavior and attempts to determine its organizing principles from the behavior alone.

In contrast to Chomsky, Piaget considered "that language cannot be considered alone; that it cannot be detached from the total context of symbolic function which entails at least four behavior patterns which appear almost simultaneously, namely deferred imitation which starts after the disappearance of the model, symbolic play, evocative memory and mental imagery" (Piaget, 1983, p. 112). Piaget's approach differs from Chomsky's in that Piaget assumes that language acquisition depends on concept acquisition, while Chomsky has language acquisition autonomous, and

Piaget directly studies the child while Chomsky attempts to describe the model—the adult's language—to determine the guides to learning.

Vygotsky's Application of Piagetian Theory to Language. *Inner Speech.* Vygotsky (1962) basically expanded Piaget's model to emphasize language, making some modifications, which Piaget incorporated into his later theory. First, he pointed out that children begin using speech in correct forms before they have use for it or understand what they are doing. At the sensorimotor stage this speech is a narration accompanying what the child is sensing and has no social function. After the sensorimotor period this egocentric speech "turns inward," and is called *inner speech.* Essentially, inner speech is the "voice inside one's head" "heard" while one is thinking. At the same time, the child learns that speech has a communicative function and begins to talk about things in order to communicate with others.

Syntax Acquisition. Subsequently there is the same pattern of development with words and syntax in the preoperational stage as there was with speech generally in the sensorimotor stage. The child correctly forms sentences but has not yet conceptualized the rules controlling the structures that are formed. The separation between sensorimotor thought and preoperational thought, between the use of speech as redundant to observation and the use of speech as communication, is marked by the child's sudden interest in learning names of things and constant request for names, a development that never occurred in the chimpanzees, nor seems to occur in any other animal. Development from preoperational speech through to formal operations is observed by dissecting the child's concept formations, one of Vygotsky's major contributions.

Category Organization and Vygotsky Blocks. To study concept formation, Vygotsky devised a system known as *Vygotsky blocks.* These are blocks differing simultaneously on several dimensions, such as color, size, shape, and so on. The child (or adult) sorts them into piles, and, clearly, can choose a number of strategies for doing this—all red ones in one pile and blue in another, or red triangles, blue triangles, red rectangles, and blue rectangles each in separate piles, and so forth.

In the preoperational stage, the child sorts into *syncretic conglomerates,* unorganized heaps created by chance. For instance, the child may touch a red triangle and put that into a pile and then add the next block touched, whatever it is. In the next phase of this stage the categories look no different when the child finishes, but the guiding principle is proximity in space, so all blocks near one are placed in one pile, all near another in another.

In the third phase, the child makes a superordinate group, which still appears unorganized but reflects the principle of hierarchical structure: First the child will make a number of groups based on spatial proximity. Then (s)he will form a new group by taking one member of each of the first groups and putting it in the new one. All groups in this stage appear unorganized to the adult because although children have acquired the notion of group and hierarchy, they have not yet acquired the ability to exploit similarities, which Vygotsky considered a higher form of reasoning than exploiting differences.

At the next stage the children's categories make more sense to the adult eye. In the first phase children group by *association.* First things are added to the group because of color, then shape, and so on. No particular attribute may serve as guiding principle for long, but the children verbalize the principles as they add blocks—"now, the blue one." Since the principle keeps changing, the result is a seemingly unorganized heap.

The next phase in this stage produces *chain complexes,* where children stick with one feature for a time before another captures their attention. So, for example, blues may go together until a blue triangle is added. At this point, the triangle aspect may be noticed, and triangles are added to the pile, regardless of color. (For Crazy Eight players, the deck at the end of the game is "organized" in chain complexes.) This will also produce apparently unorganized piles in the end, since the rule keeps changing. But note: In the last phase of syncretic conglomeration, children evidenced the notion of hierarchy; with grouping by association they indicated understanding of the notion that groups have guiding principles; now, with chain complexes, there is indication that the child has learned something about what that principle might be.

In the last phase groups emerge that look like the adult groups. However, interrogating the child about the principle produces nonadult-like responses. For example, the child may have reds in one pile and blues in another, but when asked about the piles, will note a red triangle and say the pile is all triangles. If asked to account for an error, say a blue one in the red pile, the child will neither move it nor attempt to modify the principle but will act as though there is no problem. During concrete operations, the principles become formalized in children's minds and they will make the corrections.[2]

Summary.   With respect to nativism-empiricism, Piaget and Vygotsky had similar views. They emphasized maturational changes in the child's ability to reason. But these interact markedly with environmental input—they do not just unfold but are a product of the child's active attempts to understand and the child's experience with the world. Experience does not get passively imprinted on a child the way light does on a photographic plate (or male song does in a white-crowned sparrow) but gets actively transformed by assimilation with and accommodation of the child's schemes. Moreover, what is innate or maturational, in this view, is not specific to language, but to a general program of thinking that serves the language system as well as other

2. Interestingly, Vygotsky points out that the same kinds of reasoning continue in adults, in a way. If we come across a new word in a sentence and are asked to define it, we usually paraphrase the rest of the sentence as a definition (the word or part = the whole), although we know the "formal operation" that the word must contribute a meaning to the rest. Repeated exposures to the word in new contexts will allow us to add the meanings of the contexts and eventually factor out the common contribution. In the same way, the child's principle of organization develops from all the things dumped in the same group as the "meaning" of the category, to the notion of this or that feature in common, to a correct factoring of similarity. Vygotsky also points out that if the meaning of a word is traced through a language's history, it appears to go through the same kinds of changes as in a child's thinking—metaphorical extensions get applied by an almost haphazard notice of a shared detail between the word's usual meaning and the figurative extension.

thought systems. Finally, their methodology consists of observation of the child's behavior combined with experimental probing of the reasoning underlying the behavior.

Skinner and the Acquisition of Verbal Behavior

At the other end of the nativism-empiricism continuum we find the behaviorists, and interestingly, like Chomsky, they talk little about what the child actually does and more about general principles of learning deduced from adult behaviors or (unlike Chomsky) from animals. In this approach what may be considered innate are the abilities to form associations through classical and operant conditioning , to generalize, and to discriminate. These abilities do not change through life. However, the number and quality of associations formed do change as we gather experience, and therefore, what can get conditioned has an increasingly greater base of previous associations.

Shaping Communication. Skinner (1957) saw the beginning of language acquisition as the reinforcing of "relatively unpatterned vocalizations" (p. 31). These spontaneous vocalizations have no obvious "cause"—that is, they may be innate, although Skinner did not use that word. Once they appear, their incidence is increased through reinforcement and then they are shaped toward sounds the verbal community accepts. In Skinner's view *primary* reinforcement is always food or the like, and social reinforcement, praise or attention, is *secondary* (effective because of associations with primary reinforcers. Note that money is a secondary reinforcer; secondary reinforcers may be as powerful or more powerful than primary reinforcers!). The association between social reinforcement and primary reinforcement is one of the first things the child must learn. Whether the parents in fact feed children when they vocalize is dubious, but certainly parents respond to the vocalizations with increased attention to and interest in them. If we accept this as reinforcing, there is no question that parents do "encourage" increased vocalization.

Shaping Vocabulary. Many parents also "shape" words, repeating them until the child produces them and then reinforcing the child with praise or hugs. Children's imitations of the parents' productions are variously explained in the theory. (1) Skinner suggested that children begin because they like their parents and want to do what they do (p. 164), but how "liking" fits in with other behavioristic notions he did not specify. (2) Imitations are specifically taught by the parents for educational purposes—"say___" is the discriminative stimulus for an imitation, which is then reinforced. (3) Other behaviorists suggested that imitation is "innate," self-reinforcing, a building block of association, like classical and operant conditioning.

Shaping "Symbol" Use and Syntax. After shaping the production of a word, for example, "milk," by reinforcing it with milk, the parent teaches an extension of the concept to situations where milk was present or absent, using social reinforcement. Thus, the child learns to generalize the name to the class of objects it describes. The parent also begins to reinforce more complete statements of needs so that the child will have to say "I want milk" to get it, or "there is the milk" to get social praise for naming. Correct pronunciations, correct syntax, and so on, are specifically shaped by the parents—the child hears a model over and over again and imitates it, increasing the strength of that verbal response; the parents reinforce finer and finer discriminations (or generalizations) so that the child's verbal behavior comes to match that of the community.

Summary of Theoretical Outlook. There are several points to note about this approach to language acquisition with respect to the others. First, here the child is seen as relatively passive, an emitter of behavior subject to reinforcement, including the self-reinforcement of imitation, but not as one engaging in an intentional goal-directed process. In Chomsky's approach the child derives language because of an active, if uncontrolled, biological "urge" to acquire it. In Piagetian theory, the child learns because of action on the environment and because of active internal restructuring through accommodation and assimilation. In Skinner's approach the child learns because of pressures from the parents.

Second, here parents are seen as playing an important pedagogic function. In Chomsky's approach parents are viewed as *unable* to teach because: (1) they do not have explicit knowledge of their own grammar and therefore of what model the child should be approaching, (2) they do not know what steps or "successive approximations" would be reasonable, and (3) they would be teaching performance, not competence, and competence is what transformationalists say the child acquires. In Piaget's approach, the parents passively teach in that they provide children with a model and with experience that children use to form their own ideas. Skinner's approach has parents playing a more active role. This also suggests that to study language acquisition one must look at what the parents are doing, and at parent-child interaction, an approach that has only recently been taken by experimenters in child language acquisition.

A third important conceptual distinction is in what is acquired. In the linguistic outlook, the child knows about distinctive features, words, sentences, deep structures, and transformations, and "learns" only which ones are used. The basic structural units are given. For Piagetians the unit is the word, and the child learns what words refer to and how to combine them. Skinnerians basically propose no unit from which more complex linguistic structures derive: In some cases the child begins with sounds and patterns them into words and phrases; in others the child imitates a whole phrase and later learns to separate it into components that play a role in other sentences. Phonology and syntax are seen as habit strengths. If "Ipledgeallegiance" has greater frequency than "pledge," children will use that as a unit until they are taught to distinguish the components. If "mama" is taught in isolation then that will be a unit and combining it with others into sentences will have to be acquired. In this approach there is no complex system of internalized rules, either innately given or acquired through development, but a system of habit strengths.

The main contribution of the Skinnerian approach is its concern with parental input. The main criticisms of it have been its failure to recognize the role the child plays in providing either innate structures for acquiring language, or in actively seeking to imitate, accommodate, and assimilate linguistic knowledge.

Summary of Theoretical Approaches

Four approaches to language acquisition have been outlined with respect to nativism-empiricism. The first two were based on generative grammar and argued that the basic aspects of language structure are innate and the child learns which innate rules apply to the language at hand. To discover the innate forms, one approach analyzed the adult language for structural properties not obvious from the surface representations and compared structures of languages for commonalities in form. The other analyzed children's language under various environmental conditions for similarities in the acquisition process that could indicate that the environment is not responsible for learning, and, therefore, that there are innate structures.

The third approach was Piaget's. In that formulation, the child actively studies the environmental stimulation and forms classifications. Language acquisition was seen as just a part of this general learning process, dependent on the child's cognitive growth. Study focused on the child's performance and considered changes in language as reflecting changes in the child's ability to think.

The final approach was behavioristic. The child was viewed as a passive recipient of language "lessons" provided by the parents. The parents were not considered to have a specific lesson plan but rather to provide a "perfect" model in their productions and to recognize when the child's production is in line with that of the verbal community, reinforcing the utterances that sound like the ones they hear from others. In this approach study focused on the parent-child interaction.

Methodology in Language Acquisition Studies

The approaches of interest in the context of this chapter are those that deal with the child's language specifically, since characteristics of the adult language and their relative transparency in surface structure were discussed in the first part of this book. Study of children's language acquisition is fraught with methodological pitfalls, such as what should be measured and how to interpret the measurements, and how to "equate" children to compare across subjects.

What to Measure. As an example of measurement problems, consider collecting the sounds children produce as an index of their language knowledge. We run into the competence-performance distinction head on. In many cases, it is obvious that children understand more than they produce, as when they grab at a bottle when asked if they are hungry, making no verbal response. More subtly, do children know the difference in sound between /bɔ/ and "ball" but make the former because they are not yet able to say /l/? If this is the case, do we want to argue that they have the phonological competence for this word, since it is recognized, or that they do not, since it cannot be produced? Finally, suppose children do produce something correctly, as in the second-to-last phase of category organization of Vygotsky blocks. At that point it will look like real language, but with a little probing it becomes clear that children do not understand what they have produced any more than they understood the principle of organization that they apparently used. Should we argue that they have the competence simply because the production was correct?

Production Measures. Two general techniques have been used to study children's productions. One is a simple cataloguing of the utterances, called *diary studies*. These are made either for all utterances or for specific samples of utterances, say for all utterances produced during two-hour visits every Friday. Aside from the problem of interpreting what children know given what they produce, diary studies suffer from the possibility that children may just not elect to talk using everything they know and so the diary may never contain a particular kind of utterance.

The second technique attempts to correct for this shortcoming by eliciting utterances from the child. This may be done by (1) asking the child a question, with the answer being the target production; (2) asking the child to describe a picture, or action of a puppet, with the description expected to contain the target; and (3) prompting the child with several utterances of the desired format and then presenting a new utterance for the child to complete following that format. Note that for these elicited productions, some comprehension must be involved—at least of the "instructions" for the task. Thus, a failure to complete a sentence could reflect an inability to produce the completion, a failure to recognize or comprehend the completion pattern of the example sentences, or a failure to understand the instructions. Likewise, a failure to describe a picture may stem from an inability to produce the description, to understand what the picture is about, or to recognize that the task at hand is picture description.

Comprehension Measures. Use of comprehension as an index of linguistic knowledge is also not easy. Techniques for comprehension include asking children to explain or paraphrase utterances, asking them to answer questions, or asking them to select the picture that represents a given utterance or make a doll act out the utterance. The first two of these clearly involve production, and a child's failure to answer a question can be interpreted as an inability to understand the question (comprehension) or to construct the answer (production). For the other methods, comprehension of the task and of the pictures is necessary in addition to comprehension of the sentence. For these methods either errors or reaction times are recorded.

Other Measures. Two other indices have been used to assess children's language knowledge, imitation,[3] and grammaticality judgments. In *imitation,* the child is

---

3. A common test of children's language makes use of all three measures, the *imitation-comprehension-production test (ICP)* (Fraser, Bellugi, and Brown, 1963). A particular contrast, say the plural, is represented in a pair of sentences—"The boy draws"; "The boys draw"— which are also represented by pictures. In the first part of the task, the experimenter recites the sentences and asks the child to repeat them (imitation). For comprehension, the experimenter recites the sentences and the child must pick the appropriate picture. Finally, for production, the experimenter pronounces the sentence with the picture and asks the child to "name" the picture, producing the sentence. Underlying this task is the assumption that imitation is easier than comprehension, which in turn is easier than production, and indeed that was the accuracy order Fraser et al. found. However, Bloom and Lehey (1978) noted that (1) all the sentences were short, making imitation easier than the other tests; (2) by the time the children were asked to produce a sentence they had heard it (been practiced) at least three times, perhaps making production too easy; (3) production is the hardest to score for accuracy since the range of possibilities is greatest (in contrast to the comprehension task, for instance, where in this case, chance performance is 50 percent correct); and (4) the imitation task may be hard because it is unnatural in conversation: If A says "I'm sick" B may "repeat" with "you're sick," correctly capturing the sense but incorrectly imitating. The stand we take, therefore, on ordering of difficulty of the three tasks is that, depending on the specifics of the task or utterance, any one might be harder or easier than the others.

instructed to repeat what the experimenter says. Young children often fail to repeat exactly, indicating difficulties in understanding the original utterance, in remembering it, or in producing it. This can indicate the child's language competence, however. Imagine yourself trying to imitate a sentence from a foreign language. Initially you might get some general sound, like duration, intonation, and a couple of phonemes. Once you recognize words you will be able to repeat those. Once you understand the sentence and the grammar, the sentence is likely to be reproduced in its entirety. The same is true for the child; the quality of the imitation reflects the similarity between the child's internal structures for the language and the structure of the model.

Grammaticality judgments are designed to probe the child's tacit knowledge of the language, as judgment tasks are designed to probe ours. We can judge, for example, that anomalous sentences are "better" than scrambled sentences, or that a double-embedded sentence is "worse" than a single-embedded. Can a child make similar judgments? Again, getting the child to understand the task can be tricky. And getting the child to recognize that there may be gradations of nonsense may be trickier. And, finally, with this task, as with all the others, one has the problem of dealing with children's natural curiosities, inattentiveness, and so on, perhaps best exemplified by the following frequently quoted dialogue:

> Interviewer: Adam, which is right, "two shoes" or "two shoe"?
> Adam: Pop goes the weasel.
>
> *(Brown and Bellugi, 1964, p.135)*

How to Equate Children.   Three of the four approaches to language acquisition we examined assume some change in language as a result of maturational pressures and therefore some commonalities in language acquisition across children. It is necessary to be able to equate children with respect to maturation in order to look for similarities in acquisition among different children. Moreover, even if one believes that maturation plays a small role and that the environment shapes language, it is desirable to compare and contrast children exposed to different environments to pinpoint the environmental contribution. Obviously we must find some way to equate the children with respect to environmental exposure.

A last reason to equate children is that it is inconvenient to do *longitudinal* studies, in which the same children are followed through their course of development. To look at development longitudinally from birth to age five takes five years. Hence, studies are frequently based on the alternative, comparing different children at different points of development and inferring the probable course of development from these *cross-sectional* data. Thus, one could look in the same year at newborns, one-year-olds, two-year-olds, and so on. To assume that the course of development is the same, that the newborn will later look like the one-year-old, entails the assumption that children can be equated.

Age as Measure. The first method of equating that comes to mind is equating by age, and this was done for many years. The problem with it as a measure is that children have different individual rates of development, because of maturational factors, and/or because of different environmental exposures. In any case, one can see one thirteen-year-old already past puberty, and others not reaching it until age seventeen. Would it be reasonable to assume that the thirteen-year-olds are equivalent, or that all children at puberty, regardless of age since birth, are equivalent?

MLU as Measure. To avoid the difficulty of different maturational rates, a commonly accepted method of equating children with respect to language acquisition is to scale language specifically. Brown (1973) has established the *mean length of utterance (MLU)* as a standard measure of children's linguistic age. The length is counted in morpheme number, so /bɔ/ would be one, "ball" also one, /dɚbɔ/ two, and so on. Since most syntactic complexity also increases utterance length, one can expect the MLU to increase steadily as the child becomes linguistically proficient. Syntax cannot be properly studied until the MLU is greater than one, obviously, and in the children Brown and his colleagues have studied intensively, the MLU is 1.8 between the ages of 20 and 32 months. To use the MLU as a standard, one compares production, comprehension, and so forth in children of the same MLU: For example, do children of MLU = 2 understand the passive? Are there fricatives in the productions of children of MLU = 1? Do we find abstract nouns in children before MLU = 5?

Summary

We have reviewed some different theoretical approaches to child language acquisition and some common methods used in its study. The approaches differ with respect to how much of language is considered innate, how active a role the child is seen as playing in learning, how important a role the parents are ascribed in teaching, and the extent to which the proper focus of study of langugage acquisition is considered the child's language itself. Methods for studying child language acquisiton include purely observational methods in which the child's productions are collected, and experimental methods, in which production, comprehension, or imitation is deliberately elicited. Either approach may be used in longitudinal or cross-sectional studies. The problems of measurement are that no task seems to measure purely what it is designed to measure, so comprehension can entail production and the reverse. It is difficult to interpret an incorrect response as a result. There are problems interpreting cross-sectional data because subjects are not easily equated developmentally, and we looked at some ways in which such equating has been attempted.

With this as background for theoretical and methodological frameworks guiding collection and interpretation of data from children, we turn next to look at the data themselves.

Language in the Infant, MLU < 1

At the end of the first year of life children normally utter their first words, and it is at this point that study of language development usually begins. During the first year, however, the infant does mature, learn about the environment, and exhibit behaviors, and these factors play a role in subsequent language development. Necessarily, the study of language in infancy has been concerned primarily with sound perception and production, since semantics and syntax cannot be studied until there are words.

Maturational Changes in the First Year

Physical Changes. During the first year of an infant's life there are profound neural and physical changes. At birth, and perhaps before, there is noticeable asymmetry in the size of particular areas of the left and right cerebral hemispheres associated in later life with language; the left side, subserving language in adults, is larger in most infants than the right side (Witelson and Pallie, 1973). The brain increases in weight by more than 350 percent from birth to age two, but only about 35 percent from age two to the adult weight. Most of this growth derives from proliferating neural connections, not the number of neurons, which is fixed from birth. Some of the additional connections, the additional "brain power," have been hypothesized to underlie the unfolding of an innate language program (Lenneberg, 1967).

During the first year there are also marked changes in the infant's skeletal development. The vocal tract changes shape so that a supralaryngeal, suboral cavity develops, making the infant less like the chimpanzee and more like the adult (Lieberman, 1975). The infant's mouth changes also, losing fat in the cheeks. Finally, the vocal folds grow rapidly in the first year, continuing to grow subsequently, but at a slower rate (Delack, 1976).

Stages of Sound Production. *Crying.* All children regardless of language environment go through the same stages of sound production in the first year. Initially the only vocalization is crying. While crying, the newborn vocalizes only while exhaling, producing no more than eight distinguishable sounds (you may need to review Table 6.1 to "translate" the phonetic symbols)—/æ/ (most frequent), /I/, /ε/, /ʌ/, /u/, /h/, /l/, and /ʔ/. Not all neonates produce all these sounds; the front vowels predominate for most infants and /æ/ may be the exclusive member of the phonetic repertoire. For consonants, the back sounds predominate (Irwin, 1949). Some parents have claimed to be able to distinguish cries used in different contexts, which would imply that the cries at an early age exhibit semanticity. However, experimental investigations in which the cries are taped and the sound alone played to the parents have failed to support such claims (Dale, 1976). It is important to realize that under natural conditions parents have considerable context available: They know how long it has been since the last feeding or changing and may use this to interpret their infants' cries.

Cooing. At the end of the first month the second "stage" of vocalization occurs. In addition to crying the infant makes sounds for pleasure, described as *cooing*. These consist mostly of back rounded vowels (/u/), combined with glottal stops.

Babbling. At about six months there is another change in infant speech production called *babbling*. Here the phonetic repertoire changes rapidly: Syllables are produced containing many consonants and vowels, including sounds that are not used in the adult language. The infant appears to be playing with the sounds, enjoying the tactile and auditory feel of vocalization.

Real Speech—The Sounds. The last stage is a true sound system or phonology. The transition between babbling and speech may be gradual, with ever-increasing sound production from six months to a year, with a change in frequency of the babbled sounds, dropping those sounds that are not in the language of the adults and increasing those that are. For some children the change is abrupt, with the end of the babbling stage marked by a silent period, and then real speech emerging (Dale, 1976).

Characterization of real speech, or separating it from babbling, is difficult. Some researchers have invoked an intention aspect (note that "intention" would make this a candidate for the start of communication as opposed to signaling)—in babbling, vocalization is play; in real speech, it is planned, with the baby trying to produce a particular sound (Dale, 1976). The sounds children have under deliberate control are fewer than those they can produce randomly. Generally, in the emergence of real speech, the first distinction to appear is consonant-vowel, with consonant marked by a front sound /p/, and vowel by a back sound /a/. The next distinction children control is nasal-oral, adding /m/ to the repertoire. Next they acquire labial-dental, adding /t/, along with the low-high distinction in vowels, adding /i/. Subsequently they acquire the back sounds, /u/, /g/, and /k/, and other manner distinctions such as frication. As most of us have observed, there are sounds that seem particularly difficult and over which the child may not gain control until after school age—/r/, /l/, and /w/ tend to be confused with one another, and fricatives and affricates, particularly the interdentals, /ð/ and /θ/, tend to be produced as other fricatives or as stops of the same place of articulation (e.g., the dental stop /d/) (Ingram, 1978).

Real Speech—The Rules. It is important to observe that the acquisition pattern reflects not only articulatory control but also understanding of phonological principles. Macken and Ferguson (1981) cite data from one of the diary studies showing that a child pronounced "pretty" perfectly for a year and then transformed it systematically, first to /piti/ (reducing the consonant cluster), then /bidi/ (voicing the unvoiced consonant), and finally back to /pɚIti/, as her phonological system for voicing and consonant clusters changed. Note that this process indicates that children are not just memorizing but actively producing sounds according to the rules in their schemes (cf. Piaget) or grammar (cf. Chomsky). Note also that the initial perfect production supports Vygotsky's observation that structures may appear perfect before they are completely understood.

Cross-Cultural Similarities. The pattern of difficulty and general order of acquisition of sounds appears to be universal (Jakobson, 1968); indeed, most languages have as words naming mother and father sounds that the child produces early, such as our "mama" and "papa." This probably is because the child produces these sounds and the adult takes them as names, incorporating the baby utterance into the language. Be that as it may, the universality indicates that at least some aspects of sound production are under innate and maturational control.

Suprasegmental Development. In addition to developing segmental control the infant has suprasegmentals from a very early age. In babbling the infant uses many intonation contours, the most common being the rise-fall pattern (declination). This is true across languages, and as the infant moves from babbling into real speech, the pattern becomes more frequent relative to other patterns (Delack, 1976). During babbling, infants will often mimic the intonation patterns used by adults talking to them, superimposing the pattern on their own play syllables. Intonation or stress may also be the first "feature" to be used semantically: Dale (1976) cited an instance of a child calling his mother ma'ma and his father mama', later correcting the /m/ to the /p/ in the latter. Delack (1976) showed that six- to twelve-month-olds use different contours for vocalizations made in the presence of their mothers, strangers, objects that they could see, objects that they could hear, and objects that they could touch, indicating that they discriminated the situations.

Analysis of Phonological Development in the First Year

Babbling.   The importance of cooing and babbling to the onset of real speech has been much disputed. Some investigators regard babbling in particular as necessary practice in articulation, through which children gain control over their vocal tracts. In learning theory formulations, the spontaneous babbling provides the base vocabulary for selective reinforcement by the parents. However, Lenneberg (1967) noted that children prevented from babbling because of operations on their mouths, for example, are not delayed in producing real speech and show the same sequence of development of phonetic contrasts as normal children. So babbling does not seem necessary for real speech.

Further reason to separate babbling from real speech lies in the acquisition order of the phonetic distinctions. You may have noticed that the earliest sounds, like cooing, are largely back sounds, which the child gains control over late in real speech. Similarly, in babbling the child has no difficulty with liquids and fricatives, sounds that may not be acquired until very late. If practice early during and cooing and babbling facilitates real speech development one would not anticipate a reversal in acquisition order; the sounds most practiced should be those first produced.

Whether or not babbling is an instance of *language* development, there can be no question that it is innate. All children in all cultures coo and babble at roughly the same ages, although there are individual differences in the amount of vocalization during these periods. Moreover, deaf infants, who receive no auditory feedback from their productions nor any auditory input from their parents, go through these early stages just as normal children do. For deaf children, however, vocalizations peter out after babbling (Fry, 1966).

Unfolding Innate Phonetic Features?   Another aspect of sound acquisition in the first year that has been considered innate is the order of acquisition of sounds in real speech (Jakobson, 1968). Jakobson hypothesized that sound acquisition proceeded by successive divisions of sound along distinctive feature lines—such that features high in the hierarchy (see Chapter 6 for review), providing most information—are acquired first. Sound acquisition order was presented here following a Jakobsonian framework: Note that the first sounds were "pa," representing both the consonant-vowel difference and front-back. Successive acquisitions split the consonant class into manner and place classes and added the other point vowels (/i/ and /u/). Jakobson argued further that the earliest sounds hold a special position in that they are universally found in adult languages, whereas the later sounds may be found only in some.

Generally, studies examining order of acquisition even cross-culturally have supported the description, although not necessarily the theoretical framework (Dale, 1976). In part, the order is too rigid—place differentiates in many children before manner so one sees /p/–/d/ rather than /p/–/m/. More importantly, acquisition of a phonetic feature is context-sensitive, indicating that acquisition is not of features but perhaps of phonemes or syllables. Thus, if the child has split the consonants into nasal-oral for the bilabials, one would expect to find both /d/ and /n/ entering together, once the bilabial-alveolar distinction enters. Usually, only one comes in, and then the child seems to learn the other sound anew without evidence of generalizing the manner change. Similarly, fricatives are acquired one at a time, without reflecting any experience with the place distinctions already supposedly acquired with the stops (Ingram, 1978). However, generally speaking, Jakobson's framework describes acquisition order and, as we saw, also describes production and perception data in adults. It has guided research, and thus exerted a profound influence, whether ultimately it is right or wrong.

Sound Perception in the Infant

Measurement of Perception. Although the child does not produce speech sounds until the middle to the end of the first year, from very early on infants are responsive to the sounds of their language. Responsiveness is measured by observing a change in the child's activity correlated with introduction of sounds. The activity change may be gross, as in overall body movements such as kicking and pounding the air versus relative quiescence as the child drifts off to sleep. The change may be "fine" as in change in heart rate. A sound new to the infant, which captures its attention, produces an *orienting response,* initial decreased activity and heart rate deceleration followed by increased activity and heart rate acceleration as the infant explores or studies the new stimulus. When (s)he loses interest, when it has become familiar, heart rate and activity level generally return to baseline, and if the stimulus continues, the activity level may continue to fall off as the infant becomes bored. This decrease in activity level with increasing familiarity with the stimulus is known as *habituation.* (Note that this pattern is not unique to infants. If something captures our attention we may momentarily "freeze." If it is interesting, excitement and activity level grow as we study it. As we get bored, these wane, and we may find ouselves drifting off to sleep if we continue try to attend to it.)

Using the relative changes in activity level we may determine whether an infant can discriminate between sounds. First, a sound is presented. If the infant can tell that this is a new sound, there will be an orienting response and increased activity until the infant habituates to this sound. If the infant cannot discriminate the new sound from the old, habituation should continue after the stimulus change.

Perhaps the most popular method for studying infant speech perception making use of this activity pattern is the *high amplitude sucking (HAS)* paradigm (Eimas, Siqueland, Jusczyk, and Vigorito, 1971). The activity level measured is the amount the infant sucks on an electronically wired pacifier. Each suck causes a sound to be played so that the infants in effect control how much they hear. As they study the sound, their sucking rate is great, causing many instances of the sound to be presented; as they habituate, the presentation rate tapers off. Infants, of course, suck reflexively so there is no difficulty getting the procedure started.

Results—Paralanguage and Body Language. Studies using such techniques have revealed a prodigious receptive capacity in the infant, either innate or acquired very early. By three days an infant responds differentially to its mother's voice (DeCasper and Fifer, 1980) compared with other women's—the infant will suck more for the reward of the mother's voice than another's. One-day-old infants synchronize their body movements (heard turns, kicks, . . .) with phoneme onsets in fluent adult speech but do not exhibit synchrony to isolated words or tapping sounds. Moreover, American infants synchronize as well to Chinese speech as to American English speech (Condon and Sander, 1974). Infants only a few days old discriminate and imitate adult facial expressions (Field, Woodson, Greenberg, and Cohen, 1982) and manual gestures (Meltzoff and Moore, 1977). One-month-old infants discriminate rising from falling intonation in single syllables (Morse, 1972) and syllable-initial from syllable-final stress in disyllables (ba'ba vs baba') (Spring and Dale, 1977). At six months infants look longer at films in which the soundtrack and lip movements are synchronized than at those in which they are not (Kuhl and Meltzoff, 1982), particularly when the films are shown on their right, presumably engaging the left cerebral hemisphere (MacKain, Studdert-Kennedy, Spieker, and Stern, 1983). Finally, Kuhl and Meltzoff noted that their infants babbled when the full speech signal was synchronized with the film, but when the formant frequencies were filtered out, leaving only fundamental frequency contours, they neither babbled nor showed a differential looking preference for synchronized versus unsynchronized sounds. This indicates that they were responsive to the spectral properties of the speech.

Summary.   Thus, we can see that by six months the infant has skills at speaker identification, suprasegmental recognition, imitation of facial expressions and speech, and at recognition of the correspondence between lip movements and speech.

Results—Perceiving Phonetic Distinctions.   Are very young infants similarly able to discriminate segmental information, and do they do this like adults? Recall the issue of acquired distinctiveness versus acquired similarity, raised in Chapter 7. It was found that adults perceived the consonant sounds of their own language categorically, with sharply differentiated identification functions and excellent between-category but poor within-category discrimination functions. Presented with sounds phonemic in other languages, the same adults showed slightly above chance discriminations throughout. The question raised was whether experience causes the adult to sharpen category distinctions, causing the excellent between-category discriminations (acquired distinctiveness), or whether all potential phonemes are innately distinctive, and a lack of experience with them causes discriminability to atrophy (acquired similarity).

Beginning with the seminal research of Eimas et al. (1971), researchers have for more than a decade addressed this question for a number of consonant and vowel distinctions. Of course, the answer is not simple; there seems to be evidence for both acquired distinctiveness and acquired similarity, depending on the distinction studied.

In the first demonstration, for example, Eimas et al. reported that one- and four-month old American infants discriminated the voiced-voiceless distinction in stop consonants categorically, as American adults do. The results, averaged for the four-month-olds, from the HAS procedure, are shown in Figure 9.1. Observe that infants who were habituated to a VOT of 20 msec, a /b/ in adult category, and then were

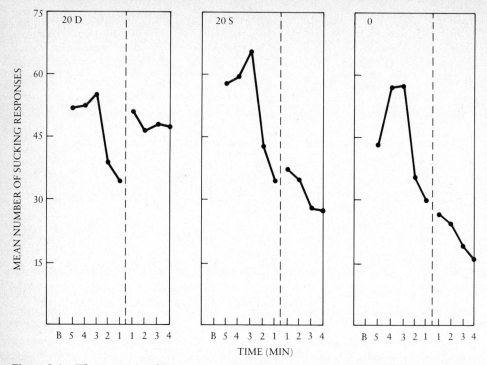

Figure 9.1   *The average sucking responses for stimuli from different adult categories (20 D), the same adult categories (20S) and the same stimulus (O). The dotted line shows the point at which the stimulus was changed.*

From "Speech perception in infants" by P. D. Eimas, E. R. Siqueland, P. Jusczyk, and J. Vigorito, 1971, in Science *171, pp. 303–306. Copyright 1971 by the AAAS. Reprinted by permission.*

shifted to a VOT of 40 msec, an adult /p/, markedly increased their sucking. When the sound shifted between VOTs of 60 and 80 msec, the same change of VOT but within-category, habituation continued. And the same infants were able to discriminate the within-category VOT values in a "nonspeech context," when the steady states were removed, as the adults are.

The results indicate that: (1) infants make the same speech-nonspeech distinctions adults do (but recall in Chapter 7 we presented data indicating that chinchillas do this as well), and (2) the voiced-voiceless boundary is either innate or learned at an extremely young age. Of course, if the boundary is innate, it may be because the *linguistic* distinction is innate or because auditory discriminability is greatest in this acoustic region, and languages have exploited this auditory constraint.

Note that in this study American infants were tested on a distinction phonemic in the language of their parents. Would they perform similarly to adults with sounds with which they had absolutely no experience? One such distinction in English is the prevoiced-voiced distinction. This difference is phonemic in many languages, but

English speakers categorize prevoiced sounds as voiced. Eimas (1975) found that American infants could discriminate this distinction but only at very large prevoicing values, larger than adults need in languages where the distinction is relevant. Streeter (1976) found that Kenyan infants raised with the Kikuyu language, in which the prevoiced-voiced distinction is phonemic but the voiced-voiceless distinction is not, were able to discriminate categorically both prevoicing from voicing and voicing from voicelessness. Moreover, the Kikuyu-speaking adults were likewise able to discriminate the voiced and voiceless categories, although they are not linguistically relevant!

Putting the results together, we conclude the following:

1. some distinctions are innate, accounting for the infants' and adults' performance with voiced-voiceless;
2. these require no experience to maintain, accounting for the Kikuyu adults' performance;
3. some distinctions must be acquired, such as prevoicing, accounting for the difference between Kikuyu infants and American infants;
4. acquisition of such distinctions occurs very early.

(This pattern should be reminiscent of the tunable blueprint model presented in the last chapter, where some features of sparrow song were innate but could be changed through exposure to a model with appropriate features during a critical period.) Again, note that in assuming that there are some innate distinctions we are not necessarily implying that the language itself is innate but that the acoustic underpinning may be. In that case, as languages have evolved through use, they would select distinctive acoustic points for their sounds, in the same way as languages may select the sounds "mama" to represent the mother because they are the sounds first produced by most infants.

Aside from some specific phonetic distinctions, other features of adult perception, such as context-sensitivity, may be innate as well. Eimas and Miller (1980) showed, for example, that infants do not respond to the absolute feature of transition length in distinguishing /b/ from /w/ but rather respond to a relative feature of transition length compared with overall duration of the syllable in discriminating the manner category. As you may recall, this kind of relative perception is what adults do. Thus, perceiving an acoustic feature in relation to context is either innate or learned very early.

Summary

By the time children have uttered their first words, they have considerable knowledge about language and communication, some of it perhaps innate. At least in play, speech sounds common to many languages have been produced, and many sounds used in speech seem to be innately perceived; discriminations of others are honed in the first year. Infants listen to relative rather than absolute features instinctively and may use this to sort sound differences into language-relevant classes. The infant imitates facial expressions, manual gestures, segmental and suprasegmental sounds; synchronizes movements with conversation rhythm; and recognizes the correspondence between facial movements and sounds. Finally, there is some evidence that the infant recognizes that sounds (at least, different intonation contours) may be used to differentiate situations, a beginning semanticity. With this base, the child is ready to sharpen articulatory control, and more significantly, to begin mastery of word meanings and syntax.

Language in the Child, MLU = 1

Between 10 and 12 months of age children utter their first words, and for the next few months show a steady increase in vocabulary. During this period words are produced one at a time, and not until the vocabulary includes about 50 words are any joined into sentences (Dale, 1976). Use of sounds as words rather than as babble can be recognized by the regularity of the pronunciation and the regularity of context that evokes them.

Most of the first words acquired (Nelson, 1973) are nouns, either general category names like "doggie" or "ball," or specific names for individuals like "Mommy" or "Spot." Next most frequent are names of actions like "give," "bye-bye," "more," or "up" and modifiers like "mine," or "dirty." Then come social words like "yes" or "no" and, finally, lowest in frequency, function words. Nelson (p. 31) pointed out that most of the words used describe objects or attributes that change (move, make noise, and so on) or actions the child can make or objects the child can act on— although "shoes" is frequent, "diaper" is not; the child sees the diaper but interacts with it only passively, while actively manipulating the shoe. Note the consistency with Piaget's sensorimotor theory.

Phonological Processes

Although words at this point have both regular pronunciation and regular meanings for the child, neither may be the same as the adult uses. With respect to pronunciation, as we have already noted, some feature values do not come into regular use until very late, so naturally they will not be represented in the first words. Phonological differences between child and adult speech fall into the following general categories (see, for example, Bloom and Lehey, 1978):

> phoneme deletion: [ɚ:t] for "hurt"
>> (":" indicates lengthening of the previous sound)
> syllable deletion: [æˈnd] for "behind"
> coalescence across syllables: [pæf] for "pacifier"
> assimilation: [gɪk] for "kiss"
>> (Note that the initial and final consonants share both place and manner of articulation in the child's production, unlike the target.)
> *reduplication* (repetition of a syllable): [tɪtɪ] for "kitty."

Three things should be noted about this categorization. First, following the transformational outlook the child's productions are *not* considered errors or mispronunciations but rather "correct" pronunciation from phonological rules different from those of the adults. Second, in most cases in the examples, the child's production reflects a modification of a phoneme or a feature of the adult system that the child does not yet produce—back sounds like /h/ or /k/ in the first two or last examples, or fricatives like /s/ in the third and fourth examples. In this regard, note further that attempts to describe the child's productions as simplifications of adult utterances fail; somtimes the child's is reduced, dropping a syllable or phoneme (as in the preceding examples), and sometimes expanded, reduplicating a syllable of an adult one-syllable word or adding one, as in "bowwow" or "doggie" for "dog," or [kɪʔkæt] for "cat." (Of course, the adult may supply these nursery words to the child, but probably at some time a child invented them.)

Third, following Vygotsky, it is interesting to note that the phonological processes the child uses are seen in the adult language in historical changes: We have phoneme deletion in h-dropping in Cockney or r-dropping in Boston; syllable deletion in "bye" for "goodbye" or "gator" for "alligator"; coalescence in "bike" for "bicycle"; assimilation, as in the match of the nasal in place of articulation with the stop in a consonant cluster such as "improbable"; and reduplication in "hoity-toity," "pell-mell," or "itsy-bitsy." Since we see these phonological processes in the first words and in the adult language, it is reasonable to assume that they occur throughout development, as indeed they do. It may also be reasonable to consider these processes as part of our innate procedures for processing linguistic input.

Meaning Processes

As children's pronunciations do not match those of the adults, neither do their meanings match. Three types of mismatch may be identified. In the first, the child uses a word an adult would use, but to define a different category. For example, Dale (1976) reported an instance of a child using "mama" to request fulfillment of a need or the presence of an absent adult, and "papa" to name a present parent of either sex.

A second meaning mismatch is *overextension,* where the child generalizes a name inappropriately to other objects with some similar perceptual attributes. For example, "daddy" may be used for *all* men; "doggie," for all mammals; "ball," for all round objects. Clark (1973) found that overextensions gleaned from diary studies were based on shared attributes of shape, size, sound, movement, taste, or texture, but rarely on color.

The third meaning change is *overrestriction,* the opposite of overextension, where a name applies to a narrower class of objects than in adult use. For example, Dale (1976) reported his daughter as using "muffin" for blueberry or blueberry muffin but not for other types of muffins. Generally, overextensions seem more common than overrestrictions in child language, but as Dale pointed out, this may be because of a bias in the recorder: It is easier to notice an overextension since a word is used inappropriately, than an overrestriction where a word is not applied where it could be. Humans have a harder time detecting the absence of something that could be present than the presence of something that should be absent.

What's in the Word?

Thus far we have merely described the child's output at the one-word stage, assuming as little about the cognitive structures underlying it as we did for the chimpanzees. There has been a great tendency in the literature on child language acquisition to *rich interpretation* of the language data, that is, inferring either from the nonverbal contexts or the prevalent linguistic theory that a complex cognitive structure underlies the simple productions. Using the design features of Table 8.5 as a guide, consider the arguments presented here to find hard evidence that children behave qualitatively differently from the chimpanzees. Remember to be consistent: What seems to be reasonable to impute to the child should be allowed also for the chimpanzee or pigeon, unless you can specify criteria that differentiate the two subjects objectively.

Holophrasis. A common description of the one-word stage is one attributing an entire sentence structure to the word. By "mama" the child could mean "Mama please come here," or "I want mama" or "There is mama" or "It was mama who dropped the bottle," depending on the nonverbal context. Similarly "sock" could be considered to reflect a request, a statement of existence, or statement of action ("it was the sock that dropped to the floor"). Expressing a *whole* sentence or *phrase* in a single word is called *holophrasis.*

The arguments in favor of holophrasis begin with the fact that during the one-word stage children seem to understand more than they produce (so do pets), so perhaps there is a linguistic competence underlying both comprehension and production, which is limited in production by performance deficiencies. Moreover, children's single-word utterances seem marked with different intonations that adults can classify with about 80 percent accuracy as declarative, interrogative, or imperative (Dore, 1975). Therefore, there seems to be some "syntax" expressed in the single word. The final argument for holophrasis comes from an assumption of innate language combined with rich interpretation of the nonverbal context in which the utterances occur. Children seem to be commenting on the world—using a single word to name an object when it falls, makes a noise, disappears, reappears, or in some other way captures their attention. It seems possible that these comments are in fact predicates. (Of course these events could just cause the child to notice the object since it has changed, rather than noticing what has happened.)

Alternative Interpretations.   Given that so much has to be inferred from the single word in order to assume that it represents the syntax for an underlying sentence, most current formulations have retreated at least in part from a holophrastic description. Instead, some researchers have suggested that the single word represents a speech act (Dore, 1975) consisting of a force (declarative, interrogative, imperative) plus a rudimentary referring expression. The expression later turns into a proposition with the development of syntax. Others have suggested that the single word represents a predicate alone or a single semantic relation, such as location. This last suggestion is interesting at least insofar as it permits classification of which semantic relations (see Chapter 4) the child might understand. The child uses object, with self as recipient; possessive as when the child says "Daddy" when looking at Daddy's slipper; patient, as in "shoe" when the shoe falls; and agent as in "Mommy" when the child wishes her to do something.

Intonation, force, and nonverbal context aside, it seems unreasonable to attribute much underlying competence to the child's single-word utterances. That does not mean that there is little there, but there seems no reason to assume from the data at hand more in the child's mind than in the linguistic ape's.

One-Word "Stage"?

Implicit in the last section is the assumption that single-word utterances constitute a stage of development. As you may recall, the Piagetian concept of stage refers to a point in development marked by a new cognitive organization. Given this definition it is reasonable to consider the single words a stage (although not one corresponding directly to any of Piaget's stages in particular)—they differ from previous utterances in intentionality or planning and seem to reflect for the first time that the child understands something about naming. Assuming that you agree that they reflect little or no syntax—that they are not holophrases—they differ from the next language developments in that they show no syntax or concept of word combination. Indeed, following the arguments of Terrace, Petitto, Sanders, and Bever (1979) in the last chapter, this concept of word combination may be critical to the definition of *human* language and a way of marking our accomplishments from those of apes. Thus, there does appear to be a critical leap from the notion of words as names to words as units to be combined. Therefore, the one-word period may be considered a stage.

It is important to note, however, that not everyone considers the one-word period a stage. The principal argument against the stage notion is that the one-word period represents a point in the continuous development of multiword utterances, with no abrupt mark between one- and two-word periods. So there are points in time when a child may be uttering predominantly single words with one or two two-word utterances, and later, points when the child is producing mostly two-word utterances with some one-word utterances still appearing (Bloom and Lehey, 1978). This suggests that there is no sudden grasp of syntax that would mark abrupt development.

Recall, however, that the stage, as Piaget defined it, does not require a sudden or abrupt change, nor that learning of a new concept or cognitive organization affects all previous schemes at once. Rather, there is gradual change, a continuity in development from one stage to the next. Indeed, babbling does not abruptly disappear, although that is usually considered a "stage." It may continue not only into the one-word period but also well beyond. Most of us have observed school children spouting nonsense and then claiming after the fact that the utterance "meant" something like someone's name or another word for some common object. They also babble nonsense rhymes (pony, plony, prony, trony) and will babble "odd" sounds like tongue trills when they (re)discover them. (So do we, perhaps, accounting for the poplarity of songs like "The Name Game": [for Bob] "Bob, bo bob, banana fana fo fob . . ."). This does not mean that babbling is not a stage, but that there is continuity between stages. Thus, it is not unreasonable to consider the change from no words to one word and from one word to two words as important changes in the linguistic thought processes.

Summary

At about the end of the first year children utter their first words. For a period each word is said alone and then, gradually, words are used in combination. The words usually represent concrete objects, actions, or attributes that the child not only perceives frequently but also actively manipulates. There has been some disagreement about whether to consider the single words as words or as reduced representations of a larger unit, like a proposition, reduced perhaps because of limited memory. There is also disagreement about whether the one-word period constitutes a special stage of thinking or a point in the continuum of language acquisition.

Language in the Child, MLU > 1

Once the child begins to put morphemes together it is reasonable to discuss the acquisition of morphology and syntax, in addition to semantics. Characterizations of children's outputs and their internal grammars have changed markedly in the last 20 years. Initially, they were based on the assumption that children have completely internalized *adult* grammars with restrictions on performance limiting their outputs. This has moved to emphasis of kinds of semantic relations the child encodes, as well as the parents' interaction with the child in expanding the utterances to "shape" adult grammar. These differences in general framework were discussed in the beginning of the chapter. Here we present samples of the children's utterances, and then accounts, both old-fashioned and new, of the competence underlying them.

MLU = 2

Table 9.1 shows sample utterances produced by children of MLU = 2. Note first that the two-word "stage" differs from the one-word primarily in the fact that words are strung together, not in what is described. The question is, what has the child learned or what is the child trying to express with the concatenations? Syntax-centered formulations have postulated that the child has put words into rudimentary grammatical categories and has learned (or knows innately) that these must be combined.

Pivot-Open Formulation.   Using a distributional analysis of the child's utterances Braine (1963), for example, noted that two-word utterances are comprised of words from a small class used frequently (the *pivot class*) together with words from a large, growing class (the *open class*). Pivot words consisted of fundamental relations like "more," "allgone," or "there"; open words, of noun categories like "Daddy" or "shoe." The child's grammar could be written as $S \rightarrow P+O$, $S \rightarrow O+P$, $S \rightarrow O+O$. Thus, we see "There Daddy," "Daddy allgone," "Daddy shoe," but never "There allgone." The child assigns words to the pivot class based on observation of order and function in adult sentences. The pivot class grows slowly because it is hard for the child to attend to order. The open class is order-independent and so can grow rapidly.

Child A	my mommy	see boy	nightnight office	do it	pretty boat	more taxi	allgone shoe
	my daddy	see sock	nightnight boat	push it	pretty fan	more melon	allgone vitamins
	my milk	see hot		close it			allgone egg

Child B	all broke	I see	no bed	more car	other bib	airplane bye	byebye ball	boot off
	all clean	I shut	no down	more cookie	other bread	siren bye	byebye car	light off
	all done	I sit	no fix	more high	other milk		papa byebye	pants off
	all dry		no mama	more sing	other piece			

Child C	want baby	it ball	get ball	see ball	there ball	that box	bunny do
	want car	it boy	get doll	see doll	there book	that dinner	daddy do
	want do	it checker	get Betty	see Steve	there doggie	that doll	momma do
	want get	it daddy			there doll		
	want up	it doll			there momma		

Table 9.1 *Sample frequent two-word utterances from three children (from Braine, 1963).*

Transformational Formulation. McNeill (1970) challenged this formulation because of its reliance on surface structure properties. In his view the pivot-open distinction was important because it emphasized the child's productivity, the spontaneous creation of utterances by rule, rather than the passive imitation of adult utterances. However, he considered the pivot and open classes to represent the major constituents from adult grammar, respectively, predicate and subject or object. In this analysis, children have a production limitation so that they cannot make the three-term actor-action-object relation that is necessary. One term, the one that seems most redundant, is dropped. In the egocentric child the most redundant term is usually the subject, the child him- or herself, since it would seem obvious to the child that his/her view as agent or perceiver was shared. "There Daddy" could be analyzed as "I see Daddy" with the "I" unstated, since in the child's view, it is redundant. What is left when the subject is dropped is the two-term action-object constituent, equivalent to P+O. When the relation or object is dropped we hear the equivalent of O+O or O+P.

In support of the logic underlying the redundancy-deletion analysis, McNeill cited evidence from adult language and cross-linguistic studies. In English, we are unlikely to announce to a crowd sharing our experience, "I see the bus we are all waiting for at last," but rather the much-reduced "At last," the same strategy McNeill claimed for the child. In Japanese, there is a morpheme that marks understood, shared subjects from explicit subjects. Japanese children, like English children, use sentences with implicit subjects first, dropping the subject, consistent with the egocentric sensorimotor activities. When they later start using explicit subjects regularly, though, they learn the morphological marker for explicit subjects before the marker for understood ones, presumably, McNeill argued, because it is not redundant and therefore catches their attention.

Bloom (1970) provided a transformational description of the utterances described by pivot-open grammar. She determined not just the two-word utterances but also the contexts in which they occurred. "Mommy sock" might be said for a context in which the adult would respond "yes, it's Mommy's sock" or "Mommy is putting on

your sock," the former being a possessive relation and the latter an actor-object relation. On this basis, Bloom claimed the child would have two different deep structures
producing the same surface structure through a deletion transformation, which
would remove, among other elements, the verb. Bloom described the child's grammar
at this stage as consisting of rules that rewrite a sentence as a combination of a noun
or demonstrative pronoun (like "that" or "there") with an adjective, verb, or participle (a verb used as an adjective, as you may recall). Note that the basic sentence
parts, NP and VP, are expressed in this analysis but not the same way as in an adults'
grammar.

Semantic Formulation.   Bloom emphasized the importance of the semantic relations the child expresses. Brown (1973) expanded her analysis and classified the following relations as occurring at least occasionally in the young child's utterances:

1. Nomination—the child names an object either in response to a question or
   spontaneously.
2. Recurrence—the child comments on or requests a repetition.
3. Nonexistent expression of negation—the child comments on the disappearance of something.
4. Agent + action—usually animate object combined with a verb.
5. Agent + object—usually animate agent combined with the object.
6. Action + object—verb + object.
7. Action + location—the verb with the place the action occurred.
8. Entity + location—thing or person and place it occupies.
9. Possessor + possession—(very frequent).
10. Entity + attribute—specifies attribute of entity that could not be known
    from the class concept alone.
11. Demonstrative + entity—same as nomination: for example, that dog.

It is interesting to note that this is a large list of two-term relations, but that there
are some others possible that children do not use, notably relations reflecting causality
such as the instrumental case (object + object-that-causes-a-change, e.g., door [open
by] key). The existence of some of the terms children use in juxtaposition (for example, Mommy shoe) indicates that their speech is productive since they are not likely
to hear such a juxtaposition from the adult models.

Summary.   From producing mostly one-word utterances the child begins spontaneously to produce two-word strings. These are usually utterances, the elements of
which are found in the parents' language, but the juxtaposition of which is a novel,
productive creation of the child. There is some disagreement about how best to
describe the syntax of these two-word strings.

"Telegraphic" Speech

Once children have acquired two-term relations, they combine them into three-term relations and more. The early three-term utterances have been described as "telegraphic" speech. Inflections are generally absent, as are the copula (the verb "to be"), auxiliary verbs, and articles. Not all function words or affixes are missing: Many prepositions and pronouns are included. These may be acquired early because they are free, not bound, because they are not inflected differently in different contexts, because they express meanings already learned, like agent or object (in pronouns), and because they may be stressed in speaking (Brown, 1973). Typical three-term early sentences are:

> See truck Mommy
> There go one
> Put truck window
> Adam make tower
> > *(McNeill, 1966)*

Once again it is important to note that the child's utterances are not simply passive imitations of adult speech, since the adult would never produce these strings. Whether the child's competence is in fact closer to the adult's than these utterances suggest is undeterminable, but at this stage children respond better to grammatical adult sentences than to sentences that mimic the structure the children produce themselves (Shipley, Smith, and Gleitman, 1969). However, imitation data seem to indicate that children's utterances conform to their grammar, regardless of the specific model. Thus for example, Brown (1973) reported a child who imitated "I showed you the book" with "I show book" (25½ months), another with "(?) book" (28½ months), and another with "I show you the book" (32½ months). Similarly, the model "I am very tall" yielded imitations of "(?) tall," "I tall," and "very tall" from the same children.

Is It Telegraphic? Some have argued that the omissions reflect performance limitations such as a small memory capacity, so that the child can retain only a few morphemes; others that the child has not yet learned the significance of the omitted morphemes, nor, in fact, noticed them in adult speech. Indeed, as observed before, Brown (1973) considered that the morphemes that appear in early child language are those that are salient either because of their meaning contribution or because of their capacity to carry linguistic stress. In most cases these are the base "content" words only, giving the speech the telegraphic appearance. One other class appears: rote expressions. Thus, Brown observed one child producing "pieceoftoast" at a time when no other prepositions of similar function were produced. Brown concluded that for this child, pieceoftoast constituted one long word, not a complex syntactic structure.

Syntactic Descriptions. Bloom and Lehey (1978) concentrated on what appears in speech at MLU>2 rather than on what is absent, true verbs as opposed to action words, like "allgone." They noted first that real verbs are very rare in one-word and two-word utterances, although, of course they are frequent in adult speech. Second, they characterized two-word utterances as having a *linear syntax*, simple concatenation of the two words, without expressing a new meaning (such as temporal relationship) by the combination. With the addition of verbs and introduction of three-term utterances, a new, higher-order meaning unit is constructed through the verb's relating the two noun phrases. Note that the difference between linear syntax and combinatorial meaning is important with respect to our language criteria: Only in the latter do we derive a hierarchical structure and duality of patterning in meaning, each word representing itself and also participating in a new unit. The chimps described in the last chapter appear to exhibit only linear syntax in creating their multiword strings.

Bloom and Lehey also analyzed the order of appearance of verbs and concluded that specific categories of verbs are acquired at different times. First, there are general verbs of simple action, like make, get, and do, which may be used with many different subjects and objects; next, verbs of location like put, take, go, sit, and fall; and finally, verbs of state like want, sleep, see, and is. Note that members of each of these verb categories have the same relation with the subject (or object if the verb takes one) as other members of the same category. It is this new relation that defines the sentence as a higher-order structure, not just a linear addition, and it is the creation of the higher-order structure that marks the MLU>2 period as distinctive, perhaps as the first emergence of language by our definition.

Semantic Change, MLU > 3. Bloom and Lehey (1978) also described the most significant development beyond MLU = 3: The child learns to put more than one proposition in a sentence, usually between ages two and three. The first connective used cross-lingually is "and" and the first multiple-thought sentences reflect simple conjunction, usually of two things occurring at the same time. This is called *coordinate relation,* as in "I put this on the train and this on the train." Subsequently, the child conjoins, creating a new meaning with the conjunction, as in *superordinance,* statements of causality, or statements of priorness or simultaneity. Causality is clearly a new relation; the time relations are new also since the conjunction indicates a temporal relation not indicated by the two clauses independently. A third type of conjunction, which also comes in late but adds no new meaning beyond that provided by the clauses alone, is *subordinance,* where a clause is added descriptively as in "a toilet where you poopoo. . . ."

As the child becomes more accomplished at expressing new thoughts and relations, obviously the length of the utterance increases. Note also that these function words, the conjunctions, at least in English, are perceptually salient and not bound— thus, as soon as the child can comprehend the underlying meaning relation, these words are noticed and incorporated into the child's syntax.

Development of Inflections

As children develop, in addition to discovering more about the world that can be expressed in new relations like causality and simultaneity and more about the language so that they know how to express these thoughts, they also start to use the grammatical markers—the inflectional morphemes—of the language correctly. There may be several reasons for this, in part depending on your philosophical orientation. One reason is that as more of the important things in language are incorporated into the language schemes, the child can free attention to the details of the language. A second possibility is that these details are the furthest removed from the language universals of LAD, and so the last to unfold. And a third possibility is that these are the last to be shaped; parents begin to attend to the details once meaningful communication is under control.

Inquiry into the acquisition of inflection began from the linguistic-nativist view. A search, initially successful, was conducted to show that the sequence of acquisition of inflections was universal across many languages and that what was acquired were rules that could be used productively, not just imitated or memorized instances. While it has been demonstrated that productive rules are acquired, the most recent findings indicate that the sequence in inflection acquisition is not identical across languages but does depend on the characteristics of the parents' language. In particular, children acquire early those inflections of the adult language used frequently, with relative consistency (few changes in form depending on context), stress, and greater meaning contribution; that is, the inflections seem to be learned from the adult model.

Order. As you should recall (see Chapter 4), English is largely a noninflected language, using word order to mark semantic relations. Inflections are used to mark tense (as in, -ed, -ing), number (-s), and person (-s is added to verbs for the third-person present tense), and case markings are used for pronouns only . No markings distinguish noun genders or cases, as they do in many other languages.

We have already noted that English-speaking children attend to word order early, even in the two-word utterances. Braine (1963) suggested that attention to order distinguished pivot from open words; Bloom (1970) and Brown (1973), that order distinguished functional roles in two-word propositions. At the three-word "stage" English children's utterances all follow the subject-verb-object (SVO) word order. Is this an innate, unmarked syntactic form or a strategy used for sentence processing?

At one time it was thought that SVO word order was a basic perceptual strategy (Bever, 1970), allowing the child a means of mapping the words heard to the important semantic relations, and providing the child a base from which to learn exceptions and inflections that could specify the same semantic relations in other orders. Much was made of the fact that children do not hear SVO order exclusively, given the prevalence of passives, questions, and negatives in English, and thus that its acquisition was independent of the linguistic environment.

That argument has lost force for several reasons. First, it turns out that in addressing children, English-speaking parents rarely use anything but simple active sentences (Hoff-Ginsberg and Schatz, 1982). Moreover, comprehension tests of active and passive sentences showed that children were capable of interpreting the passives as long as they were irreversible (Slobin, 1966a). (As you may recall, irreversible refers to sentences in which reversing the subject and the object to make the passive produces nonsense, such as "the boy was watered by the plant.") Finally, children are likely to misinterpret subject and object in active sentences if they are reversible and the "object" has been made the focus of attention through nonlinguistic means (see Chapter 5) (Strohner and Nelson, 1974).

Together the results suggest that the child's strategy is to attend to the probable semantic/pragmatic aspects of the situation and map the language to that, and only if that fails, to use the SVO strategy. If children use semantic strategies first, it seems possible that they infer SVO from previous experience with the language and adult input and the situation, rather than having this strategy instinctively.

Cross-Linguistic Evidence that Order Is Learned. The most damaging evidence against SVO order as innate came from cross-linguistic studies. Again, initial examination of children's productions in foreign, order-free languages indicated some preference either for SVO or SOV order, although other orders were possible (see Slobin, 1966b). However, continued study of both child and adult language (see Slobin and Bever, 1982, for example) showed a strong correlation between the two. Adults used certain orders less frequently than others, and those tended to be acquired later. Even if the adult language used most of the orders, in talking to children adults tended to restrict themselves to simple sentences with only one or two orders. Moreover children showed great individual differences in the word orders they would produce, although each child tended to produce only one or two orders. And at a very young age (Turkish) children were able to understand commands using any word order, provided the words were correctly inflected, even when their own productions were restricted to one or two orders. In languages with relatively free word order, the object inflection is acquired very early, which would make sense since it would mark important *semantic* and syntactic function, disambiguating agent and object in a word-order–free language.

Conclusion.   The current view, consistent with both Piaget and Skinner, is that children develop schemes for typical sentences of their language, where typicality is determined by frequency and salience (together producing differential habit strengths). What is incorporated first into these schemes are the important semantic relationships, with other characteristics either passively imitated or omitted in the child's own production. In English, most sentences spoken to children are in SVO word order—and that order is learned first by English-speaking children. The order is also important semantically, accounting for its early productive use. In other languages where order is not semantically salient or not as frequently drilled, it appears to be either passively imitated or ignored, with the more linguistically salient markers attended to.

Acquisition of Affixes.   *Evidence from Natural Production.* We have already mentioned some studies of morpheme acquisition for non-English languages—in Japanese the explicit subject marker is acquired early; in Turkish, case markers are acquired early. In both instances the morpheme carries important semantic information not otherwise clear from word order. In English, acquisition of affixes appears later than order, perhaps because affixes carry less semantic weight. Indeed, as we shall see, order of acquisition in English is predictable from semantic function.

Brown (1973) performed an extensive longitudinal study of the acquisition of 14 grammatical morphemes in three English-speaking children. The grammatical morphemes he looked at were the progressive (-ing), the third-person singular (-s), the past tense, the plural, possessives, articles, auxiliaries, and the copula. Table 9.2 displays his results. Note that there is a relatively consistent order of acquisition of the morphemes across children. The first morpheme to come in is the progressive, -ing, which marks verbs describing ongoing actions, a sensorimotor conversation topic.

Adam		Sarah		Eve	
I (2;3)		I (2;3)		I (1;6)	
II (2;6)	Present progressive *in* *on*, plural	II (2;10)	Plural *in,on* Present progressive, past irregular Possessive	II (1;9)	Present progressive, *on*
III (2;11)	Uncontractible copula Past irregular	III (3;1)	Uncontractible copula Articles	III (1;11)	*in* Plural, possessive
IV (3;2)	Articles Third person irregular, possessive	IV (3;8)	Third person regular	IV (2;2)	Past regular
V (3;6)	Third person regular Past regular Uncontractible auxiliary Contractible copula Contractible auxiliary	V (4;0)	Past regular Uncontractible auxiliary Contractible copula Third person irregular Contractible auxiliary	V (2;3)	Uncontractible copula Past irregular Articles Third person irregular Uncontractible auxiliary Contractible copula Contractible auxiliary

Table 9.2   The acquisition order for three children of fourteen English morphemes.
From R. Brown, A First Language, *1973, Cambridge, MA: Harvard University Press, p. 271. By permission.*

Later the other tense markers enter. The possessive also comes in early, and possessive meanings were clearly conveyed in two-word utterances, and possibly in one-word. The last grammatical morpheme that children begin producing is the difference between the definite and indefinite articles (the and a), perhaps because these are unstressed in speech and perhaps because their semantic function is highly abstract. The course of acquisition does not run smoothly: There is some time between the first occurrence of a form and its perfect use every time, and the interval is marked by regressions. It is important to note further that Brown found no compelling relation between the order of acquisition of the morphemes and their frequency in parental speech. It is his claim that children are learning from the adult model, but that they pick up the perceptually salient aspects of adult speech, not simply the most frequent.

There is no question that use of these forms is productive, not just passively imitated. Evidence for this comes both from examination of the children's productions over time and from experimental studies. Children initially produce what they see as unmarked, uninflected words. This may, inadvertently, include inflected words like "children" or "walked," but these indicate rote learning as did "pieceoftoast." When the child starts to attend to the inflections, they do not just appear in one or two words but in many, and they may appear in words in which they do not belong. Thus, children acquiring the past tense may correctly say talk, talked, but also say walked, walkeded, if they previously had "walked" as an internally unanalyzed verb. Since this, or "runned," would not likely be heard in the adult speech, one can infer that the child has inferred a rule and is using it productively.

Evidence from Elicited Production. Experimentally, Berko (1958) showed the productivity of morpheme acquisition in a now famous study. She created nonsense words that she illustrated with a cartoon (see Figure 9.2). She would then tell her subjects, pointing to the picture, "This a wug. Now there is another one. There are two of them. There are two ____." Or "This is a man who knows how to niss. He is nissing. He did the same thing yesterday. What did he do yesterday? Yesterday, he ____." The children were to fill in the blanks. Since the words were nonsense, subjects' responses could not derive from imitation but must reflect generative capacities. The children, taken from Boston-area middle-class schools and ranging in age from

THIS IS A WUG.

NOW THERE IS ANOTHER ONE.
THERE ARE TWO OF THEM.
THERE ARE TWO _____.

Figure 9.2 *The drawings of a "wug" used to elicit the plural from children.*
From "A child's learning of English morphology" by J. Berko in Word, 1958, p. 154. By permission.

four to seven and a half years, were tested on the plural, progressive, possessive, past, and third-person singular. They were also presented with compound words like blackboard and asked if they could say why the word named the object, to see if they were conscious of internal morphology.

Recall that in English affixing a plural, possessive, or past-tense marker can take a number of phonetic forms depending on the last phoneme of the root. Adults are very uniform in their responses, even with nonsense words, reflecting their tacit knowledge of the morphophonemic rules. The children were less consistent than adults but showed more consistency and more adultlike responses in the older age groups tested. For the plural all children added "s" or "z" where appropriate but had difficulty with the /əz/ form. Berko hypothesized that their rule was "plurals have s or z at the end" and therefore the words that already had an s or z sound (like niss) were assumed to be plural and not to need additional markers.

The same phonological constraints hold for the possessive and third-person singular endings, but there the children more often appropriately added all three variants. Thus, the difficulty with the /əz/ form cannot be articulatory or a failure to recognize the requisite context. For the past tense, performance was poorer over all than for the plural, with /əd/ again more difficult than /d/ or /t/, perhaps for the same reason. As one might expect from Brown's results, the progressive produced the best performance from the children.

Finally, most of the children tested did not give adult responses in explaining compounds. Most responded with a statement like "A blackboard is called a blackboard because you write on it" (which you might expect from Piaget's view that pre-operational children do not fully understand the relationship between words and referents), but some of the older children did separate them correctly into real (blackboard = black+board) or fanciful (Friday = the day to fry things) components. In any event, Berko's study indicates that children are using and acquiring rules productively. Their responses are not random but conform to the language structure. Finally, at the age of seven and a half, most children do not yet have an adult's understanding of morphological structure, at least in English compounds.

Cross-Cultural Evidence. This discussion has focused on English acquisition. As we have mentioned, other languages are much more complex inflectionally. Russian, for example, has three genders and six cases for nouns, and a complex system of markers for verbs. Slobin (1966b) extensively studied acquisition of inflectional morphology in Russian and found results parallel to those found for English. First, children begin to apply inflection after the two-word period. Second, the first inflections applied are those that correspond semantically to case markings (English children mark these by order). Third, children begin marking a case using one ending and later differentiate this class by gender. This is true for each case individually, suggesting that gender, like the articles in English, is semantically opaque and therefore late to emerge.

Summary. Brown (1973) summarized the acquisition process of the inflections of English as follows: Initially the verb appears in its generic, unmarked form either as an imperative (*get* book), past (book *drop*[ped]), intentional statement (Mommy [gonna] *read*), or as a progressive (fish [is] *swim*[ming]). As children acquire inflections, they use: the present progressive, -ing added with no auxiliary; past with -d or an irregular applied initially to the immediate past and later extended to more distant events; auxiliaries undifferentiated into their real forms like gonna, wanna, and hafta together with unmarked verbs. Slowly these grammatical subtleties develop into more adultlike categories in the order of their semantic distinctiveness and salience in the adult language. The early grammatical markers are semantically simple and reflect concepts with which the child is familiar early on. The copula, auxiliary, and third-person marker come in later because they are more complex semantically and because they are redundant with other meanings and so are noticed and needed later. The last of the grammatical markers to be used correctly in English are the definite and indefinite articles, since these are semantically most complex.

Acquisition of Transformations.   So far we have examined acquisition and word markings for concepts expressible by active affirmative sentences, those with surface structures derived with minimal transformation of deep structure. There have been a few studies of acquisition of complex sentences, producible by transforming the base structure. One, which we have already discussed, is the development of conjunction. Others include the development of negation, questions, embeddings, and comprehension of verbs that take irregular complements (such as promise). As we saw with inflections and word order, there are two ways to look at the development of these syntactic categories: as syntax acquisition or as concept acquisition.

Negation. Looking at negation from a syntactic perspective, Bellugi (1967) defined three stages of development into the adult form. In the first stage, the child precedes the core sentence with a negative marker: "No he bite you." As you may recall, this structure is close to the base structure in Chomsky's view for the negative sentence. At the second stage, the negative marker appears inside the sentence—"he no bite you." In the last stage, the auxiliary is added and the negation applied to that, yielding the adult form, "he won't bite you."

Interrogatives. A similar developmental pattern may be seen with questions. Initially a question is marked by beginning a sentence with a question word and applying interrogative intonation. Then auxiliaries are introduced. Finally, the main verb and auxiliary are inverted. Again it is interesting to observe that according to transformational theory, the interrogative marker and auxiliary are elements supposed to be present in the base structure, while the inversion is performed by transformation. The linguistic-nativist position predicted the base structure to be innate and therefore early, but transformations to be learned, and therefore later.

Brown and Hanlon (1970) provided additional support for a transformational-type theory of syntax acquisition. They analyzed derivationally complex questions produced by children such as "Ursula's my sister, isn't she?" They noted that such questions employ multiple tranformations internal to the question: The first clause is a simple active declarative, while the tag (in this example) is a negative question that substitutes a pronoun agreeing in gender and number with the subject of the main clause for it, and modifies number and tense of the auxiliary in the tag to agree with the auxiliary of the main clause. Analysis of this type of question alone suggests that if the child is learning to transform, we might expect to see the first clause initially produced with just a rising intonation or a tag, "huh," at the end. Subsequently, the child may add the tag but produce it incorrectly as in "Ursula's my sister, is she?" Finally, the child will produce the adult form of the question. Generating seven such predictions for derivational complexity of question forms, Brown and Hanlon confirmed most of them from the productions of three children. From this they derived a *law of cumulative complexity:* If children have a complex grammatical construction such as negative + question, then they must already have the single elements (negative, question).

Semantic Interpretation. *Negation.* Bloom and Lehey (1978) analyzed negation semantically and came up with somewhat different conclusions. They noted that negation can refer to distinct semantic concepts: nonexistence, disappearance, nonoccurrence, cessation, rejection, prohibition, and denial. As we have seen, children early refer to the nonexistence or disappearance of something whether they use a negative construction (no book) or not (allgone book). We might expect that as they acquire the syntactic negative they use it first in instances they have already recognized as negative semantically. In fact, they do—and the other negative concepts are then acquired in the order just listed. Interestingly, Bloom and Lehey (1978) point out that the same stages of syntactic transformation apply to each of the negatives as it is acquired. This implies that the procedure of moving the negative into the sentence is *not* learned as a generative rule but must be learned for each new semantic category.

Adjectives. Bloom's and Lehey's analysis of adjectives also shows acquisition dependent on semantics. Adjectives are first used, as we have seen, to restrict the noun classes ("big ball"). Next they are used as predicates in sentences ("this broken"). Finally they are understood as oppositional contrasts (as in hot vs cold, e.g.). It is clearly not the case that they come in as a syntactic class.

Embeddings. A similar trend of syntactic recognition following semantic was obtained by Caramazza and Zuriff (1978) for embedded sentences. They tested comprehension with a picture-matching task for reversible (the boy that the girl is chasing is tall), nonreversible (the apple that the boy is eating is red), and improbable (the boy that the dog is patting is fat) sentences. Children under six did very poorly on the reversible sentences, although there was substantial improvement overall in comprehension of the sentences between the ages of three and six. It appeared that they learned to interpret the embeddings but on the basis of semantics rather than on the basis of syntax.

Complements. The last syntactic acquisition we will examine is the acquisition of complements. Recall that some verbs can take other verbs as objects: "I think Bill should go," "I told Bill what to do," "I asked Bill what to do," "I promised Bill to leave," and so on. (The *complement* of "ask" is the second clause "what to do," e.g.) Most of the time the subject of the second verb is the closest noun: In the first two sentences the subjects of "go" and "do" are "Bill," which immediately precedes them. Some verbs are irregular; For "ask" and "promise" for instance, the subjects are "I" in the preceding sentences, the NPs farthest away. Do children understand these deep structure differences despite the identical surface structures?

Carol Chomsky (1969) addressed this question experimentally, having five-to eight-year-olds act out such sentences by using Disney puppets. At five and six most of the children interpreted all sentences by using a minimal distance principle: The NP closest to the verb was interpreted as its subject. So in response to "Mickey told Donald to jump" or "Mickey promised Donald to jump" the child would make Donald jump. As the children matured they were less likely to make this error. For each child, abilities to differentiate the regular verbs from the irregulars were highly correlated across verbs tested, but the exact age at which the ability developed depended on the individual child.

Summary of Syntax Acquisition.   In the early studies of language development it was assumed that much of syntax was innate and the innate rules could be used as a guide to vocabulary, other semantic acquisitions, and learning other specifics of the language. In particular, it seemed that the child might have basic relations like nouns, verbs, and sentences, and their core relationships in deep structure. What was assumed to be acquired were specific transformations and specific ways of marking these base relations using devices like word order or inflection.

Some evidence has accumulated to support at least aspects of this position. First, children seem to express initially the core relations of subject-predicate and express them as core sentences. Second, across languages first utterances seem very similar. Third, as language develops, specific grammatical devices are produced, imitated, and understood more frequently as the child learns them from exposure to the adult language.

However, the bulk of the evidence refutes a strong syntax-native position. Although the sequence of acquisition of syntax seems to be invariant across children exposed to the same language, there are radical individual differences in absolute times across children. (Of course, this does not strictly rule out a biological unfolding; puberty, which certainly is biologically controlled, can begin any time between ages nine and twenty, depending on the individual.) Across languages children show somewhat different developmental sequences, but these have been related usually to the structure of the language learned and the frequency or salience of particular types of utterance, suggesting that they were learned rather than "unfolded." The acquisition data make most sense given a primarily semantic[4] rather than syntactic framework: Across languages children talk about the same things, things the concepts for which seem already to have been grasped mentally but nonlinguistically. Thus, for English-

---

4. Gleitman and Wanner (1982) argue that the emphasis on semantics as a guide to syntax is perhaps overused in child language acquisition. They point out that learning by association of words to real-world objects is not straightforward since the word the parent uses may not match the aspect of the situation that the child has attended to. "Eat your peas" is usually uttered when peas are not being eaten, they point out. The implication is that learning does not take place by such association, but rather that with aspects of syntax innate, these can serve as a guide to resolving such semantic ambiguities. However, there is every reason to assume that children can learn associations between language and pragmatic aspects of situations. "Eat your peas" is appropriate as a command, in fact, *only* when peas are *not* being eaten and is therefore not bewildering at a discourse level. After all, the chimpanzees were able to discriminate situations where obedience to a command or answer to a question was required, and we would not want to argue that they had a LAD!

speaking children, the present progressive, the tense children would use to describe what they are currently doing, enters early. These actions are the topics of early communication.

What may be universal, therefore, is not the notion of subject and predicate or the forms NP and VP but the cognitive tendency to categorize the world in terms of agents and their effects, or nominal categories and their descriptors, and so forth. Thus, we see in syntactic development more regularity when we look at the emergence of case, causality, semantic classes of negation, and so on, than we see if we look at acquisition of abstract transformations, as the Piagetian framework concluded. That is not to say that children do not use syntax or acquire it—they *tend* to use the minimal distance principle or SVO strategy in English, they understand syntactically correct sentences from adults better than those that have child surface structures, and like adults they recall more syntactically correct than anomalous or scrambled sentences (McNeill, 1970). It just seems that the syntactic rules must be learned and mapped onto underlying innate or acquired conceptual structures. Moreover, it seems that acquisition of these rules depends on some combination of frequency of use in the adult language and perceptual or semantic salience.

As Brown (1973) summed up, language acquisition emerges as:

> [a] change in a set of probabilities rather than as the sudden acquisition of quite general rules. If our conception is correct it means that the learning of the intricate network of rules governing the 14 grammatical morphemes is more like habit formation and operant conditioning than anyone has supposed (p. 388).

Development of Word Meaning

In our discussion of syntactic development at MLU > 2, we wound up talking about acquisition of basic concepts like the past and future, what a negative is, definiteness or indefiniteness (in articles), and semantic relations. These, together with the notions of overgeneralization or overrestriction and acquisition of full meanings (such as a class concept or superordinate relation, and so on) constitute most of what is relevant about the child's acquisition of semantics. There have been empirical studies of children's strategies for learning new concepts and their development of associations, and these will be discussed here.

Word Associations. As we might expect, given Piaget's and Vygotsky's work on the formation of categories, children's word associations are very different from those of adults. If you present an adult with a noun, the association is likely to be another noun; with an adjective, another adjective, and so forth. Moreover, the associations are likely to differ from the stimulus in only one feature. (A likely association of "mother" is "father," not "plant.") And frequent associations are the polarities, hot-cold, warm-cool, pretty-ugly, and so on. This form of association is called *paradigmatic association*.

In the last section we noted that in adjectives the concept of polarity is acquired late, so we would not expect it to mark children's associations. And the concept of word class is acquired late, as are some aspects of meaning. Children's associations are usually words associated contiguously with the stimulus word (soft-pillow), rather than words from the same class. These are called *syntagmatic associations*. The other frequent type of association by children is whole-part (face-nose).

It is interesting to note that children do not make paradigmatic associations initially. If the word classes are innate, as the linguistic model proposes, and children learn early which word fits into which class, it would seem that other words in the class would be highly associated, even early on.

Brown and Berko (1960) tested the development of associations to count nouns (as in "a *glass*"), mass nouns (as in "some *milk*"), adjectives, transitive verbs, intransitive verbs, and adverbs in first, second, and third graders. There was a marked increase in paradigmatic associations as the age group increased for the count nouns and adjectives. By third grade, the children did not yet make paradigmatic associations for the other parts of speech. The results reflect either an immature ability to form abstract classes or an immature attentiveness to contiguous words. More recently, Cermack (1978) has found that children are more likely than adults to recognize falsely synonyms or rhyming words as words presented during a memory test. This similarly shows a difference in attentiveness to word features (both meaning and sound) between children and adults.

Inferences of Word Meanings.   The results are consistent with the way children seem to infer word meanings at the early grade school level. As part of their study, Brown and Berko (1960) gave the children nonsense words in sentences and asked them what they thought the word meant. For example, a sentence might be "The cat wants to niss some fish." A typical adult definition of niss would be catch or eat, reflecting the understanding that the word will add a new meaning to the other words, and, given the practical situation, what the new meaning is likely to be. The children, on the other hand, supplied other words in the sentence as "meanings" of the new word: "a niss is a fish—the cat wants a fish." Similarly Piaget (as cited by Vygotsky, 1962) noted that when asked to supply the meaning of "because" in the sentence "the child missed school because he was sick," seven- and eight-year-olds would respond with either clause but not with the relation between the two. Both results demonstrate the inability of the child to separate the part, the new word, from the whole, the rest of the sentence.

In an extensive study of meaning inference Werner and Kaplan (1950) demonstrated that this type of responding persists until at least age 12. They presented their subjects with new words in several sentences, each of which added to the meaning. For example:

1. A corplum may be used for support.
2. Corplums may be used to close off an open place.
3. A corplum may be long or short, thick or thin, strong or weak.
4. A wet corplum does not burn.
5. You can make a corplum smooth with sandpaper.
6. The painter used a corplum to mix his paints.

The child was presented with each sentence and then asked the meaning of the word. The next sentence was then presented to see how the child modified the answer. As one might expect from performance with Vygotsky blocks, children were not consistent in the same way as adults in applying meanings. They tended to take the sentence as a whole for the word meaning: For "people like to talk about the borducks of others and don't like to talk about their own" borduck was interpreted as people talk about others and not themselves; adding "people with borducks are often unhappy" produced "Say this lady hears that another lady is talking about her, so she'll get mad at her and that lady will be very unhappy."

Another method of meaning inference was to incorporate one sentence into the next. For "hudray" (grow, enlarge) two sentences were "you must have enough space to hudray your library" and "if you eat well and sleep well you will hudray." Responding to the first that "hudray" meant "to have enough space" one child explained the second as meaning if you eat well your stomach will have enough space for more food.

Other common "errors" were to change the meaning of a word in small details to tailor it to each sentence. By age 12 children seemed to reason the way the adults did. Note that this is about the age at which formal operations are supposed to begin.

One point that should be observed about the "errors" in the previous studies is that to a large extent they may be committed not because children do not understand how to reason but because they do not have the world knowledge to deduce the relation the word expressed. At what age would you expect a child to know that wood can burn, so that the corplum sentence would provide useful data? Many children's errors seem to be errors in the adult's eye because we know the real meaning or real world properties. Children's "misunderstandings" can be quite ingenious and reflect full comprehension of abstract meanings, just not ones the adult is familiar with. For instance, Bowerman (1981) reported the following dialogues:

AGE

3.1 Mother (playing with a toy): The cow would like to sing
    but he can't.
    Child (pulling the cow's string): I'm singing him.

4.3 Child (arguing about wearing a sweater): It always sweats me.

4.6 Child: Everybody makes me cry.
    Mother: I didn't make you cry.
    Child: Yes you did, you cried me.

Although these are wrong in English, their meaning is clear (substitute "cause to ____" for the odd verb, if you do not see the meaning) and these verbs, *causatives,* are used in other languages.

Metalinguistic Meaning Development. *Metaphor Comprehension.* Winner, Rosenstiel, and Gardner (1976) investigated metaphor comprehension in children between six and fourteen years old. The metaphor types they examined were psychological-physical, where the metaphor "explains" a psychological experience through comparison to a physical event, and cross-sensory, where one physical experience is expressed by means of another. For example, "the prison guard was a hard rock" refers to a personality characteristic using a physical property, and "her perfume was bright sunshine" uses a visual sensation to describe an olfactory one. The children were asked either to explain the metaphors or to select the appropriate explanation from several choices.

Winner et al. proposed several classes of response: magical, metonymic, primitive metphoric, and genuine metaphoric. In the magical response, the child interprets the metaphor literally and invents a world to account for it; for example, "The king had a magic rock and he turned the guard into another rock." Although these responses were not frequent in any age group, they were most frequent in the youngest children (six, seven and eight).

In the metonymic response, an association is formed between the two terms of the metaphor as if they were separate descriptions; for instance, "The guard worked in a prison that had hard rock walls." The primitive metaphor differs from a genuine metaphor in that the meaning of the figurative element is literally rather than figuratively applied, as in "The guard had hard, tough muscles" versus "The guard was mean and did not care about the feelings of the prisoners." The six-, seven-, and eight-year-olds made primarily metonymic and primitive metaphoric responses, but even the ten-year-olds made only 48 percent genuine metaphoric responses.

Winner et al. did not speculate on the change in strategy with development but pointed out that children produce good metaphors considerably before they appear to understand them, from this study. This may be because to comprehend another's metaphor, one is removed from the immediate sensory experience and must make the relation entirely inside one's head. In Piagetian terms, this relation of thought to thought must follow concrete operations, and formal operations usually begin around adolescence. It is interesting to consider this hypothesis in light of the purported creative abilities (e.g., stale cookie = cookie rock) of the apes discussed in the last chapter. From an anthropocentric view, it seems highly unlikely that an ape with two years' experience with language would have metalinguistic skills exceeding those of ten-year-old children. (Of course, production results only have been reported for the apes, and children do produce what are recognized as metaphors before they understand them.)

Other Metalinguistic Skills. Aside from metaphor comprehension, metalanguage skills include awareness of the structure of language, that sentences are composed of words, words of syllables, and so on. Investigators have assumed some metalinguistic awareness in even young children since children backtrack and correct themselves, indicating that they note discrepancies between the structure of their production and their intention. Tunmer and Herriman (1984) cite an example of a child trying to say "shoes": š, šI, šIš, šu, š?, šuš—finally rescued by the mother supplying the correct pronunciation.

In a similar vein, there have been numerous reports of children practicing language to themselves. Weir (described in McNeill, 1970) recorded "presleep monologues" from her child by hanging a microphone over the crib. One instance, when the child was two and half years old is "go for grasses—go for them—go to the top—

go for pants—go for shoes," an obvious example of play with the "go for ____" sentence frame. Similar monologues have been recorded from many other children (Kuczaj, 1983).

Although the practice and repairs indicate some awareness of the form of the language, it is not clear that they indicate conscious reflection on its structure. As Tunmer and Herriman (1984) pointed out, parrots engage in speech practice, and we would be loath to attribute metalinguistic awareness to a bird. Recognition of a mismatch between an intended and an actual utterance may be simply mismatch recognition, not awareness of a structural problem.

Metalinguistic skills have also been assessed directly. Children have been asked to tap in rhythm to an utterance, tapping for each phoneme, syllable, or word. Liberman, Shankweiler, Fischer, and Carter (1974) found that nursery school children were able to signal the syllables better than the phonemes, and that by first grade, performance was 90 percent for syllables and 70 percent for phonemes. This indicates that syllable understanding precedes phoneme awareness, and that sound awareness is generally late in developing. Young children (between four and seven) are also poor at tapping to words in sentences, sometimes tapping on the basis of syllables, and sometimes to content words only (Tunmer, Pratt, and Herriman, 1984). Moreover, when asked "does the word book have pages?" or to "name a large word" a significant proportion of young *adolescents* indicate confusion between the concept of a word and the thing it denotes, responding, for example, "yes" to the first question and "house" to the second. (It is important to note that these tasks have not been performed with adults as rigorously as with children, and so it is possible that many adults too respond incorrectly to these questions.)

Thus, it appears that awareness of language as a system and the ability to discuss and appreciate its structure develops through childhood and adolescence. Complete metalinguistic awareness appears only in the human adult (and perhaps not even then).

Summary of Semantic Acquisition.   Children's meanings for words and their methods of deducing word meanings change as they develop. The most significant changes reflect a change from inconsistency to consistency in reasoning and from syntagmatic to paradigmatic associations based on similarity. At least some of the changes in association or other differences between child and adult meanings are due to incomplete understanding of the relations of the objects in the world or the way the specific language describes those relations. In these instances experience teaches.

Whether any aspect of the development of reasoning or word association is innate or maturational, or whether all aspects reflect experience with the language, is unclear. It certainly seems, however, that a marked, salient feature of words is *not* their syntactic class but their sound or contiguous associations. This may facilitate learning of syntax, since similar sounds characterize inflections, and inflections are frequently reserved for one word class (e.g., verbs are those words that may end in "ed"), and since contiguities entail word order. It does suggest that attention to the part of speech is not the primary learning strategy, as the LAD position might suggest. The indication is that full knowledge of language as a system in itself, of metalinguistic awareness, does not appear until late childhood or early adolescence, around the time that Piaget proposed that formal operations, awareness of the systematicity of thought, develop.

Acquisition of Discourse Rules

Piaget's concept of egocentrism notwithstanding, from a very early age children seem to respond to the social demands of the communication situation. In infancy, as we noted, they synchronize to the parent's speech, giving some kind of feedback, and they also babble contingent on the parent's speech, again providing feedback. Later they respond appropriately to commands, indicating an understanding of what is expected of them. The first words are usually uttered not as demands but as efforts to share with another—"children talk in order to participate, to be human, not in mere imitation but in emulation . . . sociolinguistics begins in the crib" (Menn, 1981).

At MLU > 2 we see development of real interaction skills, appropriate monitoring, feedback and turn taking, and eventually, tailoring of the conversation to the audience. Children talk in simpler sentences when talking to other children than when talking to adults; they also ask more questions of adults (Bloom and Lehey, 1978). More interestingly, Bloom and Lehey reported that a two-year-old shifted readily from sign to speech when shifting conversation from a deaf parent to a hearing one. And children asked to describe something to a blind person tend to provide more details than when asked to describe something to a sighted person. All of this reflects an awareness of the conversational needs of others, and that children are not as egocentric as it might appear from the Piagetian framework.

One difference between children's discourse skills and those of adults is in the relation between sentences in conversation. Children's earliest "sentences" echo a part of the adult's previous utterance, something that rarely happens in adult discourse (Bloom and Lehey, 1978). Children's utterances also are sometimes unrelated to the adult's previous statement. And finally, those utterances that fall into neither of these categories tend to expand simply on the adult's utterance (Bloom, Rocissano, and Hood, 1976). Bloom et al. offer the following examples:

ADULT	CHILD
Noncontingent: Alright. Put the light on.	Cookie.
Imitative: Take your shirt off.	Shirt off.
Contingent: I see two.	I see two bus come here.

The differences are that for adults 90 percent of the utterances are contingent on previous sentences as opposed to 70 percent for children, and that in adults the connection is more abstract. Analyzing interviews with politicians, Bloom et al. reported the following as typical of adult contingencies:

President Ford: We watch the Miss America contest all the time.

Miss America: I sure hope you watched it this year.

Note that the topic is the same, but that all other parts of the sentence are new. The redundancy may seem greater in children's speech because so much is new to children that they may feel that the contributions they make to the conversation when echoing are as significant as they later do when adding.

Peterson and McCabe (1983) reported developmental changes in children's abilities to describe stories. As you may recall from chapters 4 and 5, adult stories (in our culture) are usually constructed as elaborations on a theme, with the topic given initially, followed by descriptive details, designed to portray the setting, the characters' feelings, the sequence of events, and the causal connections. The oldest children Peterson and McCabe examined (nine years) reflected these constraints on stories to a greater extent than younger children. Four-year-olds, for example, were more likely to omit important events or tell them out of order or to fail to give appropriate orientation, as the following example illustrates (E is the experimenter) (p. 44):

E. When I go home I have to visit my aunt who's in the hospital. She broke both of her legs ...

B. She had to have a cast on.

E. That's right.

B. *My* sister had, she's had. She broke a arm when she fell in those mini-bike.

E. Tell me what happened.

B. She broke her arm. She had, she went to the doctor, so I, my Dad gave me a spanking, and I

E. Your Dad gave you what?

B. A spanking to me.

E. A spanking?

B. Yeah. And she had to go to the doctor to get a cast on. She had to go to get it, get it off, and it didn't break again. . . .

Note the lack of explanation for the relation between the spanking, the accident, and the cast, and the failure to elaborate on any aspect of the event—the child simply jumps from one event to another.

In addition to providing less detail and omitting necessary relations, younger children are less coherent and tend to provide orienting information such as setting at the middle or the end where it is less useful. They also favor descriptive stories, with temporally linked events, over causally connected stories. Finally, younger children tell shorter stories than older ones. Contrast, for example, a four-year-old's narrative (p. 226):

E. You went to your grandma's? What happened?

S. I just said "Hiii," and then and then they, Mom said, said, "Say, *say* something." And I said, "*Nooo, I wanta go home.*" "Not 'til you say, say, say hello." "I *said* hello, Ma." And then she, and then my Mom goed back to my grandma's and then she said, "Oh, she's just a bad girl," like that.

with this nine-year-old's narrative (p. 247)

> E. What happened the last time you went [to visit your aunt]?
> D. Nothing. We went to see our aunt because she, she's getting real old and yet, she's going to die pretty soon, so we went and visited her and, my brother, he found a sh, *rattle* snake and he thought it was one of those *play* snakes, and he, he said, *"Gee, look at this play snake,"* and my Dad goes, *"That ain't no play snake, that's a real snake."* My mother, *"Drop that durn thing you, and get in here and wash your hands."*

As Peterson and McCabe conclude, more to language develops than sentence structure: Discourse coherence also develops and development is not complete at middle childhood.

Practice and the Parent as Teacher

In the course of examination of syntactic development we have observed some correlation between the acquisition of a structure or concept and its frequency in the adult language to the child (SVO in English, e.g.). This suggests that there may be language teaching taking place, either passively or actively, as the behaviorist models suggested.

Studies of practice effects in language have taken two forms: study of children's obvious practicing by themselves, as already discussed, and studies of the nature of parent's discourse with the child. Like children's practice, examination of adult interaction with children suggests that practice has an effect. The adult's language is characterized by short, simple, redundant sentences with few inflections or syntactic complexities or performance errors. Mothers have longer MLUs when talking to older children than when talking to younger ones (Seitz and Stewart, 1975). Either of these results may occur because the parent is trying to teach the child or because the parent is imitating the child. Adults tend to talk to children about what the child is currently doing; children respond in kind. Again it is not obvious who is imitating whom. Adults use more gestures and talk in basic category levels initially. When understanding has increased gesturing decreases, and finer or grosser category distinctions are made (Hoff-Ginsberg and Schatz, 1982). (As you may recall from Chapter 3, the basic level was in part defined as the level children use first. But this may be circular, if children use that level first because it is the level that adults "teach" first.)

Children's acquisition, as we have observed, also seems to reflect features they can easily pick up from adult speech. Hoff-Ginsberg and Schatz (1982) suggested that word categories could be learned by noting the similarity of inflections used; thus, verbs could be classed together as those things that take -ed. And many words, especially nouns (which enter early) are spoken by the parents in isolation. This can aid recognition. Other syntactic categories can be learned from semantic regularities, although these are not usually sufficient to differentiate all abstract, arbitrary syntactic forms. However, they can provide an initial prod (Hoff-Ginsberg and Schatz, 1982).

As a final point in favor of the child's modeling language from adult speech, researchers note that parents do "correct" aspects of child language. Generally grammar is not corrected, and generally parents respond to whatever they understand the child as saying, reinforcing the communication. Parents do tend to modify children's speech by expanding it: If the child says "there shoe" the parent may rejoin "That's right. There are your shoes." And some studies have shown that children develop syntax more rapidly when there is much expansion relative to other types of verbal input (Hoff-Ginsberg and Schatz, 1982), although that result is not consistently obtained (see Dale, 1976 for discussion).

On the negative side, there are the studies that fail to show effects of parental input, as just mentioned. And there are studies that indicate that the parents do not respond differentially to poorly formed and well-formed utterances, and so could not be serving as teachers (Brown and Hanlon, 1970). There is also the argument that the high correlation between the parents' utterances and the children's comes from the parents' matching the children rather than the other way around. This is plausible at least in part because it is not clear that most parents are conscious enough of syntactic levels to know how to scale down their speech to be effective language teachers. Finally, there are wonderful counterexamples cited to show how ineffective teaching is. McNeill (1970), for example, reports the following:

Child: Nobody don't like me.
Mother: No, say "nobody likes me."
Child: Nobody don't like me.

.
.
.

(eight repetitions of this dialogue)

.
.
.

Mother: No, now listen carefully; say
"nobody likes me."
Child: Oh! Nobody don't likes me.

So, at this time, it seems that the parents may not play an active, obvious teaching role, but in supplying language models, they provide the child with the experience necessary to develop schemes for the language.

Summary

In this section, we examined development of syntactic, morphological, semantic, and discourse concepts in children at MLU > 2. Not surprisingly, we found that there is a steady increase in language sophistication with age, and that the acquisition process is by no means over when children enter school. Transformational accounts to the contrary, it appears that language acquisition occurs through children's attention to semantically and phonologically (stressed) salient features of the language, from which syntactic structure is learned. Moreover, it appears that in interacting with children, parents do provide a model and do try to teach, which perhaps facilitates learning.

Summary and Conclusions

The chapter began with a description of several possible theoretical stands on language acquisition, ranging from innate language structure, through innate cognitive structures that interact with the environment and language, to language learned in the same manner as all other knowledge. We then examined the course of acquisition, mostly of English, but also of some other languages.

Results showed that there is considerable invariance in the order of acquisition of concepts and structures. All children cry, coo, babble, then produce words; all children perceive certain phonetic distinctions categorically, regardless of experience, and other distinctions noncategorically until they have experience. All children use the same phonological processes of reduplication, assimilation, and reduction. In syntax we see a steady progression from one word to two and more, production of the same cases initially, across languages, and attention to inflection or word order or conjunction occurring at predictable times across languages. In semantics there are reliable trends in word association and in inferring meanings from contexts.

The striking similarities in sequence across children may be due to some innate language mechanism or may be due to general cognitive changes coordinated with similar real-world environments. As Premack taught Sarah if-then (see Chapter 8) by mapping it to a conditional discrimination, children may not be able to learn conditionals (or past tenses or causality) in syntax until they understand the underlying real world situation. In any event, if there is something innate about language, few people believe now that it is specific syntactic structures, but rather more general cognitive and perceptual strategies that allow for the deduction of syntax. On the language innateness side, however, is the urge to communicate using language, the attention paid to these particular environmental noises, and the fact that syntax is acquired or used in language at all. As we pointed out in Chapter 8, communication about one's needs for food, water, social contact, and so on, can be quite effective without use of language.

Another aspect of language that might be innate is the time of acquisition. In this chapter we discussed language acquisition given normal input from two years to adolescence. Innateness was defined not only as reflex responding, which we investigated by looking for similarities across children in production, but also as a tuning of the individual to critical features in the environment at a particular time. If there is a language acquisition device it may require input to become activated. We saw that parents communicate with their children early, provide a comfortable social environment to allow expression of the sociolinguistic need, provide model utterances, and shape the children's outputs through expansions. These need not indicate exclusively that language develops from experience; it may be that experience interacts with an unfolding "tunable blueprint" to allow language development. In the next chapter we will look at severely disturbed environmental inputs to see their effects on language acquisition.

Aside from the innateness issue, this chapter was aimed at applying our language criteria objectively to children, as we did to animals. We can rule out "language" as appearing at the one-word stage since there is no evidence there for productivity (syntax). In the one-word stage we do see rapid fading, broadcast transmission and reception, interchangeability, and total feedback. Indeed, these features appear at the crying stage.

More interestingly, at the one-word stage, there is evidence of specialization, semanticity, arbitrariness, and discreteness. The two-word stage adds no new features, but once MLU > 2, we see the emergence of real language. First, children begin to talk about things that are not currently occurring, indicating displacement. Second, they seem to be regularly applying syntactic rules, indicating productivity. And third, they seem to be creating new, hierarchical units by combination, showing duality of patterning.

The other language features we discussed are either inapplicable or harder to assess from the data presented here. Traditional transmission, learnability, and simultaneity and smear clearly apply to the language acquired but not to the acquirer, and so are irrelevant. Prevarication we have not discussed; the folk wisdom is that children are less likely to lie (leading to embarrassing situations when a white lie would be expected), but there is no question that they cry sometimes to gain attention, deliberately implying a physical problem when there is none.

Metacommunication is acquired in part by the three-word stage since children can respond to questions for names and ask such questions. But ability to comprehend metaphors fully, to respond like adults to questions about segmentation of sentences or words, or to respond to linguistic aspects of words apart from their referents do not appear fully until much later, between school age and adolescence, depending on the skill.

Children transmit less information than adults, at least in our view, but that may be because of our knowledge of the redundancies of the world. Thus, when we make a contingent response, there is less redundancy with the previous utterance than when a child makes a contingent response, but that may be because the child does not observe the redundancy and so *is* transmitting more information than we would be with the same utterance. Certainly, phonetically, children and adults transmit information at similar rates.

Finally, once children start forming higher-order units, in the three-word stage they exhibit recursiveness: A sentence may be rewritten NEG S, or QUESTION S; sentences may contain conjoined sentences. Thus, with the possible exception of the metalanguage criterion once MLU > 2 we may conclude that a child "has language"; with the metalanguage criterion, we have to say that children do not "have language" until adolescence.

In sum, we have shown how language develops in children. There are common perceptual and cognitive strategies employed cross-culturally by the children, and common linguistic models provided cross-culturally by the parents. Moreover, there are common environmental events that all children are exposed to. We cannot ascertain which of these has the most important role in establishing the similarities in language acquisition we observed across children. In the next chapters we will look at language when some of these features deviate from normal to see their relative importance for occurrence of normal language.

REFERENCES

Bellugi, U. (1967). The acquisition of negation. Unpublished doctoral dissertation. Harvard University. Cited in Bloom and Lehey, 1978.

Berko, J. (1958). The child's learning of English morphology. *Word, 14,* 150–177.

Bever, T. (1970). The cognitive basis for linguistic structures. In J. R. Hayes (Ed.). *Cognition and the Development of Language,* pp. 279–362. NY: John Wiley and Sons.

Bloom, L. (1970). *Language Development: Form and Function in Emerging Grammars.* Cambridge, MA: MIT Press.

Bloom, L., & Lehey, M. (1978). *Language Development and Language Disorders.* NY: John Wiley and Sons.

Bloom, L., Rocissano, C., & Hood, L. (1976). Adult-child discourse: Developmental interaction between information processing and linguistic knowledge. *Cognitive Psychology, 8,* 521–552.

Bowerman, M. (1981). The child's expression of meaning: Expanding relationships among lexicon, syntax, and morphology. In H. Winitz (Ed.). *Native Language and Foreign Language Acquisition.* pp. 172–189. Annals of the New York Academy of Sciences, NY: New York Academy of Sciences, *379.*

Braine, M. (1963). The ontogeny of English phrase structure: The first phase. *Language, 39,* 1–13.

Brown, R. (1973). *A First Language.* Cambridge, MA: Harvard University Press.

Brown, R., & Bellugi, U. (1964). Three processes in the acquisition of syntax. *Harvard Educational Review, 34,* 133–151.

Brown, R., & Berko, J. (1960). Word association and the acquisition of grammar. *Child Development, 31,* 1–14.

Brown, R., & Hanlon, C. (1970). Derivational complexity and the order of acquisition in child speech. In J. R. Hayes (Ed.). *Cognition and the Development of Language,* pp. 11–53. NY: John Wiley and Sons.

Caramazza, A., & Zuriff, E. B. (1978). Comprehension of complex sentences in children and aphasics: A test of the regression hypothesis. In A. Caramazza & E. B. Zuriff (Eds.). *Language Acquisition and Language Breakdown,* pp. 145–161. Baltimore: Johns Hopkins University Press.

Cermack, L. S. (1978). The development and demise of verbal memory. In A. Caramazza & E. B. Zuriff (Eds.). *Language Acquisition and Language Breakdown,* pp. 277–289. Baltimore: Johns Hopkins University Press.

Chomsky, C. (1969). *The Acquisition of Syntax in Children from 5 to 10.* Cambridge, MA: MIT Press.

Chomsky, N. (1965). *Aspects of the Theory of Syntax.* Cambridge, MA: MIT Press.

——— (1968). *Language and Mind.* NY: Harcourt Brace Jovanovitch.

——— (1975). *Rules and Representations.* NY: Columbia University Press.

Clark, E. V. (1973). What's in a word? On the child's acquisition of semantics in his first language. In T. E. Moore (Ed.). *Cognitive Development and the Acquisition of Language,* pp. 65–110. NY: Academic Press.

Condon, W. S., & Sander, L. W. (1974). Neonate movement is synchronized with adult speech: Interactional participation in language acquisition. *Science, 183,* 99–101.

Dale, P. S. *Language Development.* (1976). NY: Holt, Rinehart and Winston.

DeCasper, A. J., & Fifer, W. P. (1980). Of human bonding: Newborns prefer their mothers' voices. *Science, 208,* 1174–1176.

Delack, J. B. (1976). Aspects of infant speech development in the first year of life. *Canadian Journal of Linguistics, 21,* 17–37.

Dore, J. (1975). Holophrases, speech acts, and language universals. *Journal of Child Language,* 2, 21–40.

Eimas, P. D. (1975). Speech perception in early infancy. In L. P. Cohen & P. Salapatek (Eds.). *Infant Perception,* vol 2, pp. 193–231. NY: Academic Press.

Eimas, P. D., & Miller, J. L. (1980). Contextual effects in infant speech perception. *Science, 207,* 1140–1141.

Eimas, P. D., Siqueland, E. R., Jusczyk, P., & Vigorito, J. (1971). Speech perception in infants. *Science, 171,* 303–306.

Eimas, P. D., & Tartter, V. C. (1979). On the development of speech perception: Mechanisms and analogies. In H. W. Reese & L. P. Lipsitt (Eds.). *Advances in Child Development and Behavior,* vol. 13, pp. 155–193. NY: Academic Press.

Field, T. M., Woodson, R., Greenberg, R., & Cohen, D. (1982). Discrimination and imitation of facial expression by neonates. *Science, 218,* 179–181.

Fraser, C., Bellugi, U., & Brown, R. (1963). Control of grammar in imitation, comprehension and production. *Journal of Verbal Learning and Verbal Behavior, 2,* 121–135.

Fry, D. B. (1966). The development of the phonological system in the normal and the deaf child. In F. Smith & G. A. Miller (Eds.). *The Genesis of Language,* pp. 187–206. Cambridge, MA: MIT Press.

Ginsburg, H., & Opper, S. (1969). *Piaget's Theory of Intellectual Development.* Englewood Cliffs, NJ: Prentice-Hall.

Gleitman, L. R., & Wanner, E. (1982). Language acquisition: The state of the state of the art. In E. Wanner & L. R. Gleitman (Eds.). *Language Acquisition: The State of the Art,* pp. 3–48. Cambridge: Cambridge University Press.

Hoff-Ginsberg, E., & Schatz, M. (1982). Linguistic input and the child's acquisition of language. *Psychological Bulletin, 92,* 3–26.

Ingram, D. (1978). The production of word-initial fricatives and affricates by normal and linguistically deviant children. In A. Caramazza & E. B. Zuriff (Eds.). *Language Acquisition and Language Breakdown,* pp. 63–85. Baltimore: Johns Hopkins University Press.

Irwin, O. C. (1949). Infant speech. *Scientific American,* offprint.

Jakobson, R. (1968). *Child Language, Aphasia, and Phonological Universals.* Translated by H. Keiler. The Hague: Mouton.

Kuczaj, S., III. (1983). *Crib Speech and Language Play.* NY: Springer-Verlag Inc.

Kuhl, P. K., & Meltzoff, A. N. (1982). The bimodal perception of speech in infancy. *Science, 218,* 1138–1141.

Lenneberg, E. (1967). *Biological Foundations of Language.* NY: John Wiley and Sons.

Liberman, I. Y., Shankweiler, D., Fischer, F. W., & Carter, B. (1974). Explicit syllable and phoneme segmentation in the young child. *Journal of Experimental Child Psychology, 18,* 201–212.

Lieberman, P. (1975). *On the Origins of Language.* NY: Macmillan.

MacKain, K., Studdert-Kennedy, M., Spieker, S., & Stern, D. (1983). Infant intermodal speech perception is a left hemisphere function. *Science, 219,* 1347–1349.

Macken, M. A., & Ferguson, C. A. (1981). Phonological universals in language acquisition. In H. Winitz (Ed.). *Native Language and Foreign Language Acquisition,* pp. 110–129. Annals of the New York Academy of Sciences, NY: New York Academy of Sciences, *379.*

McNeill, D. (1966). Developmental psycholinguistics. In F. Smith & G. A. Miller (Eds.). *The Genesis of Language,* pp. 15–84. Cambridge, MA: MIT Press.

———(1970). The development of language. In P. H. Mussen (Ed.). *Carmichael's Manual of Child Psychology,* pp.1061–1161. NY: John Wiley & Sons.

Meltzoff, A. N., & Moore, K. (1977). Imitation of facial and manual gestures by human neonates. *Science, 198,* 75–77.

Menn, L. (1981). Studies of phonological development. In H. Winitz (Ed.). *Native Language and Foreign Language Acquisition,* pp. 130–137. Annals of the New York Academy of Sciences, NY: New York Academy of Sciences.

Morse, P. A. (1972). The discrimination of speech and nonspeech stimuli in early infancy. *Journal of Experimental Child Psychology, 14,* 477–492.

Nelson, K. (1973). Structure and strategy in learning to talk. *Monographs of the Society for Research in Child Development, 38,* no. 149.

Peterson, C., & McCabe, A. (1983). *Developmental Psycholinguistics: Three Ways of Looking at a Child's Narrative.* NY: Plenum Press.

Piaget, J. (1952). *The Language and Thought of the Child.* NY: The Humanities Press.

———(1981). *Intelligence and Affectivity: Their Relationship During Child Development.* Translated and edited by T. A. Brown & C. E. Kaegi. Palo Alto, CA: Annual Reviews Inc.

———(1983). Views on the psychology of language and thought. In R. W, Rieber & G. Voyat (Eds.). *Dialogues on the Psychology of Language and Thought,* pp. 107–120. NY: Plenum Press.

Seitz, S., & Stewart, C. (1975). Imitations and expansions: Some developmental aspects of mother-child communications. *Developmental Psychology, 11,* 763–768.

Shipley, E. F., Smith, C. S., & Gleitman, L. R. (1969). A study in the acquisition of language: The responses to commands. *Language, 45,* 322–342.

Skinner, B. F. (1957). *Verbal Behavior.* NY: Appleton-Century-Crofts.

Slobin, D. I. (1966a). Grammatical transformations and sentence comprehension in childhood and adulthood. *Journal of Verbal Learning and Verbal Behavior, 5,* 219–227.

Slobin, D. I. (1966b). The acquisition of Russian as a native language. In F. Smith & G. A. Miller (Eds.). *The Genesis of Language,* pp. 129–148. Cambridge, MA: MIT Press.

Slobin, D. I., & Bever, T. G. (1982). Children use canonical sentence schemas: A cross-linguistic study of word order and inflections. *Cognition, 12,* 229–265.

Spring, D. R., & Dale, P. S. (1977). Discrimination of linguistic stress in early infancy. *Journal of Speech and Hearing Research, 20,* 224–232.

Strohner, H., & Nelson, K. E. (1974). The young child's development of sentence comprehension: Influence of event probability, nonverbal context, syntactic form and strategies. *Child Development, 65,* 567–576.

Streeter, L. A. (1976). Language perception of two-month-old infants shows effects of both innate mechanisms and experience. *Nature, 259,* 39–41.

Terrace, H. S., Petitto, L. A., Sanders, R. J., & Bever, T. G. (1979). Can an ape create a sentence? *Science, 206,* 891–902.

Tunmer, W. E., & Herriman, M. L. (1984). The development of metalinguistic awareness: A conceptual overview. In W. E. Tunmer, C. Pratt, & M. L. Herriman (Eds.). *Metalinguistic Awareness in Children: Theory, Research and Implications,* pp.12–35. NY: Springer-Verlag.

Tunmer, W. E., Pratt, C., & Herriman, M. L. (Eds.). (1984). *Metalinguistic Awareness in Children: Theory, Research and Implications.* NY: Springer-Verlag.

Vygotsky, L. (1962). *Thought and Language.* Edited and translated by E. Hanfmann & G. Vakar. Cambridge, MA: MIT Press.

Werner, H., & Kaplan, E. (1950). Development of word meaning through verbal context: An experimental study. *The Journal of Psychology, 29,* 251–257.

Winner, E., Rosenstiel, A. K., & Gardner, H. (1976). The development of metaphoric understanding. *Developmental Psychology, 12,* 289–297.

Witelson, S. F., & Pallie, W. (1973). Left hemisphere specialization for language in the newborn: Neuroanatomical evidence of asymmetry. *Brain, 96,* 641–646.

STUDY QUESTIONS

1. Critically compare and contrast the transformational, Piagetian, and behaviorist approaches to language acquisition. What is the major philosophical position of each with respect to the roles of innate structures and learning? In *your* view which position best represents the language acquisition data presented in this chapter? Why? Pick a few (not all!) examples.

2. Take the design features for language and communication presented in Chapter 8 and, for each, discuss when and how it appears in child language acquisition. At what age do you think children "have language?" Which (if any) design features do you therefore consider noncritical? (Be sure in your answer to present data from language acquisition, such as when and in what form children first use the vocal-auditory channel or exhibit displacement.)

3. Prepare a chart for language development. Try to assemble, with respect to rough age-groups, the phonological, semantic, morphological, syntactic, metalinguistic, and discourse skills discussed.

10

Human Communication in the Absence of a Language Model

What happens if children are neglected for 13 years or so and thus are exposed neither to the human social contact usual for developing language nor to the specific language structures during early maturation? Can they learn language? Do they go through the same pattern of acquisition at a later age when exposed to language, or have some critical periods for learning passed so that new techniques must be used for language learning? Do the adult models treat alinguistic adolescents in the same way as they treat alinguistic infants, producing the same language examples for both, or do they naturally employ different "teaching" techniques? Does it matter if the duration of social deprivation is for the first two years, the first six years, or the first 13 years?

What happens if children are not neglected, are treated lovingly, but are not exposed by parents to appropriate language—say, if the children are deaf? In this case the social situation should be appropriate to stimulate communication rather than suppress it, but specific language experience is removed. Do children spontaneously activate innate language structures? What form do these take given the absence of both the adult example and auditory feedback from the child's own productions?

In the last chapter we examined the development of human communication under normal circumstances—in a loving, caring home with native-language speaking caretakers interacting with the infant, if not actively teaching. We raised the issue of whether some aspects of language acquisition might be innate or reflexive, whether some might be innate but require environmental interaction to prime, perhaps during critical periods, or whether language was completely learned, in the same manner as other associations. We also questioned the effect of parental interaction on language development: Do parents tailor their language to the child and does this help the child learn? Do parents correct or expand the child's utterances and does this facilitate learning?

Study of normal language acquisition cannot yield definitive answers to these questions because in normal acquisition all factors are confounded: The child is cared for and given appropriate stimulation; the child receives language input from birth so it is difficult to tell whether there is a critical period; and the parents are appropriate interactive responders so we cannot tell if the child is being shaped by them or would learn language anyway. In this chapter we will look at some cases of abnormal language acquisition that can help separate these individual potential influences. Two types of abnormal input will be examined: (1) neglected, abandoned, or abused children who have been deprived both of social contact generally and language contact specifically; and (2) congenitally deaf children raised in loving homes but without specific training in manual language. (In the next chapter we will look at the language of deaf children raised by deaf parents who sign and so are provided with a language from birth, like normal hearing children, but without speech. It is important to note the difference!)

Interpreting the "Experiments": Some Cautions

The data we will be discussing in this chapter derive from case histories. Case histories are not experiments in the optimal sense of the word. In an experiment, the experimenters control potential outside influences and carefully manipulate the factor(s) they are interested in studying. An ideal although horribly unethical experiment would be to take identical triplets, raise one with normal language, one with love but no language, and one in isolation with only physical needs attended to (à la Psammetichos—see Chapter 1). In this case we would know that the subjects were genetically identical and therefore should mature at the same rate, and we would be able to attribute differences in language acquisition clearly to their environments.

In the case histories we will be examining, we have in many instances no knowledge of whether the child was normal at birth or what its experiences were before its discovery by civilization. Therefore, if the child does *not* develop language normally we do not know whether that was because the child had an innate learning disability (which might have led to its neglect or abandonment) and would never have learned language, or was too old to learn language at the point of discovery.

A second problem of interpretation lies in the fact that 13 years of neglect does not mean 13 years of no experience. Aside from the lack of social stimulation, which might deter language learning, an adolescent will have learned how to survive in whatever bizarre world has been created for it. For example, one of the children we will study, Genie, upon discovery at age 13, displayed an unnatural love of plastic objects, preferring them to other toys or objects provided for her entertainment, collecting not only plastic jewelry and toys but also plastic plates, trash cans, and so forth. One interpretation of this could be that all children innately like plastic, but most are deflected from this interest by early exposure to stuffed animals or whatever. A second interpretation might be that at the age of 13 a love of plastic unfolds in all children but is not normally noticed because so many other interests are still being pursued from earlier development. The third, and in this case obviously more likely, explanation is that something happened in this child's experience that caused an abnormal interest in plastic. In Genie's case the only objects in the room where she was confined for many years were plastic raincoats and plastic cottage cheese containers. Although in this case it seems obvious that the cause must have been Genie's prior experience, when language appears abnormal it is not always clear that the cause of the abnormality is likewise traceable to prior experience.

A similar, if less dramatic, difficulty appears in interpreting language acquisition data from deaf children raised in homes where the parents were deliberately suppressing gestural communication to encourage or force the child to learn to speak and lipread. Although the motive is benign, the suppression may "teach" the child not to try to communicate at all. Other parents of deaf children take the approach of gesturing more frequently, in the interest of teaching about the environment ("don't touch that; it will burn" must be conveyed), and this experience with manual communication can affect the child's later abilities to learn speech or lipreading.

The final problem in interpreting data on language development in older children is that the "teaching" techniques are probably not identical. When talking to an infant, adults use simpler sentences, redundant with nonverbal context, and exaggerate facial expressions and intonation, as discussed in the last chapter. When adults do not understand (because they are foreign or deaf or whatever) other adults tend to get angry and talk louder and slower but do not change syntax or vocabulary to accommodate them. It is quite possible that part of our innate response as adults to "babyishness," in addition to finding it cute and wanting to care for it, may be a simplified language pattern. Older children will not elicit the same sympathy for crying or wetting themselves; likewise they may not elicit the same sympathy by their lack of understanding or elicit the same parental language teaching program. Thus, the older child's different learning pattern could arise either from a different teaching program by the caretaker, or by a different set of skills brought to language learning by maturity or prior experience.

Feral Children

From time to time children have been discovered surviving alone in the wild and believed to have been reared by animals. Probably the best known of such stories in our society is the legend of Romulus and Remus, typical in many respects except for the ultimate stardom of the abandoned children. Romulus and Remus were twin heirs to an ancient throne, ordered drowned by a usurping uncle. Rather than drown them, their executioner set the infants in a basket and placed it in the flooding, turbulent waters of the Tiber. Some time later a pair of healthy, if grubby, infants were discovered in the den of a she-wolf, downriver, apparently suckled by the animal. Restored to civilization, the infants lived to found Rome. Similar stories, occasionally based on stronger evidence of animal rearing, have arisen in many parts of the world.

Credibility of Reports

Whether such children are in fact reared by animals or manage to survive by themselves in the wild is a moot question. As several investigators (Tyler, 1863; Zingg, 1940; Dennis, 1941, for example) have noted, there is a bias on the part of observers to attribute rearing of wild children to animals: Such children are not socialized like humans and it is assumed that they have acquired their "manners" from animals; there is a reluctance to believe that a small child can exist alone in the wild, and so it is surmised that the child has received assistance from animals; and such children are often discovered in animal dens or in the company of animals, suggesting to the discoverers that the association is customary.

However, skeptical investigators have pointed out that the animals assigned the role of foster parents vary in different regions correlated with the prevailing mythology of the region: In parts of the world where wolves are accorded near-human status (as in our concept of werewolves as repositories for condemned human souls), wolves emerge as frequent adopters. In parts of the world where bears are seen as humanlike, bears seem to rear abandoned infants more than wolves. This suggests a lack of objectivity on the part of the observers. Moreover, discovery in an animal den or in the company of animals does not necessarily imply rearing by those animals. The child may have fled from human pursuers and taken shelter in the cave of an animal but not permanently live there. Finally, reports of suckling of children for several years are incredible because most mammal mothers wean their own young after a few months and would be likely to generalize those habits to their human adoptee.

Review of Early Cases

It would be good to know whether the wild children had indeed been raised with the benefits of social company of animals or lived in isolation. However, even without that knowledge, we can look at their behavior before and after rehabilitation to society to see what deprivation of human contact in the early years produces. There is no doubt that there have been children who have suffered extreme neglect and survived, and interestingly, these children seem to show similar perceptual, social, linguistic, and cognitive capabilities on initial rescue. Some have managed total rehabilitation to society; others have never completely recovered from their early experience. Whether the differences are due to individual differences among the children, differences in their prewilderness or wilderness experience, or differences in the age at which rehabilitation began is indeterminable.

Zingg (1940) reviewed 31 such reported cases beginning in the fourteenth century. The common characteristics (aside from observer bias) were insensitivity to heat and cold, unwillingness to share, repressed sexual expression, keen eyesight especially at night, and beastlike eating habits such as sniffing food before eating, killing and eating animals raw, eating raw starches and vegetables (like potatoes), and a distaste for normal human foods like bread. Many of the children were also reported to run on all fours and to be quite scarred and calloused. Most were mute when discovered and made at most animal-like sounds. Of these 31 children, four learned to talk reasonably fluently (one became a nun), and one acquired 50 words after recovery. For two of those who acquired fluent speech there are no data about the age of rescue or methods of teaching language (this includes the nun); another of them was recovered at about age 10; the last, Kasper Hauser, was not a wild child but one imprisoned with human caretakers, and so his recovery is not as remarkable. He will be discussed in the next section. Given the paucity of data on the other children, as Zingg decided, it is unwarranted to draw conclusions about their capacities. However, we should note that most of the children who could not be rehabilitated to speak were discovered at 8–12 years of age.

The child who learned 50 words is a documented case of a child reared by animals. She was discovered in 1920 in India at about age 8. Rumors had been reported that children were seen running with the wolves, and they were tracked to a den. In the den were discovered two children, one about 8 and one about 1½, clasped together in a ball with two wolf cubs (Brown, 1958). The younger child, named Amala, died within a year after rescue, having begun to utter some sounds. The older child, Kamala, lived for about 10 years, developed social skills, and learned 50 words.

Victor—A Well-Documented Case

The wild child for whom there are the most data, Victor, was discovered more than a century before Amala and Kamala, roaming the fields of France (see Lane, 1979). He was about 13 at the time of his final rescue and return to civilization. He was entrusted to the care of Dr. Itard, who "experimented" with the child to see (1) what the condition of a man-of-nature really was (an important philosophical issue of the time), and (2) whether such a person can be rehabilitated to a "normal" life.

Perceptual Sensitivities. The same reports were made of Victor, "the wild boy of Aveyron," as of most wild children—insensitive to temperature, uncivilized appetites, running on all fours, and so on. Some of these Dr. Itard substantiated and some he refuted. Victor was able to thrust his hand into a fire to retrieve potatoes and he would eat them directly, making noises of pain, indicating that he did feel, but ignored, the heat. He was able to run naked—in fact, preferred to do so—in the dead of winter and showed no sensitivity to the cold. Generally, he sniffed his food before eating and preferred potatoes and nuts (raw) to cooked meats, bread, and vegetables. Finally, Dr. Itard never observed him going around on all fours, nor were his palms and knees particularly calloused as they would have been if this had been his usual mode of locomotion. Dr. Itard wrote that he doubted it was possible for a human to assume such a stance comfortably or efficiently.

Training Victor. Victor was trained by Dr. Itard for five years, during which time he showed considerable progress in sensory, emotional, moral, cognitive, and linguistic development. Of as much interest as Victor's progress are Dr. Itard's teaching methods, often foreshadowing the behavioristic techniques of shaping, fading, reinforcing, and punishing. His procedure has influenced current educational programs for the deaf, mentally disabled, and psychotic, and also the Montessori program of education.

Developing the Experience of Punishment and Reinforcement. The first problem was that Victor seemed relatively insensitive to outside stimulation, so that little could serve as reinforcement or punishment. Moreover, Victor seemed to have very short visual and auditory attention spans. His main motivations were to escape and to obtain physical needs like food. To increase Victor's sensitivities, Dr. Itard began a program of tactile stimulation, giving the boy long hot baths and massages. This increased not only his temperature and tactile awareness (he began to dislike going out in the cold, would test his bath water before entering it, and enjoyed stroking velvet) but also generalized to all forms of sensory stimulation. The next task was to develop, in modern terminology, secondary reinforcers, so that social praise and toys might be directly stimulating, removing Victor from the beastlike interest in food. Dr. Itard accomplished this while improving Victor's visual attention. He placed a nut (the primary reinforcer) under one of three cups and rewarded Victor with the nut if he was able to keep track of it when he moved the cups. Eventually the "shell game" became fun in and of itself and the primary reinforcer could be faded. Similarly, secondary reinforcers were mapped to trips outside and so on. Eventually, social reinforcement or punishment (a look of praise or dismay) was sufficient to control behaviors.

Developing Emotions. Dr. Itard was also interested in measuring and training emotional responses. At first Victor was never seen to cry, although sometimes he smiled or laughed. After some time in civilization he would shed tears, and interestingly, tears of joy—on reuniting with his governess after an escape, and then again, when she reproached him, in sadness, at the tone of her voice. Victor also began to exhibit more "refined" emotions. Shortly after his governess' husband had died he set the table with a place setting for the man, as had been customary. This caused an outburst of grief from the widow, which seemed to cause Victor considerable pain. He cleared the place setting and never again made that error. Another time, Dr. Itard deliberately pretended to be about to punish Victor after correct performance on a lesson, to see how Victor would respond to the injustice. Normally, Victor submitted passively to punishment, but on this occasion resisted, ultimately biting the doctor, who delighted in the exhibit of moral consciousness.

It might seem that we have digressed considerably from a discussion of language, but it is important to realize that *language serves a function of human communication in human social settings.* As such, it must be understood first that communication is possible and necessary to enable participation in a social group, and second, that interaction in the group depends on a shared understanding of "rules" within the culture. Both language and nonverbal communication depend on this shared understanding. Thus, for someone whose "culture" is 13 years of isolated living in the wild, the first step is socialization, to understand the speakers' culture. Language depends not only on the understanding necessary for communication but also on specific cognitive and perceptual skills. To understand speech, for example, hearing must be good, differential attention must be paid to vocal noises and other noises, some variations in speech sounds must be ignored and others attended to (categorical perception), and memory must be developed sufficiently to store the rapidly fading signals. After socialization, therefore, it is necessary to assess and develop cognitive and perceptual abilities before language training itself.

Teaching Speech. With respect to language development and language training, Dr. Itard noted first that Victor was neither deaf nor mute. Victor would turn when there was a sudden loud noise or the softer noise produced by cracking a nut. Victor made laughing sounds spontaneously and was induced to imitate some speech sounds. The process of teaching imitation was to strike one of three noisemakers (a bell or drum, for example) and then allow Victor the opportunity of reproducing the action. After Victor learned this task, Dr. Itard moved to reproduction of sound in the vocal tract, which took a long time, and resulted only in the acquisition of only a few vowels. Lane (1979) pointed out that Victor might have learned more speech had Dr. Itard better understood phonology; he trained by using the letters of the alphabet, which as we know have many different sound representations and thus can cause confusion in learning pronunciation. A better choice would have been to teach through articulatory features, which map more directly to the vocal gestures Victor would have been trying to make, or phonemes, for which, unlike letters, there is a straightforward sound association.

Teaching Visual Speech. Despairing at last of teaching Victor speech, Dr. Itard began to teach him language through vision, using gestural communication and written words. Victor spontaneously "gestured"—fetching coats to indicate he wanted to go out, fetching other people's coats to indicate he had wearied of their visits, and understanding when handed a pitcher that he was to go fetch water. Unfortunately, this was never worked into a sign system.

Instead, Dr. Itard trained written language, using a method of shaping. First, Victor was required to select for each of several objects the picture of that object. Victor would not do this spontaneously. To train it, Dr. Itard drew on an attention to order that he had observed in Victor's personal habits: He placed some objects in a row with their pictures behind them and then scrambled the objects, indicating to Victor that he was to put them in the order marked by the pictures (the original order). Victor complied, but Dr. Itard noted that the correct performance could have been due to a memory for the original order or to a match of the objects to the pictures. To test this he changed the order of the pictures; Victor still returned the objects to the original order. By increasing the number of pictures and objects and the frequency of their scrambling, Dr. Itard succeeded in getting Victor to attend to the pictures as representations of the objects.

Then the second stage began: mapping the letter names (written words) to the pictures. This also initially failed because Victor did not know the letters of the alphabet. Backtracking, Dr. Itard taught him the alphabet by using a *matching-to-sample* technique, where one cut-out letter was given as a sample and Victor had to select the matching alternative from a set of cut-out letters. This technique was used to train finer and finer discriminations until Victor had learned the alphabet.

Then spelling was taught on a board on which letters could be mounted, also using matching-to-sample, a technique similar to that used by Premack with Sarah more than a century and a half later. Victor was taught how to spell names of objects he frequently requested like "lait" (French for milk) so that he could use his written language to make such requests. Several such words were taught, ending the first *nine months* of Victor's return to civilization. At that time Dr. Itard made his first report on Victor's progress, in which he concluded that man's nature when deprived of civilization is nonintelligent, amoral, and savage, that social responses and social needs must be learned, that individualized training could overcome previous experience, and

> That this imitative force, whose purpose is the education of his organs and especially the apprenticeship of speech, and which is very energetic and active during the first years of his life, wanes rapidly with age, with isolation, and with all the causes which tend to blunt nervous sensitivity. We may conclude that the articulation of sounds, indisputably the most unimaginable and useful result of imitation, must encounter innumerable obstacles at any age later than early childhood.
>
> (*quoted in Lane, 1979, p. 129*)

Teaching Words. Dr. Itard continued training Victor for another 4½ years, at the end of which he wrote a second report. During this time, he taught Victor to apply the names of objects he had learned to object classes rather than to individual objects (in Skinner's term, extended tacts; see Chapter 2). To do this, he had to teach similarities between objects that had previously been considered different—for example, a knife and a razor could be individual objects that form a class of "cutting tool" or some such. Once the similarity was learned in these disparate objects, the principles of object classes formed by shared function (such as "tool"), visual similarity, or whatever, were acquired. Not only did this training give Victor the needed "rules" for forming semantic classes but it also provided a new mental flexibility: Victor in one instance took a small, curved picture down from the wall and held it horizontally as a substitute for a plate, to mand (again, using Skinner's term) food. Beyond teaching extended tacts and additional object names, during this second phase Dr. Itard taught Victor adjectives and verbs: A large book and small book were selected and Victor was taught to differentiate them using the appropriate adjective, then the adjective pair was transferred to nails to see if the concept was learned; familiar objects were manipulated differently and then their names combined with verbs indicating the manipulation, and the verbs were then transferred to manipulations of new objects.

As Victor's vocabulary and grammar grew the placement of the word names on the board became more and more cumbersome, and Dr. Itard taught Victor to write by imitation. Ultimately, Victor was able to write written words from memory and to use his writing to communicate his needs. Details about the size of his vocabulary or complexity of his grammar are not available.

Summary

There are several fascinating points to be gleaned from Victor's story (together with those of the other wild children). Probably most important is the fact that there is some language recovery even after a long period of isolation. This could be because the wild children did have some language before their life in the wild. As Dennis (1951) observed, to survive on their own in the wild the exposure of most of the children must have occurred past infancy, so that they were already mobile and eating solid foods. This suggests that they were somewhat socialized before their wild lives started. The effects of this early experience are not observable in any of the reports of wild children, arguing *against* a hypothesis of durability of early experience. On the other hand, most were not able to shed the effects of years in the wild to learn language, which most of the investigators use, illogically, to support the notion of permanence of early experience.

If Victor knew no language when abandoned, we could conclude that the critical period for such things as symbolic naming or forming simple sentences extends to the teens, if it ends ever. On the other hand, spontaneous naming, spontaneous vocal imitation, and vocalization seem to require early stimulation to emerge. (If Victor knew some language before being abandoned in the wild, we can draw similar conclusions, except that we would have to say that functions like symbolic naming do not require continuous stimulation to be maintained whereas functions like vocalization do.)

It is interesting to note also that basic social and perceptual responses need encouragement in early childhood or they either die out or are never formed. Note too that aspects of a written language may be acquired in the absence of speaking a language to "sound it out to." (It is, of course, possible that Victor's ability to perceive speech was intact and writing may have been associated to that.)

Finally, we must note the parallels and relative effectiveness between Dr. Itard's teaching techniques and those used to train chimpanzees to communicate, or to "train" normal children. There is no question that operant procedures can be effective tools for teaching language and can work as well for humans as for chimpanzees. Whether Victor learned more (or less) than Sarah as a result of his human nature (or years in the wild) is impossible to say, given the information we have available on his language. But there can be no question that he was given different and more rigorous language training than are most children, with a less beneficial effect. His poorer performance may be due to his age at first exposure, the years of neglect, the differences in training technique, or some combination of these causes.

In sum, although we are not sure about Victor's earliest experiences, the advances that he made after rescue suggest that the effects of early experience are not immutable: Either he changed twice, losing early socializing in the wild and then losing wild behavior back in civilization, or only once, with the latter. Language did not unfold in Victor or the other children once they were exposed to it, either because they were past the age for a language acquisition device to work, or because there is no such device. At late ages vocabulary, concepts, and perhaps syntax seem to be teachable at least by behaviorist techniques. This does *not* prove that such techniques are used in natural language acquisition, since it is conceivable that natural language learning may make use of some innate structures the critical period for which had passed in these children. Finally, Victor's case and Dr. Itard's success point to the importance of social environment in the development of language.

Deprived Children

In the last section we looked at language development in children socially isolated from human culture. The isolation has two obvious potential effects, both of which have to be overcome by specific training for rehabilitation. The first is the absence of appropriate social stimulation and social contact. The second is the lack of specific language training or language models during the young years. In the feral children we cannot tell if learning failures are the result of either of these causes or both.

There are several reported cases of children who are raised without a language model or normal cognitive and sensory stimulation, but who still have contact with some semblance of human society, so they do not have to fend for themselves, do not acquire savage mannerisms, and are not forming their first human affectionate contacts in their early teens. Efforts to rehabilitate these children have been far more successful than those for the wild children.

Early Cases

Kasper Hauser.   An early such case is that of Kasper Hauser, found in 1828 at about the age of 17, referred to in the previous section as one of the cases restored to fluent speech. He has been assumed to have been the heir to a throne of a small state in Germany, imprisoned at a young age in a cellar dungeon and hidden from view so the usurpers' plot would not be discovered. His memories after discovery indicate some contact with human beings: He had two hobbyhorses and a toy dog to play with and was fed on bread and water. He also spoke one sentence on discovery, quite garbled, but indicating nevertheless some language before imprisonment or some human contact thereafter. (Note the former suggests that he *forgot* his language during confinement.) He lived for only five years after rescue, in which time he recovered fluent speech and learned to read and write fluently, enough to become a legal clerk.

Unlike the wild children, there was no report for Kasper of bizarre eating habits, temperature insensitivities, and so forth. His first response to a view from a window, after years in a cellar, however, was one of horror, and he later recounted that this visual experience was completely chaotic until he had traveled outside to some extent and learned to identify certain visual sensations with buildings, animals, and other objects.

Anna.   Within this century there have been several cases of similarly deprived children (in the United States), for whom we have more data on their initial condition, their training, and their ultimate condition. Anna (Davis, 1940, 1947) was "found" when she was five years old. She had been illegitimate and her mother's father was furious at her birth. He had tried to farm her out to several foster homes, but the social welfare agency decided ultimately that she should go home. Her grandfather then kept Anna and her mother confined in the attic. Note that although deprived, she still had the social company and care of her mother (who was similarly deprived).

Anna was visited by Davis three days after her removal to an orphanage. Davis reported that her reflexes were good, that she was able to localize to sound, that she showed good touch sensitivities, and that she was able to grasp and manipulate objects with her hands. However, she displayed a general apathy and did not engage in social play but in asocial ritualistic play with her own fingers. (*Ritualistic* means repetitive— where the same movement or movement sequence is performed over and over again. Finger drumming is ritualistic as is hair twirling, both ritualistic behaviors observed in many normal adults.) A year later she was able to walk alone, respond to verbal commands, and recognize people, and she displayed some interest in getting attention from others. She was still relatively insensitive to outside stimuli, barely wincing when a blown-up paper bag was popped. Interestingly, a clinician who visited her at the time reported that her spontaneous speech was in the "babbling stage" (Davis, 1947, p. 433). It is unclear whether this means that the six-year-old was now engaging in the same kind of behavior found in six-month-olds (babbling many sounds from different languages) or was speaking unintelligibly; no other reports of babbling in isolated children at such a late age have appeared.

On Davis' last visit in 1941 Anna had regained considerable physical coordination: She was able to bounce and catch a ball and eat with a spoon. She also spoke like a two-year-old, using some simple sentences. She died the following year; so whether her language development would have continued to progress will never be known. Nevertheless, she, like Kasper Hauser and unlike the wild children, showed gains in recovering speech. This could be because of her relatively young age or because of her incomplete isolation from human society.

Anna had not been given specific, individual training as had Victor; she was placed in an orphanage and given only physical care. Her recovery might have been stronger and quicker had she been specifically treated and trained. Another child of about the same age at discovery, and at about the same time, Isabelle, made considerably greater progress, but with specific training.

Isabelle. Isabelle (Mason, 1942) was imprisoned, with her mother, by her maternal grandfather. Her mother seems to have done her best to care for her, making her social deprivation less than in the previous cases, but the mother could not provide a language model, being both deaf and mute from brain damage suffered in a traumatic accident that occurred when she was only two. Therefore Isabelle spent her first six and a half years in silence; then her mother escaped with her and had her admitted to a hospital. Perhaps because of the separation from her mother, Isabelle spent her first few days in the hospital in tears and then displayed a generally flat, apathetic affect, not uncommon for young children undergoing separation from a parent.

Mason was able to capture Isabelle's interest by lavishing attention on another child on the ward; Isabelle began to imitate what the other child was doing to get attention for herself. Mason then initiated a game of labeling body parts and jewelry to which Isabelle could point, beginning language training. Although the child was attentive to sounds and learned to respond to the different names and readily imitated gestures, she did not spontaneously imitate speech. This had to be shaped. After one month she produced single words: mama, fat, pretty, and bye, in appropriate contexts. Two months later she had progressed to short sentences, also appropriately: "That's my baby [doll]," "open your eyes," "'top it [stop it]," and "[æ]t's mine [that's mine]." At the same time she was also able to read some printed words. A year after rehabilitation began she was able to write, count, add 10, listen attentively to stories, and paraphrase the stories with her own small vocabulary.

Eighteen months after initial training her vocabulary was estimated to be 1500–2000 words and her sentence structure was complex. Examples of spontaneous questions she asked were: Why does the paste come out if one upsets the jar? What did Miss Mason say when you told her I cleaned my classroom? Do you go to Miss

Mason's school at the university? These illustrate knowledge of correct inflectional morphology, pronouns, and prepositions, and more impressively, good grasp of linguistic meaning and world knowledge and complex syntactic structure like question formation, sentence conjunction, and embedding.

It is obvious that Isabelle's recovery was spectacular, compared with that of other children we have discussed. Moreover, in her case, it is likely that she had little, if any, early exposure to language, since her mother's condition precluded that. (It is possible that her grandfather talked to her, but given his general neglect, not likely.) We can attribute the extent of her recovery to several factors: her lack of *social* isolation, since she had a strong relationship with her mother; her young age on discovery; and the specific individual training she received. Her social contacts made the trainer's task easier in that social needs did not have to be taught: Isabelle cried (recall that tears were rare in wild children until after socialization) and sought human attention; therefore attention and its removal could be used immediately as social reinforcers and punishers. Her age and training enabled her to learn speech, impossible for Victor. Still, speech acquisition seems markedly different at six and a half than at one year: There is no spontaneous imitation and no play with sounds, once produced. Grammatical and semantic skills are recoverable, and indeed, at six and a half Isabelle went from the one word "stage" to MLU>2 (and learned to read!) about 12 times faster than happens normally.

Conclusions.   Comparing Isabelle and Anna with the wild children, we can see the benefits of early exposure to language as well as early exposure to some society. There are several reasons that these children may have advanced beyond Victor. They were younger, and from the standpoint of LAD or critical periods, the innate guide or blueprint for language learning may still have been operative. From a learning standpoint, we can observe that they had less experience before socialization, which would have meant less to overcome to acquire new habits. And finally, they were younger and so what they may have been expected to learn may have better matched their capabilities.

To clarify this last point, consider the six-and-a-half-year-old Isabelle, who from a Piagetian standpoint should be either preoperational or in the concrete operation stage. She should be developing and modifying schemes for concrete objects, which would also be what her teachers would be providing labels for. Victor, at 13 and a survivor, would no longer be studying objects like potatoes and nuts to produce complete schemes for them since he already would have such schemes. Therefore when Dr. Itard would try to direct attention back to those objects to teach a label, there would be a mismatch that could retard learning. (It might be useful to compare this to our trying to learn a second language by reading a grade-school primer in that language. On the surface it seems that it should be a good way to learn vocabulary, since the syntax will not be overwhelming and there are many pictures and an easy to follow story. Unfortunately, for adults who have mastered formal operations, the task would probably be too boring to concentrate on sufficiently to learn the vocabulary.)

Thus, we might consider that the facile language learning we see in the younger children lies in their being provided labels for the things that are uppermost in their thoughts. The advanced development of Isabelle over Victor can thus be incorporated into any of our theoretical frameworks for language acquisition. By contrast to Victor's, her case supports, for whatever reason, the importance of early exposure for language learning. The two cases together emphasize the importance of social contact in language acquisition.

A Well-Documented Case: Genie

The isolated child for whom we have the most data is known as Genie (Curtiss, Fromkin, Krashen, Rigler, and Rigler, 1974; Fromkin, Krashen, Curtiss, Rigler, and Rigler, 1974; Curtiss, 1977). Discovered in 1971, she has been tested and trained according to current psycholinguistic theory and procedures, as presented in the earlier chapters of this book. Thus, her skills are most easily compared with normal language acquisition and normal adult language.

History. Genie's history resembles that of Anna and Isabelle. She was born to a weak mother and abusive father who hated children. They had had two children previously: The older had died of pneumonia from being kept in the garage; the younger was saved from a similar fate by the father's mother. Unfortunately for Genie, this woman died about a year after Genie's birth, unleashing the father's full abuse. The father preserved his mother's room as a sanctuary, and Genie was confined in the only other room on that floor. Strapped to a chair by day and bundled in a special harness at night, Genie was severely restricted in both movement and sensation. The only visual "decoration" in her room was two plastic raincoats hanging on the wall. A single window allowed light but was too high for to see out of. She also heard few sounds since the room next to hers was empty and her father, hating noise, did not allow either a television set or a radio in the house and beat Genie for any sound she made. Her food was restricted to baby foods, fed to her by spoon.

Hospital records indicate that Genie was probably normal at birth; she weighed 7½ pounds and appeared alert. She had a congenital hip dislocation, which was treated, and she was seen twice by the doctor for putting on and removing the splint. Both times she seemed normal, although at the second visit, when she was nearly a year old, she was somewhat underweight.

She was not discovered until she was 13½ when her mother, who was nearly blind, persuaded her father to be allowed to go to an eye doctor for treatment. Genie accompanied her and as soon as she was seen in public she was recognized as highly abnormal and taken to a social welfare agency. The father committed suicide the following day.

Condition on Discovery. Suffering from severe malnutrition, Genie was admitted to a hospital. Like the wild children, she was insensitive to temperature and touch. She was also completely silent, even throwing tantrums without making a sound— not surprising considering that she had been punished for every whimper. Unlike the wild children, her attitude was social: She made good eye contact and gave the impression of understanding to the hospital staff. Within one month after her removal to the hospital she recognized the words Genie, mother, walk, go, no, don't, door, jewelry, box, rattle, bunny, red, blue, green, and brown. She attended to mouth movements and tried to imitate them, soundlessly. Seven months after admission to the hospital (age 14.2) her doctor recorded the following conversations:

Dr. We have to put it back now.
G. Back.
Dr. That's hot.
G. Burn.

Language tests. *Sound Skills.* Genie was first tested formally in 1973, three years after her rescue (age 16½). She had in the meantime been discharged from the hospital and placed in a foster home, where she received informal "training" from her foster family in communication, much as any child would. (Note, however, that Genie was a teenager in appearance, therefore likely to elicit different communication behaviors from the family than would an infant.) The tests she was given were designed to measure various linguistic skills. Speech perception was measured by use of a picture selection task in which the picture names differed in only one phoneme, for example, lamb and lamp. Both initial and final consonant discrimination were measured, as was consonant cluster perception. In the entire battery, Genie made only two errors. Another test measured her mental representation of sound, not just immediate discriminations. She was presented with two pictures and an unrelated word. Her task was to select the picture whose name rhymed with the word. This task, too, presented no problems.

Imitation was good except for pitch and volume control. In spontaneous speech, however, her pitch was abnormally high and her voice very breathy, and she tended to distort the sounds, simplifying consonant clusters by deleting a consonant or by inserting schwas between the consonants, neutralizing vowels, dropping final consonants, deleting unstressed syllables, and "reducing" consonants of other manner classes to stops of the same place of articulation. Examples of her spontaneous utterances (refer to Table 6.1 for phonetic translations) are:

all → /ɔ/	blue → /bəlu/
touch → /tʌ/	stop spitting → /tapapItI/
soup → /su/	little → /lIˀ/
blouse → /bæᵘ/	

In addition, at times /z, s, ð, θ, h/ were reproduced as /d/ or /t/ and /m/ as /b/. None of the alterations Genie made were hard and fast; sometimes she would produce a word perfectly and at other times transform it.

Comprehension Skills. More important for *language* acquisition than sound production or perception are the higher language functions: syntax, morphology, and semantics. As noted earlier, Genie was attentive and responsive to the hospital staff from the first. Her comprehension of their instructions was dependent on pantomime and gestures; words alone did not suffice. One month after admission, for example, her doctor asked with appropriate context, "Do you want to look again?" and Genie looked, and subsequently, again with the nonverbal situation clear, "Look at Mrs. M. now; do you see her?" and Genie went up and touched her. Her response also included at times a vocalization, either imitative ("Is that fun?" → "/f ∧ /") or unintelligible.

Grammatical Skills. A year after placement in the foster home, specific grammatical comprehension tests were administered. Genie was tested for comprehension of negative versus affirmative sentences, adjectives, prepositions, singular versus plural nouns, conjunctions (e.g., "and" versus "or"), pronouns, comparatives (e.g., "bigger" versus "smaller"), superlatives (e.g., "biggest" versus "smallest"), tenses, actives versus passives, questions, and relative clauses. The tests required either selection of the appropriate picture (e.g., "show me the bunny that does [not] have a carrot") or manipulation of objects to fit the sentence (e.g., "put the blue fox in [on, next to, . . .] the white box").

From the first Genie was perfect or nearly perfect at differentiating affirmative from negative sentences, polar (e.g., "hot" versus "cold") and comparative (e.g., "hotter") adjectives, the pronouns "all," "one," and "they," "each other," and "themselves," and color words. The particular words "big" and "little" she interpreted first as absolute quantities, but as soon as she realized they were relative measures, her performance was perfect. Superlatives were understood about 70 percent of the time, except for "biggest," which was always correct. "Some" was confused first with "all," then with "one" and never understood properly. With the exception of those mentioned, she could not distinguish or use most personal pronouns properly. She perfectly understood "and" but consistently interpreted "or" as "and." Her performance on prepositions showed relatively steady improvement but was never perfect, with great variation between individual items. She was almost 98 percent correct on "in" from the first but only 40 percent correct on "under." Curtiss (1977) observed that opposite prepositions like "behind" and "in front of" were acquired as a pair rather than in the normal pattern of using both interchangeably for one concept. Similarly she seemed to learn polar adjectives as a pair rather than first acquiring the positive form and then the opposite.

Looking at the morphemes frequently studied in English acquisition (see Chapter 9) we find some similarities but many differences between Genie's performance and normal children's. Without specific drilling, Genie performed at chance in differentiating singular and plural items. Curtiss trained all morphophonemic variants (e.g., /s/, /z/, /əz/) of the plural, repeating them with appropriate pictures, after which Genie performed perfectly. The tenses tested were the future (will, going to), the present progressive (is -ing), and the past (regular, irregular, and finish + VP). Genie's performance was good only on the "going" form of the future and the "finish" form of the past, indicating that she did understand the meaning behind tenses but not the morphemes marking them. It is particularly interesting to contrast her performance after four years of experience with normal children who acquire the present progressive first, at about two and a half, and the rest of these forms by age four (see Table 9.2). It is also interesting to compare her performance with the six-and-a-half-year-old Isabelle, who clearly surpassed her with respect to complexity of sentence structure and semantic relations expressed.

Genie's performance was, not surprisingly, worse with derivationally complex sentences, the next level of grammar. Her comprehension of subject and object in testing was poor for *both* actives and passives; her best performances on the final tests was 74 percent on *nonreversible actives* (e.g., the boy watered the plant, where inter-preting the plant as subject is nonsensical). Similarly her performance was poor on answering wh-questions such as "what is the blue box on?" or "what is on the blue box?" with poorer performance on object-questions, such as the former, than subject-questions, such as the latter, as is found in normally reared children. She also had difficulty with relative clauses and, as is normally found, the greatest difficulty with center-embedding. The only transformation that she understood well was negation—in simple sentences, as already mentioned, and also in complex sentences such as "the book that is (not) red is on the table."

Discussion of Performance on the Tests.   It is important to observe that although her performance was poor in these tests, the testing situation was constrained. Com-paring her performance on these tests with normal children's performance in spon-taneous conversation from transcriptions, as were used for Table 9.2, puts Genie auto-matically at a disadvantage. Genie's spontaneous performance exceeded her test scores as well. In real life there are additional cues—the context usually indicates who the actor and who the object really are. In the test situation one is presented with two pictures of actors and object, either of which might be described by the sentence to be presented.

One reason to attribute a greater competence to normal children than to Genie is that their abilities to comprehend in natural situations are supplemented by their spontaneous productions. Genie's spontaneous speech was quite limited, perhaps reflecting her history of punishment for sound production, but perhaps also reflecting a limited competence. Also because her sound production was abnormal, it is hard to interpret omissions and additions in her speech. For example, since she frequently simplified consonant clusters by deleting a consonant, omission of the plural marker could reflect either a lack of internalization of the morphological rule for plurals or the application of a supplementary phonological rule deleting the /s/ (we have such a rule in writing for possessives: If a word ends in "s" possession is marked by an apostrophe indicating deletion rather than a supplementary"s"). Since she frequently broke up consonant clusters by schwa insertion, if the most common plural form in her speech were "-ez" it would reflect her own idiosyncratic rule, not knowledge of the usual rule to mark additionally a form ending in /s/ or /z/ with an inserted vowel.

Production Measures.   Initially Genie's speech consisted of single-word utter-ances and uninterpretable sounds. (Could the uninterpretable strings be what was called "babbling" in Anna?) Eight months after her discovery she began to produce two-word utterances. Her vocabulary at the time was about 200 words, compared with the 50-word vocabulary with which normally reared children usually enter the two-word "stage." Her first two-word utterances look like those of normal children:

Jones ['s] shampoo.
Yellow poster.
D. hurt.
Like powder.

(Curtiss, 1977, p. 144)

reflecting, respectively, a possessive-N, modifier-N, NP-V, V-NP structure. Like normal children, possessor-possessed was one of the first semantic relations to appear in her speech.

A year after her admission to the hospital she began spontaneous production of three-word utterances, like normal children's, of the structure NP-V, V-NP, or N-V-N. Examples are:

> Genie love M.
> Spot chew glove.
> Four teeth pull.
>
> *(Curtiss, 1977, p. 145)*

She also produced long NP strings such as "little white clear box" or "Sheila mother coat." More interesting was her production four months later of two two-word sentences, "Cat hurt. Dog hurt," followed immediately by "Cat dog hurt." (Curtiss et al., 1974), suggesting an understanding of coordination and deletion transformations. During this same period she began constructing negative sentences, as young children do, with a preposed negative particle. Her first was "no more" and later she added "not" to distinguish between refusal and other types of negatives. Unlike most children, she never learned to move the negative into the sentence, nor did she ever produce utterances potentially generated though transformations.

In the two-word period she learned to signify locations as in "play gym." As her grammar developed she would convey the same sense in prepositional phrases such as "Mama wash hair in sink."

By the following year she began using embedded sentences in her spontaneous speech (two years after rehabilitation began, at about age 15), demonstrating the acquisition of recursion. Examples are:

> Tell [M] door was locked.
> See I want you open my [your] mouth.
> I want mat [which] is present.
> Father hit Genie [who] cry long time ago.
>
> *(Curtiss, 1977, 158–160)*

Conspicuously absent from her speech were questions. Her foster family tried to drill those by modeling transformation of her spontaneous sentences into questions, but this caused tremendous confusion and random preposing of wh- forms in appropriate sentences. After the family stopped, these strange sentences disappeared. Genie never learned the question form.

As you may have observed, also absent from Genie's speech were most grammatical morphemes, pronouns, affixes, and articles; her sentences, even the complex ones, look very telegraphic. The first morpheme she used consistently, like most children, was -ing, which appeared after about two years. Six months later plural markers appeared, but only occasionally. At the same time she introduced "the" into some NPs and started to use the possessive morpheme. Past markers appeared sporadically the following year, and the third-person marker on verbs was not used even after five years of rehabilitation (age 18). The only pronouns she used reliably were "I" and "you."

Genie never engaged in language games, playing with sounds or syntactic frames, as children (or adults) do when they learn a new form. Some of her spontaneous creations were stereotypical, fitting words into set formulae such as "Help me ____" or "I want ____." However, some of her productions displayed a creativity or productivity. Protesting being taken on a trip, she wished "Little bit trip"; instructed that her mother was not old, she claimed "Mother new." She also seemed aware of the paradigms used by others, the strict subcategorization rules. Her response to a question of the form "What did you do?" was always a verb; to "What kind ____?" a noun or adjective, as appropriate.

Summary and Interpretations.   Compared with Isabelle's or with normal children's, Genie's language skills are quite poor and quite different. Abnormalities in her language development include a retarded rate of development, failures to acquire certain syntactic forms, a marked discrepancy between comprehension and production, deviant order of acquisition in some cases, and abnormal variability in applying the rules she had learned.

It is tempting to attribute her deviance to the late age at which she began learning language, 13½ years as opposed to six and a half years or six months. If there is a critical period for learning language and if this precedes puberty, then Genie's acquisition pattern may reflect language learning in its absence, without the benefit of innate tunable blueprints. Again, note that what may be missing is either blueprints for language specifically, or a match between Genie's cognitive structure at 13 and basic language instruction. Since Genie was so deprived, compared with Victor, it seems unlikely that she would have already formed schemes for many real world objects or ideas. She may, however, be missing the blueprints for developing some of these schemes—these would be general cognitive blueprints, not language-specific ones—if these unfold early in maturation.

Physiological Tests.   One striking fact suggests that there may be language-specific structures that Genie lacks. Genie is strongly right-handed but tests showed that she processed her language in the right hemisphere. As you may recall, right-handed individuals usually show a right-ear advantage in dichotic listening (see Chapter 7), believed to reflect specialization of the left hemisphere language center in the brain. (It is assumed that material traveling from one ear to the hemisphere on the same side is suppressed by material traveling from the ear opposite.) As we will see in detail in Chapter 12, more than 95 percent of right-handed individuals afflicted with damage to areas of the left hemisphere show severe language impairments, as compared with right-handers with damage to the same areas in the right hemisphere. (This suggests the left hemisphere lesions affected the language center.)

Since Genie is right-handed, there is a greater than 95 percent chance that she would have language in the left hemisphere. Genie was given several dichotic listening tests, equivalent tests in vision, brain activity tests (*evoked potential tests,* which average successive EEGs to determine the brain's response to a particular stimulus), and a battery of cognitive tests used to distinguish right-brain-damaged from left-brain-damaged patients. On all she responded like a person with left-brain damage. When presented with speech in only one ear, she performed equally well with her left and right ears, indicating no hearing loss. Under dichotic competition, however, her left ear score was perfect while her right ear score never exceeded 20 percent correct. Both the direction and magnitude of the difference are highly unusual; normally, individuals make some errors in both ears with a slightly better performance *in the right ear*. Evoked potential studies showed a greater activity in Genie's right hemisphere than in her left when she performed linguistic tasks, the reverse of what is found in normal right-handers. The visual tests showed an advantage for language presented to the right hemisphere, as opposed to the left hemisphere advantage normally found.

Genie also excelled at tasks that normally require right hemisphere involvement, such as face recognition, holistic recall of unrelated objects, and number perception without counting; she scored better than normal adults and frequently provided the highest score ever recorded. For nonlinguistic left-hemisphere tasks like counting or sequencing she was well below average. Together the results are consistent with the hypothesis of a dominant right hemisphere, which would bring different strategies to language processing than the normal left-hemisphere language-specific strategies.

Conclusions on the Critical Period.   With respect to Genie's performance and the critical period hypothesis, we may tentatively draw several conclusions. Genie's language is processed in the right hemisphere unlike most right-handers, and therefore the right hemisphere may have imposed its own processes, different from those of the normally used left hemisphere, on language acquisition. This would account for her deviant performance (and competence?). The left hemisphere may normally process language only if it is stimulated during a critical period, which could end some time before puberty. If the left hemisphere is not stimulated during the critical period, not only is it unable to learn language, but also it becomes less effective relative to the right hemisphere in all cognitive tasks.

Summary

In this section we have examined the language learning capabilities of children raised with little stimulation, especially linguistic, but with some human contact. Unlike the wild children discussed in the first section, recovery of speech and language is possible for these children provided they are given individual training and it is started at an early age. Comparing the wild children with these children suggests that some early social contact is necessary for the development of language, even if it is not very nurturing or specifically language-supporting. Comparison of both groups with normal children suggests further that specific social reinforcement for speaking may be necessary at ages under five years for children to imitate sounds spontaneously.

The difference between Isabelle's and Genie's language development indicates that exposure to language probably needs to begin before puberty for relatively normal development. In that case syntactic markers, complex sentences, and the full complement of syntactic constructions are acquired, probably using the normal language mechanism. (This is more a guess than a conclusion; we do not know whether Isabelle processed language in her left hemisphere or her right.) Otherwise language is acquired in the other hemisphere, and perhaps because of the absence of some innate language guides, there is general inattention to syntactic and morphemic rules (subject versus object, tense markers, movement transformations) as compared with general semantic functions (adjectives, negation, locatives).

Deaf Children in Hearing Homes

The children discussed in the previous two sections were deprived sensorily and socially as well as linguistically. There is another group of children that may provide data from rearing under conditions not so deprived: Profoundly deaf children raised by hearing and speaking parents (and some deaf parents) who fail to learn language normally because they can hear neither their own productions nor those of their parents.

General Social Histories

It is important to distinguish profoundly deaf children from hearing-impaired children, deaf children raised with sign language, and the earlier groups. *Deafness* is defined as the inability to hear sound in the frequency ranges of speech, < 3000 Hz. As we know from Chapter 7, we do not need two ears to understand speech nor do we need as many as three formants, so deafness in one ear, or deafness at frequencies above 1000 or 1500 Hz, will not profoundly affect speech comprehension. A child with such problems usually learns speech in the normal way, perhaps assisted by a hearing aid. If the child is binaurally deaf then (s)he will have difficulty learning speech through traditional transmission. If the parents are also deaf, sign language may be taught traditionally since this is what most deaf parents are likely to use in their everyday communication with each other and with the children. (Language acquisition of sign through traditional transmission will be discussed in the next chapter.) If the parents are hearing they frequently opt (particularly in the past) for a method of *oral education:* treating their children as though they were hearing, minimizing gestures to force them to attend to lip movements for lipreading and to whatever sounds they can also manage to hear. When the children are old enough they may be sent to a school for the deaf where speechreading and speaking skills are taught more formally.

These deaf children are not deprived except for the delay in experience with a native language and their inability to hear. They live in normal homes with appropriate visual, tactile, and taste stimulation. They also have the advantage of more communication with their parents than the children in the last section did. Parents are likely to use gesture for important concepts like "Don't touch the hot stove," so that there is little chance of misunderstanding.

Although there are sporadic reports of complete "oral successes" in the profoundly deaf, the instances are rare. More typical, around the world, are the children who struggle with the spoken language of their parents and surreptitiously sign to other children in their school (Tervoort, 1978). As Tervoort describes it (p. 173):

> Anyone who has ever visited a school for the deaf and observed its pupils, especially the younger ones, more than very superficially must have noticed the striking difference in their behavior in situations in which so-called "good" language, to be used on behalf of the hearing partner, is requested from them, and their behavior in circumstances where they are left free to communicate as they please among themselves. *In the first instance, their behavior is awkward, inhibited, and hesitant; it reminds one of a foreigner, unfamiliar with the language, who tries to utter something which he has to put together by thinking hard and using the little he knows.* In the latter case, however, the deaf children's behavior is that of partners at ease who focus upon the subject matter at hand, to be dealt with in a communicative code the use of which is a matter of course.
>
> (*italics mine*)

In fact Tervoort contends that the deaf child who emerges as an oral success is one who merged the sign language of peers with the spoken language of teachers, losing the former, not one who never signed.

Other investigators have similarly concluded that the deaf child born to nonsigning, hearing parents usually shows a language delay in speaking. Many youngsters do not acquire even the beginnings of language, whereas others acquire the basics but not the fine points of syntax. Few orally educated deaf individuals learn to read at better than the fifth-grade level, only 12 percent are considered linguistically competent, and only 4 percent rated as proficient lip readers or speakers (Schlesinger, 1978). Compared with deaf children raised by signing parents, orally raised deaf children, even those given intensive preschool academic training, are significantly poorer academically than manually trained children (Vernon and Koh, 1971). Most deaf adults do become proficient in a language, not the drilled oral language, but the sign language used by the deaf community (Schlesinger, 1978).

Of course, in interpreting the acquisition of spoken language by deaf children we must keep in mind that these children are not only learning language late and that they do so in classroom drills that are not part of "traditional transmission," but also that they are attempting to learn it from a highly impoverished signal. It is estimated that only 16 of the 40 phonemes of English are distinguishable from lipreading (Erber, 1974). Given the perceptual difficulty, it is not surprising that language acquisition is abnormal.

Spontaneous Signed Language

More interesting for our purposes than the deaf child's success (or failure) at mastering speech and language from oral education is the continual mention of signing in orally trained deaf people, either surreptitious signing in the schools or sign acquisition as adults once they are incorporated into a deaf community. Where does the sign come from and does it show languagelike characteristics?

Recently, Goldin-Meadow has examined the structure of sign spontaneously invented by deaf children (Goldin-Meadow and Feldman, 1977; Feldman, Goldin-

Meadow, and Gleitman, 1978; Goldin-Meadow, 1982) and its relation to the communication patterns of the parents (Goldin-Meadow and Mylander, 1983). The researchers studied six deaf children of hearing parents, aged from 17 to 49 months at the initial visit. The children were videotaped in one- to two-hour sessions for eight weeks. Interviews were unstructured: The child was given toys to play with and encouraged to interact freely with the toys, the parent, or interviewer during the session.

Analysis of the videotapes by two coders yielded substantial agreement on communicative gestures, gesture boundaries, and gesture concatenations, as well as gesture meaning, using rich interpretation (making inferences about what was said using the nonverbal context, as discussed in the last chapter). Two types of gestures were used predominantly: pointing gestures (which may be instances of deixis, or pointing through language, as discussed in Chapter 2) signifying objects in the environment, and *iconic* gestures (these look like what is described) signifying actions or attributes.

Gestures were spontaneously combined into "sentences"—a point at a shoe and then at the table indicated "put the shoe on the table"; at a jar and then making a hand twisting motion, that the jar was open. Some of the children maintained a rigid order between the parts of their strings, such as actor-action-object (perhaps, SVO?), with the actor always preceding the action. The children produced complex sequences of gestures as in one child's gesture at a shovel, then downstairs (where it was usually kept), then a digging motion (what it was usually used for). Gesture combinations were determined to be sentences if there was no appreciable pause between gestures or a return of the hands to neutral position. As do hearing children, these children tended to make two-"word" combinations, usually deleting the actor from a noun-verb-noun sentence.

One child analyzed extensively by Goldin-Meadow (1982) showed a further important syntactic creation, coordination, indicative of recursiveness. This child produced two types of sentences: one to request an action or comment on one, and the other to comment on a perceived attribute of an object. These two sentence types were conjoined in all possible ways. For example, two actions performed sequentially were gestured: TAKE-OUT GLASSES [and then] I [will] DON [them]. (It is customary to write English translation of signs in capital letters.) An action sentence conjoined with an attribute sentence produced a relative-clause-like construction, as in: [you] MOVE-TO [my] PALM GRAPE [which one] EATS. In the second sentence, the relative clause was not redundant since the grape in question was a toy grape and would not be eaten. Therefore the relative clause expressed additional aspects of the pretense.

Parental Gestures

Interestingly, the parents' use of these gestures was well behind the children's, indicating that the parents did not function as teachers. In fact, it seems more likely that the children taught their parents since the parents generally used the objects themselves as props, rather than referring to them as the children did, by pointing, a form of pronominal reference. Parents produced two different types of responses to the gestures: reinforcement, by smiling or complying with a request, or "punishment," by not understanding, asking for clarification, frowning, or ignoring a request. Attempts to correlate these responses with the frequency of occurrence of the gestures in the children yielded no relationship, further suggesting that the parents were not shaping the children's language.

Summary and Interpretation

Thus, it appears that children spontaneously develop language-like behavior given a supportive although nondirective social background. In these productions we see some few defining features of language as described in Chapter 8. The children actively transmit and receive, can serve in either role (interchangeable) and can monitor their own productions as well as those of others (feedback). The signals produced disappear as they are made (rapid fading) and are discrete. The signals may refer to objects not in view (displacement) and are combined productively, and at least for one child, recursively. Since the gestures in combination specify semantic relations (like the agent of the action) that they do not in isolation, they show duality of patterning. They are clearly learnable, and when the children enter school and begin formal oral training and writing, they will exhibit medium transferability. Finally, since the gestures may be expressed together with emotion in facial expression, they show some simultaneity.

However, many of our design features are missing from this communication system. Some are trivial: those that deal directly with characteristics of sound such as "sound" or "broadcast transmission and reception." But many are significant, such as arbitrariness (these gestures bear a definite nonarbitrary relation to their referents), semanticity (the relation in many cases between the gesture and the referent is almost identical—but note that the parents frequently did not understand, so that it cannot be as identical as it appears), and metalanguage (although there is not much metalanguage in any average four-year-old).

Given what is missing, we would not want to call this language, in this form, but it is still strikingly different from behaviors we see in animals. Moreover, as we shall see in the next chapter, this kind of system may grow into a complex, full-blown language, given time, an adult conceptual system, and the general force of change in language through use. It is striking that these children, unlike animals, seem to have an instinctive need to communicate about the environment for reasons other than for direct reinforcement. Given no barrier, they will invent by themselves a symbol system enabling them to so communicate, and they will spontaneously combine their symbols to form propositions.

Summary and Conclusions

We began this chapter urging caution in interpreting the data to be presented in it. As we saw, language data and data on the living conditions of abandoned, neglected, and abused children are incomplete and subject to much bias in the telling and retelling. Moreover, they are experiments of nature and as such are not rigorous; many factors may not be controlled, such as the child's starting point, previous experience in the environment, training after discovery, and so on; so we never can be sure of our conclusions. We next looked at three groups of children, those left to fend for themselves in the wild, those confined but with some human contact, and those deprived of language by a sensory deficit but not deprived of human social contact.

Keeping in mind that our conclusions can at best be tentative because of the problems in interpreting the data, we can suggest the following:

1. Complete isolation from human society suppresses the urge to communicate, the spontaneous imitation of other human behavior, and particularly the imitation of speech. Some contact with human society allows for the continued urge to communicate and imitate, allowing a better prognosis for recovery.

2. For recovery of language to be good it is necessary that training begin before puberty, in which case the child may bring to the language task special left-hemisphere language-specific skills and the less mature, more flexible brain, accelerating the normal course of language learning.

3. If training begins after puberty, communication and language skills can be taught, but successful methods seem to be radically different from normal, more like those used for operant conditioning of language (or other behaviors) in animals than like the relatively passive modeling which is the normal linguistic input to children.

4. If training begins after puberty, the language seems to have a radically different form from normal language, omitting syntactic fine points like inflections and transformations, and seems to be processed differently from normal, in a different cerebral hemisphere.

5. Given an appropriate nonconfining social situation with a responsive parent, if not one able to teach language traditionally, the urge to communicate is sufficiently great that children will invent their own symbol system, with many of the features that characterize human communication.

Thus, we saw relatively poor recovery for wild children, with practically no successes at speech recovery and intensive training necessary for recovery of language at all, as in Victor. In the neglected children, we saw poor recovery for Anna, who was not given individual attention. We saw excellent recovery for Isabelle, who received such attention, but who did not require painstaking shaping as did Victor, and who took less than two years to learn what most children learn in five. And we saw medium recovery in Genie, who was past puberty and given specific training, but who learned a symbol system markedly different from what she was taught, using different brain structures than is usual. Finally, we looked at the structure of the communication developed by young deaf children for their own use and saw that it shared many of the communication and symbol characteristics of language but not those normally attributed to the speech medium, nor the higher-level characteristics like metalanguage or perhaps arbitrariness. We suggested that these omissions were in part because of the young age of the speakers, and in part because of the young age of the language. In the next chapter we will look at such gestural communication systems when they have the benefit of adult use, language change, and traditional transmission.

REFERENCES

Brown, R. (1958). *Words and Things.* NY: The Free Press.

Curtiss, S. (1977). *Genie: A Psycholinguistic Study of a Modern-Day "Wild Child."* NY: Academic Press.

Curtiss, S., Fromkin, V., Krashen, S., Rigler, D., & Rigler, M. (1974). The linguistic development of Genie. *Language, 50,* 528–554.

Davis, K. (1940). Extreme social isolation of a child. *American Journal of Sociology, 45,* 554–565.

———. (1947). Final note on a case of extreme isolation. *American Journal of Sociology, 52,* 32–37.

Dennis, W. (1941). The significance of feral man. *American Journal of Psychology, 54,* 425–432.

———. (1951). Further analysis of reports of wild children. *Child Development, 22,* 153–158.

Erber, N. P. (1974). Visual perception of speech by deaf children: Recent developments and continuing needs. *Journal of Speech and Hearing Disorders, 39,* 178–185.

Feldman, H., Goldin-Meadow, S., & Gleitman, L. (1978). Beyond Herodotus: The creation of language by lingusiticaly deprived deaf children. In A. Lock (Ed.). *Action, Gesture, and Symbol: The Emergence of Language,* pp. 351–413. NY: Academic Press.

Fromkin, V., Krashen, S., Curtiss, S., Rigler, D., & Rigler, M. (1974). The development of language in Genie: A case of language beyond the "critical period." *Brain and Language, 1,* 81–107.

Goldin-Meadow, S. (1982). The resilience of recursion: A study of a communication system developed without a conventional language model. In E. Wanner & L. R. Gleitman (Eds.). *Language Acquisition: The State of the Art,* pp. 51–77. Cambridge: Cambridge University Press.

Goldin-Meadow, S., & Feldman, H. (1977). The development of language-like communication without a language model. *Science, 197,* 401–403.

Goldin-Meadow, S., & Mylander, C. (1983). Gestural communication in deaf children: Noneffect of parental input on language development. *Science, 221,* 372–374.

Lane, H. (1979). *The Wild Boy of Aveyron.* London: Granada Publishing Ltd.

Mason, M. K. (1942). Learning to speak after six and one-half years of silence. *Journal of Speech Disorders, 7,* 295–304.

Schlesinger, I. M. (1978). The acquisition of bimodal language. In I. M. Schlesinger & L. Namir (Eds.). *Sign Language of the Deaf,* pp. 57–93, NY: Academic Press.

Tervoort, B. T. (1978). Bilingual interference. In I. M. Schlesinger & L. Namir (Eds.). *Sign Language of the Deaf,* pp. 169–240. NY: Academic Press.

Tyler, E. B. (1863). Wild-men and beast children. *Anthropological Review, 1,* 29–32.

Vernon, M. C., & Koh, S. D. (1971). Effects of oral preschool compared to early manual communication on education and communication in deaf children. *American Annals of the Deaf, 116,* 569–574.

Zingg, R. M. (1940). Feral man and extreme cases of isolation. *American Journal of Psychology, 53,* 487–517.

STUDY QUESTIONS

1. Critically discuss the shortcomings of the case histories presented in this chapter. Why is it difficult to draw definite conclusions from these data?
2. Compare Dr. Itard's methods of training Victor with Premack's methods for training Sarah, discussed in Chapter 8. Be specific in making your comparisons!

3. Compare Genie's language acquisition with normal language acquisition. Aside from the age difference, what differences and similarities do you see in her progression of skills? (It might be helpful to consult the chart you prepared for the study questions for Chapter 9 and fit Genie in.)

4. Critically evaluate the critical period notion in language acquisition, given the data presented in this chapter. Discuss whether it is reasonable to assume special language-specific blueprints unfolding at different ages as opposed to general cognitive blueprints.

11

Sign Language as a Primary Language

In the last chapter we looked at gesture systems created by deaf children living within a hearing community. We noted that the features of these systems were impressive as indicators of native human communication abilities, but fell short of our stringent criteria for language. Of course, we were looking at productions of four-year-olds and younger, and of children who had generated their own system in the absence of reasonable adult models. When these children grow up and have children and grandchildren, will the gesture systems used in their homes as the primary mode of communication show similar impoverishment compared with spoken language? Or will the gesture system take on the semantic and syntactic complexities of human language? Linguistic complexity could develop from the pressures of dealing with an adult's world or through shaping by normal conversational use with other deaf individuals who have more sophisticated language. It could also occur because the innate language template that operated on limited input to produce the language observed in the first-generation deaf children of Chapter 10 would not have to start from scratch in the second-generation children.

As you may recall, beginning with Aristotle, something special has been attributed to speech as the vehicle for language. Aristotle considered the vocal apparatus crucial for language, and thought deafness an atrophy of hearing caused by the lack of exercise of the auditory system by language because the user was too cognitively impaired to learn language. More recently, in establishing design features for language, Hockett (1960) began with vocal-auditory transmission and followed with several features, such as broadcast transmission and reception, which are characteristic of the speech mode of communication. *Most* languages do use the vocal-auditory channels and so automatically satisfy these criteria. By definition, visual-gestural systems violate the criterion of vocal-auditory transmission and also some other criteria peculiar to speech. For example, one must choose to look at a gesture, but one has no choice but to hear a sound; gestural languages are less able to broadcast than spoken languages. Does this mean that a visual-gestural system is not a language? Or are other criteria such as arbitrariness, semanticity, recursiveness, and so forth, more central to our concept of what a language is, and so, if a visual language meets these standards, we would call it a language despite its modality? *Is* there something about the vocal-auditory system that enables language to have these special other characteristics? Or is language-as-a-symbol-system a general human cognitive skill relatively independent of the form of the input and output? In either case, how does use of the visual-gestural channel for input and output affect the characteristics of human communication?

To begin to answer these questions, in this chapter we will study the structure and processing of sign languages. Sign languages are used by deaf communities throughout the world. Because of the extensive linguistic and psycholinguistic data available, we will concentrate on American Sign Language (ASL), the system used by the deaf community in the United States. At times, we will compare ASL with other signed languages.

A Brief History of ASL

The Birth of ASL

To understand the evolution of sign language, one has to consider the population using it. For all spoken languages there is an obvious community of speakers—most people are hearing and it is simple to find people to talk to. Until the eighteenth century in the Western world, deaf children were educated on an individual basis if wealthy, and if poor, were not educated at all. For those educated, instruction was primarily in speech and reading, and communication was necessarily labored. However, the educated deaf person would become integrated into the hearing community. The uneducated deaf person would presumbly survive within the hearing community by using some *home sign,* a primitive gesture system spontaneously developed, such as those described at the end of Chapter 10. A deaf individual in a large community might meet other deaf individuals with similarly developed systems. Although there are mentions of deaf communities with gestural systems before the eighteenth century, little is known about them (Woodward, 1978).

In 1760 the Abbé de l'Épee opened, in Paris, the first school for the deaf, initiating group instruction and inadvertently establishing a deaf community. De l'Épee invented gestures to name objects; the deaf students took those "nouns" and invented their own adjectives, adverbs, and verbs to form a language (Lane, 1979). About 50 years later, an American involved in deaf education, Gallaudet, visited de L'Epee's school in Paris and took his most promising pupil, Le Clerc, back to Hartford, Connecticut, to teach in a school for the deaf he was opening there. Le Clerc's arrival and dissemination of the French Sign Language (FSL) in the United States is usually considered the birth of ASL. However, arguments have been made that a sign language must have existed before Gallaudet's return, since by 1864, 48 years after the Hartford school had opened, there were enough American deaf educated in sign to warrant the establishment of a college for signing students, Gallaudet College in Washington, D.C. (Woodward, 1978).

It is important to observe that ASL derives from FSL, not from English or the British signing system, BSL. To most people this observation comes as a surprise, in part because it is strange to think of there being many different sign languages and in part because Americans are not used to thinking about difficulties understanding British speakers. The sign languages are independent of the spoken languages, however, and a BSL user and an ASL user may need an interpreter to be able to converse with each other!

Creolization and Historical Change

The idea of a language's beginning is probably also a startling idea. We have not discussed previously the evolution of language to any great extent, noting only that new words are created sometimes by borrowing from other languages and sometimes by combining existing morphemes in the language, and that frequently used words may undergo shortening for efficiency. These presuppose an existing language to borrow from, to expand, or to abbreviate. A gestural system cannot borrow from a spoken system directly, since the sounds are not reproducible by the hands. Moreover, word-names, as we have seen, are a very small part of language: How does one create a syntax, phonology, or semantic structure? To answer this question, we will digress briefly to discuss some evidence and theory for the development of spoken languages considered analogous to the development of ASL.

Conditions for Pidgins. Of course, with spoken language no one knows what the *first* language was like, but the changes in any language over the course of a particular time frame can be and have been traced. For purposes of comparison with sign, the type of historical change that is of most interest is one caused by the domination of one multitribal and therefore many-languaged culture by a second, with the second imposing its language on all the groups of the first and forcing their intermingling. This situation has occurred many times historically. Consider, for instance, English domination of the islands of the South Pacific or Hawaii, or American domination of slaves from many tribes of Africa mixed on a single plantation. In such situations there is no common language, since the colonizers have disrupted tribal boundaries and forced different groups to work together. The colonizers interact directly with only a few natives, who in turn transmit their orders down some well-established hierarchy. The contact of the natives with native speakers of the now-dominant language is therefore minimal, but the knowledge of that language may be all the common language the natives have. This reduced, mixed language is called a *pidgin language.*

In many cases, pidgin speakers speak pidgin to their children. The children then are provided with a very impoverished language model, since the parents' language is a reduced language. What is interesting is that often in as little as one generation, there is a new language in the group, an expanded pidgin, with many of the normal features of language. This expansion is called *creolization,* and the resulting language, a *creole.* Creoles are believed to be created from pidgins in the absence of additional language models. Moreover, pidgins and creoles the world over show very similar features, regardless of the characteristics of the language of the dominating culture or of the original cultures (Bickerton, 1982, for example).

Conditions for Creoles.   Most pidgins have disappeared without record through the process of creolization. An exception is Hawaiian pidgins, and they have been studied extensively together with their creoles (Bickerton, 1982). Note that pidgin here is plural: Speakers of different native languages may each make a different pidgin, combining their original language with the now-dominant language. Because communication under such circumstances must be poor, pidgins usually amplify redundancy through repetition, and delete subtleties (which would go unnoticed anyway) like tense or case markings, articles, movement rules, embeddings, and so on. (Bickerton, 1982). Generally the syntax and phonology of each pidgin will stay close to the speaker's native language, with words borrowed from the dominating language, a process known as *relexification*. (You may note this process yourself in second language acquisition. You still speak English with your friends, but with friends from your French class you may say "it's time for déjeuner," to be cute. The use of the French word, in this case, is a trivial instance of relexification.) The reduction in morphological markings results in pidgins' relying on word order to establish grammatical relations.

According to the prevalent linguistic theory (Bickerton, 1982), the process of creolization is performed by the pidgin speakers' children since they *need* a rich, native language and find the pidgin inadequate. (The parents do not have a similar need since they each have a rich language in their native language before the domination.) The children apply their innate language knowledge to introduce features of grammatical complexity into the language. Since the parents' pidgin does not exhibit the complexities, it is argued that it could not possibly have served as model.

It should be noted that this is currently the dominant interpretation. It seems reasonable that the children do hear the parents' native languages as well as the now-dominant language from at least some more fluent speakers, and therefore that the children are not totally devoid of experience with full-blown language. It also seems probable that there may be a serious difficulty in outsiders observing use of the native languages. If the parents feel that their native languages are inferior to the dominant language, they are likely to suppress using their own languages when they are being watched by educated scientists, and to deny using it ever, if asked. The use is likely to take place at private cultural events from which the outside observers are excluded. Thus, we may be getting a false picture of the degree to which the native languages have disappeared. Indeed, it is interesting to note, particularly in light of this chapter's subject, that scientists and instructors who work with deaf children in countries with negative attitudes to signing report no gesturing among the children (Tervoort and Stroombergen, 1983), which is probably more accurately interpreted as no *observed* gesturing!

Regardless of how a creole emerges from the pidgins, all creoles tend to maintain the repetitiveness of the pidgins, sometimes repeating whole sentences, sometimes just one word for emphasis. Repetition is also a common way of marking plurals or habitually performed actions. (Repetition of a morpheme for any of these purposes is called *reduplication*.) Creoles, unlike pidgins, generally distinguish between definite and indefinite articles, mark tense and *aspect* (a morpheme indicating among other possibilities, whether an action is habitual, completed, continuous, and so on), and use relative clauses and other kinds of embeddings. Usually there are few words serving as only function words, but there are content words serving an ambiguous role sometimes as content word and sometimes as function word. For example, Bickerton (1982) reports the following from Hawaiian Creole:

1. a ded im ded → he's *really* dead. (Note repetition of "ded.")
2. dei wen go ap dea erli in da mawning go plaen → They went up there early in the morning to plant. (Note "go" for "to.")
3. so ai go daun Kiapu go push → so I went down to Kiapu to push (clear land with a bulldozer). ("Go" for "to" again.)

Finally, all creoles exhibit features novel to any of the languages in the area. For example, Hawaiian creole distinguishes between "go" as just used for successfully completed actions, and a "fo" to be used when an action was attempted but failed. In English we use "to" for both "I managed to escape" and "I failed to escape" so this distinction can*not* be borrowed from the dominating language (but perhaps is from one of the indigenous languages?).

Interpretations.   This kind of data is taken as evidence that the children are creating new structures. However, analysis of creoles has been exclusively of the adults' language, so it is not clear that it is as children, rather than as adults, that they create the new forms, as is claimed. Moreover, the children of pidgin speakers have the advantage of pidgin at home plus exposure again to the dominating language, perhaps some of the conquered languages, and the adult world. Therefore they have additional input about what might be expressible by language generally and can apply that knowledge for "creation." Nevertheless, whether as children or adults and whether with some additional input or not, it is clear that these language users restructure the input.

Signed Languages as Creoles

It has been cogently argued that ASL (and perhaps most other signed languages) constitute creoles and not full-fledged independent languages. As we have seen, FSL was introduced into the United States as the cultured, educated sign language, by virtue of its being explicitly taught in a school. This cultured emphasis makes it a dominant or high-class form. Presumably, before this introduction there were native American sign systems, perhaps many of them, created in the manner described in Chapter 10. When these multiple-native-language speakers got together for instruction in the high form, FSL, the conditions would have been perfect for development of a creole (Woodward, 1978). The second creolizing influence is, of course, the language of the dominant community, the hearing people—English. Even when sign is freely taught, instruction is continued in English for reading and writing, and the structures and semantics of English will thus continually influence sign.

The decreolizing process is likely to be slower in sign language than in spoken language because, on the one hand, the modality difference will limit the amount of incorporation of the dominant, spoken language, and, on the other hand, the social pressure from educators and parents trying to integrate the deaf into the hearing community will limit the self-containment of sign as a language. Moreover, since only 10 percent of deaf children have deaf parents, most deaf children learn sign late (in school) after some other communication system has been used; so the process of creolization, to some extent, takes place *each* generation. Continuity and progress in decreolizing can be provided only by the handful of deaf who learn ASL as their native language (Fischer, 1978).

Conclusions

If the argument about creoles applies to ASL we should expect to see features of ASL common to other creoles—reduplication, few function "words," and so forth. We would not want to use this to argue that the visual modality *per se* constrains language in this way, since in spoken creoles we have analogues in vocal-auditory languages.

If we can substantiate the argument that ASL is a creole, we will have demonstrated an important social constraint on the form of language, how relatively impoverished exposure to adult language and the necessity of communicating with speakers of different pidgins affects the nature of language, be it vocal-auditory or visual-gestural. Moreover, the process of forming pidgins, creoles, and full-blown languages has important implications for the nativist-empiricist argument. It seems that not only do children spontaneously form primitive communication systems, as we saw in Chapter 10, but, with these as input, they can also modify the systems to show more regular features of language. The general thrusts of these language changes indicate the cognitive pressures toward the most efficient type of communication for humans, language.

The Structure of ASL

Producing ASL

The Dimensions of Sign. American Sign Language is produced within a window bounded by the top of the head and the waist and about a foot on either side of the body. It consists of regularly specified movements of the hand(s), arm(s), face, and body. For the most part, it is the movements of the hands and arms that are important in distinguishing signs.

Signs are commonly differentiated along four dimensions: *movement, handshape, location* in signing space (Stokoe, Casterline, and Croneburg, 1965), and *orientation* of the palm (Battison, 1978). For example (see Figure 11.1), the sign for THINK (by convention, signs are written [or *glossed*] with all capital letters) is produced by moving the hand to the forehead with the index finger pointing to it and the back of the hand oriented toward the observer. Handshape is the index finger extended from an otherwise closed fist; movement is a touch at the forehead; location is the forehead, and orientation is the back of the hand out. THINK differs from WONDER only in movement; in WONDER the index finger traces small circles on

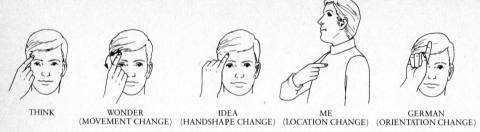

THINK	WONDER	IDEA	ME	GERMAN
	(MOVEMENT CHANGE)	(HANDSHAPE CHANGE)	(LOCATION CHANGE)	(ORIENTATION CHANGE)

Figure 11.1 *Five signs showing formational differences in one parameter from THINK. WONDER changes* movement, *tracing a circle, IDEA is* shaped with the little finger instead of the index finger, *ME is located* at the chest instead of the forehead, *and this sign for GER-MAN is* oriented *with the palm out instead of in.*

the forehead. THINK differs from IDEA only in handshape; in IDEA the little finger alone is extended. THINK differs from one sign for GERMAN only in orientation; in GERMAN the back of the hand makes contact with the forehead. If two signs differ from each other in only one dimension they constitute minimal pairs analogous to words differing in only one phoneme. Most signs, like most words, differ from one another in several dimensions simultaneously. Battison (1978) has estimated that there are 25 distinct locations, 45 distinct handshapes, 10 distinct movements, and 10 distinct orientations.

Fingerspelling.   An important subsystem of ASL is fingerspelling, which many people erroneously consider to be all of sign. (The letters of the manual alphabet are displayed in Figure 11.2.) In most fingerspelling, handshape is the only changing dimension: The dominant hand is held up, between the shoulder and the cheek, oriented for the most part with palm facing the observer. One handshape then corresponds to each letter. For example, "a" is a closed fist, thumb next to the index finger, "b" an open hand with thumb across the palm, "c" an open hand with fingers curved and thumb protruding, and so on. A few of the letters of fingerspelling contain an obvious orientation or movement change: "z" is made with the hand oriented down and index finger tracing a "z" in the air; "h" with only the second and third fingers extended and the wrist twisted so that they are horizontal to the ground and the back of the hand faces the observer.

Depending on the backgrounds of the signers, fingerspelling serves several functions in sign. If one of the signers is fluent in English and not in ASL, conversation may consist entirely of spelled words. Usually, though, fingerspelling is reserved for particular English words for which there is no corresponding ASL sign or for which one or the other of the signers may not know a sign. This occurs most often when one of the signers is nonnative; native language users who think in the language usually can find a way to express a concept for which there may not be a word in the language, using phrases as descriptors. Finally, as with the borrowing of foreign words into English, words may be borrowed from English into ASL, and then they are fingerspelled.

It is in borrowing from English that we see incorporation of fingerspelling into

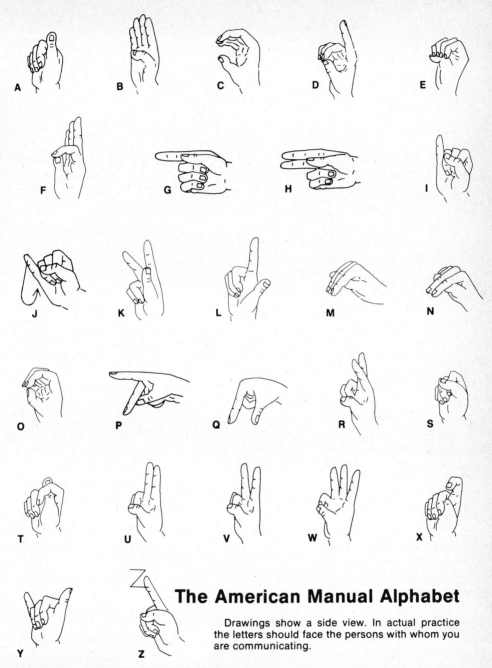

The American Manual Alphabet

Drawings show a side view. In actual practice the letters should face the persons with whom you are communicating.

Figure 11.2 *From L. L. Riekehof,* The Joy of Signing, *1978, p. 15. Copyrighted by Gospel Publishing House, 1445 Boonville Avenue, Springfield MO 65802. Used by permission*

pure ASL, in two ways. In fingerspelling *formulae* (Battison, 1978; Akamatsu, in press) the spelling pattern for words becomes conventionalized. The words are usually short, although there are some long words that also are fingerspelling formulae. *Conventionalization* refers to changes in the fingerspelling pattern that make it look less like discrete letters and more like a sign of the language. For example, fingerspelled J-O-B is produced with three almost separate motions, as you can see if you make the three letters with the help of Figure 11.2. In contrast, JOB is *signed* with a fluid motion going from "j" to "b" (with the "o" never fully realized), and the "b" is produced with the back of the hand facing the observer. The result is one sign with two handshapes, the "j"-hand in initial position and a modified "b"-hand in final position. *Fluidity of motion* or *flow* refers to motion in a single direction, with blending of separate hand configurations in a smooth movement (Frishberg, 1975).

In *initialization*, the second use of fingerspelling within true ASL, a sign is created by using the handshape corresponding to the fingerspelled first letter of an equivalent English word. For example, one sign for computer is made by making a "c" handshape with the dominant hand and moving it along the forearm of the nondominant hand. (The sign may be derived as a stylization of the computer light panel, with the forearm representing the panel, and the moving hand, the changing light display.) Initialized signs are usually words borrowed from English and may be avoided by signers wishing to dissociate themselves from influences of the hearing community (Battison, 1978).

It is interesting to note that British Sign Language uses a completely different system of fingerspelling, one way of demonstrating the independence of the two languages. In BSL, fingerspelling is two-handed, with one hand pointing to locations (fingers or different places on the palm) of the other hand. Each location corresponds to a different letter.

Constraints on Sign Formation. A particular interest in studying signed language lies in its being so different from most of our natural language experience that we are tempted to pose questions about it that we would never think to ask of oral language, but that are just as applicable. For example, in the preceding discussion, you might have thought "*why* is that the sign for computer?" or "*why* does BSL use two-handed fingerspelling?" When you catch yourself asking such questions turn them around and apply them to your own language. Why are computers called computers? Why does the word for computers begin with a /k/ sound rather than a /g/? Or even, why do we use our voices alone to indicate words, only rarely supplementing our vocal articulatory repertoire with hand gestures? At times the answer to such questions may be a simple "why not?" but at other times the answer may tell us something very important about why language is the way it is.

Take, for example, the difference between one-handed and two-handed fingerspelling. You might be tempted to argue, if you are an efficient one-handed speller, that two-handed fingerspelling is *in*efficient: It ties up both hands, involves coordination of the two hands, and requires more movement. If you are a two-handed fingerspeller you would rebut with the observation that movements are more visible on two hands than on one or that you get to use the flexible index finger more and need not rely on the clumsier fourth and pinky fingers. In either case, what you are considering are production and perception *constraints* on the form of the language: If a gesture is too hard to see or too hard to make, you assume it will not or does not exist. Obviously, for fingerspelling *either* one-handed or two-handed methods (since both exist) must fall within the bounds of reasonably perceptible and reasonably producible, although in different ways.

Visibility of Signs. What constraints can we observe in sign production? Obviously, no sign would occur that had to be signed behind the back or the head since it would not be visible. Similarly, no sign would occur that had to be produced by bending down or stretching since those require too much production effort. In fact, the window in which signs are produced is exactly the area in which it is easiest to move the arms, and which is, at the same time, the most visible area to an observer looking at the face of the transmitter. (Notice that for speech there are probably similar constraints: The first three formants lie in the frequency range to which the ear is most sensitive, and all articulatory gestures are producible without great effort.)

It is in "looking at the face" that we see a second interesting set of constraints on sign production. In natural face-to-face conversation people make eye contact and use it to signal turn-taking, social interest, and so forth. Eye contact is also something that develops very early in social infants and presumably is a universal aspect of human contact. Is eye contact also made in a gestural language, where the temptation might be to watch the moving objects, the hands? The answer is yes—fluent signers watch each other's faces, and probably for that reason we see an interesting pattern in sign production (Siple, 1978): Signs with location on the face or neck are more finely differentiated in handshape and location than signs produced in the lower part of the window. Note, for example, that fingerspelling (which entails fine handshape discriminations) is done at a location near the side of the face. If one is gazing at the face, one's central vision (which is more acute than peripheral vision and which is thus more capable of making fine differentiations) encompasses this area. Signs that fall in the periphery tend to be much grosser, usually using two hands (thereby increasing the redundancy in that part of the visual channel where there is more likely to be a perceptual error) and involving larger movements than signs made at or near the face. Moreover, on the face very small differences in location, such as between the forehead and the nose, may be "phonemic," that is, signal different signs; whereas on the body much larger distances distinguish "phonemes," for example, the shoulder versus the heart. So here we see an apparent match between the perceptual capacity of the visual system and the demands made on the system by the language.

Producibility of Signs. The third constraint on signing has to do with manual coordination. Try to make your two hands do separate things simultaneously (such as drumming *different* rhythms with the fingers of each hand, simultaneously, on the table). Then coordinate them so they are doing the same thing. As you can see it is much easier to move both hands if they are doing the same thing, or to move one hand while the other is doing nothing, than to have them act independently. These are the basis of the *dominance* and *symmetry* constraints in ASL (Battison, 1978): If both hands are used in making a sign either one is passive and the other acts on it (dominance), or the two hands move together with the same handshape, and so on (symmetry).

One way of proving that these constraints serve as phonological *rules* is to look at what happens to signs introduced into the language that violate the constraints. Historically, there were signs that were made on the face with two hands that were made asymmetrically, or that were made on the body with one hand. Signs are also regularly introduced by educators of the deaf that may violate the constraints, having been invented by nonnative speakers. Frishberg (1975) and Battison (1978) have looked at the course of change of signs in the language and described general principles of historical change in ASL (there are films of signing from the early 1900s that were consulted for this purpose):

1. Signs made in contact with the face
   (a) tend to become one-handed.
   (b) tend to displace from the center of the face away from direct contact with the sense organs, to the periphery of the face.
2. Signs made without contact on the face
   (a) tend to become two-handed.
   (b) tend to centralize about the line of bilateral symmetry and move up toward the hollow of the throat.
3. Two-handed asymmetric signs become symmetric in handshape and movement.
4. One-handed signs that become two-handed also become symmetric.

Examination of these rules should show clearly, in most cases, their relation to the constraints just outlined. We see also historically a tendency to minimize the productive effort in signing, akin to the phenomenon described by Zipf (see Chapter 2) for spoken languages. BIRD, for example, was originally signed by making the index and forefinger form a beak at the lips and then spreading the arms to flap wings. Over the course of time the second movement has been deleted, illustrating the tendency for two-handed signs to become one-handed if there is facial contact, and obviously saving productive effort (Frishberg, 1975). In sign, it is easy to see the effects of perceptual and production limitations; they exist also for spoken languages, as we have indicated. Try to think of some examples.

Face and Body Movements in Sign Production. In addition to moving the hands and arms, signers are able to move their faces, heads, and bodies to communicate. Nonmanual gestures serve linguistic functions in sign, sometimes redundantly with manual gestures. They also serve nonlinguistic functions, like those they serve in oral language (Baker and Padden, 1978). Examples of linguistic functions are: making searching movements with the eyes while signing SEARCH (Baker and Padden, 1978), blinking at constituent boundaries (Baker and Padden, 1978), raising the eyebrows while making subordinate clauses (Liddell, 1980), flapping the tongue to intensify a point (Davies, 1983), or accompanying a sign produced on the neck with a raising of the head to expose the neck. Nonlinguistic functions of face and body movements in sign fall into the same general categories as in spoken language: eye gaze used to indicate turn-taking in conversation, blinking or eye narrowing to indicate emotional distress, and so forth. (Baker and Padden, 1978).

It should be noted that there are many signs produced by some combination of facial or head movement with the hand movement. The sign for MENSTRUAL PERIOD, for example, has a manual gesture accompanied by the puffing of one cheek. To WHISPER the sign in mixed company, the hand movement may not appear at all, with the meaning conveyed only by puffing the cheek (Baker and Padden, 1978). The old sign for WONDER had the head moving in small circles, while the index finger pointed to the forehead. As the sign changed, the movement of the head was transferred to the hand, the usual direction of change in sign (Frishberg, 1975). This is perhaps most dramatically seen in the sign for YES, which is made with a closed fist bobbing at the wrist, imitating a head nodding. Although the head can nod too, either alone or with the hand, the meaning can be conveyed by the hand alone.

Signs and Meaning

It is very difficult to equate a particular aspect of ASL with an aspect of spoken language. However, as a beginning, let us say that each sign roughly corresponds to a word of spoken language. As we discuss sign and meaning, you will see that this is a gross simplification and generalization, but we need to begin somewhere. We start with the word level partly because as English speakers we think about language with respect to words most easily, and partly because so do the sign dictionary makers. If you thumb through a dictionary of sign you will note signs corresponding to many English content words. If the dictionary is a real ASL dictionary you may also note a strange absence of function words or inflections. This absence led early investigators to consider sign "primitive"; we will suggest instead that it indicates that the word may be the wrong level of comparison.

Content Words as Function Words.   A few observations may be made concerning the lack of function words. First, as we saw earlier, some have argued that sign is a creole and that creoles as a class have few words serving only grammatical function. Creoles tend to employ content words as function words, as in the example where "go" was used for "to." If sign is a creole we might find a similar pattern. Indeed FINISH may be used as a time marker in ASL (Fischer, 1978): An English translation for TOUCH+FINISH EUROPE, YOU? is "Have you been to Europe?" (It is important to recall that word-for-word translation from any language can produce strange-looking English. Take TOUCH, here—a reasonable metaphorical extension of "touch," which we do not use, is "visit"; we use something close as in "I touched down in England." Do not be put off by the glosses—the real *translation* is "have you been to Europe"; what is in capitals is a sign-to-word glossing.)

Facial Expression as Function Words.   The second and third explanations for the failure to find function signs derive from where one looks in the sign signal. Recall our discussion of "simultaneity and smear" from chapters 7 and 8. We pointed out that any one segment of the speech signal can convey a number of things—consonant, vowel, speaker identity, emotion, syntax—and also that the cues for any one of these appear across many segments of the signal. If you have been picturing sign production, you probably have already observed a similar situation, at least for simultaneity. We can move our faces and hands at the same time, and both hands at the same time. Hearing people looking at the language have a tendency to dismiss what happens on the face as *para*linguistic, since facial movements accompanying oral language are not considered real language. For this reason, it was assumed for many years that there were no function words in sign at all. However, in our discussion of facial markers in sign, we observed that the eyebrows are raised during subordinate clauses, and that the tongue is flapped as an intensifier. Is it reasonable to exclude these as function words, or would it be wiser to note the eyebrow raise and gloss it as "that" or "which"? (It is possible that these facial expressions may some day be conveyed on the hands, following the historical trend of lexical information shifting from the face to the hands.)

"Subtle" Morphology as Function Words. *Gender.* So we might give as the second explanation for the missing function words that the sign lexicographers omitted the function words carried on the face. The third explanation also rests on a failure to notice critical aspects of sign that differ from (many) spoken languages, but in this case that *do* occur on the hands, facts that have been collected only recently (Klima and Bellugi, 1979). Because of the bias toward the English way of doing things, linguists studying sign began looking for separate signs to convey each word of English, without noticing *parts* of signs that could have consistent morphological function, like inflections used in English and other languages. For example, GIRL is produced with closed fingers, thumb extended, and touching the cheek; BOY is produced with a similar, though not identical, handshape at the forehead. MOTHER, GRANDMOTHER, and LADY share location with GIRL while FATHER, GRANDFATHER, and GENTLEMAN share location with BOY. MOTHER and FATHER share all parameters but location, as do GRANDMOTHER and GRAND-FATHER, and GENTLEMAN and LADY. One way to analyze this situation is to argue that location here is a morpheme for gender, something that we overtly mark in English only in pronouns but something that is marked in many other languages overtly by function words or inflections. Indeed, signs introduced into the language that refer to things with obvious gender, historically, will migrate to conform to these gender markings (Frishberg, 1975).

Pronouns. A second example concerns ASL's treatment of pronouns (Bellugi and Klima, 1982); again, most are not marked by separate signs. "I" and "you" have specific signs, a point to the appropriate body. "He" and "her" are "variable" signs, created during conversation in what is called *indexing.* When a person is first mentioned (s)he is named with a sign, and if the signer expects to continue to talk about him/her, the signer will either gaze at a particular horizontal position at about waist level when the person is named, point to that approximate position, or terminate the name with the hand coming to rest in that position. The (fluent) observer now records the position on the invisible stage as representing that named individual. From then on in the narrative, the signer can sign any verb in that position and convey that it is the previously named person performing it without rementioning the person specifically. (We do something like this in speech when we look to where we last saw a person when we talk about him/her.) So the location could be considered as indicating (indexing) pronominal reference.

Note the subtlety for translation, though! The dictionary form of GIVE is: one-handed, open, palm up, moving away from the signer, occurring between the chest and the waist. In conversation that form is best translated as I GIVE YOU. In "you give me," the sign is performed almost identically; the difference is that the direction of movement is reversed. If the signer has previously been talking about Jane (stage right) and Dick (stage left), "she gives him" is signed by making GIVE move from right to left, and "he gives her" by making it moving from left to right. Technically, though, the different propositions "I give you," "you give me," "he gives her," "she gives him" are each produced with only *one* sign—an inflected variant of GIVE.

Tense. We have just seen that previously established positions in space can identify a person and that place of articulation on the face can mark gender. Position in space from the back of the signer to the front can mark tense. Signs produced immediately in front of the signer represent events of the near present, extended in front are of the future, and near the shoulder (as back as can be comfortably produced) and behind the eyes are of the past. Gestures pointing over the shoulder signify distant past. This tense marking may be put on a verb by producing it in any of these locations, or it may be appended to the sentence as with YESTERDAY (at the shoulder), which would indicate a past tense for the whole sentence (Frishberg, 1975).

Classifiers. In the examples given so far, I have shown how movement or location can be a function marker and I have restricted examples to morphological markings that have equivalents in English. In the next example, handshape conveys the grammatical function, and the equivalent part of speech cannot be found in English but is found in some oral languages of the American Indians such as Navajo (Newport and Bellugi, 1978). These are *classifiers,* markers indicating a single abstract dimension of a group of possible referents. ASL uses classifiers for, among others: person, regardless of age or sex (index finger alone raised), vehicle regardless of type—car, boat, sled—(hand horizontal, thumb, middle and index fingers extended and spread), and small, thin objects (little finger alone extended). Classifiers are used as pronouns are used.

Inflections. As a last example of ASL morphology, we will look at aspect markings in sign, which utilize differences in movement. Like tense, aspect makes a temporal modification of the sentence, but rather than locating it at a specific time, aspect marks how an action occurs over time: Is the action a one-time occurrence? Is it habitual? Is it discrete but repetitive? With the exception of the progressive "-ing," aspect is not overtly marked by inflection in English (though it is in many other oral languages) so examples may seem strained to most readers. However, English examples of the concept could be: I gave at the office (and will not give again); I am a giving person (this is a continual quality); I always give at the office (it is not continual but repetitive, say at yearly intervals); I give to fifteen different charities (each is one-time but they happen serially). Note that in English, we do not inflect the verbs usually to reflect this kind of temporal property. Rather we add content words (or change the verb to an adjective) to convey the concept.

ASL directly marks the verb for aspect (Klima and Bellugi, 1979) in much the same way as it marks some verbs with indexes indicating subject and object. Handshape is maintained but the movement of the verb changes depending on aspect (see Figure 11.3, which displays some of the inflections discussed here). To mark contin-

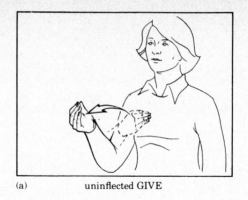

(a)   uninflected GIVE

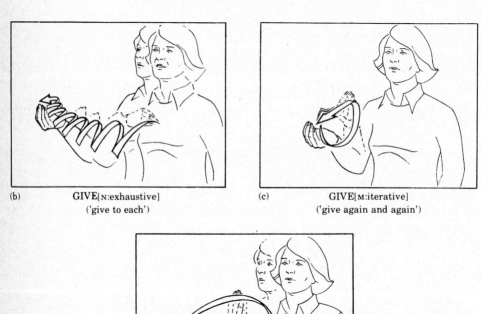

(b)   GIVE[N:exhaustive]
         ('give to each')

(c)   GIVE[M:iterative]
         ('give again and again')

(d)   GIVE[[N:exhaustive]M:iterative]
('give to each, that act of giving occurring again and again')

Figure 11.3 *Some inflected forms of GIVE.*
Originally appeared in Klima, E. S. & Belugi, U. The Signs of Language, Cambridge, MA: Harvard University Press, 1979. Reprinted by permission.

uous aspect, the verb movement is repeated (note the reduplication), with each repetition being a long, slow ellipse. To mark iterative (repetitive) aspect, the verb movement is also reduplicated, but each repetition is an abrupt movement out, a halt and then a slow movement back. To indicate multiple actions (giving to each) the verb is repeated quickly in multiple locations in the space directly in front of the signer. (This is not a complete list of inflections of ASL, but should suffice for illustration. For additional information see Klima and Bellugi, 1979.)

Discussion of Function Words.   Initial observation (by English speakers) of ASL produces the impression that it is devoid of function words, and that signs map rather directly to content words. This impression and a strong pro-English bias has led many educators to consider sign an impoverished language, incapable of expressing the abstractions of normal, oral language. However, as we have seen, ASL does make use of functors, although not at the word or discrete sign level. With classifiers and aspect markings ASL displays a morphology richer than that of English. The differences between English and ASL in terms of the grammatical categories they mark morphologically is further evidence that they are separate languages.

At the beginning of the section on meaning, we said that signs only roughly correspond to words. The reason for this should be clear now. Depending on the inflections, *one* sign can represent an entire sentence, complete with agent (I), verb (give), adverb (repeatedly), recipient (to you). Combining that with facial expression, we can make this single sign a subordinate clause (= addition in English of the relative pronoun "that"). And if we add another adverb (tongue waggle—"really"), while it will appear to a naive observer that we are making only "give" and repeating it, the fluent signer will understand something equivalent to "That I really keep giving to you . . . ," a rather complex clause. Note how much can be transmitted simultaneously in one gesture!

It is interesting to observe the extensive duality of patterning in sign. The four dimensions used to produce sign were presented as articulatory descriptions without meaning. In some cases that is a reasonable way of viewing them. In others, as we have seen here, it is not: Handshape, movement, or location can be meaningful. Classifiers are distinguished in handshape. Pronouns, gender markers, and the roots of some words (consider THINK, WONDER, and IDEA, for example) are distinguished by location. Aspect is distinguished by movement. Thus, the parameters have an articulatory (meaningless) role as well as morphemic (meaningful) role. Therefore sign, like spoken language, exhibits duality of patterning.

Iconicity in Sign Language.   Examination of a sign dictionary or consideration of some signs mentioned here (e.g., THINK, BIRD) shows another apparent important difference between sign and spoken language besides the absence of function words. Frequently signs look like what they are supposed to represent: THINK points to the head, BIRD forms a beak. This property is called *iconicity,* and signs that look like their referents are called *iconic.* The existence of iconicity, *if* it is prevalent in sign, could be an important distinction between sign and spoken language: (1) It would indicate that sign is not arbitrary (arbitrariness is a high-level feature of language!), and (2) it could suggest a major *processing* difference between sign and spoken language, since sign would be more transparent. We will return to the issue of processing differences as a result of iconicity in more detail in the section on psycholinguistics and sign; for now, let us note only that there is very little evidence that it is used in *processing* the language.

With respect to arbitrariness, it is important to recall that words in spoken language are seldom totally arbitrary if we look to their origins, as in Box 2.4. "Invention" of a word usually takes place by making novel combinations of morphemes (which we know or think we know a meaning for), or extending the use of some other word (which also had a well-defined meaning). A cartoon is *not* completely *non*arbitrary: It abstracts the aspects of the scene that it tries to emphasize, interpreting the scene. The difference between spoken language and sign language comes in describing visible objects. Sound can reflect appearance only occasionally (onomatopoeia and sound symbolism), whereas the visual modality can directly reflect appearance. Mostly what humans seem to discuss are things they *see,* allowing a greater opportunity for iconicity in a visual language. When we name sounds, we get the same effect in spoken language: roar, growl, snarl, chirp, grunt, hiss, gong, tinkle, and so on.

Also, by analogy to spoken language, we see that iconicity plays a small role in the maintenance of sign structure. Although all spoken languages have onomatopoeia, no two use exactly the same sounds. English roosters say *cockadoodledoo*; French, *cokeriko*—the sounds the language uses to mimic will follow its phonological constraints, and these override the attempt to mimic. Moreover, the onomatopoetic words must be learned through traditional transmission; they are not so obvious as to be reinvented by each generation or instantly understood.

These properties hold true in sign language also, which is why there is no universal sign (nor universal speech). Each language has its own set of formational rules and modifies its depiction of the outside world with respect to them. Historically, the sign STEAL was made with the hand opening and closing in a grasp, clearly iconic and nonarbitrary. As it developed in the language, the handshape changed to bent index and middle fingers, less iconic but more in keeping with the "phonological" structure of the language. Indeed, Frishberg (1975) noted a historical trend in ASL away from iconicity. The result is that stories signed in one sign language are not comprehensible to users of another (Jordan and Battison, 1976).

It is worthwhile to consider previously iconic signs. GIRL, for example, we have already described as produced with a fist, thumb extended, brushing the side of the cheek. In a classroom demonstration I asked naive observers what they thought the sign meant, giving no hints. Someone tentatively suggested "shaving" and was happy at accepting a meaning of "boy," extending from that concept. The class was quite confounded by the real meaning. Supposedly, the sign derives from an Old French Sign Language sign for girl, which may have indicated the bonnet strings worn by women at the time (Klima and Bellugi, 1979). Now, in our culture, it has lost its iconic reference but not its power as a symbol. Moreover, GIRL's association with location, as was pointed out, has been incorporated into the morphological structure of sign, as a completely arbitrary gender marker.[1] It should be noted that more formal tests of transparency of iconic signs with nonsigners show that the meanings are usually difficult to fathom, although once told the meaning, people are quick to make up probable sources (Hoemann, 1975; Klima and Bellugi, 1979).

Poetry and Word Play.   One place where iconicity plays an important part in the language is in signed poems. The "literature" in sign is much smaller than literature in English: Sign is relatively new as a language, it is newer still as an accepted language of the educated classes, and it has no written form with which to preserve literary creations. (Ironically, that means that sign literature must be preserved by an "oral tradition.") There is currently a National Theatre for the Deaf that renders literature in English into sign and creates its own signed plays, and there are individuals who also write ASL poetry (Klima and Bellugi, 1979). Since poetry, as we are used to it, is more image evocative than prose and uses the evocativeness of sound more than prose, it is not surprising that sign poetry would use the potential image evocativeness of iconic signs.

Before seeing an example, it will help to understand something about the structure of the poetry, so that the exaggerated iconicity may be understood in context. As we have noted, some signs are one-handed and some are two-handed. In normal signing, a signer tends to use the dominant hand for one-handed signs, although there are grammatical reasons that the hands might switch (an aside or parenthetical comment is often made with the other hand, while the dominant hand holds a marked position in space). In the signed poetry we will discuss, the hands are used symmetrically, with signs flowing between them, creating a rhythm in the alternation. A second rhythmic feature derives from the tendency to shorten or lengthen individual signs in the poem to provide a beat or stress pattern. These two patterns structure the poetry. Then, within it, as in spoken poetry, there are devices like repetition of a handshape (alliteration?), exaggeration of the iconic qualities, and so forth.

As an example let us look at a verse of a poem written in both English and ASL by Dorothy Miles, a person fluent in both. The English version is structured as a Haiku:

> Green depths, green heights, clouds
> And quiet hours, slow, hot
> Heavy on the hands.
>
> *(Dorothy Miles, quoted in Klima and Bellugi, 1979).*

Remember as we discuss the sign version that it is not a translation of the English but a poem in sign. Figure 11.4 shows the poem. First, note that in the first line the left hand is maintained as a base throughout the line. This is a distortion of the cita-

---

1. It may be reasonable to question the arbitrariness of the gender markings. Note that the male marking is higher than the female, perhaps iconically suggesting dominance or greater height. The male marker is also made in the "THINK" location, perhaps giving it a connotation of intelligence the female marker lacks.

Figure 11.4   *A signed poem.*
Originally appeared in Klima, E. S. & Belugi, U. The Signs of Language, *Cambridge, MA: Harvard University Press, 1979. Reprinted by permission.*

tion forms of some of the signs; the *base hand* (a passive hand that the other hand produces the sign on) would normally occur only in DEEP, BELOW, and ABOVE; its maintenance creates a balance and cohesion of the elements in the first line. Next, observe how few handshapes are used, the index finger alone, two fingers alone and five fingers spread; only three of the 45 or so estimated possible. A third point, which cannot be observed in the sketch, is that in signing the poem, Miles uses roughly the same time for each line by lengthening and shortening some signs compared to the way they would be produced in normal conversation. And this brings us to the last point—one of these lengthenings is a hold on SLOW, increasing its temporal length iconically.

Of the kinds of word play, poetry is probably the most interesting for us because it is formal and has its own structural properties. There are, of course, other kinds of word play in sign, and, to reinforce the concept that sign language has the creative power of spoken language, these are worth a brief mention. Some examples are found in Klima and Bellugi (1979). (1) The sign for THIRTEEN is very close in form to the sign for EJACULATE. Knowing this, one signer articulated EJACULATE in the sentence "You know he's a man when he's ejaculate years old," an obvious pun. (2) A student at a school for the deaf was asked why he and his fellow students were so happy. He began his response with the sign TC (fingerspelled "t" on the left hand, while the right-hand makes a fingerspelled "c" [see Figure 11.2]. Note that this is a relatively recent and nonnative introduction into the language, and is asymmetric.) TC stands for Total Communication (see following), a method of deaf education where signing is done simultaneously with speaking to increase the available language channels. The sign SMOKE is made with a t-handshape touching the lips, and DRINK with a c-handshape also in the mouth area. TC is made at chest level, but this student transformed TC into SMOKING (marijuana) and DRINKING, by alternating his hands from the TC location back and forth to his mouth.

Ritualized word games also occur in sign. One such game, an alphabet game, is to produce the letters of the alphabet in turn, but in doing so use the handshapes to pantomime a coherent story. For example, one might begin with the a-hand (closed fist, thumb up) representing a bottle, then take the spread, flat b-hand to wipe the mouth as a napkin, and so on. Another game involves producing all signs with a *single* handshape, distorting most of the signs, for a game of comprehension, which, surprisingly, is possible (except of course in fingerspelling).

Asking deaf informants for other such games, I found that no one remembered playing any as children, but they were happy to try to invent some. The two games they came up with were first, to use one hand, forefinger only extended, as a representation for the body, and make all signs on locations on that finger rather than the body; and second, to sign producing all movements in reverse.

Whether their inability to come up with children's language games means that none are played is questionable. It may be that this particular group had not used any, or that they do not remember what they did. Alternatively, deaf children born into hearing homes very quickly become involved in the "game" of inventing a language; and deaf children of deaf parents are, by the age of six, involved in the very difficult "game" of trying to learn English through lipreading. These "games" may allow them little interest in more frivolous language games!

The Syntax of ASL

Because English is relatively uninflected, with syntax and syntactic categories determined mostly by word order, the search for syntax by English speakers usually starts with a search for order restrictions. Early examination of sign resulted in the observation that it was relatively unstructured (no syntax). We have already seen in our discussion of meaning in sign that this cannot be true: Markers of subject and object may be incorporated into the verb, with their referents having been *previously* established either by convention (I, you) or indexing (John—stage left); subordinate clauses are marked with a special facial expression; verbs are inflected for tense and aspect, and so forth. These observations tell us that there is a syntax capable of conveying pronominal reference, subject and object, embeddings and tense. (Since we have already discussed these devices, we will not discuss them further.) These facts have been revealed slowly in only the last decade, during and after much of the debate on whether ASL has syntax.

Order. Initial observations of ASL suggested that word order was relatively free, but more recent work has indicated that, in fact, the basic structure of ASL is subject-verb-object (SVO), with other orders permitted only under special conditions

(Fischer, 1975; Liddell, 1980). To some extent this change in view represents a change in the language, since it seems to have been order free at the turn of the century. This change may have occurred through continued influence of English on ASL. To some extent the change in understanding of ASL as order free to order restricted has arisen from increased sensitivity on the part of outside observers to inflections articulated on the face, which mark pauses and sentence structure nonmanually.

Native signers presented with NNV and VNN sequences can interpret them, provided there are well-defined pauses: NNV is interpreted with object as topic, subject-verb; VNN as verb-object, subject with the subject, or verb phrase as topic. The topic is marked by a break between it and the rest of the sentence. The language reflects the SVO basic order in that "a very simple rule predicts the location of the subject and the object on either side of the 'intonation break,' if the subject or object accompanies [is adjacent to] the verb, the subject precedes the verb and the object follows the verb" (Liddell, 1980, p. 70).

Aside from intonation altering the SVO word order, the basic order may be altered to accommodate "phonological" or semantic constraints. For example, Liddell (1980) cited the sentence "the woman put the pie in the oven," which is preferentially signed WOMAN PIE PUT-IN-OVEN (SOV). In this case, PIE is made with one hand flat, as a base, and this iconically may be "put in the oven" if it is signed first. In other examples, with verbs that move between subject and object already indexed in space, there is a similar semantic constraint (establishing reference for the pronoun first); the S and the O loci are established first, and then the verb moves between them. Finally, locations are usually signed first in sentences, and if location is the grammatical focus (as in "the accident happened on the bridge"), it (bridge, in this example) is signed first. Thus, we can see that although basically SVO, ASL permits OSV or SOV orders more frequently than English but still under rule-governed conditions.

Semantic Relations.   The verbs that we have discussed thus far are all capable of free movement in space and all capable of having subjects and objects. Not all verbs in ASL can move freely in space, and interestingly, those that cannot do so express different semantic relations from those that can. We have already encountered the verbs THINK and WONDER, which require contact with or near the forehead. LOVE is produced by crossing the arms at the chest, a modified self hug; SURPRISE by flicking the forefinger off the thumb near the eye. These verbs cannot take objects in ASL and in fact, express a particular relationship between the subject and the verb, not an action the subject makes, but an experience the subject feels. (In case grammar this subject is called an *experiencer*.) To express who it is that is the experiencer in ASL, once the "stage" has been set up, the signer produces the verb with a body tilt indicating the position of the experiencer: If John (stage left) is supposed to be surprised, the signer will make SURPRISE with the head inclined left, looking right, from John's perspective.

Setting the Stage.   We have already seen how characters are placed on a "stage" in ASL, with a look or a point to a position after an individual is named. The "stage is set" in other ways too, which provide the basic structure of ASL stories and sentences. Edge and Hermann (1977) note that telling a story or describing an event usually begins with a description of the setting, the location. After that is established the topic is given and then possibly the time. Finally, the predicate or comment on the action is made. Descriptions of both settings and characters are conveyed by *listing,* mentioning the noun and then piling adjective descriptors on, painting in the details. This structure carries over from discourse to sentences: To sign "the bird flew out of the tree" the signer would begin with TREE (location), make a marker for BIRD, locating it on the tree, thus establishing the setting and the topic, and then provide the predicate, FLEW, directionally moving the verb from the tree. For a sentence constructed by a native deaf signer that translates into "The cat knocked over the spaghetti" the signer made an evocative list of descriptive verbs: "ONE CAT CARELESS WALK-WRONG PUSH POUR-OUT SPREAD SPAGHETTI CHAOS" (from Tartter and Fischer, 1982).

Other Signing Systems. We have been discussing ASL almost exclusively here, and it is important at least to mention that other signing systems exist in the United States. These were constructed to facilitate learning of English. Earlier, as part of a sign joke, TC was mentioned—a method where speaking and signing are produced simultaneously. If you think about it, it should bother you that this is possible with ASL; if order does not conform to English, if aspect is marked in ASL but not in English, if pronouns (he, she) are used in English and not in ASL, and so on, signing and speaking English simultaneously means producing two languages at once.

The fact is that TC does not employ ASL but rather signed English. In signed English, structure is determined by English (strict SVO), inflections are omitted and their senses conveyed instead by separate signs created for that purpose. In strict versions of signed English (e.g., Signing *Exact* English), signs are used for English inflections like -ing, -ed, or -s and then appended to the verb. Clearly, in these systems there are function signs. The advantage of such systems is that they can allow easy transfer from a manual system to English, which facilitates interaction with the hearing community as well perhaps as development of English reading and writing skills.

It is too early to say for sure whether signed English systems are effective either as a language themselves, or for teaching English. There are clearly some problems with them. First, as designed, artificial languages they do not get shaped by the constraints of a natural language, so we see difficult-to-make, asymmetric signs like TC in the language. Second, most often signed English is used only within the school in formal settings when someone is watching; as soon as the children are out of sight they will use the more comfortable, naturally evolved ASL. Third, signed English systems are often taught by native English speakers, not native signers, so the teachers are not communicating in the same language as the students. Finally (in my view) there would be a natural but incorrect tendency on the part of less skilled teachers to interpret a sign as its gloss and a sign sequence as its gloss in English (since this is the way the teachers learn sign), and since the citation form of the sign and the dictionary definition do not convey use, there would be continual misunderstandings.

This is not the place to discuss or criticize such systems. They are mentioned in part because sign dictionaries frequently show signs for signed English, which are not in common use in ASL, and in part to underscore the difference in structure between ASL and English as it is conveyed on the hands. It is worth thinking about the validity of trying to translate literally a language shaped by the oral-aural modality into a visual-gestural modality, a question we will discuss later in this chapter. Do written sentences (visual and not rapid fading) have identical structure to spoken sentences of English, or are they longer and more convoluted, with more distant references, reflecting the absence of constraints produced by rapid fading? Should a modality with as many spatial channels as the visual modality—eyes, head, two hands, body— be constrained to use a strict temporal order expressed by only the hands, as spoken languages are constrained by the single channel vocal articulators? Consider this on your own now; it will come up repeatedly in sign processing.

Summary

We have reviewed some salient aspects of the structure of ASL, showing it to be a rich language capable of expressing what spoken language expresses, although differently. With respect to sign production, there are four formational parameters: location, handshape, movement, and orientation, values of which specify every sign. At one level these parameters are meaningless; at another they may serve as morphemes, marking gender, tense, aspect, or pronouns. Combinations of parameters are constrained phonologically, and also, in part, by ease of production and perception. Signing also uses facial expression and body movements productively, as supplements to signing, as conveyers of paralanguage, and as syntactic markers.

Meaning seems to be conveyed in sign as it is in spoken language. There are signs, corresponding to content words, that occasionally appear nonarbitrary and iconic but nevertheless must be learned. Moreover, there is a historic tendency away from iconicity. There is a noticeable lack of specific separate function word signs, but this seems to be because those meanings are conveyed by inflection incorporated into the sign or made on the face. Sign is capable of expressing abstract, arbitrary, and figurative meanings (as are all known languages).

The syntax of sign is markedly different from English. Word order may vary depending on facial expression and inflection. Reference must be established before the verb; location, setting, and topic seem to be established before the predicate also. Adjectives usually follow nouns. Descriptors may be in vivid succession, called listing. Embeddings are marked by a facial expression serving as a "function word." Tense, aspect, and, for many verbs, subject and object are not marked independently of the verb but incorporated into it.

Given the difference in structure between ASL and English, and the difference in modalities, which may impose different perceptual and production constraints, it seems that ASL might be processed differently from English, or more generally, that signed languages may be processed differently from spoken languages. We turn next to consider the evidence bearing on this issue.

Processing of Sign Language by Normal Adults

In the last sections we discussed the structure of ASL. We noted that, in terms of articulation, ASL can be described as a combination of values on four formational parameters together with movements of the head and body. If ASL is processed like speech we might expect to see some indication of perception of ASL in terms of these formational dimensions. We might also expect that all of the information from the visual signal is not extracted, but rather that recognition of sign can be triggered by some set of cues abstracted from the sign signal. And we might expect to find context-sensitivity in perception and production of sign, rather than invariance. Finally, with respect to perception, we might ask to what extent the face and body movements contribute to normal sign processing, and to what extent they are redundant and perhaps not attended to, as "body language" is frequently ignored in speech.

With regard to the organization of meaning in ASL and of signs within sentences and discourse, we noted that frequently each sign contains information *simultaneously* about a number of elements of meaning that would be conveyed *successively* in English, in sequentially spoken words or morphemes. Given this difference, we might ask whether there is any reason in terms of processing ease that sign employs simultaneity and speech sequentiality. We might also ask whether what we English speakers consider separate elements are extracted separately from a sign, or whether all that a sign conveys is processed as a whole. Another difference that we noted between the depiction of meaning in ASL and in English is an apparent iconicity or nonarbitrariness in sign. Will this affect the processing of meaning in ASL, or is it just an additional dimension of sign that has no particular psychological effect?

In this section we will look at the existing research on these issues for normal native-signing adults. In the next section we will examine child acquisition of sign. We will begin with perception and production of sign, since it seems that sign processing is likely to differ most from spoken language processing at the level where modality has the greatest effects.

Production of ASL

We have evidence on the production processes of ASL from three sources: studies that have measured signing rate (Bellugi and Fischer, 1972; Grosjean, 1977; Akamatsu, in press), studies that have been performed on motor movements in normal signing (Poizner, Newkirk, and Bellugi, 1983), and studies that have looked at the equivalent of slips of the tongue for sign, *slips of the hand* (Klima and Bellugi, 1979; Newkirk, Klima, Pederson, and Bellugi, 1980). The evidence suggests that signing is subject to articulatory constraints different from those of speech, but that, in signing, the main ideas are transmitted at the same rate as speech, and that signs are not produced as undifferentiated wholes but, rather, have formational components. Like speech, some aspects of sign production are linguistically meaningful and some irrelevant, allowing for individual variation in production.

Rate of Signing and Speech.   Bellugi and Fischer (1972) asked subjects who were bilingual in sign and English to tell a story under three conditions: in ASL, in English, and simultaneously signing and speaking. Subjects were not given a script, so stories differed somewhat in form and content. The overall duration of the stories minus the pauses was measured and then the number of words in each story was counted. For sign, a single sign, irrespective of any inflections, was counted as one word. For the individually signed and spoken stories, signing rate (exclusive of pauses) was *half* (i.e., sign is much slower) the speaking rate. This difference held also for the simultaneously signed and spoken story (pause duration increased here, perhaps reflecting the greater cognitive load) and has also been found in the production of memorized narratives (Grosjean, 1977).

Bellugi and Fischer proposed that this difference might result from the fact that the arms cannot move as fast as the vocal articulators. They also noted that in counting a sign as a word without considering the meanings of its inflections, sign is at a disadvantage. So in a second analysis they counted the number of propositions rather than the number of signs/words in their stories. Propositions were determined by totaling the number of predicates. Under this analysis, sign and speech are produced at nearly the same rate! Moreover, when instructed to speed up or slow down, signers and speakers have available the same range of rates (Grosjean, 1977). Thus, it seems that sign may be under control of some general language device with fixed output rates, and that sign may have evolved to use simultaneity as a way to compensate for the slowness of the articulators, to conform to the constraint of this language device. In other words, *a cognitive constraint of optimal rate of proposition transmission may affect the structure of language.*

There is one more study to consider with respect to the question of signing rate: a study of fingerspelling (Akamatsu, in press). How reasonable is it to consider a language communicating at the rate of spelling? (Try it yourself for spoken English.) As we said earlier, because fingerspelling is used in ASL in formulae, there is modification of both handshapes and movements to increase fluidity (real fingerspelling is used only to sign English and so is a kind of derivative language). Akamatsu measured the rate to sign fingerspelled formulae, comparing it with the rate to spell the words named in the formulae. She reasoned that if each letter was made individually, the more letters there were, the longer it would take to spell a word. This was true for real fingerspelling, but producing the formulae showed no change in duration with increase in the number of letters and was faster for all lengths than the fingerspelled words.

Akamatsu argued that in producing formulae, the hand configurations and movements outline a shape in the air; this whole shape is both the target (so letters are not produced as individuals) and the percept (so letters are not seen as individuals). Indeed, an anecdote supports the point. A deaf informant reported that in his childhood his mother used to shop at Safeway, which she spelled at him. He used the formula too, beginning at a very young age, and only at the age of nine did he realize it looked like S-A-F-E + W-A-Y. When he tried spelling it to himself he recognized that his mother's formula had in fact been a sequence of letters all the time. She never noticed a change in his production; the approximation he made by tracing the shape in space when he was young was equivalent to the sequential spelling he used after his realization.

The production and perception of spelled words as whole patterns can account generally for the otherwise remarkable ability of young deaf children to spell. It also indicates how a system can modify an awkward code to make it conform to perceptual and cognitive constraints. Although vocally spelling English is impossible to follow, as you must have realized if you tried it, we too have our formulae, "e.g." "S.A.T.," "Ph.D.," which we produce and perceive as "words," unlike our producing or perceiving t-h-e.

Motor Movements. To measure motor movements Poizner et al. (1983) have filmed signers wearing small incandescent lights at the major joints of the arm, using a computer system that reconstructs the three-dimensional coordinates of each light. Characteristics of the movement, such as amplitude (size), final position, or pauses have been independently examined or manipulated in the reconstruction. Typically, Poizner et al. have studied verbs under various forms of inflection so as to understand the components of inflectional movements. Final position in space and overall tension exhibit less variation than amplitude and starting position in well-formed inflections. Since there is independent evidence that final position and tension are more easily controlled motorically than is amplitude, this constraint on language production probably reflects a general articulatory constraint.

Slips of the Hand. The last line of evidence on the nature of production of sign comes from unintentional errors made in the course of signing. Klima and Bellugi (1979) and Newkirk, Klima, Pederson, and Bellugi (1980) have assembled a small corpus of sign slips of the hand (131) to determine the units of production. Few signs were substituted entirely for other signs (only 9 of the 131), indicating that signs are not produced as undifferentiated wholes. Few errors yielded combinations of formational values not permitted in ASL; instead most errors preserved phonological constraints such as symmetry of two-handed movement. The vast majority of errors involved substitutions of one value of a formational dimension for the correct one while maintaining the target values on the other dimensions; for example, substituting one handshape for another. There was also some indication that the values on the formational dimensions might be further analyzed. For example, in one error the index and middle fingers were extended relative to the other fingers, as they should have been, but retained a bent shape from an earlier sign. The corpus was too small to determine whether these features occur regularly.

As Klima and Bellugi (1979) concluded, the pattern of slips of the hand mirrors the pattern in slips of the tongue: Sign errors reveal an arbitrary, sublexical structure, indicating a duality of patterning (meaningless elements combining to form meaningful units). The errors also show that sign, like speech, has productive "phonological" rules, allowing for some combinations and arbitrarily disallowing others, and that these rules govern the errors. Finally, note that both sign and speech productively use a small number of articulatory features to form a large vocabulary. The productive use of a limited number of elements may reflect the operation of a constraint on human information processing: *Employ only enough features to keep words from being confused and not so many as to create a burden for learning.*

Perception of ASL

The study of low-level ASL perception has employed three methods borrowed from studies of speech: confusions in noise, judgments of similarity between signs, and identification and discrimination of signs produced by minimal cueing. These studies indicate further that formational dimensions have a psychological reality, that the dimensions may be analyzed into smaller, perceptually valid features, and that a much-reduced signal for sign is intelligible, all findings comparable to those for speech perception. There have also been studies of higher-level perception in sign, duplicating the methods and effects found in study of short-term memory for speech and shadowing of well-formed utterances.

Confusions in ASL. The studies of confusions in ASL are based rather directly on the classic study of confusions in speech performed by Miller and Nicely (1955, see Chapter 7). As you may recall, in that study nonsense syllables were presented in various noise conditions for identification, and it was found that speech sounds tended to be confused with other sounds with which they shared distinctive features. With this as a model, Lane, Boyes-Braem, and Bellugi (1976; see also Klima and Bellugi, 1979), Poizner and Lane (1978), and Stungis (1981) attempted to discover what might be a distinctive feature level in sign. "Nonsense" signs that varied principally in one dimension, handshape (Lane et al., 1976; Stungis, 1981) or location (Poizner and Lane, 1978) were presented for identification of that dimension value. Values on the other dimensions were constrained to very few of those possible. "Noise" was created by superimposing *video snow*, the kind of signal television produces when the dial is set between channels.

Results showed that confusions increased with the noise level but were not random. Multidimensional scaling (for review, see Chapter 3 on factor analysis in the semantic differential) showed that handshape confusions divided into three principal clusters: closed or partly closed fist versus extended fingers, and then within the extended fingers group, prominent thumb and index finger versus other finger extensions. Within these groups there were also clusters, but that breakdown is probably too detailed to warrant further discussion here. Stungis (1981) found that these confusion patterns were predictive of performance on discrimination tasks; the more confusable the two handshapes, the less discriminable they were. Discrimination did not look categorical, however, with respect to these features, since small changes between features were discriminable.

Clusters were also found for location. The most important division was between signs made anywhere on the upper face, and anywhere else on the body. Within the second category, confusions revealed areas of central body, palm-wrist-forearm, and neck and lower face.

Together the studies suggest what some of the salient features for sign perception are. They indicate that signers do not treat all variations in production equally (e.g., the difference between full and partial closure of the hand is less relevant than that between partial closure and extension) but divide both handshape and location into salient areas. This is an additional similarity with speech, although it seems that handshape, at least, does not produce as marked a division into perceptual categories as do the consonants in spoken language.

Judgments of Similarity of Signs. In studying the perception of movement only, Poizner (1981) asked subjects to judge which two of three presented signs seemed most similar. As with confusion data, similarity data may be used for multidimensional scaling to obtain clusters of similarity (or confusability). What was particularly interesting about this study was that Poizner used both subjects naive to sign and native signers to see if knowledge of the language structure changed perception. For both groups of subjects the most important bases for judging similarity were: (1) whether or not the movement was repeated, (2) whether the sign was made in the vertical or transverse plane with respect to the signer's body, (3) how curved the movement was, and (4) whether the sign was to the left or the right of midline. However, in making these judgments the deaf subjects relied much more heavily on the movement dimensions (1 and 3) than on the location dimensions (2 and 4), whereas the hearing subjects did the opposite. The results suggest therefore, that movement may also be analyzed into discriminable features, and more important, that which features are discriminable depends on which features are distinctive *linguistically*. This is similar to categorical perception, in that language categories affect low-level perception.

Sufficient Information for Perceiving ASL.   Since the invention of the telephone it has been known that it is possible to transmit speech by using a small percentage of the normal frequencies present in the voice. The visual signal on a television set is much richer than the audio signal we hear on the telephone; it would take about 1000 telephone lines to transmit the information carried on a black and white TV screen (cf. Tartter and Knowlton, 1980). This has two important implications for ASL. First, we may ask whether all that extra information is necessary to perceive ASL; if so, this result would suggest processes fundamentally different from those used in speech. Second, with respect to studying sign, we must recognize that videotaping equipment has been far more advanced at the early stages of sign research than audio equipment was at the early stages of speech research. The relatively poor audio equipment encouraged people to ask how much and in what way the speech.signal could be distorted and remain intelligible. The advanced video technology has made the equivalent question unnecessary to ask in sign. To study perception, therefore, it is necessary to impoverish the signal, as by adding video snow, so that people make errors, and then see what kind of information they might be using. If impoverishing the signal does not produce errors we may conclude that the information that had been discarded was not necessary for perception.

Aside from superimposing snow, the most popular technique for degrading the sign signal has employed a method used in vision research to study motion perception. Johansson (1973) attached small light bulbs or special reflective tape (bicycle tape) to the major joints of subjects and filmed them under lighting conditions such that only those points were visible. As long as the people were in motion observers spontaneously organized the illuminated points (like fill-in-the-dots) as groups, and the movements of the subjects were identified easily as walking, running, dancing, and so on. (Cutting and Kozlowski [1977] have in fact demonstrated that placement of only two lights, on the hip bones, is sufficient to allow judgments of the sex of the subject, if [s]he is walking.)

Applying this technique to sign, Tartter and Knowlton (1980, 1981) found that sustained, comfortable conversation was possible in sign when the participants were viewing each other only as light configurations. In this case, the lights were placed on gloves, with a protruding light on top of each finger and lights on the back knuckles and around the wrists. In addition, one spot was placed on the nose for reference. In all, no more than 23 spots were visible at any one time, and nevertheless, conversation was possible, without training!

This study has several important implications for the perception of ASL. As you may have already realized, the face is not visible under these conditions. Signers continued to make facial expressions, but they were not received. Clearly the face is not necessary for comprehension, then, although under normal conditions, information conveyed on the face may be used. It is possible that the facial information is conveyed redundantly, in something that the light configurations would transmit. For example, in questioning, we furrow our brows, and usually also move our heads forward and to the side. Head movement would show up in movement of the nose spot. Some facial movements may also be conveyed on the hands. For example, one of the pairs of subjects became involved in an argument, during which one of the participants repeated herself three times, with increasing anger. Of course, her face reflected the increasing emotion, but so did her sign: The movements became exaggerated and tense to the point of almost shaking, and the final movement, a touch of the index finger on the wrist of the passive arm, changed from a touch to a slap with her increasing anger.

A second important implication of the study is that perception of sign does *not* use considerably more information than speech. Tartter and Knowlton (1980) estimated that the moving light displays would require about a half a telephone line to be transmitted (as opposed to the equivalent of 1000 lines of a black-and-white TV). The first two formants, which we have seen are sufficient to convey most of the distinctions of speech, also would use about a half a telephone line.

As Bellugi's and Fischer's (1972) study showed that sign does not transmit information more slowly than speech at the proposition level, Tartter and Knowlton's study shows that at low perceptual levels, sign may not transmit more information per second than speech. Given that sign and speech use such different modalities, *the fact that their transmission rates are similar suggests that the rate may be a basic human constraint on language.*

Minimal Cues to ASL.   Using the illumination technique just described, Poizner, Bellugi, and Lutes-Driscoll (1981) and Tartter and Fischer (1982) tried to determine specifically what linguistic information was conveyed in moving light displays. Poizner et al. were interested in the recognition of different types of movements—movements distinguishing lexical items, and movements signaling inflections. They placed lights on each signer's head, shoulders, elbows, wrists, and index fingertips. The signers were then filmed for stereoscopic projection (like a 3-D movie) to ensure perception of depth. Subjects were asked to compare the light configurations with normal videotaped signs to assess whether the configuration represented the same movements. They also were asked to label the light configuration alone. Subjects were quite good at the task, although somewhat better for inflections than lexical movements. Poizner et al. also asked subjects to try to recognize the movements from only three sets of lights, removing one set from one of the four positions at a time. Only removal of the fingertip light severely impaired performance; as long as it was present along with reference lights on the head, shoulder, or arm, movement identification was possible.

Tartter and Fischer (1982) asked subjects to identify signs made by using the configuration tested by Tartter and Knowlton (1980). Pairs of signs were selected that differed in only one of the formational dimensions and then were embedded in identical ASL sentence frames. Subjects had to select from two cartoons, each of which represented one of these two sentences, the cartoon that depicted the sentence they had viewed. For example, the ASL translations of "he had a bad headache" and "he had a bad toothache" contrast only in the location used for the "ache," the head or the mouth. The question was, with no redundancy available from the context, would such minimal differentiations be possible, and, if not, which were less discriminable? Subjects again were given little practice, and for location and orientation differences performed only slightly worse than they did using normal videotape displays. Movement distinctions were seen somewhat more poorly, and handshape distinctions only slightly better than chance. In a followup, Fischer and Tartter (in press) modified the configuration by adding a line on the thumb, and this improved handshape discriminations to the level of the other dimensions. Note that differentiation of the thumb was found to be a salient feature preventing confusions in situations where signing was viewed through video snow.

Together the results suggest that the fingertips plus some anchor are sufficient to convey movement (Poizner et al., 1981), that an anchor on the nose (separating upper and lower face) and spots on the hands (separating face from body) are sufficient to convey location, and that marking the fingertips, back knuckles, and thumb specifically is sufficient to convey handshape (and orientation). The results also suggest that additional information carried on the face or in a full video signal may supplement communication but is not necessary for sign perception.

Top-down Perception of Sign.   Thus far in discussing perception of sign we have considered only the lowest levels, perception of formational features and meaningless "cues" in the visual signal. As you may recall from Chapter 7, in speech a considerable portion of the perceptual process is "top-down," with words, meaning, and syntax shaping perception of the incoming signal. Some of the procedures used to study top-down processing in speech have also been used to study top-down processes in sign.

Grosjean (1980) applied a gating procedure to determine when a sign was recognized. In this procedure, a clock is started at the onset of the sign and stopped at intervals during its production. After each interval subjects are asked to guess the sign, and as he reported finding in speech, subjects have a good idea of what the item is long before production is complete. Subjects are first able to guess location and orientation correctly, a little later to guess handshape, and need the most time (but not the entire duration of the sign) to guess movement and recognize the sign. The fact that recognition is possible before production of the entire sign indicates that the signal is redundant and also that subjects use their knowledge of possible forms in the language to guide their perception. The selection seems to take place through a process of narrowing down the sign, dimension by dimension.

Grosjean also reported two studies performed by using a shadowing task. (As you may recall, shadowing is the procedure in which the subject repeats as closely in time as possible the speaker's utterance.) McIntyre and Yamada (1976) asked fluent signers to shadow videotaped signed narratives. The lag behind the model was 200 to 800 msec, comparable to that found for speech (Marslen-Wilson, 1975). The errors also were comparable, being *appropriate* semantic or syntactic substitutions. This type of error would be unlikely if copying were done only at a perceptual level, without processing the sense and form of the narrative. Mayberry (1977) reported similar shadowing results, even when the model's face was blacked out, pointing again to redundancy of facial information with information conveyed by head movement or the hands.

Is Speech Special?

In Chapter 7 arguments were presented that there may be something special about speech processing. The arguments are that speech sounds (at least consonants) are categorically perceived, produce a right ear advantage in dichotic listening (perhaps because of special processing by a left hemisphere language center), and show greater short-term memorability than print (perhaps because of a special auditory memory). If these effects occur for speech particularly, they suggest special processing that may give auditorially presented material an advantage or that may have evolved to deal with vocal communication in particular. Where would that leave sign?

Categorical Perception.   As we have already seen for sign, handshape, at least, does not appear to be categorically perceived: Although there were confusions among clusters of handshapes corresponding to features, gradations between the features were still discriminated (Stungis, 1981).

Further evidence supporting the noncategorical perception of handshape has been provided by Newport (1982). She showed that naturally produced signs varying in small increments between two signs differing only in handshape were assigned to distinct categories with an abrupt shift at the category boundary. Discrimination functions, however, did not look categorical but showed good discriminability throughout. Reduction of visibility through brief presentation impaired discriminability but not more so within-category than between-category. Thus, handshape, at any rate, is not categorically perceived.

There is, however, evidence that once a feature of sign is perceived linguistically, it is perceived in terms of *linguistic* features, as we already discussed (Poizner, 1981). This is a weak form of categorical perception, since although it captures the intent that categorizing affects perception, it does not satisfy the predictability requirement of identification for discrimination (see Chapter 7). Of course, neither did speech completely, which was why separate mechanisms such as auditory memory were invoked. And not all linguistically relevant speech is categorically perceived; vowels are continuously perceived. So it is an open issue whether sign and speech differ critically in that only speech is strictly categorically perceived. Given that there seems to be a tendency to perceive sign differently if one perceives it linguistically, and given that the observation of categorical perception in consonants has been variously interpreted (see Chapter 7), it seems that the more conservative conclusion is that there is not a special *speech* processing mechanism but a special language mode, perhaps resulting from the vast experience one has with linguistically relevant distinctions.

Laterality and Sign.   In Chapter 7 we described how simultaneous presentation of different speech sounds (consonants) to both ears (dichotic listening) yields a greater accuracy in report of the sounds presented to the right ear than to the left.

This has been correlated with results obtained from brain-damaged individuals to suggest that the right ear information has privileged access to a special left hemisphere language processor. In the next chapter we will present the evidence from brain-damaged native signers. For now, let us note that speech and signing show very similar patterns in brain damage. In the visual equivalent of dichotic listening, though, the similarity is not so striking (Poizner and Battison, 1980), but this may result from difficulties in the stimulus presentation.

The visual system is organized so that each eye projects to both hemispheres. If a line is drawn down the middle of each eye, the information to the right of the lines (the *right visual field*) goes to the left hemisphere, and the information to the left of the lines (the *left visual field*) goes to the right hemisphere. So, to create privileged access to one hemisphere, one must present two stimuli simultaneously to the same eye. Obviously this is easiest to do if the stimuli are stationary and brief, since they will not cross the visual fields. However, stationary stimuli are not very "signlike" and so may not be processed in the same manner as natural sign.

Overall, the results indicate a small right field advantage (left hemisphere) for moving signs and left field advantage for stationary stimuli (see Poizner and Battison, 1980). Since the moving stimuli have more signlike properties, it is more reasonable to assume that they reflect natural sign processing. More compellingly, the brain-damage evidence also shows left hemisphere processing of sign, as we will see in the next chapter. Therefore we might tentatively conclude that sign is processed by the left hemisphere language mechanism and therefore that laterality effects probably do not support a special speech processor.

Short-term Memory for Sign. As discussed in Chapter 7, short-term memory for lists of English words typically fits a bow-shaped curve, with recall of the initial (primacy) and final (recency) items better than recall of the middle items. This is true particularly for auditory presentation; if the lists are written, the recency effect is smaller and sometimes nonexistent. This difference is the so-called "modality effect." The recency effect for auditory presentation may be eliminated by presenting an additional, not-to-be-remembered item at the end of the list if this extra item is acoustically similar to the list items (suffix effect). These results have been taken to indicate a special memory of short duration capable of holding a limited amount of speech. Since the effects are not obtained with written lists it has been assumed that this memory is auditory.

Once again we may ask whether speech, because it is speech, has a special processing advantage that sign does not have. Shand (1980, 1982; Shand and Klima, 1981) made tests of short-term recall for sign by native signers. As with speech, recall was in writing and lists were presented in two conditions: signed or written. Across experiments both recency and suffix effects were measured. Shand found that signed lists showed typical "auditory" effects: pronounced primacy and recency advantages, with the recency effects eliminated by a signed suffix. Written tests, although also visual, showed the usual absence of recency effects. Since both written and signed lists were visual, Shand concluded that the recency and suffix effects do not derive from a modality-specific memory that is responsible for the effect, but rather from a memory specific for the subject's native language. In essence, there is a processing advantage for material presented in the language form one thinks in, and this advantage is reflected in the recency effect. (It should be noted that in one of the "signed" conditions Shand's stimuli were line drawings of signs, and these too showed a recency effect. Thus, the effect for sign does not depend on either perceived movement in the stimulus or length of presentation.)

Other Short-Term Recall Effects for Sign. Researchers in memory have demonstrated that for *both* auditory and written English lists, recall is better if the lists are phonologically distinct than if they are not (Wickelgren, 1965, for example). For instance, a list of rhyming letters (v, g, d) is harder to recall than a list of unrelated letters (f, c, h), and the errors in the recall of rhyming lists are intrusions of other similar-sounding letters. The effect for written lists too depends on phonological similarity, not similarity in appearance.

Short-term recall studies of sign have shown sign-based coding analogous to the phonetic coding indicated by the preceding results. Lists of formationally similar signs (all sharing the same handshape, for instance) are harder to recall than formationally distinct lists (Bellugi, Klima, and Siple, 1975; Poizner, Bellugi, and Tweney, 1981; Shand, 1982). Moreover, written lists show the same effect for deaf subjects as do signed lists, suggesting that, in reading, signers sign silently as we might silently say the words to ourselves. Some signers are able also to use a phonological code (Shand, 1982), given their intensive training in English and lipreading, and this group may also show phonological confusions. Indeed, in performing the task one subject noticed that some lists sounded alike and others looked alike and hit upon the effective strategy of mentally signing the former and mentally speaking the latter to avoid confusions (Shand, personal communication)!

Summary. The effects that have been claimed to indicate specialized speech processing are categorical perception, left hemisphere processing, recency advantage for auditory presentation, and phonological confusions in both spoken and written memory lists. For the most part, these effects seem to transfer across modality and occur for sign in native speakers of that visual language. There is evidence that experience with the language affects low-level perception, that there is left hemisphere processing of sign, that recency effects occur for signed but not written lists, and that short-term memory for signed or written lists is in terms of the articulatory features of ASL. These results, together with the results for speech, suggest that it is not speech that makes spoken language special, but rather language that makes speech special. As Whorf (1956, p. 42) said, "language is the great symbolism from which other symbolisms take their cue," and once we think in a language, whatever its form, we use that language code to interpret incoming information.

Semantic Processing in ASL

In discussing semantic processing of English we looked at three models of meaning organization within an abstract verbal system (prototype, network, and feature) and two models of less abstract systems (imagery and motor movements). Research on meaning processing in sign has been limited and has chiefly addressed the question of the role of iconicity or nonarbitrariness in extracting meanings from sign. The evidence indicates that although sign is obviously amenable to image and motor codes, it is nevertheless processed in terms of abstract meanings and abstract characteristics of the language.

We have already seen indications of this in the studies of short-term memory just mentioned. In these studies sign lists seem to be recalled in terms of abstract formational dimensions, just as spoken words are recalled with respect to phonetic features. Poizner, Bellugi, and Tweney (1981) tested short-term recall for highly iconic lists against recall for highly imageable lists, semantically similar lists (items from the same semantic category), formationally similar lists, and random lists as a control. Compared with the control, formational similarity severely depressed recall and semantic similarity slightly depressed recall, as is found in spoken lists for hearing subjects. Highly imageable lists were better recalled than the others, again as is found for English. But iconicity of the sign itself to its referent had no effect on recall nor did it affect recall of signs of more or less imageable referents. Thus, memory studies indicate that signs are encoded in terms of abstract formational parameters, as are spoken words, and stored in terms of semantic factors such as imageability and category membership, again as are spoken words. There is no obvious effect of the nonarbitrariness of the word on encoding or storage.

Another finding from short-term recall studies of sign shows that the uninflected form of the sign (called the *base*) and its inflections are separately encoded and stored, despite their simultaneous production (Poizner, Newkirk, Bellugi, and Klima, 1981). Intrusion errors in this study revealed that the inflections were transposed to different base forms within a list more often than whole signs (base + inflections) were transposed. As with the previously mentioned studies the results indicate a coding of sign in terms of abstract linguistic, formational properties rather than in terms of iconic or holistic properties of the sign itself.

One study of semantic organization within sign looked at the structure of the language from the prototype/basic level view described by Rosch, Mervis, Gray, Johnson, and Boyes-Braem (1976, see Chapter 3). In this framework, categories are considered to be formed of objects that share some perceptual features, and the basic level of the category is defined as the level that most differentiates category members from members of other categories while best capturing the similarities among members of the category. In the taxonomy tool-screwdriver-Phillips screwdriver, screwdriver is considered the basic level, since tool contains too much diversity among category members, and Phillips screwdriver is too precise to capture the similarity among all types of screwdrivers. In their study Rosch et al. (1976) claimed that signs show a different taxonomy than English words, almost exclusively representing words at the basic level.

Newport and Bellugi (1978) reinvestigated the structure of sign to verify this claim. They noted that most single signs are at the basic level but that syntactic processes in sign allow for combinations of elements to represent superordinates and subordinates. The properties of these combinations are interesting both for what they say about category perception generally and for what they indicate about sign specifically. To form superordinate categories, such as "fruit" or "jewelry," signs for category members are strung together, as in

APPLE BANANA ORANGE or RING BRACELET NECKLACE

Not all category members may be used to form such compounds; those that can be so used are invariably prototypical items. The compound itself has formational properties different from those of a list: There is smoothing of movement and hand-shape between the individual signs, a special rhythm or stress pattern on the compound, and an invariant order in which the members must be listed. Similar constraints on articulation apply to forming compounds for subordinates, but here the prototype name is combined with a modifier as in SCHOOL TRUCK for school bus (notice that the English translation is also a compound that has a different stress pattern than in "school, bus, . . ."). It is interesting that what seem to be used as prototypes for naming super- and subordinate categories are those items that seem to be prototypical in English. According to Rosch, as you may recall, prototypicality is not language specific but rather arises from structural similarities of objects and so should be the same across languages, as it appears to be here. It is also interesting to note that the notion of basic level is so directly reflected in the semantic structure of sign.

Summary. The few studies that have been performed on semantic processing of ASL indicate that there are more similarities than differences to processing of spoken language. Although signs of ASL themselves are iconic, this property of sign does not appear to affect encoding or retrieval. Rather, signs seem to be stored and recalled in terms of abstract formational properties and "abstract" linguistic properties like semantic similarity, morphological structure, and concreteness or abstractness of the referent. Sign categories seem to be formed of prototypes at the basic level but are hierarchically organized, as are categories of spoken language.

Syntactic Processing in ASL

There have been few studies of syntactic processing in ASL. In the sections on perception and semantic processing, we have already discussed processing of inflections and root verbs, so this will not be discussed again here. We also mentioned that studies of shadowing of sign have shown attentiveness to the syntactic structure of the narrative, with errors usually consistent with that structure. Further evidence for syntactic processing in ASL was provided by Tweney, Heiman, and Hoemann (1977), who showed that good ASL sentences could be more easily recognized, despite disruption by frequent interruption, than syntactically correct but semantically anomalous sentences, and that these were more resistant to disruption than random sign strings. As with English strings, this result confirms that syntax is used in the processing and recall of incoming sentences, although it does not say how.

Grosjean and Lane (1977) attempted to specify the syntactic processing units of ASL by examining pauses between and within sentences produced at normal and slowed rates. In normal signing (of an assigned story), there is a marked pause between sentences, suggesting the sentence is a syntactic processing unit at least for production of nonspontaneous narratives. (It is also possible that these pauses are used in perception to isolate sentences, but this was not tested.) When signing is slowed, pauses also appear between constituents, suggesting a psychological reality to constituent structure in ASL. For example, the first sentence of the story was

LONG-TIME-AGO GIRL SMALL DECIDE WALK IN WOODS
40   0   60   30   0   0

Below the sentence are the pause durations in milliseconds. LONG-TIME-AGO is a manner adverb and one sign. It is separated from the NP GIRL SMALL by a break, but there is no break between the constituents of the NP. The largest pause occurs between the NP and the rest of the sentence, the usual major constituent boundary between subject and predicate. There is a pause also between DECIDE and WALK, the main sentence and the embedded sentence, but not between WALK, IN, and WOODS, a unitary embedded clause. Except for the lack of an expected break between WALK and IN WOODS, the pause structure does reflect the constituent structure we would have assigned the sentence. Thus, at least in the production of ASL, there does seem to be a psychological reality of constituent structure.

Summary. For the few studies performed on the syntactic processing of ASL, the results are consistent with the studies of syntactic processing of spoken language. Syntactic structure seems to be recognized and the redundancy it provides used when the sign signal is disrupted. Signers are at least tacitly aware of constituent structure and demonstrate this awareness by pausing between constituents, not within them. And, on another level, signers seem to produce and perceive inflections separately from the signs—a reality of morphological structure.

Summary

Processing of sign generally manifests more similarities to processing of speech than differences. We have seen that perception of signs is affected by linguistic experience to some extent, and that the sign signal may be greatly reduced without severely impairing intelligibility. Effective communication presumably requires the same rate of idea transmission in sign as in speech, and this has apparently modified ASL to facilitate efficient communication. ASL, like spoken language, is perceived and remembered with respect to abstract formational properties, but demonstrates effects of imageability, semantic similarity, and prototypicality, like spoken language. Syntactic structure seems to govern production of sentences and is used in perception, at least under difficult viewing conditions, perhaps for top-down processing. Finally, the processing differences obtained between speech and nonspeech, which have been used to argue that speech was special, seem to obtain also between sign and other visual signals, suggesting the specialness is in the language, not the modality.

Child Acquisition of Sign

At first glance it might seem that ASL would be an easy language to acquire. There is considerable use of pointing, iconicity, and "pantomime" of motion, which might make it less abstract and thus easier for a child than spoken language. In fact, at least initially, this is the strategy adults acquiring ASL as a second language use— to try to recall vocabulary items by using iconic mnemonic strategies, such as GIRL refers to the "softness of the cheek," an incorrect etymology. Our discussion of the structure of sign and its processing by adults suggests, alternatively, that there might be little difference between the acquisition of sign by children of signers and the acquisition of spoken language by hearing children. If there is no difference between acquisition of sign and speech it suggests that children bring to language learning a bias toward a particular kind of organization, a strong line of evidence supporting the idea of an innate language blueprint.

Earliest Stages of Sign Production

One difference that does seem to be consistently reported is that the first signs are usually made earlier than the first words (Bonvillian, Orlansky, and Novack, 1983). Bonvillian et al. found that the majority of their subjects produced their first sign by the age of nine months (11–14 months for the first word) and had about 10 signs by the age of one year. First sign combinations were also made earlier, at 17 months (as opposed to 18–21 months for speech). Most of the signs that were produced were not iconic. Some that might be considered iconic by adults were unlikely to be seen as such by children: MILK is produced by opening and closing the hand, resembling milking a cow, but this procedure for getting milk is not likely to be understood by most modern, urban infants.

The precocious development of sign as compared with speech is usually attributed to earlier motor coordination of the hands than the vocal articulators, the direct visual feedback possible in sign but not in speech, and the opportunity the parents have to mold the children's hands and arms, an opportunity not available in speech. The earlier acquisition of sign has not been universally accepted, however; Volterra (1983; Volterra and Caselli, 1983), for example, argued that gestures are made earlier than words but that it is necessary to distinguish between signs-as-gestures and signs-as-symbols. In terms of symbolic or generalized reference, she noted that signs and spoken words seem to be used at about the same time.

As might be expected, there is a regular developmental sequence in the ability to form signs. The earliest handshapes make use of the opposition of the thumb, then the extension of one or more fingers, and finally finger contact with the thumb (McIntyre, cited in Hoffmeister and Wilbur, 1980). Presumably the sequence is shaped by motor development and similar sequences exist for other formational dimensions. S. Supalla (1980) noted that there are strict phonological rules governing acceptable combinations of dimension values on signs of people's names and that these rules are internalized at a very early age. Young children who are not yet able to make a particular name sign will change it to one they can make, but always also one that conforms to the restrictions of the name-sign system (S. Supalla, personal communication). This suggests that children are observing the rules of the language and that the limiting factor on performance is motor skill.

Acquisition of Meaning in ASL

Meaning acquisition in ASL has been studied with respect to the order in which specific semantic relations appear in sign as compared with speech, and with respect to the effect that iconicity in particular has on acquiring ASL. In the few studies that compare semantic stages in English and ASL, no difference has been found: Deaf children express possessor-possessed, object-attribute, agent-object, action-object, and so forth, as do hearing children and at the same ages (see, for example, Newport and Meier, in press; Hoffmeister and Wilbur, 1980).

For the iconicity issue several specific features have been addressed: whether verbs that look like the actions they symbolize are acquired more easily than arbitrary verbs (Meier, 1982), how pointing is incorporated into the linguistic system (Hoffmeister and Wilbur, 1980), whether pronouns with reference conveyed by pointing are acquired differently from noniconic pronouns (Petitto, 1983), and whether inflecting verbs that move between subject and object are learned earlier than noniconic inflections, like aspect markings (Fischer, 1973; Meier, 1982). Generally, as we have seen with adults, iconicity has been found to play a surprisingly small role in processing of sign by children.

Some signs for verbs look very much like their actions. DRINK, for example, is made by cupping the hand and touching it to the mouth. Other verbs are more abstract; LOOK-AT is made with the index and middle fingers extended to form a "v." Examining productions of three deaf children, Meier (1982) found no difference in age of acquisition of the base forms of iconic and noniconic verbs, nor in the acquisition of inflections for them.

Hoffmeister (Hoffmeister and Wilbur, 1980) found that deaf children tend to use pointing for expression (note that they are also using nonpointing signs during this period) but use it symbolically and show the same constraints on length of utterance as hearing children. In the first stage, utterances use two points, as to a toy and the child, perhaps indicating "my toy," or to the toy and a toy chest, perhaps indicating the usual location for the toy. At the next stage three-point gestures are used, indicating additional case relations, as hearing children develop from two-word to three-word utterances. Sometimes the three-point utterances use a sign and two points. As children learn sign, they will change from using just an index finger point to pointing with the whole hand or the thumb and little finger only, handshapes common in ASL. There is no indication that being able to point to the object directly rather than using an abstract word for it speeds acquisition of the underlying concepts or case relations, suggesting that the emergence of the points reflects the growing conceptual structure of the child rather than obvious features of the environment.

Another linguistic structure that might be expected to be acquired early in ASL is pronominalization, since the pronouns for "I" and "you" are made by pointing at the individual. Interestingly, once again this does not seem to facilitate acquisition. Petitto (1983) found that children of less than a year freely pointed to objects and people but stopped pointing to people just before the age at which hearing children begin to use "me." The deaf children at this time used proper names for people, and over the next few months, reintroduced points to people into their repertoires. First the sign for "you" was used but in situations where the meaning "me" was clearly intended. Note that if the parent is indicating the child with a pronoun, (s)he will be pointing at the child; if children *imitate* this gesture to indicate themselves, they will be pointing back at the parent, incorrectly making YOU. Once the child realizes that pronouns are variable and not names—that is, once that child has the concept of deixis—the gesture imitation will cease, and the child will correctly point at the appropriate referent. This happens in deaf children, as in hearing children, at about two years of age.

What is particularly interesting about this result is that it indicates that pointing is not transparent; as Wittgenstein said (see Chapter 2), a gesture at two nuts could indicate nut, two, or the group. A gesture at the child could mean you, the child's name (in which case it should be imitated), or some aspect of the child. Initially children seem to use points to indicate objects; as they become familiar with the idea that signs stand for objects, their concept of pointing changes, and they stop pointing. Once it is clear what a point means, it is reintroduced as the correct pronoun.

Morphology and Syntax Acquisition

In ASL, as we observed, much of the grammar is conveyed through morphological markings rather than word order. Newport and Meier (in press) observed that there has been little study of syntax acquisition apart from study of acquisition of morphological inflections. They noted that although word order is relatively free in ASL as compared with English, most children begin signing SVO word order (this is the most frequent order in ASL). Acquisition of negation in ASL also resembles acquisition of negation in English: The first use of negation is the sign NO or a headshake preceding the utterance; subsequently the negation sign is moved into the sentence, perhaps accompanied by the headshake. Acquisition of other complex syntactic structures such as relative clauses has not been studied.

Acquisition of morphological markers has been studied with respect to inflectional morphemes, marking semantic relations such as subject or object, deictic reference in discourse, and derivational morphemes, changing nouns to verbs. Meier (1982) looked at the acquisition of verbs for which the movement changed to indicate subject, object, indirect object, and so on. He specifically examined only the contexts in which the referents were present in the environment so that there was no need for the children to remember or set up reference; rather they could just make the verb with respect to the objects. The youngest children did not attempt to inflect the verb at all. When slightly older, they inflected some verbs but not others, suggesting that these inflected verbs had been learned as unanalyzed rote forms. Still later, inflections appeared slowly, across verbs, indicative of the learning of inflections as part of the linguistic system. By the age of 3½ all the children correctly used the inflections.

Meier's results are consistent with an early finding of Fischer's (1973) that at two years of age verbs are used without inflection, and subject or object is indicated by a separate point, and at three years the inflections are used but generalized to verbs that are not inflected in the adult language. The overgeneralization indicates acquisition and application of a rule. Meier (1983) showed, in addition, that the first inflections used are those required for grammaticality; optional inflections are acquired later. This, too, suggests that children are learning general features of a linguistic system, not individual items.

Together the results indicate a similarity in the acquisition process of deaf and hearing children. There does not seem to be a processing advantage incurred from the iconicity inherent in the language. The similarity in acquisition, despite the apparent differences in representation of speech and sign, suggests that *the limiting factors for language acquisition are basic cognitive abilities in symbolizing.* Moreover, it appears that *the process of symbolizing is arbitrary, regardless of whether the symbol, the word or the sign, is itself arbitrary.*

Meier had looked at use of space for deictic reference at a sentence level. Loew (1980) looked at children's acquisition of deixis at a discourse level, in storytelling. Recall that to enable subsequent pronominal reference in ASL, the narrator, on first mentioning someone, indicates a position on an imaginary stage by moving the hand, head, or eye toward that point. This position then can be used to indicate that person, or body movements from that position can be used to indicate the person's perspective. To establish consistent use of position requires not just recognition of this rule, but also memory for where an individual had been assigned and recognition of whether the "listener" is likely to remember that assignment. Loew found that beginning at about 3½ years, children would use the stage but not systematically; *all* characters would be piled up in the same location. At this time children would use facial expression appropriately to indicate what a character was feeling but would not be able to use spatial positions to indicate who the character was. At 4½, the use of space was somewhat better in that characters were distributed across locations, not just piled in one place, but a given location was not maintained throughout the story for a particular character. For the children Loew examined, proper attention to who was assigned where was given by the age of four years and nine months.

One study has looked at the acquisition of derivational inflections. Launer (1982) examined children's knowledge of a morphological rule that can convert nouns to verbs in ASL as our stress rule could "cónvert" a "convért" (see Chapter 6 for other such examples in English). In ASL, verbs and nouns derived from them share handshape, location, orientation, and many aspects of movement. However, the movement for the verb is more stressed, and for the noun, more restrained and invariably repeated (Supalla and Newport, 1978). Launer found that initially children do not differentiate nouns and verbs at all; they seem to be simply acquiring vocabulary items. At age two to three, nouns and verbs are occasionally marked appropriately but not with any regularity. Between three and five, the rule seems to be internalized to the extent that children now extend it to new items, "verbing their nouns" (see Box 4.2) creatively. The distinction indicated by productive application of the movement difference between verbs and nouns suggests a knowledge of nouns and verbs as syntactic categories.

Summary.   From the small amount of work done on syntax acquisition in ASL there appears to be a developmental sequence consistent with that obtained for hearing children with spoken language. At first, vocabulary items are acquired as unanalyzed wholes, independent of function or inflection. Inflections are acquired by rule, so that initially they are used only if they are rote-learned; subsequently they may be used productively, but not in all the instances they should be; and finally, they are used correctly, as the adult uses them. Processes that make more cognitive demands, such as those that require memory of multiple locations, seem to be acquired later than processes that require a smaller cognitive load.

Parent-Child Interaction

The two principal differences between signing parents' and speaking parents' interactions with their children involve the greater manipulability of sign: Signing parents frequently sign directly on their infants' bodies rather than on their own, and signing parents frequently "correct" a production by molding the child's hands into the proper position (Hoffmeister and Wilbur, 1980). This additional sensory stimulation may account in part for the earlier acquisition of the first word. In other respects, signing parents seem to play the same "teaching" role as speaking parents: signing grammatically but simply (showing few inflections) and exaggerating intonation markers and, on occasion, iconicity (Newport and Meier, in press).

As far as corrections, expansions, or tailoring utterances to the child's level are concerned, indications are that there is no difference between signing parents and speaking parents, nor any difference in the effects that these alterations have on the children. Launer (1982) found that the parents did not make the noun-verb morphological distinction to the youngest children in the study, intentionally simplifying. Parents also occasionally exaggerated the iconicity, repeated and elaborated for the youngest children, but stopped this as the children became older. Parents of older children used more complex and morphologically marked sentences. Petitto (1983) reported a mother's repeated correction of a young child's pronoun to no avail: The child picked up her own bathing suit and signed to her mother YOUR SWIMSUIT. The mother, somewhat embarrassed, signed NO. YOUR SWIMSUIT, and they went back and forth, with no indication that the child understood the error.

Thus, it seems that parents are sensitive to the emergent linguistic abilities of their children and tailor their language accordingly. Whether this in fact assists children in language acquisition is not clear, nor is it clear in spoken language.

Summary

Acquisition of a signed language does not appear very different from acquisition of a spoken language. The first sign seems to precede the first word, but subsequently articulation, vocabulary acquisition, and acquisition of inflections and syntax follow similar patterns, with age of acquisition dependent on processing difficulty. Somewhat surprisingly, transparency of sign in both semantics and syntax (the semantic relations marked by iconic, deictic inflections are transparent) does not aid acquisition, suggesting that the observation and internalization of the rules are abstract linguistic processes.

Summary and Conclusions

In this chapter we have looked at structure and processing of a system with very different surface characteristics from spoken language. Like spoken language, sign appears to be formed through a combination of a small number of distinctive features, which mediate perception and memory for sign. Like some spoken languages, ASL marks cases using a system of inflections, and these seem to be acquired, produced, perceived, and remembered somewhat independently of the base sign. Like spoken language, sign has the capability for expressing complex linguistic relations like anaphoric reference, embedding, and figurative language. Sign appears to show similar laterality, short-term memory, and perhaps categorical perception effects as spoken language and appears to be perceived through redundant minimal features, as is spoken language.

Although sign is visual and not auditory it seems to contain most of the features we consider defining characteristics of language. Hockett's features of vocal-auditory channel, broadcast transmission and reception, and specialization of the channel are not met by sign. However, sign like speech is rapid fading and allows interchangeability and total feedback. More importantly, sign shows semanticity, arbitrariness and discreteness (at least in processing), displacement, productivity, duality of patterning, traditional transmission, learnability, metalanguage, medium transferability, simultaneity and smear, recursiveness, and the human information transmission rate.

Thus, the comparison of ASL and spoken language not only suggests that ASL is a language, since it meets our most important criteria, but also, *because ASL has potential for being so different and is nonetheless similar, suggests that there are real cognitive/linguistic pressures affecting the shape of language.* In chapters 12 and 13 we will look at the shape of language when some of these pressures are removed or altered—by brain damage or psychological disease.

REFERENCES

Akamatsu, C. T. (in press). Fingerspelling formulae: A word is more or less the sum of its letters. In W. Stokoe (Ed.). *Proceedings of the Third International Symposium on Sign Language.* Washington, D.C.: Gallaudet University Press.

Baker, C., & Padden, C. A. (1978). Focussing on the nonmanual components of American Sign Language. In P. Siple (Ed.). *Understanding Sign Language through Sign Language Research,* pp. 27–57. NY: Academic Press.

Battison, R. *Lexical Borrowings in American Sign Language.* Silver Spring, MD: Linstok, 1978.

Bellugi, U., & Fischer, S. D. (1972). A comparison of sign language and spoken language. *Cognition, 1,* 173–200.

Bellugi, U., & Klima, E. S. (1982). From gesture to sign: Deixis in a visual-gestural language. In R. J. Jarvella & W. Klein (Eds.). *Speech, Place and Action: Studies of Language in Context,* pp. 297–313. Sussex: Wiley and Sons Ltd.

Bellugi, U., Klima, E. S., & Siple, P. (1975). Remembering in signs. *Cognition, 3,* 93–125.

Bickerton, D. (1982). Learning without experience the creole way. In L. Obler & L. Menn (Eds.). *Exceptional Language and Linguistics,* pp. 15-29. NY: Academic Press.

Bonvillian, J. D., Orlansky, M. D., & Novack, L. L. (1983). Early sign language acquisition and its relations to cognitive and motor development. In J. Kyle and B. Woll (Eds.). *Language in Sign,* pp. 116-125. London: Croom Helm.

Cutting, J. E., & Kozlowski, L. T. (1977). Recognizing friends by their walk: Gait perception without familiarity cues. *Bulletin of the Psychonomic Society, 9,* 353-356.

Davies, S. (1983). "The tongue is quicker than the eye": Nonmanual behaviors in American Sign Language. Paper presented at the Third International Symposium on Sign Language Research, Rome.

Edge, V. L., & Hermann, L. (1977). Verbs and the determination of subject and object in American Sign Language. In L. Friedman (Ed.). *On the Other Hand,* pp. 137-179. NY: Academic Press.

Fischer, S. D. (1973). Verb inflections in American Sign Language and their acquisition by the deaf child. Paper presented at the Winter Meetings, Linguistic Society of America.

Fischer, S. D. (1975). Influences on word order change in American Sign Language. In C. N. Li (Ed.). *Word Order and Word Order Change,* pp. 3-25. Austin: University of Texas Press.

Fischer, S. D. (1978). Sign language and creoles. In P. Siple (Ed.). *Understanding Language Through Sign Language Research,* pp. 309-331. NY: Academic Press.

Fischer, S. D., & Tartter, V. C. (in press). The dot and the line: Perception of ASL under reduced conditions. In W. Stokoe (Ed.). *Proceedings of the Third International Symposium on Sign Language Research,* Washington, D.C.: Gallaudet University Press.

Frishberg, N. (1975). Arbitrariness and iconicity: Historical change in American Sign Language. *Language, 51,* 696-719.

Grosjean, F. (1977). The perception of rate in spoken and sign languages. *Perception & Psychophysics, 22,* 408-413.

Grosjean, F. (1980). Psycholinguistics: Psycholinguistics of sign language. In H. Lane & F. Grosjean (Eds.). *Recent Perspectives on American Sign Language,* pp. 33-59. Hillsdale, NJ: Lawrence Erlbaum Associates.

Grosjean, F., & Lane, H. (1977). Pauses and syntax in American Sign Language. *Cognition, 5,* 101-117.

Hockett, C. F. (1960). The origin of speech. *Scientific American, 203,* 88-96.

Hoemann, H. (1975). The transparency of meaning of sign language gestures. *Sign Language Studies, 7,* 151-161.

Hoffmeister, R., & Wilbur, R. (1980). Developmental: The acquisition of sign language. In H. Lane & F. Grosjean (Eds.). *Recent Perspectives on American Sign Language,* pp. 61-78. Hillsdale, NJ: Lawrence Erlbaum Associates.

Johansson, G. (1973). Visual perception of biological motion and a model for its analysis. *Perception & Psychophysics, 14,* 201-211.

Jordan, K., & Battison, R. (1976). A referential communication experiment with foreign sign languages. *Sign Language Studies, 10,* 69-80.

Klima, E., & Bellugi, U. (1979). *The Signs of Language.* Cambridge, MA: Harvard University Press.

Lane, H. (1979). *The Wild Boy of Aveyron.* London: Granada Publishing Ltd.

Lane, H., Boyes-Braem, P., & Bellugi, U. (1976). Preliminaries to a distinctive feature analysis of American Sign Language. *Cognitive Psychology, 8,* 263-289.

Launer, P. (1982). "A plane is not to fly": Acquiring the distinction between related nouns and verbs in American Sign Language. Unpublished doctoral dissertation, City University of New York.

Liddell, S. (1980). *American Sign Language Syntax.* The Hague: Mouton.

Loew, R. C. (1980). Learning American Sign Language as a first language: Roles and reference. Paper presented at the Third National Symposium on Sign Language Research and Teaching, Boston.

Marslen-Wilson, W. (1975). Sentence perception as an interactive parallel process. *Science, 189,* 226–228.

Mayberry, R. (1977). Facial expression, noise and shadowing in American Sign Language. Paper presented at the First National Symposium on Sign Language Research and Teaching, Chicago. Reported in Grosjean, 1980.

McIntyre, M. & Yamada, T. (1976). Visual shadowing: An experiment in American Sign Language. Paper presented to the Linguistics Society of America, Philadelphia, 1976. Reported in Grosjean, 1980.

Meier, R. P. (1982). Icons, analogues and morphemes: The acquisition of verb agreement in American Sign Language. Unpublished doctoral dissertation, University of California at San Diego.

Miller, G. A., & Nicely, P. E. (1955). An analysis of perceptual confusions among some English consonants. *Journal of the Acoustical Society of America, 27,* 338–352.

Newkirk, D., Klima, E. S., Pederson, C. C., & Bellugi, U. (1980). Linguistic evidence from slips of the hand. In V. A. Fromkin (Ed.). *Errors in Linguistic Performance: Slips of the Tongue, Ear, Pen, and Hand,* pp. 165–197. NY: Academic Press.

Newport, E. L. (1982). Task specificity in language learning? Evidence from speech perception and American Sign Language. In E. Wanner & L. R. Gleitman (Eds.). *Language Acquisition: The State of the Art,* pp. 450–486. Cambridge: Cambridge University Press.

Newport, E. L., & Bellugi, U. (1978). Linguistic expression of category levels in a visual-gestural language: A flower is a flower is a flower. In E. Rosch & B. B. Lloyd (Eds.). *Cognition and Categorization,* pp. 49–71. Hillsdale, NJ: Lawrence Erlbaum Associates.

Newport, E. L., & Meier, R. P. (in press). Acquisition of American Sign Language. In D. I. Slobin (Ed.) *The Cross-Linguistic Study of Language Acquisition.* Hillsdale, NJ: Lawrence Erlbaum Associates.

Petitto, L. A. From gesture to symbol: The relation between form and meaning in the acquisition of personal pronouns in American Sign Language. In *Proceedings from Stamford Child Language Conference.*

Poizner, H. (1981). Visual and "phonetic" coding of movement: Evidence from American Sign Language. *Science, 212,* 691–693.

Poizner, H., & Battison, R. (1980). Neurolinguistic: Cerebral asymmetry for sign language: Clinical and experimental evidence. In H. Lane & F. Grosjean (Eds.). *Recent Perspectives in American Sign Language,* pp. 79–101. Hillsdale, NJ: Lawrence Erlbaum Associates.

Poizner, H., Bellugi, U., & Lutes-Driscoll, V. (1981). Perception of American Sign Language in dynamic point-light displays. *Journal of Experimental Psychology: Human Perception and Performance, 7,* 430–440.

Poizner, H., Bellugi, U., & Tweney, R. D. (1981). Processing of formational, semantic, and iconic information in American Sign Language. *Journal of Experimental Psychology: Human Perception and Performance, 7,* 1146–1159.

Poizner, H., & Lane, H. (1978). Discrimination of location in American Sign Language. In P. Siple (Ed.). *Understanding Language Through Sign Language Research,* pp. 271–287. NY: Academic Press.

Poizner, H., Newkirk, D., & Bellugi, U. (1983). Processes controlling human movement: Neuromotor constraints in American Sign Language. *Journal of Motor Behavior, 15,* 2–18.

Poizner, H., Newkirk, D., Bellugi, U., & Klima, E. S. (1981). Representation of inflected signs from American Sign Language in short-term memory. *Memory & Cognition, 9,* 121–131.

Rosch, E., Mervis, C. B., Gray, W., Johnson, D., & Boyes-Braem, P., (1976). Basic objects in natural categories. *Cognitive Psychology, 8,* 382–439.

Shand, M. A. (1980). Short-term coding processes of congenitally deaf signers of ASL: Natural language considerations. Unpublished doctoral dissertation, University of California at San Diego.

Shand, M. A. (1982). Sign-based short-term coding of American Sign Language of signs and printed English words by congenitally deaf signers. *Cognitive Psychology, 14,* 1–12.

Shand, M. A., & Klima, E. S. (1981). Nonauditory suffix effects in congenitally deaf signers of American Sign Language. *Journal of Experimental Psychology: Human Learning and Memory, 7,* 464–474.

Siple, P. (1978). Visual constraints for sign language communication. *Sign Language Studies, 19,* 95–110.

Stokoe, W. C., Casterline, D., & Croneburg, C. (1965). *A Dictionary of American Sign Language on Linguistic Principles.* Washington, D.C.: Gallaudet University Press.

Stungis, J. (1981). Identification and discrimination of handshape in American Sign Language. *Perception & Psychophysics, 29,* 261–276.

Supalla, S. (1980). ASL name signs do not have to be iconic. Working paper, Salk Institute.

Supalla, T., & Newport, E. (1978). How many seats in a chair? The derivation of nouns and verbs in American Sign Language. In P. Siple (Ed.). *Understanding Language Through Sign Language Research,* pp. 91–132. NY: Academic Press.

Tartter, V. C., & Fischer, S. D. (1982). Perceiving minimal distinctions in ASL under normal and point-light display conditions. *Perception & Psychophysics, 32,* 327–334.

Tartter, V. C., & Knowlton, K. C. (1980). Sign language communication over telephone bandwidth channels: A proposal. In B. Frokjaer-Jensen (Ed.). *The Sciences of Deaf Signing,* pp. 141–147. Copenhagen: The University of Copenhagen.

Tartter, V. C., & Knowlton, K. C. (1981). Perception of sign language from an array of 27 moving spots. *Nature, 289,* 676–678.

Tervoort, B. T., & Stroombergen, M. (1983). The situation of sign in Europe. Paper presented at the Third International Symposium on Sign Language Research, Rome.

Tweney, R. D., Heiman, G. W., & Hoemann, H. W. (1977). Psychological processing of sign language: Effects of visual disruption on sign intelligibility. *Journal of Experimental Psychology: General. 106,* 255–268.

Volterra, V. (1983). Gestures, signs and words at two years, or when does communication become language? In J. Kyle and B. Woll (Eds.). *Language in Sign,* pp. 109–115. London: Croom Helm.

Volterra, V., & Caselli, C. (1983). From gestures and sounds to signs and words. Paper presented at the Third International Symposium on Sign Language Research, Rome.

Whorf, B. L. (1956). *Language, Thought, and Reality.* J. B. Carroll, (Ed.). Cambridge, MA: MIT Press.

Wickelgren, W. A. (1965). Acoustic similarity and intrusion errors in short-term memory. *Journal of Experimental Psychology, 70,* 102–108.

Woodward, J. (1978). Historical bases of American Sign Language. In P. Siple (Ed.) *Understanding Language Through Sign Language Research,* pp. 333–348. NY: Academic Press.

STUDY QUESTIONS

1. Discuss the role of iconicity in the structure of sign language and in its processing. Why is this issue interesting?

2. Compare ASL sentence structure with that of English. Consider differences and similarities in the use of content and function words, order and inflection as syntax

markers, and indexing and explicit reference. Is there any reason to consider one device better or more advanced than its counterpart in the other language? Discuss.

3. There is a long history of considering speech special, both in terms of its processing and in terms of its effect on language. Given what you know about sign, discuss whether speech is special. Consider issues such as categorical perception and auditory memory (among others of like ilk), as well as issues such as the information rate, simultaneity and smear, and broadcast transmission (and others of like ilk) as special characteristics of language as derived from speech.

12

The Dissolution of Language: Brain Damage

Underlying most of our discussion of language has been the explicit assumption that language is structured, and structured on many levels. As we discussed, the task for children as they develop is to acquire the structure, by unfolding an innate scheme for it and/or by inferring it from the sample utterances to which they are exposed. Once the organization is acquired, in the adult, it is used to produce and understand language; the rules inferred are productive.

What happens if the organization is disrupted either in development or in adulthood? Do we see a total loss of language skills? Or is only a part of the language "machine" broken, with the other parts functioning—maybe producing words but without syntactic structure, or producing sounds but no recognizable words? Can we learn from what remains after disruption something about the prior organization of the language? Is it possible, for example, to lose *only* the "a" section of the mental dictionary, or all superordinate associations of canary, or the ability to make or understand passive sentences, or the ability to understand but not to speak? If any particular aspect of language behavior could be selectively damaged without affecting the rest of language behavior, we might infer that that aspect had been an independent unit of language processing. What would language look like *without* the "a" section of the mental dictionary, transformational rules, or any other structural component? Would it still appear organized? Would it still satisfy our criteria for language? Or would the system begin to look like chimpanzee sign language, with a word or two here and there but no syntactic structure? Once the structure has been disrupted, is it possible to recreate it, to teach the individual language again?

In this chapter we will examine some aspects of language after disruption arising from obvious brain damage caused by trauma, stroke, or tumor. We will look at this in two respects: briefly, what the language impairments can tell us about brain organization, and then, more substantially, what the impairments together with the location and severity of the damage imply about language organization in normal people.

In the next chapter we will examine very different kinds of language dissolution, those caused by personality disorders, as a comparison with dissolution from brain damage.

Introductory Remarks on Brain Organization

The search for a pattern in language dissolution from brain damage has been studied with respect to what it can tell about underlying brain organization, and also what it can tell about underlying language organization. It is the second of these approaches that we are most interested in, but it is worth mentioning the conceptual frameworks and methodologies of the first, since we will encounter them from time to time.

Anatomy of the Brain

Looking at a human brain from above as in Figure 12.1a, we see two large sections, the left hemisphere and the right hemisphere. If the brain is turned so we would be looking at one ear, as in Figure 12.1b, we can see other anatomical structures: the cerebellum, at the back, and the brain stem. We will be interested here in the rest of the brain, the *cerebrum,* which is also divided into sections according to major grooves such as the *central sulcus,* which divides the *frontal lobe* from the *parietal lobe,* and the *lateral cerebral sulcus,* which separates the *temporal lobe* from the frontal and parietal lobes. In addition, one other region is marked on the figure, a bump at the back, above the cerebellum, called the *occipital lobe.*

Figures 12.1a and b depict the surface of the brain. If the brain is sliced down the middle of the top of the head to the chin, we see layers of anatomical structure as in Figure 12.1c. We will be discussing primarily the effects of damage to the top layers of the structure, the "curly" surface, called the *cortex* (for the cerebrum, the cortex is called the cerebral cortex), and the region depicted just below it, in Figure 12.1c, the *corpus callosum.*

The brain may be divided into regions exclusively on the basis of anatomy, that is, which cells are connected to which. The corpus callosum, for example, stretches between the left and right hemispheres, and each nerve cell has a connection in each hemisphere. The cells of the occipital lobe connect to cells in the midbrain, in a region of the *thalamus,* which in turn connect to, among other regions, the nerve cells of the eye, the rods and cones. A different region of the thalamus receives connections from the nerve cells of the ear and makes connections with a different region of the cortex, near *Heschl's gyrus.*

Functional *Architecture and Localization versus Mass Action*

It is tempting to assign function to the regions of the brain simply on the basis of knowing their connections. Given that the corpus callosum stretches between the right and left hemispheres, for example, you might assume that the corpus callosum transfers information between them. Given that the occipital cortex connects with

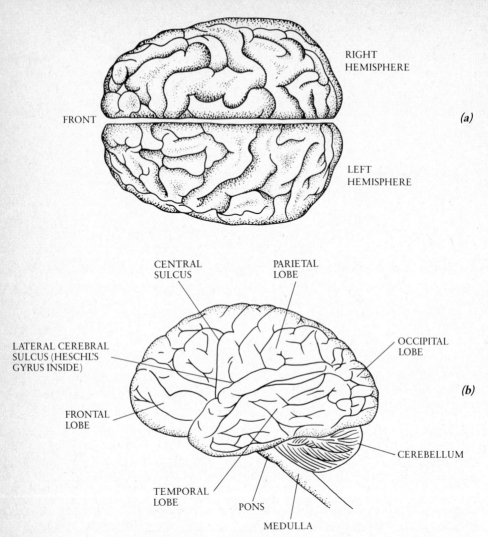

Figure 12.1 *Three views of the brain. (a) shows the brain from above. (b) shows the surface of the brain from the side. (c) shows a slice through one hemisphere, from the side. Major structures are marked in (b) and (c).*

the rods and cones, and that the *auditory cortex* connects with the nerve cells of the ear, you might assume that they are respectively involved with seeing and hearing; that is, you are assuming that different locations of the brain have different functions. This is the *localization hypothesis*.

Although most people today subscribe to some form of a localization model, it is by no means universally accepted. (We will come to an alternative shortly.) Philosophically, it is possible to see problems with it as soon as we turn from specific perceptions like vision and hearing (which seem to be separate experiences) to general mental functions like memory and attention. Consider, for example, your memory of a particular event, like getting up this morning. You should be able to recall quite a

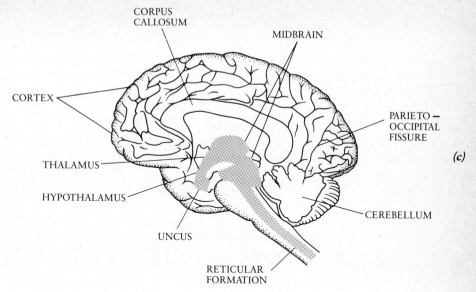

CORPUS CALLOSUM

MIDBRAIN

CORTEX

PARIETO — OCCIPITAL FISSURE

(c)

THALAMUS

HYPOTHALAMUS

CEREBELLUM

UNCUS

RETICULAR FORMATION

Figure 12.1 *(Continued)*

number of details about that event: the sequences of things that happened, the sound of the alarm, the warmth of the covers, the smell of breakfast, the glare of the sunlight, and so forth. Many of these memories come from different modalities of experience, clearly. Are they stored in separate locations of the brain by modality? If so, how are you able to evoke them together as a memory of a single event?

You can argue that since there are connections among sections of the brain, that information about the "event" may be distributed in several places, all interconnected to conceive of that event. Or you could argue that the event was remembered in one location, independent of the modality of the component experiences, and that successive events in time were stored in successive locations. The advantage of the second kind of approach is that we seem to do a fair job of recalling sequences of events in time: You may have started with the alarm going off, then considered what your next moves were, in order, and in fact, been able to reconstruct the entire day like that. And we might note that memory for order, regardless of shared modality, may be important in many tasks, such as perceiving or producing syntax in English, or learning or producing a chain of motor responses. Therefore, we might expect recognition or memory for order to have a functional location in the brain. The difficult with this is that it suggests that visual memories, for example, are distributed throughout the cortex, associated with each event.

Organization in terms of event memory with successive events stored in successive locations and organization in terms of aspects of cognitive functions like visual memories or order recognition are still localization models. Such models predict that damage to specific areas of the brain has well-specified effects. The event organization suggests that it would be possible to destroy memory for the events of perhaps a month of one's life, while the cognitive function organization suggests that it would be possible to destroy order recognition generally across many cognitive abilities, such as syntax, counting, and learning a chain.

There is a logical difficulty with localization models that may now be clear. As we have seen, language skills involve memory, memory for events or memory for order. Memory also involves language; for example, we recall word strings better if they are grammatical and sensible than if they are random or anomalous, and we are more likely to confuse items in short-term recall if they share phonetic features. So, in this case, we see memory dependent on language and language dependent on memory, a *mutual dependence of cognitive functions*. Such a mutual dependence seems to suggest that destroying a part of the brain responsible for language should affect short-term memory, and destroying a portion responsible for short-term memory should affect language skills. So, will it be possible to tie one part of the brain to a particular cognitive function?

An alternative (see, for example, Pribram, 1971) is to assume that most portions of the brain, indeed most cells, have some, but not all, information about all skills and memories; that is, that one memory or skill is "smeared" across the brain, (as acoustic features underlying a single linguistic feature are smeared across the speech signal). This would suggest that activation of any one cell or region would simultaneously activate many memories and skills, but complete information about any one memory or skill would derive only from activation of the whole brain, or at least a large region of it. This approach to modelling brain structure is called *mass action*, or *holographic* memory. The advantage of simultaneity and smear in brain organization is the same as in pattern recognition: There is a built-in redundancy so that destruction of a portion of the brain, like destruction of a portion of the acoustic signal, does not result in loss of all "cues" to a particular pattern, memory, or skill. A second advantage to mass action models is that they take into account flexibility in learning, thinking, and behavior generally. Mass action proponents point out that in localization models, associations are permanent, a property of permanent connections. In mass action, a particular association arises from a particular pattern of neural activity, and the association may be altered without altering the connections of the cells themselves but rather altering those that are contributing to the neural response; that is, those firing at a particular time.

As we said earlier, most people subscribe to at least some form of a localization hypothesis. For example, destruction of a particular portion of the left hemisphere always results in right-sided paralysis, whereas destruction of the same portion of the right hemisphere always results in left-sided paralysis. (It may result in a weakening rather than a complete paralysis, called then *left* or *right hemiparesis*.) This suggests that control of the two halves of the body is located on different sides of the brain, a localization view. The question is whether we can similarly localize general or specific cognitive functions, whether the actions controlled by a region of the brain will correspond to "meaningful" structures or processes like the mental dictionary, short-term memory, a year in one's life, and so on.

On Interpreting Loss of Function from Brain Damage

Is it reasonable to conclude that since damage to the back of the frontal lobe (the *premotor* region) of the left hemisphere causes right-sided paralysis, the premotor region is responsible for sensation and/or motor coordination of the left side of the body? At first glance it may seem reasonable; but consider, if we damage the heart, thinking stops—is it reasonable to conclude that the heart is responsible for thinking? From the mass action approach, minor brain damage should cause loss of the most abstract, complex skills (those for which complete representation occurs only when most cells are activated), while greater damage will cause loss of additional, less abstract skills, and so on. The mass action model predicts that the same pattern of language loss should occur regardless of the location of damage, determined only by the number of cells destroyed. As we will see, this does not happen; rather, specific language losses seem to be correlated with specific sites of damage.

From the localization approach, the correlation between destruction of a particular region of the brain and loss of a particular skill is subject to several interpretations: The lost skill may be represented in the damaged portion of the brain, the damaged portion of the brain may bridge the representation and the execution of the lost skill, or the damaged portion of the brain may be responsible for a skill that underlies the lost skill. Since any of these possibilities is reasonable, one must be cautious in assigning a single explanation to a pattern of loss from brain damage.

Summary

In this section we have discussed some concepts and theories of brain organization: According to one theory, each region of the brain may subserve a specific function (localization); according to another, all regions may overlap in coding material so that functional damage depends not on a specific region but on the severity of impairment (mass action). We also pointed out the logical difficulties of tying structure to function on the basis of brain damage. As we said initially, the study of brain damage and language may be undertaken either to try to assign brain locations to functions, or to determine how language is normally organized and how it is reorganized after normal organization is impaired. Although we will use a standard assignment of brain location to function in describing language after brain damage, our principal interest is in language organization, not the brain.

Aphasia

It has been known since antiquity that brain damage can cause language impairments, although these were improperly understood as sensory disorders (effect on hearing). In the nineteenth century, Broca and Wernicke each described the language symptoms of patients who had come to autopsy and whose region of brain damage was therefore known. Figure 12.2 shows the side view of the brain marked with the areas Broca and Wernicke discovered, and other areas that we now know also result in language impairments if damaged. Box 12.1 lists some passages of conversation with patients suffering a lesion in Broca's or Wernicke's area.

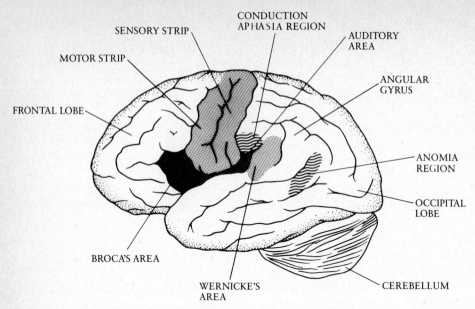

Figure 12.2 *A side view of the left hemisphere with regions marked which, when damaged, result in characteristic aphasias.*

Box 12.1 **Examples of Aphasic Language**

The following are excerpts of speech of brain-damaged patients. They are presented randomly, without regard to where the damage is. Do you see some that seem similar or different from others? Try to sort the passages into two categories and see if you can characterize the qualities of the language that are guiding your sorting.

1. But I figured that if I defective my my talking see my talking itself I I get my tongue back again to where I can talk from what they say why then it's liable to that will straighten me out again and bring me back to where I can hear something see and until I talk I under talk I got to do the interfering has got to act with me for a while see because it doesn't it won't interfere with me properly now now I hear them talking you know.

   (deVilliers, 1978, p. 131).

2. Well I had trouble with ... oh, almost everything that happened from the ... eh, eh ... Golly, the word I can remember, you know, is ah ... when I had the ... ah biggest ... ah ... that I had the trouble with, you know ... that I had the trouble with, and I still have a ... the ah ... different ... The things I want to say ... ah ... The way I say things, but I understand mostly things, most of them and what the things are.

   (Goodglass, 1973, p. 186).

3. [Describing a picture of a boy standing on a stool stealing cookies from a cookie jar, with a girl helping him on the left, and a woman on the right, washing dishes, distracted by water overflowing in the sink]

a. Cookie jar . . . fall over . . . chair . . . water . . . empty . . . ov . . . ov . . .
[examiner: "overflow?"]
Yeah.

b. Well, this is . . . mother is away here working out o'here to get her better, but when she's working, the two boys looking in the other part. One their small tile into her time here. She's working another time because she's getting, too.

(Blumstein, 1982, pp. 204–205.)

4. [Patient Peter Hogan explaining what brought him to the hospital] Yes . . . ah . . . Monday . . . ah . . . Dad and Peter Hogan, and Dad . . . ah . . . Hospital . . . and ah . . . Wednesday . . . Wednesday nine o'clock and ah Thursday . . . ten o'clock ah doctors . . . two . . . two . . . an doctors and . . . ah . . . teeth . . . yah . . . And a doctor an girl . . . and gums, and I.

[Answering about his former work in a paper mill]

Lower Falls . . . Maine . . . Paper. Four hundred tons a day! And ah . . . sulphur machines, and ah . . . wood . . . Two weeks and eight hours. Eight hours . . . no! Twelve hours, fifteen hours . . . workin . . . workin . . . workin! Yes, and ah . . . sulphur. Sulphur and . . . Ah wood. Ah . . . handlin! And ah sick, four years ago.

(Goodglass, 1973, p. 185).

5. Boy, I'm sweating, I'm awful nervous, you know, once in a while I get caught up, I can't mention the tarripoi, a month ago, quite a little, I've done a lot well, I impose a lot, while, on the other hand, you know what I mean, I have to run around, look it over, trebbin and all that sort of stuff.

(Gardner, 1975, p. 68)

6. (E) Were you in the Coast Guard?
(P) No, er, yes, yes . . . ship . . . Massachu . . . chusetts . . . Coastguard . . . years. [Raises hands twice indicating "19"]
(E) Oh, you were in the Coast Guard for nineteen years.
(P) Oh . . . boy . . . right . . . right.
(E) Why are you in the hospital?
(P) [Points to paralyzed arm] Arm no good. [Points to mouth] Speech . . . can't say . . . talk, you see.
(E) What happened to make you lose your speech?
(P) Head, fall, Jesus Christ, me no good, str, str . . . oh Jesus . . . stroke.
(E) Could you tell me what you've been doing in the hospital?
(P) Yes sure. Me go, er, uh, P. T. nine o'cot, speech . . .
two times . . . read . . . wr . . . ripe, er, rike, er, write . . .
practice . . . get-ting better.

(from Gardner, 1975, p. 61)

Types of Aphasia

Aphasia refers to brain damage that causes a language disturbance, and traditionally applies only to left hemisphere damage in the regions shown in Figure 12.2. Left hemisphere damage in these areas produces aphasia in nearly all right-handed individuals and in many left-handed individuals. Some left-handers may become aphasic only after damage to the right hemisphere, some only after damage to the left hemisphere, and others after damage to either hemisphere, indicating a more distributed language representation than that found among most right-handers.

Broca's Aphasia.   *Broca's aphasia* (called *aphemia* by Broca) is produced by damage to the premotor region. It is characterized by disfluent speech: many pauses, hesitations, word-finding difficulties, and a telegraphic style, as some of the protocols in Box 12.1 suggest. Because of the telegraphic style, the noticeable absence of function words, Broca's aphasics are sometimes called *agrammatic*. Broca's aphasics give the impression in conversation of understanding the speech of others, and also of awareness of their own disfluencies. They seem frustrated at talking in a perpetual tip-of-the-tongue state and usually report knowing what they want to say although unable to express it. Broca's aphasia is therefore sometimes characterized as an *expressive disorder* or *nonfluent aphasia*.

In addition to word finding difficulties and the absence of function words, the speech of Broca's aphasics is abnormal, containing many errors or slips of the tongue as well as phonetic distortions affecting both sound segments and speech melody. These are known as *paraphasias*. As we have seen in normal speech errors, a slip may involve a single phoneme or feature, called a *literal* (one-letter, if you will) *paraphasia*, or may involve an entire word substitution, called *verbal paraphasia*.

Because Broca's area borders on the left motor cortex, Broca's aphasia is frequently accompanied by right-sided paralysis. It is important to recognize that articulatory difficulties found in speech production do not result directly from this paralysis. Broca's aphasics usually can perform nonverbal tasks using the articulatory apparatus without difficulty. They can, on command, pantomime blowing out a match or brushing their teeth. (Difficulty with such tasks, when it occurs, is called *apraxia*.) Moreover, they usually show the same problems in writing as they do in speech, indicating that it is not exclusively a motor-articulatory deficit producing the speech errors. In Box 12.1, the Broca's aphasics are represented by extracts 3a, 4, and 6.

Wernicke's Aphasia.   Conversation with a Wernicke's aphasic is substantially different from conversation with a Broca's aphasic. Wernicke's aphasics speak fluently, without obvious effort and without particular distress at what they are saying. The difficulty in talking to Wernicke's aphasics comes in trying to interpret what they have said: The speech, although fluent-sounding, does not go anywhere; there are few content words with substance (there are empty words like "thing," however), and no obvious development of ideas. It may be difficult to stop a Wernicke's aphasic from speaking, to ask a question, and it is frequently not clear that the response is, in fact, an attempt to answer the question. Because it is difficult to elicit appropriate responses from Wernicke's aphasics, their problem has been at times interpreted as reflecting an inability to understand the question. Therefore Wernicke's aphasia is considered a *receptive* or comprehension disorder. Because their output is fluent they are also called *fluent aphasics.*

Wernicke's area is located in the temporal lobe, as can be seen in Figure 12.2, behind (*posterior* to) Broca's area. Because Wernicke's area does not border on the motor areas, Wernicke's aphasics rarely show a paralysis. However, if the damage is extensive, it may extend into the occipital lobe, creating visual disturbances. At the cortical level, a visual disruption does not necessarily produce blindness, in the sense that the individual may still be able to detect the presence or absence of light, and, for example, be able to walk around a room, appropriately avoiding articles of furniture. (Inability to detect light may result from cortical damage, depending on the area of the cortex affected. Some visual signals go to areas of the brain other than the cortex, so cortical damage may not destroy all light sensation.) Cortical disturbances usually mean that individuals are unable to recognize what something is from the visual input alone; the light pattern has lost all meaning. Recognition failure is called *agnosia;* if the failure is in visual recognition, it is visual agnosia, if in auditory recognition, auditory agnosia.

Characterizing Wernicke's aphasia as a comprehension disorder can be misleading with respect to the quality of the productions. Wernicke's patients are represented in passages 1, 2, 3b, and 5 of Box 12.1. As you can see, there are problems in speech output. First, substantive content words are missing, as has already been indicated. Second, although the flow is smooth with few hesitations, there are still slips of the tongue, paraphasias. Again these may be either phoneme or whole word slips. In phoneme substitutions, in Wernicke's aphasics, the error may be so extreme as to render the word unrecognizable, particularly if there are several phoneme substitutions in one word. (This could arise if the phonological representation of the word is not accessed, or if it is accessed and then mispronounced.) The word then looks like nonsense and is called a *neologism,* like "tarripoi" in extract 5. Patients who produce frequent neologisms are called *jargon aphasics*—their speech is like Lewis Carroll's "The Jabberwocky" ("'Twas brillig and the slithy toves ... "), syntactically interpretable but nonsense because of the inclusion of meaningless lexical items. Word substitutions by Wernicke's aphasics are characterized by *perseveration* (the tendency to repeat a word once it has been used), as the passages in Box 12.1 demonstrate. They also may result in ungrammatical sentences, by substitution, for example, of a conjunction for a noun or verb as in "to that," in the first passage. So we see in the productions of Wernicke's aphasics problems on the phonological, semantic, and syntactic levels.

Other Types of Aphasia.   We have described classical, stereotypical Broca's and Wernicke's aphasias. It is important to realize that the descriptions are idealized and that in fact no two patients are ever exactly alike, although patterns are observable in the disruption. The individual differences observed may be due, in part, to individual differences in organization before the damage, and in part, to differences in severity and location of the damage.

In addition to the "classical" Broca's and Wernicke's aphasias, there are other regions of brain damage that have been categorized according to their effects on language. Patients with damage principally in Broca's (*anterior* or front) area, but with greater comprehension deficits than usual for Broca's aphasia (perhaps because there is a wider area of damage), are known as *mixed anteriors*. If there is great damage to both anterior and posterior portions, the patient is a *global aphasic,* who may have no apparent comprehension, and production reduced to *only* a single word (like "hello" or an obscenity) or phrase, produced repetitively. Patients with large lesions surrounding Broca's and Wernicke's areas—but not directly affecting them—have *isolation of the speech areas* and may be unable to produce (*transcortical motor aphasia*) or understand (*transcortical sensory aphasia*) spontaneous, meaningful speech, since the language area is effectively detached from other areas of meaning association. These patients, however, are good at repetition and often display *echolalia,* repeating or echoing whatever is said to them.

Damage to the brain may also spare large regions of Broca's and Wernicke's areas, leaving more language function intact. If the damage occurs between Broca's and Wernicke's areas (severing the neural pathway connecting the regions), the patient is a *conduction aphasic.* Comprehension and production are both likely to be good, but the patient will have great difficulties with repetition, since to repeat, presumably, a sentence must be processed in Wernicke's area and then passed to Broca's area for production, and the "passage" is blocked. A small *lesion* (area of damage) in an area adjacent to Wernicke's area, the *angular gyrus* (see Figure 12.2), can result in difficulty naming objects in isolation. This is known as a *pure naming deficit* and in its purest form is very rare. These patients frequently are able to come up with word names in fluent speech but not in isolation. After being prompted to say the word "no," the patient may exclaim in frustration, "No, no, I told you I can't say 'no!'" and still not be able to produce the word in isolation (Gardner, 1975, p. 78).

A lesion behind Wernicke's area, marked in Figure 12.2, produces mostly naming problems, but these arise in recalling names in spontaneous speech as well as in isolated naming tasks. This deficit is known as *anomia,* and patients with it are sometimes called *amnestic aphasics.* The speech of such patients is described as *circumlocutory,* since to communicate a concept for which they cannot recall a word, the patients frequently detour around that word, substituting vague words such as "that thing" for specific concepts, or using ingenious but nonverbal ways of communicating. For example, one patient tried to refer to his daughter's wedding, did not have the word, and said "'And then, she, you know ... dum-dum-dedum' to the tune of the melody of the wedding march" (Goodglass, 1980, p. 647).

Summary. In this section we have discussed classic aphasic symptoms. Broca's aphasia, produced by a lesion in the premotor cortex, is characterized by slow, hesitant, errorful speech, a telegraphic style, and seemingly good comprehension. Wernicke's aphasia, produced by a lesion in the temporal lobe, is characterized by fluent speech, full of function words and complex structure, but devoid of content words and sense, and poor comprehension. Conduction aphasia, produced by a lesion between Broca's and Wernicke's areas, permits good comprehension and production but impairs repetition. Patients with scattered lesions in Broca's and Wernicke's areas show a variety of comprehension and production deficits depending on the nature and extent of the lesions.

Effects on Language of Other Brain Damage

In the last section we discussed the effects of damage to the "language hemisphere" in adults who had normal language before the damage. For most of this century it was thought that the right hemisphere was not involved in language processing at all, and therefore that damage to the right hemisphere had no effect on language. More recently it has been shown that the right hemisphere is not completely "silent," and that there are observable deficits as a result of right hemisphere damage. In this section we will discuss the effects of right hemisphere damage on language, and the effects on language of damage to the corpus callosum, of severing the connections between the hemispheres. Finally, we will briefly consider the results of damage to any portion of the brain on acquisition of language in the child.

Right Hemisphere Lesions. For people with language-dominant left hemispheres, lesions in the right hemisphere do not dramatically disturb either production or comprehension of language: Patients are able to construct sentences, repeat, find words, and respond to sentences on the basis of semantic and syntactic content. However, right hemisphere damage can produce a variety of cognitive impairments, some of which, at least indirectly, affect language skills. Particular agnosias are associated with right hemisphere damage, such as the inability to recognize faces, which of course means that a patient cannot produce a person's name from the sight of the face alone. Right hemisphere damage also can produce severe disorientation, inability to locate one's self in space, read maps, and so forth. It can result in a loss of musical skills, called *amusia*. (Amusias may also be associated with left hemisphere damage.) Finally, right hemisphere damage can produce an odd attentional disturbance, known misleadingly as *left visual neglect*, in which a patient thoroughly ignores the left side of space, copying only the right sides of pictures, dressing or shaving only the right side of the body, etc. Although it is called "visual," it is important to note that the attentional disturbance is not just visual but involves a tactile neglect as well.

Aside from difficulties in naming or describing experiences to which they no longer attend, right hemisphere patients do exhibit abnormalities of language. In particular, prosody and emotional content in language is disturbed. Intonation contours may be flat, and repetitions of sentences differing in tone of voice (a sentence said angrily, happily, with surprise, etc.) may not express the emotional quality (Ross, 1982; Ross and Mesulam, 1979). In addition, patients may be unable to describe their own feelings, although they may remember previous ones. Thus, for example, Ross reported a patient who spoke of being "broken-hearted" at the arrest of her brother some years before her stroke, but who used no emotional vocabulary to describe her own current condition. Other patients who clearly showed symptoms of depression did not describe themselves as depressed, nor report any change of feeling when treated with antidepressants that clearly changed their moods. Because they cannot express their emotions either in content words or in intonation changes in the sentences, right hemisphere patients may have difficulty in making others respond to them appropriately. Finally, patients with difficulties expressing emotion through intonation showed impairment in other noncontent communication behavior: Facial expressions were flat, gestures were not indicative of emotional content, and patients were unable to pantomime effectively (Ross and Mesulam, 1979). Together the results suggest a right hemisphere control of emotional expression in communication, regardless of modality.

The emotional impairment of right hemisphere patients not only affects paralinguistic behavior, as just described, but may also affect high-level linguistic behavior in interesting ways. Winner and Gardner (1977) tested some right hemisphere patients in an extensive study of aphasics' metaphor processing abilities, which will be discussed later. The patients were given sentences such as "he had a heavy heart" and asked to paraphrase their meanings and to select among pictures representing the concrete meaning of the sentence (someone carrying a heavy heart on his back), the real meaning, and the meanings of individual words. Right hemisphere patients paraphrased the sentences normally, indicating intact language comprehension, but were as likely to select the funny/strange picture of the literal meaning as the less bizarre picture of the metaphorical meaning. Presumably, when presented with two choices that were equally reasonable in terms of the sense of the words, they were unable to rule out one that should have been viewed as a "joke," an emotional disturbance affecting metaphor comprehension.

It is interesting to note that the paralinguistic deficits may be analyzed according to location of damage (Ross, 1981), and show a comparable pattern of breakdown to the linguistic deficits in left hemisphere patients described in the last section. Unfortunately, few right hemisphere patients have been tested with respect to production, repetition, and comprehension of intonation contours and emotional expression, so the similarities noted in each instance are for no more than three right hemisphere patients. Nevertheless, the pattern is striking. Patients with right hemisphere lesions in the equivalent of Broca's area were unable to mimic spontaneously or produce emotional overtones in their speech, but were able to identify emotions in the speech of others. Patients with lesions in the right hemisphere equivalent of Wernicke's area could speak with emotional overtones, but were not able to recognize emotionality in others' speech.

Examination of the patterns of behavior of patients with unilateral right or left hemisphere damage has led to the overly simplistic conclusion that the two hemispheres have different specialties in cognitive processing. The left hemisphere is often considered specialized for detailed linguistic analysis of segments and their combinations. This underlies production and perception of sequential phonetic elements and also production and perception of sequential morphemes for syntactic processing. The left hemisphere also appears to be the seat of both the dictionary (meaning store) and the lexicon (name store—see Chapter 3 for the distinction), such that damage to the left side may disrupt both semantic processing and word finding. The right hemisphere is considered specialized for spatial processing and recognition or production of global characteristics, the overall effect of the sequential combination of auditory or visual displays (see, for example, Springer and Deutsch, 1981, p. 4; Zaidel, 1978, p. 14). Thus, damage to the right hemisphere disturbs map reading, visual pattern recognition, and production or perception of intonation contours. In addition, it is tempting to conclude that the anterior regions of both hemispheres are involved in production, while the posterior regions are involved in comprehension or perception.

It is important to note, however, that this characterization of the skills and function of the regions of the brain is somewhat misleading. As we have seen, phonetic and grammatical elements are arranged not just sequentially but also hierarchically and are "smeared" in production and perception. In some sense it is as hard to isolate a segment corresponding to a "b" as it is to isolate a segment corresponding to a happy feeling. In addition, right hemisphere damage produces disturbances in music recognition and production, and certainly sequencing of elements, organization into hierarchies, and so on, is as characteristic of music as it is of language. Finally, left hemisphere damage disturbs at least production of intonation since Broca's aphasics cannot produce cohesive melodic word strings. So the division of labor commonly assigned to the hemispheres is clearly somewhat simplified.

Split-Brain Patients. As was pointed out earlier, it is somewhat suspect to draw conclusions about normal brain functions from the skills that are deficient following brain damage. When looking at a right-brain damaged patient's performance, for example, we see the results of damage to the right hemisphere as well as the effects of communication breakdown between the two hemispheres. We cannot therefore assume that a change in performance reflects normal right hemisphere control of that skill. For that reason, an important converging line of evidence about brain functions is provided by patients who have a lesion of the corpus callosum, so that communication between the hemispheres is disrupted without damage to the hemispheres themselves. These patients are called *split-brain* patients. Carefully designed stimuli may be used with such patients to determine the cognitive functions of each of the cerebral hemispheres.

As with other types of brain damage, a lesion of the corpus callosum may arise spontaneously. In addition, as treatment for severe cases of epilepsy, the corpus callosum has been deliberately severed surgically (Sperry, 1982). In all cases, the effects of the lesion are not immediately obvious, since usually stimuli are processed automatically by both hemispheres.

As we have already discussed in dichotic listening, for example, the right ear seems to have more direct access to the left hemisphere, and the left ear to the right hemisphere. Each ear does connect, however, to both hemispheres, and unless earphones are worn, any sound stimulus affects both ears anyway. When both ears are stimulated simultaneously through earphones, however, there is evidence that the information traveling from one ear to the hemisphere on the same side is suppressed en route by information traveling to that hemisphere from the ear opposite (see Milner, Taylor, and Sperry, 1968; Rosenzweig, 1951; and for somewhat conflicting results, Sparks and Geschwind, 1968; Bryden and Zurif, 1970). Thus, in split-brain patients, processing by only one hemisphere may be assessed since we may be reasonably sure under some conditions that the stimulation is not reaching the other hemisphere.

As we have already seen with normal visual stimulation, eye movements usually stimulate both halves of the retina, and therefore both hemispheres, with information about a particular visual scene. Information may be restricted to one half of the retina by causing the scene to move with the eye (by projecting an image onto a contact lens, for example [Zaidel, 1978, 1983] or by presenting a stimulus that is too short to allow an eye movement). In such cases, in split-brain patients, only one hemisphere will be able to process the stimulus.

Finally, tactile information automatically divides between the hemispheres according to the side of the body receiving it: The left hemisphere receives information from the right hand, and the right hemisphere, from the left hand. In split-brain patients contributions of each hemisphere may be independently assessed by allowing only one side of the body to touch an object. Since normally both ears, hands, and visual fields are stimulated by the same object, a split-brain patient can use the processing capacities of both hemispheres. Differences between them emerge only in subtle tests.

In most instances, testing of split-brain patients has confirmed the pattern of cerebral specialization observed with unilateral brain damage. When objects are presented to the right hand, right ear, or right visual field (left hemisphere), the patient is able to name or describe the object. When presentation is to the left side of the body, the patient *reports* sensing nothing but is able to match what was presented by pointing and may give an appropriate emotional response (as of surprised laughter to a presentation of a picture of a nude woman [Gazzaniga, 1967]). In other words, the patient is able to sense and recognize the object but not describe it verbally (Gazzaniga, 1967). After practice in testing, patients may become adept at cueing the verbal hemisphere. Gazzaniga (1967) reports one person who, when receiving stimulation only to the right hemisphere, would frown when he heard his left hemisphere giving the wrong answer, and the frown's feel would cue the left hemisphere to change the response to the correct one.

Support for cerebral specialization for particular functions has been obtained in split-brain patients by using stimuli that convey a different impression on the left and the right sides, called *chimeric stimuli.* If one focuses on the "*," "LA*LL" will send "LA" to the right hemisphere and "LL" to the left.[1] Instructions to match the stimulus with "LADY" or "BALL" should set up competitive responses, with the right hemisphere wanting to match "LADY" and the left hemisphere wanting to match

1. Note that the mapping of visual fields to hemispheres is confusing. Information on the *left* side of the *visual world* or left visual field goes to the *right* half of the retina (and conversely, the right visual field maps to the left half of the retina). Information from the right half of the retina then goes to the right hemisphere (with some stops along the way). Therefore if you are looking at the * in LA*LL, the LA is falling on the right side of the retina and the right hemisphere. You may demonstrate the retinal mapping to yourself by closing one eye, and then *gently, through the lid,* pressing on the eyeball of the other. If you are pressing on the temple side, you should have the sensation of a darkish circle near the nose. The visual sensation may be enhanced by moving your finger. The reason for the visual sensation is that you are causing the retinal neurons to fire by pressure stimulation, and when those neurons fire one has the sensation of seeing. The reason the sensation seems to be coming from near the nose is that the neurons near the temple normally respond to light from the opposite side of the visual world, the nasal side.

"BALL." Which response is made will indicate which hemisphere dominates in the decision. Chimeric stimuli may use verbal material, as in the example, or emotional material, as in (☺), which should send a smile to the left hemisphere and a frown to the right.

Using such stimuli, Levy and colleagues (Levy and Trevarthen, 1977; Levy, 1983) have shown that the right hemisphere dominates in recognizing complex visual patterns such as faces or line drawings. This includes recognition of written words, provided recognition is measured by matching the visual chimeric pattern to a normally written word. If recognition requires comprehension as in pointing to the object named by the word, or saying the word, the left hemisphere view of the stimulus dominates. This suggests that the left hemisphere does not efficiently use visual pattern recognition except for linguistic purposes. The right hemisphere's dominance in visual and spatial perception is also supported.

Although in most cases the capabilities of the right hemisphere reflected by callosal severing are the same as those suggested by hemispheric damage, the area of linguistic ability is a notable exception, still rife with controversy (see, for example, Sperry, 1982; Gazzaniga, 1983; Levy, 1983; Zaidel, 1983). Initial tests showed that if only the right hemisphere is presented with pictures, it can correctly match the pictures to spoken words. However, if presented with simple written commands such as "smile" or "frown" it is not able to respond. This led to the hypothesis that the right hemisphere is limited to a vocabulary of concrete nouns.

Subsequent tests of split-brain patients and one patient who had had her left hemisphere removed at a young age indicated additional right hemisphere linguistic skills. Zaidel (1978, 1983) has shown that the right hemispheres of select patients are capable of making semantic associations to words (such as selecting a superordinate), of understanding who is the actor and who is acted upon in short simple sentences, and of recognizing words in noise—about as well as a child between the ages of two and six years can. He also found the right hemispheres to have the skill of young adults in recognizing and understanding frequently used words from various grammatical classes.

Gazzaniga (1983) pointed out, however, that the good linguistic performance of the right hemisphere is found for only a small subset of split-brain patients. These particular patients, he suggested, may have unusual right hemisphere capabilities because of early onset of brain damage (see the next section) leading to development of linguistic skills in the right hemisphere. He also cautioned that insufficient care may have been taken in preventing cueing of the left hemisphere in testing these patients.

Whether Zaidel's claims are warranted or not, there is evidence that the right hemisphere plays some role in language understanding and production. It seems to have some vocabulary, either of concrete nouns or high-frequency words (which, of course are often one and the same), some ability to recognize words as visual patterns, and some ability to recognize spoken words in simple sentences. When noise is added or the sentences are long, the right hemisphere experiences difficulties, suggesting that the right hemisphere may not be able to perform either phonetic or syntactic processing or have extended memory for temporal order. The right hemisphere does seem to be specialized for paralinguistic analysis.

Brain Damage in Children.   By and large, studies of the left and right hemisphere capabilities of adults show distinct patterns of specialization of function. Since brain cells do not grow back, damage to the brain is permanent, leaving the patient with the opportunity to recover function only through the undamaged portions of the brain, which, in many cases, may have little linguistic skill at the time of the damage. Attempts to reteach language, to establish linguistic skills in regions where there had been none before the damage, are for the most part unsuccessful, although small improvement may be made (Schuell, in Sies, 1974; Lenneberg, 1967). Usually language recovers somewhat during the first few months after the injury, but this seems most likely to result from a reduction in the swelling caused by the damage, with recovery of prior physiological and psychological function rather than from learning in an undamaged site.

Since some mass action theories might hold, for example, that the different aphasic syndromes arise because of the size and not the locations of the lesions, it is important to note that the recovery process does *not* reflect a transition from Broca's to Wernicke's aphasias (or conversely) but an improvement in skills within the domain of the initial lesion. A patient with severe Broca's aphasia initially may develop less hesitation and greater ease of production as the swelling from the damage recedes but will not change from a telegraphic style to a fluent style lacking content words. This suggests that aphasic symptoms are tied at least in part to location of the lesion of the brain, not just to the extent of the damage (Goodglass, 1978).

The pattern of recovery is markedly different if brain damage occurs in childhood: Even in cases of total removal of the left hemisphere, recovery of language is excellent. There is some question regarding the age at which the excellent recovery chances diminish, but there is no question that after puberty prognosis is poor (Searleman, 1977). If the injury is sustained after the child has begun to acquire language, there is usually a period of silence, and then a reacquisition of language, proceeding through all the usual stages (babbling, single word, two word, ...). If the injury occurs after the child has acquired language, the child exhibits aphasic symptoms, which diminish gradually if the child is prepubescent (Lenneberg, 1967). The aphasic symptoms in childhood are not as differentiated with respect to location as in the adult (Goodglass, 1980).

It is important to recognize that the two hemispheres of the brain do not begin as equals at birth. Witelson and Pallie (1973) have shown that even in newborns there is a region in the left hemisphere that is usually larger than the corresponding region in the right and that in adults seems to be associated with language. According to current theory, however, the two hemispheres are each potentially capable of learning language at birth, but under normal conditions, the left hemisphere will take over this function and perhaps suppress the right hemisphere's capability (Lenneberg, 1967; Searleman, 1977). Damage to the left hemisphere during this period will allow the right hemisphere to assert its linguistic capacity, and this may allow the child to recover language function. It has also been suggested that for a period both hemispheres learn language, and that it is the result of this early right hemisphere language acquisition that is seen in the language capabilities of adult right hemispheres. (Zaidel [1983] has argued that this is unlikely since the right hemisphere language capacity is not consistent with any one age but varies depending on the skill tested.) Alternatively, it has been argued that those patients who demonstrate exceptional right hemisphere language skills may have suffered left hemisphere damage when they were young, allowing a partial right hemisphere takeover (Gazzaniga, 1983).

Summary and Conclusions. Studies of right-handed adults and right-handed children who have sustained either left hemisphere damage, right hemisphere damage, or callosal severing suggest an innately determined separation of cognitive functions. At birth the hemispheres may be considered equally capable. If development is normal, the left hemisphere becomes dominant for most language functions, perhaps suppressing language learning in the right hemisphere. There may be a period when both hemispheres acquire language, providing a redundant store for high-frequency, concrete content words (those learned early). While the left hemisphere dominates for most language skills, the right hemisphere dominates in other domains such as spatial reasoning and emotion recognition. If there is brain damage before cerebral specialization is complete, the intact hemisphere will take over function; if the lesion occurs after specialization, recovery of cognitive function is unlikely. The length of the critical period for cerebral specialization is disputed but does not extend beyond puberty.

Besides providing information on brain maturation, the studies discussed thus far suggest some division of language processes. Since the right hemisphere appears to dominate in paralinguistic (emotion, intonation, etc.) processing, and the left hemisphere in linguistic processing, we have evidence for separation of these two communication components. There also appears to be separation between comprehension and production in both right- and left-sided language processes. Finally, there is evidence for separate processes involved for content and function words and for concrete nouns and other words: Broca's aphasics retain the content words and lose the function words; Wernicke's aphasics retain function words and empty content words like "thing," losing meaningful content words; and the right hemisphere processes concrete content words in addition to the left, but only the left hemisphere processes other types of words. In the next section we will examine the results of studies of aphasics' language comprehension and production designed to determine specifically the independence and interactions of language processes.

Language Processing and Aphasia

As we have described aphasia thus far, there are several general types: Broca's aphasia, which seems to be an expressive disorder, preserving comprehension and content words but otherwise producing agrammatic speech; Wernicke's aphasia, which seems to be a receptive disorder, preserving production of fluent sentences but omitting all but empty content words and lacking comprehension; conduction aphasia, which is characterized by relatively preserved language skills except in repetition; and anomia, which preserves comprehension and fluent production but disturbs naming. Other types of aphasia are combinations of these, produced by scattered or large lesions in several areas. In addition, we have noted language deficits from right hemisphere damage, characterized by a loss of paralinguistic, suprasegmental information either in production, comprehension, or both. For the left hemisphere patients in particular, this characterization of the language deficit derives principally from clinical observation, not from careful analysis of the structure of the patients' speech, nor from careful experiments in production or comprehension. In this section we will look more closely at language processing after different kinds of brain damage.

Semantic Processing in Aphasia.   In discussing normal semantic processing, we considered four types of processes: basic concept organization (semantic memory), interfacing of concepts with word names, figurative and literal uses of word names, and integration and interaction of concepts in sentence processing. Each of these areas has been studied with aphasics. The processes indicated in brain damage provide support for some of our conclusions concerning normal semantic processes.

Conceptual Structure. Conceptual structure has been studied in aphasics using word association, picture selection in response to words, and similarity clustering. Schuell (in Sies, 1974) noted that verbal paraphasias (substitutions) were not random in aphasia but represented close associations of the target word, such as saying "man" for "boy," "table" for "chair," or "June" for "July," but never "table" for "July." In fact, nearly all verbal paraphasias she recorded fit into categories for word associations found in normals. However, when patients are asked specifically to make word associations, Broca's aphasics show essentially the same pattern as normals, but Wernicke's and other patients with posterior lesions make radically different associations not readily amenable to classification (Howes, 1973). This indicates that the *organization* of the mental dictionary is not disrupted for Broca's aphasics, but that for some reason, ability to retrieve an item or suppress retrieval of activated but incorrect items is disturbed. It is possible that the organization is disrupted in patients with posterior lesions.

Additional support for the hypothesis that semantic organization is intact in patients with anterior lesions comes from a modified association study by Goodglass and Baker (1976). They tested patients with anterior or posterior lesions together with non-brain-damaged controls. Subjects were shown a set of pictures; with each picture a word was presented. If the word was associated with the picture the patient was instructed to squeeze a response bulb, thus avoiding a verbal response. The pictures (e.g., of an orange), were either unrelated to the word (e.g., shoe), or named by the word (identity, e.g., orange), or the word was the superordinate category (e.g., fruit), an attribute (e.g., juicy), another member of the same category (e.g., apple), an associated action (e.g., eat), a situation in which the item was likely to be found (e.g., breakfast), or a sound-alike (e.g., arrange).

All patients and controls responded equally quickly to the identity condition, suggesting that they can understand the experimental task and can name. For the other conditions, the anterior patients again showed similar results to the nonaphasic patients, while the posterior patients showed deviant responses. The anterior patients and controls responded fastest to superordinate categories, attributes, actions, and situations. They also responded to other category members, but more slowly. Posterior patients deviated most markedly in a failure to recognize actions or contexts, although recognition of all associations was slower than normal. Again this suggests a disruption in semantic structure in posterior patients; since they respond well on the identity trials, they can recognize the words. Since they could not easily recognize associations, it suggests that they do not understand what the words mean.

In another study (cited in Caramazza and Berndt, 1978), patients were presented with pictures of cups varying in features (such as shape) to form a continuum between cups, glasses, and bowls. The pictures, in addition, contained contextual information, such as a box of breakfast cereal, appropriate for a bowl but not for a cup or a glass. The patients were asked to name the picture, and anterior patients, like normals, labeled the prototypical pictures well, had difficulty with pictures of stimuli at category boundaries, and used context to decide the identity of these peripheral members. Posterior patients were inconsistent in naming irrespective of typicality and did not appear to use context to disambiguate.

Zurif, Caramazza, Myerson, and Galvin (1974) tested semantic organization in aphasics by using a similarity measure. They presented patients with twelve high-frequency stimulus words: snake, trout, dog, tiger, turtle, crocodile, mother, wife, cook, partner, knight, husband—which could be categorized into a semantic hierarchy with the highest-level feature human-animal, and then these subdivided, respectively, into the features male-female, fish-mammal-reptile. Subjects were presented with three words at a time and asked to select the two words that seemed most similar. Patients with anterior lesions, like normals, seemed to structure their answers with respect to the human-nonhuman dimension (although clustering "dog" more often with the humans than the animals, perhaps as a household member). The anterior patients did not divide the members of the animal kingdom along biological lines, as did the normals, but rather clustered shark, crocodile, and tiger together—all ferocious and wild, apart from the other tamed, perhaps edible, animals. However, the clusters within the human terms looked normal, with husband and wife or wife and mother being most frequently associated, for example. In contrast, posterior patients showed no hierarchical organization of their semantic associations, not even showing the breakdown between human and nonhuman. Thus, although both sets of patients show some abnormalities of semantic organization, the posterior patients are more severely impaired. The disturbance for the anteriors may in fact reflect a normal highly salient association, which normals suppress in favor of another salient association that seems more intellectual.

The results thus far suggest that Wernicke's aphasics are more severely impaired than Broca's aphasics with respect to semantic organization, and in fact, may have little residual semantic structure. There are some data that suggest moderating this conclusion. Results from recent lexical decision tasks indicate that there may be still some associative structure intact in Wernicke's aphasics.

As you may recall from Chapter 3, in a lexical decision task subjects are presented a group of letters and their reaction times are measured to decide whether the letters form a word or not. Lexical decision times may be speeded by presenting a semantic association of the word before the letter group, priming it. The effects of priming on lexical decisions were measured for both visual (Milberg and Blumstein, 1981) and auditory (Blumstein, Milberg, and Shrier, 1982) lexical decision tasks in a variety of brain-damaged groups. The normal group was faster for all decisions, primed or not, than the brain-damaged groups, and the Wernicke's aphasics were much slower than other brain-damaged patients. However, all patients showed the same priming effects:

A semantically related prime speeded decisions. This suggests that at some level the Wernicke's aphasics still had access to semantic properties, and thus perhaps that their dictionaries were not completely destroyed.

There have also been studies indicating that anterior aphasics' semantic comprehension of function words is impaired. Examination of Box 12.1 shows that whereas fluent aphasics have no difficulty in appropriate use of function words, those are largely missing from productions of Broca's aphasics. There have been some indications that Broca's aphasics have selective impairments in function word comprehension as well. Zurif (1980), for example, found that anterior aphasics took longer to recognize low-frequency function words than high-frequency function words. Normals usually are faster on function words than on content words and do not show a response time dependent on frequency. Zurif concluded that there might be a special anterior process for function words that recognizes them as guides to syntax in addition to a posterior process that catalogues them in the mental dictionary and that the anterior process is disrupted in Broca's aphasia. However, Gordon and Caramazza (1982) have suggested that the results may not indicate a difference in processing of content and function words but rather a processing difference for words of exceptionally high frequency (as are most function words and relatively few content words).

Naming in Aphasia. Up to this point we have discussed semantic processing and comprehension independently of naming, and from the evidence in aphasia there is good reason to assume that naming and semantic organization are separate processes (Caramazza and Berndt, 1978). Nearly all brain-damaged patients experience word-finding difficulties, analogous to those normal people experience from time to time, but increased in severity. The increased severity is manifested not just in a quantitative increase in word-finding problems but also in qualitative changes. In brain damage, word-finding problems can affect words of all different grammatical classes and frequencies, while for normals it usually occurs only for low-frequency words. In brain damage the problem may occur for a word just provided to the patient, while for normals, a tip-of-the-tongue state rarely occurs for a recently heard word. And in brain damage the word-finding problem may be very sharply categorized so that all words of one category, such as color names, are lost, or words are lost from speech but can be retrieved in writing (Goodglass, 1980).

Goodglass, Klein, Carey, and Jones (1973) reported a study of word-finding problems in 135 patients. The patients were asked either to name a picture or to point to the picture when the name was provided. The pictures represented either objects, actions, letters, numbers, or colors. The most interesting finding was that for each patient, classes easy to name were not the same as those easily comprehended, indicating a dissociation between the naming ability and the ability to recognize an object from the name. Objects, which have high-frequency names, were among the best comprehended words and most poorly produced. Letter names were poorly comprehended but well-produced, and so forth. Since the ability to comprehend the name was not predictive of the ability to produce it, one can conclude that the two skills are separate. In addition to the dissociation between name production and name comprehension, the study also showed that naming skills varied with location of the lesion: All aphasics were equally poor at object naming, Broca's aphasics were relatively poorer at number and letter naming, and Wernicke's aphasics were relatively better at letter naming.

There have been various attempts to correlate the accessibility of names with properties of the lexicon or of the referents. As already mentioned, unlike word-finding difficulties in normals, naming difficulties in aphasics are not readily attributable to frequency. The relative inability of Wernicke's aphasics to come up with object names rather than letter names suggests that naming difficulties cannot be related only to concreteness either. And there are case studies of aphasics who have exclusively lost the ability to name colors of objects (Spreen, 1973), indicating that naming difficulties do not exclude picturable items. Nevertheless, *across* studies, frequency, concreteness, picturability, and manipulability of the referent have all been shown to affect naming ability in aphasia (Caramazza and Berndt, 1978). Generally one can conclude that the richer the associations to the object name, the more sensory modalities over which the referent may be experienced, the more frequent the experience, and so on, the more likely it is that the name will be accessible, perhaps because damage to one link between the concept and the name can be offset by the other links. None of these factors, however, is exclusively responsible for loss or preservation of naming.

Using the pattern of naming results from aphasia, Goodglass (1980) has hypothesized that naming is a two-stage process. The first stage is quick and involves access of a direct link between the concept of an object (or whatever) and its name. If for some reason that link is disturbed, as in the normal tip-of-the-tongue state, a slower associative process takes over in which the individual attempts to self-prompt, using, for example, associated concepts or sounds. In brain damage it is assumed that some of the direct links between concepts and names are impaired, accounting for the across-the-board word-finding difficulties. The associative links used in the second stage are differentially affected for different types of aphasias. For anterior aphasics, the associative network is largely intact so items like object or action names that are associatively rich may be well-retrieved compared with letter or number names. For posterior aphasics, the associative network (or access to it, to account for the results of Milberg and Blumstein discussed earlier) is disturbed and so this second stage process does not assist in naming. The disturbance in use of the associative network is reflected also in the inability of posterior aphasics to use context to disambiguate pictures or to recognize featural similarities between concepts named. Note also that the reliance on the slower second stage process could account for the slow, tortured speech of Broca's aphasics.

Grammatical Morphemes in Aphasia. In discussing semantic processing with brain damage thus far we have considered words as the unit of processing. It is reasonable to ask whether brain-damaged language reflects morphological processes: Are only word roots preserved in brain damage? Are words used together with their inflections? Are all grammatical morphemes equally available?

Examination of the protocols in Box 12.1 should indicate that grammatical morphemes are preserved in fluent aphasics but are lost at least in part in agrammatic aphasics. In Broca's aphasia, the plural and progressive morphemes tend to be used. As the protocols show, these aphasics have difficulty with pronouns: In one case (no. 4) the patient referred to himself by name, "Peter Hogan," to avoid using the pronouns; in another (no. 6), the patient improperly used "me" as the subject form. Formal studies of frequency of grammatical morphemes in nonfluent aphasia have shown the order of difficulty to be (from easiest to hardest): progressive, plural, contractible "be" form (e.g., isn't), noncontractible "be" form, articles, negative past, irregular past, and third-person singular (de Villiers, 1978). Broca's aphasics have also been shown to be more likely to omit the possessive "s" than the plural "s" and less likely to notice the omission of the possessive than the plural in the speech of others (Goodglass, 1973).

Additional evidence on morphological processes comes from examination of specific aphasic cases. Kehoe and Whitaker (1973) reported cases of aphasics who have particular difficulties with verbs and use in their stead nouns derived from them, such as "decision" for "decide." They also reported one patient who was able to produce derived words correctly but paused between the root and the derivational morpheme, decomposing "bandaged" to "bandage+ed" and "bacteriological" to "bacteriology+ical," for example.

The pattern of breakdown in grammatical morphemes in aphasia has interesting implications for normal processing. First, the fact that Broca's aphasics lose some inflectional and derivational morphemes while preserving content morphemes suggests that inflecting or deriving may be active processes, that words are not always stored in all possible forms. This is supported also by the case study in which the root and derivational morpheme seemed to be independently produced. Second, the fact that at times a patient may have access to one form of a word (like "me" or the noun) but not others, suggests that not all morphological changes are actively produced, but that there may be direct storage of some inflected forms.

Finally, it is interesting to observe that at least in some cases the grammatical morphemes better preserved in aphasia are not the ones earliest acquired. In particular, the past-tense markers usually precede use of the copula (the verb "be" in identity relations, such as "I am happy") in acquisition, and are more likely to disappear in dissolution than the copula (de Villiers, 1978). Since the acquisition order has been attributed to semantic or phonetic salience, the pattern in breakdown is clearly not just a result of low salience, since it is not identical to the pattern in acquisition.

Summary and Conclusions. Analysis of semantic processing at the word and morpheme levels in aphasia suggests a separation between naming and the concept network, with breakdown possible in either or in the link between the two. The conceptual network appears to be particularly affected by posterior lesions, resulting in a diminished ability to make normal associations or to use associative cues to word retrieval. In addition, it appears that individual semantic categories such as colors or letters may be specifically and exclusively affected, perhaps indicating a separate storage or process for these categories.

Generally it seems that the richer the associations for particular words are—as in high frequency words with imageable, concrete, manipulable referents—the more likely the word is to be retrieved in Broca's aphasia, perhaps because of some slow, associative, self-prompting process. The good preservation of content words in Broca's aphasia and function words in Wernicke's aphasia suggests that the content-function distinction reflects a psychological separation of the two classes in mental structure and process. Finally, the pattern of grammatical marking found in brain damage suggests that in some cases, the morphological derivatives may be stored as unanalyzed wholes, while in others the root is stored and alternative forms are produced actively. We will look at semantic processing at the sentence level for both figurative and literal interpretations in the discussion of syntactic processes, since they require integration and interpretation of meanings from syntactic combinations.

Syntactic Processes in Aphasia. As we have already seen, Wernicke's aphasics seem unable to integrate information from either pictorial or verbal-associative contexts to disambiguate the meaning of a picture or a word. Broca's aphasics are nearly normal in that respect. However, Broca's aphasics do not produce syntactically integrated sentences, do not process function words separately as a class, and fail to use many grammatical markers in both production and perception. In these respects, the speech of Wernicke's aphasics looks more normal. In fact, examination of the extracts in Box 12.1 of speech of Wernicke's aphasics should reveal complex sentence structure, complete with embedding in almost every instance. To what extent are syntactic processes preserved in aphasia, and to what extent do aphasia data indicate that syntactic processing can be divorced from semantic processing?

Caramazza and Berndt (1978) argued that aphasia presents strong evidence for the independence of syntactic processes from lexical processes, since in anterior aphasia only the former seem to be affected, while in posterior aphasia only the latter are affected. This is true in spontaneous speech, but as they argued, the force of the statement must be mitigated somewhat by the apparently good comprehension by Broca's aphasics. If they can in fact understand sentences, then they must be making use of syntax to narrow word-meanings and also to derive basic sentential relationships. Of course, as we have seen with research with normal adults and children, some of the information in sentences may be derived from semantic processes alone: "The plant was watered by the boy" (irreversible passive) conveys the identities of actor and patient (object) both through syntax and through knowledge of real world events. Is the apparently good comprehension of Broca's aphasics a result therefore of semantic or syntactic processing?

To answer this, investigators have given patients sentences that may be unambiguously interpreted semantically or syntactically, such as "the bicycle the boy is holding is broken," or through only syntax, such as "the lion that the tiger is chasing is fat," and asked them to indicate comprehension by selecting a picture that best represents the meaning (Caramazza and Zurif, 1976). (Note that two of the pictures at least would contain the subjects of both clauses, but one would have the lion, for example, as fat, and the other, the tiger.) For both kinds of sentences posterior aphasics were poorer than anterior aphasics, but showed no worse performance on the reversible embeddings than on the nonreversible ones. For anterior patients (and conduction aphasics) performance was close to 90 percent correct on the semantically unambiguous sentences but near chance on the syntax-only sentences, indicating a clear syntactic impairment. Since language is normally redundant both extralinguistically with real-world events and intralinguistically with semantics, the patients may appear to have good comprehension—without syntactic processing.

Similar deficits have been found in Broca's aphasics with reversible passive and reversible active sentences (Schwartz, Saffran, and Marin, 1980) and with sentences like "he showed her baby the pictures" versus "he showed her the baby pictures," which require syntax to comprehend (Heilman and Scholes, 1976). For such sentences, invariably, Broca's aphasics' comprehension is still better than Wernicke's aphasics' comprehension but is impaired compared to normal. These results indicate that even in comprehension Broca's aphasics fail to make use of most syntactic information, even the basic "SVO" interpretation of active sentences. When correct, their responses thus must be based on semantic or contextual comprehension strategies.

Broca's aphasics have been found to have some difficulties with other aspects of grammatical comprehension. Blumstein, Goodglass, Statlender, and Biber (1983) reported that Broca's aphasics had difficulty comprehending pronouns that referred to distant nouns when gender and number (singular-plural) markings were absent. The gender and number markings may be considered lexical cues, and with these present anterior aphasics comprehend sentences with pronouns most easily. Thus, for example, in "the woman watching the man bandaged herself," the referent of "herself" is clear from gender alone. If lexical cues are absent, as in "the boy watched the man bandage him," anterior aphasics have greater difficulty. In this sentence, there are conflicting cues to the referent of "him." The absence of the "-self," which would be required if "him" were to refer to the man, indicates that the referent is "the boy" or some other male. On the other hand, the minimum distance principle, which says that usually pronouns refer to the nearest possible noun, in this case incorrectly signals "the man" as referent. Neither Broca's nor Wernicke's aphasics relied particularly on the cue provided by the "-self" or on normal parsing operations, but they used the minimum distance principle preferentially. Broca's aphasics used gender and number information over the minimum distance principle, if they were available.

Zurif and Blumstein (1978) reported a study that tested Broca's aphasics for comprehension of determiners. The patients were asked to "select (a, the) black one" when there were one or several black ones to choose from. Mild aphasics and normal adults took longer and showed confusion if the determiner was inappropriate ("the" when there are many or "a" when there is only one), while Broca's aphasics showed no indication of noticing the discrepancy. This is consistent with the hypothesis that Broca's aphasics do not comprehend the syntactic (or semantic) function of function words and are processing only the content words, just as they produce only the content words.

However, Linebarger, Schwartz, and Saffran (1983) pointed out that Broca's aphasics can understand the difference between "in" and "on," so they are not just failing to attend to function words, and they can recognize the ungrammaticality of sentences with inappropriate function words. For example, their subjects could recognize that "the policeman was talking a woman" was wrong (the function word "to" is omitted) although "the policeman was lecturing a woman," with similar semantic interpretation and syntactic structure, was acceptable. They contended that Broca's aphasics have not lost their grammatical skills totally but fail to use this information to construct representations of sentences, perhaps because of processing overload.

If Broca's aphasics have sufficient grammatical competence to recognize ungrammaticality in some instances, it seems clear, nevertheless, that they do not use it to derive a syntactic representation of the sentence. Using a clustering procedure, Zurif, Caramazza, and Myerson (1972) directly measured the ability of aphasics to comprehend the hierarchical organization of sentences. To understand their procedure one must be aware that brain-damaged patients cannot respond appropriately to abstract instructions like "diagram a sentence." Instead, each patient was shown a sentence, such as "he hit the ball," which was kept in view throughout the task. Then the subject was given three words from the sentence like "ball, he, the" and asked to select the two that went best together. Normal subjects usually select words that are part of the same constituent, so in this case would pick "the ball." Across many trials for a single sentence, thus, the selection pattern will illustrate constituent structure; words that belong to most of the same constituents will go together often, while words that belong only to the sentence constituent (one from the subject and another from the predicate) will be grouped together seldom.

In this task, posterior aphasics showed random grouping of the words. Anterior aphasics' groupings reflected constituent structure for the content words. However, depending on the patient, either the function words were grouped together across boundaries or were ignored. Based on results such as these, some have tried to write a grammar for Broca's aphasics' productions, arguing that the basic syntactic categories and their relationships are retained, but each is represented only by a single word or word part (such as the uninflected N in a NP or PP) (Kean, 1980; Lapointe, 1983).

It is important to recognize that even if Broca's aphasics have few syntactic strategies left, they are not restricted to deriving sentence meanings only by "adding" likely meanings of individual words. Winner and Gardner (1977) tested brain-damaged patients for comprehension of figurative speech—sentences such as "a heavy heart can make a difference." (We have already looked at their results for right-brain–damaged patients.) The sentence was given along with pictures showing someone depressed, someone carrying a heavy heart (the sentence meaning but literal and strange), or showing just a heart or just a weight. If the patient used only individual word meanings, either of the last two pictures would be as likely to be selected as the first. Normals, of course, chose mostly the figurative meaning pictures. As might be expected, Wernicke's aphasics performed generally very poorly on the task. Broca's aphasics, like normals, chose the figurative pictures, indicating comprehension of the entire sentence *and* of figurative speech.

The discussion of syntax thus far has concentrated primarily on comprehension processes in Broca's aphasics and has demonstrated severe impairment. Of course, Broca's aphasics also are impaired syntactically in production. This is obvious from the protocols: They omit function words and inflections, leaving the speech telegraphic, for example. But more serious grammatical problems have also been noted. Saffran, Schwartz, and Marin (1980) elicited productions from Broca's aphasics and discovered a marked inability to order the noun phrases in the sentences appropriately when both NPs were animate or both were inanimate. Production was elicited by presenting the patients with pictures that could be described by a single sentence, such as "the girl runs to the man," (action relation, both NPs animate), "the pencil is in the sink" (location relation, both NPs inanimate), "the girl runs to the house" (action relation, one NP animate), or "the bird is in the sink" (location relation, one NP animate). Subjects made some errors on all types of sentences, but the majority of errors occurred when both subject and object shared "animacy," in which case over one-third of the time, their order was reversed (e.g., for the first example sentence, "the man ran to the girl"). Moreover, in a follow-up task, where the subjects were given the words on cards and asked to order them appropriately for the pictures, a similar confusion emerged.

The results suggest that the most salient feature of a lexical item for a Broca's aphasic is whether or not it is likely to serve as an actor, and that underlies ordering all lexical items. In sentences where there is one animate and one inanimate noun, the animate one is usually the actor, resulting normally in good comprehension. On other sentences the strategy provides no information. Thus, the syntactic deficit in Broca's aphasics' productions is not limited to "the little words" but extends to the most fundamental sentential relationships.

Assessment of syntax in Wernicke's aphasics is difficult in comparison with Broca's aphasics, since the semantic abilities of Wernicke's aphasics are significantly impaired. Therefore, naturally, they have difficulty with picture verification tasks or word clusterings apart from any syntactic impairments. It is important to observe, however, that just as Broca's aphasics show comprehension difficulties with respect to syntax, Wernicke's aphasics show production deficits with respect to syntax: There are violations of both subcategorization rules (e.g., using a noun or verb in adjective position) and selection restrictions (e.g., using an inanimate word like "thing" when an animate one is required) (Caramazza and Berndt, 1978). Coupled with the repetitions of items, these give a strange syntactic appearance to Wernicke's aphasics' productions. Finally, compare the productions of the Wernicke's aphasics in Box 12.1 to the approximations of English produced by scrambling sentence chunks in Chapter 5. You should note a strange similarity. The scrambled sentences of course still have substantive content words, but fail to hang together even at the higher orders because there is random association between chunks of the string. Likewise, Wernicke's aphasics seem to be randomly splicing large chunks of words like "I figured that," "it's liable to," "I had trouble with," and so on, which have internal consistency and structure, perhaps because they are stored as a unit. When they are combined there is a superficial apparent structure, as in the English approximations, not necessarily because they have been productively generated, but perhaps because they have been randomly linked in a chain.

Summary. In this section we have looked at syntactic processing in brain-damaged patients. We have seen that even in patients for whom comprehension is good and concept structure is preserved, there are comprehension problems when sentence meaning may be obtained only through syntax. Usually this does not create a problem because of the redundancy of the language: Broca's aphasics are able to use semantic processing strategies to recover basic sentence relations, or to use general processing strategies like the minimum distance principle without performing a complete syntactic analysis. They also seem to be able to recognize some subtleties of grammar, to judge ungrammaticality, even if they cannot use these subtleties to recover structure. For aphasics for whom comprehension is normally poor, it is difficult to judge the extent to which they are able to process syntactically.

Phonological Processing in Aphasia.   At various times it has been proposed that the problem in aphasia is not necessarily conceptual dissolution but inability to recognize the incoming sounds or to generate a sound representation in response to a picture or written word (see, for example, Luria, 1973). At the same level, one might attempt to explain Broca's aphasia by arguing that difficulties arise not in representation of function words, for example, but in production of unstressed syllables (most inflections and function words are not stressed) or in production of long sequences. (Wernicke in fact argued that Broca's aphasia was a disturbance of the "motor image" of words [Sies, 1974].) Certainly if there is a breakdown at these low levels of processing, it will have ramifications at the higher levels.

Speech Production. We have already noted that all aphasics are likely to make "slips of the tongue," and these include literal paraphasias, and single phoneme slips, as well as verbal paraphasias. One might ask whether there is a pattern in these mispronunciations that reflects the regular operation or change in phonological rules, and whether there is a pattern of correctly pronounced items.

Blumstein (1973a, 1973b) analyzed the speech of Broca's, Wernicke's, and conduction aphasics from tape recordings made of free conversations to discover such patterns. For all aphasics, regardless of the locus of the lesion, the frequencies with which the phonemes were produced mirrored the frequency of occurrence in normal language. The aphasics made fewer errors on high-frequency phonemes than on low-frequency ones. Errors were made by substituting one phoneme for another (most usual e.g., "book" → /gʊk/), deleting a phoneme (e.g., "prince" → /pIns/), accommodating a phoneme to the phonemic environment (as in assimilation, e.g., "Crete" → /tɚit/), and addition of a phoneme (least common, e.g., "boot" → /blut/). The relative frequency of each type of error was the same for all aphasic groups. More single-feature changes were made than multiple-feature changes, and the feature most likely to be altered was place of articulation. The main difference in terms of production between groups of patients was in "fluency": Broca's aphasics needed more time to make a set number of phonemes than did Wernicke's aphasics, and Broca's aphasics had flatter intonation contours.

Since the pattern for Broca's and Wernicke's aphasics is similar at the phoneme level, we cannot argue that the production deficit for Broca's aphasia lies in loss of skills for producing particular phonemes. However, one might argue that the particular deficit in Broca's aphasia comes in organizing these individual motor programs into hierarchies of motor commands—into syllables, words, and phrases. Indeed, usually the speech of Broca's aphasics is emitted in bursts of less than four words (Goodglass, 1973), and this has been attributed to:

> an increased threshold for initiating and maintaining the flow of speech—either after a silence or as a combination of sequences already in progress. . . . in order to produce any speech, the patient with this disorder must find the salient point in his intended utterance, which is ordinarily the significant noun or verb. As a result, his speech issues in short bursts, each centered about a salient verbal element with rarely more than one unstressed morpheme before or after it. The normal melodic intonation and rhythm are thus destroyed.
>
> (Goodglass, 1973, p. 204)

It is possible that the patient consciously uses this strategy because of some awareness of an inability to organize motor commands into higher-order units, or that this is the result of the reduced ability to produce those units but normal strategies obtain. In either case, the pattern of speech production in Broca's aphasia is consistent with the notion of a hierarchy in motor organization (see Chapter 7 for discussion), with the upper levels of the hierarchy requiring greater processing. It also suggests that a basis for each unit of organization, wherever in the hierarchy, might be the syllable that receives the main stress.

There is one last point to observe in the production patterns in aphasia, and that is that the breakdown usually preserves the phonemes and phonological rules of the native language. Because of disruptions of intonation, the patients may not sound like native speakers, and there are anecdotes of patients suffering embarrassment when their speech acquired a foreign accent . . . from an enemy country (Critchley, 1973). These anecdotes are rare and seem to occur because of intonation changes rather than segmental changes. The reason this is important is that it suggests that even in the extreme cases of the neologisms of Wernicke's aphasics, the phonological structure is operative; they are not the product of random groupings of articulatory features.

Speech Perception in Aphasia. Identification and discrimination of individual speech sounds have been measured in Broca's and Wernicke's aphasics. Perhaps surprisingly, perception in Broca's aphasia is impaired as well as in Wernicke's aphasia, again indicating that Broca's aphasics do not have purely expressive disorders. Both types of patients have difficulties responding to nonsense syllables as compared with real words (Blumstein, Baker, and Goodglass, 1977), and, for Broca's aphasics, as you may recall, in naming letters (like "b" or "p") compared with naming objects. Therefore, perception tasks must be somewhat modified for use with brain-damaged people—as in using a /bæt/-/pæt/ contiuum rather than /bæ/-/pæ/. The difficulty in perception of or response to nonsense syllables may indicate an increased dependence on top-down processing in brain damage, of "guided" listening from items still available in semantic memory or the dictionary.

Blumstein, Baker, and Goodglass (1977) tested aphasics' abilities to differentiate words distinguished by voicing (pear-bear), place (pin-tin), or both (pen-den), syllables (prescribe-describe), and phoneme order (main-name). All aphasics showed some impairments in these abilities and in reasonably predictable patterns: Two-feature differences were easier to discriminate than single-feature differences, place differences were harder to discriminate than voicing differences (for posterior aphasics only), and phoneme order and unstressed syllables were difficult to distinguish for all groups. Generally the performance of Broca's aphasics was better than that of Wernicke's aphasics.

Synthetic speech continua have also been used to isolate the perceptual difficulties in aphasia and on occasion to try to manipulate the speech cues to improve aphasics' performance. Blumstein, Cooper, Zurif, and Caramazza (1977) tested identification and discrimination of voicing (VOT) by using synthetic speech and found that patients fell into three groups: One showed normal identification and discrimination functions; one, random identification functions but normal discrimination with a peak at the phoneme boundary; and one showed poor identification and discrimination. Note that if the patients could identify the stimuli then invariably they could discriminate them, but that discrimination ability did not necessarily indicate identification ability. (This precedence of discrimination argues against one model for categorical perception in speech, that the shape of the discrimination function derives from subjects' labeling and then using the labels for discrimination [see Chapter 7], since here subjects were able to discriminate when they could not label.) Generally in perception of voicing, Broca's aphasics performed better than Wernicke's aphasics but showed a larger impairment in production of the correct voicing value (Blumstein, Cooper, Goodglass, Statlender, and Gottlieb, 1980): In the patients tested in this study, VOT production was good for the Wernicke's aphasics, although they could not label and sometimes could not discriminate VOT, but they greatly deviated from normal values for the Broca's aphasics, who were able to perceive normally.

Comparable results have been obtained for aphasics' perception of place of articulation (Blumstein, Tartter, Nigro, and Statlender, 1984). What is interesting in the tests of place of articulation perception is that various cue combinations enhance perceptibility for aphasics. Blumstein et al. (1984) for example, showed a greater consistency in performance across patients for stimuli containing both burst and transition information than for stimuli in which place of articulation was cued by transitions alone. Tallal and Newcombe (1978) found that lengthening the transitions, so that the rate of information change was slower, enhanced perceptibility of this consonant distinction in aphasics, although their results have not been consistently replicated (see Blumstein et al., 1984). Both results suggest ways of improving speech mechanically to enhance aphasics' comprehension. They also suggest support for models of speech perception that implicate several cues in the perception of place of articulation rather than just one.

Summary. Studies of speech production and perception in aphasia have shown impairments in both these low-level language abilities across aphasic groups and support for most current theories of speech processing. In both articulation and perception there are more likely to be single-feature errors than multiple-feature errors, and the feature most likely to be mistaken is place of articulation, the lowest level of the feature hierarchy. Errors occur also in syllable processing and phoneme ordering. Broca's aphasics show a disturbance in production of particular feature values in VOT and in producing higher-level units of organized segments. Labeling and discrimination of phonetic feature differences in synthetic speech are relatively normal in Broca's aphasia, but higher levels of speech perception, as in differentiating phonemes or syllables, are impaired. Wernicke's aphasics are able to produce voicing contrasts normally but show impairment in identification and sometimes also in discrimination. Finally, there is some evidence that redundancy in cueing feature differences, as in having both burst and transition or in lengthening transitions, facilitates perception in aphasia.

Aphasia and Exceptional Language Skills. Thus far we have discussed the patterns of breakdown of language when a single spoken language was the native language. It should be noted that although in most cases here the discussion was of English, these patterns are not exclusive to English: Broca's patient was French and Wernicke's German, and research in aphasia has been conducted across the world, with comparable results to those reported for English. In this section, we will not discuss any other spoken language specifically, but rather, briefly, the pattern of breakdown in multilinguals and with sign language.

Aphasia and Multilingualism. Although there are problems calibrating an individual's experience with multiple languages, it is interesting to consider whether two languages known by the same individual share a conceptual structure and thus show equivalent deficits in Wernicke's aphasia, share syntactic operations, and thus show equivalent syntactic deficits, and so on. At this point, the most common conclusion is that aphasia is likely to affect both languages in the same way, if both are native and fluency is equal in both. Usually also, the more internalized language—and thus the more native or the more frequently used language—is better spared in brain damage. Finally, it should be observed that there are also "exceptional" patterns—people who lose one, presumably native language completely, and retain mastery of another (Vaid and Lambert, 1979; Kinsbourne, 1981).

Aphasia and Sign Language. Testing the effects of brain damage on sign language is fraught with many difficulties. As you may recall, the signing community is comprised of people who have had various exposures to sign language: Some learn it at birth from fluent signing parents, others learn it at school after using a homemade gestural communication system until then, still others do not learn it until much later, being trained in lipreading at school. Therefore with deaf people who suffer brain damage, it is difficult to determine how abnormal a lack of fluency or grammaticality is for them specifically. A second problem is that most people who work with or study aphasics are not also schooled in sign language so that testing is difficult, since the testers are speaking and assessing a foreign language. For these reasons, there are few reliable case studies of deaf aphasics, and caution must be applied in generalizing from the few cases there are.

Despite these reservations, sign language presents an interesting contrast for spoken language with respect to brain damage. Sign is a *spatial language*—and spatial processing is considered primarily right hemisphere based. So a question immediately presents itself about whether signers will show aphasic symptoms with left hemisphere damage or with right hemisphere damage. (This question too is partially confounded with the age of acquisition—remember Genie showed right hemisphere language, perhaps because she learned language after the critical period for left hemisphere language.) As with people fluent in several spoken languages, we might also want to ask whether a deaf person schooled in speech and sign shows similar impairments in both. Finally, since sign has a more simultaneous than sequential organization in comparison to speech, it is interesting to ask whether the pattern of deficits for Broca's and Wernicke's aphasias occurs for sign also.

In a recent set of studies Poizner and colleagues (Poizner, Bellugi, and Iraqui, 1984; Poizner, Kaplan, Bellugi, and Padden, 1984) have investigated linguistic and nonlinguistic processing in four brain-damaged deaf individuals. All had hearing parents but learned sign at a young age. Two were born deaf, one became deaf at five years, and one became deaf at six months. Three of the patients suffered left hemisphere brain damage, and one (congenitally deaf), right hemisphere damage. Of the left hemisphere patients, one was described as a Broca's aphasic, one as a mixed anterior, and one as a Wernicke's aphasic.

The first point of interest is that the left-hemisphere-damaged patients had no difficulties arranging blocks, copying or producing drawings, or recognizing faces, while the right hemisphere patient showed marked impairment in these tasks. The right hemisphere patient also exhibited a left visual neglect in copying, which the left hemisphere patients did not. Therefore, lateralization of nonlinguistic function appears the same in these patients as in hearing patients.

Organization of language also seems comparable in these patients to organization in hearing patients. The right hemisphere patient remained fluent in sign. The left visual neglect, however, affected her sign, although it usually does not affect speech. Specifically, for signs that required movements in both sides of space, such as SQUARE, which is made by tracing a square with the index finger, the left side was omitted. The patient also exhibited difficulties using the left side of space as in "setting the stage" for pronoun reference (see Chapter 11). Thus, here, general language processing appeared intact, but a specifically spatial component of it was impaired by the spatial neglect.

The left hemisphere patients demonstrated severe aphasic symptoms. As with speaking aphasics, they made many production errors, had word-finding (that is, sign-finding) difficulties, and were limited in comprehension of complex constructions. For those who wrote English as well as signed, their writing looked like their signing, with similar deficiencies. The Broca's aphasic was nonfluent, unable to produce more than one sign at a time. Since there is no content-function word distinction in sign, we might not expect a differential breakdown in aphasia. However, she also had difficulties with inflections but not uninflected base forms, indicating the same general pattern of breakdown as is seen in spoken language. In this case, the suggestion is that grammatical morphemes disappear not because of the form they are in (word or unstressed syllable) but because of the nature of their function within the language, as syntax markers rather than meaning carriers. The posterior aphasic's output resembled that of posterior speaking patients, with fluent but uninterpretable signing. The mixed anterior was relatively fluent, with little aphasic impairment aside from word-finding problems, paraphasias, and failure to make index references clear.

The other cases reported in the literature (Schuell, in Sies, 1974; Poizner and Battison, 1980 for review) also point to the comparability of aphasic symptoms in sign language with those in speech. Given the basic differences in modality and organization of the two languages, the similarity in breakdown is particularly striking, supporting similar underlying brain organization and processing operations. Since the languages seem so different it is tempting to conclude that the similar brain organization derives from an innate predisposition for that organization and processing of language.

Summary and Conclusions

The studies of language processing in brain damage have important implications for the development, organization, and processing of language normally. First, they suggest that there is a special left hemisphere mechanism for processing *language,* regardless of modality or form. This left hemisphere capability appears to be specified at birth, and if development is normal, will take over phonetic, semantic, and syntactic processing of language by the age of puberty, while the right hemisphere specializes in paralinguistic processes. If development is abnormal, if there is brain damage early, the right hemisphere appears capable of assuming language processing. The critical period for lateralization of language function appears to be before puberty, and lateralization does not depend on spoken language input.

A second important conclusion that may be drawn from studies of brain damage concerns "modules" of language processing:

1. Since right hemisphere impairments produce paralinguistic deficits while left hemisphere impairments produce linguistic deficits, we have evidence for the psychological reality of separating paralinguistic from linguistic processing.

2. The impairment of naming as opposed to comprehending words in Broca's aphasia supports the notion of separating a dictionary with word-meaning from a lexicon with word-names and pronunciation rules (see Chapter 3): Either can be selectively impaired.

3. The differential effects of brain damage on content and function words, on syntactic processes generally relative to semantic processes, suggest the psychological reality to separating these language processing components: Some function words (or some inflections in sign) may have a dual role as meaning items and as syntax guides, and the latter function only is destroyed in Broca's aphasia. This accounts for the inability of the patients to organize function words with respect to the sentence, the perhaps abnormal frequency dependence of function words in lexical decisions, and the loss of inflection in the speech or sign of Broca's aphasics. Moreover, the ability of Broca's aphasics to comprehend semantically unambiguous sentences but to fail to comprehend sentences rendered unambiguous only through syntax indicates a selective impairment of syntax and separation of syntactic and semantic processing.

4. Finally, studies of the speech of aphasics indicate an independence of speech processing difficulties from semantic and syntactic difficulties: All patients show similar impairments in speech production and perception regardless of their comprehension and fluency skills. Thus, for all patients, more frequently used phonemes show less disruption than less frequently used phonemes, place of articulation differences are harder than differences in other features to perceive or produce, and deleting phonemes is easier than adding them. All patients seem to benefit from redundancy: Synthetic speech is more reliably processed when there are multiple cues to a feature than when there is one, multiple-feature differences are easier to distinguish than single-feature differences, and feature differences are easier to distinguish in real words than in nonsense syllables. This last result may indicate an increased reliance on top-down processing. The research in aphasics' speech, in addition, indicates that Broca's aphasics may have a special impairment in combining lower-level motor programs into higher-order ones and in producing particular voicing values.

Examination of language breakdown in multilinguals and sign language users shows no startling differences from language breakdown in a single spoken language, a result that may be startling in itself. Despite its spatial nature, sign language seems to be organized in the brain as is spoken language, suggesting a predisposition for language organization independent of the modality of processing. The variety of patterns obtained for aphasic multilinguals may be interpreted by using several generalizations. First, what is best known seems to be best preserved, where best known means most frequently used. Second, processing of later-learned languages may depend on the structures and processes established for the first language and so be derivative rather than primary. In that case, later languages will be at least as impaired as the first language.

As a last conclusion it is worthwhile to raise the philosophically interesting issue, given our criteria, of *when* after brain damage we can say that an individual no longer has language. Obviously some global aphasics, who are reduced to uttering a single word, no longer have language; they have lost productivity, recursiveness, metalinguistics, hierarchical organization, and duality of patterning at least, and perhaps also semanticity in the sense that the relation between word and referent is no longer clear.

To some extent, the same argument may be made for less severe types of aphasia. We noted in Wernicke's aphasia, for example, that there seems to be a limited use of hierarchical organization in syntax; rather large chunks of language seem to be simply chained together. Broca's aphasics, too, lack some normal hierarchical language abilities, breaking down in speech production in the organization of speech into large units and faltering in syntactic analysis in the comprehension of hierarchical constituent structure. There are also difficulties in some symbolic aspects of language at least in Wernicke's aphasia. And finally, learnability is damaged if the aphasia strikes in adulthood, since learning alternative systems or relearning the original system is impaired. Thus, we might have to conclude, if we use our criteria consistently, that most adult aphasics no longer "have language."

In this chapter we have examined dissolution of language as a result of observable brain damage. We have seen how language "tests" may be used to diagnose clinical pathology, and, further, how clinical pathology may be used to support theories about normal and aphasic language processing. In the next chapter, we turn to examination of language breakdown in the absence of obvious physical damage—in the language of individuals with personality disorders. Again, we will see that language tests may be used for diagnosis, and that diagnostic groups may show different patterns of dissolution, informative about the normal processing of language.

REFERENCES

Blumstein, S. (1973a). Some phonological implications of aphasic speech. In H. Goodglass & S. Blumstein (Eds.). *Psycholinguistics and Aphasia,* 124–137. Baltimore: Johns Hopkins University Press.

Blumstein, S. E., (1973b). *A Phonological Investigation of Aphasic Speech.* The Hague: Mouton.

Blumstein, S. E., (1982). Language dissolution in aphasia: Evidence from linguistic theory. In L. Obler & L. Menn (Eds.). *Exceptional Language and Linguistics,* pp. 203–215. NY: Academic Press.

Blumstein, S. E., Baker, E., & Goodglass, H. (1977). Phonological factors in auditory comprehension. *Neuropsychologia, 15,* 19–29.

Blumstein, S. E., Cooper, W. E., Goodglass, H., Statlender, S., & Gottlieb, J. (1980). Production deficits in aphasia: A voice-onset time analysis. *Brain and Language, 9,* 153–170.

Blumstein, S., Cooper, W., Zurif, E., & Caramazza, A. (1977). The perception and production of voice-onset time in aphasia. *Neuropsychologia, 15,* 371–383.

Blumstein, S. E., Goodglass, H., Statlender, S., & Biber, C. (1983). Comprehension strategies determining reference in aphasia: A study of reflexivization. *Brain and Language, 18,* 115–127.

Blumstein, S. E., Milberg, W., Shrier, R. (1982). Semantic processing in aphasia: Evidence from an auditory lexical decision task. *Brain and Language, 17,* 301–315.

Blumstein, S. E., Tartter, V. C., Nigro, G., & Statlender, S. (1984). Acoustic cues for the perception of place of articulation in aphasia. *Brain and Language, 22,* 128–149.

Bryden, M. P., & Zurif, E. B. (1970). Dichotic listening performance in a case of agenesis of the corpus callosum. *Neuropsychologia, 8,* 371–377.

Caramazza, A., & Berndt, R. S. (1978). Semantic and syntactic processes in aphasia: A review of the literature. *Psychological Bulletin, 85,* 898–918.

Caramazza, A., & Zurif, E. B. (1976). Dissociation of algorithmic and heuristic processes in language comprehension: Evidence from aphasia. *Brain and Language, 3,* 572–582.

Critchley, M. (1973). Articulatory defects in aphasia: The problem of Broca's aphemia. In H. Goodglass & S. E. Blumstein (Eds.). *Psycholinguistics & Aphasia,* pp. 51–68. Baltimore: Johns Hopkins University Press.

de Villiers, J. G. (1978). Fourteen grammatical morphemes in acquisition and aphasia. In A. Caramazza & E. B. Zurif (Eds.). *Language Acquisition and Language Breakdown,* pp. 121–144. Baltimore: Johns Hopkins University Press.

Gardner, H. (1975). *The Shattered Mind.* NY: A. A. Knopf.

Gazzaniga, M. S. (1967). The split brain in man. *Scientific American, 217,* 24–29.

———. (1983). Right hemisphere language following brain bisection. *American Psychologist,* 525–537.

Goodglass, H. (1973). Studies on the grammar of aphasics. In H. Goodglass & S. E. Blumstein (Eds.). *Psycholinguistics & Aphasia,* pp. 183–215. Baltimore: Johns Hopkins University Press.

———. (1978). Acquisition and dissolution of language. In A. Caramazza & E. B. Zurif (Eds.). *Language Acquisition and Language Breakdown,* pp. 101–108. Baltimore: Johns Hopkins University Press.

———. (1980). Disorders of naming following brain injury. *American Scientist, 68,* 647–655.

Goodglass, H., & Baker, E. (1976). Semantic field, naming, and auditory comprehension in aphasia. *Brain and Language, 3,* 359–374.

Goodglass, H., Klein, B., Carey, P., & Jones, K. J. (1973). Specific semantic word categories in aphasia. In H. Goodglass & S. E. Blumstein (Eds.). *Psycholinguistics & Aphasia,* pp. 251–266. Baltimore: Johns Hopkins University Press.

Gordon, B., & Caramazza, A. (1982). Lexical decisions for open- and closed-class words: Failure to replicate differential frequency sensitivity. *Brain and Language, 15,* 143–160.

Heilman, K. M., & Scholes, R. J. (1976). The nature of comprehension errors in Broca's, Wernicke's, and conduction aphasics. *Cortex, 12,* 258–265.

Howes, D. (1973). Some experimental investigations of language in aphasia. In H. Goodglass & S. E. Blumstein (Eds.). *Psycholinguistics & Aphasia,* pp. 231–249. Baltimore: Johns Hopkins University Press.

Kean, M. (1980). Grammatical representations and the description of language processing. In D. Kaplan (Ed.). *Biological Studies of Mental Processing,* pp. 239–268. Cambridge, MA: MIT Press.

Kehoe, W. J., & Whitaker, H. A. (1973). Lexical disruption in aphasia: A case study. In H. Goodglass & S. E. Blumstein (Eds.). *Psycholinguistics & Aphasia,* pp. 267–279. Baltimore: Johns Hopkins University Press.

Kinsbourne, M. (1981). Neuropsychological aspects of bilingualism. In H. Winitz (Ed.). *Native Language and Foreign Language Acquisition. Annals of the New York Academy of Sciences,* pp. 50–58. NY: New York Academy of Sciences, *379.*

Lapointe, S. G. (1983). Some issues in the linguistic study of agrammatism. *Cognition, 14,* 1–39.

Lenneberg, E. (1967). *Biological Foundations of Language.* NY: John Wiley and Sons.

Levy, J. (1983). Language, cognition, and the right hemisphere: A response to Gazzaniga. *American Psychologist,* 538–541.

Levy, J. R., & Trevarthen, C. (1977). Perceptual, semantic, and phonetic aspects of elementary language processes in split-brain patients. *Brain, 100,* 105–118.

Linebarger, M. C., Schwartz, M. K., & Saffran, E. M. (1983). Sensitivity to grammatical structure in so-called agrammatic aphasics. *Cognition, 13,* 361–392.

Luria, A. R. (1973). *The Working Brain.* Hammondsworth, Middlesex: Penguin Books.

Milberg, W., & Blumstein, S. E. (1981). Lexical decisions and aphasia. *Brain and Language, 14,* 371–385.

Milner, B., Taylor, L., & Sperry, R. W. (1968). Lateralized suppression of dichotically presented digits after commisural section in man. *Science, 161,* 184–185.

Poizner, H., & Battison, R. (1980). Neurolinguistic: Cerebral asymmetry for sign language: Clinical and experimental evidence. In H. Lane & F. Grosjean (Eds.). *Recent Perspectives on American Sign Language,* pp. 79–101. Hillsdale, NJ: Lawrence Erlbaum Associates.

Poizner, H., Bellugi, U., & Iraqui, V. (1984). Apraxia and aphasia in a visual-gestural language. *American Journal of Physiology: Regulatory, Integrative, and Comparative Physiology, 246,* R866–R883.

Poizner, H., Kaplan, E., Bellugi, U., & Padden, C. A. (1984). Visual-spatial processing in deaf brain-damaged signers. *Brain and Cognition, 3,* 281–306.

Pribram, K. H. (1971). *Language of the Brain: Experimental Paradoxes and Principles in Neuropsychology.* Englewood Cliffs, NJ: Prentice-Hall.

Rosenzweig, M. R. (1951). Representation of the two ears at the auditory cortex. *American Journal of Physiology, 167,* 147–158.

Ross, E. D. (1981). The aprosodias. *Archives of Neurology, 38,* 561–569.

———. (1982). The divided self. *The Sciences,* 8–12.

Ross, E. D., & Mesulam, M. M. (1979). Dominant functions of the right hemisphere? *Archives of Neurology, 36,* 144–148.

Saffran, E. M., Schwartz, M. F., & Marin, O. S. M. (1980). The word order problem in agrammatism: II. Production. *Brain and Language, 10,* 263–280.

Schwartz, M. F., Saffran, E. M., & Marin, O. S. M. (1980). The word order problem in agrammatism: I. Comprehension. *Brain and Language, 10,* 249–262.

Searleman, A. (1977). A review of right hemisphere linguistic capabilities. *Psychological Bulletin, 84,* 503–528.

Sies, L. F. (Ed.). (1974). *Aphasia Theory and Therapy: Selected Lectures and Papers of Hildred Schuell.* Baltimore: University Park Press.

Sparks, R., & Geschwind, N. (1968). Dichotic listening in man after section of neocortical commisures. *Cortex, 4,* 3–16.

Sperry, R. (1982). Some effects of disconnecting the cerebral hemispheres. *Science, 217,* 1223–1226.

Spreen, O. (1973). Psycholinguistics and aphasia: The contributions of Arnold Pick. In H. Goodglass & S. Blumstein (Eds.). *Psycholinguistics & Aphasia,* pp. 141–170, Baltimore: Johns Hopkins University Press.

Springer, S. P., & Deutsch, G. (1981). *Left Brain, Right Brain.* San Francisco: W. H. Freeman.

Tallal, P., & Newcombe F. (1978). Impairment of auditory perception and language comprehension in dysphasia. *Brain and Language, 5,* 13–24.

Vaid, J., & Lambert, W. E. (1979). Differential cerebral involvement in the cognitive functioning of bilinguals. *Brain and Language, 8,* 92–110.

Winner, E., & Gardner, H. (1977). The comprehension of metaphor in brain-damaged patients. *Brain, 100,* 717–729.

Witelson, S. F., & Pallie, W. (1973). Left hemisphere specialization for language in the newborn: Neuroanatomical evidence of asymmetry. *Brain, 96,* 641–646.

Zaidel, E. (1978). The elusive right hemisphere of the brain. *Engineering and Science,* (Sept.–Oct.) 10–32.

———. (1983). A response to Gazzaniga: Language in the right hemisphere, convergent perspectives. *American Psychologist,* 542–546.

Zurif, E. B. (1980). Language mechanisms: A neurophysiological perspective. *American Scientist, 68,* 305–312.

Zurif, E. B., & Blumstein, S. E. (1978). Language in the brain. In M. Halle, J. Bresnan, & G. A. Miller (Eds.). *Linguistic Theory and Psychological Reality,* pp. 229–245. Cambridge, MA: MIT Press.

Zurif, E. B., Caramazza, A., & Myerson, R. (1972). Grammatical judgments for agrammatic aphasics. *Neuropsychologia, 10,* 405–417.

Zurif, E. B., Caramazza, A., Myerson, R., & Galvin, J. (1974). Semantic feature representations for normal and aphasic language. *Brain and Langauge, 1,* 167–187.

STUDY QUESTIONS

1. Discuss the differences between Broca's and Wernicke's aphasias with respect to syntactic, semantic, and speech processing. Which aspects of language seem to be affected by anterior lesions and which aspects by posterior? Given these data, is it reasonable to say that the normal brain's parser, for example, is in Broca's area? Why or why not?

2. To what extent is it reasonable to argue that the left hemisphere has a tunable blueprint for language? In discussing this question, consider evidence from childhood brain damaged and deaf aphasics as well as evidence from earlier chapters. Make clear why each piece of evidence is relevant to the question.

3. Given the pattern of breakdown in Broca's and Wernicke's aphasias, discuss how language processes are normally performed. Consider which aspects of language processing seem relatively independent of one another (because of independent effects in brain damage) and which of our earlier proposals about syntactic, semantic, or speech processing seem to be psychologically real from the studies in brain damage.

13

Language Changes from Personality Disorders

The preceding chapters began with the assumption that all human beings bring the same fundamental processes to language, in everyday use, in acquisition, and in regularly enumerable ways, in breakdown. Of course, there are individual differences in language and in language processing. In this chapter we will begin with this assumption, exploring some of these differences as personality indicators and as indicators of the range of processes normally available.

We have argued that somehow language is related to thought. How is language affected by profound thought changes as in deep depression, a "personality split," or schizophrenia? Do such abnormal psychological states alter conceptual structure generally, linguistic structure specifically, or physical structure (such as hormones or brain function) with secondary effect on language? If there are either primary or secondary effects on language from personality disruption, are they the result of a language-specific change as in aphasia or of a more general social/communication disturbance? Are individual differences in topic, vocabulary, or grammar merely individual differences in "style," or are they derivative of distinct language processes?

For the final introductory question, we must note that schizophrenics and Wernicke's aphasics have occasionally been mistaken for each other, as the title of a recent article, "Schizophrenic and aphasic language: Discriminable or not?" (Rausch, Prescott, and DeWolfe, 1980), suggests. Is the confusion justified based on either their language output or their language processing? Or can we specify criteria that will separate schizophrenic and aphasic language?

In this chapter we will investigate individual differences in language as a result of personality disorders. As in the the last chapter, we approach this from two standpoints: (1) how language reflects or may be used to diagnose the personality disorder, and (2) how the language change indicates organization and processing of language normally. The former is analogous to using language impairments to diagnose regions of brain involvement; the latter to using language breakdown to ascertain relative independence of the parts of the language "machine." We will discuss the first briefly and concentrate on the second.

Personality Disorders

Brain damage is a well-defined physical abnormality—the existence, location, and extent of the damage may be measured by using a variety of objective techniques. The damage may then be associated with clinical impressions of behavior and with specific tests of language abilities, as we saw in the last chapter.

In contrast, personality disorders are not clearly defined physically, and therefore there is no conclusive way to assign patients to diagnostic categories independently of their behavior. Categorization is accomplished through a combination of clinical judgment and behavior tests, both of which are less reliable than the physical tests used to diagnose many other diseases. Physical correlates of personality disorders such as brain abnormality, or imbalance of hormones or *neurotransmitters* (the chemicals brain cells use to communicate with one another) have been found (see Seidman, 1983, for review of such findings in schizophrenia), but these are not consistently present in all patients with the same diagnosis. Since the assignment of individuals to clinical categories is more variable in personality disorders than in brain damage, we may expect to find less consistent patterns of language breakdown here than we did in aphasia.

The search for reliable behavior patterns in personality disorder is confounded further by the fact that there is no generally accepted classification system. In this chapter, we will be looking primarily at schizophrenia, a form of psychosis. *Psychoses* are characterized by a loss of touch with reality. A psychotic may experience hallucinations (in any modality—see things, hear voices, feel things crawling on the skin). A psychotic may also experience delusions, a thought system removed from reality. For example, one might believe himself to be Jesus Christ, or believe that there are enemy agents plotting against him. The first is a *delusion of grandeur,* the second, *paranoia.* A psychotic may also display emotions independent of obvious external cause, such as wild fits of laughter.[1]

Schizophrenia is only one form of psychosis, and there may be many forms of schizophrenia. Bleuler (1911/1950) identified four forms of schizophrenia based on behavior of patients. The first is *simple schizophrenia,* characterized by withdrawal from society, and no other particularly dramatic symptoms. A second form is paranoid schizophrenia; as already discussed, its principal distinctive symptom is a delusion of persecution. A third form is *catatonia,* in which patients assume a rigid posi-

---

1. The other major division of personality disorder is *neurosis,* believed to be caused by anxiety or one's defenses against it. Neurotics are not out of touch with reality to the same degree as psychotics, although there may be a similarity of symptoms. A neurotic might have an unrealistic fear of heights, for example, while a psychotic fears a delusional enemy. The neurotic is aware usually that the fear is unfounded in reality although unable to control it, while the psychotic is unaware that there is a discrepancy between the experience and reality.

tion—possibly resisting being moved—for extended periods. The last form is *hebephrenia* and corresponds most closely to the stereotypical portrayal of insanity: a loss of interest in personal appearance and cleanliness, wild, inappropriate mood swings, fits of talking or laughter, and so on. Clearly, from descriptions of these different types, the term "schizophrenia" is applied to a very wide range of psychotic behavior.

The forms of schizophrenia described by Bleuler are not consistently accepted today. For purposes of prognosis, many diagnosticians prefer to look at the origin of the symptoms rather than their nature. Schizophrenics are thus divided into two groups: (1) those whose history indicates a sudden onset of disease, perhaps deriving from a traumatic incident, called *reactive* schizophrenics; and (2) those who showed a slow deterioration over a long period, called *process* or *chronic* schizophrenics. The former are more likely to benefit from treatment by drugs or other forms of psychotherapy. This grouping, obviously, generalizes across Bleuler's behavior categories.

In studying schizophrenic language, researchers sometimes treat patients as a homogeneous group, sometimes consider patients with respect to either of the classification systems described, and sometimes select only a few individuals for intensive study without considering whether they are representative of any particular population. An analogous situation would be if language in brain damage were studied without regard to location or extent of the lesion, with the attempt to draw reliable conclusions sometimes looking at the relatively unimpaired right-brain-damaged patients and at other times looking at global aphasics as examples of the same disease! Obviously, this inconsistency in patient selection will limit our ability to find definitive, consistent language patterns across studies of schizophrenic language. Thus, from the outset, we may expect to draw less compelling conclusions about both schizophrenic language and normal language processes as reflected in the personality breakdown than we did in the last chapter.

Language as a Diagnostic Indicator

Much of psychiatry in this century has used language both as an integral part of therapy and as an important tool in diagnosis. Psychoanalysis, for example, effects a personality change in part by increasing one's self-awareness through the verbalizing of unconscious preverbal experiences (Forrester, 1980). Since language is an easily measured behavior and indicates conceptual structure, it has also been studied in psychiatry as an indicator of underlying, perhaps disturbed, emotional and conceptual structure. Before proceeding with our main topic—language disturbance in schizophrenia—we will describe some clinical procedures and theories directly relevant to psycholinguistics.

Freud's Analysis of Speech Errors

We have already looked at slips of the tongue and the tip-of-the-tongue phenomenon from a linguistic standpoint, in which the item actually uttered or the parts of it recalled are analyzed with respect to structural similarity to the target. Freud (1901/

1960, 1917/1961) analyzed these speech lapses from a different standpoint, as indicators of the presence of some unconscious wish.

Slips of the Tongue.   Freud argued that a slip of the tongue (*parapraxis,* using his term) reflects the existence and incomplete suppression of a message in competition with the target message. The slips in which he took the greatest interest (and that he claimed erroneously to be the most common) were slips in which the target word was replaced by its opposite—as in "Gentlemen, I take note that a full quorum of members is present and herewith declare the sitting *closed*" (Freud, 1917/1961, p. 33). In this case, the argument is that the wrong word appeared because the speaker wished to end the meeting although obliged to begin it. This created competing messages, one of which he unsuccessfully attempted to suppress.

In terms of language processing, Freud's analysis may be quite reasonable. Suppose that at any given time we are thinking several different thoughts. Obviously, only one may be vocalized at a time. There is more likely to be intrusion of one of the other thoughts if it is highly salient to the individual—the point Freud emphasized— or if it is formationally similar to the target. In the latter case we can consider that the intruding word receives some extra activation through sound association that causes the incompleteness of suppression. Note that first letters and rhymes are effective prompts for a word (see Chapter 3) and so must have strong connections to it. Similarly, we can expect activation by close meaning associations and thus intrusion by semantically related words. Indeed, Freud's focus on opposites reflects this type of intrusion, since, for example, "open" and "close" are likely to share many semantic links including their disjunction.

Thus, if we consider that all slips of the tongue reflect the incomplete suppression of another message we may account for their occurrence: Suppression is most difficult when the person has a strong urge to speak the message—when attention lags through fatigue, for example, or when there is extra activation spread by structural or semantic associations. For the purposes of personality analysis, what is of interest is the existence of the competing message.

Tip-of-the-Tongue States.   In our earlier discussion of the tip-of-the-tongue phenomenon we concentrated on two aspects: the apparent potential dissociation between a name and its semantic representation and the kind of information still available when the name seems to have disappeared. Psychoanalytic interest in tip-of-the-tongue phenomena focuses on *why* a particular word is forgotten and again points to unconscious feelings as the reason. Freud (1901/1960) distinguished between two types of tip-of-the-tongue states: those in which the forgotten name touched directly on something unpleasant, and those in which the forgotten name was associated with another word that in turn touched on something unpleasant. In either case, the task for the analyst is to discover the unpleasant association and bring it to the patient's awareness. In indicating potential trouble spots for the individual, the tip-of-the-tongue phenomenon takes on clinical significance.

Word Associations

We have discussed word associations extensively in earlier chapters in relation to the organization of the semantic network in normal and brain-damaged individuals and in language acquisition. It is interesting to note that among the first experimental studies of and norms for word association were those designed for clinical purposes (Jung, 1905/1973).

Jung measured the reaction time to make an association as well as which words were given as associations. Associations were elicited under normal conditions and also under conditions of "stress," where there was acoustic distraction (noise) or where the individual was fatigued. In addition to producing associations, subjects were also asked to recall previously produced associations.

We have already noted Jung's primary results: Under normal conditions, adults usually make paradigmatic associations; that is, the words they produce match in grammatical class the stimulus word and usually differ from it semantically in only one feature (e.g., mother → father, plant → animal). Other frequent responses included syntagmatic associations, words that frequently follow the stimulus word in ordinary speech, such as Christmas → tree. He also noted intrusions in associations, where the word produced might be a carryover (a perseveration) from an earlier word in the list. Finally, under conditions of stress, when subjects are not fully attentive to the task, a tendency emerges to produce associations of sound only, either repeating the stimulus word or producing a rhyme. This Jung considered the lowest form of association, a carryover from childhood.

For clinical purposes, Jung's principal interests were in abnormal responses, either associations that took an unusually long time to produce, or associations that were highly idiosyncratic, pointing to a salient event in the individual's experience. For example, one of his subjects made the unusual association ring → garden, and upon questioning revealed that he had found a ring in the garden of the place where he worked, the owner of which had still not claimed it. Another subject, who was in love with a woman from a different religion, came up with a cluster of unusual associations to words dealing with love, such as wedding → misfortune, to love → is useless, and to kiss → never.

If the stimulus word or its associations were emotionally troublesome, reaction times to produce the associations were longer than if the words were neutral. Thus, a particularly long reaction time could be indicative of a clinically interesting area, even if the association produced ultimately was normal. An interesting example of the use of this indicator is Jung's selection of stimulus words marginally related to a crime one of his subjects was suspected of committing. The subject's responses to these words were abnormally slow, and when this was pointed out to him, together with the suspected reason, he confessed his complicity.

As one might expect from Freud's analysis of tip-of-the-tongue phenomena, associations connected to emotionally troublesome areas are more poorly recalled than neutral ones, another emotional indicator in word association. And emotionally troublesome words tend to produce more sound associations than neutral words, indicative of their stressfulness. Finally, stress, such as fatigue or distracting noise, tends to accentuate the differences in association to neutral and emotionally charged words. Thus, we again find a straightforward psycholinguistic task highlighting areas of clinical significance.

The Semantic Differential

As you may recall from Chapter 3, in the semantic differential an individual is given words like "mother" and asked to rate them with respect to polar adjective scales like warm-cold, hard-soft, and so forth. Responses are then analyzed to determine clusters, which almost universally fall along dimensions describable as evaluative (good vs bad), potency (strong vs weak), and activity (active vs passive). Based on these data, Osgood, Suci, and Tannenbaum (1957) argued that the connotative portion of semantic space was organized in relation to these dimensions, and that individuals' conceptual organizations could be measured by seeing where particular concepts were located relative to the norm.

It should be obvious how this can be used as a clinical measure. In fact it has been used twice to describe the conceptual spaces of each personality of a split personality: once, the famous case known as "the three faces of Eve" (Osgood, Suci, and Tannenbaum, 1957), and more recently, in another triple split personality who was called Evelyn (Osgood, Luria, Jeans, and Smith, 1976). (Split personality is a different clinical disorder than schizophrenia!) In both cases the patient was asked in each of her three personalities to rate a number of concepts such as love, child, my mother, or my father, on a number of scales such as valuable-worthless, clean-dirty, or tasty-distasteful. In both cases the psychiatrist administered the test and the results were analyzed by other people who had no familiarity with the patient or her history (a *blind* analysis). In addition to describing the organization of the conceptual space for each personality, Osgood et al. attempted to make clinical inferences such as which personality was more "real," under what conditions the split had occurred, how the patient was progressing in therapy, and so on. These were then compared with the psychiatrists' independent evaluations. They were surprisingly similar.

There are several points of interest in the cases. Probably the most interesting is that each of the (two) individuals was able to access her conceptual space differently for her three personalities, thereby allowing the differential to be an effective clinical tool. This was so true that Osgood et al. (1976) commented, "It is easy . . . to forget that we are dealing with a single human being with a single brain" (p. 286).

An alternative interpretation of the data is that each individual maintained three separate conceptual networks, one for each of her personalities. This seems unlikely, since after therapy the personalities were integrated, and we would not want to assume that this resulted from a massive brain reorganization or loss of several conceptual networks. Moreover, there is other evidence that the individual personalities have access to a single semantic network but select to access it differently. Each of us could, for example, follow instructions to rate words as we would if we were a "goody two-shoes" or an irresponsible "playboy." Osgood et al. (1957, 1976) noted that when individuals assume a "role" (are not "real"), their use of semantic space as indicated by the differential is very rigid, showing little of the variability normally shown and fitting closely along the major axes. For some of the personalities assumed in the splits, the researchers noted this type of rigidity, indicative of role-playing rather than a different conceptual structure. Indeed, recognition of the pretense from the rigid use of semantic space formed the basis of the diagnosis of which of the personalities was "real."

The third point of interest is exactly how the patients responded in each of their personalities. We will not present this in detail here. However, as an indication, consider two of Eve's faces—Eve White and Eve Black. Eve White was described by the clinician as retiring, demure, feminine, and industrious, a competent wife, mother, and housekeeper with some anxieties about her performance in these roles. It was Eve White who sought therapy. In one session she complained of a headache and reaching her hands to her head, became Eve Black, a "party girl," shrewd, vain, deceptive, and sexy. (Neither Eve White nor Eve Black remained after therapy.) On the differential, Eve White rated doctor, child, mother, father, love, job, and peace as very positive, with sex, me, spouse, and sickness as negative, and fraud and hatred as maximally negative. From this Osgood et al. concluded that Eve White looked "normal" except for low self-esteem, and had a wide discrepancy in view of love and sex. Eve Black rated doctor, me, peace, father, hatred, and fraud very positively on the evaluation scales, mother and control negatively, and child, sex, love, job, spouse, confusion, and sickness as most negative. Osgood et al. called particular attention to the reversal in view of the parents in the two personalities, and the obvious abnormal positive evaluation of fraud and hatred and negative evaluation of love.

Summary. Standard psycholinguistic techniques may be used to assess individual differences for clinical diagnosis and indicate that personality differences do not alter basic language processing: All individuals make slips of the tongue, form similar kinds of word association, and organize their concept evaluations with respect to evaluativeness, activity, and potency. Moreover, all individuals seem to show similar effects of emotional stress, increasing reaction time, decreasing memory, and producing rigid, artificial responses in word association or word rating. In fact, it is the commonality of processing that permits clinical diagnosis through psycholinguistics; one can be assured, for example, in word association that no matter how idiosyncratic the response is, there is a memory linking the stimulus word and the response, and therefore that deviant responses are worth following up. Conversely, clinical use of psycholinguistic techniques has added to our understanding of normal language processing by demonstrating reliable effects of stress on language. Thus, for example, we might be tempted to explore the mental processes contributing to the long reaction times for emotionally stressful word associations. Are the normal associations actually harder to access as a result of stress, causing a less salient and therefore slower association to be aroused? Or is the increase in reaction time a result of several processes, such as retrieval and rejection of the normal association, followed by retrieval of another?

Vocal Indicators

As was indicated in the appendix to Chapter 7, physical and physiological factors contribute to tone of voice. The size of the individual's vocal tract and larynx affects the formant frequencies and pitch. Facial expressions, like smiling, which alter the vocal tract, also affect the voice in predictable and audible ways. Since the facial expression can indicate mood, this change could be used as a personality diagnostic. Studies of the effect of emotion *per se* on the voice have shown that stress, anger, and heightened arousal generally increase vocal pitch and speech rate, while sadness decreases pitch and slows the rate. These changes presumably result from a combination of altered breathing pattern, vocal cord tension, and fluids in and around the mouth.

Aside from use as indications of temporary mood changes, vocal changes have been correlated with long-term personality characteristics. For this use it is important to note that categorization by clinicians or other listeners made on the basis of tone of voice alone does not reliably predict diagnosis from other means. Moreover, across studies of vocal indicators of psychopathology there are frequently conflicting results (Scherer, 1979). However, the most consistent results (see Scherer, 1979, for review) show that compared with normals, chronic depressives have abnormally low pitch with staccato, step-wise intonation contours rather than smooth ones, as well as reduced range in loudness contour and lack of emphatic stress, and slower, more halting speech. Schizophrenics are reported to have unusual vocal qualities, but depending on the individual, these are occasionally manifested as increased pitch range and occasionally as decreased pitch range. For other vocal dimensions similar variation has been reported, suggesting no specific vocal pattern for schizophrenia. The results in general suggest that although the voice may be affected both by personality and mood, individual variation is sufficiently great that vocal cues may not be used as reliable indicators of psychological state.

Summary

In this section we have discussed the use of some common psycholinguistic measures as diagnostic indicators of personality. For the most part, the aspects of language that have been employed in personality research are those that either measure conceptual processing or seem to measure physical changes as might be reflected in the voice, while syntactic measures are notably absent. Reliable linguistic changes with personality changes are difficult to discover, in part because personality assessment by other means is not reliable compared with, for example, brain damage assessment.

Nevertheless, the studies and explanations of language change with personality change indicate common processing mechanisms between normal individuals and those suffering personality disorders. Chronic depressives show slower, more low-pitched speech than normal, but normal individuals experiencing a temporary sadness reflect the same direction of vocal change. Study of slips of the tongue, word forgetting, word association, and use of the semantic differential show similar conceptual processes in normal and disturbed individuals. For the most part, the ability to access the conceptual network is not impaired.

However, for both normal and chronic upsets these studies also illustrate the effect of emotional disturbance on language processing: Words associated with unpleasant experiences are more likely to be forgotten, harder to make associations to, and may cause disruption of other messages; stereotyped personalities, assumed for role-playing or from trauma in personality splits, show less than normal flexibility and variability in concept access. These common patterns can be used by clinicians to diagnose conceptual trouble spots.

In the next section we will look at language processing in one particular personality disorder, schizophrenia. From time to time, particular attention has been paid to the language of schizophrenics; indeed, language is among the most studied psychological processes in schizophrenia (Rubin, Doneson, and Jentons, 1979). We will examine the language and performance in language tasks of schizophrenics to see if their language processing is disturbed, and also to see what their language processing strategies can tell us about normal language processes.

Language Breakdown in Schizophrenia

Since language is intimately associated with thought, the breakdown of thought in psychosis should produce a breakdown of language. In fact, a pronounced characteristic of schizophrenia, a form of psychosis, is deviant language. Schizophrenic language has been studied in some detail to assess the nature of the thought disturbance. In this section we will look at the structure and processing of language in schizophrenia, to make inferences about normal processing, to determine the nature of the language dissolution, and to compare the dissolution with that in aphasia. Unlike the previous section, this section will consider language itself, not the use of language deviation for diagnosis.

Do Schizophrenics Have a Language Disturbance?

Before beginning our discussion of schizophrenic language processing we should note that there is some controversy over whether there is a linguistic deficit in schizophrenia. On the one hand, the speech of some schizophrenics is described as *word salad,* "a senseless ungrammatical succession of words" (Brown, 1958, p. 293)—as in "the house burnt the cow horrendously always" (cited by Chaika, 1974, p. 266). In such cases it would seem that language processing must be severely disturbed.

On the other hand, it has been frequently claimed, beginning with Bleuler (1911/1950), that the disturbance is not in language processing but rather in language content. Indeed, Brown (1973) concluded that reports of word salad were considerably exaggerated and that schizophrenic language was in fact normal, except in the areas where there was thought disturbance, as part of the delusion. For example, one patient with whom Brown conversed appeared normal, until claiming that when he left the hospital he would be starring in the movie version of *Fiddler on the Roof,* to be filmed in Scotland. The language used to make this claim was all fine; in fact, Brown commented that if the patient had begun the claim with "I dreamt that . . . " there would be no deviance at all. The difficulty was in real-world knowledge: He was too young for that part, the film was not being made, and if the film were being made Scotland would have been an unlikely location. Thus, the content of the speech was disturbed, but there was no apparent disturbance of language processing, of language specifically.

Brown's suggestion is that schizophrenics have intact language and intact comprehension but for one delusional area. Others have suggested that schizophrenics have normal language processes, but *autistic* or egocentric communication skills, a failure to recognize the need for making things clear to others. One patient (Whitehorn and Zipf, 1943), for example, referred continually and cryptically to "airplane messages" that she was receiving, causing the nurses to monitor her when airplanes passed overhead. Eventually her meaning was deciphered—she did not mean "airplane" but "air plain" (plain as air), and she failed to recognize (perhaps deliberately) that this was a private and ambiguous usage. Note that the derivational process she used was grammatical within English; we have compounds like "dog tired," "lily white," or "ice cold" that derive from the same structure as "air plain."

With regard to communicability of schizophrenic messages Whitehorn and Zipf (1943) compared the frequency and range of words used in the speech of schizophrenics with those of normals. In their view, optimal communication occurs within the bounds of sufficient repetition or redundancy for clarity and sufficient diversification for informativeness. If too many different kinds of words are used the repetition boundary is broken and communication is poor, and if too few are used, the diversification criterion is violated and the message is not informative. They found that normals and schizophrenics use the same number of different words, but that schizophrenics crowd "an inconveniently large number of meanings onto a relatively small number of words," (p. 844), overusing their most frequent words relative to normals, and thus rendering their speech less informative. Simultaneously, schizophrenics also tended to have a greater diversity of words that they used only once relative to normals: Schizophrenics, "inconsiderate of others, might indulge in a diversified polysyllabic discourse, using such a large and unfamiliar vocabulary as to be incomprehensible to most" (p. 844). This feature makes their language less redundant than normal and thus more difficult to follow. Thus, with respect to both redundancy and informativeness, schizophrenic language is impaired relative to normal.

In this kind of analysis the deviance in schizophrenia is attributed not so much to language processes as to communication processes. Patients do not take into account the needs of others in designing their speech, perhaps because of an inability or deficit in perceiving those needs, or perhaps because of a deliberate desire to be less well understood. In Brown's analysis the disturbance is in neither language nor communication but rather in one delusional thought area.

Alternatively, it may be reasonable to consider the disturbance a linguistic one. Box 13.1 shows some samples of schizophrenic language that have appeared in the literature. As you can see, although the language is odd, it is not particularly disturbed syntactically, compared with Broca's aphasia, for example. Not only are the sentences well constructed, but also both content words and function words are used and used appropriately. The features to observe in the language, which make it deviant, are the neologisms, like "pupped" and "subsicates" (1), the repetitions of "frank" (2b), "Joseph Nemo," and "for my nose" in 3, and the sentence anomalies in most of the passages. You may also note the inappropriate use of inflection in the first passage, but this is atypical and has thus far been rarely reported. Because there is little disturbance in phonology or syntax and most investigations have not found significant deviance in these areas in schizophrenia, we can quickly review these areas and then concentrate on semantic processing in schizophrenia.

As we examine studies of schizophrenic language processing consider whether they are compelling in showing a language impairment. We will return to this question later. Whether or not they indicate deficiency in the language mechanisms, the deviations from normal can be informative about the components and functionings of the normal language mechanism.

Box 13.1 Examples of Schizophrenic Language

The following are examples of language written or spoken by schizophrenics. There are many different types of schizophrenia and also vast individual differences in schizophrenics. Do not try to organize these into groups but consider if they are similar to or different from aphasic language.

1a. I don't like the way I'm pupped today (p. 226).

b. ... with syndicates organized and subsicates in the way that look for a civil war (p. 226).

c. I'm write letters in self defense and have been write for 25 years already. Russia and Israel is try to drive me to approve of war against Canada I'm not interested in become a socialist (p. 230).

d. Hawaiians are very sick mental way people (p. 231).

(Herbert and Waltensperger, 1982, one patient)

2a. I like coffee, cream, cows, Elizabeth Taylor. (p. 9)

b. [translated from German] It is from the Imperial House, they have it from ancestors, from the ancestral world, from the preworld. Frankfort-on-Main, there are the Franks, Frankfurter sausages, Frankenthal, Frankenstein. (p. 9)

c. [define "fable"]

Trade good sheep to hide in the beginning. (p. 13)

(Maher, 1972, three different patients)

3. Kindly send it to me at the hospital. Send it to me Joseph Nemo, in care of Joseph Nemo and me who answers by the name of Joseph Nemo will care for it myself. Thanks everlasting and Merry New Year to Metholatum Company for my nose, for my nose, for my nose, for my nose, for my nose, for my nose.

(Maher, 1972, p. 14)

4. The subterfuge and the mistaken planned substitutions for that demanded American action can produce nothing but the general results of negative contention and the impractical results of careless application, the natural results of misplacement of mistaken purpose and unrighteous position, the impractical serviceabilities of unnecessary contradictions.

(Maher, 1972, p. 13)

> 5. [Complete the sentence "I get warm when I run because . . . "]
> Quickness of blood, heart of deer, length
> Driven power, motorized cylinder, strength.
>
> *(Cameron, 1951, p. 61)*
>
> 6. In spite of the fact of that you insist on exercising your patriarchal influ-
> ence, my mind (even if not my pocket-book) is emancipated from that feu-
> dal conception of parental domination. No doubt you can arouse a certain
> amount of public sympathy from such narrow-minded goops as the Dovers
> and the Clarks, but it only goes to prove the futility of the development of
> intelligence and makes me realize that this is an unredeemable civilization
> of grocery men and fishmongers.
>
> *(Whitehorn and Zipf, 1943, p. 845)*

Speech Processing in Schizophrenia

Paralanguage.   The few reports of speaking disturbances in schizophrenia have
been concerned primarily with paralanguage and show little consistent disturbance
across patients. Bleuler (1911/1950), for example, described schizophrenic speaking
patterns as

> abnormally loud, abnormally soft, too rapid or too slow. Thus one patient speaks in
> a falsetto voice, another mumbles, a third pants. A catatonic speaks in precisely the
> same fashion during inspiration as during expiration. . . . When the patients think of
> themselves as different persons, they utilize a correspondingly different tone of voice
> (p. 148).

Although this description indicates that there is speech deviance, it does not indicate
that it is caused by an inability to control motor programs or to create melodic speech
units, as we saw in aphasia. In fact, the ability to speak on the inhale or to create
different voices for different characters suggests good control of speech skills. The
deviance stems from the failure to follow conventional conversational practices, not
from inability to organize speech.

Goldfarb, Goldfarb, and Scholl (1966) reported disturbances in pitch, loudness,
and rate in the speech of schizophrenic children, and these disturbed intelligibility.
For these aspects of the voice, the problems were that the modulations were inappropriate: Increased loudness did not correspond to syllable stress or emotional stress,
and similarly, pitch changes occurred independently of syntactic or mood changes.
Since syllabic stress was inappropriately marked, the speech took on a slurred quality.
(This points to the importance of suprasegmental information in guiding normal
speech interpretation.) In some patients, overall intonation was also deviant, either
excessively high-pitched or excessively monotonic.

Segmental Deficits.   Pathology in production of speech segments likewise does
not indicate difficulty in motor programming of speech. Two deficiencies have been
described, however. First, like Wernicke's aphasics, schizophrenics may produce

neologisms, such as "subsicates" (1b). Those produced, however, generally conform to the phonological structure of the native language (Chaika, 1974), indicating both proper internalization of the phonological rules and appropriate use of them in production. The neologisms may occur because the patient was deliberately avoiding using an intelligible word. Alternatively, as in aphasia, the neologism could occur because the patient has tried unsuccessfully to access the phonological representation of a particular word or has accessed it and unsuccessfully implemented it, producing multiple slips of the tongue.

Arguing against the correct access theory is the fact that schizophrenics rarely try to correct these pronunciations, as a normal individual might with speech errors (Chaika, 1974). In favor of the interpretation of deliberate word creation is a schizophrenic's self-report:

> I used some words in order to express a concept entirely different from the usual one. Thus, I blithely employed the word *mangy* to mean gallant. If I could not immediately find an appropriate word to express the rapid flow of ideas, I would seek release in a self-invented one, as for example, *wuttas* for *doves*.
>
> *(Bleuler, 1911/1950, p. 150)*

The impairment here seems to be in understanding *why* people talk—to *communicate* (which implies an awareness of the receiver, as you may recall), not simply to *express* an idea—rather than in understanding *how* one talks.

The second commonly noticed deficiency in the speech of schizophrenics is their perseveration on particular sounds, called *klang associations*. Most frequently these occur for the beginning syllables of a word, as in the "frank" example in Box 13.1, or more subtly, in the fourth example as in "*sub*terfuge" and "*sub*stitution" (there are others in that extract that you might try to find). It may occur at word ends, as in the repetition of "tion" (in 4) or in the rhyme of "length" and "strength" in the next extract. It clearly occurs not only on the morpheme level but also on the word and phrase levels, as in "Joseph Nemo" and "for my nose." Aside from these abnormalities however, segment production seems normal.

Speech Perception. Low-level speech perception has not been tested in schizophrenics, but there is no reason to expect it to be abnormal. Nevertheless, Maher (1972) reported that schizophrenics were more likely to make slips of the ear than normals, to hear one word when another had been spoken. As we will see there are reports that schizophrenic responses to word association tasks are abnormal, and Maher has contended that such findings are results of misperceptions, not bizarre associations: When it is clear that the patient has correctly heard the word, the word associations are normal (see Moon, Mefferd, Wieland, Pokorny, and Falconer, 1968). The misperceptions could derive from a failure in top-down processing. If patients have trouble attending to the speech and deciphering the message, an incorrect expectation could lead them to encode the wrong words.

In other tests, top-down processes have been shown to be more influential in schizophrenics than in normals. Carpenter (1976) played sentences with clicks superimposed on them to schizophrenic and normal subjects, with instructions to write the sentence and record the position of the click. As you may recall, in normal subjects there is a bias to perceive or report the click as occurring at the major syntactic boundary of the sentence (see chapters 5 and 7), perhaps indicating an effect of syntactic structure on perception. Carpenter found the same tendency for schizophrenic subjects, but even more pronounced than for normals. The study indicates not only a strong top-down effect in the speech perception of[2] schizophrenics but also normal syntactic processing at least in determining the major constituent boundary.

Syntactic Processing in Schizophrenia

Syntax Reception.   We have just seen that schizophrenics are able to detect the major consituent boundary within a sentence, and to that extent, to parse normally. Carpenter (1976) also showed that like normals, schizophrenics demonstrated better recall of clauses if they were contained within the same sentence than if they were expressed as separate sentences. This shows a normal sensitivity to sentence boundaries as a guide to parsing. Other studies find that, like normals, schizophrenics better recall meaningful sentences than anomalous sentences, and anomalous sentences that are syntactically correct than random word strings (Koh, 1978), although overall, their performance is worse than normals. This suggests that they make use of the redundancy provided by syntax to aid recall, and therefore that they parse appropriately.

A somewhat more sensitive test required schizophrenics and normals to unscramble sentences that had been scrambled to look like random word strings (Rausch, Prescotte, and DeWolfe, 1980). The task is better in that it tests generative capacity while not making strong memory demands, since the words are visible at all times. In this task, for almost all syntactic structures tested, schizophrenic and normal subjects performed equally well. The single exception could probably be attributed to semantics rather than syntax: a confusion in placement of the last noun phrases in sentences like "the boy gave the girl the book," which normals would correctly arrange, but which schizophrenics would sometimes organize to "the boy gave the book the girl." (The examples are mine.) The grammatical distinction is between *direct object* and *indirect object,* or in case grammar terms, between patient and recipient. It should be noted that the failure may be at the level of selectional features—that humans or animate objects are unlikely to be given and that inanimate objects are unlikely to receive. The general sentence structure and subcategorizations are not impaired; verbs are not used where nouns are called for. Alternatively, it may be that the patients did not notice the absence of the grammatical marker "to" and ordered the words of the sentence as if it were there.

Thus, on tests measuring the use of syntax in comprehension, schizophrenics

---

2. It is not clear, as you may recall, that the click study measures perception. Subjects must recall the sentence and the click position and write both down, so there are potential effects of memory and response organization. For the schizophrenics it is possible that they have failed to attend to the click in perception and guessed its position at the clause boundary, or they may have been unable to recall both click position and sentence. Attention and memory have both been considered to be impaired in schizophrenia (Schwartz, 1978).

appear normal, with the possible exception of a lesser sensitivity to grammatical markers such as prepositions. Usually their performance is poorer than that of normals, particularly if memory or attentional demands are great, but on tasks that normals find more difficult, schizophrenics have proportionally greater difficulty, so the pattern of results looks similar. This suggests that syntactic processing is not particularly impaired in schizophrenia. The one deficit noted, between comprehension of direct and indirect object, might be used as evidence to separate selectional features from syntactic processing, since otherwise there is no indication of parsing difficulties. As we will see, there is other evidence of semantic or conceptual deficits in schizophrenia. And it is not unreasonable to consider selectional restrictions part of the semantic system.

Syntactic Deficits in Spontaneous Production.   For the most part, schizophrenic productions also suggest no profound syntactic impairments. Schizophrenic language "rarely (if ever) includes hard instances of agrammatism or word-finding deficits" (Cohen, 1978, p. 1). However, many investigators have been struck by an apparent abnormality in structure, at least at the discourse level in schizophrenic speech, which some have attributed to a syntactic disruption.

Consider, for example, the sentence "I like coffee, cream, cows, Elizabeth Taylor." Although the sentence is syntactically well-formed, the items included in the list reflect no common membership in a higher-order category, as is reflected in the more normal sentence "I like coffee, tea, and cocoa." This suggests that there might be fewer constraints on word selection in the schizophrenic utterance than normal. In fact, this has been assessed directly by using a technique called the cloze procedure.

In the *cloze procedure* a passage of speech is obtained usually through a prompted interview, and then words are systematically deleted from it; for example, every fifth word is removed (Pavy, 1978; Maher, 1972; Salzinger, Portnoy, and Feldman, 1978). The butchered word strings are then given to other individuals (normal or schizophrenic) to see if they can fill in the gaps. The greater the constraints from the context are on their identity, the more easily the missing elements should be guessed. As we might expect from the word count results cited earlier (Whitehorn and Zipf, 1943), it should be harder to guess the missing words from schizophrenic speech, since their word choice involves more repetition and more one-time use than normal.

The technique has yielded several interesting results. First, as expected, it is harder to guess elements missing from schizophrenic speech than it is from normal speech, providing empirical support for the observation that there are fewer constraints and less redundancy than normal in schizophrenic utterances. Second, the results showed that the speech of schizophrenics is less predictable at the ends of the passages than at the beginnings, perhaps because the prompt that triggered the response is farther away in time and therefore exerts less control. The difference in redundancy between beginnings and ends of passages is not found in normal speech, and this suggests that schizophrenics may be less limited by distant contextual constraints than normals. Third, schizophrenics are poorer at guessing the missing elements from the speech of other schizophrenics than are normals—arguing against a myth (see, for example, Brown, 1973 for discussion and critique) that schizophrenics have a common language. Finally, examination of the responses of schizophrenics to gaps produced by the cloze procedure indicates that their guesses are determined primarily by constraints from the immediately preceding word rather than the whole sentence or passage (Salzinger et al., 1978).

It is interesting to consider the findings from the cloze procedure as reflecting a finite state grammar generation of schizophrenic speech. As you may recall from Chapter 4, in a finite state grammar each element is determined only by the immediately preceding element, as the term "Thursday" might be determined only by the production "Wednesday" in a list of days of the week. It has been argued that normal human language cannot be modeled by finite state grammars, since constraints on morpheme selection apply across many words—the choice of a pronoun, for example, may be determined by a noun appearing sentences earlier. It is precisely the absence of distant constraints that the cloze technique reveals as characteristic of schizophrenic speech, as does the absence of hierarchical structure in the list "coffee, cream, cows, Elizabeth Taylor." The *contrast* between normal speech and schizophrenic speech, in this regard, underscores the observation that normal speech cannot be generated by a finite state grammar.

The question is whether schizophrenia reduces the operation of the mental syntax processor to a more primitive finite state grammar level, or whether the processor is normal in schizophrenia but some of the utterances are describable by finite state grammar. There have been relatively few investigations of schizophrenic language undertaken from a transformational grammar standpoint (Pavy, 1968), so it is difficult to ascertain whether there are important deficiencies in, for example, the implementation of certain transformations. Moreover, those studies that have examined syntax from a more sophisticated view are subject to several interpretations.

Chaika (1974), for example, analyzed the speech of one patient, comparing her output with other cases mentioned in the literature. The comparison yielded what Chaika considered to be defining characteristics of schizophrenic speech, some of which were syntactic disruptions: failure to limit the meanings of a word through the context (as in "my mother's name was Bill ... and coo"), the structuring of both sentences and discourse around individual word-meanings or sounds rather than around a topic, and the failure to apply appropriately redundancy rules such as the replacement of the second occurrence of a noun by a pronoun.[3] It is important to note, however, that none of these failures produces a profound structural deviance as would the omission of a predicate or substitution of a noun for a verb. Rather, they each contribute to a problem of cohesiveness, perhaps reflecting the operation of a finite state grammar rather than a context-sensitive grammar. Alternatively, this

---

3. The other characteristic features she described we have already discussed: the inability to match semantic features with word-names (her interpretation of the existence of neologisms), inappropriate attention to the sound of the words (as in klang associations), and failure to correct mispronunciations. Fromkin (1975) argued that none of these characteristics was peculiar to schizophrenia, nor was the combination; all can be found, although with less frequency, in the speech of normals.

might reflect an extralinguistic problem of coordinating ideas (Fromkin, 1975) rather than a syntactic disruption at all.

Herbert and Waltensperger (1982) presented a single patient who might be analyzed as showing syntactic impairments. Some examples of his utterances are given in the first passage of Box 13.1. According to the researchers, his language indicated confusions of tense and aspect (as in "organized and subsicates"), violations of subcategorization rules (as in his persistent substitution of "I'm" for "I"), and failure to use common inflections (as in substitution of the content word "way" for the adverb inflection "-ly"). Unfortunately, they did not describe his linguistic background and although his speech does not look like normal English, with the exception of the neologisms, it does look like a normal language *process,* creolization, as you may recall from Chapter 11. Moreover, as the researchers point out themselves, these particular linguistic peculiarities are highly atypical of schizophrenic language and so cannot be used as descriptive of the breakdown, as, for example, the function word omission is descriptive of Broca's aphasia.

As a final comment on schizophrenic syntax, it is perhaps instructive to examine the last extract in Box 13.1, an excerpt from a letter written by a highly educated schizophrenic patient. There is no question that this passage employs well-formed, elegant, and complex syntactic structure, although the point of the passage is obscured by the abundance of words and convoluted style. It seems that if there were an impairment in syntax *per se,* such a passage could never have been penned by a schizophrenic: In the last sentence, for example, the "it" is appropriately a singular pronoun, referring to the entire last clause and controlling the third-person singular marking on the verbs "goes" and "makes," despite their distance and the intrusion of some plural nouns. So, there clearly is context-sensitivity in the syntax beyond the single word. The passage also illustrates use of sentence-embedding, complex constituent structure, inflection, and so on—all instances of difficult, high-level syntactic operations.

Thus, it appears that if schizophrenia results in language oddities, it is not because there is damage to a syntactic processor, but rather because the patients do not use the normal syntactic strategies they have available to produce coherent discourse. This may be described possibly as a semantic failure, since meaning is not appropriately put into words; a communication failure, since meaning is not appropriately structured for transmission; or a thought failure, since meaning is not appropriately conceptualized. We turn next to studies of schizophrenics' processing of linguistic meaning to consider whether there is, in fact, evidence of semantic disruption.

Semantic Processes in Schizophrenia

Most investigators of schizophrenia agree that schizophrenics show disturbances in thought or conceptual structure. The level of language most likely to reflect disruption in schizophrenia, therefore, is the semantic system. As we shall see, semantic deficits have been noted in schizophrenics in categorization, in word selection, in rating word pairs, and also in determining sentence meanings. However, there is no agreement on how best to describe these deficiencies, nor whether they are deficiencies in underlying semantic organization, in semantic processing, or in strategies applied to normal semantic organization and processes. We will investigate the results of experiments in semantic processing in schizophrenia within the context of some of the hypotheses proposed to explain or describe the deviance.

Concreteness and Immediacy Hypotheses. We have already observed that schizophrenic productions seem to be organized as a chain, with links between immediately adjacent words only. This characteristic of sentence construction also seems to be characteristic of schizophrenic thought, sometimes referred to as the *immediacy hypothesis* (Salzinger et al., 1978) or reflecting a *concrete attitude* rather than an abstract, logical one (Goldstein, 1951). What is hypothesized is that the schizophrenic's attention is captured by some immediate feature of the environment, either of the nonverbal context or of the last word uttered. For example, Angyal (1951) reported a patient who, when asked where her husband was, responded that he was in the wedding picture present in the room. Because the controlling stimulus is some aspect of the immediate environment, this response may be considered a reflection of the immediacy. Because the response is selected on the basis of some specific and concrete characteristic like visibility rather than on the basis of the symbolic meaning, it is considered to reflect a concrete attitude.

Other manifestations of the concrete attitude are overinclusiveness or overgeneralization of objects in categories, a relative paucity of use of general category names, and a use of words as names rather than symbols. Goldstein (1951) cited one patient, for example, who described a group of green objects individually as "bright green, bell green, baby green," and so on, as if he did not see the abstract similarity in color. The word "green" was used as though it were a proper name for each object.

If the problem in schizophrenia is an underlying difficulty in abstract thinking or in using nonimmediate information, we should expect schizophrenics to have deficits in semantic categorization, and these might be reflected in tests of word association, perception of semantic similarity, recognition of semantic classes, and sentence comprehension, which would involve abstraction of relevant meanings from the individual words. These abilities have been measured in schizophrenics. (There are other effects that problems in semantic categorization might produce that have not been measured; e.g., a null effect of semantic similarity in verification of false sentences, since the similarity is not noticed. Try to generate other hypotheses for breakdown given what you know of normal semantic organization and the possible debilitating effects of immediacy and concreteness.)

Word Association and Immediacy. The responses given by schizophrenics in word association tasks fall within the normal range, provided care is taken to ensure that the stimulus word is correctly perceived (Moon, Mefferd, Wieland, Pokorny, and Falconer, 1968; Maher, 1972). However, there have been a number of reports of lack of continuity or "loosening" of association in schizophrenia (Bleuler, 1911/1950), caused by words losing their most salient meaning features and thus failing to reflect their abstract meaning. Moreover, schizophrenics have been occasionally reported to emit rare associations (Pavy, 1968; Schwartz, 1978 for review), perhaps reflecting a failure to make or use the abstract associative network. Finally, as we have already noted, associations suggested by intrusions in the spontaneous speech of schizophrenics are indeed deviant. There are klang associations, in which the immediate sound of the word seems to capture attention, and chained associations based on a single concrete semantic feature as in the "coffee, cream . . . " example, rather than on membership in the same abstract category.

To account for the variety of results, it has been proposed that there are two types of association available: a normal, logical, abstract association, and a personal idiosyncratic association, based on concrete, immediate experience. We should note that these types of association are not just found in schizophrenia: We have seen concrete, idiosyncratic association in normals in the "ring-garden" example, and we have also seen sound associations in normals. Schizophrenics may be less able or less willing to suppress this type of association in favor of the abstract, conventionalized ones than normals, but they do not appear unable to produce the abstract ones.

Semantic Similarity and Concreteness. Schizophrenics' observation of semantic similarity has been measured in recall and direct ratings. Koh (1978) presented normal and schizophrenic subjects with lists of words to recall. The lists consisted of either semantically similar items, which are better recalled by normals, or unrelated items. Note that there should be a difference of recall of the lists only if the subject is able to abstract the similar semantic feature from the different list items. The schizophrenics did not benefit by the organization in the list. In fact, their performance was poorer on semantically similar lists than random lists. That there was an observable effect of semantic similarity suggests that the schizophrenics were able to abstract it from the list items; however, it should have helped recall rather than hurt it.

One possible explanation for the poorer performance on semantically similar lists derives from the concreteness hypothesis. When asked to add items to a list like "trot, gallop, ____," normal response is "canter," which shares both the horse and movement aspects of the other words. The response of schizophrenics to this example is "horse," which is a strong association to each of the other words but misses in abstracting the movement feature they have in common (Pavy, 1968). Suppose that "trot, gallop," and so on, were words presented in a short-term memory list. We might expect an intrusion error from the schizophrenic subjects of "horse," making their performance poorer than on random lists. Thus, it is possible that their poorer performance on semantically similar lists derives from intrusion errors from a related semantic category. These, in turn, could derive from a failure to block immediate associations or to abstract fully the relevant semantic features.

Chapman and Chapman (1965) specifically measured the ability of schizophrenics to abstract semantic similarity by asking them to rate pairs of words with respect to the similarity between members of the pair, and later to choose from a pair of words the word most similar to a target word. For the first task, they found that schizophrenics tended to overrate the similarity of all the word pairs relative to normal, but that with decreasing similarity between the words as determined by normal ratings, the schizophrenic ratings also decreased. That the subjects recognized the similarity indicates that they do have abstraction abilities, and that the ratings decreased with decreasing similarity indicates appropriate sensitivity to abstract word-meaning. Moreover, in the second task the schizophrenics exhibited normal responses.

Categorization and Concreteness. To measure semantic categorization in schizophrenia two tasks have been used: (1) giving subjects a criterion and asking them to generate or select instances conforming to it, and (2) giving subjects words and asking them to sort them into categories. An example of the first is the feature "has a head," and correct responses include most animals and also inanimate objects like "hammer," "nail," or "beer," for example. Normal people are able to generate or recognize atypical instances, but schizophrenics are more "concrete" in their definitions and typically use only the animate examples (study cited by Pavy, 1968).

Davis and Blaney (1976) presented subjects with a category name and then a set of related words. Subjects had to decide whether the related words were part of the definition of the category. For example, defining features of "bird" might be feathers, beak, two feet, egg-laying, while a merely related feature might be small size. Normal subjects consistently separated the features into two classes, while the schizophrenic subjects checked all related words. This difference was interpreted as a tendency to overgeneralize, and thus as a deficit in categorization.

It should be noted that schizophrenics do not just overgeneralize; they also over-discriminate. Chapman and Chapman (1965) reported patients who labeled some vegetables as fruits (overgeneralization), and others who could not say why a dog and lion were similar since one barked and the other roared (overdiscrimination). Over-generalization seems to involve abstraction, an observation of similarity, while over-discrimination reflects a concrete thought process. Deviance from normal in either, though, indicates a problem with the abstraction process.

Larsen and Fromholt (1976) gave subjects a list of words to sort into categories. The subjects were not told how many categories to make nor were they given any rules for categorization. They were not permitted to examine their sortings, so at all times they could see only the top word in the category. After the sorting, the words were shuffled and the subjects were asked to duplicate their sorts. Ninety-two percent of the normal subjects were able to reconstruct their work, whereas only 71 percent of the schizophrenic subjects could. The categories that the two groups made were not structured differently, but the schizophrenics tended to change the number of categories they were using while sorting, and the normals did not.

Generally the results suggest that schizophrenics and normals have the same conceptual bases for organizing the words, but that schizophrenics are more variable in the criteria they apply at any given instant. This could be interpreted as support for the immediacy hypothesis in that schizophrenics may be distracted from applying a rule that they had used before by a minor change in the immediate conceptual environment (such as a new order that would put different words near one another).

Metaphor Interpretation and Concreteness. The last way we suggested looking at immediacy and concreteness as modes of thinking that affect language in schizophrenia was in derivations of meaning from word combinations. An early test was proverb interpretation, which not only looked at sentence processing generally but also at figurative reasoning specifically. Benjamin (1951) reported that schizophrenics were impaired at this task. In mild instances, they would give a literal interpretation, as in "when nobody's around they do things they wouldn't do if the cat was there" for "while the cat's away the mice will play." Note that the literal interpretation implies a concrete attitude, an inability to make an abstract meaning. In more severe cases, the interpretation bore little relation to either the literal or figurative meaning, as in "that means feline absence and rodential job which has its sources in the nature of the Savior, divine forgiveness, Heaven, Hell and inscrutability."

Others have also reported disturbances in figurative interpretation (Pavy, 1968) but the reports are inconsistent (Maher, 1972). Vigotsky (1934) proposed that schizophrenics could interpret proverbs they were familiar with from childhood, presumably because the meaning of the proverb did not have to be generated but just recalled, but that they failed to provide interpretations for new ones for which they would have to abstract meaning.

Summary. Generally speaking, there does not seem to be strong or exclusive support for either a concrete attitude or the immediacy hypothesis as governing schizophrenic language disturbances. In controlled settings, schizophrenics are capable of sorting words into categories, in many instances of replicating their performance despite a reshuffling of the words with new possibilities for chained associations, of recognizing semantic similarities between words, and even of making figurative interpretations.

Of course, there are also indications that semantic skills are impaired:

1. as a group, schizophrenics were less able to repeat their categorizations than normals,
2. they were less able to keep track of the number of categories they were using (both of these might suggest a memory deficiency rather than a semantic one),
3. they were more influenced by characteristic features in categorizing than were normals,
4. they produced erratic word associations occasionally,
5. and they had occasional difficulties with figurative interpretations.

If Vigotsky's observation is true, the difficulties with figurative interpretations may arise only when they need to generate the interpretation, not when they need to recall it. In general, it seems that impairment on semantic tasks in schizophrenia does not result from deviant language *processing*, as would be reflected by concrete rather than abstract thinking. The difficulty may come from inappropriate cognitive *structures*—which features define a particular category. Alternatively, it may derive from deviant general cognitive processes like attentional or memory mechanisms.

The Dominance Hypothesis. Chapman and Chapman (1965; and Daut, 1976) suggested that the underlying semantic organization of schizophrenics may be normal, as might be their general semantic processing, but that their deficiency arises from an inability to attend to any but the dominant meaning of a word or dominant association to a word. Given our discussion of semantic organization, this could occur if the spread of activation was limited so that fewer associations than normal were aroused, or if the mechanism for deciding which concept had received the most activation from all sources was defective and so could consider only the link most highly weighted initially.

To test the dominance hypothesis, Chapman et al. (1976) presented subjects with ambiguous words in a disambiguating sentence context. Subjects were instructed to select the best meaning for the word, given three choices. One choice was the usual meaning of the word, which should be expected to be most strongly activated in the absence of context. A second was a less usual meaning, but one that the context preferentially activated. A third choice was irrelevant, simply a control for guessing. For example, for the sentence "when the farmer bought a herd of cattle he needed a new pen" the choices were:

a. he needed a new writing implement (strong word meaning)
b. he needed a new fenced enclosure (weak word meaning, but correct given context)
c. he needed a new pickup truck (irrelevant).

In this task schizophrenics ignored the information provided by context and uniformly selected the dominant meaning. Note that this could arise either because they did not know the weaker meanings or because they were not able to select the weaker meanings using the context. The first alternative Chapman et al. ruled out by giving the patients the words in isolation and asking them to select *all* possible meanings for each. The schizophrenics were able to do this, indicating that all meanings were available. Thus, their performance in the first task suggests an inability to weigh the contextual information appropriately.

The dominance hypothesis can account for some of the results we have observed already. First, in schizophrenic sentence production we may consider that chained associations occur through arousal of dominant associations rather than through a synthesis and abstraction of meanings as a whole (Maher, 1972). Second, the difficulty with interpretation of unfamiliar proverbs could arise because each word in the proverb arouses a dominant association that cannot be integrated with those aroused by the other words. For familiar proverbs, the dominant association could be the figurative meaning of the whole sentence.

The dominance hypothesis fails to account for results that indicate that schizophrenics have access to nondominant meanings, as they must to judge words of medium similarity as similiar. Moreover, it is inconsistent with some results supporting the immediacy hypothesis, such as the patient's selection of a picture of her husband to answer a question about his whereabouts, since the dominant association should be the individual, not his photograph. In fact, this example suggests that patients can make use of immediate context to modify meanings, albeit strangely.

Since the results as a whole suggest that schizophrenics have access to nondominant associations as well as dominant associations, the semantic system seems to be intact, and spreading activation from a concept to related but nondominant associations must occur. That schizophrenics do not always use the better association suggests that their deficit lies in judging which is better; that is, which was more activated in a particular circumstance. The deviance in selection from, or comparison of, a competing response has been discussed as a mechanism for schizophrenic language and is known as the *self-editing* hypothesis.

Abnormalities in Self-Editing. As we have observed, it is possible to explain schizophrenics' selection of dominant word-meanings in multiple choice disregarding context as a problem in editing. There are other results that support this explanation. For one thing, schizophrenics' performance on recall tasks, where they must generate the response, is poorer than that of normals, but on recognition tasks, where items are selected for them, they show no deficit in memory (Cohen, 1978). This difference suggests that memory is not impaired, but the ability to select a given memory spontaneously is. For another, in production tasks that require careful selection among alternatives, schizophrenics perform much worse than normals.

In one such task, two people are shown a pair of stimuli, and one is told which of the pair is the target. The task is to communicate the target to the other person. Cohen (1978) used colors as stimuli and varied the difference between them. Red and green would be easy to signal between, but two shades of pink would require finer verbal tuning, a careful selection from among irrelevant, noncommunicative responses. The close colors were more difficult for normal subjects, but with extra time they correctly signaled the target. With the pink example, for instance, a normal subject initially gave the clue "salmon," and then realized both choices were salmon-colored, and added "the pinker one." When schizophrenics elaborated, generally the addition was not helpful: Also beginning with "salmon," one subject continued "from the can."

Smith (1970) used a similar task, but with stimuli entirely from a verbal domain. Subjects were paired and then each was shown a word pair such as "robber-thief." One of the subjects was also told which of the words in the pair was the target, for example, "robber," and the task was for that subject without directly mentioning the target word to make the other subject say it as in a game of Password. Abilities to select a good clue can be measured in this task for both the transmitter and the receiver. Note that for the example here, a clue like "one who steals" is ineffective since it prompts both words equally. A better clue for "robber" might be "baron," and for "thief," "jewel," because of the associations "robber baron" and "jewel thief." Note also that the task should be difficult for schizophrenics if the words share a dominant meaning, since then the transmitter might not be able to ignore it to provide an effective clue.

In selecting the target from the clues given, schizophrenics performed like normals in receiver position, suggesting once again that their associative structures are intact. They were considerably worse as transmitters, at cueing the target, however, indicating either an inability to generate the clues spontaneously or to select among clues they had generated.

To differentiate these possibilities, Smith gave the same subjects a forced-choice task in which they were to select the better of two clues provided for a given word of a word pair. If they performed normally here, when the clues were given to them, then it could be concluded that their difficulty lay in generating possible clues. Difficulties in this task would focus the problem on selection of the better of alternative clues.

The schizophrenics were able to select the better clue only when it related strongly to the target word, and were impaired if the better clue was a weak association of the target. As an example, consider the pair "below-beneath," with "below" as target and "under" and "belt" as possible prompts. "Under" is a stronger association of "below" than is "belt," but it is also a good prompt for "beneath." The association of "belt" to either "below" or "beneath" occurs only in the expression "below the belt" and therefore uniquely signals "below." Since "under" relates to both words, "belt"—although weakly related to "below"—is a better clue for it. Schizophrenics had trouble selecting this kind of clue, apparently unable to assess the *difference* in the association of the two clues to the potential targets. Thus, their problem appears to be in selecting among (editing) clues and also appears to be limited to a particular kind of selection.

Description of the processes necessary to perform well on this task is reminiscent of a model of metaphor comprehension discussed in Chapter 3. In that model it was proposed that subjects looked for similarities between the topic and ground of the metaphor (for example, between "billboards" and "warts of the landscape") beginning with the most highly weighted features of the topic. The similarities were then judged *against the background of differences.* The forced-choice task described here requires a similar kind of weighting, not a simple judgment but a complex comparison of the similarity of each clue to the possible targets, judged against a background of the difference. The difficulty in the editing task is suggestive of potential difficulties with proverb and metaphor interpretation.

Be that as it may, it is important to observe that schizophrenics are as able as normals to select the target from the clue given (to act as receiver) and so must be performing the comparisons properly. The failure they exhibit is a failure to communicate, which may be construed either as a failure to select among the clues, to recognize the perspective of the other, or as a failure in *motivation* to be clear. As we have already seen, the speech of schizophrenics is egocentric—that could be from a desire to be cryptic as easily as from idiosyncratic definitions (a problem in semantic structure) or semantic processes, or from neglect of the other person's position (an attention problem). Most of the hypotheses that we have entertained consider breakdown in definitions or in semantic processes, but, as we have suggested, many researchers consider schizophrenia a problem in communication generally, not language specifically (Whitehorn and Zipf, 1943; Brown, 1973; Cohen, 1978, to name a few).

Summary and Conclusions

Our examination of schizophrenic communications reveals a number of abnormalities. We will review these here to consider whether there is reason to assume that they derive from a breakdown in language processing. In schizophrenia there may be an unrealistic set of concepts (a delusion), but this is often appropriately expressed in words, suggesting that there is not a linguistic problem. On the other hand, schizophrenics may use words idiosyncratically and may structure their communications to be less informative than normal either by increasing or decreasing the redundancy necessary for optimal communication. It is unclear whether this is a linguistic deficit or a failure to take the other's perspective, perhaps deliberately, to be cryptic.

Schizophrenics seem to have a greater tendency than normals to mishear words spoken to them and a greater tendency to perseverate on, or attend to, the sounds of the words rather than the meanings in constructing their speech. Although it is tempting to argue that this reflects a dissociation between the name store and the meaning store, as we argued for Wernicke's aphasics, it is important to recall that Jung found a tendency for sound-based associations in normals when the stimulus word was associated with psychological distress or when they were experiencing physical stress. Schizophrenia may produce stress as a disease, or may be a psychological reaction to stress, and so the abnormalities in sound production and perception may be an outgrowth of normal linguistic processes together with the normal reaction to stress.

In aphasia we discussed a dissociation between sound and meaning stores. Broca's aphasics seemed to use a slow system of semantic association to prompt a name, indicating intact associative processes with disturbance of the normal fast association between a name and its referent. Wernicke's aphasics seemed to have lost their access to the associative store altogether. The breakdown between naming and association is far more tenuous in schizophrenia—the schizophrenics can and do make normal associations, both with respect to producing the words and with respect to the meaning relation between them. The problem is that they fail to do this sometimes, but the occasionalness of the disturbance does not indicate damage, as in aphasia.

Schizophrenics seem to have normal abilities to parse sentences spoken by others, and their own sentences frequently use high-level syntactic operations like embedding and recursion. However, their spontaneous discourse reflects fewer constraints than normal, as we saw with the difficulty in guessing words deleted from schizophrenic utterances. In some instances, the speech of schizophrenics does not appear to be hierarchically structured but rather structured as a chain. This problem, however, does not indicate a breakdown in the syntactic ability to form higher-order constituents, since the looseness of association it suggests never produces ungrammatical sentences but rather, at worst, semantically anomalous ones. Thus, at present, there is no evidence that there are syntactic processing disturbances in schizophrenia.

We might consider the unusual choice of words for constituents producing the anomalies to reflect a semantic problem. Other semantic deviations include an occasional failure to use selectional restrictions appropriately (e.g., selecting an inanimate noun as recipient), a less-than-normal ability to use extended, distant, or weaker meanings of words (e.g., difficulty with "pen" as enclosure), and a difficulty in dissociating from strong but irrelevant associations aroused either verbally (e.g., "pen" as writing instrument) or nonverbally (e.g., the picture in the immediate environment as husband).

However, none of these instances suggests damage to the language structures or processes *per se,* as there appears to be in aphasia, where, for example, names of concrete nouns may be inaccessible and therefore replaced by appropriate charades like the tune of the wedding march for the word "wedding" (see Chapter 12). Rather, the disruption lies in whether and how the patients make use of the language knowledge they have accessible. In this respect, the language "deficit" is similar to the semantic deficit for split personalities, not a deviant semantic organization but a deviant use of semantic organization, consciously or unconsciously. Indeed, perhaps because language structures and processing are not impaired, it is reasonable to use tests relying on language to assess personality, and to do personality therapies through language, as in psychoanalysis.

Our examination of schizophrenic language is informative about the nature of language normally. First, it demonstrates dramatically the effect of loosening of the powerful constraints of context on word selection in sentences. Normal language does not look like a schizophrenic chain. Second, it demonstrates the importance of considering language as communication: When the audience is not taken into account by speakers, productions are measurably abnormal and may cease to look like language because of too high or too low an information rate. Finally, comparing schizophrenic language with aphasic language we see dramatically the difference between an intact but oddly accessed language machine and a broken one. There is a tendency to credit aphasics with intact language competence but a deficit in performance, to assume that there is an ideal speaker-hearer imprisoned by damage to the brain (see, for example, Gardner, 1975, for discussion). Such a description may be applicable to the schizophrenic or split personality but, by contrast, seems unlikely for the aphasic.

Summary and Conclusions

In this chapter we have examined some effects of personality disorder on language processing. We began by noting the effects of emotional stress on normal language processing. Competing messages may produce intrusions in word selection (and nonsense words as a result). Stressful associations may cause temporary loss of memory for a word, or stress may cause a normal individual to produce idiosyncratic or sound-based associations to a word. Pretense may produce rigid use of the semantic differential. Finally, emotion changes may affect vocal quality. We then discussed some personality disorders and how they affect language behaviors with respect to some of these measures and others discussed in earlier chapters.

Comparison of language skills in personality upset (schizophrenia, in particular) with language processing after brain damage indicates a very different pattern of disruption. Schizophrenics may make idiosyncratic associations, perseverate on the sound of a word or a semantic feature seemingly irrelevant to the current context, and be less informative and less redundant than necessary for normal discourse. However, careful tests indicate that their semantic categories are normal, that their associations are normal provided that they correctly hear the stimulus words, and that even under the unusual conditions of psycholinguistic testing they "play" word "games" like the variant of Password correctly. The disturbance seems to be in which features of the language they select to attend to (sometimes idiosyncratic meanings, sometimes sound, sometimes a meaning suggested by immediate context, and so on), the kind of language "disturbance" seen in normal people when experiencing emotional stress.

The abnormality found in schizophrenic language underscores the importance of language as a communication system—when there is a loss (perhaps deliberate) of the perspective of the other in constraining transmission, there is noticeable deviance.

For the most part, schizophrenic language meets our language criteria, sho ving recursiveness, metalanguage, arbitrariness, and so on. The deficit seems to be in communication, perhaps in aspects of interchangeability, since schizophrenics perform normally as receivers in many tasks we discussed, but not as transmitters. Moreover, they seem to show a reluctance to alter their own mental structures around what is being transmitted to them, and an inattention to whether they are successful in altering others' structures when they transmit, both required for true communication.

We began this chapter by pointing out that there have been confusions of schizophrenics with brain-damaged patients. From language behavior alone it seems that it should be easy to differentiate the groups. In brain damage we would expect to see particular problems with syntax, especially in deriving constituent structures and in producing complex sentences with embeddings, which we would not expect to see in schizophrenia. In brain damage we would expect to find problems with a linguistic category of words, function words in Broca's aphasia and substantive content words in Wernicke's aphasia, while in schizophrenia word-related abnormalities may appear without regard to linguistic or semantic structure. In Wernicke's aphasia, but not in schizophrenia, we should find impairment of access to the associative network. And there are other possible linguistic and psycholinguistic differentiators, which you might try to find.

In sum, comparison of schizophrenic language processes with aphasic language processes suggests that the disorders should be easily discriminable, and moreover, that the schizophrenics' difficulties are not primarily linguistic. Perhaps the best way to demonstrate that the breakdowns are different is to examine Box 13.2 and realize how easy it is to label the schizophrenic and the aphasic "language."

Box 13.2 Schizophrenic or Aphasic Language?

The following passages are taken from a schizophrenic patient (Bleuler, 1911/1950, p. 156) and a Wernicke's aphasic (Gardner, 1975, p. 68). Can you tell which is which?

1. Oh sure, go ahead, any old think you want. If I could I would. Oh, I'm taking the word the wrong way to say, all of the barbers here whenever they stop you it's going around and around, if you know what I mean, that is tying and tying for repucer, for repuceration, well, we were trying the best that we could while another time it was with the beds over there the same thing . . .

2. At Apell plain church-state, the people have customs and habits taken partly from glos-faith because the father wanted to enter new f. situation since they believed the father had a Babeli comediation only with music. Therefore they went to the high Osetion and on the cabbage earth and all sorts of malice, and against everything good. On their inverted Osetion Valley will come and within thus is the father righteousness.

REFERENCES

Angyal, A. (1951). Disturbances of thinking in schizophrenia. In J. S. Kasanin (Ed.). *Language and Thought in Schizophrenia*, pp. 65–90. Los Angeles: University of California Press.

Benjamin, J. D. (1951). A method for distinguishing and evaluating formal thinking in schizophrenia. In J. S. Kasanin (Ed.). *Language and Thought in Schizophrenia*, pp. 65–90. Los Angeles: University of California Press.

Bleuler, E. (1911/1950). *Dementia Praecox or the Group of Schizophrenias*. Translated by J. Zinkin. NY: International Universities Press.

Brown, R. (1958). *Words and Things*. NY: The Free Press.

———(1973). Schizophrenia, language, and reality. *American Psychologist*, 395–403.

Cameron, N. (1951). Experimental analysis of schizophrenic thinking. In J. S. Kasanin (Ed.). *Language and Thought in Schizophrenia*, pp. 50–64. Los Angeles: University of California Press.

Carpenter, M. D. (1976). Sensitivity to syntactic structure: Good vs bad premorbid schizophrenics. *Journal of Abnormal Psychology, 85*, 41–50.

Chaika, E. (1974). A linguist looks at schizophrenic language. *Brain and Language, 1*, 257–276.

Chapman, L. J., & Chapman, J. P. (1965). Interpretation of words in schizophrenia. *Journal of Personality and Social Psychology, 1*, 135–146.

Chapman, L. J., Chapman, J. P., & Daut, R. L. (1976). Schizophrenic inability to disattend from strong aspects of meaning. *Journal of Abnormal Psychology, 85*, 35–40.

Cohen, B. D. (1978). Referent communication disturbances in schizophrenia. In S. Schwartz (Ed.). *Language and Cognition in Schizophrenia*, pp. 1–34. Hillsdale, NJ: Lawrence Erlbaum Associates.

Davis, K. M., & Blaney, P. H. (1976). Overinclusion and self-editing in schizophrenia. *Journal of Abnormal Psychology, 85*, 51–60.

Forrester, J. (1980). *Language and the Origins of Psychoanalysis*. NY: Columbia University Press.

Freud, S. (1901/1960). *The Psychopathology of Everyday Life*. Translated by Alan Tyson and edited by James Strachey. London: Ernest Benn, Ltd.

———(1917/1961). *Introductory Lectures on Psychoanalysis*. Toronto: Clark, Irwin, & Co.

Fromkin, V. A. (1975). A linguist looks at "A linguist looks at 'schizophrenic language.'" *Brain and Language, 2*, 498–503.

Gardner, H. (1975). *The Shattered Mind*. NY: A. A. Knopf.

Goldfarb, W., Goldfarb, N., & Scholl, H. H. (1966). The speech of mothers of schizophrenic children. *American Journal of Psychiatry, 122*, 1220–1227.

Goldstein, K. (1951). Methodological approach to the study of schizophrenic thought disorder. In J. S. Kasanin (Ed.). *Language and Thought in Schizophrenia*, pp. 17–40. Los Angeles: University of California Press.

Herbert, R. K., & Waltensperger, K. Z. (1982). Linguistics, psychiatry, and psychopathology: The case of schizophrenic language. In L. Obler & L. Menn (Eds.). *Exceptional Language and Linguistics*, pp. 217–246. NY: Academic Press.

Jung, C. G. (1905/1973). *Experimental Researches*. Translated by L. Stein in collaboration with D. Riviere. Princeton: Princeton University Press.

Koh, S. D. (1978). Remembering of verbal materials by young schizophrenic adults. In S. Schwartz (Ed.). *Language and Cognition in Schizophrenia*, pp. 55–99. Hillsdale, NJ: Lawrence Erlbaum Associates.

Larsen, S. F., & Fromholt, P. (1976). Mnemonic organization and free recall in schizophrenia. *Journal of Abnormal Psychology, 85*, 61–65.

Maher, B. (1972). The language of schizophrenia: A review and interpretation. *British Journal of Psychiatry, 120*, 3–17.

Moon, A. F., Mefferd, M. B. Jr., Wieland, B. A., Pokorny, A. D., & Falconer, G. A. (1968). Perceptual dysfunctions as a determinant of schizophrenic word associations. *Journal of Nervous and Mental Disease, 146,* 80–84.

Osgood, C. E., Luria, Z., Jeans, R. F., & Smith, S. W. (1976). The three faces of Evelyn: A case report. *Journal of Abnormal Psychology, 85,* 247–286.

Osgood, C. E., Suci, G. J., & Tannenbaum, P. H. (1957). *The Measurement of Meaning.* Urbana, Illinois: University of Illinois Press.

Pavy, D. (1968). Verbal behavior in schizophrenia: A review of recent studies. *Psychological Bulletin, 70,* 164–178.

Rausch, M. A., Prescott, J. E., & DeWolfe, A. S. (1980). Schizophrenic and aphasic language: Discriminable or not? *Journal of Clinical and Consulting Psychology, 48,* 63–70.

Rubin, A. I., Doneson, S. L., & Jentons, R. L. (1979). Studies of psychological function in schizophrenia. In L. Bellack (Ed.). *Disorders of the Schizophrenic Syndrome,* pp. 181–231. NY: Basic Books.

Salzinger, K., Portnoy, S., & Feldman, R. S. (1978). Communicability deficit in schizophrenia resulting from a more general deficit. In S. Schwartz (Ed.). *Language and Cognition in Schizophrenia,* pp. 35–53. Hillsdale, NJ: Lawrence Erlbaum Associates.

Scherer, K. R. (1979). Nonlinguistic vocal indicators of emotion and psychopathology. In C. E. Izard (Ed.). *Emotions in Personality and Psychopathology,* pp. 493–530. NY: Plenum Press.

Schwartz, S. (1978). Language and cognition in schizophrenia: A review and synthesis. In S. Schwartz (Ed.). *Language and Cognition in Schizophrenia,* pp. 237–274. Hillsdale, NJ: Lawrence Erlbaum Associates.

Seidman, L. J. (1983). Schizophrenia and brain dysfunction: An integration of recent neurolinguistic findings. *Psychological Bulletin, 94,* 195–238.

Smith, E. E. (1970). Associative and editing processes in schizophrenic communication. *Journal of Abnormal Psychology, 75,* 182–186.

Vigotsky, L. S. (1934). Thought in schizophrenia. Translated by J. Kasanin. *Archives of Neurology and Psychiatry, 31,* 1063–1077.

Whitehorn, J. C., & Zipf, G. K. (1943). Schizophrenic language. *Archives of Neurology and Psychiatry, 49,* 831–851.

STUDY QUESTIONS

1. Discuss the use of standard psycholinguistic techniques as personality diagnostics. Consider the relation of language to thought in your discussion with respect to why linguistic indicators may be effective diagnostics.

2. Review the analyses of the language abnormalities in schizophrenia. Be critical and consider whether you feel that there is a language deficit indicated by the disorder. Support your position with results from the literature, and consider how to incorporate conflicting results with your position.

3. Suppose a person were presented to you whose speech was fluent but seemed nonsensical. To diagnose whether the individual was psychotic or aphasic, which features would you look for in the speech? Which tests would you consider performing? Discuss which results you would expect for each disorder. Try to come up with your own tests, based on earlier chapters, in addition to those suggested specifically in this chapter.

14

Retrospectives on Language

Since antiquity we humans have been interested in our language, speculating that it reflects or possibly even shapes thought, that it separates us from animals, that it is the fire Prometheus stole from the heavens to give us civilization. Historically we have wondered whether language is part of our biological makeup, questioning whether children raised in isolation would be able to develop language and whether biological dysfunction produces language dysfunction.

With ideas such as these we began our explorations of language and language processing, as they have emerged from research in this century. In this century several breakthroughs have enabled us to take a fresh look at the age-old speculations about language:

1. The concept of evolution, which pushed thinking toward a more equal view of humans and our place in the animal kingdom (see Chapter 8).
2. The concepts of behaviorism, which suggest methods of learning and teaching common to all animals (see chapters 2, 4, and 8, in particular).
3. The tools of cognitive psychology, which have enabled us to study scientifically mental processes (see chapters 3, 5, and 7, in particular).
4. The tools of computer science, which have allowed testing and modeling of structural and processing descriptions of language (see chapters 3 and 5).
5. The methods and findings of linguistics and anthropology, which have generated and compared descriptions of languages the world over to find universals (and particulars) (see especially chapters 2, 4, 6, 9, and 11).
6. The increased knowledge of neural mechanisms, which has allowed us to consider issues of brain and language specifically (see chapters 10, 12, and 13).

Summary of Our Exploration

As we saw in the first half of this book, use of these breakthroughs has built on previous research to produce a good picture—albeit one with many parts still missing—of language structures and processes. This picture suggests three interacting levels of structure and process: formational (the articulatory and perceptual levels in speech and sign), semantic/meaning, where formational units are related abstractly to characteristics of the outside world, and structural/syntactic, where formational units are related to one another. Each of these levels may be described by its own system of rules and its own set of processes, but because of the combination of bottom-up and top-down processing, no level is completely autonomous.

Thus, we find for speech (chapters 6 and 7) that a reasonable descriptive system of structure includes acoustic features like bursts and transitions. These map directly to phonetic features like voicing and place of articulation, which combine to form phonemes, syllables, and multisyllabic words. The mapping and combination is not straightforward. There is context-sensitivity in both articulation and perception so it is virtually impossible to discuss even the lowest-level mapping, acoustic to phonetic features, without considering influences of higher levels. Moreover, we found good reason to suppose that syntactic and semantic knowledge guide both production and perception.

For meaning and meaning processing (chapters 2 and 3) we observed a similar interdependence of levels of structure. We began discussing the analysis of linguistic meaning with units like morphemes, words, and phrases, but found that the interpretation of these individual units is affected profoundly by their combination. Likewise, decomposing category meaning into characteristic features and defining features produced difficulty since our mental categories do not directly map to extralinguistic features. So we turned to describing the mental representation of meaning as a massive, interacting associative network of features. This network maps word names to word representations at one level, representations (denotations) to evocative feelings (connotations) at a second level, and representations to perceptual features of the environment at a third level. These word representations are also mapped to other word representations within the network at many other levels. The result is that there is no starting place for meaning. A "simple" concept like "dog" is defined mentally in terms of many other "simple" concepts, like "bark" and "setter," each of which has, as part of its definition, "dog." Since linguistic meaning is in part self-defined and is not isomorphic with extralinguistic thought, it constitutes a special sign system—a symbol system—and it can influence internalization and acquisition of new knowledge.

In syntax and syntactic processing (chapters 4 and 5) we found the need to hypothesize the existence of at least two levels of structure: (1) a deep structure or proposition level, which specifies the meaning of a sentence and the relationships of constituents of the sentence to one another; and (2) a surface structure level that Implements the deep structure through the conventions of the language. We discussed

various interactions between these levels, including tacitly understood transformations and perceptual or semantic strategies. Transformations are a purely syntactic
means of relating deep and surface structure, while the others reflect the influence of
semantic and formational strategies on the most abstract linguistic domain, syntax.
We found for syntax, as for the other levels of language, good reason to hypothesize
top-down processes, or at least processes that worked simultaneously on several linguistic units.

Finally, in the second half of the book, we investigated some of the conditions
necessary to produce this complex symbol system. In Chapter 8, we discussed various
evolutionary mechanisms that might have contributed to our language growth, such
as sexual selection and genetic specification of a "blueprint" for the vital features of
a communication system. We compared our main communication system with other
aspects of human communication and with animal signal and communication systems to see that language develops as part of a particular social community, expressing particular needs and using particular cognitive structures.

In Chapter 9 we found evidence in human beings specifically for innate language
blueprints and also saw how these interact with the language environment to permit
children to learn language. We found that uniformity of language learning across
children derived in part from such blueprints, in part from uniformity in exposure
(parents talk the same way to infants cross-culturally), and in part to the operation of
the same general cognitive and perceptual strategies.

In Chapter 10, we looked at language acquisition under abnormal conditions,
when the environmental exposure was deficient and the social setting for communication was disrupted. Here we found additional evidence for a blueprint for language,
together with evidence for critical periods in language learning, and also saw strong
evidence for an innate urge to communicate (in deaf children born in hearing homes
where sign language is not used by the parents), given a social setting conducive to
normal interaction.

Chapter 11 demonstrated that the basic features of language derive from cognitive constraints: Sign language structures and processes bear an amazing similarity to
spoken language structures and processes, despite the modality difference.

In Chapter 12 we discussed the neural underpinnings of these cognitive structures, demonstrating how brain damage affects language processing and language
structures. We found that brain damage can have a selective effect, damaging one
level of language independently of others. And we saw some examples of what language-based communication looks like in the absence of syntactic processing or
access to the meaning-associative network.

Finally, in Chapter 13 we saw how language processes can be stretched. With
personality disorder we see a break between language and communication, with language intact but odd because of its dissociation from its principal social function.

Now that we have looked at the findings and theories about language structure
and processing, it is time to return to the initial questions: What is the relation of
language and thought? Is language or any aspect of it innate? What is language? Is
language something special for us? These questions will allow us to sum up and see
where the research has taken us.

Language and Thought

Evidence for Thought without Language

Whereas we cannot conclusively address the issue of language's relation to thought, there are several lines of evidence we have examined that can be brought to bear, each of which points to a form of thought that is not specifically linguistic. For one, there is the equivocal evidence of image processes in normal adults and of dual-coding into imagery and propositional representations. This suggests that there is at least a form of thought that is nonverbal. Perhaps more compellingly, there is the evidence of right hemisphere cognitive processes, which indicates nonlinguistic forms of thought for spatial tasks, object recognition, and so on. There is the dissociation in aphasia between naming and concept organization and between basic syntactic processes and concept organization, indicating language processes that are affected by brain damage, together with some processes that are not. Each of these lines of evidence suggests that in adults with language skills there are still nonlinguistic modes of thought.

We also find evidence for nonlinguistic thought in language acquisition. It seems that words or word strings map onto concepts that the child has already acquired. So for example, object permanence precedes naming, and the initial words and word strings reflect sensorimotor activity and thinking. This suggests not only that there is nonlinguistic thought, but that it precedes and shapes linguistic thought.

Looking at nonhuman animals, we find very little evidence that they have language and no compelling evidence that they can learn it. However, there is no question that many animals exhibit complex cognitive behavior, suggesting that such behavior does not require language-based thought.

And finally, we find little experimental support for the strong form of the Whorf-Sapir hypothesis. Despite cross-cultural differences in specific linguistic or cognitive *structural* categories, the same basic cognitive *processes* are manifested—in categorizing, forming prototypes, and so forth. Together these findings suggest that there is thought independent of language and that language maps onto thought.

The Influence of Language on Thought

That is not to argue that language or language structure plays no role in shaping conceptual structures. We have seen that the formational characteristics of speech (articulatory features) or sign language (formational dimensions) affect short-term recall and that there is a tendency to make associations by language sounds rather than conceptual meanings. There is also evidence that normal conceptual organization is based at least in part on linguistic associations such as semantic relatedness or part of speech. These may or may not relate to the physical characteristics of the referents but clearly derive from associations of the referents' names in the language.

This ability to "think through language" accounts for much that is philosophically wonderful and troublesome about meaning. It allows us to say that lions and tigers are both similar in ferociousness although we may never have seen either beast awake or outside a zoo. It also allows us to create unicorns and say that they are like horses, although we have certainly never experienced one. Thus, through linguistic thought we can create new conceptual categories, without any further nonlinguistic influences.

There is also evidence that linguistic experience can influence development and organization of nonlinguistic thought. Concepts that are more codable in language are more memorable and produce quicker reactions than concepts that are not easily coded in language. Phonetic features that have been reinforced through experience in language use are perceived differently from those not so reinforced. We see evidence in adult concept organization that the first words may map to specific concepts from which a linguistic structure is deduced, but that, subsequently, similar concepts are then acquired with respect to this structure, producing partial cognitive economy. In this case it looks like thought can both precede and follow language.

Thought for Language

There is, of course, also a part of the conceptual structure devoted specifically to language, the part responsible for our tacit knowledge of language structure and our metalinguistic knowledge. In Wernicke's aphasia this may be preserved while much of the rest of the conceptual structure is destroyed, allowing for apparently good syntax and fluent production but empty propositions. Our at least tacit awareness of linguistic aspects of conceptual structure shapes our behavior in the creation of language games, creation of words, and creation of false personas in split personalities. In this last case we find that in employing an artificial conceptual structure, the individual sticks to the axes of a normal conceptual space without the normal variability, indicating a tacit awareness of the dimensions of that space.

Summary

Thus, with respect to the question of thought's relationship to language we may consider that in humans thought precedes language with language mapping onto it, but that complex thoughts are possible without language in both humans and animals. Once we have acquired language, linguistic thinking may be a dominant mode of thought, or at least of thought by one cerebral hemisphere, shaping additional knowledge acquisition.

Language as a Biological Heritage

Evidence from Language Acquisition

There are several lines of evidence suggesting that something about language development is innate. First, all children raised in normal environments acquire language. They internalize formational rules and more importantly, meaning structure and syntax. In contrast, attempts at teaching at least syntax to animals, that are either reared like human children or given special training, are not anywhere near as successful.

Second, studies of the effects of brain damage at different ages indicate that there is a critical period for language acquisition and that there are biological structures that seem to be innately determined to serve language. If the child's language learning is interrupted by injury to the language areas of the brain, acquisition of language begins again, taking the same route as it had initially. If the brain is damaged after language acquisition is completed, there is an unrecoverable loss of language skills.

Additional evidence for the biological predetermination of language structures is provided by contrasting Genie's language acquisition with that of the younger neglected children. Genie began language training after puberty, had difficulty learning language (but not learning generally), acquired abnormal language skills ultimately, and showed a highly abnormal pattern of cerebral specialization. These facts together suggest strongly that there is a critical period for language learning, analogues for which we see throughout the animal kingdom in communication and perceptual development. The critical period ends by puberty, but during the sensitive period there are some "innate guidelines" to focus our attention on language structures.

Evidence from Brain Damage

Another line of evidence suggesting aspects of language as innate comes from examination of language (and thought) patterns after brain injury in adults. For nearly all right-handed adults, damage to some particular region of the brain has a predictable effect on language. The pattern of language impairment as a result of brain damage indicates that "production" is disturbed by injury to the front of the left hemisphere, "comprehension" to the rear, that function words have a dual representation in both front and rear, and that concrete words have a dual representation in the left and right hemispheres. Syntactic strategies are disturbed by damage to the front of the left hemisphere. Conceptual structure is spared by damage to the front of the left hemisphere. Word naming may be impaired independently of conceptual structure, indicating that the names are mapped to, but dissociated from conceptual structure.

That this pattern occurs again and again, and seems to be recurring in as formationally different a language from English as ASL, suggests that the mapping of brain structures to linguistic functions may be predetermined biologically. The increased size of the language regions even in fetal brains supports this contention.

Evidence from Language Universals

Cautions for Interpretation.   The last and most controversial line of evidence for innate characteristics of language derives from an examination of languages the world over and the resultant discovery of universal features. This line of argument is tricky, since what might seem to be a universal feature, may, in fact, reflect common environmental features or contamination from exposure to other languages, or chance, rather than an innate endowment.

The possibility of common environmental features producing common language structures we discussed with respect to the notion of basic objects (prototypes) and natural categories: All the world's people have similar visual systems and see through sunlight, and we might expect, therefore, not only that all the world's languages will contain a word for sun as it appears against the blue sky, but also that all people will process color similarly. In the same vein, recognition of basic category features like human versus nonhuman, animate versus inanimate, and so on, might be expected to prevail not because those concepts are innate as such, but because those categories are perceptually distinct.

This environmental commonality may account for the similarity of children's language acquisition around the world: All babies are exposed to mothers and milk and are fascinated by objects appearing and disappearing from sight (allgone, bye-bye, peek-a-boo). Because infants are provided similar environments, first language acquisition beginning long after infancy, as with Genie, may be expected to be markedly different. The exposures and perceptual foci of older children will be different from those of infants.

The second possibility, of contamination by other languages, intrudes in two ways: by one language influencing the other, and by the knowledge of one language influencing the investigations of the other. For instance, some of the similarities in structure between ASL and English, such as the move from free word order to SVO order, may derive from the continual cross-fertilization of the deaf community with the English-speaking community. So to conclude that there is an innate tendency toward SVO would be imprudent.

The questions that investigators of other languages raise often reflect the categories of the investigators' own languages: How is tense expressed? How is causality expressed? How is actor-action-object expressed? Such questions presuppose that there will be tense, causality, and actor-action-object expressed somehow in the other language. Given that orientation, it is likely that these categories will be found in the other languages, even if they do not represent a structure that linguists raised in that language would themselves produce. Some of this natural bias and its correction are reflected in the changing views on universality of word order in child language acquisition or existence of grammatical structure in ASL, for example.

Communication and Articulatory Structure Universals.   Be that as it may, we might *cautiously* suggest some features that seem universal and therefore perhaps innate. The first is the urge to communicate (which is probably present for all social animals, *at least* during mating season). We see this most clearly in the children who develop their own symbol system, and we also see it in the fact that all human cultures have developed a language. The second is the use of the vocal-auditory system, if available, for communication. Again, all cultures—except deaf cultures—seem to use an oral language as preferred communication, although sign systems have been developed secondarily among speaking peoples. Within the oral language systems the world over we find the same speech features, innately determined by the characteristics of the auditory system and the possibilities for articulation. Analogous perceptual and motor constraints apply in sign systems so that all use, for example, the same formational dimensions and fine-tuning of articulation on the face. Thus, they look superficially alike in all cultures.

Higher-Level Language Universals.   At perhaps more interesting linguistic levels we find units corresponding to words and sentences in all languages, perhaps indicating an innate tendency to categorize and construct proposition-like representations. We also see, universally, the *symbolic* use of words rather than a signaling use. No culture uses words rigidly to refer to single concrete objects in a stereotyped fashion. All cultures have a mythology and mythical beasts, demonstrating symbolic use of words. From the data we have examined, the tendency for symbol use is probably best demonstrated in the spontaneously created language of children and the change by deaf children in the use of nonarbitrary gestures, like indexing or pointing, to symbolic gestures of pronominal reference. Although this occurs also as hearing children internalize the spoken linguistic system, it is perhaps more striking in sign language where the "word" that is used symbolically iconically stands for the referent. Of course, this tendency to use language symbolically also occurs for arbitrary words throughout the world and thus may be innate.

Another general feature of language (and perhaps of all human information processing) that may be universal and innate is hierarchical organization. We see this at all levels of English structure and processing. There exists hierarchical organization of motor commands in speech production, hierarchical organization of speech perception reflected in part through the interaction of top-down and bottom-up processing, hierarchical organization of categories in conceptualization, and hierarchical organization of words into phrases, phrases into sentences (sentences into [embedded] clauses and back into sentences), sentences into cohesive discourse, and so on. Although these levels interact in processing, there is evidence as well for individual psychological representations of each: of words in semantic memory, of semantic relations within propositions, of mental propositions, and of connections between propositions connected in meaning.

It is perhaps in hierarchical organization that we see the greatest difference between natural language processes and contrived processes. Chimpanzees certainly have been taught to use words, may use them symbolically, and may string them together. They do not (at least as yet) create a higher-order unit using these skills or exhibit hierarchical structuring. Or, as a second example, the early attempts at modeling human language by machine produced good language *approximations* (provided one did not look too closely) from programming whole chunks of language into the machine into which words could be inserted, or by programming meaning for individual words, with no attempt at unifying them into hierarchical structure. It was not until hierarchical structures were modeled—which put words into phrases, phrases into functional categories, functional categories into relations within a proposition, and propositions into organized text—that anything like human use of language appeared.

Finally, we see in language breakdown, both in aphasia and in some instances of schizophrenic language, the nonlanguage-like look resulting from a loss of hierarchical structures. A chain composed of either the main words of the thought (Broca's aphasia), overlearned syntactic "fillers" like "it is likely that" (Wernicke's aphasia), or of partially associated but nonintegrated concepts (schizophrenia) is noticeably bizarre and nonlanguage-like. It is only when the pieces are integrated, hierachically, that the output looks like language. Since the hierarchical organization occurs at all levels of language and in all languages, we may want to suggest that it is innate, either for language specifically or for human thinking generally.

Processing Universals. This observation brings us to our last suggestion for innateness in language: human processing capabilities. In considering sign language and spoken language we noted two striking similarities against a background of differences. First, rate of information transmission was similar with respect to both speed of production of propositions and the amount of information sufficient to transmit intelligible reduced signals. Second, recognition and use of the physical and meaning features of the languages were similar. These similarities were striking, since different modalities are used to convey the two languages and the tongue is quicker than the hand. Also one of the physical characteristics of sign is often a mimicry of a physical feature of the referent, and this is rarely true in spoken language. That none of these factors seems to make a significant difference in language processing suggests that there are innate processes for language that interpret linguistic input regardless of its form. These may, of course, also affect the shape of the language, as in compensating for the slowness of individual sign articulation by simultaneous production of several morphemes to result in a uniform proposition rate.

Other Universals? Many investigators have suggested more features of language as innate. For example, it has been suggested that there are innate ideas like time and motion, innate syntactic rules like the concept of transformations and the forms transformations may take, and innately perceived phonetic feature distinctions. (There are of course investigators who think very little is innate, with only the basic abilities to form associations predetermined.)

It is of course possible that some or all of these language characteristics are innate and specific for language, but the evidence does not compellingly point only in this direction. Consider, for example, for some phonetic distinctions categorical perception seems to be either inborn or acquired in the first month of life; it seemed that SVO word order was understood earlier than other orders even if it was not an order exclusively used by the language; and under strained communication conditions (those good for producing pidgins and creoles) inflections disappear and word order is used to express semantic relations. This evidence does suggest innateness. However, closer examination has revealed that there are some phonetic distinctions not perceived categorically by the neonate (and some that are by chinchillas). An SVO order is only preferentially understood if it is more frequently used than other orders in the language. And the loss of inflection in pidgins and creoles may be explained by the fact that inflections are usually unstressed and carry less meaning than roots and therefore are harder to perceive and less necessary for communication. (In regard to the last, note that we saw in ASL that inflections are remembered [or forgotten] separately from the roots, and so we can attribute their loss under difficult conditions to an attention/perception failure combined with a memory failure.)

Therefore, the evidence for "universal" language features like categorical perception, SVO order, and inflection loss in pidgins can be explained, respectively, by reference to regions of general auditory hypersensitivity that languages have mapped onto, frequency of experience, and constraints imposed by general attention and memory mechanisms. We may explain both the relative universality of time and motion as ideas and the movement transformation as a syntactic device by a similar appeal to general perceptual and cognitive processing constraints combined with commonality of outside experience.

Summary.   So, for now, at least until evidence suggests more strongly otherwise, we suggest that innate determinants of language include:

1. the urge to communicate,
2. use of the vocal-auditory system if possible for communication,
3. some general idea of what language looks like (words, etc.),
4. the tendency to make *symbolic* associations,
5. a period of learning sensitivity to language with a general blueprint for neural organization of language,
6. some general psychophysical processing constraints imposed by articulatory abilities (vocal or gestural), perceptual abilities (auditory or visual), and general cognitive abilities (attention, memory, and information processing preferences as in hierarchical organization).

As they evolve, languages will move toward optimizing these determinants. Thus, they share features we can attribute to the common restrictions imposed by the human mind and body and the common experiences provided by nature.

What Is Language?

In Chapter 1, language was defined as the way humans communicate. As we have looked at communication processes in this book and deduced them from language structure, that definition may not seem as trivial as it might have at first. Human beings, through their cognitive and perceptual structures, have shaped their communication system. To define what it is that makes language unique, therefore, we must consider the biological makeup of its creators and users.

To many readers, the use of human biological makeup to define language may seem unfair and unnecessary. We will return to this point at the end of this section, but here we will raise the issue of why we should bother to define language at all. As was pointed out in chapters 1 and 8, there are two reasons people have given for undertaking the process of defining language: (1) to prove that we are specially and better endowed than other organisms, and (2) to be able to recognize what is and what is not language—a pattern recognition problem—given a newly encountered communication system. The first reason, although interesting philosophically, is not of concern here. From our evolutionary perspective, we consider that all species are specially and uniquely (although not necessarily optimally!) endowed for their biological niche. It is the second reason that is of interest to us, and, thus, it is as important to specify human characteristics in language structure and processing as it would be to specify "feathers" in defining bird flight apart from, for example, airplane flight.

Low-Level Design Features

In the last section we presented some characteristics of language specifically and human information processing generally that might be innate and determine the shape of language. Most of these contribute to the design features for language discussed in Chapter 8.

An innate push to use the vocal auditory channel for communication, combined with some innate constraints on information processing, could underlie the language features of rapid fading, broadcast transmission and reception, total feedback, specialization, and, given our biological makeup, interchangeability. (Transmission and reception are not sex-linked, for example, as they are in many birds.) If our information processing system were incapable of handling rapidly fading messages—as it would be if we had more limited short-term memory—we could not use such a system without increasing redundancy.

Because humans attempt to use the vocal-auditory channel innately for communication, most human languages share these low-level design features, which are thus characteristic of much of language. Clearly, such features as rapid fading and specialization are not necessary for higher-level language features, such as the complexity of the concepts we communicate or of the syntactic structures we employ. We find similar complex structures and concepts transmitted in writing and visual-gestural languages lacking the features peculiar to the vocal-auditory system.

If we wish to define language as special because of what it communicates, features like rapid fading, and so on, may be dropped. However, if we consider language as a function of its users, the vocal-auditory system (and its characteristics) seems to be the primary mode for language, although we are flexible enough to use other modes. Therefore, although the characteristics of language determined by its usual modality may not help to define whether language is a special symbolic process, they do define it, in part, as a species-specific communication system.

Higher-Level Design Features

An information-processing influence on language that we have considered innate is the tendency for symbolic thinking. In language, this could underlie the proposed features of semanticity, arbitrariness, discreteness, and displacement. Once an association between two physical events is recognized (e.g., between a word and its referent, a phonology and a geographical location, a clothing style and a time period, lightning and thunder), the direct association or even generalized association is transcended to allow for additional idea manipulation. This means words are used symbolically rather than referentially, as may be other characteristics of behavior like clothing or dialect, to stand for a culture. It also means that unobservable associations may be sought, like the nature of lightning and the causes of sound, and so on.

Within language this innate tendency for symbolic thought means that no matter how concrete the initial association (association rather than identity implies semanticity), as in iconic signs or onomatopoeia, within a few uses the observation of concreteness is not attended to, and the word (or whatever) is processed as arbitrary and discrete. Once this occurs it may be used to discuss displaced events. (Note that for us and other species symbolic thinking has influences outside language.)

Another suggestion for an innate force in language, derived from general cognitive constraints, was the tendency for hierarchical organization. Together with symbolic thought this accounts for many of our design features: productivity, duality of patterning, deception, metalanguage, simultaneity, and recursiveness. If information processing occurs in hierarchically arranged stages, one element may be considered simultaneously on many levels: as a sound, as a morpheme or word, as a contributor to syntactic structure of the sentence. This phenomenon we called duality (actually, multiplicity) of patterning. The most efficient use of the hierarchical processes would be to consider each element on all these levels at once, so that processing at the highest level is not waiting for output from lower levels. This leads to simultaneity. Once an element has been recognized, at any level, it can be used as a symbol itself and be processed through the same hierarchy, leading to productivity, use of words for deception, and recursiveness. And once the elements can be recognized simultaneously, at different hierarchical levels, as having an existence as elements as well as associations to their referents, metalanguage—words like "word," "phoneme," "language," and "metalanguage"—may develop so we can talk about the elements of processing *as* elements of processing.

Other Design Features

In the last section we noted also that an innate determinant of language may be a critical period for language learning. This may underlie Hockett's last design feature, traditional transmission. Finally, we might note that the innate human information processor is imperfect—there are lapses of attention and memory, regions of hypersensitivity (and therefore regions of less sensitivity), and so forth. These characteristics produce our last design features, smear and the human thought transmission rate. We need redundancy because of imperfect processing and this is accomplished through smear. We cannot incorporate new thoughts at excessively rapid rates or maintain attention at excessively low rates, and so simultaneity, sequentiality, and smear are balanced in the language to produce an optimal transmission rate.

Language Defined as Unique to Us

By founding our criteria for language in the biology of its human users, we have eliminated the possibility that chimpanzees or any other animal could use or learn language or that computers (as they exist today) could use language as we know it. It is worthwhile considering whether this anthropocentric conclusion is warranted.

Turing (1963) proposed a test to determine whether human intelligence had been truly simulated by machine. If a human questioner was allowed to address any questions (s)he wanted to a machine and could not tell from the answers whether the machine was "manned" by a computer or by a human, artificial intelligence would have been achieved. The Turing test may be considered from two points of view: whether the answers themselves seem human and whether the way that they are generated seems human. With respect to language it seems possible that at some point either a nonhuman animal or a machine might produce answers that could not be differentiated structurally or symbolically from human answers. However, it is highly unlikely that the *process* of deriving the answer could not distinguish the imposter from the human. Now, we might ask: Is there a way to get at the process rather than the answer? The answer is yes, and this book is full of such ways: lexical decision times, ratings of semantic relatedness, reaction time for processing derivationally complex sentences, likely occurrence and (re)starting places for slips of the tongue and false starts, categorical perception of speech or nonspeech sounds, effects of a bullet wound to a particular spot in the "brain," and so forth. Any and all of these tests could be administered (barring ethical considerations for the last) to draw the conclusion that that machine (or animal) may be clever but is no human.

Some may protest (as Turing did) that this is not a particularly interesting criterion for language simulation or artificial intelligence. After all, the important thing is flying, not doing it with feathers. That is fine, and in that case, probably we do not need most of our design features for language. And probably we would consider that language now, already, is not unique to us. If we define the "task" as communicating, we do that no better than the "lowest" of animals in terms of communicating social needs and surviving. If we define the task as use of symbols and syntax (using the middle-level design features—semanticity, . . . , recursiveness), we can also conclude that language is not unique to us. Computers already use symbols, syntax, hierarchical processing, and recursiveness, in even simple "nonintelligent" programs.

Thus, we seem to be in a position either of forfeiting what we perceive as unique about language *as a pattern* or of conceding that the "specialness" derives from particular properties housed within a particular biological medium, and therefore that reasonable tests for language include processing tests, which in all likelihood no machine or other animal can pass, by definition. As we said, there are two reasons to try to define language: One is to recognize language as a pattern, in which case the Turing test using processing is fair, and the other is to try to use it to argue that we are in some particular way special. For the second purpose, it seems only honest to be clear about being self-serving, and so define language with respect to "special" human qualities.

Concluding Remarks

Remaining Questions

At this point it may seem as though we have answered all questions, but realize that in this chapter we have addressed only the ones we began with. Along the way other questions have been raised, and it is important to keep in mind in summarizing that we know more about the way language is *not* structured and *not* processed than we do about the way it is. At the basic level we do not know how speech is perceived, whether there are invariants, whether we compensate for variability using a specialized speech processor or top-down processing, and where or how this takes place in the brain. At higher language levels we do not know if connotation is processed differently from denotation, figurative language from literal language, concrete words from abstract words, and so on. Although we have discussed an underlying conceptual structure to which linguistic units map, the nature of that structure (word-concept, proposition, nonverbal form) is not specified. We do not know how to define categories or whether there are defining features of categories at all. And we do not know whether we perform syntactic processing in the absence of semantic strategies by unwinding transformations or by using general strategies that approximate the undoing of the derivational process.

This is just a brief and necessarily incomplete summary of questions left to answer. Every chapter has raised many more.

Applications of Available Answers

In closing it seems worthwhile to mention the use to which many of the discoveries about language have been put, for better or for worse; that is, to mention areas of application of psycholinguistic research.

One important consequence of linguistic and psycholinguistic research has been the recognition that there are no inferior languages in terms of structure or processing, and therefore that it is not imperative that all children be made to conform to a specific language or dialect. This has caused a gradual move from considering sign language as a crude gestural system to recognition that it is a complex and beautiful language, resulting in the establishment in 1983 of Swedish sign language along with Swedish as the official language of Sweden.

Structural analysis of what is now termed Black English (see, for example, Labov, 1972) has showed similarly that this is a *non*standard and not *sub*standard language, and that although it shares many words with standard English, it is different structurally (syntactically) and so is not identical to standard English. This has permitted understanding of why ghetto children (like deaf children) may have problems learning to read—they are almost learning to read in a foreign language! The solution to this problem is far from settled, since there are social stigmas attached to being taught a nonstandard dialect in schools. However, the recognition of the problem and the importance of language in forming conceptual structures has permitted increased tolerance for the notion of bilingual education.

Aside from modifying attitudes toward language, research in language has been applied to techniques of teaching or reteaching language, and in testing linguistic competence. There have been changes in foreign language instruction from rote memorization of vocabulary items and overt grammatical rules to concentration on language *as used* with emphasis on acquisition of tacit knowledge of structure. Language rehabilitation programs for aphasics not only give practice in the person's original language skills but also try to recruit what are believed to be spared cognitive functions by teaching language through song or visual patterns (see Gardner, 1975, for example). Finally, in new approaches to intelligence tests (see Sternberg, 1979, for example) there is an increased emphasis on processes in verbal reasoning (as needed for metaphor comprehension, creation, and appreciation, for example) rather than on verbal knowledge (as needed in vocabulary tests). Moreover, the processes used to solve the verbal problems are studied specifically, rather than just the answers, by formulating each problem with respect to component processes and testing for each of these separately. (This is analogous to the task decompositions we saw in Chapter 13 for studying schizophrenic language. For various tasks, the patients were asked to produce an answer and then to do follow-up problems to see if their failure lay in production of possible responses, the underlying knowledge for some of the responses, or the ability to select among those responses. In this way processing tasks can be used to differentiate among abilities of creation, memory, and editing, for example, and this type of subtask assessment is being advocated now in intelligence testing.)

As a result of our increased knowledge of language and language processing (combined with technological advances), and despite the great gaps in knowledge, there are now adequate reading machines for the blind (they take text and convert it to speech), computer programs that correct or teach spelling and grammar, and automated knowledge bases that can be accessed for information as diverse as store inventories, moon rocks, location of information in libraries, or availability of tickets for theaters or airlines. Although humans may have to modify their language somewhat to interact with these systems, the systems are becoming increasingly "user-friendly"—requiring less adaptation on the part of the human users. A computer that can pass the Turing test (regardless of processing differences) may still seem to be a long way in the future, but machines that require us to think in order to figure out how to trick them into failing the Turing test are already here.

Conclusion

We still have a long way to go to understand language and its processing, and many exciting years of research ahead. But we have come a long way since Psammetichos!

REFERENCES

Gardner, H. (1975). *The Shattered Mind.* NY: A. A. Knopff.

Labov, W. (1972). *Language in the Inner City: Studies in the Black English Vernacular.* Philadelphia: University of Pennsylvania Press.

Sternberg, R. J. (1979). The nature of mental abilities. *American Psychologist, 34,* 214–230.

Turing, A. M. (1963). Computing machinery and intelligence? In E. A. Feigenbam & J. Feldman (Eds.). *Computers and Thought,* pp. 11–35. NY: McGraw-Hill.

Glossary

See also the appendix to Chapter 4 for definitions of grammatical terms like noun, verb, or instrumental case.

absorption   the trapping of sound frequencies in an object.

abstract   as opposed to concrete. Concepts difficult to point at, such as "democracy."

abstract surface structure   in new transformational theory, the level at which meaning interpretation is performed. It contains the surface structure relations together with markers designating where elements have been moved from deep structure.

ABX task   a discrimination task in which two different stimuli are presented, followed by a third, and subjects must decide which of the two the third matches.

accommodation   the change of a mental structure around new information that does not fit into existing mental structures.

acquired distinctiveness   the assumption that at birth all speech sounds are continuously perceived, but that those used in the language become categorically perceived as a result of practice.

acquired similarity   the assumption that all possible speech sounds are categorically perceived at birth, but that the ability to discriminate those not in the language diminishes as a result of the lack of practice.

active   with respect to communication, deliberate.

activity   one of three factors to emerge in semantic differential analyses. Measures liveliness.

acute   see grave.

adaptation   decreased sensitivity to a stimulus produced by repeated exposures to it.

affricate   a consonant that begins as a stop and then releases partially into a fricative, like the "ch" in "church."

agnosia   an inability to recognize a pattern as a result of brain damage and without sensory disturbance.

agrammatic   a term characterizing aphasics who have lost use of syntax rules, at least in production.

alveolar   the ridge on the roof of the mouth just behind the teeth. Also refers to a consonant produced with closure in the area of the alveolar ridge.

allophones   two sounds that native speakers identify as members of the same phonemic category, but that are, in fact, different.

ambiguity   a single language unit with more than one meaning.

amnestic aphasia   see anomia.

amplitude   the height of a wave, from peak to trough.

amusia   brain damage resulting in a loss of musical skills.

analysis-by-synthesis   a model for perception in which it is assumed that a guess is made at the identity of the signal, the signal is then mentally synthesized, and the synthesis is compared to the input signal. If there is a match, then the identity of the input is known.

analytic   a linguistic entity that can be verified within the context of the language alone, without external reference.

anaphora   reference to something earlier.

angular gyrus region of the cortex, that when damaged, produces naming problems.

anomia a loss of ability to recall names in spontaneous speech or naming tasks.

anterior front.

anthropocentrism the view of the world and its inhabitants from the perspective that humankind is the pinnacle of creation.

anticipation errors intrusions from words or actions that an individual expects to perform in the future.

antiformants see zeros.

antiresonances see zeros.

apex the tip of the tongue.

aphasia brain damage resulting in loss of language skills.

aphemia see Broca's aphasia.

apraxia brain damage resulting in a disturbance in the ability to mimic actions.

arbitrary when there is no obvious relation between a sign and what it represents.

articulatory features see phonetic features.

aspect a verb marking indicating, among other things, the regularity or nature of occurrence of the action, as in whether it is habitual, continuous, over and done with, etc.

aspiration the breathy noise resulting from partial closure or sudden release in speech.

assimilation (1) the incorporation of new information into existing structures. (2) a change in the language whereby pronunciation of a sound becomes more like the other sounds in its context. For example, the nasal of the in-prefix matches place of articulation with the following consonant as in *im*possible or *in*discriminable.

attribute-value pair a primitive "concept" programmed in artificial intelligence, that consists of the name of a property (the attribute) like color and then the value of that property taken by the current concept. For example, the flower "rose" might have as part of its definition the pair, "colored: red."

auditory cortex see Heschl's gyrus.

augmented transition network (ATN) a method of modifying finite state grammars to allow them to express dependencies across several elements and give them memory. Essentially each state of an ATN may be used as a starting point to jump to a new ATN and execute a subsidiary operation before returning.

aural auditory, of the ear.

autistic language like egocentric language in that the individual's communication does not reflect the perspective of the other. However, this is used to indicate severe abnormality.

autoclitics verbal behaviors controlled by other verbal behaviors (called function words, in linguistic terminology).

babbling the sound productions of infants at about 6 months of age. It consists of syllables with phonemes found in all languages.

backformation a method of word formation where the derivation of the word is incorrectly supposed and a new word derived by removing supposed morphemes. For example, "editor" was a single morpheme at one time and the word "edit" derived by removing a "suffix" from it.

bandwidth the range of frequencies around a central frequency.

basic level the level in a taxonomy with the highest information content that also captures best the feature correlations within the category. See also prototype and focal color.

behavioral disposition tendency to act in a certain way in response to a stimulus.

between-category discriminations perceived differences between stimuli that subjects identify differently.

bilabial see place of articulation.

bipolar scale   a rating scale marked on each end by one of two opposites; e.g., hot—cold.

bit   a measure of information equal to the amount necessary to decide a yes-no question when yes and no are equally likely.

bleat   a nonspeech pattern produced by presenting only one formant from a speech syllable.

blind analysis   when the person doing the analysis is unfamiliar with the goals of the experiment, the way the data were collected, and/or the characteristics being assessed, so the analysis is not influenced by prior bias.

blocking   in experimental design, when trials of the same kind are presented together.

body language   the set of arm and hand movements, facial expressions, and head and body movements that are part of human communication and signaling but are not language.

bottom-up processes   processes that begin with the data at the lowest level and work up toward a conceptual representation.

bound morpheme   a morpheme that cannot be uttered in isolation; it must be connected to another.

branching   the way choice is indicated in a finite state diagram, by alternative routes starting at the same point.

breathy voice   see register.

broadcast transmission and reception   a design feature for language that refers to the fact that we can produce a signal that may be picked up by anyone within hearing distance.

Broca's aphasia   aphasia characterized by slow, halting speech and a telegraphic style, and a loss of syntax in production and comprehension.

burst   a short, high-energy bit of noise characterizing released stop consonants.

case   see semantic relation.

catatonia   a form of schizophrenia in which a symptom is the person's assuming a rigid position for extended periods.

categorical perception   the assumption that stimuli are discriminated by reference to the category names and so discrimination cannot be better than identification. It usually involves a sharp division into categories in identification, peak discriminability between categories, and near chance discriminability within a category.

category size effect   it takes longer to retrieve the information that something is not a member of a category if the category is large than if it is small.

causative   a type of verb that implies causation. We express the idea usually through the verb "make" as in "it makes me feel warm." This could be expressed as "it warms me," with "warms" then being a causative.

center-embedding   when a clause is embedded in a sentence such that it is inserted between the subject and the verb, as in "The dog that bit the man had rabies."

central sulcus   the brain groove that divides the frontal and parietal lobes.

centralization   the tendency for sounds to become articulated with the least deviance from the mouth's resting position.

cerebellum   the lobe of the brain behind and under the cerebrum.

cerebrum   the major mass of the brain, not counting the brain stem or cerebellum.

chain   a sequence of behaviors in which each behavior signals performance of the next and is in turn reinforced by the next. A Markov model of behavior.

chain complexes   a second level of organization in preoperational children's sortings of Vygotsky blocks. Here the child takes one feature and applies it for a time before attending to another feature. The ultimate categories will look unorganized to the adult.

characteristic features   as opposed to defining features. Aspects that most category members, or at least typical category members, share but which are not necessary to have to be a member of the category.

chest register   see register.

chimeric stimuli   stimuli designed to send conflicting messages to the two visual fields (and brain hemispheres) when focus is at a certain point.

chirps   nonspeech sounds produced by removing the steady states from a consonant-vowel or vowel-consonant syllable.

chronic schizophrenia   a form of schizophrenia characterized by gradual onset and steadily worsening symptoms.

circumlocutory   talking around the subject. In brain damage this may arise because the individual does not have access to the words needed.

classical conditioning   a form of learning where a stimulus is paired with an innate stimulus-response connection so that it comes to elicit a response similar to that innate response.

classifier   a part of speech found in ASL and some other languages. Classifiers are morphemes indicating some shared physical characteristic of objects. For example, two-legged or long and thin.

Clever Hans phenomenon   refers to the possibility of an experimenter unconsciously cueing the subject about the right answer.

closed-class words   see also function words. Refers to a class of words that is limited in growth; there are a certain number in the language and they do not usually get supplemented.

cloze procedure   a technique to assess the redundancy in speech and/or people's abilities to make use of it. Words are deliberately and systematically deleted from utterances and subjects are asked to guess their identity.

codability   the ease of access a word has to its mental meaning. Measures of codability include word length, reliability of judging instances of a category, reaction time to make such judgments, among others.

code system   see signaling.

cognitive economy   an assumption in some memory models that information is stored only once, with a superordinate rather than with each category member, thereby saving storage space. It is retrieved by inference from the member to the superordinate.

cohort (model)   the assumption that as people listen (or read) they guess words as likely input on the basis of available information, narrowing down the guesses as additional information becomes available until only one is left. The candidates that are potential choices form the cohort. The information may be the sequential sounds, meanings suggested by context, etc.

comment   see rheme.

commitments   a measure of processing load in sentence interpretation. Each word is hypothesized to set up expectation of more words ("the" suggests at least a noun to follow, for example). The sum of the expectations across a sentence equals the commitment.

communication   the active transfer of information from one to another.

compact   in one linguistic theory, a feature used to differentiate sounds with large cavities in front of the constriction relative to behind the constriction. Diffuse is the opposite.

comparative linguistics   the study of several languages to discover common features.

comparison theory (of metaphor interpretation)   shared features of the tenor and vehicle are derived.

competence   the knowledge that all native speaker-hearers have of their language. See also performance.

complement   a verb taken as an object by another verb, as in "I promised Bill *to go*."

compound   a new word created by combination of free morphemes accompanied usually by a change in stress pattern.

conceptually driven processes   see top-down processes.

concrete   a concept of a real-world object that can be easily imaged.

concrete attitude   one characterization of schizophrenic thought. Here it is assumed that the individual has difficulty recognizing abstract similarities.

concrete operations   a third stage in Piaget's cognitive development theory in which the child has an organized system of thought for concrete referents.

conduction aphasia   damage between Broca's and Wernicke's areas affecting primarily the ability to repeat.

connotation   contrast with denotation. What is left over in word-meaning once reference is removed. "Lady" and "woman" have different connotations, with the former implying someone well-bred, and the latter, nowadays, someone liberated. However, their denotations are the same.

conservation task   a test of cognitive development in which the child is shown a mass of object (a lump of clay or a volume of water) and asked to determine whether it has the same mass when formed into a new shape.

constituents   members of a structural class.

content words   those words that carry meaning external to the language—nouns, verbs, adjectives, and adverbs.

context-sensitive   an element or a rule that does not have a single form but changes depending on surrounding elements.

contiguous   occurring together in time. One way associations are believed to be connected.

continuous perception   the assumption that stimuli will be discriminated proportionally to their physical difference.

contradiction   the opposition in meaning of two words.

conventionalization   changes in fingerspelling that make it look less like a combination of discrete letters and more fluid.

cooing   the pleasure sounds produced by infants of about one month of age. They consist of back vowels and glottal stops.

coordinate relation   a form of conjunction in which there is no new relation as a result.

copula   the verb "to be" used in identity relations.

coreferential   two words that refer to the same thing.

core sentence   a statement in the form of a simple, active sentence, before transformations introduce surface complexities.

corpus   a collection of language samples used to determine language structures.

corpus callosum   a nerve fiber tract connecting the left and right cerebral hemispheres.

correlation   a statistical measure of the degree and direction of relatedness of two variables. A positive correlation implies that when one increases so does the other; a negative correlation, that when one increases, the other decreases.

cortex   the surface layers of cells in the human brain (and that of other "higher" animals), responsible for cognitive processes.

creaky voice   see register.

creole   the stage in historical development of some languages, following pidgins. The creole is more expanded, with regular syntax.

creolization   the process of changing a pidgin to a creole.

critical period   a genetically programmed time when it is easiest to learn something. Often attempts at learning outside the critical period are unsuccessful.

cross-sectional study   a study of development in which children at different ages are compared to assess the probable course of development across age.

cue   a portion of a signal or pattern that provides (partial) information to the identity of the pattern.

cued recall a memory task in which an item is indicated from the memory set by providing a prompt.

cumulative complexity (law of) a child acquires the elements of a hierarchical structure before the structure. If the child has the structure, (s)he must also have the elements.

damping the loss of energy in sound frequencies as a result of interaction with objects.

data-driven processes see bottom-up processes.

daughters members of a category dominated directly by the category.

deafness a hearing loss that extends into the speech frequency range.

decibel a unit measuring the loudness of sound.

declination effect the usual intonation contour is a fall-off in pitch at the end of the sentence, unless the speaker chooses to specially mark the utterance. This appears to be a language universal.

deep structure the underlying relationships expressed in a sentence, regardless of the surface form of the expression.

default a value that is used when no particular value is otherwise specified.

defining features as opposed to characteristic features. Characteristics that an instance *must* have to be a member of a category.

deixis "pointing" through language, as in pronouns, for example.

delusion of grandeur a psychotic delusion in which the individual believes (s)he is some great person like Jesus Christ or Napoleon, or has access to important information.

demand characteristics the cognitive requirements of an experiment. They may influence the subjects' normal processing strategies.

denotation contrast with connotation. The aspect of word-meaning that refers.

dental see place of articulation.

derivational complexity the relative number of transformations required to produce the surface form from the deep structure.

derivational morphemes morphemes that change the part of speech of a word.

detector a cell or cell group that is responsible for picking out a particular stimulus feature and indicating the presence of the stimulus by changing its response rate.

deterministic a processing routine that does not backtrack or attempt operations that will be later discarded for another set if they do not work.

diary studies observational measures of a child's language development in which the child's utterances are catalogued.

dichotic listening when two different sounds are presented (nearly) simultaneously, one to each ear.

dictionary as opposed to lexicon. The associative mental meaning network.

difference threshold the minimum physical difference between stimuli that can be detected by an individual.

diffuse a feature in one linguistic theory of sounds that describes sounds produced with a large region behind the closure relative to the region in front of the closure. Contrasts with compact.

diphthong a sound that speakers consider one vowel but that consists of two vocal gestures, one very much reduced in relation to the other.

direct object see "patient" in the appendix to Chapter 4.

discrete a design feature for language indicating that the signal does not mirror the continuous nature of many referents; it does not get longer to indicate greater length, for example.

discrimination a psychophysical task in which subjects are asked to indicate whether items are the same or different, or decide which one of a group is different.

discriminative stimulus in operant conditioning, the stimulus that is used to signal which of a number of operants (responses) is the appropriate one for reinforcement.

disjunctive association a link between two words that indicates they are different; for example, birds and fish are different types of animals.

displacement a design feature for language indicating that the topic may be distant in time and/or space.

dissimilation when pronunciation changes historically to increase the differences between sounds produced together. For example, the addition of the schwa to words already ending in "s" (as in "horse") to mark the addition of the "s" for the plural.

distinguishers aspects of meaning that make a word unique.

distributional analysis a procedure used in linguistics to define language categories by noting the relative distribution of elements of the language.

domination the superordinate's relation to its constituents.

dominance constraint if both hands are moving in sign language, either they do the same thing (symmetry) or one acts on the other (dominance).

dominance hypothesis one explanation for the deviance in schizophrenic communication in which it is assumed that the individual's attention is abnormally restricted to the usual, dominant word-meaning and thus cannot be released for rarer meanings or modifications by context.

double blend errors when two sounds differing by two features are presented dichotically and both are reported incorrectly such that the feature values are incorrectly combined. For example, "p" and "d" differ in voicing and place. The double blend would be "t" and "b," which have the same voicing and place features, but combined differently.

dual-code model (speech perception) in perceiving sounds we have access to a crude auditory representation of the sound as well as a phonetic feature label.

dual-code theory (meaning) word meaning is represented in two ways, abstractly and also as a mental image.

duality of patterning a design feature of language indicating that a given aspect of the signal may play a role in many levels; for example, as a meaningless sound and also as a meaningful word.

dyadic interaction conversation between two people.

echoes the reflection of sound frequencies by objects.

echolalia a speech disorder where the patient repeats meaninglessly what is said.

egocentric the assumption that receivers share the transmitter's viewpoint and therefore that aspects of it need not be made explicit. A frequent feature in the speech of young children.

embedding see center-embedding.

empirical learned through experience.

encoded refers to the fact that consonant identity is not readily available from any set of cues in the speech signal but must be abstracted across many.

eng the sound written "ng" at the end of "sing."

ethnolinguistics a branch of linguistics that compares languages across cultures, with special reference to the culture in which the language is used.

evaluation a requirement for true communication by which the transmitter is monitoring for feedback from the receiver and comparing the feedback with some expectation.

evaluative factor one of three factors usually found through semantic differential analysis. Measures good vs. bad.

evoked potential surface recording of the combined action of many nerves.

excitation an increase in a neuron's discharge rate over spontaneous levels.

experiencer   in case grammar, the case denoting the one who is feeling some emotion expressed in the proposition.

expressive disorder   a language disturbance primarily affecting production.

extended tact   a generalized tact referring to a class concept rather than a specific object.

extralinguistic   knowledge about events, concepts, etc. from the real world, apart from language.

factor analysis   a statistical technique for determining multiple correlations of items to discover meaningful clusters.

fading   a technique in operant conditioning in which a stimulus controlling a response is gradually removed, allowing the response to come under the control of a different stimulus.

falsetto   see register.

fan effect   description of a memory retrieval finding. The more items learned in connection with a subject, the more items that activation must spread to (fan out over) from that subject, and the longer retrieval takes, under some conditions.

figurative   representing one concept in terms of another to create new meanings.

filter characteristics   the effect that an object has on sound waves; these include resonance, reflection, and absorption.

finite state grammar   a language model in which it is assumed that each word (or constituent) is determined by only the immediately preceding word (or constituent).

flap   a consonant made with brief but complete closure with fast release, as is the sound in the middle of "ladder" or "latter."

flow   see fluidity of motion.

fluent aphasia   see Wernicke's aphasia.

fluidity of motion   in sign language, movement in a single direction with blending of separate hand configurations into a smooth gesture.

focal color   the best example of a color category cross-culturally, presumably because it best captures similarities among members of its category while maintaining maximal distance from other categories. See also basic level and prototype.

focus   see rheme.

formal operations   the final stage of Piaget's cognitive development theory in which the thought system itself is systematically conceived.

formant frequencies   the resonant frequencies of the vocal tract. Also used to refer to the dark bands on a spectrogram that represent the vocal tract resonances.

formational dimensions   in sign language, this refers to the hand feature classes that distinguish signs. The four dimensions are handshape, hand movement, location in space, and hand orientation.

formulae (fingerspelling formulae)   the conventionalized fingerspelling pattern that develops for frequently spelled words in sign language, which may develop into a sign for that word.

frames   see script.

free morpheme   a morpheme that can stand alone as a word.

frequency   the number of repetitions in a unit of time. Inversely proportional to wavelength.

frication noise   a relatively long duration noise segment accompanying the release in fricatives.

fricative   see manner of articulation.

front vowel   a vowel produced with the highest point of the tongue at the front of the oral cavity.

frontal lobe   a part of the cerebrum.

functional structure the structure of a sentence as determined by the roles that constituents play in it.

function words words that have little meaning outside the language, serving within the language to specify connections between words. Includes prepositions, articles (determiners), and conjunctions.

fundamental frequency the largest frequency shared by members of a complex. Also called pitch.

garden path sentences sentences that we attempt to parse incorrectly, like "the horse raced past the barn fell."

generalization where more is learned than the specific stimulus or response that is being trained.

global aphasia aphasia in both Broca's and Wernicke's areas leaving the patient with virtually no language skills.

gloss writing in translation.

glottal see place of articulation.

glottis the air space between the vocal cords.

graded continuous, as opposed to discrete or categorical.

grammaticality judgments a test of tacit knowledge in which the subject is asked to judge whether a sentence is acceptable in the language.

grave a distinctive feature in speech characterizing a large and undivided mouth cavity. Contrasts with acute.

ground the relation between the tenor and the vehicle in a metaphor.

habituation a decrease in activity level as a result of increased familiarity with a stimulus.

handshape see formational dimensions.

harmonic complex a group of frequencies in which each is a multiple of some base frequency.

hebephrenia a schizophrenia characterized by wild fits of laughter, sudden mood swings, and apparent disregard for one's appearance.

hedge a word used to direct interpretation of the meaning of a clause, as in "loosely speaking, . . ."

hemiparesis a weakening of half the body due to brain damage in the motor areas of the cerebral hemispheres.

hertz (Hz) the unit measuring frequency. 1 Hz = 1 cycle per second.

Heschl's gyrus a groove deep in the cortex where auditory information is processed.

heuristic a processing strategy that is organized with respect to the likelihood of success.

high-amplitude sucking paradigm a means of testing infants' discrimination abilities, by putting the stimulus in the infants' control, so that when the infant sucks on a special nipple the stimulus is presented. After a time the infant habituates, decreasing sucking. If the stimulus is changed so that the infant can discriminate the change, sucking will then increase.

holographic memory see mass action.

holophrasis a description of child language when children's mean length utterance = 1. Using rich interpretation, some investigators believe these single morphemes to represent whole phrases (= holo + phrasis).

home sign a sign language system developed within a family and not shared by a large community. Usually, such a system is less rich than a real language.

hypothesis-driven processes see top-down processes.

iconic signs that look like what they represent.

identification a psychological test in which subjects are asked to provide labels for stimuli.

illocutionary force   in speech act analysis, the portion of an utterance that indicates speaker intent.

imitation-comprehension-production (ICP) test   a test of child language acquisition in which each of the skills named by the test are measured for each linguistic structure, in order.

immediacy hypothesis   one explanation for the deviance in schizophrenic language, which holds that a schizophrenic's attention is captured to an unusual extent by features of the immediate environment.

implication   a linguistic entity that logically entails another.

implosive   see ingressive.

indexing   a method of marking pronoun reference in ASL. The individual is assigned a location in the space in front of the signer by a hand movement or eye movement to that location. Signs subsequently made from that location refer to that individual.

indirect object   see "recipient" in the appendix to Chapter 4.

infix   a bound morpheme that occurs inside a word.

inflections   morphemes that mark grammatical relations such as tense, aspect, number, or gender.

information   with respect to information theory, a reduction of uncertainty.

ingressive   a sound produced by sucking air in rather than expelling it.

inhibition   a decrease in a neuron's discharge rate below spontaneous levels.

initialization   the process by which a sign in ASL, usually borrowed from English, uses as handshape the shape of the fingerspelled first letter of the English word. Such signs are initialized.

innate   inborn; instinctive; not requiring learning.

inner speech   the result of the turning inward of egocentric speech; the beginning of pure thought.

interaction theory (of metaphor interpretation)   the tenor and the vehicle are not simply related but create a tension that enables a new insight.

interchangeability   a design feature for language indicating that we may play the role of transmitter or receiver equally well.

interdental   see place of articulation.

invariant   a cue or set of cues that does not change with context.

irreversible   when interchanging the subject and object of a sentence produces nonsense.

isolation of the speech areas   patients with damage around Broca's or Wernicke's areas resulting in poor production or comprehension but good repetition.

isolation peep   the call of the squirrel monkey that identifies it as an individual and a member of a particular group, and that is used when the individual becomes separated from the group.

jargon aphasics   aphasics (usually Wernicke's) who produce many neologisms.

kernel sentence   see core sentence.

keyword   a word used to trigger a response in automated data retrieval.

klang association   word association based on sound. A characteristic feature of schizophrenic word association and spontaneous speech.

labiodental   see place of articulation.

language acquisition device (LAD)   the innate rules, structures, and strategies hypothesized by Chomsky and other transformationalists to be part of every persons' biological endowment.

larynx   the organ containing the vocal cords. The Adam's apple.

lateral   see manner of articulation.

lateral cerebral sulcus   the brain groove that divides the temporal lobe from the frontal and parietal lobes.

lax   see vowel features.

learnability   a design feature for language indicating the ability to learn many different language systems.

left visual field   see visual field.

left visual neglect   a symptom of some right hemisphere damage where the patient seems to ignore visual and tactile information from the left side of space.

lesion   region of damage to tissue.

lexical decision (task)   where a subject is presented with a letter string and must decide whether or not it is a word. Usually reaction time to make the decision is measured.

lexicon (as opposed to dictionary)   the mental name store together with pronunciation rules.

linear syntax   a description of children's sentences implying that words are strung together without forming a hierarchical relation.

linguistic determinism   see linguistic relativity hypothesis.

linguistic relativity hypothesis   in its strong form, that language determines thought.

literal paraphasia   a speech error involving a slip of a single phoneme or phonetic feature.

localization hypothesis   a theory of brain organization that maps different cognitive functions to different brain locations.

listing   in ASL, a grammatical device for description.

literal   language used in its usual sense.

loan word   a word taken as is from a foreign language into another language.

location   see formational dimensions.

logical empiricists   see logical positivists.

logical form   the relationships expressed in deep structure.

logical positivists   a group of philosophers of language who attempted to define a system of rules that would derive all grammatical statements and eliminate all ungrammatical ones.

longitudinal study   a study of development in which the same subjects are followed for the duration of the developmental period of interest.

lookahead   a processing routine that uses a scan of later information to determine the structure or sense of the current information.

looping   the way repetition of a state is indicated on a finite state diagram, with a path from one point back to the same point.

macrostructure   in discourse analysis, the characteristics of the entire discourse.

magnitude estimation   a psychological task in which subjects guess how large their response is to a given stimulus. The task is to assign a number to the response as it is experienced, *not* to guess the size of the stimulus.

male song   the mating song of the white-crowned sparrow.

mand   a verbal behavior that is reinforced by an action on the part of the listener (a comMand).

manner of articulation   a phonetic feature differentiating the way closure is made: completely (stop consonants or plosives), completely but with air leaking through the nose (nasals), completely by the tongue tip but with air leaking around the side (laterals), partially with turbulence (fricatives), partially with no turbulence (liquids and semivowels).

Markov process   a sequence of elements in which a given element is determined only by the element directly preceding it.

masking   the decreased perceptibility of a signal when another signal is presented near it in time.

mass action   a theory of brain organization in which it is assumed that cognitive functioning is distributed across many cells and that a given function is determined by the pattern of cells firing.

matching-to-sample   a testing technique in which one item is given as a sample and the subject must select from two other items the best match.

mean length of utterance (MLU)   one measure of a child's language development, in which the average number of morphemes per utterance is calculated.

medial   a sound occurring between two others. For example, the vowel in a consonant-vowel-consonant syllable is a medial vowel.

mediating response   some set of responses, which come between the stimulus and the overt response that can be used as "meaning" for the stimulus.

medium transferability   a design feature for language indicating that we may learn to communicate in many modalities, writing as well as speaking, for example.

metacommunication   communicating about communicating.

metalanguage   language used to talk about language; for example, the word "word."

metaphor   a figure of speech in which one thing is given the characteristics of another.

metonymy   a figure of speech in which part of a word's meaning is used to stand for the whole concept or the reverse.

microstructure   in discourse analysis, the relation between individual propositions.

minimum distance principle   a strategy of sentence processing in which the individual attempts to select the closest possible syntactic unit as potential filler in an ambiguous structure: A pronoun is assumed to refer to the nearest noun, a verb to have as subject the nearest noun, etc.

minimal pair   two words identical but for one formational feature. In English an example would be bat-pat; in ASL, the signs THINK-IDEA.

mixed anteriors   aphasics with a lesion in Broca's area but substantial comprehension deficits as well.

modal structure   in meaning interpretation, the interpretation provided at the deep structure level to specify the scopes of quantifiers.

modality effect   the finding of a greater recency effect for spoken sounds than for written words.

morpheme   the smallest unit of language that conveys meaning. Can be a word or a part of one; "s" in some contexts, for example, is a morpheme indicating the plural.

morphophonemic rule   a rule governing sound production in certain meaning contexts. For example, a stress change can change a noun to a verb in English.

motor theory (in meaning)   the hypothesis that movements normally accompanying an action serve as mediating responses for interpreting the meaning of the name of the action.

motor theory (in speech)   the assumption that speech is identified through recognition of the articulatory movements the listener would have had to have made to produce the sound heard.

movement   see formational dimension.

nasal   see manner of articulation.

nasal murmur   a low-frequency energy characterizing nasal consonants.

native   innate, inborn, instinctive.

natural selection   a process in evolution where traits are continued or eliminated across generations by their effect on the organism's ability to compete for the essentials of life, such as food, water, or access to mates.

necessary   a set of cues that must be present to recognize a pattern.

neologism   a newly created "word."

neuron   a nerve cell.

nesting see center-embedding.

neurosis a class of personality disorders deriving from anxiety or one's defenses to it and not involving a loss of touch with reality.

neurotransmitter chemicals that brain cells use to communicate with one another.

new information see rheme.

noise a random combination of frequencies.

nondeterministic a processing routine that backtracks when it recognizes it has made a false start.

nonfluent aphasia see Broca's aphasia.

nonterminal string the result of application of rewrite rules, when more are still needed to produce a sentence that could be uttered.

nonverbal communication a branch of communication studies that deals with information not conveyed by language—usually body language and paralanguage.

normalization a process of compensating for individual differences in speaking, whereby a speaker's frequency range is calibrated and then mental adjustments are made to translate it to the space occupied by some idealized voice. Identification then takes place with respect to the idealization. For example, a high pitch might be mentally lowered.

nth order approximations strings of words generated by combining subjects' responses to a prompt of n − 1 words. Thus a second-order approximation would take two-word strings so produced and combine them to the desired utterance length.

numerosity a test of cognitive development in which the child is presented with rows of objects differing in number or spatial arrangement and asked to determine which has more.

object permanence the awareness that objects do not cease to exist when they can no longer be directly sensed. Object permanence is necessary for conceptualizing things.

obligatory transformations that must be performed to convert the deep structure to a terminal string.

occipital lobe a part of the cerebrum, responsible for vision.

old information see theme.

onomatopoeia words that sound like their referent; for example, "splash."

open class (1) in child language acquisition in one formulation of the syntax of two-word utterances, the class of words that seem to grow and are combined either with one another or words in the pivot class. (2) In adult language, open class words are roughly equivalent to content words; the class that can get new members as new concepts are invented or learned.

operant conditioning a form of learning where a behavior is followed by a stimulus that increases or decreases the probability of its recurring. See also reinforcement and punishment.

optional transformations or portions of rewrite rules that do not have to be performed to result in a grammatical string.

oral education a method of teaching deaf children to communicate using exclusively speech and lipreading.

orientation see formational dimension.

orienting response the set of behaviors made by an organism when its attention is attracted. In infants this includes initial heart rate decrease followed by an increase.

overextension in child language acquisition, this refers to children's generalizing meanings incorrectly, as in using "daddy" to refer to all men.

overrestriction in child language acquisition, this refers to the child's overdiscriminating the meaning of a word, as in using "muffin" to refer only to the blueberry variety.

oxymoron   a poetic device pairing opposites, as in "hot ice" to refer to an improbability.

paired associate task   when two items are presented to a subject who is to learn them as a pair. Either may then be used to prompt the other.

palatal   see place of articulation.

paradigmatic association   word association based on semantic feature and grammatical class, as in mother-father.

paralanguage   see suprasegmental.

parallel processing   processing operations performed at the same time. As opposed to serial processing.

paranoia   a schizophrenia characterized by a delusion of persecution.

paraphasia   a speech error or melodic disturbance accompanying aphasia.

parapraxis   Freud's term for slips of the tongue or temporary memory lapses.

parietal lobe   part of the cerebrum.

parse   analysis of a structure into its components.

performance   as opposed to competence, what speakers of a language actually do in understanding or producing sentences. It may contain mistakes, false starts, etc.

periodic   regularly occurring.

perseveration errors   intrusions from actions the individual has made in the past.

persistence of set   use of a familiar strategy in an inappropriate situation.

phasic level   in one system of classifying communication, a low level in which signals are tied to a particular state of the organism but change when that state changes.

phoneme   the smallest unit of sound that can be used to differentiate words.

phonemic restoration effect   the finding that deleting or masking a sound in the speech stream does not prevent subjects from thinking it was there along with "noise" somewhat removed from its real location.

phonetic   a description that reflects precise articulation of the sound rather than the use the sound plays in the language (as in phonemic).

phonetics   a branch of linguistics studying the sounds of a language to determine the system of rules governing their production, perception, and combination.

phonetic features   articulatory or acoustic distinguishers of allophones.

phonology   see phonetics.

phrase marker   the tree diagram used to illustrate phrase structure.

phrase structure   the expression of the hierarchical constituent relationships expressed in a sentence.

pidgin language   the language system that emerges when adults with no common language are forced to live and work together under the rule of speakers of a distinct, dominating language. The result is word combinations from the potpourri of languages, with very reduced syntax.

pitch contour   the ups and downs in pitch of an utterance.

pivot class   in child language acquisition, the words used in the two-word stage as relations or predicates. These are added to slowly and combined with open-class words.

place of articulation   a phonetic feature describing the place of constriction for consonants. Bilabial = at the lips, labiodental = with a lip and the teeth, dental = at the teeth, interdental = between the teeth, alveolar = at the alveolar ridge, palatal = at the soft palate, velar = at the velum, and glottal = behind the velum, in the throat.

plosive   see manner of articulation.

point vowels   the vowels /i, a, u/ pronounced with the most extreme differences in tongue height and tongue position.

polar   semantic features that signal opposites, like male-female.

potency   one of three factors to emerge usually from semantic differential analysis. Measures strength vs. weakness.

power spectrum   a graphic display of the amount of energy or amplitude (y-axis) at each frequency (x-axis).

pragmatics   the study of the practical use of signs and symbols.

precategorical acoustic store (PAS)   one explanation of the modality effect, in which it is assumed that there is a special short-term, limited capacity memory, the PAS, for auditory material only.

predicate   the verb and modifiers of a sentence, including the object. Called the verb phrase in transformational grammar.

prefix   a bound morpheme that attaches to the front of the root.

premotor region   the back of the frontal lobe, where Broca's area is.

preoperational stage   Piaget's second stage of cognitive development, in which thought is rudimentary. There are schemes, but adding to them occurs unsystematically.

presupposition   an unstated fact that is assumed in generating a sentence but not stated in the sentence.

prevoiced   see voicing.

primacy effect   in short-term recall, the finding that the first items presented are better recalled than later items.

primary reinforcement   a stimulus that will act as a reward (increase the preceding behavior) because it satisfies a primary need like hunger or thirst.

priming   when a subject is given a clue to the identity of a stimulus that should facilitate its recognition.

primitive   the smallest unit of psychological meaning, in terms of which all other meanings are composed.

process schizophrenia   see chronic schizophrenia.

productive   a rule or distinction that generates many meaningful units of a language.

projection rules   in one semantic system (see Chapter 2), the portions of the system that map word-meanings onto syntactic structures.

prompts   stimuli that elicit particular responses.

proposition   the core relationships of a sentence, subject-verb-object-location-manner. Many consider it the meaning of a sentence in memory, a breakdown into those interconnected relations. It is roughly equivalent to deep structure.

propositional content   in speech act analysis, the meaning of a sentence apart from speaker intent.

prototype   a typical or average instance of a category. See also focal color and basic object.

psychoses   personality disorders characterized by a loss of touch with reality.

punishment   the form of operant condition where the frequency of occurrence of a behavior is decreased by the following stimulus.

pure naming deficit   a rare form of aphasia resulting only in the patient's inability to name in isolation.

quantifier   a word that specifies the relative amount, like "each," "all," or "neither."

reaction time   a common measure of mental processing. The time it takes between stimulus presentation and the response.

reactive schizophrenia   schizophrenia characterized by sudden onset, perhaps in response to some emotionally traumatic incident.

received pronunciation (RP)   the upper-class British dialect that makes use of the creaky voice register.

recency effect in short-term recall, the finding that the last item presented is better recalled than all earlier items but the first.

receptive aphasia see Wernicke's aphasia.

receptive field the set of stimuli that a neuron responds to, either through excitation or inhibition.

recognition one way to test memory, by presenting a stimulus and seeing if the subject can tell whether or not it has been presented previously.

recursiveness a function that can name itself. "This sentence is false" becomes paradoxical because the sentence is recursive.

redundancy in information theory, a duplication of signal in such a way that no new information is provided. This may help if there was information loss through noise.

reduplication repetition of a morpheme as a syntactic marker, for example, to intensify.

referent what a symbol refers to in the real world. The referent of "dog" would be any animal correctly named by the word.

reflection the bouncing back of sound waves, producing echoes.

registers vocal changes produced by manipulation of the tension pattern on the vocal cords. For example, falsetto (more tension than normal), chest (normal), creaky voice (uneven tension), breathy voice (partial tension accompanying an air leak).

reinforcement the form of operant conditioning where the frequency of occurrence of a behavior is increased by the following stimulus.

release when, after making a constriction, it is loosened, allowing air to leak through.

relexification the process of borrowing words from a dominating language while retaining the syntax and phonology of the native language.

reliability consistency in getting the same result each time a test is performed.

repetition effect the phenomenon of faster retrieval of an item from memory when it has been recently activated.

resonance the sympathetic vibration of objects in response to sound frequencies. An object does not vibrate to all frequencies; those that it does vibrate to are its resonant frequencies.

retroflex a sound produced by turning the tongue back on itself (the English "r" for example).

reversible a sentence in which the subject and object may be reversed without resulting in nonsense.

rewrite rules rules for substituting constituents for one another to generate sentences.

rheme the new information a sentence provides with respect to the topic or theme.

rich interpretation in studying language acquisition, when the investigator assigns meaning to an utterance based not only on what was said but also on the context.

right ear advantage (REA) in dichotic listening, the finding that speech sounds presented to the right ear are more accurately reported than those presented to the left ear. Assumed to reflect the right ear's superior access to the language area of the left hemisphere of the brain.

right visual field see visual field.

ritualistic behavior repetitive actions that have no real, external purpose.

schema see script.

scheme a mental structure.

schwa the neutral vowel, produced with the least movement from the tongue's resting position.

scope the size and type of constituent a transformation works on. Also the size of a linguistic unit a quantifier applies to.

script an organization of knowledge used in artificial intelligence. For example, one script might be "restaurant" and contain all information about what might be found in a restaurant, the usual behavior at one, etc.

secondary reinforcement   a stimulus that serves as a reward (increases the occurrence of a preceding behavior) after it is associated with a primary reinforcer. Money, for example, is a secondary reinforcer of extraordinary power because of its associations to so many primary reinforcers.

segments   the individual speech units that are combined to form meaningful units. Can be phonetic features, phonemes, or syllables.

selectional restrictions   conditions specifying which words may combine with which others on the basis of semantic features so that sentence anomalies are avoided.

self-editing hypothesis   one explanation for the deviance in schizophrenic language in which it is assumed that the individual cannot select appropriately among alternative interpretations or word choices.

semanticity   a design feature for language indicating that the relation between word and referent must be learned.

semantics   the branch of linguistics concerned with meaning.

semantic differential   a technique for measuring connotative meaning. Words are rated on bipolar scales and then the ratings are factor-analyzed to determine meaningful organizational dimensions.

semantic markers   general meaning features shared by many words, such as human, animal.

semantic relatedness   a measure of the strength of association between two words, which may be determined by the number of shared associations or frequency of conjoint production.

semantic relation   the function of a noun or noun phrase with respect to a verb.

semivowel   see manner of articulation.

sensorimotor stage   the first stage in Piaget's framework for cognitive development, where the child's schemes are derived directly from physical experience with the environment.

serial processing   processing operations performed sequentially. See also parallel processing.

serial recall   a recall task requiring duplication of the stimuli in the order they were presented.

setting a flag   an expression in programming signifying that some operation is noted.

sexual selection   a process of evolution whereby certain traits are propagated because they enhance the possibility of attractiveness to a mate.

shadowing   a task in which subjects are asked to repeat a message as it is being transmitted as closely as possible in time with the transmission.

sign   an element that indicates another. Words are a special type of sign, called symbols.

signal level   in one system of classifying communication, a high level, where transmission begins only in the presence of another and the transmitter is monitoring for feedback.

signaling   as distinct from real communication, this refers to a coordinated system of symptom emission and recognition on the part of the transmitter and receiver. The connection between signal and response is known as the code system.

sign stimulus   a characteristic feature of an object or animal that causes a reflex response.

signal level   in one system of analyzing communication, communications that take place because the transmitter becomes aware of the receiver.

simile   a figure of speech in which the novel use of a word is signaled by "as" or "like."

simple schizophrenia   a form of schizophrenia involving withdrawal from society but no other dramatic symptoms.

simultaneity   a design feature of language referring to the fact that at any single instant of transmission, many different patterns are signaled.

single-cell recording a method of measuring the sensitivity of an individual neuron by recording its discharges to various stimuli.

slip of the ear misperceiving a correctly uttered word.

slip of the hand the analogue of a slip of the tongue, for sign language.

smear a design feature of language referring to the fact that cues to a particular language pattern are spread in time across the signal.

social markers clues in verbal or nonverbal communication as to the transmitter's social group.

soft palate the soft part of the roof of the mouth.

sound symbolism where the sound of a word is used to convey meaning.

specialization a design feature for language indicating that our signals are only for language; they are not a symptom of some bodily state that they "name."

spectrograph a machine that produces a spectrogram.

spectrogram a graphic display of the energy present at each frequency (y-axis) with respect to time (x-axis).

speech act a language unit that takes into account the speaker's intention for action on the part of the listener, regardless of the structure of the utterance. "Would you pass the salt?" is a demand for salt, not a question, for example.

split-brain patients people who have had the corpus callosum severed, stopping cortical communication between the cerebral hemispheres.

spontaneous activity the discharge rate of a neuron in its natural resting state.

spreading activation the method by which one memory is hypothesized to arouse others. All links to the given memory are aroused in proportion to their distance from it.

stage a time in development characterized by a particular mode of thought.

steady state unchanging frequency in a formant, usually considered a cue to vowel quality.

stimulus-driven processes see bottom-up processes.

stop consonant see manner of articulation.

subcategorization (strict subcategorization rule) assignment of words to major syntactic categories (parts of speech). The rules specify how the categories may be combined. Violation produces ungrammaticality.

subject (of a metaphor) see tenor.

subject (of a sentence) the words governing the verb; usually the actor in a sentence.

subordinance conjoining sentences by using one sentence as added description of another.

subphonemic feature see phonetic features.

substitution theory (of metaphor interpretation) a grammatically sensible sentence is interpreted in place of the anomaly suggested by the metaphor.

sufficient a set of cues to a pattern that will cause it to be identified but that may not always be present when the pattern is recognized.

suffix a bound morpheme that comes after the root.

suffix effect the finding that for spoken lists, the recency advantage may be eliminated by presenting an item similar to the list items following the list but not to be recalled.

superordinance conjoining sentences and thereby adding a new meaning, such as their temporal relationship.

superordinate in a taxonomy, a category that subsumes other categories.

suprasegmental information in speech that is not contained in the segments but derives from their combination, such as loudness or intonation contour.

surface structure see phrase structure.

syllable a unit of speech consisting of only one vowel or diphthong.

symbol an element that refers to another without indicating it directly, as words refer to underlying concepts.

symmetry constraint see dominance constraint.

symptom (in communication) a physical or behavioral change emitted passively by an organism that may be interpreted by an observer.

syncretic conglomerate the unorganized piles a preoperational child makes when asked to sort Vygotsky blocks.

synonym a word that denotes the same thing as another.

syntagmatic association connection of events or ideas because they occur sequentially. For example, milk-shake.

syntax the branch of linguistics concerned with the rules underlying combination of words. Roughly synonymous with grammar.

synthetic a statement that can be verified only with reference to extralinguistic information.

synthetic speech continuum a set of speech stimuli produced by a machine with values that are acoustically intermediate between two phonemes.

tacit knowledge knowledge that we have but of which we are not consciously aware.

tact a verbal behavior that describes the external environment.

tautology a self-evident truth.

taxonomy a category hierarchy.

temporal lobe a part of the cerebrum.

tenor what a metaphor is about.

tense (1) a morpheme marking the relative time of occurrence of the action. (2) See vowel features.

terminal string the sequence of language units as it could be uttered, without any additional operations necessary.

thalamus a midbrain structure that receives input, in different locations, from the sensory systems.

timbre the quality of a sound.

theme what the sentence is about.

tip-of-the-tongue state when an individual knows an item but cannot recall it at the moment, although frequently, (s)he may be able to say quite a bit about it.

tone language a language that uses vocal pitch phonemically.

tongue height see vowel features.

tongue position see vowel features.

tonic level in one system of classifying communication, a low level, in which an aspect of state is signaled continuously through a bodily process.

top-down processes processes that begin with the abstract concept and use it to guide data interpretation.

topic see tenor (metaphor) p. 000, or theme (sentence).

total feedback a design feature of language indicating that we can monitor our own transmissions as well as receive feedback from others.

trace a marker in abstract surface structure indicating elements that have been moved by transformation of deep structure.

traditional transmission a design feature for language indicating that it is passed on through learning across generations.

transcortical motor aphasia isolation of the speech area producing problems in spontaneous speech production.

transcortical sensory aphasia isolation of the speech area producing problems in spontaneous speech comprehension.

transfer function   a representation of the filter characteristics of an object showing the relative enhancement and damping of each frequency.

transformations   context-sensitive rules that apply first to deep structure, and then cyclically, to transformed structure to produce the surface form of the sentence.

transition   change in frequency over time in a formant. Usually considered to cue manner and place of articulation.

transitional probability   the likelihood that any particular path will be chosen in a finite state grammar.

trill   a manner class not used in English, produced by repetitive openings and closings.

undershoot   the assumption that in producing a vowel, a speaker has as ideal the steady state formant frequencies of the isolated vowel, which are missed because of modifications by

unit   an indivisible element.

universal grammar   the innate language structures or rules that can be found in all languages. Roughly the same as the language acquisition device.

universals   features found in all languages presumably because they are innate.

variance   the sum of the squares of the difference between a number of scores and an average score. A measure of dispersion around a center.

vegetable level   in one system of ranking communication, the lowest level, in which one inter-actant responds to another solely as a stimulus.

vehicle   the means through which a metaphorical comparison is achieved.

velar   see place of articulation.

velum   the area of the mouth near the uvula, the flap hanging down at the back.

verbal paraphasia   a speech error involving a whole word slip.

verification task   where sentences are presented and subjects must decide whether they are true or false. Reaction time to make the decision is usually measured.

video snow   the picture a television set produces when between channels. It is used as a mask for visual signals.

visual field   in the human visual system, if a line is drawn down the center of the retina, information from the right half of the retina goes to the right cerebral hemisphere and information from the left half, to the left cerebral hemisphere. Information from the right side of space, or the right visual field, falls on the left half of the retina and information from the left visual field, on the right half of the retina.

voice onset time (VOT)   a set of acoustic features underlying the voicing distinction. These include the amount of aspiration noise, the relative length of the first formant transition, and the relative onset of periodic pulsing to signal onset.

voiced   see voicing.

voiceless   see voicing.

voicing   a phonetic feature distinguishing when the vocal cords start vibration relative to the release of air. If the vibration precedes release, the sound is prevoiced; if it is simultaneous, voiced; and if it follows the release, voiceless.

vowel features   vowels are produced with no closure. Tongue height refers to the peak height of the tongue in the vowel; tongue position to where that peak occurs; tense-lax, to vowel "length" and stress.

vowel harmony   a property of some languages in which all the vowels of a word are the same with the particular vowel value morphemic.

Vygotsky blocks   a set of blocks differing along several perceptual dimensions, which may be arranged in groups according to any of the dimensions.

wavelength   the distance between two peaks or two troughs in a wave. Inversely proportional to frequency.

Wernicke's aphasia aphasia characterized by fluent but empty speech and comprehension problems.

Whorf-Sapir hypothesis see linguistic relativity hypothesis.

within-category discriminations perceived differences between stimuli that are labeled the same.

word salad a term used to describe unusually disturbed schizophrenic language, in which the words in a "sentence" seem to be randomly selected.

zeros frequency regions that have been absorbed.

INDEX